Colorado Constitutional Law and History

AF693230

Second Edition

Colorado Constitutional Law and History, Second Edition

David B. Kopel, adjunct professor of constitutional law, University of Denver, Sturm College of Law; research director, Independence Institute; adjunct scholar, Cato Institute.

Colorado Constitutional Law and History, Second Edition

David B. Kopel

Published by:

Vandeplas Publishing, LLC – January 2022

801 International Parkway, 5th Floor
Lake Mary, FL. 32746
USA

www.vandeplaspublishing.com

Copyright © 2022 by David B. Kopel

All rights reserved.

No part of this book may be reproduced, stored in a retrieval system, or transmitted by any means, electronic, mechanical, photocopying, recording, or otherwise, without written permission from the author.

978-1-60042-548-6

Dedication

To the memory of my grandparents, Cornelius and Bess Blanke, for emigrating to Colorado, and for supporting my mother's decision to become a lawyer.

To my mother, Dolores Kopel, and to the memory of my late father, Jerry Kopel. In many decades of involvement in government and civic affairs, they worked hard to help Colorado fulfill its constitutional values of liberty and the rule of law.

Summary of Contents

Contents

List of figures

List of tables

Preface

To gain admission to the Colorado Bar, a person must take seven oaths. The first oath is: "I will support the Constitution of the United States and the Constitution of the State of Colorado." Persons who take an oath should be well-informed about what that oath means.

In Colorado, public school teachers at all levels must swear to support the state constitution. So must the civil officers of all the myriad levels of government. Regarding oaths, Colorado is like other states.

Yet law schools too often leave students unprepared to understand the oath they are taking, and without the tools to carry out that oath. Although as least one class on the United States Constitution is mandatory at U.S. law schools, many schools do not offer any classes on state constitutional law.

All constitutions are part of the living history our sovereign federal republic and our sovereign states. Almost every high school graduate in the United States will take at least one survey class in American history. Yet state history is often overlooked in secondary and post-secondary education. Civics education—to the extent it exists at all—has deteriorated so badly that students are barely informed about the founding principles and constitutional form of government of the United States of America, rendering students ignorant about their own state's principles and government structure.

This textbook aims to fill the educational gap in Colorado. Although written for law school instruction, is also accessible to lay readers and usable as reference manual.

The textbook begins with chapters on the early history of Colorado, and how that history shaped the 1876 Colorado Constitution. The chapters elucidate the foundational rules of Colorado government: sovereignty of the people, natural rights, and a republican form of government.

Thereafter, the chapters cover one or more articles of the Colorado Constitution. The chapters proceed through each article section by section—first providing the constitutional text, and then history and analysis. Leading judicial opinions on a section are summarized.

A common defect of books on constitutional law is the assumption that "constitutional law = judicial opinions." Judicial opinions are very important in shaping the application of constitutional provisions. Yet they are not the only source of constitutional understanding. For example, long-standing and unchallenged legislative practices often create *de facto* precedents that are later accepted by the courts.

At times, a constitutional provision may be disdained, ignored, or nullified by the judiciary or by other branches. Subsequently, popular opinion, elections, and changes in elite opinion may result in greater respect for that provision. This textbook examines how constitutional text may be applied or negated, including by the judiciary.

Within the time available for a one semester course, textbooks must be selective. This textbook pays close attention to constitutional text and history, and only occasionally delves into lengthy excerpts of judicial opinions. The mandatory first year classes in law school, as well as many upper-level electives, are very good at teaching students how to analyze judicial opinions. This book aims to develop a different skill, that of understanding a constitution comprehensively, in whole and in part.

Self-government is far from universal in today's world, and in world history it has been the exception rather than the rule. How can a people create a sustainable, enduring system of self-government? *Colorado Constitutional Law and History* examines the successes and failures of the people of Colorado in their attempts to retain and exercise their sovereignty.

Conventions and editorial choices

Any material in [brackets] within quoted text is added by me, except as noted. Material in (parentheses) is original to the quoted source, unless otherwise noted.

<u>Colorado Constitution text that is underlined has been partly or fully nullified by the judicial, legislative, or executive branches</u>. The highlighted text does *not* include Colorado constitutional text that was found to violate the U.S. Constitution; the underlining is for constitutional text that is still formally valid, but which has been judicially or otherwise filleted by Colorado actors.

Titles for the Colorado Constitution's 29 articles mostly follow those in the 1876 Constitution. Unless otherwise noted, bolded headings on constitutional sections have been added by me; they are so indicated in the paragraph before the constitutional text.

The publisher of this book, Vandeplas Publishing, requires minimalist capitalization. For example, government offices and titles are generally not capitalized. Exceptions are sometimes made in the interests of clarity, especially on the first use of a term.

The citations mainly follow *The Bluebook: A Uniform System for Citation*. However, some citations have been modified for easier understanding. Certain formatting choices may vary between sections, again in the interests of clarity or readability.

Case names may vary from one reporter to another, so the case name in the textbook may not be identical to the name in the online link in the ebook version of this textbook

This book gives relatively little attention to Colorado Constitution provisions that have been held to violate the United State Constitution. Although the cases raise interesting issues, this book focuses on how Coloradans create and enforce their Constitution within the boundaries of the U.S. constitutional system of distributed sovereignty.

Background

My mother's family moved from their farm in Iowa to Colorado Springs in the 1940s. At the University of Colorado, my mother, Dolores Blanke, met my father, Jerry Koplowitz, a Baltimore native who had emigrated to Colorado following service in the Army Corps of Engineers. As a Journalism major, he had been advised by the department head to find another field, but he persisted and became managing editor of the campus newspaper, the daily *Silver and Gold.* My mother was a reporter, and many of their dates consisted of preparing the next day's edition.

She attended the University of Denver's law school, because DU law school welcomed prospective female students and CU law school did not. Meanwhile, my father began a career in journalism, starting at the *Walsenberg World-Independent*, and moving to the *Rocky Mountain News*. Because the *Rocky* was a morning paper, journalists had to work every evening. Dissatisfied with rarely seeing Dolores, Jerry began attending DU law school part-time. They were both outstanding students. After he graduated in 1958, they shortened their last names and formed the Kopel & Kopel law firm. They practiced civil law, specializing in bankruptcy. Seeing how many bankrupts had been exploited by predatory lending practices led them to become champions of consumer credit reform. Their other great issue was civil rights. In northeast Denver, they were leaders of the Park Hill Action Committee, which worked successfully for the racial integration of Park Hill.

Early in his career, Jerry worked part-time for the Colorado state archives, and then for the Colorado attorney general as a legislative drafter. Some of the photographs of documents you will see in chapter 1 are those that he saved from being disposed by fire. Burning extra copies of books did not seem right to him, especially at the state archives.

In 1964, Jerry was elected as a Colorado state representative from northeast Denver. In the following decades, he compiled an 11–2 election record, and completed his final term of service in 1992. As a Democrat, he was in the minority for 9 of his 11 terms, but still passed many important bills. Among his early accomplishments were expanding Colorado's Fair Housing Act (1965) and strengthening of the Uniform Consumer Credit Code (1971). With experience, he developed new insights into how laws can work against consumers. For example, licensing laws often operate to enrich incumbents and exclude potential competitors, thus raising prices for consumers and preventing people from following a trade or calling. So Jerry Kopel wrote the first Sunset Law in the United States (1975). Widely copied in other states, Sunset Laws declare that regulatory agencies for occupations automatically cease to exist after a term of years, unless affirmatively renewed by the legislature. He followed up with the first Sunrise Law, to control the creation of new regulatory agencies. He strongly favored regulation to protect consumers, and strongly opposed misuse of regulation to harm consumers.

As the best-informed lawyer in the legislature—and one of the very few legislators who read every bill in full before voting—he made countless amendments to Colorado statutes. He worked quietly with Democratic, Republican, and Independent legislators to improve the language of their bills and avoid unintended conflicts with other statutes.

He didn't write the Martin Luther King holiday bill; representative Wilma Webb did that. Jerry's expertise in parliamentary procedure made the bill pass, with Jerry's three-step trap on a series of parliamentary motions. At step two, the bill's supporters called out, "No, Wilma, that's wrong." So it seemed, until step three sprang the trap.[1]

Perhaps most relevantly for readers of this book, Jerry Kopel shepherded more constitutional amendments than anyone else in Colorado history. All his amendments were to remove obsolete constitutional provisions. While the Colorado Constitution is one of the longest in the United States, it would be even longer without him.

At the suggestion of the dean of DU law school, Jerry created a program to help students prepare for the Colorado bar exam. Together, Jerry and Dolores ran their Colorado Bar Refresher for a quarter century. For students on the cusp of passage, he provided personal tutoring to improve their essay answers.

One of the first female lawyers in Colorado, Dolores Kopel in 1972 organized a seven week "Women in the Law" seminar at the University of Denver College of Law. A bankruptcy expert, she was appointed as the first regional U.S. Trustee in a pilot program created by the Bankruptcy Reform Act of 1979. The program was later adopted nationally. Dolores's region comprised the federal bankruptcy courts of Colorado and Kansas. She oversaw the largest bankruptcy in the U.S. at the time, Storage-Tek in 1984.

She also served as first public member of the Colorado Real Estate Commission and of the Collection Agency Board. Jerry and Dolores Kopel were the first married couple on the Board of Governors of the Colorado Bar Association.

They were ardent Colorado patriots. He was Jewish and she was Methodist, and they knew that there was much more tolerance of mixed marriage in Colorado than in the places they had come from. They were both individualists and thrived in Colorado's freer spirt. They paid it forward.

In the 1992 legislative session, when Jerry announced that he would not seek reelection, the *Rocky Mountain News* described some of the causes for which Kopel & Kopel had fought:

---

[1] For the House's consideration of the Senate's amendments to the bill, Rep. Webb's motions were, in order: the House should adhere to its version of the bill; the House should request a conference committee; the House should concur in the Senate amendments. In the written note that rep. Kopel gave rep. Webb: "ADHERE, CONFER, CONCUR." *See* Jerry Kopel, *Passing the Martin Luther King Holiday*, available on the home page of jerrykopel.com (1st published as *Using rules to pass Martin Luther King bill*, COLO. STATESMAN, Feb. 5, 1993).

> State Rep. Jerry Kopel hopes to end his legislative career the same way he launched it 27 years ago: Prohibiting governments from seizing private property without due process of law.
>
> Ask the Denver Democrat what bill he's proudest of and he immediately cites the first one he pushed through the legislature as a freshman in 1965. It prohibited creditors from going to court and garnisheeing wages without a hearing. Until then, they could attach your pay at the same time they filed their complaint.[2]
>
> This year, his last at the legislature, Kopel is again confronting a greedy government. His HB 1219 would prohibit state law enforcement agencies from keeping the cars, cash and other goodies they seize from suspects unless they get a conviction.
>
> . . .
>
> "I think he was the most intellectually honest guy I ever served with," [former Republican state senator Steve] Durham said.

Peter Blake, *Kopel Fights to Last for Libertarianism*, Rocky Mountain News, Feb. 10, 1992 (1992 WLNR 441816).

My parents never thought of themselves as libertarians. They were John F. Kennedy liberal Democrats, optimistic about the ability of affirmative government to promote the common good. They were also constitutionalists, and they well knew how big government can rob the little guy.

In the words of U.S. rep. Diana DeGette (D-Denver), "Jerry and Dolores have had a distinctive lifetime at the forefront of Colorado politics, policy, and history and their commitment to public service and the betterment of their fellow Coloradans serves as a sterling example for younger generations and those entering public policy careers." 154 Congressional Record E1229, E1230 (June 12, 2008).

They inspired me. Perhaps some of the great Coloradans you meet in this book will inspire you.

Acknowledgements

This book reprints, with revisions, some articles that Jerry Kopel wrote for the *Colorado Stateman* newspaper in the two decades after he retired from the legislature.[3] Some of this material also appears in Jerry Kopel & David Kopel, Rules for State Legislators: Jerry Kopel's Guide (2015). The website jerrykopel.com has the originals of these articles and hundreds of others, as well as biographical information about Jerry and Dolores Kopel.

Chapter 15 is adapted in part, with permission, from Robert G. Natelson, *The Colorado Taxpayer's Bill of Rights*, Independence Institute, Issue Paper no. 3-2016.

Thank you to all my Independence Institute colleagues for their support.

Uncredited photos and illustrations are from Shutterstock. The English language and German language Colorado Constitution photos are by Tyler Massey of the Independence Institute. The chapter 21 photos of the Capitol rotunda are by Greg Walcher. Ten photos from History Colorado are credited in their captions. All photos and illustrations are used by permission or license.

Many thanks to my excellent interns Alexander Adams, Clayton Calvin, Nathaniel DeMelis, and Jacob Fogleman for their hard work in preparing this manuscript for publication.

---

[2] A garnishment is a court order that an employer withhold some of an employee's wages and give those wages to a creditor of the employee.

[3] The *Colorado Statesman* used to be the *Colorado Democrat* and is today *Colorado Politics.* Jerry Kopel's columns won seven awards from the Colorado Press Association.

Colorado Constitution Frame of Government

Essentials

- Boundaries. Art. I.
- Principles of government and rights. Art. II.

The three branches of state government

- Separation of powers. Art. III.
- Executive offices: governor, lieutenant governor, attorney general, treasurer, secretary of state. Art. IV.
- Legislative power: general assembly, people's powers of initiative and referendum, redistricting. Art. V.
- Judiciary. Art. VI.

Elections

- Art. VII.

Key institutions

- State institutions: educational; reformatory and penal; insane; blind, deaf, and mute; higher education. Seat of government. Art. VIII.
- Education. Art. IX.

Taxes and debt

- Taxes, including Taxpayer's Bill of Rights. Art. X.
- Debt. Art. XI.

Other structural elements for effective and good government

- Rules for state officers, state personnel system. Art. XII.
- Impeachment. Art. XIII.
- Counties and special districts. Art. XIV.

Particularly important substantive laws

- Corporations. Art. XV.
- Irrigation, mining. Art. XVI.
- Militia. Art. XVII.
- Other key topics. Homestead exemption, forests, gambling, marijuana, term limits, minimum wage, more. Art. XVIII.

Amendment or new convention

- Art. XIX.

Amendments to 1876 Constitution

Note: there are many interpolative amendments to the original articles I-XIX.

- Home rule. Additional powers to local governments. Art. XX.
- Recall. Art. XXI.
- Repealed amendments on alcohol prohibition and publication of legal notices. Arts. XXII & XXIII.

Old Age Pension Fund. Art. XXIV. The only constitutional state-level fund still in existence in the U.S.
Public utilities. Art. XXV.
Nuclear detonations. Art. XXVI.
Great Outdoors Colorado. Uniquely in the U.S., state lottery revenues are dedicated to outdoor recreation. Art. XXVII.
Campaign finance. Art. XXVIII.
Gifts to government employees. Art. XXIX.

Schedule. Adopted as part of the Constitution in 1876, the Schedule provided the mechanics of the transition from territorial to state government. Some sections have continuing legal effect today.

Part I
Foundations

CHAPTER 1

Creation of the State of Colorado

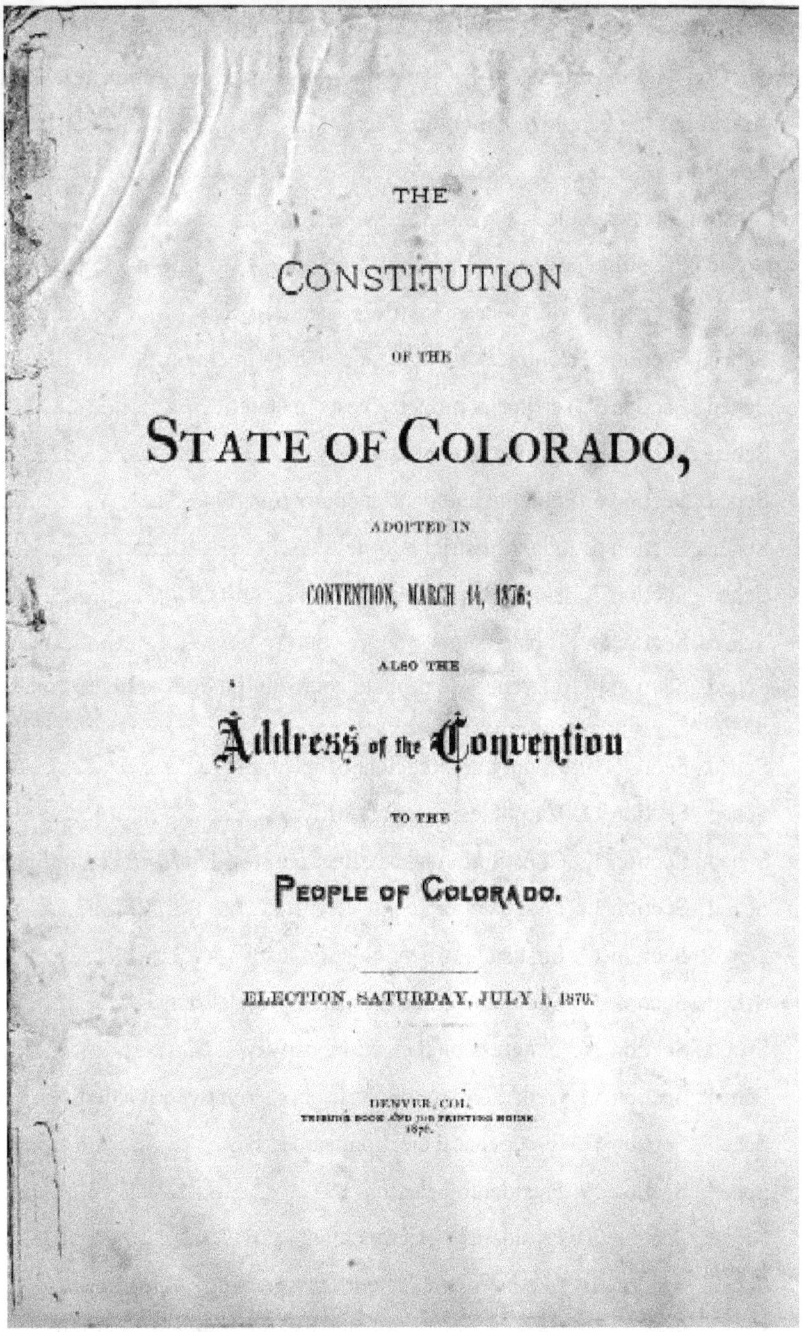

THE

CONSTITUTION

OF THE

STATE OF COLORADO,

ADOPTED IN

CONVENTION, MARCH 14, 1876;

ALSO THE

Address of the Convention

TO THE

PEOPLE OF COLORADO.

ELECTION, SATURDAY, JULY 1, 1876.

DENVER, COL.
TRIBUNE BOOK AND JOB PRINTING HOUSE
1876.

Figure 1. 1876 Constitution & Address to the People.

> Every constitution uses principles of design for achieving the kind of life envisioned by its authors, and the principles will vary according to that vision . . . The constitution describes what that life should be like and the institutions by which will be achieved that way of life. A constitution enunciates the values that support the good life, thereby providing a definition of justice [and] includes an enumeration of political offices, the duties of each, how each is to be filled, how the offices interact to reach collective decision, and who is eligible to hold office—in effect, a design for the distribution of power.[1]

This chapter covers the creation of the Colorado state government. The people of Colorado adopted the Colorado Constitution by a 3:1 majority on July 1, 1876.

Part A provides the foundational legal documents: the United States Constitution sections regarding the admission of new States, and the Colorado Enabling Act. The Enabling Act was the law passed by the U.S. Congress specifying the conditions for Colorado's admission to the Union. The Enabling Act continues to govern certain aspects of Colorado law today.

Part B tells the story of the Colorado Convention, of the proposed Constitution's approach to governance, and of the popular vote ratifying the Constitution. Part B includes the Convention's Address to the People of Colorado, explaining the proposed constitution.

Part C is the Constitution's Schedule, which governed the transition from territorial government to state government, and which continues to have legal effect today.

Part D is the Preamble to the Colorado Constitution.

Part E explains how Colorado got its shape. It begins with article I of the Constitution, which specifies the State of Colorado's boundaries. Those boundaries are the same as boundaries of the Colorado Territory, which was created by Congress in 1861.

The rest of part E is the history of sovereignty and boundaries. In the centuries before statehood, over a dozen groups contended for the area, including the Apache, Comanche, Kiowa, Pawnee, Cheyenne, Arapahoe (also spelled without the *e*), Ute, Spanish, French, Mexicans, Texans, and Americans. Each group exercised sovereignty in some sense in parts of Colorado, at different times.

When the Gold Rush of 1858–59 brought large-scale settlement in Colorado from "the States," the settlers found themselves on the periphery of the periphery. There was no government at all, except what they could provide for themselves. So governments were created by the people themselves, with no legal authorization other than the natural right of self-government. Colorado's early experience in self-government helped set a tone of people's rights that has always been part of the Colorado ethos.

Finally, Part E summarizes the 1861 congressional legislation that created the Colorado Territory. It explains why Congress drew the particular boundaries.

---

[1] DONALD S. LUTZ, THE ORIGINS OF AMERICAN CONSTITUTIONALISM 7 (1988).

A. Foundational Documents

U.S. Constitution, Article IV

> Section 3 (Admission Clause):
> New States may be admitted by the Congress into this Union; but no new State shall be formed or erected within the Jurisdiction of any other States; nor any State be formed by the Junction of two or more States, or Parts of States, without the Consent of the Legislatures of the States concerned as well as of the Congress.
>
> Section 4 (Guarantee Clause):
> The United States shall guarantee to every State in this Union a Republican Form of Government, and shall protect each of them against invasion; and on Application of the Legislature, or of the executive (when the legislature cannot be convened) against domestic violence.

The Constitution of the United States aims to unite many States in perpetuity. All the original states were republics. They wanted union only with fellow republics. If some states could have absolute monarchies (*e.g.*, like North Korea or Oman), or military dictatorships (*e.g.*, Cuba), then free states could not share a federal government with them.

The word *republic* comes from the Latin *res publica*—the people's affair. So, the first characteristic of a republican form of government is that the citizens rule. They can rule by direct vote or through elected representatives. Under the Colorado Constitution, they do both.

The second characteristic of a republican form of government is no monarch. A monarch might exercise limited powers (such as the United Kingdom's Queen Elizabeth II), or a monarch might reign tyrannically (such as Kim Jong Un).

While Queen Elizabeth and Kim Jong Un both inherited their positions, a monarchy does not *have* to be hereditary. The Roman emperorships often passed from hand to hand, by force of whoever had the strongest army faction. The English word *monarchy* comes from the Greek *monos* (alone) plus *arkhein* (to rule). Any system in which a lone person rules is a monarchy—and is therefore prohibited by the Guarantee Clause.

The third essential characteristic of a republican form of government is the rule of law. *See* Robert G. Natelson, Guarantee Clause, *in* THE HERITAGE GUIDE TO THE CONSTITUTION (2d ed. 2014).[2]

The Colorado Enabling Act, next, carries out Congress's article IV powers, by requiring the State of Colorado to have a republican form of government.

Colorado Enabling Act

An Act to enable the People of Colorado to form a Constitution and State Government, and for admission of said State into the Union on an equal footing with the original States
18 Statutes of the United States 474 (March 3, 1875)

---

[2] Many of the hyperlinks in this textbook to U.S. Constitution provisions are to the relevant section of the *Heritage Guide*, which provides a succinct analysis of background, original meaning, and subsequent application for every clause of the U.S. Constitution.

The admission of Colorado to the Union was authorized by act of Congress in 1875, on the final day of the session. The Enabling Act provides the terms, conditions, and procedures for Colorado's admission to the union:

- On an *equal footing* with the other States. § 1.
- Within specified lines of latitude and longitude. Longitude is measured from Washington, D.C. § 2.
- Setting up elections for a constitutional convention; delegates to be elected in districts by the people. § 3.
- Conditions for the convention and the constitution. § 4. This is the most important section of the Enabling Act.
    - Within 60 days after the election, the convention delegates must assemble.
    - The Convention "shall declare, on behalf of the people of said Territory, that they adopt the Constitution of the United States."
    - After adopting the U.S. Constitution, the convention will proceed to drafting a Colorado Constitution.

People who wish to become part of the United States must adopt the United States Constitution. The rule is true for individuals, such as persons who become naturalized citizens. Their Oath of Allegiance declares, "I will support and defend the Constitution and laws of the United States of America against all enemies, foreign and domestic; that I will bear true faith and allegiance to the same." Communities that wish to join the United States must likewise declare their adherence to the U.S. Constitution.

According to the Enabling Act, the Colorado Constitution must have certain characteristics. All relate to essential elements of national citizenship:

- The Constitution must have a republican form. This is required by the Guarantee Clause ("Republican Form of Government") in article IV, § 4 of the U.S. Constitution.
- The Colorado Convention must create certain laws that may never be revoked, unless Congress *and* the people of Colorado consent to revocation:
    - No distinction on account of race.
    - Perfect religious toleration.
    - The State must disclaim any right to unappropriated federal lands.
    - Lands belonging to non-residents may not be taxed at a higher than the rate for residents.

The next section of the Enabling Act requires that the Convention's proposed Colorado Constitution be ratified by a vote of the people. § 5.

Decades later, in 1910, the direct democracy rights of initiative and referendum would be added to the Colorado Constitution (Chapter 9). But thanks to the Enabling Act, direct democracy has always been part of the structure of the Colorado Constitution. Section 4 of the Enabling Act required that certain guarantees of fundamental rights be irrepealable without a vote by the people themselves (plus consent by Congress). Pursuant to section 5, the Constitution proposed by the Convention could only become law if approved by the people in a direct vote.

Section 6 provides for the first Colorado representative in the U.S. House of Representatives, and for the replacement of federal territorial officers with State of Colorado officers.

The remainder of the Enabling Act relates to lands. Certain federal lands are donated to the State for enumerated purposes: common schools, state buildings, a penitentiary, and a university. §§ 7–10. Revenues from sale or lease of the common schools' lands must be kept in a perpetual fund for the common schools (*i.e.*, public schools). § 14.

Two forms of land received individualized treatment: the U.S. government did not grant any mineral lands. § 15. The new state could select up to 12 salt springs on federal lands to be transferred to the state. The transfer rights did not apply to privately-owned land. § 11. Five percent of the revenue from federal sales of land within Colorado shall perpetually be given to the state for internal improvements. § 12.

The Enabling Act's careful attention to land ownership was wise. In the American system, the federal government and the states each have sovereignty within their respective spheres. To avoid conflict, it is important to set out in advance whose land is whose.

The boldface headings are by Kopel, and not part of the Enabling Act text.

Territory made a State on equal footing

[Sec. 1] Be *it enacted by the Senate and House of Representatives of the United States of America in Congress assembled,* That the inhabitants of the Territory of Colorado included in the boundaries hereinafter designated be, and they are hereby, authorized to form for themselves out of said Territory, a State government, with the name of the State of Colorado; which State, when formed, shall be admitted into the Union upon equal footing with the original States in all respects whatsoever, as hereinafter provided.

Boundaries

Sec. 2. That the said State of Colorado shall consist of all the territory included within the following boundaries, to wit: Commencing on the thirty-seventh parallel of north latitude where the twenty-fifth meridian of longitude west from Washington crosses the same; thence north, on said meridian, to the forty-first parallel of north latitude; thence along said parallel west to the thirty-second meridian of longitude west from Washington; thence south on said meridian, to the thirty-seventh parallel of north latitude; thence along said thirty-seventh parallel of north latitude, to the place of beginning.

Election for constitutional convention

Sec. 3. That all persons qualified, by law to vote for representatives at first election to the general assembly of said Territory, at the date of the passage of this act, shall be qualified to be elected, and they are hereby authorized to vote for and choose representatives to form a convention under such rules and regulations as the governor of said Territory, the chief justice, and the United States attorney thereof may prescribe; and also to vote upon the acceptance or rejection of such constitution as may be formed by said convention, under such rules and regulations as said convention may prescribe; and the aforesaid representatives to form the aforesaid convention shall be apportioned among the several counties in said Territory in proportion to the vote polled in each of said counties at the last general election as near as may be; and said apportionment shall be made for said Territory by the governor, United States district attorney, and chief justice thereof, or any two of them; and the governor of said Territory shall, by proclamation, order an election of the representatives aforesaid to be held throughout the Territory at such time as shall be fixed by the governor, chief justice, and United States attorney, or any two of them, which proclamation shall be issued within ninety days next after the first day of September, eighteen hundred and seventy-five, and at least thirty days prior to the time of said election; and such election shall be conducted in the same manner as is prescribed by the laws of said Territory regulating elections therein for members of the house of representatives; and the number of members to said convention shall be the same as now constitutes both branches of the legislature of the aforesaid Territory.

Meeting of convention to form state constitution. Constitution must have republican form, no distinction on account of race, and perfect religious toleration. State must disclaim right to unappropriated federal lands. Lands belonging to non-residents may not be taxed at

higher than the rate for residents.

Sec. 4. That the members of the convention thus elected shall meet at the capital of said Territory, on a day to be fixed by said governor, chief justice, and United States attorney, not more than sixty days subsequent to the day of election, which time of meeting shall be contained in the aforesaid proclamation mentioned in the third section of this act, and, after organization, shall declare, on behalf of the people of said Territory, that they adopt the Constitution of the United States; whereupon the said convention shall be, and is hereby, authorized to form a constitution and State government for said Territory:

Provided, That the constitution shall be republican in form, and make no distinction in civil or political rights on account of race or color,

And provided further, That said convention shall provide, by an ordinance irrevocable without the consent of the United States and the people of said State, first, that perfect toleration of religious sentiment shall be secured, and no inhabitant of said State shall ever be molested, in person or property, on account of his or her mode of religious worship; secondly, that the people inhabiting said Territory do agree and declare that they forever disclaim all right and title to the unappropriated public lands lying within said Territory, and that the same shall be and remain at the sole and entire disposition of the United States, and that the lands belonging to citizens of the United States residing without the said State shall never be taxed higher than the lands belonging to residents thereof, and that no taxes shall be imposed by the State on lands or property therein belonging to, or which may hereafter be purchased by the United States.

Constitution to be submitted to a popular vote

Sec. 5. That in case the constitution and State government shall be formed for the people of said Territory of Colorado, in compliance with be limited to the provisions of this act, said convention forming the same shall provide, by ordinance, for submitting said constitution to the people of said State for their ratification or rejection, at an election, to be held at such time, in the month of July, eighteen hundred and seventy-six, and at such places and under such regulations as may be prescribed by said convention, at which election the lawful voters of new State shall vote directly for or against the proposed constitution; and the returns of said election shall be made to the acting governor of the Territory who, with the chief justice and United States attorney of said Territory, or any two of them, shall canvass the same; and if a majority of legal votes shall be cast for said constitution in said proposed State, the said acting governor shall certify the same to the President of the United States, together with a copy of said constitution and ordinances; where-upon it shall be the duty of the President of the United States to issue his proclamation declaring the State admitted into the Union on an equal footing with the original States, without any further action what-ever on the part of Congress.

U.S. Representative; transition for territorial officers

Sec. 6. That until the next general census said State shall be entitled to one Representative in the House of Representatives of the United States, which Representative, together with the governor and State and other officers provided for in said constitution, shall be elected on a day subsequent to the adoption of the constitution, and to be fixed by said constitutional convention; and until said State officers are elected and qualified under the provisions of the constitution, the territorial officers shall continue to discharge the duties of their respective offices.

School lands

Sec. 7. That sections numbered sixteen and thirty-six in every township, and where such sections have been sold or otherwise disposed of by any act of Congress, other lands, equivalent thereto, in legal subdivisions of not more than one quarter-section, and as contiguous as may be, are hereby granted to said State for the support of common schools.

Land for public buildings

Sec. 8. That, provided the State of Colorado shall be admitted into the Union in accordance with the foregoing provisions of this act, fifty entire sections of the unappropriated public lands within said State, to be selected and located by direction of the legislature thereof, and with the approval of the President, on or before the first day of January, eighteen hundred and seventy-eight, shall be, and are hereby, granted, in legal subdivisions of not less than one quarter-section, to said State for the purpose of erecting public buildings at the capital of said State for legislative and judicial purposes, in such manner as the legislature shall prescribe.

Penitentiary

Sec. 9. That fifty other entire sections of land as aforesaid, to be selected and located and with the approval as aforesaid, in legal sub-divisions as aforesaid, shall be, and they are hereby, granted to said State for the purpose of erecting a suitable building for a penitentiary or State prison in the manner aforesaid.

State university

Sec. 10. That seventy-two other sections of land shall be set apart and reserved for the use and support of a State university, to be selected and approved in manner as aforesaid, and to be appropriated and applied as the legislature of said State may prescribe for the purpose named and for no other purpose.

Salt springs

Sec. 11. That all salt-springs within said State, not exceeding twelve in number, with six sections of land adjoining, and as contiguous as may be to each, shall be granted to said State for its use, the said land to be selected by the governor of said State within two years after the admission of the State, and when so selected to be used and disposed of on such terms, conditions, and regulations as the legislature shall direct: *Provided,* That no salt-spring or lands the right whereof is now vested in any individual or individuals, or which hereafter shall be confirmed or adjudged to any individual or individuals, shall by this act be granted to said State.

5% of revenue from certain federal land sales to be given to state for internal improvements

Sec. 12. That five per centum of the proceeds of the sales of agricultural public lands lying within said State which shall be sold by the by the United States subsequent to the admission of said State into the Union, after deducting all the expenses incident to the same, shall be paid to the said State for the purpose of making such internal improvements within said State as the legislature thereof may direct: *Provided,* That this section shall not apply to any lands disposed of under the homestead-laws of the United States,[3] or to any lands now or hereafter reserved for public or other uses.

Unexpended territorial funds to be used to pay for constitutional convention

Sec. 13. That any balance of the appropriations for the legislative expenses of said Territory of Colorado remaining unexpended shall be applied to and used for defraying the expenses of said convention and for the payment of the members thereof, under the same rules and regulations and rates as are now provided by law for the payment of the territorial legislature.

---

[3] The 1862 Homestead Act, 12 Stat. 392, distributed over 80 million acres of federal land to settlers over the next four decades. A settler could acquire up to 160 acres for free, by continuous residence and improvement of the land. Or after six months, a settler could buy the land for $1.25 per acre.

The Colorado Constitution (art. XVIII, § 1) required the state legislature to enact "liberal" homestead laws, for settlers on state-owned lands.

Revenues from sale of school fund lands

Sec. 14. That the two sections of land in each township herein granted for the support of common schools shall be disposed of only at public sale and at a price not less than two dollars and fifty cents per acre, the proceeds to constitute a permanent school-fund, the interest of which to be expended in the support of common schools.

Enabling Act does not apply to mineral lands

Sec. 15. That all mineral-lands shall be excepted from the operation and grants of this act.

The Branson case and the federal land trust for public schools

As sections 7 and 14 of the Enabling Act specify, certain lands were donated to Colorado in trust, for the support of public schools. Until 1996, Colorado's sales or rentals of such lands were conducted to maximize revenue for the schools. As of 1996, Colorado still owned almost 3 million acres of the original 4.6-million-acre grant. That year, Colorado voters amended section 10 of the Colorado Constitution's article IX (education) to change the policy. Now, instead of revenue maximization, the objective was only "reasonable and consistent income over time." Moreover, 300,000 acres were removed as revenue sources, and are to be held as "Stewardship Lands" in perpetuity to "enhance the beauty, natural values, open space, and wildlife habitat."

Three school districts in the San Luis Valley, and two schoolchildren (represented by their parents) in Washington County brought a federal suit claiming that the new lands policy violated the Enabling Act. *Branson School District RE–82 v. Romer,* 161 F.3d 619 (10th Cir. 1998).

The first issue for the Tenth Circuit was whether plaintiffs had standing. They had indeed suffered "injury in fact." As public-school districts and public-school students, they were the beneficiaries of the land trust. As such, they were entitled to the undivided loyalty of the trustees. But the new environmentalist land management policies had given the trustees a competing set of loyalties.

In general, federal court standing doctrine is hostile to entertaining lawsuits against a parent state by one of its political subdivisions. However, the Tenth Circuit ruled that the doctrine was only for individual rights; as intended beneficiaries of the land trust, the school districts were not stripped of standing by the political subdivision doctrine. Later decisions by the Tenth Circuit have narrowed the exemptions to the political subdivision doctrine, and the Tenth Circuit clarified the doctrine in the en banc *Kerr v. Polis* case (discussed in chapter 15).

Finally, the state did not have sovereign immunity under the U.S. Constitution's Eleventh Amendment, which, as interpreted, bars many but not all federal court lawsuit against states. Here, the plaintiffs were seeking only injunctive relief, not monetary damages.

On the merits, the specificity of the language in the Enabling Act did manifest a congressional intent to create an enforceable legal trust.

However, the Tenth Circuit held that the new land management policies were not facially inconsistent with the trust. Managing for a reasonable income stream might amount to the same thing as managing for maximum income. Perhaps the Stewardship Lands could be leased for income. There would only be clear conflict if Colorado eventually reduced its trust lands to only the 300,000 acres in the Stewardship Trust and was unable to generate revenue from them. On the whole, the amendment changing land management policies was not so clearly contrary to the trust created by the Enabling Act as to be illegal.

B. The Colorado Convention and the ratification of the Colorado Constitution

Pursuant to the Enabling Act, the people of Colorado held elections in districts for delegates to the constitutional convention. The people elected 39 delegates—24 Republicans and 15 Democrats.

The delegates convened on December 20, 1875, at 15th and Blake Streets in downtown Denver. The met in the Odd Fellows Hall, above the First National Bank. The convention finished its work by unanimously adopting a proposed constitution on March 14, 1876.

The Colorado Constitution was the longest of any state constitution to date. Today it remains among the longest, thanks to continuing amendment by the people.

The 1876 Colorado Constitution was lengthy because of distrust of legislatures. The Colorado territorial legislature, like legislatures in other states and territories, had wasted public resources by subsidizing corporations, especially railroads. The corporations made big promises about public benefits, but many promises were broken.

Thus, the Constitution repeatedly forbade corporate welfare. To ensure transparency and accountability, the Constitution was replete with anti-corruption provisions, including strict controls on the legislative process.

The original effort to protect taxpayers and to check corruption has continued ever since, via amendments. As will be discussed in later chapters, the legislature, governor, and judiciary have sometimes evaded or nullified the protections against misgovernment. In response, constitutional amendments have, over time, tended to become longer and more detailed, to reduce the possibilities of nullification by hostile interpretation.

The Constitution was immigrant friendly. When the proposed Constitution was sent to the people for ratification, it was printed in English, German, and Spanish. Likewise, the Constitution required that until at least 1900, state statutes be printed in Spanish and German, as well as English, for "inhabitants who speak those languages and who may be unable to read and understand the English language." COLO. CONST. 1876, art. XVIII § 8.[4] The multilingual policy followed the practice of the Colorado territorial legislature.[5] However, very few people requested the Spanish or German versions of the statutes. A century later, long after the trilingual statute printing provision was legally obsolete, it was repealed, as part of textual cleanup. Although Colorado's Constitution is long, it has often been trimmed by the repeal of obsolete provisions.[6]

---

[4] The 1876 Constitution is available at https://legisource.net/wp-content/uploads/2018/01/1876-Colorado-Constitution.pdf.

[5] *See*, e.g., ESTATUTOS REVISADOS DE COLORADO, EN FUERZA DE LEY DESPUES DE LA SUSPENSION DE LA SESION NOVENA DE LA ASEMBLEA LEGISLATIVA (E. T. Wells & Fred. J. Stanton eds., 1872) (Spanish). For a German text, see ALLGEMEINEN GESETZE DES STAATES COLORADO (William M. Clark ed., 1877).

The convention delegate behind the mandate for multilingual publication of statutes was Casimiro Barela, who had sponsored the bill in the territorial legislature for Spanish language statutory publication. JOSÉ E. FERNÁNDEZ, THE BIOGRAPHY OF CASIMIRO BARELA 16-18, 38-42 (A. Gabriel Meléndez trans., 2003) (1911). Barela was elected to the first statehood Senate in 1876 and served as a state senator until defeated in the 1916 election. Id. at xviii–xxix.

[6] Some other obsolete constitutional provisions that have been repealed by voters are: prohibition against duelists holding public office, eight-hour workday exceptions, educational qualifications for voters, denying appropriations for the 1976 Winter Olympics, state employment preferences for veterans of the 1898 Spanish-American War, provisions for the now-abolished offices of constable and of justice of the peace, eligibility to serve in the first general assembly, denying future legislative benefits to railroads that fail to file a certificate accepting the 1876 Constitution, setting the dates for 1877 and 1878 elections, prohibiting voting by people who have resided in Colorado fewer than one year or fewer than three months

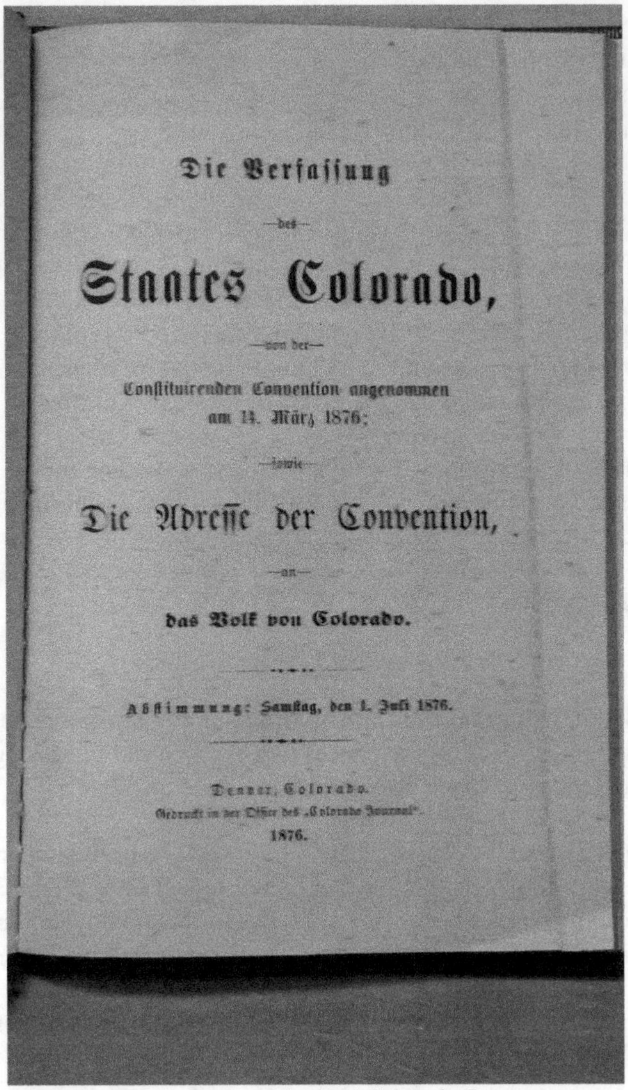

Die Verfassung

—des—

Staates Colorado,

—von der—

Constituirenden Convention angenommen
am 14. März 1876;

—sowie—

Die Adresse der Convention,

—an—

das Volk von Colorado.

Abstimmung: Samstag, den 1. Juli 1876.

Denver, Colorado.
Gedruckt in der Office des „Colorado Journal".
1876.

Figure 2. German edition of the 1876 Colorado Constitution.

Along with the proposed Constitution, the Colorado constitutional convention wrote an *Address to the People* explaining the various provisions of the proposal. The following excerpt addresses issues that have continued to vex the people of Colorado:

[following *Dunn v. Blumstein*, 405 U.S. 330 (1972) (three month minimum residence for voting violates Equal Protection)], limiting the elective franchise to persons at least 21 years old [invalid under U.S. 26th Amendment, ratified 1971], authorizing state elections on whether women should have suffrage, controlling appropriations for the state capitol, establishing the territorial seal as the state seal, consolidating multiple school districts in Denver into a single district, requiring that election ballots identify candidates whose voting records "disregarded voter instruction on term limits" [held to violate Elections Clause of U.S. CONST., art. I, § 4, cl. 1, in *Cook v. Gralike*, 531 U.S. 510 (2001)], allowing property tax exemptions for increases in land value resulting from "the planting of hedges, orchards and forests," prohibiting the importation of "spurious poisonous and drugged liquors," and the constitutional repeal of state alcohol prohibition statutes.

The various repeals are covered in the relevant chapters of this textbook. As a state representative, my father, Jerry Kopel, was responsible for legislative passage of referenda to allow the people to vote on repeal of obsolete provisions.

- legislative evasion of restraints on lawmaking,
- funding for public education,
- welfare for corporations and other special interests, and
- public debt.

The *Address* also discusses women suffrage. Under the Constitution, women could vote in school board elections. The question of broader suffrage would be decided by popular vote. As described in chapter 11 (art. VII, elections), voters rejected women suffrage in 1877, and then adopted it in 1893, with Colorado being the first state to do by popular vote. The Wyoming territory legislature and the Utah territory legislature had adopted female suffrage earlier; the Utah statute was overturned by Congress, as the statute had the effect of increasing the voting power of polygamous Mormons.

The *Address* points out the advantages of the straightforward system for amending the Constitution. Most importantly, with a state constitution, Colorado would enjoy the benefits of self-government, no longer dependent on often corrupt federal territorial government.

Address to the People of Colorado

Legislative Department

The evils of local and special legislation being enormous, the passage of any law not general in its provisions is prohibited—thus saving the State from expenses usually incurred in passing and publishing laws secured by combinations to advance private interests, and to create dangerous monopolies.

To afford protection from hasty legislation, it is required that all bills shall be printed; that only one subject shall be embraced in each bill, which shall be clearly expressed in its title; that it shall be read on three different days in each House before being passed, and that no bill shall be introduced, except for the general expenses of the government, after the first twenty-five days of the session.

We invite your special attention to section twenty-five of the article on legislation, wherein are enumerated the many cases in which the General Assembly is prohibited from passing any local or special laws.

To provide against extravagance we have prohibited the passing of any law giving extra compensation to any public officer, servant, agent or employee, after services rendered, without previous authority of law; nor is any officer of the State to be in any way interested in any contracts or awards by which the legislative and other departments of government are furnished with stationery, printing, paper and fuel.

It is further provided that no appropriation shall be made to any denominational, sectarian or any other institution not under the absolute control of the State.

Attention is also directed to sections twenty-seven and twenty-eight, providing against the corruptions heretofore complained of in legislative bodies, and prescribing punishments therefor.

Education

The maintenance of free public schools, and the gratuitous instruction therein for all children between the ages of six and twenty-one years, is forever guaranteed.

It is declared that the public school fund shall forever remain inviolate and intact; that neither the State, nor any county, city, town or school district shall ever make any appropriation, not pay from any public fund anything in aid of, or to help support, any school or institution of learning of any kind controlled by any church or sectarian denomination whatsoever; that no religious test shall ever be required as a condition for admission into any of the public schools, either as pupil or teacher; that no religious or sectarian dogmas shall ever be taught in any of the schools under the patronage of the State.

Corporations

Probably no subject has come before the Convention causing more anxiety and concern than the troublesome and vexed question pertaining to corporations. The legislatures of other States have, in most cases, been found unequal to the task of preventing abuses and protecting the people from the grasping and monopolizing tendencies of railroads and other corporations. Experience has shown that positive restrictions on the powers of the legislature in relation to these matters are necessary.

To this end we have provided for the wiping out of all dormant and sham corporations claiming special and exclusive privileges. We have denied the General Assembly the power to create corporations, or to extend or enlarge their chartered rights by special legislation, or to make such rights and privileges irrevocable; but in case it shall be found that the exercise of such rights and privileges proves injurious to the people, then the General Assembly shall have power to alter, revoke or annul such charters, when that can be done without injustice to the corporators.

We have declared that railroad corporations shall be liable as common carriers, and that to avail themselves of the benefits of future legislation, they must subject themselves to all the provisions and requirements of the Constitution. We have forbidden the consolidation of parallel and competing lines, and of all unjust and unreasonable discriminations between individual in their business with such corporations.

We have carefully guarded the right of eminent domain, requiring a just compensation to be paid in cash when private property is taken, and have required all foreign corporations, as a condition of their doing business here, to have one or more known places of business, and an agent or representative within the State, upon whom the process of our courts can be served at any and all times.

We have also retained the jurisdiction of our courts in case of consolidation of a corporation with the State with any foreign corporation, over that part of the corporation property with the limits of this State.

We are aware that these provisions do not cover the whole ground, but it must be remembered that while some of sister States have not gone far enough in placing restrictions on the legislative power, others have gone too far, and have had to recede. We have endeavored to take a middle ground, believing it to be more safe, and in the end that it will give more general satisfaction.

Public Indebtedness

By provisions of this article we have prohibited the Legislature from lending the credit of the State in aid of any corporation, either by loan or becoming a subscriber to any stock, or a joint owner with any party, except in case of forfeitures and escheats; also, from assuming any debt or liability of any party, and have also required appropriations to be kept within the limits of our resources, and that no appropriations be made unless assessments are also made sufficient to meet them, and at the same session of the Legislature.

The same principles are applied to counties, cities, towns, and school districts, as far as applicable, with the additional safeguard that to increase the indebtedness which may be contracted by counties, we have endeavored to make a classification that would not cripple counties having small resources, and at the same time restricting those of larger resources to prevent extravagance.

Suffrage and Elections

By this article we have given the right of suffrage to every male person over the age of twenty-one years, imposing such restrictions only as required by the Constitution of the United States, and upon questions pertaining to schools in the several districts of the State no person is denied the right to vote on account of sex. The question of female suffrage having been strongly urged upon the Convention by petitions numerously signed and otherwise, and the Convention thinking it unwise to hazard the adoption of the Constitution upon the decision of this question, but recognizing the right of the people to express their will there-on, have required the General Assembly, at their first session, to submit the question to a direct vote of the people at the next general election thereafter.

Miscellaneous

We have provided for the printing of this Constitution in Spanish as well as laws passed by the General Assembly until the year 1890, thus giving the Spanish-speaking population of the State an equal opportunity of being fully informed on the provisions of the fundamental law, as well as all laws passed in compliance therewith.

We have provided liberally for the amending of the Constitution, thus giving to the people frequent opportunities of changing the organic law when experience and public policy may require it.

Who is there among you that would not rather be a citizen of an independent sovereign State, than a mere settler upon the public lands of the Territory, governed by satraps[7] appointed and removed at pleasure, as best serves the whims and purposes of political rings and cliques—beggars, asking pittance at the gate of the nation; poor wards dependent upon the charity of Congress, living in a sort of penal colony, the Botany Bay[8] of political servitude? Now that the golden opportunity if afforded, shall this state of things longer exist? We confidently believe it will not. Let us cherish, then, this occasion with more than ordinary zeal, actuated by the memories of the past, and inspired by the rewards for us in the future; let us arouse ourselves to the responsibilities of the hour, and, as citizens of a free republic, become, in fact, as well as in name, citizens of the American Union of Sovereign States.

The Vote

The people of the Colorado Territory adopted the Colorado Constitution on July 1, 1876: 15,443 in favor and 4,052 opposed. Voter turnout was low because opposition was almost nonexistent. 2 FRANK HALL, HISTORY OF THE STATE OF COLORADO 328 (1890) (noting that farmers and miners were in peak activity periods).

As in the Illinois vote to adopt a new constitution in 1870, support for Colorado 1876 Constitution was based on: 1. the bipartisan nature of the new constitution's advocates, and 2. dissatisfaction with the current system of government. *See* Jeremy Walling, *Understatement and Development of Illinois Constitutionalism, in* THE CONSTITUTIONALISM OF AMERICAN STATES 411 (George E. Connor & Christopher W. Hammons eds., 2008) ("strong public support was a result of negative public sentiment regarding the state government in general and support for the apparent spirit of bipartisanship under which the document was written"); JANET CORNELIUS, CONSTITUTION MAKING IN ILLINOIS, 1818–1970, at 73, 83 (1972) (two main factors in overwhelming approval of the 1870 Constitution were "dissatisfaction with the performance of the Illinois state government" and the proposed constitution being "a bipartisan document").

---

[7] A provincial governor in ancient Persia. More generally, a subordinate official, usually with a negative connotation.

[8] The British penal colony established in Australia in the late 18th century.

On August 1, 1876, president Ulysses Grant issued the proclamation making Colorado the 38th state. Colorado is called "the Centennial State," but that is not precisely accurate. As Grant's proclamation noted, Colorado became a state in the year "of the independence of the United States of America the one hundred and first." If you start counting from July 4, 1776, the hundredth year ended July 3, 1876; Colorado became a state four weeks later, during the one hundred and first year.

Grant's proclamation observed that the Colorado Constitution complied with all the terms that had been required by the congressional enabling act. These included that "perfect toleration of religious sentiment shall be secured, and no inhabitant . . . shall ever be molested in person or property on account of his or her mode of religious worship."

President Grant's proclamation concluded: "I have herewith set my hand and have caused the seal of the United States to be affixed. Done at the city of Washington this first day of August, in the year of our Lord, 1876, and of the independence of the United States of America the one hundred and first." Ulysses S. Grant, Proclamation 230—Admission of Colorado Into the Union (Aug. 1, 1876), in Gerhard Peters & John T. Woolley, The American Presidency Project. August 1 is celebrated as Colorado Day.

C. Colorado Constitution, schedule

The final part of the Colorado Constitution was the Schedule. It set forth the procedures for transition from territorial government to state government. Like the preamble to the Colorado Constitution and the 19 articles of the original Constitution, the schedule was adopted by the people of Colorado in a popular vote on July 1, 1876. The vote was yes/no on whether to adopt the Colorado Constitution as a whole, containing the preamble, the articles, and the schedule. The Schedule is and always has been part of the Colorado Constitution. It is part of the supreme law of the State, and equal in every respect to the other parts of the Constitution.

Today, many portions of the Schedule no longer have practical application. For example, the assets of the Territory of Colorado have become assets of the State of Colorado. The Schedule's provisions for the transfer of assets have done all the work that they could do. Some sections, however, have present applicability. In particular, section 1 states that all laws of the territory of Colorado remain in effect until repealed. Section 1 appeared in a variety of cases through the early twentieth century, and today it is the reason why the city of Georgetown legally exists.

Section 20 perpetually guarantees the right of the people of Colorado to choose their U.S. presidential electors by direct election. As will be described below, the legislature has nullified this right.

Many provisions of the schedule were applied in cases after statehood, but by the twenty-first century were no longer relevant. These are: Contracts and obligations of the territory and of local governments continue to be enforceable. COLO. CONST., Schedule § 2. Property belonging to the Colorado Territory becomes property of the State of Colorado. § 3. The new legislature must enact legislation carrying out the schedule processes. § 4. Transitions for judges, county officers, and so on are specified. §§ 5–11. The Constitution takes effect upon the president's proclamation of Colorado's entry into the Union. § 12. Procedures for the first elections to U.S. House of Representatives and the Colorado legislature are set forth. §§ 13–18. Any remaining unpaid expenses of the Colorado Convention shall be paid by the legislature. §§ 21–22.

Sched., Preamble

> That no inconvenience may arise by reason of the change in the form of government, it is hereby ordained and declared:

Sched., Section 1. All laws remain till repealed

> That all laws in force at the adoption of this constitution shall, so far as not inconsistent therewith, remain of the same force as if this constitution had not been adopted, until they expire by their own limitation or are altered or repealed by the general assembly; and all rights, actions, prosecutions, claims and contracts of the territory of Colorado, counties, individuals or bodies corporate (not inconsistent therewith) shall continue as if the form of government had not been changed and this constitution adopted.

Section 1 continues to have legal effect in the twenty-first century. The town of Georgetown operates pursuant to its 1868 charter from the territorial legislature; the official title of the town's laws is "Territorial Charter and Municipal Code of the Town of Georgetown, Colorado." If the schedule somehow were no longer in legal effect, Georgetown would have no legal existence, and would have to start over with a process of incorporation. The validity of the past and present action of the Georgetown government would be in serious doubt. Anyone who contends that the schedule has no continuing legal effect should be prepared to explain on what date the schedule ceased being part of the Constitution, and the government of Georgetown therefore ceased to have any legal authority.

Early twentieth century cases

A 1912 constitutional amendment eliminated the phrase "justices of the peace" from article VI, § 1 (judicial department). Did the amendment mean that the office of justice of the peace had ceased to exist in Colorado? Certainly not, said the Colorado supreme court. The office of justice of the peace had been created by territorial statute. The territorial law had never been changed or repealed. So justices of the peace could continue to perform their duties. *W.H. Courtright Pub. Co. v. Bray*, 67 Colo. 588, 189 P. 30 (1920).

A few years before, section 1 had been discussed in a challenge to a state statute allowing the state board of equalization to raise the assessed valuations that had been made by county assessors. Assessment in Denver were notoriously low, and the city was plainly shirking its duties to pay its fair share of state taxes. Could the legislature expand or contract the duties of the county constitutional officers who are named in article XIV? A 4–3 majority of the Colorado supreme court held in the affirmative. As part of the discussion, the court observed that that "the constitutional schedule continued such duties [of county officers] in force 'until they were altered or repealed by the General Assembly.'" *State Bd. of Equalization v. Bi-Metallic Inv. Co.*, 56 Colo. 512, 514–15, 138 P. 1010 (1914). The U.S. supreme court, in a unanimous opinion by justice Oliver Wendell Holmes, held that the broad imposition of a valuation increases in Denver did not violate any of the parties' due process rights. *Bi-Metallic Inv. Co. v. State Bd. of Equalization,* 239 U.S. 141 (1915).

Alferd Packer

In 1885, the court heard a criminal appeal by the infamous Colorado cannibal Alferd Packer. *Packer v. People,* 8 Colo. 361 (1885). Back in the winter of 1874, when Colorado was still a territory, Packer was part of a six-man expedition that became lost in the San Juan Mountains in Hinsdale County. Only Packer came out alive; he confessed to having survived by eating the flesh of another member of the party. He escaped from jail, fled, and was recaptured in 1883. HAROLD SCHECHTER, MAN-EATER: THE LIFE AND LEGEND OF AN AMERICAN CANNIBAL (Amazon Pub. 2015). Thereupon he was tried and convicted of premeditated murder. *Packer*, 8 Colo. at 362.

The Colorado supreme court held that Packer could not be convicted of murder because the state legislature had changed the murder statute in a way that made it inapplicable to Packer. *Id.*

at 363. However, at a new trial, Packer could be charged with voluntary manslaughter. The territorial legislature had enacted a statute against manslaughter, and state legislature had not amended the manslaughter statute. The territorial manslaughter statute was still good law pursuant to the Colorado Constitution Schedule. And because the manslaughter statute had no statute of limitations, Packer could be prosecuted in 1886 for what he had allegedly done in 1874. *Id.* at 364.

Moreover, section 2 of the schedule specifically provided that crimes committed before statehood could still be prosecuted after statehood. *Id.*

According to the *Packer* opinion:

> The first and second sections of the Schedule to the Constitution of Colorado are necessary savings clauses and proper to be inserted in a constitution; for, while it is not the business of the framers of a constitution to prepare and submit to the people a code of laws, it is their duty to preserve existing law until the legislature, the proper law-making body, can be convened to amend or repeal such existing laws as they deem proper, and to prepare such new laws as they deem necessary for the benefit of the new state.

Id.

Sched., Section 2. Contracts, recognizances, indictments

> That all recognizances, obligations and all other instruments entered into or executed before the admission of the state, to the territory of Colorado, or to any county, school district or other municipality therein, or any officer thereof, and all fines, taxes, penalties and forfeitures due or owing to the territory of Colorado, or any such county, school district or municipality, or officer; and all writs, prosecutions, actions and causes of action, except as herein otherwise provided, shall continue and remain unaffected by the change of the form of government. All indictments which shall have been found, or may hereafter be found, and all informations which shall have been filed, or may hereafter be filed, for any crime or offense committed before this constitution takes effect, may be proceeded upon as if no change had taken place, except as otherwise provided in the constitution.

The Colorado Constitution, which entered into effect on August 1, 1876, provides that a grand jury shall consist of 12, of whom nine shall be necessary to issue an indictment. A grand jury indictment issued earlier in the year, when a territorial statue provided for different numbers of grand jurors, was still valid. *Wilson v. People*, 3 Colo. 325 (1877).[9]

Sched., Section 3. Territorial property vests in state

> That all property, real and personal, and all moneys, credits, claims and choses in action, belonging to the territory of Colorado at the adoption of this constitution, shall be vested in and become the property of the state of Colorado.

---

[9] The opinion by chief justice Thatcher could have been better written. It mistakenly cites the Grand Jury section as being part of section 1 of the Schedule, when in fact the section is in section 2. The opinion cites the general continuity principle of Schedule section 1, but omits discussion of section 2, which specifically provides for continuity in indictments.

Sched., Section 4. Duty of general assembly

> The general assembly shall pass all laws necessary to carry into effect the provisions of this constitution.

You wouldn't think this would have to be said, but it was necessary. Despite the section 4 order, the general assembly does not always pass the laws necessary to effectuate the Constitution. Laws to de-effectuate portions of the Constitution are sometimes enacted.

Sched., Section 5. Supreme and district courts transition

> Whenever any two of the judges of the supreme court of the state elected or appointed under the provisions of this constitution shall have qualified in their office, the causes theretofore pending in the supreme court of the territory, and the papers, records and proceedings of said court, and the seal and other property pertaining thereto, shall pass into the jurisdiction and possession of the supreme court of the state; and until so superseded the supreme court of the territory and the judges thereof shall continue with like powers and jurisdiction as if this constitution had not been adopted. Whenever the judge of the district court of any district elected or appointed under the provisions of this constitution, shall have qualified in his office, the several causes theretofore pending in the district court of the territory, within any county in such district, and the records, papers and proceedings of said district court, and the seal and other property pertaining thereto shall pass into the jurisdiction and possession of the district court of the state, for such county, and until the district courts of the territory shall be superseded in manner aforesaid, the said district courts and the judges thereof shall continue with the same jurisdiction and powers to be exercised in the same judicial districts respectively as heretofore constituted under the laws of the territory.

When a territorial judge (with a particular geographic jurisdiction) became a state district judge (for a partially overlapping region), the criminal prosecution against a defendant within the old and new courts' jurisdictions could continue seamlessly. *Wilson v. People*, 3 Colo. 325 (1877).

Sched., Section 6. Judges, district attorneys

> The terms of office of the several judges of the supreme and district courts and the district attorneys of the several judicial districts first elected under this constitution, shall commence from the day of filing their respective oaths of office in the office of the secretary of state.

Sched., Section 7. Seals of supreme and district courts

> Until otherwise provided by law, the seals now in use in the supreme and district courts of this territory are hereby declared to be the seals of the supreme and district courts respectively of the state.

Sched., Section 8. Probate courts, county courts

> Whenever this constitution shall go into effect, the books, records, papers and proceedings of the probate court in each county, and all causes and matters of administration pending therein, shall pass into the jurisdiction and possession of the county court of the same county, and the said county court shall proceed to final decree or judgment, order or other determination, in the said several matters and causes, as the said probate court might have done if this constitution had not been adopted. And until the election of the county judges provided for in this constitution, the probate judges shall act as judges of the county courts within their respective counties, and the seal of the probate court in each county shall be the seal of the county court therein until the said court shall have procured a proper seal.

Sections 8 and 9 show that county judges are county officers. Accordingly, pursuant to a (later-repealed) constitutional section, the legislature could not pass a law providing them with a new source of compensation. *In re Compensation of County Judges*, 18 Colo. 272, 32 P. 549 (1893).

Sched., Section 9. References to probate courts and judges apply to county courts and judges

> The terms "Probate Court" or "Probate Judge", whenever occurring in the statutes of Colorado territory, shall, after the adoption of this constitution, be held to apply to the county court or county judge, and all laws specially applicable to the probate court in any county, shall be construed to apply to and be in force as to the county court in the same county, until repealed.

Upon adoption of the Constitution, county courts were given all the powers that had belonged to the territorial probate courts. *Keystone Min. Co. v. Gallagher*, 5 Colo. 23 (1879). Later, by constitutional amendment (art. VI, § 9), probate jurisdiction was transferred to district courts.[10]

Sched., Section 10. County and precinct officers

> All county and precinct officers, who may be in office at the time of the adoption of this constitution, shall hold their respective offices for the full time for which they may have been elected, and until such time as their successors may be elected and qualified in accordance with the provisions of this constitution, and the official bonds of all such officers shall continue in full force and effect as though this constitution had not been adopted.

Sched., Section 11. Vacancies in county offices

> All county offices that may become vacant during the year eighteen hundred and seventy-six by the expiration of the term of the persons elected to said offices, shall be filled at the general election on the first Tuesday in October in the year eighteen hundred and seventy-six, and, except county commissioners, the persons so elected shall hold their respective offices for the term of one year.

[10] Except in Denver, where the later-adopted article XX authorizes the City and County to creates its own probate courts. The revised text of article VI recognizes the constitutional status of Denver's probate courts.

Sched., Section 12. Constitution takes effect on president's proclamation

> The provisions of this constitution shall be in force from the day on which the president of the United States shall issue his proclamation declaring the state of Colorado admitted into the Union; and the governor, secretary, treasurer, auditor and superintendent of public instruction of the territory of Colorado shall continue to discharge the duties of their respective offices after the admission of the state into the Union, until the qualification of the officers elected or appointed under the state government; and said officers, for the time they may serve, shall receive the same compensation as the state officers shall by law be paid for like services.

Thus, the Colorado Constitution came into force the moment that president Grant signed the proclamation of statehood, on Aug. 1, 1876.

Sched., Section 13. First election, contest

> In case of a contest of election between candidates, at the first general election under this constitution, for judges of the supreme, district or county courts, or district attorneys, the evidence shall be taken in the manner prescribed by territorial law; and the testimony so taken shall be certified to the secretary of state, and said officer, together with the governor and attorney-general, shall review the testimony and determine who is entitled to the certificate of election.

If there were post-election contests for the 1876 elections, the territorial laws about election contests would govern. Section 13's rule is implicit in section 1's general rule, about continuity of law. Given the importance of elections, it was prudent to specifically state the continuity of law for election contests.

The next four sections also provide in continuity of territorial election laws, for the 1876 elections.

Sched., Section 14. First state officer election, canvass

> The votes at the first general election under this constitution for the several officers provided for in this constitution who are to be elected at the first election shall be canvassed in the manner prescribed by the territorial law for canvassing votes for like officers. The votes cast for the judges of the supreme and district courts and district attorneys shall be canvassed by the county canvassing board in the manner prescribed by the territorial law for canvassing the votes for members of the general assembly; and the county clerk shall transmit the abstracts of votes to the secretary of the territory acting as secretary of state, under the same regulations as are prescribed by law for sending the abstracts of votes for territorial officers; and the aforesaid acting secretary of state, auditor, treasurer, or any two of them, in the presence of the governor, shall proceed to canvass the votes, under the regulations of sections thirty-five and thirty-six of chapter twenty-eight of the Revised Statutes of Colorado Territory.

Sched., Section 15. State senators, representatives, districts

> Senators and members of the house of representatives shall be chosen by the qualified electors of the several senatorial and representative districts as

established in this constitution until such districts shall be changed by law; and thereafter by the qualified electors of the several districts as the same shall be established by law.

Sched., Section 16. Congressional election, canvass

The votes cast for representatives in congress at the first election held under this constitution shall be canvassed and the result determined in the manner provided by the laws of the territory for the canvass of votes for delegate in congress.

Sched., Section 17. General assembly restrictions removed for first session

The provision of the constitution that no bill, except the general appropriation bill introduced in either house after the first twenty-five days of the session shall become a law, shall not apply to the first session of the general assembly; but no bill introduced in either house at the first session of the general assembly after the first fifty days thereof shall become a law.

Colorado's article V (legislative power) has always had constitutional rules against general assembly bills introduced late in a session. Section 17 provided an exemption to the standard 25-day rule in the 1876 Constitution. For the first session only, bills could be introduced in the first 50 days of a session.

In the 1876 Constitution, article V had originally limited legislative sessions to 40 days, except for the first session of the first general assembly, which had no time limit.

Sched., Section 18. First general election, canvass

A copy of the abstracts of the votes cast at the first general election held under this constitution shall by the county clerks of the several counties be returned to the secretary of the territory immediately after the canvass of said votes in their several counties; and the secretary, auditor and treasurer of the territory, or any two of them, shall on the twenty-fifth day after the election, meet at the seat of government and proceed to canvass the votes cast for members of the general assembly and determine the result thereof.

Sched., Section 19. Presidential electors 1876

The general assembly shall, at their first session, immediately after the organization of the two houses and after the canvass of the votes for officers of the executive department, and before proceeding to other business, provide by act or joint resolution for the appointment by said general assembly of electors in the electoral college, and such joint resolution or the bill for such enactment may be passed without being printed or referred to any committee, or read on more than one day in either house, and shall take effect immediately after the concurrence of the two houses therein, and the approval of the governor thereto shall not be necessary.

For the 1876 presidential election only, the new general assembly will choose the presidential electors. The bill to choose the electors does not need to follow some of the standard rules of article V, such as the requirement for reading on three separate days in each house.

Although article II of the U.S. Constitution clearly allows state legislature to choose presidential electors, the last time any state legislature actually exercised the power was in the 1876 presidential election.

Thereafter, each state's presidential electors have always been chosen by direct vote of the people. Colorado is the only state whose constitution guarantees the right of the people to direct election of the presidential electors, pursuant to section 20.

Sched., Section 20. Presidential electors after 1876

> The general assembly shall provide that after the year eighteen hundred and seventy-six the electors of the electoral college shall be chosen by direct vote of the people.

Throughout this book, Colorado constitutional provisions that have been in practice nullified by one or more branches of the state government are marked with underlining.

When the Colorado Convention met, it was clear that statehood would be achieved before the 1876 presidential election. States have great latitude in how to choose presidential electors. "Each State shall appoint, in such Manner as the Legislature thereof may direct, a Number of Electors . . . " U.S. CONST., art. II, § 1, cl. 2. In presidential elections, state legislatures have sometimes picked the electors themselves, and sometimes left the selection of electors to a direct vote of the people of the state, either at large or in districts. Direct election is the practice in all states today.

According to the Colorado Constitution Schedule, Colorado's presidential electors for 1876 would be chose by the state legislature. Schedule § 19. Thereafter, section 20 provides that Colorado's presidential electors must be chosen by vote of the people.

The 1876 legislature choose three Republican electors, who helped Republican Rutherford B. Hayes defeat Democrat Samuel Tilden; Hayes won 185 electoral votes to Tilden's 184. Had the electors been chose by the Colorado voters in 1876, the election probably would have had the same result, since Republicans narrowly won most of the statewide elections that year.[11]

Until 2019, the general assembly scrupulously obeyed section 20. Then in 2019, the general assembly adopted the National Popular Vote Compact. Once the compact gains the adherence of states with 270 or more electoral votes, Colorado electors will not be chosen by direct vote of the people.[12]

---

[11] The election was held Oct. 3, 1876. Here are the results:
Governor: John Routt (R) 14,154. Bela Hughes (D) 13,316.
Lt. governor: Lafayette Head (R) 14,191. Michael Beshoar (D) 13,093. Republican lieutenant governor Lafayette Head would be the first and last elected state official in Colorado named "Lafayette."
Secretary of state: William Clark (R) 14,582. James Smith (D) 12,843.
Auditor: David Crawford (R) 12,843. J.F. Benedict (D) 13,295.
State treasurer: George Corning (R) 14,038. Thomas Field (D) 13,310.
Attorney general: A.J. Sampson (R) 13,310. G.Q. Richmond (D) 13,182.
Supt. public instruction: Joseph Shattuck (R) 14,304. G.B. Groesbeck (D) 12,473.

Besides winning the auditor race, Democrats also won some of the seats on the Colorado supreme court.

Republicans won the state legislature. The Senate had 26 members and the House 49 members. Quickly convening, the new state legislature chose three Republican presidential electors. For U.S. Senators (who were chosen by state legislatures until the U.S. Seventeenth Amendment was ratified in 1913), the legislature picked Republicans Henry Teller and Jerome Chaffee.

[12] The system goes into operation once states with a collective total of 270 electoral votes join the compact. However, "No State shall, without the Consent of Congress, . . . enter into any Agreement or Compact with another State, or with a foreign Power . . ." U.S. CONST., art. I § 10, cl. 3 (Compact Clause). Modern

Instead, the Colorado secretary of state will appoint Colorado's presidential electors. The competing slates of electors pledged to the Democratic, Republican, Libertarian, Green, etc., presidential candidates will still be chosen by the parties, pursuant to party rules. The Colorado secretary of state will appoint a particular slate of electors based on the secretary's determination, in conjunction with secretaries in other compact states, about which candidate won the most popular votes in all the compact states combined.

Whatever the policy merits of the NPV, it violates section 20. Colorado's electors must be chosen by "direct vote." The only people who can possibly cast a direct vote for Colorado presidential electors are Colorado voters.

When New Yorkers voted for president in 2016, the majority chose a slate of 29 New Yorkers who were pledged to Hillary Clinton. When Coloradans voted in 2016, they chose a slate of 9 Coloradans pledged to Hillary Clinton. Coloradans and New Yorkers cannot vote for the same slate of electors. The individual electors in each state are different from the electors in every other state.

In the 2020 general election, there was a referendum on the National Popular Vote Compact (Proposition 113). The voters chose to retain the statute entering into the NPV compact by 52% to 48%. However, a statute cannot trump the Constitution. The proper approach for Colorado NPV advocates would be to propose the constitutional repeal of section 20. Given the closeness of the vote on the NPV statute, it is not certain that Coloradoans would have supported relinquishing one of their constitutional rights if the constitutional question had been presented.

Under the Colorado Constitution, the National Popular Vote system is of plainly unconstitutional. The system deprives the people of Colorado of their express constitutional right to choose their own presidential electors by direct vote.

However, an 1892 U.S. supreme court case held that state legislatures have plenary power to determine the mode of choosing the electors of their state. In dicta, the court said that not even a state constitution could constrain a state legislature's power. Although the opinion did not mention Colorado's section 20, the opinion can be read as implicitly nullifying it. *McPherson v. Blacker,* 146 U.S. 1 (1892).

Further reading: David B. Kopel & Hunter Hovenga, *The National Popular Vote Violates the Colorado Constitution*, DENVER L. REVIEW FORUM (22-Sept.-2020).

Sched., Section 21. Expenses of Convention

> The general assembly shall have power at their first session to provide for the payment of the expenses of this convention if any there be then remaining unpaid.

Sched., Section 22. Recognizances, bonds, payable to People continue

> All recognizances, bail bonds, official bonds and other obligations or undertakings, which have been, or at any time before the admission of the state shall be made or entered into, and expressed to be payable to the people of the territory of Colorado, shall continue in full force notwithstanding the change in the form of government, and any breach thereof, whenever occurring, may after the admission of the state be prosecuted, in the name of the people of the state.

---

judicial interpretation still requires states get congressional permission for foreign compacts. But the need for permission for domestic compacts has been nullified by Supreme Court precedent. *U.S. Steel Corp. v. Multistate Tax Commission*, 434 U.S. 452, 471 (1978) (domestic state compacts only need congressional approval if they "encroach upon the supremacy of the United States"). Because the Supremacy Clause (U.S. CONST. art. VI, cl. 2) already forbids state violations of federal supremacy, the domestic Compact Clause has no additional legal effect.

D. Colorado Constitution, preamble

> We, the people of Colorado, with profound reverence for the Supreme Ruler of the Universe, in order to form a more independent and perfect government; establish justice; insure tranquility; provide for the common defense; promote the general welfare and secure the blessings of liberty to ourselves and our posterity, do ordain and establish this constitution for the "State of Colorado".

As in the U.S. Constitution's preamble, the term "more perfect" means "better"—that is, closer to perfection.

The Colorado preamble mostly tracks the U.S. preamble, with two differences. The U.S. preamble's first purpose is "to form a more perfect Union," whereas Colorado's is "to form a more independent and perfect government."

Second, the Colorado preamble states the people's "reverence for the Supreme Ruler of the Universe." The Colorado Convention spent considerable time debating whether to mention God in the Preamble. Some Protestants and Catholics favored doing so, whereas advocates of strict separation of church and state were opposed. The enacted language is the compromise.

E. Article I. Boundaries and the Early History of Colorado

> The boundaries of the state of Colorado shall be as follows: Commencing on the thirty-seventh parallel of north latitude, where the twenty-fifth meridian of longitude west from Washington crosses the same; thence north, on said meridian, to the forty-first parallel of north latitude; thence along said parallel, west, to the thirty-second meridian of longitude west from Washington; thence south, on said meridian, to the thirty-seventh parallel of north latitude; thence along said thirty-seventh parallel of north latitude to the place of beginning.

Why is longitude measured from D.C.?

Colorado's southern boundary is the 37th parallel of latitude, and the northern boundary is the 41st parallel of latitude.[13] The zero parallel of latitude is the Equator, because the Equator is the center plane of the earth's axis of rotation.

The eastern and western longitude boundaries are expressed in degrees west of Washington, D.C. This seems odd to a modern reader; today, everyone counts longitude from Greenwich, England, which is longitude zero. In modern terms, Colorado's eastern boundary is the 102nd meridian west (of Greenwich, England), and Colorado's western boundary is the 109th meridian.[14]

Following a proposal adopted at an 1884 conference, people and governments started switching to Greenwich as the prime meridian. Before that, different peoples used different prime

---

[13] The 40th parallel is Baseline Avenue in Boulder. The 39th parallel is a little south of Grand Junction. The 38th parallel is La Junta to just north of Telluride.

[14] 103rd meridian: approximately the western boundaries of Colorado counties that border Kansas. 104th: approximately the western borders the next group of counties, moving westward from the Kansas line. 105th: Denver. 106th: Fairplay-Salida-Conejos. 107th: Pagosa Springs. 108th: a little west of Durango.

To be precise, the Colorado meridians, as measured from Greenwich, England, are 102 degrees and 3 minutes, and 109 degrees and 3 minutes.

meridians (the zero degree of longitude). Often, a given country's prime meridian would be set in an important location of the country.

When Congress passed the Colorado Enabling Act in 1875, there was no generally accepted prime meridian. So, for clarity, the Enabling Act specifies boundaries based on degrees west of Washington, D.C.

In 1919, New Mexico brought a suit pointing out that Colorado-New Mexico border in some areas did not really follow the 37th parallel. The 1868 survey that had been used to establish the border, and which was accepted by New Mexico when it joined the Union in 1912, was incorrect. A more recent survey showed that certain Colorado lands were south of the 37th parallel. The supreme court ruled that the 1868 survey line had been long established and relied on by everyone, including New Mexico. It was too late to adjust state boundaries. *New Mexico v. Colorado*, 267 U.S. 30 (1925).

Why does Colorado have its size and shape?

Colorado's boundaries, like Wyoming's, are a perfect rectangle. Colorado got its shape because of the *equality of states*. As section 1 of the 1875 Enabling Act provides, Colorado would be admitted on an "equal footing" with the other states. All new states admitted to the Union enjoy exactly as much sovereignty as do the original thirteen.

To implement the principle of the equality of states, Congress has followed the urging of Thomas Jefferson to make the size of new states as nearly equal as possible. Initially, this was difficult. England's 1606 Royal Charter to the Virginia Company, and 1620 Royal Charter to the New England Company had purported to cover all land from the Atlantic to the Pacific. The future northern Colorado was part of the New England Colony, and southern Colorado part of the Virginia Colony. Obviously, no Englishman had the ability to enforce any claim so far inland from the Atlantic strip of settlements.

The 13 original states had complicated and sometimes overlapping boundaries, derived from charters granted by English monarchs. For example, what we today call "Illinois" belonged to Virginia. By 1800, all of the original states with western land claims had ceded those claims to the United States.

New states such as Kentucky and Tennessee were in the second row towards the interior. Their boundaries were usually derived from the old states from whence they had sprung: Kentucky from Virginia, Tennessee from North Carolina, Alabama from Georgia, and so on. As the new nation moved westward, into areas where no original state had continuing claims, creating boundaries became more flexible, and the principle of territorial equality of states was easier to apply.

West of the Mississippi, there is much less rain and water, so there were few mighty rivers that had to be natural boundaries for states. Many western states are approximately equal in height, breadth, or both. MARK STEIN, HOW THE STATES GOT THEIR SHAPES TOO: THE PEOPLE BEHIND THE BORDERLINES 54–55 (2011). Colorado and Wyoming are the perfection of the principle of territorial equality, being almost exactly the same size.

Four flags over Colorado

As of about 1700, Utes controlled most of Colorado west of the continental divide, as they had for centuries. The Jicarilla Apache held the area around the San Luis Valley. On the eastern plains, there were Pawnee in the northeast, the Plains Apache in the east central, and the Comanche in the southeast. The Apache had migrated from subarctic Canada and established themselves in

Colorado around 1525. They were driven off the plains by the Comanche in the first half of the eighteenth century.[15]

By 1830, warfare had further altered the possession of the land. The San Luis Valley was predominantly in the hands of the Utes. The northeastern and north central plains were now held by the Southern Arapaho and Southern Cheyenne, who had taken them from the Comanche. The Cheyenne and Arapahoe had come the upper Great Lakes area and had moved to escape the bullying of the Sioux, who eventually conquered vast parts of the upper Midwest.

The southeast, below the Arkansas River, was the territory of the Comanche and their Kiowa allies. Tribes often crossed into other areas for hunting expeditions. For example, the Ute hunted as far east as Oklahoma.[16] The plains tribes hunted in the mountains. Intertribal warfare was endemic.

In Colorado—as everywhere—the ability to exercise sovereignty over land has depended on the ability to take or hold that land by force. Whereas the Apache had held the Colorado plains for about two centuries, and the Comanche for about one century, the Arapaho and Cheyenne would be able to maintain their plains ascendancy for only a few decades, as other powers were beginning to cast an eye on Colorado.

Between 1803 and 1850, the United States obtained claims to the future Colorado territory from France, Spain, Mexico, and Texas. All of Colorado had for a time been part of New Spain.

France's colonization of the Louisiana colony began with the land claim asserted by explorer René-Robert Cavelier, Sieur de La Salle ("La Salle") in 1682. The Louisiana never proved profitable to France; the expenses of territorial administration, based in New Orleans, and military garrisons outweighed the trading revenue.

France conveyed Louisiana to Spain in the 1762 Treaty of Fontainebleau. Spain secretly retroceded Louisiana to France in 1800 in the Third Treaty of San Ildefonso. At the time, American tensions with France were high. The United Kingdom and France were at war, and neither nation respected the neutrality of American merchant shipping. From 1798 to 1800, the U.S. was fighting an undeclared naval war with France, the Quasi-War. The Convention of 1800, signed on September 30, brought the end of the Quasi-War.

Figure 1. Cross of Burgundy, major flag of New Spain.

Yet the very next day, on October 1, France reacquired Louisiana in the Treaty of San Ildefonso. The French threat in the Atlantic Ocean had been replaced by one in the American mainland. At the time, the terms of the treaty were secret, but the retrocession of Louisiana became known when the French flag and French officials returned to the Louisiana.

The American Revolution had ended with the 1783 Treaty of Paris, by which Great Britain recognized the independence

Figure 2. Fleur de Lis, major flag of New France.

[15] THE GALE ENCYCLOPEDIA OF NATIVE AMERICAN TRIBES 149, 258–59 (Sharon Malinowski ed., 1998).

[16] The map of Ute territory in the Ute Indian Museum in Montrose, Colorado, depicts the widest range of Ute hunting expeditions as if it were the same as the area over which the Ute were the dominant tribe.

of the United States, with territory stretching from the Atlantic seaboard to the Mississippi River. If a foreign power could block use of the Mississippi, and of the port of New Orleans, development of the western U.S. would be impossible.

Spain, which had been the dominant global power in the sixteenth century, was in obvious decline, and had not seemed to pose much danger to the new United States. France, however, was ruled by the military dictator Napoleon Bonaparte, who was rapidly gobbling up Europe. At its height, Napoleon's empire extended from the Atlantic to Moscow.

President Thomas Jefferson dispatched envoys to Paris to negotiate for the purchase of New Orleans, or at least enough of it to be used by American shipping. Although Jefferson was no admirer of Great Britain, Jefferson believed that if New Orleans remained under exclusive French control, the United States would inevitably have to ally with Great Britain in war against France.

Astonishing everyone, Napoleon offered to sell the entire Louisiana to the United States. First, he needed the money. More importantly, he viewed Louisiana as impossible to hold against the superior British navy. Better to sell it to the neutral Americans than to have it taken by the British.

The 1803 Louisiana Purchase doubled the size of the United States. The Colorado portion of the Louisiana Purchase is approximately the land north of the Arkansas River, and east of the Continental Divide. Treaty Between the United States of America and the French Republic, Fr.-U.S., Apr. 30, 1803, 8 Stat. 200.

The remainder of Colorado was part of the Spanish colony of New Spain. In 1819, the Adams-Onís Treaty was negotiated by U.S. secretary of state (and future president) John Quincy Adams and Spanish foreign minister Luis de Onís y González-Vara. Treaty of Amity, Settlement, and Limits, Between the United States of America and His Catholic Majesty, Spain-U.S., art. 3, Feb. 22, 1819, 8 Stat. 252. Besides providing for Spain's sale of Florida to the United States, the treaty also ascertained the boundary in Colorado between the U.S. (the Louisiana Purchase) and New Spain. The U.S. was north of the Arkansas River, and New Spain was to the south. Previously, Spain had contended that its territory included the northern drainage of the Arkansas. THOMAS J. NOEL, COLORADO: A HISTORICAL ATLAS 56 (2015).

Figure 3. First flag of the United States of Mexico, 1821–23.

The United States of Mexico won its independence from Spain in 1821. The same year, Americans led by Stephen Austin began settling in Texas, a region in northern Mexico. The region included southeastern and southcentral Colorado. Nearly all the settlement in Texas was in the Texan southeast, not too far from New Orleans. Most of Texas—like much of the rest of Mexico and the future state of New Mexico—remained under the control of the Comanches, who for many years blocked attempted expansions by Spain, France, Mexico, Texas, and the United States. *See* PEKKA HÄMÄLÄINEN, THE COMANCHE EMPIRE (2008).

Soon, the constitutional republic in Mexico was overturned by a military dictatorship. General Antonio de Padua María Severino López de Santa Anna y Pérez de Lebrón obliterated the right of self-government that republican Mexico had guaranteed to Texan settlers. Santa Anna did the same to the rights that had been guaranteed to all Mexicans by the 1824 Constitution of the United States of Mexico.

The Texans sent Stephen Austin to Mexico City to ask that Texas be admitted to the Mexican Union as a state and that Texans' rights under the Mexican Constitution be respected. The dictatorship imprisoned him for four months. All the Texans' peaceful petitions for redress of grievances were met with contempt.

Figure 4. The Gonzalez flag that began the Texan War of Independence.

Several Mexican states revolted against the dictatorship. To the north, the Texan War of Independence began at Gonzales, Texas. The dictatorship tried to seize a small cannon that the settlers had used to scare away Indians.

The Texans were armed with knives, pistols, and rifles. Their flag dared, "Come and Take It." Santa Anna's army tried, then retreated. The 1836 Texas Declaration of Rights included principles that had been stated by earlier U.S. state constitutions, and which would also appear in later ones, such as Colorado's. For example:

> All political power is inherent in the people, and all free governments are founded on their authority and instituted for their benefit; and they have at all times an inalienable right to alter their government in such manner as they may think proper.

This restates the second paragraph of the United States Declaration of Independence.

The Republic of Texas won independence in 1836. The boundaries of Texas were the Arkansas River on northeast, and the Rio Grande River on the west and south. Texas also claimed the land stretching north in-between the headwaters of those rivers: a strip of central Colorado and southern Wyoming. THOMAS J. NOEL, COLORADO: A HISTORICAL ATLAS 56 (2015).

Following a crushing defeat on April 17, 1836, at the Battle of San Jacinto, the Mexican dictatorship gave up trying to conquer Texas, but it refused to acknowledge Texan independence or Texan boundaries.

Figure 5. Republic of Texas flag, now the statehood flag.

After 1836, Colorado west of the Rio Grande (approximately the western quarter of the future state) was indisputably Mexican. Central and southeast Colorado had both Mexican and Texan claims. In practice, sovereignty over all of Colorado belonged to the Indians who lived there. American, Texan, or Mexican holdings in Colorado amounted, at most, to some small settlements or trading posts, and occasional forts.

The most notable American settlement was Bent's Fort, a trading post in southeastern Colorado. It carried on a thriving trade with the plains Indian tribes. DAVID LAVENDER, BENT'S FORT 15 (1954).

The long-running wars of the Cheyenne-Arapahoe alliance against the Comanche-Kiowa alliance ended with an 1840 peace treaty. It set the Arkansas River as the boundary, with the Cheyenne and Arapahoe on the north side. The treaty allowed for free trade and free travel. So

Bent's Fort flourished even more as a commerce center for buffalo robes, firearms, horses, and many other goods.[17]

The Utes, of western Colorado, were not parties to the 1840 treaty, and their warfare with the tribes continued. The Pawnees, who were at perpetual war with all other tribes, and who ranged into northeastern Colorado, were also not part of the peace treaty. Decades later, the U.S. army would learn to employ Pawnee scouts in warfare against other tribes.

In 1845, Texas chose to join the United States. Because Santa Anna refused to accept Texan boundary claims, the Mexican War began. It lasted until 1848 and ended when outnumbered U.S. forces captured Mexico City.

Although some Americans wanted to annex all of Mexico, U.S. president James K. Polk opted for milder terms. In the 1848 peace Treaty of Guadalupe Hidalgo, Santa Anna accepted Texan sovereignty and Texans' choice to join the United States. Further, he sold off a large portion of Mexico's neglected far north. This included the western quarter of Colorado—the area west of the Rio Grande River and its headwaters.

As of 1848, all of Colorado belonged to the United States or to the State of Texas. Or at least the U.S. government and the Texan-Americans thought so. As of 1848, a detached observer would have to say that the Colorado Indians tribes exercised much more practical sovereignty than did anyone else.

Texas sold its far north and west to the United States, as part of the Compromise of 1850. Some of the former Texan land is now the Oklahoma panhandle. Some became part of New Mexico. Some is now southeastern and central Colorado.

Figure 8. American states and territories before creation of the Colorado Territory. Wikimedia Commons.

---

[17] Bent's "Adobe Empire" of trade stretched into all the (future) states adjacent to Colorado, plus far northern Texas. See LAVENDER, at inside cover (map). Bent's Fort was a partnership of brothers William and Charles Bent, plus Ceran St. Vrain. *See* RONALD K. WETHERINGTON, CERAN ST. VRAIN: AMERICAN FRONTIER ENTREPRENEUR 10 (2012). The latter was a former trapper. He built another trading post, Fort St. Vrain, near the northern Front Range.

Before the Colorado Territory

In 1850, Congress organized the territories of New Mexico and Utah, and in 1854 the territories of Kansas and Nebraska. All of Colorado was in the peripheral lands of these territories. Colorado was the periphery of the periphery.

Western Colorado was part of the Utah Territory (based in Salt Lake City). Far southeast and southcentral Colorado belonged to the New Mexico Territory (based in Sante Fe). The northeastern plains were in the Nebraska Territory (based in the far eastern part of the territory). Much of the front range and most of the eastern plains were in Kansas Territory (also based in the territory's far east). "Thus in 1860 Breckenridge was in Utah, Conejos in New Mexico, Boulder in Nebraska, and Denver in Kansas." LEROY R. HAFEN, COLORADO: THE STORY OF A WESTERN COMMONWEALTH 134 (1933).

When the Gold Rush began in 1858–59, the American settlers established homes in what would become the most populous parts of the state (the Denver-Golden-Boulder region and Colorado Springs), in farms, and in mining towns, such as Georgetown, Central City, and Black Hawk. Technically, most of this was part of the Kansas Territory. But the settlers quickly found that Kansas had almost no ability to establish a semblance of government in Colorado, and the other territorial governments had none at all.

So as will be detailed in chapter 6 (Fighting for Survival), the first Colorado governments were created by the people themselves, as "miners districts" in the mountains, as "claims clubs" in farming areas, and as "town companies." These voluntary associations recorded and certified property ownership, provided courts for settling disputes, and organized vigilance committees for law enforcement. Some towns elected their own legislatures. In the Fall of 1859, the people created their own territorial government, the Territory of Jefferson.

The quasi-governments were of questionable legality. Especially questionable was the Jefferson Territory, since only Congress has the legal power to create a U.S. territory. Coloradans, though, relied on the U.S. Declaration of Independence for the inherent, inalienable right of self-government. Coloradans had no alternative but to govern themselves. If the governments they created had the consent of the governed, that was good enough for the Coloradans.

Later, when the Colorado Constitution was written in 1876, the first three sections of its Bill of Rights would strongly affirm Coloradans' rights of self-government. No other state constitution, before or since, has so forcefully declared the rights of self-government of the people of the state. For example, section 2 of the Colorado Bill of Rights announces:

> The people of this state have the **sole and exclusive right of governing themselves, as a free, sovereign and independent state**; and to alter and abolish their constitution and form of government whenever they may deem it necessary to their safety and happiness, provided, such change be not repugnant to the constitution of the United States.

COLO. CONST., art. II, § 2 (bolding added).[18]

Coloradans' strong consciousness of their rights of self-government shaped Colorado constitutional law. Protecting self-government is why the 1876 Constitution contained so many restraints on the legislature, and why more restraints have been added since then. Self-government is why Colorado became one of the first states to constitutionalize the people's rights of initiative and referendum. Later, the people would enact the Taxpayer's Bill of Rights, to ensure that the people, and not the government, would decide how much the people could be taxed and how fast government spending could grow.

---

[18] Section 2 will be examined in more detail in chapter 2.

A people confident in their "sole and exclusive" right to govern themselves would become a people who defied federal law by constitutionally legalizing marijuana, and even ordering their state government employees to commit major federal felonies by serving as accessories to facilitating the marijuana trade. *See* chapter 30 (Vices?).

The Colorado Territory

In February 1861, Congress officially created the Colorado Territory, with the same boundaries as the future state. 1 FRANK HALL, HISTORY OF THE STATE OF COLORADO 244–45, 258–63 (1889) (describing the bill's journey through Congress).[19] Sidestepping an issue that would soon cause the American Civil War, the Organic Act said nothing in regard to slavery in Colorado. There was no black slavery in Colorado, but in the 1860s, the Utes and Comanches ran a slave trade in southern Colorado, selling captives of any race to buyers of any race. The Indian slave trade continued in Colorado until 1865, when president Andrew Johnson issued a proclamation outlawing Indian slavery and the Indian slave trade. VIRGINIA MCCONNELL SIMMONS, THE UTE INDIANS OF UTAH, COLORADO, AND NEW MEXICO 33, 121 (2d ed. 2000); chapter 4 (Bill of Rights, § 26, slavery prohibited).

When the Organic Act was introduced, the new territory was to have been called Idaho, but the bill as enacted named the territory for the Colorado River. STEPHEN J. LEONARD & THOMAS J. NOEL, DENVER: MINING CAMP TO METROPOLIS 23 (1990).[20]

Far eastern Utah Territory became the far west of Colorado. Congress did not look favorably on Brigham Young's theocratic government of Mormon Utah, and so took the opportunity to reduce Utah's size.

The southern boundary line of the former Utah lands was extended eastward. This put sparsely settled far northern New Mexico into Colorado and began to give Colorado the Hispanic influence that it retains to this day.

The Nebraska Territory's far southwest (*e.g.*, Julesburg, Sterling) was more closely tied economically to Denver and the Front Range than it was to Nebraska, so it too became part of Colorado.

Kansas, meanwhile, had just become a state, and the majority of Kansans wanted the capital to be in the east, so they were content with letting go of their far west. A Kansas that stretched to the continental divide would have needed a capital well west of Topeka. *See* Francis H. Heller & Paul D. Schumaker, *The Kansas Constitution: Conservative Politics through Republican Dominance*, in THE CONSTITUTIONALISM OF AMERICAN STATES at 490, 496–97; Calvin W. Gower, *Kansas Territory and Its Boundary Question: "Big Kansas" or "Little Kansas,"* 33 KAN. HIST. Q. 1, 3, 8 (1967).

The boundaries of the new State of Colorado were logically the first article of the Colorado Constitution. Next in order of importance were the fundamental principles of free government and liberty. They are expressed in the next article of the Constitution, the Bill of Rights. The placement reflected the American principle, stated in the second paragraph of the Declaration of Independence, that rights precede government; the essential purpose of government is protect pre-existing inherent, natural rights.

---

[19] The four-volume *History of the State of Colorado* by territorial secretary Frank Hall is the most comprehensive early history, especially for politics in the pre-statehood period.

[20] Legally, what we call the Colorado River was the Grand River until Congress changed the name in 1921. EUGENE H. BERWANGER, THE RISE OF THE CENTENNIAL STATE: COLORADO TERRITORY, 1861–76, at 6 n.3 (2007). That is why the name for the county that contains the river's headwaters is Grand County. However, the settlers had called the river the "Colorado" since early days. *Id.*

CHAPTER 2

Rights Come First. art. II, preamble & sections 1–3

Figure 6. Casimero Barela, territorial legislator, sheriff, Colorado convention delegate, Colorado's longest-serving state senator, 1876–1916, "father of the Senate." History Colorado-Denver, Colorado.

Mr. COOLEY, in his Constitutional Limitations, p. 47, thus speaks of the functions of a state constitution:

> *It is not the beginning of a community nor the origin of private rights. It is not the fountain of law nor the incipient state of government. * * * It grants no rights to the people; but is the creature of their power, the instrument of their convenience. Designed for their protection in the rights and powers which they possessed before the constitution was made, it is but the frame-work of the political government, and necessarily based upon the pre-existing condition of laws, rights, habits, and modes of thought.*

Packer v. People, 8 Colo. 361, 364–65 (1885) (quoting THOMAS COOLEY, A TREATISE ON THE CONSTITUTIONAL LIMITATIONS WHICH REST UPON THE LEGISLATIVE POWER OF THE STATES OF THE AMERICAN UNION (1868)). Michigan supreme court justice Thomas Cooley wrote the leading state constitutional law treatise of the latter 19th century.

Decades later, Colorado governor Carr stated, "The individual is supreme and government is established only to protect and foster his rights . . . the people were sovereign and the government and its administrators were their servants, and not their masters." ADAM SCHRAGER, THE PRINCIPLED POLITICIAN: THE RALPH CARR STORY 74, 109 (2008).

Today, the Ralph L. Carr Judicial Center is the home of the Colorado supreme court, the Colorado court of appeals, and the office of the attorney general. Governor Carr was a budget-balancing Republican, opponent of the New Deal, and ardent advocate of states' rights. During World War II, when the federal government was removing American citizens of Japanese descent from the West Coast, many states refused to allow them to come in. Governor Carr did allow their settlement in Colorado, at Camp Amache. The decision was politically unpopular at the time and might have cost him the next election. He is now recognized as Colorado's exemplar of justice.

A. The Colorado Convention's principles of government

In 1875 the people elected twenty-four Republicans and fifteen Democrats as delegates to the Colorado Constitutional Convention. At the time, southern Colorado was more Democratic and

Catholic, while the north was more Republican and Protestant. The dividing line was the Palmer Divide, an east–west ridgeline north of Colorado Springs.[1]

On most issues, including the Bill of Rights, partisan divisions were not important. Wilbur Fiske Stone—a Democrat, delegate, and future Colorado supreme court justice—recalled "there was no politics in it at all."[2] As Stone put it, the "lines between Democrat and Republican were very lightly drawn in those days."[3] E.T. Wells, a Republican delegate and a territorial judge, wrote that on "no occasion whatever" did "personal acrimony or partisan feeling" impede the Convention.[4] On issues where there was controversy—such as votes for women or whether to acknowledge the deity in the preamble—the divisions did not break down along party lines.[5]

The fundamental problem for the convention was not a partisan one. Rather, it was the inherent tension in what the delegates wanted. They knew they did not want a "do nothing" government. To the contrary, their constitution ordered the creation of state institutions for higher education, for care for the insane, and for the blind, deaf, and mute.[6] The delegates required the establishment of "a thorough and uniform system of free public schools," and that such schools not be racially segregated.[7] The Framers created a commissioner of mines, and ordered the general assembly to enact laws prohibiting child labor in mines, and for safe working conditions in the state's most important industry.[8] The Convention wrote the first American constitution to mention forests, instructing the general assembly to "enact laws in order to prevent the destruction of, and to keep in good preservation, the forests upon the lands of the state."[9] This was an early manifestation of the Colorado ethos of conservation.[10] The conservation imperative

[1] It divides the drainages of the South Platte and Arkansas Rivers.

[2] Donald Wayne Hensel, A History of the Colorado Constitution in the Nineteenth Century 101 (Aug. 9, 1957) (Ph.D. thesis in History, University of Colorado) (citing an interview with Stone in the *Denver Post* from Oct. 22, 1911).

[3] *Id.* Newspapers agreed that partisan politics had played no role in the Convention. *Id.* at 101 n.27 (citing DENVER TIMES (Mar. 8, 1976); DAILY ROCKY MOUNTAIN NEWS (Mar. 8, 1876); COLO. BANNER (Boulder) (Mar. 16, 1876); COLO. TRANSCRIPT (Golden) (May 24, 1876)). The *Daily Rocky Mountain News* was a Republican newspaper, while the Boulder and Golden newspapers were Democratic. *Id.*

[4] LEGISLATIVE, HISTORICAL AND BIOGRAPHICAL COMPENDIUM OF COLORADO 166 (Denver, C.F. Coleman's Publ'g House 1887); 2 FRANK HALL, HISTORY OF THE STATE OF COLORADO 295 (1890) (after the Convention officers were elected, "no spectator could have supposed, from anything seen or heard in the assembly or in any outer room, that party politics had ever been so much as dreamed of in the loft of the mansard roof occupied by the convention."); *id.* at 296 (the Convention heeded its President's admonition against the "slightest semblance of partisanship or sectional spirit." It has neither "time, opportunity, or inclination to rethresh the oft cudgeled sheaves of party politics").

[5] Taking a middle position, the Preamble begins, "We, the people of Colorado, with profound reverence for the Supreme Ruler of the Universe . . ." COLO. CONST. pmbl.

[6] *Id.* art. VIII, §§ 1, 5.

[7] Art. IX, §§ 2, 8.

[8] Art. XVI, §§ 1–2. The General Assembly was also allowed (but not mandated) to enact laws for mine drainage, and to provide for the science of metallurgy and mining to be taught in state institutions of learning. *Id.* §§ 3–4.

[9] Art. XVIII, § 6. Consistent with the environmental ethos expressed in 1876, the people of Colorado amended the Constitution in 1992 to provide that lottery revenues would be used for public lands. Art. XXVII ("Great Outdoors Colorado"). Colorado is the only state to dedicate its lottery revenues to the outdoors. Most other states use the money for the general fund or education. Vicky Bollenbacher, *Two Sides of Colorado, Amplified Through Constitutional Redesign, in* THE CONSTITUTIONALISM OF AMERICAN STATES 602 (George E. Connor & Christopher W. Hammons eds., 2008).

[10] The first game laws were enacted in 1877 and 1883, setting seasons and bag limits for some animals. VIRGINIA MCCONNELL SIMMONS, THE UTE INDIANS OF UTAH, COLORADO, AND NEW MEXICO 205 (2d ed. 2000). Game wardens were appointed starting 1891. *Id.* at 206. Starting in 1903, the Colorado Fish and Game Commission began charging one dollar for hunting licenses and using the revenue to promote

may have resulted in part from knowledge of how the Indians (and, later, U.S. settlers and travelers) had overused the woodlands along the rivers of the plains.[11]

The new constitution further provided that the general assembly "shall" enact "liberal homestead and exemption laws,"[12] "shall" pass arbitration laws,[13] and "shall" enact laws against "spurious, poisonous or drugged spirituous liquors."[14]

Yet while the Convention had a list of things it mandated the legislature to do, the Convention profoundly distrusted the legislature. In the words of one scholar, "The delegates created a legislature and then, as though they regretted their work, they took most discretionary authority from it."[15]

The 1876 Convention was meeting in "the post-Civil War era, when popular distrust of legislatures was at its height."[16] The early American state constitutions had been terse statements of principles, with only a broad outline for the structure of government—similar to the U.S. Constitution.[17] At the federal level, the short constitution seemed to be working well enough, since Congress could only exercise the enumerated powers that it had been granted. At the state level, though, legislatures could legislate on almost any topic. Special legislation for the benefit of powerful interests—especially, railroads—had been rampant. Starting in the 1830s, the new state constitutions and the new constitutions adopted in older states were much more active about constraining legislative discretion.[18]

The Colorado Constitution went especially far to hem in the government, with the longest state constitution up to that point in American history. As amended, the Colorado Constitution remains the one of the longest, reflective to Coloradans' inclination to instruct their government exactly what it must do and cannot do.

For example, article V, creating the Colorado House of Representatives and Senate, is much longer than article I of the U.S. Constitution, which creates the Congress. Article V contains many procedural restrictions on the process of enacting legislation.[19] Legislative sessions were

---

hunting and to conserve species at sustainable levels. STEPHEN J. LEONARD & THOMAS J. NOEL, DENVER: MINING CAMP TO METROPOLIS 153 (1st ed. 1990).

[11] Discussed in chapter 6 (Fighting for Survival).

[12] COLO. CONST. art. XVIII, § 1.

[13] *Id.* art. XVIII, § 3.

[14] *Id.* art. XVIII, § 5 (repealed 2008).

[15] Hensel at 133. One gets the sense that the Convention wished that it didn't have to create a legislature. DALE A. OESTERLE & RICHARD B. COLLINS, THE COLORADO STATE CONSTITUTION 4 (1st ed. 2001).

[16] G. ALAN TARR, UNDERSTANDING STATE CONSTITUTIONS 199 (1998).

[17] *Id.* at 61–62, 66.

[18] *Id.* at 118–21.

[19] COLO. CONST. art. V, § 6 (General assembly may not fix its own compensation); art. V, § 8 (legislators may not hold other office); art. V, § 9 (no changes in salaries or per diem to be effective until a new legislature takes office) (repealed 1974); art. V, § 14 (sessions must be public); art. V, § 17 (no bill may be altered from its original purpose); art. V, § 19 (no bills except appropriations may be introduced after twenty-fifth day of session; no bill to take effect for ninety days, except for emergency legislation with supermajority approval) (amended 1950); art. V, § 20 (no bill may be passed unless heard by a committee); art. V, § 21 (bills, except general appropriations, may contain only a single subject, clearly expressed in the title); art. V, § 22 (bills must be read at length, on three separate days, in each house; amended in 1950 to allow first reading by title only); art. V, § 23 (no accepting of amendments or conference reports except by recorded vote, to be published in the house's journal); art. V, § 24 (no amendment or revisions of laws by reference to title; full text must be published); art. V § 25 (no local or special laws on twenty-three specified subjects, including "granting to any corporation, association or individual any special or exclusive privilege, immunity or franchise whatever"); art. V, § 28 (no bill giving extra compensation to a public officer or contractor); art. V, § 29 (legislature and other government departments must use low bid for supplies; no public officer may have an interest in supply contracts); art. V, § 30 (no extending the terms of

limited to forty days, with no legislative sessions in even-numbered years.[20] Several constitutional provisions outlawed taxing, spending, or borrowing on behalf of corporations or other private interests.[21] Later, the first constraints on the legislature would be bolstered by amendments, adopted by the people.[22]

As one historian summarized, the Convention believed "that permitting too much freedom to govern was a far greater threat than possibly clogging the government's effectiveness in order to shield the people from their own rules. If the turnstiles blocked efficiency, they also checked exploitation and rascality."[23]

B. Rights are at the beginning

The 1875–76 Colorado Convention looked carefully at the constitutions of other states. Missouri's new 1875 constitution was closely studied, and it provided a model for several provisions, including the right to arms. When Missouri's original 1820 constitution was written, Missouri was entering the Union as a slave state. The Bill of Rights was the last article in the constitution. But when Missouri adopted a new constitution in 1875, rights came first: "Clearly, limiting government had taken precedence over establishing political institutions and distributing political power to those institutions."[24]

The new approach was more consistent with the theory of government in the Declaration of Independence. As paragraph two of the Declaration explains, all people have inherent rights "endowed by their Creator."[25] The purpose of government is to protect those rights. If a government harms rights instead of protecting them, then the people can replace the old government with a different one:

> That to secure these rights, Governments are instituted among Men, deriving their just powers from the consent of the governed, —That whenever any Form of Government becomes destructive of these ends, it is the Right of the People to alter or to abolish it, and to institute new Government.

---

public officers) (repealed 1974); art. V, § 31 (revenue bills must originate in House); art. V, § 32 (general appropriations bill must contain only the ordinary expenses of the three branches; other appropriations may have only a single subject); art. V, § 33 (no money to be paid from state treasury, except by appropriation); art. V, § 34 (no appropriations to organizations not under state control); art. V, § 35 (no delegation of power to supervise municipal functions); art. V, § 36 (no bill may authorize certain investments by trustees); art. V, § 38 (no obligation or liability of a person or corporation can be diminished by the general assembly); art. V, § 40 (no vote-trading on bills); art. V, §§ 41–42 (no influence-selling); art. V, § 43 (legislators may not vote on matters in which they have a personal interest).

20 COLO. CONST. art. V, § 6 (1876) ("No session of the General Assembly, after the first, shall exceed forty days."); *id.* art. V, § 7 (alternate year sessions only, except when the governor calls a special session). Exempted from the forty-day limit, the first general assembly sat for 140 days. 2 HALL at 362.

21 *See, e.g.*, COLO. CONST. art. X, § 13; art. XI, § 1; art. XV, § 12.

22 Most importantly: Initiative and referendum, COLO. CONST. art. V, § 1; GAVEL (Give a Vote to Every Legislator), art. V (several sections); and the Taxpayer's Bill of Rights, art. X, § 20.

23 Hensel at 120.

24 RONALD BRECKE & GREG PLUMB, *Missouri Constitutionalism: Meandering Toward Progress, 1820–2004*, *in* THE CONSTITUTIONALISM OF AMERICAN STATES 205 (George E. Connor & Christopher W. Hammons eds., 2008). Similarly, when Ohio replaced its 1802 constitution in 1851, the Bill of Rights was moved to the beginning of the document. "[B]efitting the Jacksonian model, the bill of rights precedes both the letter and the spirit of the parts of the constitution granting power to the different branches." JAMES J. WALKER, *The Ohio Constitution: Normatively and Empirically Distinctive*, *in* THE CONSTITUTIONALISM OF AMERICAN STATES, at 455.

25 THE DECLARATION OF INDEPENDENCE para. 2 (U.S. 1776).

"First come rights and then comes government," summarizes Randy Barnett.[26]

Colorado and Missouri agreed. Their article I defines the boundaries of the state.[27] Their article II declares the Bill of Rights.[28] Before creating any structure for government, Colorado and Missouri gave priority to the inherent rights of the people.

The structure of Colorado's constitution suggests that when there is a close question between the rights of Coloradans and the powers of their government, the former should prevail.

Unlike the federal Bill of Rights, the Colorado Bill of Rights does not begin by enumerating specific freedoms. Instead, the Bill of Rights first declares the principles of government.[29] These are meant to inform the understanding of everything that follows—namely the enumerated rights, and then the structure and operation of the government.

C. Rights and duties go together. art. II, Preamble

Article II is the only article of the Colorado Constitution with a preamble: "In order to assert our rights, acknowledge our duties, and proclaim the principles upon which our government is founded, we declare:"[30]

Rights and duties are closely linked. The right to a jury trial cannot exist if citizens fail to perform their duty of jury service. A good citizen has the duty to pay taxes. At the same time, citizens have the right not to be taxed in violation of the constitutional rules for taxation. The American Revolution began in part because Americans asserted their right not to be taxed without their consent.[31] The Colorado Constitution provides the system for obtaining consent for taxation.[32]

A governmental system that was all duties and no rights would have no liberty; it would be the antithesis of legitimate government. A governmental system that was all rights and no duties would soon collapse, thus endangering the rights that every legitimate government is created to defend.

D. The sovereign right to alter the government

After the preamble, article II, section 1 states:

> All political power is vested in and derived from the people; all government, of right, originates from the people, is founded upon their will only, and is instituted solely for the good of the whole.[33]

---

[26] RANDY E. BARNETT, OUR REPUBLICAN CONSTITUTION: SECURING THE LIBERTY AND SOVEREIGNTY OF WE THE PEOPLE 63 (2016).

[27] COLO. CONST. art. I; MO. CONST. of 1875, art I.

[28] COLO. CONST. art. II; MO. CONST. of 1875, art. II.

[29] COLO. CONST. art. II, §§ 1–3. The Ninth Amendment (guarantee of unenumerated rights) and Tenth Amendment (reservation of powers by the people and the States) to the U.S. Constitution provide interpretive principles for the document as a whole, copying the British style of placing interpretive rules at the end of a document.

[30] COLO. CONST. art. II, pmbl.

[31] *See, e.g.*, THE DECLARATION OF INDEPENDENCE para. 19 (U.S. 1776) ("For imposing Taxes on us without our Consent").

[32] *See* COLO. CONST. art. X.

[33] COLO. CONST. art. II, § 1.

The people, not the government, possess the sovereignty. The government is the delegated agent of the sovereign people. Popular sovereignty has been the bedrock principle of American government since 1776.[34] It is very different from the views in some other nations, where the government is considered to possess the sovereignty.[35] According to the U.S. supreme court:

> [James Madison's] premise was that the Constitution created a form of government under which 'The people, not the government, possess the absolute sovereignty.' The structure of the government dispersed power in reflection of the people's distrust of concentrated power, and of power itself at all levels. This form of government was 'altogether different' from the British form, under which the Crown was sovereign and the people were subjects. 'Is it not natural and necessary, under such different circumstances,' he asked, 'that a different degree of freedom in the use of the press should be contemplated?' Earlier, in a debate in the House of Representatives, Madison had said: 'If we advert to the nature of Republican Government, we shall find that the censorial power is in the people over the Government, and not in the Government over the people.' 4 Annals of Congress, p. 934 (1794).

New York Times Co. v. Sullivan, 376 U.S. 254, 274–75 (1964).[36]

Section 2 of the Bill of Rights affirms the sovereign people's right to alter or abolish the government:

> The people of this state have the sole and exclusive right of governing themselves, as a free, sovereign and independent state; and to alter and abolish their constitution and form of government whenever they may deem it necessary to their safety and happiness, provided, such change be not repugnant to the constitution of the United States.[37]

This is the universal human right asserted by the U.S. and Texan Declarations of Independence.[38] Section 2 rejects the notion that government is prior to the people or that the government receives its authority from God. Instead, government exists only by the choice of the

---

[34] *See, e.g.*, THE DECLARATION OF INDEPENDENCE para. 2 (U.S. 1776) ("[T]hat whenever any Form of Government becomes destructive of these Ends, it is the Right of the People to alter or to abolish it, and to institute new Government."); U.S. CONST. pmbl. ("WE THE PEOPLE of the United States . . . do ordain and establish this CONSTITUTION for the United States of America.").

[35] *Cf.* Noriho Urabe, *Rule of Law and Due Process: A Comparative View of the United States and Japan*, 53 LAW & CONTEMPORARY PROBLEMS. 61, 69 (1990) (contrasting meaning of the "Rule of Law" in the United States and Japan; in the former, the phrase implies the subordination of the government to the people; in the latter, it refers to the people's obligation to obey the government, and is thus "an ideology to legitimize domination").

[36] The *New York Times* Court was quoting from Madison's 1798 report to the Virginia legislature about state resistance to the unconstitutional federal Sedition Act of that year. State resistance, including to the Sedition Act, is discussed in chapter 5 (Vertical Separation of Powers).

According to the *New York Times* case, a government officer may recover damages for libel only if the publication was made with "actual malice." Legally speaking, "actual malice" does not mean malign intent; rather "actual malice" is a factual misstatement that was made with knowing or reckless disregard for the truth. The principle was later extended to include "public figures" who are not government workers.

[37] COLO. CONST. art. II, § 2.

[38] THE DECLARATION OF INDEPENDENCE para. 2 (U.S. 1776); TEXAS DECLARATION OF INDEPENDENCE para. 4 (Tex. 1836).

people, as their agent to carry out certain functions that the people choose, and in the manner they, as sovereigns, specify.

The principle of the power to alter government is expressed in many other state constitutions.[39] Colorado's language is similar to the 1875 Missouri Constitution.[40]

What could an altered government be like?

While many state constitutions have Alteration Clauses, Colorado's clause is one of the few that specifies what the altered government would be like. When Texas had adopted a new constitution

---

[39] *See, e.g.*, in order of statehood: DEL. CONST. pmbl. ("[T]herefore all just authority in the institutions of political society is derived from the people, and established with their consent, to advance their happiness; and they may for this end, as circumstances require, from time to time, alter their Constitution of government."); N.J. CONST. art. I, § 2 ("All political power is inherent in the people. Government is instituted for the protection, security, and benefit of the people, and they have the right at all times to alter or reform the same, whenever the public good may require it."); S.C. CONST. art. I, § 1 ("All political power is vested in and derived from the people only, therefore, they have the right at all times to modify their form of government."); OHIO CONST. art. I, § 2 ("All political power is inherent in the people. Government is instituted for their equal protection and benefit, and they have the right to alter, reform, or abolish the same, whenever they may deem it necessary . . . ."); ARK. CONST. art. 2, § 1 ("All political power is inherent in the people and government is instituted for their protection, security and benefit; and they have the right to alter, reform or abolish the same, in such manner as they may think proper."); IOWA CONST. art. I, § 2 ("All political power is inherent in the people. Government is instituted for the protection, security, and benefit of the people, and they have the right, at all times, to alter or reform the same, whenever the public good may require it."); CAL. CONST. art. II, § 1 ("All political power is inherent in the people. Government is instituted for their protection, security, and benefit, and they have the right to alter or reform it when the public good may require."); MINN. CONST. art. I, § 1 ("Government is instituted for the security, benefit and protection of the people, in whom all political power is inherent, together with the right to alter, modify or reform government whenever required by the public good."); ORE. CONST. art. I, § 1 ("[T]hat all power is inherent in the people, and all free governments are founded on their authority, and instituted for their peace, safety, and happiness; and they have at all times a right to alter, reform, or abolish the government in such a manner as they may think proper."); NEV. CONST. art. 1, § 2 ("All political power is inherent in the people[.] Government is instituted for the protection, security and benefit of the people; and they have the right to alter or reform the same whenever the public good may require it."); N.D. CONST. art. I, § 2 ("All political power is inherent in the people. Government is instituted for the protection, security and benefit of the people, and they have a right to alter or reform the same whenever the public good may require."); MONT. CONST. art. II, § 2 ("The people have the exclusive right of governing themselves as a free, sovereign, and independent state. They may alter or abolish the constitution and form of government whenever they deem it necessary."); IDAHO CONST. art. I, § 2 ("All political power is inherent in the people. Government is instituted for their equal protection and benefit, and they have the right to alter, reform or abolish the same whenever they may deem it necessary . . . ."); WYO. CONST. art. 1, § 1; ("All power is inherent in the people, and all free governments are founded on their authority, and instituted for their peace, safety and happiness; for the advancement of these ends they have at all times an inalienable and indefeasible right to alter, reform or abolish the government in such manner as they may think proper."); UTAH CONST. art. I, § 2 ("All political power is inherent in the people; and all free governments are founded on their authority for their equal protection and benefit, and they have the right to alter or reform their government as the public welfare may require.").

[40] MO. CONST., art. II, § 2 (1875) ("That the people of this state have the inherent, sole and exclusive right to regulate the internal government and police thereof, and to alter and abolish their constitution and form of government whenever they may deem it necessary to their safety and happiness, provided such change be not repugnant to the Constitution of the United States.").

in 1873, the Alteration Clause stated that anything about the government could be changed—except that there always had to be "a republican form of government."[41]

Two years later, the new Missouri Constitution broadened the language, and Colorado copied it. According to the Missouri and Colorado text, the new, altered government would have to be "not repugnant to the constitution of the United States."[42]

The U.S. Constitution requires that all states have a "republican form of government."[43] Thus, the Colorado and Missouri language affirms that any new state government would be republican in nature. With different language, the same is true in Texas.

Colorado and Missouri went further, however, in attempting to protect rights even in a post-alteration government. Because the altered government may not be "repugnant to the constitution of the United States," the altered state government could not do things that the U.S. Constitution expressly forbids states to do—such as coin money, enact ex post facto laws, or grant titles of nobility.[44]

Mississippi (1890, revised constitution) and Oklahoma (1907, statehood constitution) would adopt similar language.[45]

A republican form of government is based on universal human nature

Insistence on a republican form of government is based on a particular view of human nature: what humans have in common is far more important than the differences among them. Any other view is incompatible with a republican form of government.

As political scientist Donald Lutz explains:

> Today, any philosophical perspective that views humans as having a nature, or an essence, is termed "essentialist." There has been a sustained attack on essentialist philosophy during the modern era. Racists and ethnocentrists have denied that all human humans share a single nature and have either emphasized the effects of culture on human identity or argued for genetic or "blood" differences between groups of humans. Moral relativism under various guises, including its recent manifestation as "postmodernism," has attacked essentialism as a cover for privilege and elitism. Although it is true that some elitists have misapplied essentialist ideas for their own political ends, it is difficult to see how any position that argues for an inherent psychological moral similarity among humans can support either elitism or moral relativism. It is also difficult to see how one can establish and maintain any political order approaching constitutional republicanism without resorting to some minimally essentialist position. Indeed, modern constitutionalism began with, and continues to rest upon, a notion of human equality that is grounded in one essentialist position or another. Within this philosophical frame humans exist and are fully human prior any government, so the government must always be matched to the people.

---

[41] TEX. CONST. art. I, § 2 ("All political power is inherent in the people, and all free governments are founded on their authority, and instituted for their benefit. The faith of the people of Texas stands pledged to the preservation of a republican form of government, and, subject to this limitation only, they have at all times the inalienable right to alter, reform or abolish their government in such manner as they may think expedient.").

[42] COLO. CONST. art. II, § 2; MO. CONST., art. 1, § 3.

[43] U.S. CONST. art. IV, § 4.

[44] U.S. CONST. art. I, § 10.

[45] MISS. CONST. art. III, § 6 ("Provided, Such change be not repugnant to the constitution of the United States."); OKLA. CONST. art. II, § 1 (same).

LUTZ, PRINCIPLES OF CONSTITUTIONAL DESIGN, at 187.

The contrary view is expressed by tyrannies of various types. For example, Communist China's first ambassador to Indonesia, Pa Jen, was purged for writing that love, the pursuit of happiness, and admiration of gallantry were "all things common to mankind." To the contrary, the Chinese Communist Party informed him, "There is fundamentally no such thing as sentiment common to mankind, nor as common human nature . . . There is no such thing as 'human love.'" VALENTIN CHU, TA TA, TAN TAN: THE INSIDE STORY OF COMMUNIST CHINA 134 (1963).[46]

The fight for the right to alter

Contrast Colorado's section 2 with the "No Alteration Oath" that had been required in Great Britain, by which the swearer abjured "taking arms" against the king's government and swore "that I will not at any time endeavour any alteration of the government either in church or state."[47] Similarly, the mandatory "Non-Resistance Oath" stated "I A.B. do declare and believe that it is not lawful upon any pretence whatsoever to take arms against the king."[48] The American Founders were familiar with the Church of England's teaching that people must always submit to government, and that active resistance (such as armed revolution) was immoral, and so was passive resistance (nonviolent disobedience, such as practiced by some Quakers).[49]

Thus, only a year after the British had signed the treaty conceding American victory in the American Revolution, New Hampshire's constitution (1784) felt the need to argue the point about nonresistance. New Hampshire specifically denounced the "doctrine of nonresistance" as "absurd, slavish, and destructive of the good and happiness of mankind."[50] Tennessee copied this language for its 1796 Constitution.[51]

During the years leading to the Revolution, and during the Revolution, Great Britain had asserted that even if Americans had inherent rights, including the right to alter the government (by force if necessary), Americans had voluntarily surrendered those rights to the British

---

[46] The anti-human views of the Chinese Communist Party dictatorship of Mao Zedong (1949–76) are examined in David B. Kopel, *The Party Commands the Gun: Mao Zedong's Arms Policies and Mass Killings*, in NICHOLAS J. JOHNSON, DAVID B. KOPEL, GEORGE A. MOCSARY, E. GREGORY WALLACE & DONALD KILMER, FIREARMS LAW AND THE SECOND AMENDMENT: REGULATION, RIGHTS, AND POLICY 1863–1964 (2021 3d ed.) (online supplemental ch. 19.D.3).

[47] 1 MARK GOLDIE, ROGER MORRICE AND THE PURITAN WHIGS: THE ENTRING BOOK OF ROGER MORRICE 1677–1691, at 520 (2007). The oath was imposed on Dissenting ministers (non-Anglican Protestants) starting in 1665. *Id.*

[48] *Id.* at 519; *see also* 13 Charles II, ch. 1, § 2 (1661) (Gr. Brit.) (imposed on borough officeholders); 14 Charles II, ch. 3 (1662) (Gr. Brit.) (imposed on militia); 14 Charles II, ch. 4 (1662) (Gr. Brit.) (imposed on clergy); 17 Charles II, ch. 2 (1665) (Gr. Brit.) (imposed on former members of Dissenting clergy).

[49] *See, e.g.*, JOHNSON ET AL, at 221–36 (discussing rejection of nonresistance by American Revolutionaries; and influential ministers such as Jonathan Mayhew and Simeon Howard, who explicated the religious expression of duty to resist tyranny); DAVID B. KOPEL, THE MORALITY OF SELF-DEFENSE AND MILITARY ACTION: THE JUDEO-CHRISTIAN TRADITION 319–46, 383–96 (2017) (American Revolution, Quakers).

[50] N.H. CONST. pt. 1, art. 10 ("Government being instituted for the common benefit, protection, and security, of the whole community, and not for the private interest or emolument of any one man, family, or class of men; therefore, whenever the ends of government are perverted, and public liberty manifestly endangered, and all other means of redress are ineffectual, the people may, and of right ought to reform the old, or establish a new government. The doctrine of nonresistance against arbitrary power, and oppression, is absurd, slavish, and destructive of the good and happiness of mankind.").

[51] *See* Lewis L. Laska, *The Tennessee Constitution: An Unlikely Path Toward Conservatism, in* THE CONSTITUTIONALISM OF AMERICAN STATES, at 359. The language is retained in the present constitution, from 1870. TENN. CONST. art. I, § 2.

parliament. The Declaration of Independence retorted that such rights were "unalienable."[52] Many state constitutions in the Founding Era and Early Republic followed suit, specifically stating that the right to alter was "indubitable," "inalienable," or "indefeasible." Or sometimes all three.[53] This continued through 1819.[54] The 1819 constitutions were adopted just a few years after Americans re-won their independence in the War of 1812, which ended in 1815 with Andrew Jackson's victory at the Battle of New Orleans.[55]

Thereafter, American constitutions kept affirming the right to alter the government, but apparently did not feel the need to put the argument defending this right into state constitutions. The one exception was West Virginia, which seceded from Virginia during the Civil War. The West Virginia Constitution copied the Virginia Constitution's point that the right to alter is "indubitable, inalienable, and indefeasible."[56] That West Virginians for two and half centuries had consented to be part of Virginia did not deprive them of their right to change their minds.

Three state constitutions have language not adopted in Colorado, which seems to rule out armed revolution as a last resort. South Dakota specifies that the alteration of the government

---

[52] THE DECLARATION OF INDEPENDENCE para. 2 (U.S. 1776).

[53] VT. CONST. ch. I, art. 6 ("That government is, or ought to be, instituted for the common benefit, protection and security of the people, nation, or community, and not for the particular emolument or advantage of any single person, family, or set of persons, who are a part only of that community; and that the community hath an indubitable, unalienable, and indefeasible right, to reform or alter government, in such manner as shall be, by that community, judged to be most conducive to the public weal." (copying language from 1777 Constitution of the Republic of Vermont)); VA. CONST. art. 1, § 3 ("That government is, or ought to be, instituted for the common benefit, protection, and security of the people, nation, or community; of all the various modes and forms of government, that is best which is capable of producing the greatest degree of happiness and safety, and is most effectually secured against the danger of maladministration; and, whenever any government shall be found inadequate or contrary to these purposes, a majority of the community hath an indubitable, inalienable, and indefeasible right to reform, alter, or abolish it, in such manner as shall be judged most conducive to the public weal.").

[54] ALA. CONST. art. I, § 2 ("That all political power is inherent in the people, and all free governments are founded on their authority, and instituted for their benefit; and that, therefore, they have at all times an inalienable and indefeasible right to change their form of government in such manner as they may deem expedient." (adopted 1819, carried forward into later constitutions, including 1875 and the current constitution, from 1901); CONN. CONST. art. I, § 2 (adopted 1818, "All political power is inherent in the people, and all free governments are founded on their authority, and instituted for their benefit; and they have at all times an undeniable and indefeasible right to alter their form of government in such manner as they may think expedient."); ME. CONST. art. I, § 2 ("All power is inherent in the people; all free governments are founded in their authority and instituted for their benefit; they have therefore an unalienable and indefeasible right to institute government, and to alter, reform, or totally change the same, when their safety and happiness require it." Adopted 1819, effective 1820).

[55] *See* ROBERT V. REMINI, THE BATTLE OF NEW ORLEANS: ANDREW JACKSON AND AMERICA'S FIRST MILITARY VICTORY (1999). The battle took place two weeks after a peace treaty had been signed in Belgium—unbeknownst to the combatants. If the British had captured New Orleans, they might have refused to leave, just as they refused to evacuate forts in the American West, notwithstanding their 1783 peace treaty with the United States.

[56] W. VA. CONST. art. III, § 3 ("Government is instituted for the common benefit, protection and security of the people, nation or community. Of all its various forms that is the best, which is capable of producing the greatest degree of happiness and safety, and is most effectually secured against the danger of maladministration; and when any government shall be found inadequate or contrary to these purposes, a majority of the community has an indubitable, inalienable, and indefeasible right to reform, alter or abolish it in such manner as shall be judged most conducive to the public weal."); Robert E. DiClerico, *The West Virginia Constitution: Securing the Popular Interest*, *in* THE CONSTITUTIONALISM OF AMERICAN STATES at 221 (noting that section 3 is nearly verbatim from 1776 Virginia Declaration of Rights).

must be by "lawful and constituted methods."[57] North Carolina's 1868 Constitution stated that any alteration "shall be exercised in pursuance of law," essentially promising not to make a second armed attempt at secession.[58] Rhode Island in 1842, based on unique historical circumstances, made a similar point, although more elliptically.[59]

Unquestionably, seeking alteration through the ordinary legal channels is to be preferred. Yet as the American and Texan Revolutions had demonstrated, a government that does not want to rule by consent may prohibit peaceful alteration, leaving the people no recourse but forcible resistance. The American revolutionaries had considered their armed resistance to be lawful under the highest principles of natural law and the common law.[60] Of course the British government did not agree. Section 2 adopts the American point of view.

E. The sole and exclusive right of governing themselves

While affirmations of the right to alter the government are common, the Colorado Constitution makes a unique declaration: "The people of this state have the sole and exclusive right of governing themselves, as a free, sovereign and independent state." Art. II, § 2 Three states have similar language, but there are important differences. The Mississippi, Missouri, and North Carolina constitutions assert the sole and exclusive right "to regulate the internal government and police thereof."[61] In contrast, the Colorado right of self-governance is not limited to certain things. The Colorado right is the full right "of governing themselves." Art. II, § 2.

---

[57] S.D. CONST. art. VI, § 26 ("All political power is inherent in the people, and all free government is founded on their authority, and is instituted for their equal protection and benefit, and they have the right in lawful and constituted methods to alter or reform their forms of government in such manner as they may think proper.").

[58] N.C. CONST. art. I, § 3 ("The people of this State have the inherent, sole, and exclusive right of regulating the internal government and police thereof, and of altering or abolishing their Constitution and form of government whenever it may be necessary to their safety and happiness; but every such right shall be exercised in pursuance of law and consistently with the Constitution of the United States.").

[59] R.I. CONST. art. I, § 1 ("In the words of the Father of his Country, we declare that 'the basis of our political systems is the right of the people to make and alter their constitutions of government; but that the constitution which at any time exists, till changed by an explicit and authentic act of the whole people, is sacredly obligatory upon all.'"). George Washington did not mean revolution was always wrong. As of 1775, the British Constitution was widely considered the freest in the world; that did not stop Washington from leading a revolutionary army.

After independence from Great Britain in 1776, Rhode Island did not adopt a constitution. Instead, it relied on its colonial charter. This served to keep Rhode Island government under the control of a narrow group. A constitution was not adopted until 1842, following an attempted revolution, the Dorr War. The 1842 Rhode Island Constitution implicitly rebukes the defeated revolutionaries.

[60] *See* THE DECLARATION OF INDEPENDENCE (U.S. 1776). The Declaration of Independence sets forth a legal argument as to why the British government has forfeited its legal right to rule America: by injuring rather than defending the inherent human rights that all legitimate governments must protect.

[61] MISS. CONST. art. III, § 6 ("The people of this state have the inherent, sole, and exclusive right to regulate the internal government and police thereof, and to alter and abolish their constitution and form of government whenever they deem it necessary to their safety and happiness; Provided, Such change be not repugnant to the constitution of the United States."); MO. CONST. of 1875, art. I, § 2 ("That the people of this State have the inherent, sole and exclusive right to regulate the internal government and police thereof, and to alter and abolish their Constitution and form of government whenever they may deem it necessary to their safety and happiness: Provided, Such change be not repugnant to the Constitution of the United States."); N.C. CONST. art. I, § 3 ("The people of this State have the inherent, sole, and exclusive right of regulating the internal government and police thereof, and of altering or abolishing their Constitution and form of government whenever it may be necessary to their safety and happiness; but every such right shall be exercised in pursuance of law and consistently with the Constitution of the United States.").

Colorado's Sole and Exclusive Clause adds something else unique: Colorado is a "free, sovereign and independent state." *Id.*

The "sole and exclusive" language was not meant to be taken hyper-literally. Coloradans recognized that laws of the United States would govern Coloradans, sometimes. If somebody tried to rob a U.S. post office, the federal laws against interference with U.S. mail would govern.

Sovereignty in Colorado was necessarily mixed.[62] Under the U.S. constitutional system, the federal and state government are each delegated portions of the sovereignty possessed by the people. The Sole and Exclusive Clause does not mean that Colorado can issue patents, tax imports, or create lower federal courts; all such powers belong to sovereign functions of the federal government.

The Sole and Exclusive Clause is the right of governing *themselves*. In a union of free states, some decisions, such as whether to go to war, should be made collectively. *See, e.g.*, U.S. CONST., art. I, § 8, cl. 11 (congressional power to declare war). Other decisions, such intrastate matters, are part of states' rights, as long as Colorado complies with the baseline provisions of the U.S. Constitution. No other state constitution expresses states' rights as firmly as Colorado.[63]

Coloradans had long exercised their rights to govern themselves, starting with the *ad hoc* governments created during the gold rush. In the territorial period, Coloradans strongly opposed the appointment of federal territorial officers from elsewhere. "Coloradans fervently believed that no outsider could understand them."[64]

Today, defying federal statutes based on an (arguably overbroad) interpretation of the congressional power "[t]o regulate Commerce . . . among the several States,"[65] Colorado has created a strictly regulated system for the lawful cultivation and retail sale of medical and adult marijuana.[66] Colorado's statutes aim to ensure that Colorado marijuana commerce will be only intrastate.[67] In the spirit of the Sole and Exclusive Clause, Colorado's marijuana regulations govern something that in 1876 was considered a state matter, far beyond Congress's enumerated powers.[68]

---

[62] *See, e.g.*, THE FEDERALIST, No. 51 (James Madison) (Because in the proposed Constitution the people divide sovereignty between federal and state governments, "a double security arises to the rights of the people.").

[63] One of the 1859 guidebooks for emigrants had forecast that the West would "open a new field for the elucidation of the great principle of squatter sovereignty"—that is, the people who settle a land will govern it themselves. GEO. S. BLANCHARD, PEARMAN'S MAP AND PARSON'S GUIDE TO THE NEBRASKA AND KANSAS GOLD REGIONS 51–52 (2d ed. 1859). When the people were ready to take their place among the States, they would say to the Americans of the Atlantic and Pacific shores, "Behold our mountain land! the place where Freedom first seeks a refuge from the wiles of tyranny, and from which she will last be driven out—Patriotism and heroism are at their highest standard in mountain lands!" *Id.* at 53–54. Geography does influence political culture and individual character. No one can deny that outdoorsmanship—which has always been central to the Colorado way of life—fosters a spirit of self-reliance and independence.

[64] EUGENE H. BERWANGER, THE RISE OF THE CENTENNIAL STATE: COLORADO TERRITORY, 1861–76, at 57 (2007); *see also id.* at 137.

[65] U.S. CONST. art. I, § 8, cl. 3.

[66] COLO. CONST. art. XVIII, §§ 14, 16.

[67] *E.g.*, C.R.S. § 18-18-406.3 (setting forth anti-diversion provisions for medical marijuana use); § 24-32-117 (awarding state grants to local governments for diversion prevention); § 24-32-119 (awarding state grants to law enforcement to support investigation and prosecution of gray and black market marijuana activity); § 24-33.5-516(2)(f) (requiring Division of Criminal Justice to study diversion out of state); § 25-1.5-106(1)(d) ("The general assembly hereby declares that it is imperative to prevent the diversion of medical marijuana to other states."); § 39-28.8-101 (establishing a registration system for marijuana retailers, designed to prevent diversion).

[68] *See* Robert G. Natelson & David Kopel, *Commerce in the Commerce Clause: A Response to Jack Balkin*, 109 MICH. L. REVIEW FIRST IMPRESSIONS 55, 56, 59 (2010) (under original public meaning, interstate commerce power does not encompass sales of products within a single state).

When the voters of Colorado adopted constitutional amendments for the regulated sale of medical marijuana (2000) and for adult use marijuana (2012), the voters in essence ordered state government officials to conspire to violate the federal Controlled Substances Act.[69] Given the total quantities involved in this "conspiracy" (tons of marijuana, and many millions of dollars), the Colorado government officials are, arguably, committing federal felonies that qualify them as drug "kingpins," subject to very severe mandatory sentences.[70]

Yet consistent with the "sole and exclusive right" of Coloradans to govern themselves, state executive branch officials and the Colorado general assembly have obeyed the Colorado Constitution, and created a carefully controlled, highly taxed, government-supervised system for the production and retail sale of marijuana. "Sole and exclusive" indeed.

Quantifying popular control

One scholar's analysis of comparative constitutional systems of popular control gave Colorado a 9.05 on a scale from 0 to 11.95. This is somewhat higher that the 7.15 for the U.S. Constitution. Colorado earns the highest possible scores in some categories for having:

- an elected constitutional convention,
- a constitution approved in a popular referendum by an absolute majority,
- revisions that can be proposed and approved by an absolute majority (since 1910, as detailed in chapter 9 "Initiative and Referendum"),
- a specific statement recognizing the sovereignty of the people,
- officeholding based on requirements for citizenship, residency, and age, and not for party nomination or membership, property ownership, class, or caste,
- direct election of all three branches by the people. (Colorado judicial officers are appointed by the governor or municipal executives but are subject to periodic retention elections. COLO. CONST., art. VI.), and
- provisions for recall, initiative, and referenda.

Colorado had less than the maximum score because it allows elections to be won by a plurality candidate rather than the winner of an absolute majority. (Some municipalities, including Denver, have run-off elections if no-one wins a majority in the first round.) DONALD S. LUTZ, PRINCIPLES OF CONSTITUTIONAL DESIGN 103–05 (2006).[71]

F. Natural Rights

The final part of the Colorado Constitution's trilogy of core principles is section 3 of the Bill of Rights:

---

[69] *Compare* COLO. CONST. art. XVIII, §§ 14, 16, *with* 21 U.S.C. § 812 (2012) (listing "Marihuana" as a Schedule I controlled substance).

[70] 21 U.S.C. § 848.

[71] All the Colorado calculations are my own. Lutz's book analyzed national constitutions, not state ones. His text says the maximum score is 13.20, but this seems to be a computation error.

Colorado also scored poorly for ratio of population compared to the number of members in its House of Representatives. Colorado's representation ratio score, as of 2020 (5,845,530 population; 65 state representatives) is .12 under Lutz's formula, which in his system is rounded to the nearest .05 (that is, a score of .10). A perfect 1.0 in this category would be achieved by 65 representatives for a population of 10,195.

> All persons have certain natural, essential and inalienable rights, among which may be reckoned the right of enjoying and defending their lives and liberties; of acquiring, possessing and protecting property; and of seeking and obtaining their safety and happiness.[72]

Colorado's article II, section 3, restates a provision that first appeared in the 1776 Virginia and 1780 Massachusetts Constitutions. It is the classic American formulation of the nature of government, found in many state constitutions:

> All people are born free and equal and have certain natural, essential and unalienable rights; among which may be reckoned the right of enjoying and defending their lives and liberties; that of acquiring, possessing and protecting property; in fine, that of seeking and obtaining their safety and happiness.[73]

Colorado is one of thirty-five states whose constitutions expressly affirm that human rights are inherent, natural, or otherwise *not* the mere creation of positive law. Often, the affirmations of inherent rights specifically include self-defense.[74]

---

[72] COLO. CONST. art. II, § 3.
[73] MASS. CONST. pt. I, art. I.
[74] ALA. CONST. art. I, § 1 (describing the equality and rights of men and their "inalienable rights . . . life, liberty and the pursuit of happiness"); ALASKA CONST. art. I, § 1 ("[A]ll persons have a natural right to life, liberty."); ARK. CONST. art. 2, § 2 ("All men . . . have certain inherent and inalienable rights; amongst which are those of enjoying and defending life and liberty."); CAL. CONST. art. I, § 1 ("All people . . . have inalienable rights. Among these are enjoying and defending life and liberty."); DEL. CONST. pmbl. ("Through Divine goodness, all people have by nature the rights . . . of enjoying and defending life and liberty."); FLA. CONST. art. I, § 2 ("All natural persons . . . have inalienable rights, among which are the right to enjoy and defend life and liberty."); HAW. CONST. art. I, § 2 ("All persons are free by nature and are equal in their inherent and inalienable rights. Among these rights are the enjoyment of life, liberty."); IDAHO CONST. art. I, § 1 ("All men . . . have certain inalienable rights, among which are enjoying and defending life and liberty."); ILL. CONST. art. I, § 1 ("All men . . . have certain inherent and inalienable rights among which are life, liberty."); IND. CONST. art. 1, § 1 ("[A]ll people are . . . endowed . . . with certain inalienable rights; that among these are life, liberty."); IOWA CONST. art. I, § 1 ("All men and women . . . have . . . inalienable rights . . . of enjoying and defending life"); KAN. CONST. bill of rights, § 1 ("All men are possessed of equal and inalienable natural rights, among which are life, liberty."); KY. CONST. § 1 ("All men are, by nature, free and equal, and have certain inherent and inalienable rights, among which may be reckoned: . . . The right of enjoying and defending their lives and liberties."); ME. CONST. art. I, § 1 ("All people . . . have certain natural, inherent and unalienable rights, among which are those of enjoying and defending life."); MASS. CONST. pt. I, art. I ("All men . . . have certain natural, essential, and unalienable rights . . . enjoying and defending their lives."); MO. CONST. art. I, § 2 ("[A]ll persons have a natural right to life."); MONT. CONST. art. II, § 3 ("All persons . . . have certain inalienable rights . . . and the rights of . . . defending their lives."); NEB. CONST. art I, § 1 ("All persons . . . have certain inherent and inalienable rights; among these are life . . . and the right to keep and bear arms for security or defense of self, family, home, and others."); NEV. CONST. art. 1, § 1 ("All men are by Nature free and equal and have certain inalienable rights among which are those of enjoying and defending life."); N.H. CONST. pt. 1, art. 2 ("All men have certain . . . inherent rights--among which are . . . defending life."); N.J. CONST. art. I, § 1 ("All persons . . . have certain natural and unalienable rights, among which are those of . . . defending life . . . ."); N.M. CONST. art. II, § 4 ("All persons . . . have certain natural, inherent and inalienable rights, among which are the rights of . . . defending life."); N.C. CONST. art. I, § 1 ("[A]ll persons . . . are endowed by their Creator with certain inalienable rights; that among these are life."); N.D. CONST. art. I, § 1 ("All individuals . . . have certain inalienable rights . . . defending life . . . to keep and bear arms for the defense of their person, family, property, and the state."); OHIO CONST. art. I, § 1 ("All men are, by nature, free and independent, and have certain inalienable rights, among which are those of

The Colorado supreme court has relied on section 3 to uphold rights of contractual choice, use of property, or the practice of professions.[75] A modern application has been the right to move about freely, including via automobile.[76]

Section 3 resolves an issue that has been subject to debate under the U.S. Constitution, following the *District of Columbia v. Heller* decision about the U.S. Second Amendment.[77] *Heller* upheld the right to keep and bear arms for self-defense.[78] Could a government prohibit *unarmed* self-defense, such as fighting back with hands and feet? Or could a government prohibit self-defense entirely, and thereby remove the predicate for the right to arms? A unanimous Seventh Circuit panel made the latter argument.[79]

I have argued that the Second Amendment implicitly guarantees the right of self-defense (armed and unarmed), just as the First Amendment implicitly guarantees the right of association.[80] Whatever is the correct answer under the Second Amendment, the answer in Colorado is clear: self-defense is a natural right.

One modern application of section 3 has been in regard to the licensed carrying of concealed handguns. Colorado's constitutional right to keep and bear arms expressly exempts concealed carry from the right.[81] Accordingly, the 2003 Concealed Carry Act states that one purpose of the new law is to protect self-defense rights, which are guaranteed in section 3.[82]

---

enjoying and defending life."); OKLA. CONST. art. II, § 2 ("All persons have the inherent right to life."); PA. CONST. art. I, § 1 ("All men . . . have certain inherent and indefeasible rights . . . defending life."); S.D. CONST. art. VI, § 1 ("All men . . . have certain inherent rights . . . defending life."); UTAH CONST. art. I, § 1 ("All men have the inherent and inalienable right to enjoy and defend their lives and liberties."); VT. CONST. ch. I, art. 1 ("That all persons . . . have certain natural, inherent, and unalienable rights, amongst which [is] . . . defending life."); VA. CONST. art. I, § 1 ("That all men . . . have certain inherent rights, of which, when they enter into a state of society, they cannot, by any compact, deprive or divest their posterity; namely, the enjoyment of life."); W. VA. CONST. art. III, § 1 ("All men . . . have certain inherent rights . . . [t]he enjoyment of life."); WIS. CONST. art. I, § 1 ("All people . . . have certain inherent rights; among these are life."); WYO. CONST. art. 1, § 2 ("In their inherent right to life.").

[75] *See Olin Mathieson Chem. Corp. v. Francis*, 301 P.2d 139, 147, 149, 152 (Colo. 1956) (Fair Trade Act may not be used to control the price at which a retailer sells ammunition; the legislature may not abridge the right to contract); *Chenoweth v. State Bd. of Med. Exam'rs*, 57 Colo. 74, 141 P. 132, 134–36 (Colo. 1914) (physician's license to practice may not be revoked because he advertised); *Willison v. Cooke*, 130 P. 828, 831–32 (Colo. 1913) (ordinance may not require consent of nearby property owners for the construction of a store that complies with all building code and zoning rules).

[76] *People* ex rel. *J.M.*, 768 P.2d 219, 221 (Colo. 1989); *People v. Nothaus*, 363 P.2d 180, 214 (Colo. 1961); *cf. Dominguez v. City & Cty. of Denver*, 363 P.2d 661 (Colo. 1961) (arguing that a person behaving innocently may not be ordered to give an explanation for why he is on the streets at a late hour), *overruled by Arnold v. City & Cty. of Denver*, 464 P.2d 515, 517 (Colo. 1970).

[77] 554 U.S. 570 (2008).

[78] *Id.* at 635.

[79] "Suppose a state were to decide that people cornered in their homes must surrender rather than fight back—in other words, that burglars should be deterred by the criminal law rather than self help. That decision would imply that no one is entitled to keep a handgun at home for self-defense, because self-defense would itself be a crime, and *Heller* concluded that the [S]econd [A]mendment protects only the interests of law-abiding citizens. Our hypothetical is not as far-fetched as it sounds." *Nat'l Rifle Ass'n of Am., Inc. v. City of Chicago*, 567 F.3d 856, 859 (7th Cir. 2009) (citation omitted), *rev'd sub nom. McDonald v. City of Chicago*, 561 U.S. 742 (2010).

[80] *See* David B. Kopel, *The First Amendment Guide to the Second Amendment*, 81 TENN. L. REVIEW 417, 449–51 (2014); David B. Kopel, *The Natural Right of Self-Defense: Heller's Lesson for the World*, 59 SYRACUSE L. REVIEW 235 (2008).

[81] COLO. CONST. art. II, § 13.

[82] COLO. REV. STAT. § 18-12-201(1)(e) ("[T]he issuance of a concealed handgun permit is based on a person's constitutional right of self-protection.").

More broadly, section 3 shows what "law" means in Colorado. People have "natural, essential and unalienable rights." An "unalienable" right cannot be alienated. That is, it cannot be surrendered to government. Governments can make provisions for the orderly civil exercise of natural rights, but no legitimate government has the power to take away natural rights. Accordingly, there is no moral obligation to obey laws that destroy natural rights. In a constitutional sense, there is perhaps a duty not to obey them. Dr. Martin Luther King, Jr., explained:

> You express a great deal of anxiety over our willingness to break laws. This is certainly a legitimate concern. Since we so diligently urge people to obey the Supreme Court's decision of 1954 outlawing segregation in public schools, at first glance it may seem paradoxical for us consciously to break laws. One may ask, "How can you advocate breaking some laws and obeying others?" The answer lies in the fact that there are two types of laws: just and unjust. I would be the first to advocate obeying just laws. One has not only a legal but a moral responsibility to obey just laws. Conversely, one has a moral responsibility to disobey unjust laws. I would agree with Saint Augustine that "an unjust law is no law at all."

Martin Luther King, *Letter from Birmingham Jail*, Apr. 16, 1963.

King's position had a solid basis in Western intellectual history. The Roman lawyer Cicero, the Jewish legal scholar Philo of Alexandria, and the Christian philosopher St. Augustine of Hippo had all said that tyrannical, usurping government is no different from robbery.[83] The American Revolution was legally predicated on the point. Arguing that the British parliament had no legitimate legal power to legislate concerning the internal affairs of the American colonies, the Declaration of Independence denounced Parliament's "pretended legislation." United States, Declaration of Independence (1776) ("He has combined with others to subject us to a jurisdiction [British Quebec] foreign to our constitution, and unacknowledged by our laws; giving his Assent to their Acts of pretended Legislation").

A similar point was made in an early Supreme Court case, stating that an ex post facto criminal law was no law at all: "An ACT of the Legislature (for I cannot call it a law) contrary to the great first principles of the social compact, cannot be considered a rightful exercise of legislative authority." *Calder v. Bull*, 3 U.S. (3 Dall.) 386, 388 (1798) (seriatim opinion of justice Chase)

The U.S. Constitution's Fifth and Fourteenth Amendment guarantees of "due process of law" contain the natural law principle that some government enactments, even if regular in form, are so contrary to right and justice that they cannot be considered "law."

The concluding chapter of this textbook will return to the subject of natural, unalienable rights. The conclusion rejects the notion that the Colorado state government has "plenary power" to legislate on any matter, subject only to express limits in the Constitution. To the contrary, section 3 itself informs us that no government has, or lawfully could have, powers against "natural, essential and unalienable rights."

The preamble and opening sections of the Colorado Constitution Bill of Rights do not purport to grant any new rights. Rather, they declare rights that are inherent in human nature. In doing so, they echo the Declaration of Independence. On July 4, 1926, president Calvin Coolidge gave a speech in Philadelphia commemorating the 150th anniversary of the Declaration. While some persons had said that the Declaration and natural rights were outmoded, President Coolidge disagreed:

---

[83] *See* DAVID B. KOPEL, THE MORALITY OF SELF-DEFENSE AND MILITARY ACTION: THE JUDEO-CHRISTIAN TRADITION 10, 217 n.173 (2017).

> About the Declaration there is a finality that is exceedingly restful. It is often asserted that the world has made a great deal of progress since 1776, that we have had new thoughts and new experiences which have given us a great advance over the people of that day, and that we may therefore very well discard their conclusions for something more modern. But that reasoning can not be applied to this great charter. If all men are created equal, that is final. If they are endowed with inalienable rights, that is final. If governments derive their just powers from the consent of the governed, that is final. No advance, no progress can be made beyond these propositions. If anyone wishes to deny their truth or their soundness, the only direction in which he can proceed historically is not forward, but backward toward the time when there was no equality, no rights of the individual, no rule of the people. Those who wish to proceed in that direction can not lay claim to progress. They are reactionary. Their ideas are not more modern, but more ancient, than those of the Revolutionary fathers.

The principles in sections 1 through 3 are the foundation of government in Colorado. They are prior to everything except the boundaries of the state. They must be kept uppermost in mind when interpreting what follows in the Colorado Constitution.

Further reading: HEINRICH A. ROMMEN, THE NATURAL LAW: A STUDY IN LEGAL AND SOCIAL HISTORY AND PHILOSOPHY (Liberty Fund 1998) (1st pub. 1936, as *Die Ewige Wiederkehr des Naturrechts*).

CHAPTER 3

Distribution of Powers, art. III

> The powers of the government of this state are divided into three distinct departments,—the legislative, executive and judicial; and no person or collection of persons charged with the exercise of powers properly belonging to one of these departments shall exercise any power properly belonging to either of the others, except as in this constitution expressly directed or permitted.

The principle of the separation of powers is central to the United States Constitution but is not expressly stated. The Colorado Constitution does state the principle. The most typical use of article III in judicial opinions is to bolster specific separation arguments that can be based on other provisions of the Constitution.

The separation of powers developed historically as power was devolved from strongmen (kings, dictators, pharaohs, etc.). The separation of powers comprised four elements:

- popular consent,
- separation of functions among elements of government,
- representation (an elective body to share power), and
- federalism (local decision-making).

DONALD S. LUTZ, PRINCIPLES OF CONSTITUTIONAL DESIGN 111 (2006). Lutz's comparative study of 75 nations found a "strong correction between the Popular Control Index and the Separation of Powers Index." *Id.* at 139. "Thus, if popular sovereignty is the *sine qua non* of constitutionalism, and separation of powers converts popular control into popular sovereignty, separation of powers is also at the heart of constitutional design." *Id.* at 140.

Colorado's article III separation of powers is fortified by the prohibition against the general assembly delegating power to any special commission, private corporation, or association. Art. V, § 35. When you read subsequent chapters, consider how other Colorado Constitution provisions address the separation of powers.

As James Madison explained in Federalist No. 10, "faction" is inevitable in human affairs. The objective of a constitution is to prevent oppression by factions. Oppressive factions can be either majorities or minorities. Federalist 10 rejected the conventional political wisdom of the time: that enduring republics had to be small—like the city-states of Renaissance Italy or ancient Greece. Rather, argued Madison, a large "extended republic," such as the United States, was the best protection against tyranny of the majority or the minority. In large and diverse nation like the United States, any one faction, even if comprising a majority in one or several states, would be checked by the diverse national population. The separation of powers within the federal government (Federalist No. 63) and between the States and the federal government (Federalist No. 51) provided further security against oppression, Madison argued.

However, Madison's explanation of the safeguards inherent in the U.S. government does not perfectly transpose to state governments. First of all, any given state is much less diverse than the U.S. as a whole, so domination by a majority faction is easier—as in present-day Colorado, when the majority of electoral power is concentrated in large metropolitan areas on the Front Range.

Second, local governments within a state (*e.g.*, county or municipal governments) are relatively weak compared to the state. The states, after all, pre-existed the U.S. government by a century and a half. In contrast, local governments are generally viewed as mere creations of the state government, with no pre-existing sovereignty—although effective county government preceded effective state, territorial, or colonial government in much of the U.S., including Colorado. Subsequent chapters will examine county (art. XIV) and municipal government (*e.g.*, Denver home rule, art. XX) powers.

Even "in the absence of an extended republic," whatever separation of powers does exist is "the primary ancillary means for preventing majority tyranny." LUTZ, PRINCIPLES OF CONSTITUTIONAL DESIGN at 141–42.

In the federal courts, the doctrine of standing is based on U.S. article III's grant of judicial power to hear "Cases" and "Controversies." Colorado's standing doctrine is based partly on Colorado's article III, in the sense that a court that heard a case where there was no standing would not be exercising the judicial power and would thus be violating article III. *See* Glenn Warren Merrick, *Standing to Sue in Colorado*, 60 DENVER L.J. 421 (1983).

Notable decisions

Administrative powers and delegation

Legislative committees may not exert administrative powers. *Anderson v. Lamm*, 579 P.2d 620 (Colo. 1978) (the legislature's Joint Budget Committee).

Workmen's compensation cases are decided by executive branch administrative law judges, rather than by article VI elected judges. The system does not violate the separation of powers. The "separation of powers doctrine does not require a complete division of authority among the three branches, however, and the powers exercised by different branches of government necessarily overlap." The judicial function is sufficiently protected by the availability of judicial review of ALJ decisions for errors of law or abuse of discretion. *Sanchez v. Industrial Claims Office*, 411 P.3d 245 (Colo. App. 2017).

The Colorado legislature "may delegate to a Colorado administrative agency the discretion to promulgate regulations that substantively modify state statutes." *Amica Life Insurance Company v. Wertz*, 350 F. Supp. 3d 978, 998 (D. Colo. 2018). The delegation need not be express but may be implied. *Id.* at 1,000 (attempting to discern how the Colorado supreme court would rule). Via interstate compact, the Colorado legislature may delegate the same power to an interstate agency. *Id.* at 998. The Colorado attorney general had argued that whenever the Colorado government enters an interstate compact, all governmental actions pursuant to the compact are immune from control by the Colorado Constitution and Colorado statues. The court rejected the argument.

Delegating the power to define crimes

The legislature may not delegate to administrative entities the power to define crimes. *People v. Lepik*, 629 P.2d 1080 (Colo. 1981) (statute criminalized introducing undefined "contraband" into a correctional facility; in effect, correctional administrators had the power to define the scope of the criminal law).

Colorado law contrasts with the U.S. supreme court's approach to the federal constitution, which *does* allow administrative agencies to define criminal offenses. *Touby v. United States*, 500 U.S. 160 (1991) (administrative agency may decide which drugs are criminalized).

Prison regulation

At the beginning of the CoVid-19 pandemic, the Colorado ACLU brought a lawsuit asking the courts to order governor Polis to improve prison conditions to reduce the risk of prisoners becoming infected. Reversing the district court, the court of appeals held that courts had jurisdiction to hear a case asking for remediation of unconstitutional conditions of confinement under the Colorado Constitution. The court of appeals acknowledged that a court could not order "prison depopulation," since the Colorado Constitution give the governor the exclusive power to issue reprieves, commutations, or pardons. COLO. CONST. art. V, § 7. However, a court could issue a declaratory judgement regarding conditions of confinement. The case was remanded for fact finding. *Winston v. Polis*, 2021 COA 90 (Colo. App. 2021).

Control of courts and legal practice

The Colorado supreme court, and not the legislature, has supreme authority over the practice of law. *Unauthorized Practice of Law Comm. v. Employers Unity, Inc.*, 716 P.2d 640 (Colo. 1986).

And over the rules for contempt of court. *In the Interest of J.E.S.*, 817 P.2d 508 (Colo. 1991) (declaring unconstitutional a statute that forbade jail sentences for contempt of court; in this case, a 45-day jail sentence for repeated contempt, by a 13-year habitual truant who defied court orders to attend school).

Conversely, the judiciary has no power to control the decisions of prosecutors. *E.g.*, *People v. Thorpe*, 641 P.2d 935 (Colo. 1982) (district attorney's statutory discretion about whether to charge a juvenile as an adult).

Further reading: Russell Carparelli, *Separate Powers—Shared Responsibility: Constructing Avenues of Interbranch Communication*, 85 DENVER U.L. REVIEW 267 (2007) (Court of appeals judge offers ideas for how branches can inform each other about their work and its challenges); Courtland H. Peterson, *Rules Making in Colorado: An Unheralded Crisis in Procedural Reform*, 38 U. COLO. L. REVIEW (1965–66) (history of the long-running fight between the supreme court and the general assembly over control of court rules—a battle that has continued to the present).

CHAPTER 4

Bill of Rights, article II

Figure 7. John Routt, Colorado's final territorial governor and first statehood governor. History Colorado-Denver, Colorado.

In nineteenth century terminology, there were several categories of rights, which sometimes overlapped:

- Natural rights. Persons have these even if they do not have a government in common. For example, freedom of conscience and religion; the right to the fruits of one's labor. These rights exist in a state of nature but may be insecure since their only protection may be the natural right of self-defense.
- Civil rights. Government-created protections for natural rights. One gains these by entering into society. For example, the right to testify in court, or the right to trial by jury.[1] Also, including the right to government enforcement of natural rights, such as of the right to execute and enforce contracts or of the right to own and convey property.
- Political rights. Participation in the political structure. For example, voting, jury service, holding civil office. Denied to children, the mentally infirm, and (often but not always) aliens. At times in the past, these rights were denied to adult women, under the theory that they were more like children (in need of special protection, and incapable of exercising some rights) than like adult males.
- Social rights. Free association with persons of one's choosing. *E.g.*, choice of who to invite to one's house for dinner. Whom to marry. Violated by Jim Crow laws and by other statutes that compel unwanted association or that forbid voluntary association.

[1] "Trial by jury cannot be considered as a natural right, but a right resulting from a social compact which regulates the action of the community, but is as essential to secure the liberty of the people as any one of the pre-existent rights of nature." James Madison, speech introducing the Bill of Rights in the U.S. House, The Annals of Congress, House of Representatives, First Congress, 1st Session, 448–60 (1789).

- Legal rights. Enforceable by the legal system. Includes all civil rights, and anything else established by common law or positive law.

In general, courts are required to conduct an inquiry as to whether rights in the Colorado Constitution are broader than their federal counterparts. The inquiry focuses on the constitutional text, and on the history and traditions of the people of Colorado. *See Bock v. Westminster Mall Co.*, 819 P.2d 55 (Colo. 1991) (since city provided corporate welfare for shopping mall development, mall is a public forum and must allow nonviolent political speech in its common areas).

Below, and throughout this book, constitutional text that has been fully or partially nullified by judicial decisions is underlined.

Art. II, Section 1. All political power derives from the people

> In order to assert our rights, acknowledge our duties, and proclaim the principles upon which our government is founded, we declare:
>
> All political power is vested in and derived from the people; all government, of right, originates from the people, is founded upon their will only, and is instituted solely for the good of the whole.

Discussed in chapter 2 (Rights Come First). Some short observations:

Properly understood, rights and duties are not opposites; they are partners. The Constitution defines the essential terms of this partnership.

The principle that government "is instituted solely for the good of the whole" is carried out by the numerous constitutional safeguards against special legislation, such as those in articles V (legislative power), X (taxes), and XI (debt). Articles XXVIII (campaign finance) and XXIX (gifts to government employees) are attempts to reduce special influence on government.

It is true that many Colorado Constitution provisions have been nullified by the Colorado supreme court. Yet in the long run, government officials, including judges, may abandon the misconduct of their predecessors, and recur to the document that is the sole legitimate source of the power they wield.[2] The Equal Protection Clause of the Fourteenth Amendment was nullified during the Jim Crow era. Not until the 1930s did the U.S. supreme court begin active defense of the First Amendment. Even then, it took three more decades for the court to find that a federal statute violated the First Amendment. *Lamont v. Postmaster General*, 381 U.S. 301 (1965) (restrictions on postal delivery of communist propaganda). Likewise, the U.S. supreme court often said nice things about the Second Amendment, but never lifted a finger to protect the right until 2008.[3] As these examples show, constitutional provisions that have been left for dead by the courts may later be respected by the courts—as long as those provisions remain alive in the hearts and minds of the people. One purpose of a written constitution is to encourage the people to remember and cherish their rights.

---

[2] *Cf. Reid v. Covert*, 354 U.S. 1. 5-6 (1957)) (Black, J., plurality op.) (spouses of American soldiers stationed in England may not be tried by a military court) ("The United States is entirely a creation of the Constitution. Its power and authority have no other source. It can only act in accordance with the limits prescribed by the Constitution.").

[3] For the Court's previous statements on the Second Amendment, see David B. Kopel, *The Supreme Court's Thirty-five Other Second Amendment Cases*, 18 ST. L.U. PUBLIC L. REVIEW 99 (1999).

Art. II, Section 2. People may alter or abolish form of government

> The people of this state have the sole and exclusive right of governing themselves, as a free, sovereign and independent state; and to alter and abolish their constitution and form of government whenever they may deem it necessary to their safety and happiness, provided, such change be not repugnant to the constitution of the United States.

This is the universal human right asserted by paragraph two of the United States Declaration of Independence, and by the Texan Declaration of Independence. It rejects the notion that government is prior to the people, or that the government receives its authority from God. Instead, government exists only by the choice of the people, as their agent to carry out certain functions which the people choose, and in the manner they, as sovereigns, specify.

The right has been fortified by:

- amendments guaranteeing the rights of initiative, referendum, and recall, at the state, county, and municipal levels of government;
- the Taxpayer's Bill of Rights, Great Outdoors Colorado, and other provisions controlling and directing taxing and spending;
- many guarantees for the free and direct election of constitutional officers, including those in article VII.

Art. II, Section 3. Natural, essential, and inalienable rights

> All persons have certain natural, essential and inalienable rights, among which may be reckoned the right of enjoying and defending their lives and liberties; of acquiring, possessing and protecting property; and of seeking and obtaining their safety and happiness.

Cases or laws relying in part on section 3 are summarized in chapter 2 (Rights Come First). Natural rights precede government. While governments may specify the contours for orderly exercise of natural rights, no government has legitimate authority to violate or infringe natural rights. Being "inalienable," natural rights are not and cannot be surrendered by the people's decision to create a government.

Art. II, Section 4. Freedom of religion

> The free exercise and enjoyment of religious profession and worship, without discrimination, shall forever hereafter be guaranteed; and no person shall be denied any civil or political right, privilege or capacity, on account of his opinions concerning religion; but the liberty of conscience hereby secured shall not be construed to dispense with oaths or affirmations, excuse acts of licentiousness or justify practices inconsistent with the good order, peace or safety of the state. No person shall be required to attend or support any ministry or place of worship, religious sect or denomination against his consent. Nor shall

> any preference be given by law to any religious denomination or mode of worship.

Much more detailed than the Free Exercise and Establishment Clauses of the U.S. First Amendment, section 4 expresses well-settled interpretations of those clauses. In general, the interpretation of section 4 has not differed from the federal First Amendment.

A notable deviation from the historic pattern involved a baker who was prosecuted under Colorado civil rights statutes; the baker served all customers regardless of sexual orientation but did not want to make a custom cake specifically for a ceremony in which his religion forbade him to participate. The Colorado Civil Rights Commission's decision against the baker was upheld by the Colorado court of appeals. *Craig v. Masterpiece Cakeshop, Inc.*, 370 P.3d 272 (Colo. App. 2016), and the Colorado supreme court denied certiorari. 2016 WL 1645027 (Colo. 2016). The U.S. supreme court, however, reversed; justice Kennedy's opinion for the court focused mainly on the overt anti-religious bigotry expressed by some members of the commission during the hearing. *Masterpiece Cakeshop, Ltd. v. Colorado Civil Rights Commission*, 138 S.Ct. 1719 (2018). The supreme court opinion provided only limited guidance for more typical cases, in which government officials have the self-control not to express their anti-religious animus out loud.

For federal laws, the 1993 Religious Freedom Restoration Act (RFRA), 42 U.S.C. §§ 2000bb et seq., requires that substantial infringements on the free exercise of religion be upheld only if the government can justify them by passing the test of strict scrutiny. That was the test the U.S. supreme court had used starting in the early 1960s, but which was abandoned in *Employment Division v. Smith*, 494 U.S. 872 (1990); under *Employment Division*, generally applicable statutes that reduce religious freedom are constitutional unless there is evidence that the restrictions were intended to target religion.[4] *See Church of the Lukumi Babalu Aye, Inc. v. Hialeah*, 508 U.S. 520 (1993) (city's ban on certain animal killings was targeted to suppress only the animal sacrifices of a particular religion).

As enacted, the federal RFRA applied to all arms of the federal government (*e.g.*, Congress, executive, D.C. Council) *and* to all state and local government. But the supreme court held that the state and local application exceeded Congress's powers under section 5 of the Fourteenth Amendment—the section that grants Congress power to enact legislation against state or local violations of Americans' national constitutional rights. The court held that section 5 legislation must be "congruent and proportional" to the underlying problem, and the RFRA was too broad to be congruent and proportional. *City of Boerne v. Flores*, 521 U.S. 507 (1997). RFRA's application to federal government activities was upheld because Congress has plenary power to set rules for the operation of the federal government.

Some states have enacted their own RFRAs, but Colorado is not among them. RFRAs were uncontroversial in the 1990s, when Congress enacted the federal RFRA nearly unanimously. More recently, they have become controversial, particularly because of opposition by some LGBT groups; it might be difficult, for example, to prove that the state of Colorado has a compelling interest in forcing a cake artist to participate in gay weddings against his conscience.

Several provisions of the Colorado Constitution provide additional, specific protections for religious freedom. To protect the conscience of state officers who have religious scruples against oaths, the Constitution provides that such officers may take an "oath or affirmation" to support the U.S. and Colorado Constitutions. COLO. CONST., art. XII, § 8; *see also* C.R.S. § 24-12-101 (same). Partly to reduce the risk of government interference, state aid to "sectarian" institutions is prohibited. COLO. CONST., art. XII, § 7. Public educational institutions may not impose any

---

[4] The Colorado court of appeals followed the *Smith* approach: an ordained minister of the Hawaii Cannabis Ministry could still be convicted of violating the statute against distribution of large quantities of marijuana. *People v. Torline,* 2020 COA 160 (Colo. App. 2020).

religious tests on faculty or students and may not require the attendance at any religious service. *Id.* § 8.

Art. II, Section 5. Freedom of elections

> All elections shall be free and open; and no power, civil or military, shall at any time interfere to prevent the free exercise of the right of suffrage.

Article VII provides many specific protections of the right of free elections.

According to the Colorado supreme court, section 5 goes no further than does federal constitutional election law. *MacGuire v. Houston*, 717 P.2d 948 (Colo. 1986) (upholding statute preventing unaffiliated voters and members of minor parties from serving as election judges).

Some notable applications:

- Striking a ban on write-in votes. *Littlejon v. People ex rel. Desch*, 52 Colo. 217, 121 P. 159 (1912) ("it coerces the elector into voting for one who has filed a notice of his intention to be a candidate, and prohibits the free choice of the elector as to whom he shall have to serve him as a public officer, and thereby prevents 'the free exercise of the right of suffrage.'").
- Against employer coercion of voting and against coal "company town" bans on political activity by political opponents of the coal companies. *Neelley v. Farr*, 61 Colo. 485, 158 P. 458 (1916).
- In favor of interpreting voting statutes so as to sustain votes, unless there are problems of fraud or doubtful intent. Substantial compliance with election statutes is sufficient. So, for a write-in candidate: count the ballot that wrote the last name only (even though the state statute requires a first name or initial too); don't count the ballot with an incorrect first name or first initial; don't count the ballot that writes the name on the wrong line (for a different office). *Meyer v. Lamm*, 846 P.2d 862 (Colo. 1993).

Art. II, Section 6. Equal and open justice

> Courts of justice shall be open to every person, and a speedy remedy afforded for every injury to person, property or character; and right and justice should be administered without sale, denial or delay.

Section 6 does not by itself create a cause of action in Colorado courts. *In re Marriage of Hartley*, 886 P.2d 665 (Colo. 1994) (in custody case, child wished to fire his guardian ad litem, who was acting contrary to child's wishes; child has no right to choose his own counsel).

The section has been applied to some restrictions on judicial review or access to the courts. The most significant recent case held that "Parties are constitutionally entitled to judicial review of an administrative agency's decisions that affect their substantive statutory rights." A statute was unconstitutional because it allowed workmen's compensation appeals from decisions of the Industrial Claims Appeals office only by a petition to the court of appeals for a discretionary writ of certiorari, which is not the same as review on the merits. "[T]he need for providing judicial review on the merits of agency decisions is clear: specialized administrative tribunals, although efficient, are not always as willing or able as state courts to protect individual rights." *Allison v. Industrial Claims Appeals Office*, 884 P.2d 1113 (Colo. 1994)

Section 6 does not prevent a court from enjoining a pro se defendant not to file further complaints without judicial permission. Pro se litigants have section 6 rights, but there are also "the interests of other litigants and of the public in general in protecting judicial resources from the deleterious impact of repetitious, baseless pro se litigation." *Karr v. Williams*, 50 P.3d 910, 913 (Colo. 2002).

Further reading: Jonathan M. Hoffman, *By the Course of the Law: Origins of the Open Courts Clause of State Constitutions*, 74 OREGON. L. REVIEW 1279 (1995) (39 states have such as clause, and "The courts are in total disarray over how to interpret it.").

Art. II, Section 7. Security against searches and seizures

> The people shall be secure in their persons, papers, homes and effects, from unreasonable searches and seizures; and no warrant to search any place or seize any person or things shall issue without describing the place to be searched, or the person or thing to be seized, as near as may be, nor without probable cause, supported by oath or affirmation reduced to writing.

Similar in wording to the U.S. Fourth Amendment, and rarely interpreted differently. Search warrants are in C.R.S. §§ 16-3-301 to 311, and Colo. R. Crim. Pro. 41.

The Colorado supreme court has sometimes gone beyond the U.S. supreme court in holding that certain types of surveillance are searches, and thus a warrant is required. *People v. Oates*, 698 P.2d 811 (Colo. 1985) (beeper attached to chemical drum) (dissent: "I am troubled by the majority's failure to articulate any intent on the part of the framers of the Colorado Constitution or any circumstances unique to this state that would justify a result different from that reached [by the U.S. supreme court] in *Karo*."); *In re Sporleder*, 666 P.2d 135 (Colo. 1983) (warrant needed for pen register, which records the incoming and outgoing numbers for telephone calls, but not the content of the call).

The court also held that the North Metro Drug Task Force (a joint federal-local operation) could not use a Drug Enforcement Agency administrative subpoena to obtain a bookstore's records about the books ordered by a particular customer. The Colorado Constitution "requires a more substantial justification from the government than is required by the Fourth Amendment when law enforcement officials attempt to use a search warrant to obtain an innocent, third-party bookstore's customer purchase records." *Tattered Cover, Inc. v. City of Thornton*, 44 P.3d 1044 (Colo. 2002) (also stating that booksellers have standing to assert the constitutional rights of book buyers).

Further reading: H. Morley Swingle, *Electronic Search Warrants in Colorado*, 44 COLO. LAWYER 45 (June 2015); Kevin C. McAdam & John R. Webb, *Privacy: A Common Law and Constitutional Crossroads*, 40 COLO. LAWYER 55 (June 2011) (Judge Webb retired from the Colo. Ct. App. in 2020).

Art. II, Section 8. Prosecutions by indictment or information

> Until otherwise provided by law, no person shall, for a felony, be proceeded against criminally otherwise than by indictment, except in cases arising in the land or naval forces, or in the militia when in actual service in time of war or public danger. In all other cases, offenses shall be prosecuted criminally by indictment or information.

The Fifth Amendment requires grand jury indictments in federal criminal cases. The U.S. supreme court has *not* made it applicable to the states via the Fourteenth Amendment. *Hurtado v. California*, 110 U.S. 516 (1884).

The "otherwise provided by law" language allows the general assembly to provide that even felony cases may be commenced by information or preliminary examination, rather than by indictment. *In re Dolph*, 17 Colo. 35, 28 P. 470 (1891); *Falgout v. People*, 170 Colo. 32, 459 P.2d 572 (1969). Today, very few Colorado criminal cases use grand juries. Indictment and information rules are at C.R.S. §§ 16-5-201 to 209; Colo. R. Crim. Pro. 6-9. Proceeding by information rather than indictment is the norm in most Western states. Along with the U.S. Seventh Amendment (right to jury trial in civil cases, generally for causes of action for which a civil jury was available in 1791), the Fifth Amendment's indictment clause is very unlikely to be incorporated against the states by the U.S. supreme court, for fear of excessive interference in routine state court operations.

Art. II, Section 9. Treason, heirs, estates of suicides

> Treason against the state can consist only in levying war against it or in adhering to its enemies, giving them aid and comfort; no person can be convicted of treason, unless on the testimony of two witnesses to the same overt act, or on his confession in open court; no person can be attainted of treason or felony by the general assembly; no conviction can work corruption of blood or forfeiture of estate; the estates of such persons as may destroy their own lives shall descend or vest as in cases of natural death.

The treason material parallels article III, § 3 of the U.S. Constitution, which was cognizant of abuses of treason laws in Great Britain. There, many forms of political dissent had been classified as treason. The Colorado treason statute parallels follows the U.S. Constitution's text: "A person commits treason if he levies war against the state of Colorado or adheres to its enemies, giving them aid and comfort. No person shall be convicted of treason unless upon the testimony of two witnesses to the same overt act or upon confession in open court." C.R.S. § 18-11-101(1).

The ban on "corruption of blood" also parallels U.S. CONST., art. III, § 3. In other words, if an individual is convicted for a felony, the conviction imposes no disabilities on the person's relatives ("corruption of blood").

The suicide provision does not have a parallel in the U.S. Constitution. It eliminates an old common law rule by which the king could seize the estates of suicides. The policy rationale was to deter suicide, while monarchs liked the rule as a revenue source not dependent on parliamentary appropriation.

By interpretation, the term "forfeiture of estate" applies only to forfeitures like the English abuses, and not to the civil forfeiture of an individual's property under a public nuisance statute. *People v. Milton*, 732 P.2d 119 (Colo. 1987). Enacted as part of the "war on drugs," Colorado's very lax statutes for civil forfeiture were later reformed by the legislature, in stages.

Further reading: Taylor Mcconkie, *State Treason: The History and Validity of Treason Against Individual States*, 101 KENTUCKY L. JOURNAL 281 (2012-13); Conrad Imel & Katie Ruedebusch, Colorado Legislative Council Staff, *Civil Asset Forfeiture*, Issue Brief 17-30 (Aug. 2017).

Art. II, Section 10. Freedom of speech and press

> No law shall be passed impairing the freedom of speech; every person shall be free to speak, write or publish whatever he will on any subject, being responsible for all abuse of that liberty; and in all suits and prosecutions for libel the truth thereof may be given in evidence, and the jury, under the direction of the court, shall determine the law and the fact.

The Colorado supreme court has many times stated that section 10 is broader than "the freedom of speech or of the press" guarantees of the U.S. First Amendment. *E.g.*, *Colorado Educ. Ass'n v. Rutt,* 184 P.3d 65 (Colo. 2008).[5]

One area where the broader standards have made a difference has been in defamation (oral) or libel (written) claims brought by private persons. *Diversified Management, Inc. v. The Denver Post, Inc.*, 653 P.2d 1103 (Colo. 1985) (applying "actual malice" standard even when First Amendment does not require it).[6] Another case where the Colorado Constitution perhaps had an effect was *Browne v. City of Grand Junction,* 136 F. Supp. 3d 1276 (D. Colo. 2015) (impressionistic opinion striking ordinance against aggressive panhandling).

Colorado is unusually restrictive at denying the public access to court records, and the supreme court has held that the restrictions do not violate section 10. *People v. Owens*, 420 P.3d 257 (Colo. 2018).

Patterson v. Colorado

205 U.S. 454 (1907)

Background to the case:

The *Rocky Mountain News* was Colorado's leading Democratic paper, and its owner, Thomas Patterson, was Colorado's Democratic U.S. senator. Patterson also published *The Denver Times,* an afternoon paper that competed with the then-solidly Republican *Denver Post*. *See generally* SYBIL DOWNING & ROBERT E. SMITH, TOM PATTERSON: COLORADO CRUSADER FOR CHANGE (1995).

---

[5] *See also Tattered Cover, Inc. v. City of Thornton*, 44 P.3d 1044 (Colo. 2002) (search of bookstore's sales records for a customer); *Bock v. Westminster Mall Co.*, 819 P.2d 55 (Colo. 1991) (right to non-violent political speech in shopping mall operated with government assistance); *People v. Ford*, 773 P.2d 1059 (Colo. 1989) (upholding obscenity statute, but imposing stricter test than required by First Amendment); *Parrish v. Lamm*, 758 P.2d 1356, 1365 (Colo. 1988) (upholding restrictions on chiropractor advertising); *People v. Seven Thirty-Five East Colfax, Inc.*, 697 P.2d 348, 356 (Colo. 1985) (obscenity statute may only ban that which is intolerable, rather than that which is indecent); *People v. Berger*, 185 Colo. 85, 521 P.2d 1244 (1974) (under "more protective" section 10, there must be some "abuse" for speech to be prohibited; here, obscenity statute was not violated by photographs of non-turgid genitalia); *In Re Hearings Concerning Canon 35 of the Canons of Judicial Ethics*, 132 Colo. 591, 296 P.2d 465 (1956) (striking absolute prohibition of television or radio in the courtroom).

[6] Under modern U.S. Supreme Court doctrine, government officials and "public figures" may only win a libel case if they prove that 1. The statement was factually false; and 2. The statement was made with "actual malice." The term "actual malice" means that the defendant either knew the statement was false or was recklessly indifferent to truth or falsehood. The federal constitutional libel doctrine does not apply to private individual plaintiffs who are not public figures. A person may be a "public figure" in general (*e.g.*, a celebrity), or a "limited purpose public figure" (someone who enters the public arena in a limited way, such as by becoming an activist on a local controversy). The Colorado case applied the above standards to a libel plaintiff who was not a "public figure" in any way, but whose business dealings were a matter of "public concern."

On June 24, 1905, the *News* headlined "Supreme Court Holds that the People Cannot Amend Constitution so as to Express their Will." The divided court had just invalidated the election of Democrats to various City of Denver offices and had installed Republicans in their place. Denver had recently become a home-rule "city and county" via a 1902 amendment to the state constitution. The court ruled that Denver did not have the authority to schedule a spring election for certain municipal offices, because these "city" officials were also "county" officials, which made them state officials, and state officials may be elected only in biennial November general elections.

The *News* accused the supreme court of treating a constitutional amendment as a mere statute. For the next week, the front pages of the *News* and the *Times* ran scathing editorials and cartoons, castigating the Colorado supreme court as the corrupt tool of corporations. Patterson alleged a deal in which Republican governor James H. Peabody had stolen the 1904 election from Democrat Alva Adams, the state Senate had been stolen from the Democrats, and Peabody had sold two supreme court appointments to corporations.[7]

Particularly outrageous, in the view of the *Denver Post*, was a front-page Sunday *News* cartoon that depicted the supreme court executing Democrats. The *Post* urged that Patterson be prosecuted for contempt of court. At the behest of the chief justice, Colorado's attorney general filed charges.

Patterson refused to retreat. He penned another editorial stating he had personally written or approved every one of the attacks on the Colorado court.

An attorney, Patterson represented himself in the contempt hearing before the supreme court. He insisted that everything he had written about the court was true, and that truth ought to be a defense to charges of criminal contempt.

To punish newspapers for criticizing courts, said Patterson, would empower "a chosen body of men who may commit any crime, who may falsify justice, who may defy constitutions and spit upon the laws, and yet no man dare make known the fact."

Patterson was contemptuous of the court, but was he in contempt of court? The common law power of judges to punish contempt of court had been created to prevent interference with judicial proceedings, not to prevent criticism of judges.

Patterson insisted that he would take whatever punishment the court meted out, which could include imprisonment for as long as the justices wanted to keep him locked up. No matter what, he would devote himself to eradication of the "tyrannical power, of such just and dangerous prerogative" that would subject newspapers to punishment for publishing the truth about courts.

Sitting as a self-interested judge in its own case, the Colorado supreme court rejected precedents that limited the contempt power. The court declared the broadest possible reading of its authority. *People ex rel. Attorney General v. News-Times Pub. Co.*, 35 Colo. 253, 84 P. 912 (1906). Patterson was fined $1,000 (equivalent to more than $30,000 in current dollars)—a tolerable amount for a man of Patterson's wealth, but large enough to intimidate many other publishers.

Dissenting, justice Robert Wilbur Steele[8] wrote that the majority's "infinitely" greatest mistake was "in holding the truth to be immaterial." He carefully explicated recent precedents

---

[7] As discussed in chapter 7 (Executive Power, art. IV), the 1904 gubernational election was marred by widespread fraud on both sides; the general assembly eventually fashioned a comprise by which Adams and Peabody each briefly served as governor, and the remainder of the term was served by Republican lieutenant gov. Jesse McDonald.

[8] Not related to Robert Williamson Steele, the "Father of Colorado" and governor of the Provisional Territory of Jefferson (1859-61).

and the procedural abuses in the persecution of Patterson. Justice Steele also examined Anglo-American legal history, including England's infamous Star Chamber.[9]

He discussed the case of John Peter Zenger, printer *New York Weekly Journal*. When Zenger was prosecuted for libeling the royal governor in 1735, defense attorney Andrew Hamilton (no relation to Alexander) told the jury it could acquit—although the judge had instructed the jury that the determination of whether the *Journal*'s content was libelous was a decision for the judge, not the jury. The jury acquitted Zenger.[10] The case remains a symbol of advances in freedom of the press and jury rights—two rights that the Founders and many others have considered to be closely connected.

Rocky Mountain News publisher Thomas Patterson filed a writ of error to the U.S. supreme court. At the time, this was the typical writ for the supreme court to review a state court judgment. The court dismissed the writ, on grounds that the court lacked jurisdiction; in the majority view, Patterson had not come close to showing any violation of his U.S. Constitution rights.

Patterson v. Colorado
205 U.S. 454 (1907)

MR. JUSTICE HOLMES delivered the opinion of the Court.

. . .

The defense upon which the plaintiff in error most relies is raised by the allegation that the articles complained of are true, and the claim of the right to prove the truth. He claimed this right under the Constitutions both of the state and of the United States, but the latter ground alone comes into consideration here, for reasons already stated. *In re Kemmler,* 136 U. S. 436 [1890] [no writ of error should be granted when the petitioner would clearly lose on the merits; petitioner had argued that being executed by the electric chair is unconstitutional] . . .We leave undecided the question whether there is to be found in the Fourteenth Amendment a prohibition similar to that in the First. [Later, the Court did incorporate the free speech clause of the First Amendment. *Gitlow v. New York*, 268 U.S. 652 (1925).] But even if we were to assume that freedom of speech and freedom of the press were protected from abridgments on the part not only of the United States, but also of the states, still we should be far from the conclusion that the plaintiff in error would have us reach. In the first place, the main purpose of such constitutional provisions is "to prevent all such previous restraints upon publications as had been practiced by other governments," and they do not prevent the subsequent punishment of such as may be deemed contrary to the public welfare. *Commonwealth v. Blanding,* 3 Pick. 304, 31314 (Mass. 1825); 1 U. S. 325. *The preliminary freedom extends as well to the false as to the true; the subsequent punishment may extend as well to the true as to the false. This was the law of criminal libel apart from statute in most cases, if not in all. Commonwealth v. Blanding*, ubi supra;[11] 4 Blackstone's Commentaries 150.

---

[9] England's High Court of Star Chamber was abolished by parliament in 1641 because King Charles I (1625–49) was using its loose procedures to criminally prosecute religious dissenters people who libeled the government ("seditious libel"), such as by truthful criticism. At the time, truth was no defense to a libel prosecution. See Daniel L. Vande Zande, *Coercive Power and the Demise of the Star Chamber*, 50 AM. J. LEGAL HIST. 326 (July 2008-2010). As of May 2021, "Star Chamber" appears in 83 U.S. Supreme Court opinions, always as an example of an abusive justice system.

[10] *See* JAMES ALEXANDER, A BRIEF NARRATIVE OF THE CASE AND TRIAL OF JOHN PETER ZENGER (Stanley Nider ed., 1963).

[11] In *Commonwealth v. Blanding,* 3 Pick. 304 (Mass. 1825), a man had been convicted of criminal libel for writing in a newspaper that an innkeeper had poisoned someone. The Massachusetts Supreme Judicial

In the next place, the rule applied to criminal libels applies yet more clearly to contempts . . .

. . . It is objected that the judges were sitting in their own case. But the grounds upon which contempts are punished are impersonal. *United States v. Shipp,* 203 U. S. 563, 203 U. S. 574. No doubt judges naturally would be slower to punish when the contempt carried with it a personal dishonoring charge, but a man cannot expect to secure immunity from punishment by the proper tribunal by adding to illegal conduct a personal attack. It only remains to add that the plaintiff in error had his day in court and opportunity to be heard. We have scrutinized the case, but cannot say that it shows an infraction of rights under the Constitution of the United States or discloses more than the formal appeal to that instrument in the answer to found the jurisdiction of this Court.

Writ of error dismissed.

Figure 8. Oliver Wendell Holmes, Jr., U.S. supreme court associate justice 1902–32.

MR. JUSTICE HARLAN, dissenting:

Court, in an opinion by chief justice Parker, upheld the conviction under the principle that truth is no defense to libel (except in certain situations not relevant to the case at bar).

However, justice Holmes' simple cite to *Blanding* ignored *Blanding*'s explanation of the rule involving public officials: "if the truth only is told of public elective officers, or of acknowledged candidates for offices, in a decent manner and with a view properly to influence an election, it is justifiable," and cannot be prosecuted as criminal libel.

Incidentally, *Blanding* appears to recognize the right to arms as a personal, rather than a collective right: "The liberty of the press was to be unrestrained, but he who used it was to be responsible in case of its abuse; like the right to keep fire arms, which does not protect him who uses them for annoyance or destruction."

The "Pick." in the citation is for Octavius Pickering, who was the reporter of decisions for the Massachusetts Supreme Judicial Court, 1822–37. Such reporters were usually entrepreneurs who published the decisions at no charge to the court, and who made their living by selling volumes of the decisions. So "3 Pick." is Pickering's third published volume.

The U.S. Supreme Court used *nominative reporters* starting with A.J. Dallas in 1790, and ending with John William Wallace in 1874. So the original cite for the Supreme Court's most famous case was *Marbury v. Madison*, 1 Cranch 137 (1803). William Cranch was the reporter for 1801–15. Today, the U.S. Supreme Court has retroactively turned the nominative reports into volumes of U.S. Reports. So the modern citation is *Marbury v. Madison,* 5 U.S. (1 Cranch) 137 (1803). Be aware that most opinions written before 1990 will cite only the nominative reporter.

Fortunately for Colorado lawyers, Colorado opinions never used nominative reporters. The first Colorado cases are in 1 Colo. Later, the Colorado supreme court and court of appeals stopped publishing their own reports, and turned the whole business over to West Publishing, so that published Colorado reporters were only available in the Pacific Reporter series. Presently, both courts publish their opinions online. A cite for 2018 COA 45 is to the 45th case decided by the Colorado court of appeals in 2018. For the Colorado supreme court, the cite would be CO.

I cannot agree that this writ of error should be dismissed.

By the First Amendment of the Constitution of the United States, it is provided that "Congress shall make no law respecting an establishment of religion, or abridging the freedom of speech, or of the press, or of the right of the people peaceably to assemble and to petition the government for redress."

In the *Civil Rights Cases,* 109 U. S. 1, 109 U. S. 20, it was adjudged that the Thirteenth Amendment, although in form prohibitory, had a reflex character in that it established and decreed universal civil and political freedom throughout the United States. In *United States v. Cruikshank,* 92 U. S. 542, 92 U. S. 552, we held that the right of the people peaceably to assemble and to petition the government for a redress of grievances—one of the rights recognized in and protected by the First Amendment against hostile legislation by Congress—was an attribute of "national citizenship." So the First Amendment, although in form prohibitory, is to be regarded as having a reflex character, and as affirmatively recognizing freedom of speech and freedom of the press as rights belonging to citizens of the United States—that is, those rights are to be deemed attributes of national citizenship or citizenship of the United States. No one, I take it, will hesitate to say that a judgment of a federal court, prior to the adoption of the Fourteenth Amendment, impairing or abridging freedom of speech or of the press, would have been in violation of the rights of "citizens of the United States" as guaranteed by the First Amendment—this for the reason that the rights of free speech and a free press were, as already said, attributes of national citizenship before the Fourteenth Amendment was made a part of the Constitution.

Now the Fourteenth Amendment declares, in express words, that "no state shall make or enforce any law which shall abridge the privileges or immunities of citizens of the United States." As the First Amendment guaranteed the rights of free speech and of a free press against hostile action by the United States, it would seem clear that, when the Fourteenth Amendment prohibited the states from impairing or abridging the privileges of citizens of the United States, it necessarily prohibited the states from impairing or abridging the constitutional rights of such citizens to free speech and a free press. But the Court announces that it leaves undecided the specific question whether there is to be found in the Fourteenth Amendment a prohibition as to the rights of free speech and a free press similar to that in the First. It yet proceeds to say that the main purpose of such constitutional provisions was to prevent all such "previous restraints" upon publications as had been practiced by other governments, but not to prevent the subsequent punishment of such as may be deemed contrary to the public welfare. I cannot assent to that view if it be meant that the legislature may impair or abridge the rights of a free press and of free speech whenever it thinks that the public welfare requires that to be done. The public welfare cannot override constitutional privileges, and if the rights of free speech and of a free press are, in their essence, attributes of national citizenship, as I think they are, then neither Congress nor any state, since the adoption of the Fourteenth Amendment, can, by legislative enactments or by judicial action, impair or abridge them. In my judgment, the action of the court below was in violation of the rights of free speech and a free press as guaranteed by the Constitution.

I go further and hold that the privileges of free speech and of a free press, belonging to every citizen of the United States, constitute essential parts of every man's liberty, and are protected against violation by that clause of the Fourteenth Amendment forbidding a state to deprive any person of his liberty without due process of law. It is, I think, impossible to conceive of liberty, as secured by the Constitution against hostile action, whether by the nation or by the states, which does not embrace the right to enjoy free speech and the right to have a free press.

MR. JUSTICE BREWER, dissenting:

While not concurring in the views expressed by MR. JUSTICE HARLAN, I also dissent from the opinion and judgment of the Court. The plaintiff in error made a distinct claim that he was denied that which he asserted to be a right guaranteed by the federal Constitution. His claim cannot be regarded as a frivolous one, nor can the proceedings for contempt be entirely disassociated from the general proceedings of the case in which the contempt is charged to have been committed. I think, therefore, that this Court has jurisdiction, and ought to inquire and determine the alleged rights of the plaintiff in error. As, however, the Court decides that it does not have jurisdiction and has dismissed the writ of error, it would not be fit for me to express any opinion on the merits of the case.

Art. II, Section 11. No laws ex post facto, or impairing obligation of contracts, or granting special irrevocable privileges

> No ex post facto law, nor law impairing the obligation of contracts, or retrospective in its operation, or making any irrevocable grant of special privileges, franchises or immunities, shall be passed by the general assembly.

The first two clauses parallel federal Constitution restrictions on states. U.S. CONST., art. I, § 10 (ex post facto, obligation of contracts).

Although section 11 refers to "the general assembly," it covers all laws, such as those from local governments or the Public Utilities Commission. *E.g., Colorado Office of Consumer Counsel v. Public Service Co. of Colorado*, 877 P.2d 867 (Colo. 1994) (retroactive ratemaking by PUC, since it exercises powers delegated by the general assembly).

The three clauses of section 11 all prevent a government body from acting outside its own time zone. A past act that was lawful at the time cannot be retroactively criminalized. The terms contracts that were previously previously agreed cannot by altered by government. Today's government cannot bind future governments by creating irrevocable special privileges.

Ex post facto

Under U.S. supreme court doctrine, the federal ban on ex post facto laws only applies to criminal laws, not civil laws. *Calder v. Bull*, 3 U.S. 386 (1798 (no application to retroactive change in inheritance law). The U.S. ex post facto rule also applies to *some* changes in criminal procedure—such as increasing the penalty that applied when the crime was committed or reducing the elements that the prosecution had to prove, as those elements existed at the time of the crime. Thus, the Colorado provision against "retrospective" laws is of considerable importance because also it covers civil laws.

Because of Colorado section 11, Colorado civil statutes are interpreted as being prospective only—unless the legislative intent for retroactivity is undeniable. In which case the statute is unconstitutional. The Ex Post Facto rule applies only to vested rights or the creation of new obligations, duties, or disabilities; it does not apply to procedural or enforcement changes. *In re Estate of DeWitt*, 54 P.3d 849 (Colo. 2002) (upholding retrospective effect of Uniform Probate Code, since party had no vested rights at the time the Code was enacted).

Further reading: Grant T. Sullivan & Patrick R. Thiessen, *The Dewitt Test: Determining the Retroactivity of New Civil Legislation in Colorado*, 40 COLO. LAWYER 73 (July 2011).

Obligation of contracts

The federal prohibition on state laws that impair the obligation of contracts was one of the most common reasons for judicial invalidation of state laws in the nineteenth century. Today, the federal Contracts Clause has been considerably narrowed, but still has application. *See Allied*

Structural Steel v. Spannaus, 428 U.S. 234 (1978) (state government cannot retrospectively increase businesses' pension obligations for people who are not current employees). The U.S. Contracts Clause is today most often used when a state or its agents attempt to evade contracts to which they are parties. *Energy Reserves Group, Inc. v. Kansas Power & Light Co.*, 459 U.S. 400 (1983).[12]

A statute that expanded the boundaries for areas in which an automobile dealer could exclude competition from a new dealer of the same type of vehicles did not violate the Contract Clause or the Ex Post Facto Clause; the would-be competitor's rights to operate in a certain territory were not vested rights, but were simply established by statute, and so the statute could be changed without impairing vested rights. *DC Automotive, Inc. v. Kia Motors America, Inc.*, 411 F. Supp. 3d 1137 (D. Colo. 2019).

Irrevocable special privileges

As for the provision about "special privileges," it has been cited for the point that the city's grant of a utility franchise for a term of years does not create a permanent right for that utility. *City of Englewood v. Mountain States Telephone & Telegraph Co.*, 163 Colo. 400, 431 P.2d 40 (1967).

Section 11 has been held not to forbid legislation providing long term tax favors and other benefits as part of a corporate welfare deal with a business. *In re Interrog. by Gov. Romer*, 814 P.2d 875 (Colo. 1991). The case involved special tax and other benefits offered by the general assembly and Denver to entice United Airlines to build a maintenance facility. The United deal is discussed further in relation to Article X, § 9, which forbids relinquishment of the power to tax corporations.

Note that article XV, § 12, contains a separate ban on retrospective laws that benefit corporations.[13] In an employment discrimination case, that section was held, "[f]or purposes of this case," not to go beyond the requirements of art. II, § 11. *Continental Tire Co. v. District Court*, 645 P.2d 1310 (Colo. 1982) (upholding retrospective changes in procedures for employment discrimination cases).

Art. II, Section 12. No imprisonment for debt

> No person shall be imprisoned for debt, unless upon refusal to deliver up his estate for the benefit of his creditors in such manner as shall be prescribed by law, or in cases of tort or where there is a strong presumption of fraud.

In practice, section 12 provides little protection for defendants who fail to pay court-ordered judgments when they have the ability to pay. It does protect against imprisonment of indigent, non-fraudulent persons who are unable to pay their debts or judgments.

Unlike much of the rest of the Bill of Rights, section 12 has been held not to be self-executing. *Kinsey v. Preeson*, 746 P.2d 542 (Colo. 1987) (upholding the principle of body execution against a tortfeasor who is able to pay a judgment and refuses to do so; but since the

---

[12] Test: Is there a "substantial impairment"? If no, the case is over.

If yes, does the state have "a significant and legitimate public purpose"? If no, the case is over.

If yes, "the next inquiry is whether the adjustment of rights and responsibilities of contracting parties is based upon reasonable conditions and is of a character appropriate to the public purpose justifying the legislation's adoption."

[13] "The general assembly shall pass no law for the benefit of a railroad or other corporation, or any individual or association of individuals, retrospective in its operation, or which imposes on the people of any county or municipal subdivision of the state, a new liability in respect to transactions or considerations already past."

statute for execution does not account for ability to pay, it violates the U.S. Fourteenth Amendment); *Coryell v. Lawson*, 25 Colo. App. 432, 139 P. 25 (1914) (not self-executing; body execution statute was improperly applied to enforce a tort verdict, because the jury had not specifically found the statutorily required element of evil intent by the defendant).

Further reading: Nino Monea, *A Constitutional History of Debtors' Prisons*, 14 DREXEL L. REV. __ (forthcoming) (history of the spread of state constitutional provisions against imprisonment for debt).

Art. II, Section 13. Right to keep and bear arms

> The right of no person to keep and bear arms in defense of his home, person and property, or in aid of the civil power when thereto legally summoned, shall be called in question; but nothing herein contained shall be construed to justify the practice of carrying concealed weapons.

The Colorado Convention delegates drew on a variety of state constitutions for models, especially Illinois (1870), Missouri (1875), Nebraska (1875), and Pennsylvania (1873).[14] Nebraska and Illinois had many provisions that were adopted in Colorado, but neither state had a right to arms. Indeed, of the thirty-seven states that had joined the Union prior to Colorado, twelve did not have a constitutional right to arms in 1876.[15] Apparently the Colorado Convention did not want a constitution without the right, and the Convention turned to Missouri for a model. The 1875 Missouri Constitution right to arms was the longest such provision in any state constitution at the time. Missouri integrated several features that Colorado wanted:

- the strongest available language for guaranteeing the right,
- distinguishing personal defense from community defense,
- specifying that the right to arms protects both purposes,
- making it clear that community defense is not only through militia service,
- making it clear that community defense was to be led by appropriate legal officials, and not by freelancing,
- and authorizing restriction or prohibition of the carrying of *concealed* arms.[16]

Like the U.S. Bill of Rights, the Colorado language does not treat rights as a gift from the government. Rather, rights preexist government. As in the phrasing of the Second Amendment,

---

[14] Donald Wayne Hensel, A History of the Colorado Constitution in the Nineteenth Century 105–06, 220 (Aug. 9, 1957) (Ph.D. thesis in History, University of Colorado). Delegates also discussed the constitutions of Alabama, Arkansas, Connecticut, Delaware, Massachusetts, Michigan, Minnesota, New Hampshire, Oregon, Texas, Vermont, West Virginia, and Wisconsin. *Id.* at 106 n.8, 220 n.17. Hensel's thesis remains the best scholarly analysis of early Colorado constitutional history.

[15] Much of this section is adapted from David B. Kopel, *The Right to Arms in Nineteenth Century Colorado*, 95 DENVER LAW REVIEW 329 (2018). Some footnotes are omitted or condensed.

Nebraska, the state that joined just before Colorado, was the last state not to have a right to arms in its original constitution. All 12 states that joined after Colorado had a right to arms from the start. Of the dozen states that had no right to arms as of 1876, half of them (including Nebraska and Illinois) later amended their constitutions to guarantee the right.

[16] *See* MO. CONST. of 1875, art. II, § 17 ("[T]he right of no citizen to keep and bear arms in defense of his home, person and property, or in aid of the civil power, when thereto legally summoned, shall be called in question; but nothing herein contained is intended to justify the practice of wearing concealed weapons.").

the phrasing of the Colorado Constitution treats the right to arms as already in existence.[17] The text safeguards the right to arms but does not create it.

"The right of no person"

Like the rest of the Bill of Rights, the right to arms was not controversial. The Colorado Convention made only one significant change from the Missouri model. Colorado expanded the guarantee to cover every "person," not just the "citizen."[18]

The change was consistent with the immigrant-friendly attitude of the Convention. The Constitution required that until at least 1900, state statutes be printed in Spanish and German, as well as English, for "inhabitants of the State who speak those languages and who may be unable to read and understand the English language."[19] Likewise, the proposed Constitution itself was printed in English, Spanish, and German.

Another alien-friendly provision of the Bill of Rights was section 27, which guaranteed aliens the same property rights as citizens.[20] It was hoped that the provision would attract immigrant capitalists.[21] By statute, immigrants would be allowed to vote as soon as they declared their intent to naturalize.[22]

Consistent with the text of the Constitution, the Colorado supreme court has enforced the arms rights of noncitizens. There is no doubt that a state may reserve the fish and game of a state for the benefit of its citizens.[23] After World War I, under the influence of xenophobia and the Ku Klux Klan, many states adopted gun control laws aimed at legal resident aliens. In 1921, the Colorado legislature banned gun ownership by aliens, ostensibly to prevent them from hunting.[24]

---

[17] *District of Columbia v. Heller*, 554 U.S. 570, 592 (2008); *United States v. Cruikshank*, 92 U.S. 542, 553 (1875) (right to arms is not "in any manner dependent upon [the U.S. Constitution] for its existence").

[18] PROCEEDINGS OF THE CONSTITUTIONAL CONVENTION HELD IN DENVER, DEC. 20, 1875, at 90, 204–05 (1907).

[19] COLO. CONST. art. XVIII, § 8 (amended 1990). The territorial legislature had done the same. *See, e.g.*, ESTATUTOS REVISADOS DE COLORADO, EN FUERZA DE LEY DESPUES DE LA SUSPENSION DE LA SESION NOVENA DE LA ASEMBLEA LEGISLATIVA (E. T. Wells & Fred. J. Stanton eds., 1872) (Spanish); ALLGEMEINEN GESETZE DES STAATES COLORADO (William M. Clark ed., 1877) (German).

The convention delegate behind the mandate for multilingual publication was Casimiro Barela, who had sponsored the bill in the territorial legislature for Spanish language statutory publication. JOSÉ E. FERNÁNDEZ, THE BIOGRAPHY OF CASIMIRO BARELA 16–18, 38–42 (A. Gabriel Meléndez trans., 2003) (1911). Barela was elected to the first statehood Senate in 1876 and served as a state senator until he was defeated in 1916. *Id.* at xviii–xxix.

[20] COLO. CONST. art. II, § 27.

[21] Hensel at 135. In contrast, California's 1879 constitution had an entire article titled "Chinese." It authorized the legislature to remove Chinese from cities and towns or to limit Chinese to certain areas therein, forbade corporations to employ "any Chinese or Mongolian," and forbade governments to employ Chinese. The stated rationale was that the presence of foreigners who are ineligible for citizenship (per U.S. law at the time) was dangerous. CAL. CONST. art. XIX (repealed 1952).

[22] EUGENE H. BERWANGER, THE RISE OF THE CENTENNIAL STATE: COLORADO TERRITORY, 1861–76, at 148 (2007).

[23] *See, e.g.*, *Baldwin v. Fish & Game Comm'n of Montana*, 436 U.S. 371, 390–91 (1978) (higher elk hunting license fees for non-Montanans are constitutional); *Corfield v. Coryell*, 6 Fed. Cas. 546, 549–50 (C.C.E.D. Pa. 1823) (No. 3230) (New Jersey may prohibit oyster harvesting by people from other states).

[24]

> That from and after the passage of this act, it shall be unlawful for any unnaturalized foreign-born resident to hunt for or capture or kill, in this state, any wild bird or animal, either game or otherwise, of any description, excepting in defense of persons or property; and to that end it shall be unlawful for any unnaturalized foreign-born resident, within this

In the 1936 case *People v. Nakamura*,[25] the Colorado supreme court struck down the ban on alien arms.[26] The Colorado attorney general had argued that the right to arms is only a "collective" right and not a "personal" one.[27] Obviously, the argument was difficult to square with the text of section 13. *Nakamura* is also discussed Bill of Rights section 27, on alien property rights.

In modern case law, bans on legal resident aliens keeping or bearing arms have been held to violate the Equal Protection Clause of the Fourteenth Amendment.[28] Bans on *unlawful aliens* keeping or bearing arms have been upheld under the Second Amendment.[29]

"to keep and bear arms in defense of his home, person and property,"

Like the Second Amendment, the Colorado Constitution uses the phrase "keep and bear arms." One earlier case in Tennessee had stated that the phrase "bear arms" has a military-only connotation, so that "bear arms" means only carrying arms while in militia, and not carrying arms for personal defense.[30] The Colorado Constitution does not take this approach. In Colorado, the right to bear arms is for every "person" in defense of "home, person, or property."

"or in aid of the civil power when thereto legally summoned"

After affirming the right to possess and carry arms for defense of home, person, and property, the Colorado Constitution adds a separate reason why arms are protected: so that persons will be able to come to the aid of the civil power.

In Colorado, the need for the militia was freshly in mind. Preventing a repetition of the near conquests of the 1860s would be one benefit of a strong constitutional right to arms. Able to arm themselves, Coloradoans would be better able to defend their state, in the militia.

To Coloradans, the grave danger of an insufficiently armed public was not theoretical. Between 1861 and 1862, Colorado had been menaced by the slave power of the Confederacy. Barely, Coloradans had obtained enough arms and armed men to retain their sovereignty.

> state, to either own or be possessed of a shotgun or rifle of any make, or a pistol or firearm of any kind. Each and every person violating any provisions of this section shall be guilty of a misdemeanor, and, upon conviction thereof, shall be punished by a fine of not less than twenty-five dollars ($25) nor more than two hundred and fifty dollars ($250), or by imprisonment in the county jail not less than ten (10) days or more than three (3) months, or by both such fine and imprisonment; *Provided*, That in addition to the before-named penalty all guns of the above-mentioned kinds found in possession or under control of an unnaturalized foreign-born resident shall, upon conviction of such person, be declared forfeited to the state of Colorado, and shall be sold by the fish and game commissioner as hereinafter directed.

COMPILED LAWS OF COLORADO 1921 § 6882, at 1775 (1922).

[25] 62 P.2d 246 (Colo. 1936).

[26] *Id.* at 247.

[27] *Id.* at 246–47.

[28] *See, e.g.*, *Fotoudis v. City & Cty. of Honolulu*, 54 F. Supp. 3d 1136, 1141–42 (D. Haw. 2014) (striking firearms prohibition for legal aliens); *cf. Fletcher v. Haas*, 851 F. Supp. 2d 287, 303 n.20, 305 (D. Mass. 2012) (striking prohibition on carry permits for legal aliens under the Second Amendment, incorporated to the states via the Fourteenth Amendment).

[29] David B. Kopel & Joseph G.S. Greenlee, *The Federal Circuits' Second Amendment Doctrines*, 61 ST. LOUIS U. L.J. 193, 246–48 (2017).

[30] *Aymette v. State*, 21 Tenn. (2 Hum.) 154, 156–58 (1840). The U.S. Supreme Court expressly rejected *Aymette*'s "odd reading" of the phrase. *District of Columbia v. Heller*, 554 U.S. 570, 613 (2008).

Throughout the 1860s, the Colorado settlers were under Indian attack, and in 1864 and 1865, they had nearly been wiped out. *See* chapter 6 (Fighting for Survival). A prudent, forward-thinking policy would aim to ensure that the people's militia would never again be scarce of arms.

The militia is not the only means by which the civil power may summon aid. Another is the posse comitatus. The constitution mandates that there be county sheriffs, elected by the people.[31] Under common law, they could summon the posse comitatus, as needed.

As intended, the constitutional right to arms has helped to keep the civil power functioning effectively. Today, seventeen Colorado county sheriffs have formal posses, composed of volunteers who receive special training.[32] They aid the sheriff on everything from security at the county fair to road control during weather emergencies to hostage situations.[33]

The Missouri–Colorado language thus guarantees the ownership of arms that are suitable for posse or militia service, and not solely the types of arms that might be suitable for personal self-defense. There is a good argument that arms suitable for the one are also well-suited for the other. But to the extent that there is any divergence, Missouri and Colorado protect both.

Donald Lutz, an eminent scholar of state constitutional law, has written that "constitutionalism is an advanced technique for handling conflict."[34] In Colorado, one of the advanced techniques is that persons will be armed, to defend themselves in an instant, and to defend their communities when lawfully summoned to do so.

The constitutional language "in aid of the civil power when thereto legally summoned" presumes that there is functioning civil power capable of summoning. The Colorado Constitution was intended to create enduring civil power—to defend civil liberty and to foster public goods such as education. If civil power ceased to exist, then whatever people did to defend themselves or their communities would be beyond the scope of what the Colorado Constitution addresses. People would simply be exercising the natural rights recognized in sections 1–3 of the Bill of Rights.

"shall be called into question;"

This language is somewhat similar to the Second Amendment's "shall not be infringed." It is nearly the same as the language of the Fourteenth Amendment, ratified in 1868:

> The validity of the public debt of the United States, authorized by law, including debts incurred for payment of pensions and bounties for services in suppressing insurrection or rebellion, shall not be questioned.[35]

This states the matter firmly. There are many things that the U.S. government may do. Repudiating its debt is not one of them. Unless Section 4 of the Fourteenth Amendment is repealed or revised, the U.S. government cannot fail to perform its legal obligation to pay its debts. There is no wiggle room for evading debt if the government argues that debt repudiation would pass intermediate scrutiny, or some other standard. The question is off the table. The Fourteenth Amendment's language has served the nation well, by assuring creditors that U.S. debts will always be repaid, no matter what.

---

[31] COLO. CONST. art. XIV, § 8.

[32] *See* David B. Kopel, *The Posse Comitatus and the Office of Sheriff: Armed Citizens Summoned to the Aid of Law Enforcement*, 104 J. CRIM. L. & CRIMINOLOGY 761, 810–11 (2014).

[33] *Id.* at 817–23; chapter 19 (discussing Colo. Const. art. XIV, § 8).

[34] DONALD S. LUTZ, THE ORIGINS OF AMERICAN CONSTITUTIONALISM 14 (1988).

[35] U.S. CONST. amend. XIV, § 4.

"but nothing herein contained shall be construed to justify the practice of carrying concealed weapons."

In Colorado, the right shall not be "called in question." With some small differences in phrasing, the language had originated in Pennsylvania in 1790 and been followed by Kentucky in 1792.[36] Given the strong language, in 1822, the Kentucky highest court, the court of appeals, declared unconstitutional a ban on carrying concealed weapons. The court acknowledged that open carry was still allowed, but that did not matter:

> [T]o be in conflict with the constitution, it is not essential that the act should contain a prohibition against bearing arms in every possible form—it is the right to bear arms in defense of the citizens and the state, that is secured by the constitution, and whatever restrains the full and complete exercise of that right, though not an entire destruction of it, is forbidden by the explicit language of the constitution.[37]

Given "the explicit language of the constitution," the only means to justify a concealed carry ban was to have explicit language allowing such a ban. When creating a new constitution in 1850, Kentucky included such language.[38] Missouri did the same in 1875.[39] The strong language against questioning the right had an express exception for concealed carry. The chairman of the Missouri Convention's Bill of Rights committee explained that the express exception was necessary because the Kentucky supreme court had held that "a provision in the Constitution declaring that the right of any citizen to bear arms shall not be questioned, prohibited the Legislature from preventing the wearing of concealed weapons."[40]

Under the canon of construction *expressio unius est exclusio alterius*, the express mention of one thing excludes another.[41] Expressly giving the government power over *concealed* bearing of arms means that the government does not have a similar power over *openly* bearing arms, or over *keeping* arms.

"[N]othing herein contained shall be construed to justify the practice of carrying concealed weapons" means that nothing contained in the right to arms section is a legal justification for carrying a concealed weapon. This leaves the legislature free to regulate, prohibit, or liberally allow concealed carry, as it sees fit.[42] Thus, at various times Missouri has prohibited concealed carry, has allowed it only with a license, has revised the licensing system. Today it allows lawful

---

[36] *See* PA. CONST. of 1790, art. IX, § 21; KY. CONST. of 1792, art. XII, § 23.

[37] *Bliss v. Commonwealth*, 12 Ky. (2 Litt.) 90, 91–92 (1822).

[38] *See* KY. CONST. of 1850, art. XIII, § 25.

[39] MO. CONST. of 1875, art. II, § 17.

[40] 1 DEBATES OF THE MISSOURI CONSTITUTIONAL CONVENTION OF 1875, at 425, 439 (Isidor Loeb & Floyd C. Shoemaker eds., 1930) (referring to *Bliss*, 12 Ky. (2 Litt.) 90); *see also* David B. Kopel, Clayton Cramer, & Scott Hattrup, *A Tale of Three Cities: The Right to Bear Arms in State Supreme Courts*, 68 TEMP. L. REVIEW 1177, 1205 (1995).

[41] *Cain v. People*, 327 P.3d 249, 253 (Colo. 2014) (articulating the meaning of *expressio unius est exclusio alterius* and demonstrating its application).

[42] Colorado had copied the 1875 Missouri constitutional text, but Colorado said "shall be construed," whereas Missouri had said "is intended." The Missouri Supreme Court, interpreting language that is functionally identical to Colorado's, rejected the argument that concealed carry constitutional text forbade the 2003 Missouri legislature from enacting a system for licensing the carrying of concealed arms by qualified persons. *See Brooks v. State*, 128 S.W.3d 844, 846–48 (Mo. 2004); *see also* David B. Kopel, *The Licensing of Concealed Handguns for Lawful Protection: Support from Five State Supreme Courts*, 68 ALBANY LAW REVIEW 305 (2005) (analyzing *Brooks* and similar cases from other states).

adult firearms owners to carry concealed without a license, although in fewer places than where open carry or licensed concealed carry is allowed.[43]

In 2003, a Colorado reform law, similar to a statute earlier adopted in Missouri and many other states, made licensing uniform statewide, with licenses to be issued by county sheriffs. Standards for obtaining a license were made stricter, while persons who met the standards were guaranteed that they would be issued a license.[44] The legislature explained that it was acting to better effectuate self-defense rights, which are guaranteed in article II, section 3.[45]

Leading cases

Besides *Nakamura*, here are other major cases interpreting the Colorado constitutional or statutory rights to keep and bear arms.

City of Lakewood v. Pillow, 180 Colo. 20 (1972). When Lakewood enacted broad restrictions on firearms transportation, the court unanimously held them unconstitutional. Adopting language from the U.S. supreme court's civil liberties cases, the Colorado court stated:

> A governmental purpose to control or prevent certain activities, which may be constitutionally subject to state or municipal regulation under the police power, may not be achieved by means which sweep unnecessarily broadly and thereby invade the area of protected freedoms.

Pillow was cited by several other state courts for interpretation of their own state arms right guarantees.

Robertson v. City & Cty. of Denver, 874 P.2d 325 (Colo. 1994). In 1989, Denver enacted a ban on so-called "assault weapons." After private plaintiffs sued, Colorado attorney general Duane Woodard exercised his statutory right to intervene in the case.[46] Following cross-motions for summary judgement, the Denver district court ruled the gun ban unconstitutional. In Colorado, if a state or local law is ruled unconstitutional, the losing government may appeal directly to the Colorado supreme court. C.R.S. § 13-4-102. The supreme court upheld the gun ban 6–1. The court reasoned that because the ban only applied to a relatively few guns, and so many other guns were still available, the ban was permissible.

Students for Concealed Carry on Campus, LLC v. Regents of University of Colorado, 271 P.3d 496 (Colo. 2012).[47] After the general assembly in 2003 enacted the Concealed Carry Act, the University of Colorado, relying on an opinion from attorney general Ken Salazar, asserted that the university did not have to comply, because the statute had not specifically said that the university did have to comply. When the Mountain States Legal Foundation challenged the university policy, the district court sided with the university, but the court of appeals ruled the university's policy illegal. The Colorado supreme court unanimously affirmed the court of

---

[43] MO. REV. STAT. § 571.030.1(1) (2017) (concealed carry is unlawful only in certain locations); *id.* § 571.030.4 (location restrictions not applicable to persons with concealed carry permit); *id.* § 571.101.2(1)–(3) (procedures for issuing permits to all qualified adults, mostly recently amended by S.B. 656, 2016 Gen. Assemb., 2d Reg. Sess. (Mo. 2016)); KEVIN L. JAMISON, MISSOURI WEAPONS AND SELF-DEFENSE LAW 122–31 (2003) (describing history of restrictions on concealed carry in Missouri, prior to the 2003 enactment of a "Shall Issue" law).

[44] COLO. REV. STAT. § 18-12-201(3); *id.* § 18-12-203(1).

[45] *Id.* § 18-12-201(1)(e); *see* COLO. CONST. art. II, § 3.

[46] I represented the Office of the Attorney General. After Democrat Woodard was defeated by Republican Gale Norton in November 1990, General Norton continued the A.G.'s participation.

[47] An amicus brief by County Sheriffs of Colorado pointed out the sheriffs had been the authors of the Concealed Carry Act, and that the act reflected their specific intent to authorize licensed carry on public college campuses.

appeals decision. The supreme court relied upon the unmistakable preemptive intent of the Concealed Carry Act and did not address the constitutional right to arms.

State v. City and County of Denver, 139 P.3d 635 (Colo. 2006). Under Colorado's municipal home rule amendment, COLO. CONST. art. XX, § 6, courts divide legislative subjects into three categories: statewide concern, where state authority is exclusive; local concern, where home rule cities such as Denver enjoy exclusive authority; and mixed state and local concern, where both states and localities can legislate, but state law wins if there is a conflict. When Colorado in 2003 enacted a firearms preemption statute (restricting local gun controls), and a Shall Issue law for concealed carry licenses, Denver sued for a declaration that its municipal ordinances were not preempted by the statutes. Applying the home rule amendment, a district court upheld Denver's bans on

> (1) open carry of handguns,
> (2) the possession of certain semi-automatic firearms designated as "assault weapons," and
> (3) the retail sale of so-called "Saturday Night Specials" (small inexpensive handguns).

The court struck down

> (1) some of Denver's restrictions on carrying firearms in automobiles,
> (2) some restrictions on firearms possession by juveniles, and
> (3) prohibition of licensed concealed carry in Denver city parks.

City and County of Denver v. Colorado, 2004 WL 5212983 (Colo. Dist. Ct. Nov. 5, 2004). On appeal, the Colorado supreme court affirmed this ruling by an equally divided court (3 to 3), with the seventh justice recused from the case. *State v. City and County of Denver*, 139 P.3d 635 (Colo. 2006). The Colorado rule is that when the supreme court splits, the lower court decision is affirmed as it were an opinion of the supreme court.

Solicitor general Alison Eid had presented the oral argument in support of the preemption statute before the Colorado supreme court. When justice Rebecca Love Kourlis later resigned from the supreme court, governor Owens appointed Eid to fill the vacancy. Chief justice Mary Mullarky took advantage of the transition to delay a decision in the case until Eid was on the court, so she would have to recuse herself.

In 2018, the Boulder city council enacted a ban on firearms that it dubbed "assault weapons" and also a ban on magazines that are legal under state statute. Under *State v. Denver*, the local "assault weapon" ban would be permissible, and the magazine ban would not, since magazines are comprehensively regulated by state law. However, the supreme court had issued new decisions on preemption since the 3-3 no-decision in 2006. Based on newer precedents, a state district court held the Boulder ordinance to be entirely preempted. *Chambers v. City of Boulder*, 18CV30581 (Boulder Dist. Ct., Mar. 21, 2021).

Not long after, a criminal who lived in Arvada bought a firearm there and used it to murder 10 people at a King Soopers grocery store in Boulder. The crime might be seen as an example of the inefficacy of local gun bans. The legislature, however, used the crime as a rationale to wipe out almost all state preemption of gun laws. Even on matters where state law is comprehensive, localities are authorized to enact additional laws, provided that those laws are more severe than state law. Further, localities were authorized to ban licensed carry in buildings and other areas by posting signs. Authority to prohibit licensed carry was also granted to the more than 3,000 special districts in Colorado. (Special districts are covered in chapter 19.) What remains of Colorado preemption is: 1. sheriffs' offices must still issue carry permits to qualified applicants, and 2. localities may not criminalize firearms possession in one's automobile. SB 21-256.

Cracking down on licensed carriers was an odd decision, if the motive were to reduce crime in general or mass shootings in particular. Licensed carriers are vastly more law-abiding than is the general population of Colorado.[48]

People v. Carbajal, 328 P.3d 104 (Colo. 2014). Although laws prohibiting convicted felons from possessing arms are not *per se* unconstitutional, the court since the early 1970s had held that such a statute may not be enforced against a person whose possession of a firearm was for lawful self-defense. The precedents were drastically narrowed in 2014, as *Carbajal* implausibly stated that the previous precedents only applied to arms possession while actually engaged in self-defense, and not to possessing an arm that is intended to be used in case self-defense becomes necessary.

Rocky Mountain Gun Owners v. Polis, 2020 CO 66, 467 P.3d 314 (Colo. 2020). A 2013 statute banned the acquisition of magazines holding more than 15 rounds. A federal court case, raising only federal constitutional issues, was brought by 55 County sheriffs, joined by other plaintiffs.[49] Ultimately, the Tenth Circuit ruled that no plaintiff had standing on any issue. *Colorado Outfitters Ass'n v. Hickenlooper*, 823 F.3d 537 (10th Cir. 2016).

Also in 2013, Dudley Brown's Rocky Mountain Gun Owners—an organization with considerable success in direct mail fundraising but no record of passing Colorado legislation to advance arms rights—brought a state court case on state law issues only. The Colorado supreme court unanimously upheld the statute and declared a new standard of review: all gun control laws are valid unless they are proven beyond a reasonable doubt to be unreasonable. This is quite a different standard from the constitutional text, which provides that "The right of no person. . . shall be called into question." The court did not formally overrule *Pillow*, but it stated the *Pillow*'s rights-protective language only applied to First Amendment rights.

The court's opinion mainly consisted of rejecting plaintiffs' argument that the court should adopt the federal standard of review for the Second Amendment—namely the tiers of strict or intermediate scrutiny used by the Tenth Circuit and most other federal courts. The court also restated at length the court of appeals' statement of the evidence, ignored all evidence and briefing about the inefficacy of magazine bans, the need for magazines over 15 rounds in some defensive situations, and the availability of control systems less extreme than prohibition (such as a licensing system).

---

[48] By statute, Colorado sheriffs have discretion to revoke concealed carry permits, and typically do so when a person is arrested. In 2013–17, there were 233,918 permits (including new permits and renewals in the five-year permit cycle). There were 1,627 permit revocations (excluding revocations for permit-holders no longer residing in the county.), including 1,128 for arrest. Annual reports of issuances and revocations are available at the County Sheriffs of Colorado website, under "Resources." The data are reported annually to the legislature. C.R.S. § 18-12-206(4). The arrest rate for Coloradans in general is about 50 times higher, with 234,409 Colorado adults arrested in 2017 alone. FBI, CRIME IN THE UNITED STATES 2017, table 69. While the two sets of arrest data might not be precisely comparable, the enormity of the difference indicates that if one were looking for way to reduce crime in Colorado, laws against licensed carry would not be the first thing to consider.

If the objective is to reduce deaths from mass shootings, banning licensed carry may be counterproductive. A 2018 *Washington Post* factcheck reported that 86% of mass shootings that are perpetrated in places other than a residence take place in areas where licensed carry is prohibited. Meg Kelly, *Do 98 percent of mass public shootings happen in gun-free zones?* WASHINGTON POST, May 10, 2018. Mass shooters are sometimes stopped because lawfully armed citizens who happen to be present at the scene intervene. In Colorado, that happened in June 2021 at the Olde Town center in Arvada, in 2017 at a Walmart in Thornton, and in December 2007 at the New Life Church in Colorado Springs. Sam Tabachnik, *"True hero" Johnny Hurley shot Olde Town Arvada gunman, witness says*, DENVER POST, June 23, 2021; Thomas Hendrick, *Security Guard: "God Guided Me and Protected Me,"* KMGH-TV Denver, Dec. 10, 2007; Associated Press, *Colorado Church Gunman Had Grudge Against Christian Group, Cops Say*, FOX NEWS, Dec. 10, 2007 (Pastor Brady Boyd said, "she probably saved over 100 lives.").

[49] I represented the sheriffs.

An amicus brief from the Colorado Law Enforcement Firearms Instructors Association and 32 County sheriffs had argued, *inter alia*, that the magazine ban interfered with the constitutional right "to keep and bear arms . . . in aid of the civil power when thereto legally summoned." For example, the ban prohibited members of sheriffs' posses from having appropriate arms. The court stated, "Because Plaintiffs did not address this theory in their complaint, on appeal, or in their briefing to this court, we do not review it." 467 P.3d at 318 n.3.

Appellate courts often refuse to consider amicus argument unless a party brief makes at least some reference to them; the U.S. supreme court though, is often willing to consider any argument from anyone. Given the tenor of the Colorado supreme court's *RMGO* decision, the court's express nondecision on the Aid of the Civil Power Clause was the most nonharmful result possible on that issue.

Further reading: Colorado firearms law statutes are mainly in title 18, article 12, but a few gun laws are scattered in other titles and articles. The best guide to Colorado state gun laws is STANLEY MARKS, DOUGLAS RICHARDS & CHRISTOPHER FERRARO, COLORADO GUN LAW: ARMED AND EDUCATED (2016). However, the spate of gun control laws enacted by the general assembly in 2020-21 are not included in the 2016 book. Also: David B. Kopel, *The Right to Arms in Nineteenth Century Colorado,* 95 DENVER LAW REVIEW 329 (2018); David B. Kopel, Clayton Cramer & Scott Hattrup, *A Tale of Three Cities: The Right to Bear Arms in State Courts*, 68 TEMPLE LAW REVIEW 1177 (1995) (analysis of the *Robertson* case, and of similar cases in Ohio and Oregon).

Art. II, Section 14. No taking property for private use

> Private property shall not be taken for private use unless by consent of the owner, except for private ways of necessity, and except for reservoirs, drains, flumes or ditches on or across the lands of others, for agricultural, mining, milling, domestic or sanitary purposes.

Unlike the U.S. Constitution, the Colorado Constitution allows some taking of private property for private use. Of course, just compensation must still be paid. Idaho has a similar provision. IDAHO CONST., art. I, § 14. Private purposes takings were seen as necessary to mining development, especially to quartz mining, which is large scale and capital-intensive. G. ALAN TARR, UNDERSTANDING STATE CONSTITUTIONS 117 (1998); DENNIS C. COLSON, IDAHO'S CONSTITUTION: THE TIE THAT BINDS 104–05 (1991).

The Colorado Constitution's authorization of private takings is limited to two specific situations: 1. Private ways of necessity. 2. Water use.

The classic "private way of necessity" is for a landlocked landowner who has no means of ingress or egress to a public road, except via someone else's land. A private way of necessity is not allowed if the prospective condemnor can use an acceptable alternate route of access. *Glenelk Ass'n, Inc. v. Lewis*, 260 P.3d 1117 (Colo. 2011). The condemnor is not required to use an alternate route that is impractical, unreasonable, or cost-prohibitive. The burden of proof is on the landowner seeking to block the private way of necessity. *Tieze v. Killam*, 179 P.3d 10 (Colo. App. 2007). The property owner's willingness to lease an access route over his land is insufficient to defeat an action for condemnation. *Bear Creek Development Corp. v. Genesee Foundation*, 919 P.2d 948 (Colo. App. 1996).

A landowner cannot condemn a private way to necessity for an easement to connect his natural gas well for a natural gas pipeline. *Akin v. Four Corners Encampment*, 179 P.3d 139 (Colo. App. 2007). Nor could a state statute authorize a tramway to carry mining ore over private property without consent. *People ex rel. Aspen Mining & Smelting Co. v. Dist. Court, Pitkin County*, 11 Colo. 147, 17 P. 298 (1888).

Specific, separate language in section 14 allows for eminent domain to construct water channels, consistent with similar language from article XVI (Irrigation and Mining).

Perversely, the U.S. supreme court allows the taking of private property for private use, under the theory that the promised economic activity will be of public benefit. *Kelo v. City of New London*, 545 U.S. 469 (2005); ILYA SOMIN, THE GRASPING HAND: "KELO V. CITY OF NEW LONDON" AND THE LIMITS OF EMINENT DOMAIN (2015) (woman's home taken by the government to give to a pharmaceutical company that promised to build a factory, but never fulfilled the promise, leaving the property a wasteland).

Colorado courts do the same, under the theory that economic activity by a business is a public purpose, so the government can condemn the property and then give it to the business. The result is contrary to section 14's very specific creation of limited eminent domain powers for private parties. It is contrary to the text and to original meaning, as expressed in the *Aspen Mining and Smelting* decision.

After *Kelo* became one of the most broadly condemned U.S. supreme court decisions in history, the Colorado legislature joined the trend in many states to enact laws against taking property for private businesses. According to the Colorado statute, "'public use' shall not include the taking of private property for transfer to a private entity for the purpose of economic development or enhancement of tax revenue." C.R.S. § 38-1-101(b)(I).

But the statute has proven easy to evade. In a 2019 Colorado supreme court case, the owner of two-thirds of an acre of land near Parker, Colorado, did not want to sell to a developer for the developer's offered price. With the connivance of the Parker municipal government, the developer created a "metropolitan district," staffed entirely by employees of the developer. (Colorado's over three thousand special districts are discussed in chapter 19.) The "district" then condemned the land, for the price that the developer wanted to pay. The "district" kept the property for itself, to be developed in conjunction with the developer's plans for nearby properties. According to the supreme court, the statute against taking for "private use" was inapplicable because the new owner (the district) did not convey the land to the developer. Although the developer did benefit, there were public uses in the sense of use of some of the land for public rights of way or for storm water drainage. *Carousel Farms Metropolitan District v. Woodcrest Homes, Inc.*, 2019 CO 51, 442 P.3d 402 (2019); Vincent Carroll, *Colorado's high court gives metro districts power to seize property*, COMPLETE COLORADO, Nov. 29, 2019.

"Kleptocracy" is rule by thievery. It comes from the Greek kléptēs ("thief") and kratía ("power, rule").

Further reading: Robyn W. Kube, *Access at Last: The Use of Private Condemnation*, 29 COLO. LAWYER 77 (Feb. 2000).

Art. II, Section 15. Taking property for public use—Compensation

> Private property shall not be taken or damaged, for public or private use, without just compensation. Such compensation shall be ascertained by a board of commissioners, of not less than three freeholders, or by a jury, when required by the owner of the property, in such manner as may be prescribed by law, and until the same shall be paid to the owner, or into court for the owner, the property shall not be needlessly disturbed, or the proprietary rights of the owner therein divested; and whenever an attempt is made to take private property for a use alleged to be public, the question whether the contemplated use be really public shall be a judicial question, and determined as such without regard to any legislative assertion that the use is public.

Section 15 is more protective than the Takings Clause of the federal Fifth Amendment, at least compared to early interpretation of the latter. Notably, Section 15 applies to "damage" to property, as opposed to the nineteenth century doctrine that the Fifth Amendment's Taking Clause was only implicated by physical invasion. As interpreted by the courts, the damage must be something particularly related to the property, rather than a harm suffered by the public in general.

Diminution in property value is insufficient to prove damage. *City of Northglenn v. Grynberg*, 846 P.2d 175 (Colo. 1993). Government actions that block access to land have been one type of successful claim.

The majority view in the United States is that a taking in violation of a restrictive covenant requires compensation. The majority of the Colorado supreme court disagrees. Within a subdivision that had a restrictive covenant requiring residential use only, the government could take land to build a water tower. *Forest View Company v. Town of Monument*, 2020 CO 52, 464 P.3d 774 (2020).

Section 15 functions as a waiver of sovereign immunity. As a result, property owners can bring a suit for inverse condemnation, alleging that the government's actions constitute a taking, even when the government is not attempting to acquire title to the land.

A statutory remedy for some regulatory impairments of property rights is provided by C.R.S. §§ 29-20-201 to 205. Eminent domain is covered in title 38, article 1, parts 1 and 2.

Art. II, Section 16. Criminal defendant rights

> In criminal prosecutions the accused shall have the right to appear and defend in person and by counsel; to demand the nature and cause of the accusation; to meet the witnesses against him face to face; to have process to compel the attendance of witnesses in his behalf, and a speedy public trial by an impartial jury of the county or district in which the offense is alleged to have been committed.

Much of section 16 parallels the text of the U.S. Sixth Amendment: Right to counsel Clause, Arraignment Clause, Confrontation Clause, Speedy and Public Trial Clause, and Jury Trial Clause. Section 16 also includes specifics that were later held to be implicit in the U.S. Sixth Amendment: *Faretta v. California*, 422 U.S. 806 (1975) (right to represent oneself at trial); *Illinois v. Allen*, 397 U.S. 337 (1970) (right to be present at trial). Section 16 has not usually been interpreted differently than the Sixth Amendment.

The constitutional jury trial right does not include petty offenses. *Austin v. City & County of Denver*, 178 Colo. 448, 462 P.2d 600 (1969) (unlawful use of a traffic lane, resulting in a 90-day jail sentence) .

By statute the general assembly has provided for jury trials for all misdemeanors and petty offenses, including in municipal courts, upon defendant's request. C.R.S. § 13-10-101 (preempting the field); § 13-10-114 (municipal petty offense defendant shall have jury upon request).

A "petty offense" is 1. any crime or offense designated as a "petty offense"; 2. or an unclassified crime that is punishable by no more than six months in jail or a fine of not more than

$500, or both; 3. any municipal ordinance violation not based on a common law crime. It does not include municipal traffic ordinances that are non-criminal and not punishable by imprisonment. C.R.S. § 16-10-109(1). *See also Roalstad v. City of Lafayette*, 363 P.3d 790 (Colo. App. 2015) (enforcing statutory jury trial right for municipal law imposing fine for ownership of a vicious animal, even though city Lafayette did not formally classify the ownership as a crime).

Figure 9. Pitkin County courthouse.

A city's home rule charter cannot create an exemption from the jury trial statute. *Hardaman v. Municipal Court*, 178 Colo. 271, 497 P.2d 1000 (1972).

Panels of the Colorado court of appeals have offered mixed answers as to whether section 16 provides greater protection than the U.S. Constitution against the use of nontestimonial hearsay in a criminal trial. *See* Christopher G. Breidenbach & Joseph G. Michael, *Confronting Nontestimonial Hearsay: Colorado's Split from the Sixth Amendment and What It Means in Practice*, 45 COLO. LAWYER 21 (May 2016).

Section 23 of article II also covers juries, including the minimum size for criminal juries.

Art. II, Section 16a. Criminal victim rights

> Any person who is a victim of a criminal act, or such person's designee, legal guardian, or surviving immediate family members if such person is deceased, shall have the right to be heard when relevant, informed, and present at all critical stages of the criminal justice process. All terminology, including the term "critical stages", shall be defined by the general assembly.

This 1992 amendment came during a time when many states were creating crime victims' Bills of Rights. The implementing statutes are C.R.S. §§ 24-4.1-302 to 304. For crime victims who are witnesses, Section 16a appears to conflict with a trial court's ordinary authority to bar witnesses from watching courtroom proceedings before they testify. Colo. R. Evid. 615.

By statute, a "critical stage" does *not* include the hearing on a prosecutor's motion to dismiss charges. *Gansz v. People,* 888 P.2d 256 (Colo. 1995). Section 16a does not create any judicial review of a prosecutor's discretionary decision to dismiss charges. *People v. Herron*, 888. P.2d 256 (Colo. 1995). The rights in section 16a are for victims to be informed, not for them to control a prosecution.

Further reading: Paul G. Cassell, *Protecting Crime Victims in Federal Appellate Courts: The Need to Broadly Construe the Crime Victims' Rights Act's Mandamus Provision*, 87 DENVER

U.L. REVIEW 599 (2010);[50] Ethan D. Feldman & Meghan P. Saleebey, *Victim's Rights and Defendants' Rights: Is There a Conflict?* 36 COLO. LAWYER 45 (April 2007).

Art. II, Section 17. Imprisonment of witnesses for depositions

> No person shall be imprisoned for the purpose of securing his testimony in any case longer than may be necessary in order to take his deposition. If he can give security he shall be discharged; if he cannot give security his deposition shall be taken by some judge of the supreme, district or county court, at the earliest time he can attend, at some convenient place by him appointed for that purpose, of which time and place the accused and the attorney prosecuting for the people shall have reasonable notice. The accused shall have the right to appear in person and by counsel. If he has no counsel, the judge shall assign him one in his behalf only. On the completion of such examination the witness shall be discharged on his own recognizance, entered into before said judge, but such deposition shall not be used if in the opinion of the court the personal attendance of the witness might be procured by the prosecution, or is procured by the accused. No exception shall be taken to such deposition as to matters of form.

The 1876 Colorado Constitution was the first state constitution to provide this protection.

Further detail about the taking of depositions in criminal cases is provided by C.R.S. § 16-9-101 (subpoena to compel attendance of witnesses in criminal cases); Colo. R. Crim. Pro. 15 (depositions), 17 (subpoenas).

Art. II, Section 18. Compelled self-incrimination, double jeopardy

> No person shall be compelled to testify against himself in a criminal case nor shall any person be twice put in jeopardy for the same offense. If the jury disagree, or if the judgment be arrested after the verdict, or if the judgment be reversed for error in law, the accused shall not be deemed to have been in jeopardy.

Self-incrimination

The first sentence parallels the Self-Incrimination Clause of the U.S. Fifth Amendment. Colorado's provision has been interpreted the same as its federal counterpart. Indeed, the Colorado supreme court's decisions on self-incrimination often do not even cite Section 18, and instead rely entirely on the Fifth Amendment; as result, several widely criticized Colorado decisions of the late 1980s were overturned by the U.S. supreme court. RICHARD COLLINS & DALE A. OESTERLE, THE COLORADO STATE CONSTITUTION 67 (2d ed. 2020); *Colorado v. Spring*, 479 U.S. 564 (1987), *rev'g People v. Spring*, 713 P.2d 1985 (Colo. 1985) (murder suspect thought he was just going to be questioned about illegal firearms trafficking; his unawareness of the impending trap did not vitiate the voluntariness of his waiver of his right to remain silent);

---

[50] A professor at the University of Utah and a former federal district judge, Paul Cassell is a leading advocate of victims' rights. He also writes for the Volokh Conspiracy, a law professor weblog hosted by *Reason* magazine.

Colorado v. Connelly, 479 U.S. 157 (1986), *rev'g People v. Connelly*, 702 P.2d 722 (Colo. 1985) (mentally ill murderer walked up to a police officer and confessed; although the actions of a mentally ill persons may not be "voluntary," as long as there is no coercion by government, the confession does not violate Fifth Amendment rights against self-incrimination).

Had the Colorado court developed a distinct jurisprudence on Section 18, the Colorado decisions would have been based on *independent and adequate* state constitutional grounds, and thus immune from U.S. supreme court review. But it might not have made a difference. *Connelly* and some other criminal procedure decisions from the Colorado supreme court sparked so much outrage that governor Dick Lamm warned two justices—whom he had appointed—that if they stayed on the court he would campaign against them in their retention elections. Justices Jean Dubofsky and George E. Lohr resigned in 1987.

Note that in election contests, there are special rules for when testimony may be compelled. Art. VII, § 9.

Double jeopardy

The second sentence is similar to the Double Jeopardy Clause of the Fifth Amendment. The textual exceptions specified in the Section 18 are consistent with judicial interpretation of the Fifth Amendment.

A huge loophole in the federal Double Jeopardy Clause is the judicial doctrine that allows a person to be retried by a separate sovereign. For example, the defendant is acquitted in state court, but is then prosecuted in federal court for essentially the same conduct. The second prosecution is permitted as long as one element of the crime is different—such as the federal statute having a predicate about interstate commerce. The dual sovereignty doctrine was recently reaffirmed 7–2. *Gamble v. United States*, 139 S.Ct. 1960 (2019) (Justices Ginsburg & Gorsuch dissenting).

In Colorado, however, statute bars state prosecution following an acquittal in a court of "the United States, or another state, or of a municipality." Except when the second prosecution requires proof of a different fact and "the law defining each of the offenses is intended to prevent a substantially different harm or evil." C.R.S. § 18-1-303; *People v. Morgan*, 785 P.2d 1294 (Colo. 1990) (applying statute after prosecution in Navajo Tribal Court). The statute has been held inapplicable when the first prosecution was in another nation. *People v. Garcia*, 2021 COA 65 (Colo. App. 2021).

The Colorado supreme court likewise goes beyond the federal minimum: "we have interpreted the Double Jeopardy Clause of the Colorado Constitution more expansively than the United States supreme court's construction of its federal counterpart. Under Colorado case law, a judgment of acquittal after the attachment of jeopardy precludes a retrial of the defendant even though the judgment was improper and was based on grounds unrelated to factual guilt." *People v. Serravo,* 823 P.2d 128, 141 (Colo. 1992).

Art. II, Section 19. Right to bail, detailed exceptions

> (1) All persons shall be bailable by sufficient sureties pending disposition of charges except:
>
> > (a) For capital offenses when proof is evident or presumption is great; or
> >
> > (b) When, after a hearing held within ninety-six hours of arrest and upon reasonable notice, the court finds that proof is evident or presumption is great as to the crime alleged to have been committed and finds that the public would be placed in significant peril if the accused were released on bail and such person is accused in any of the following cases:

(I) A crime of violence, as may be defined by the general assembly, alleged to have been committed while on probation or parole resulting from the conviction of a crime of violence;

(II) A crime of violence, as may be defined by the general assembly, alleged to have been committed while on bail pending the disposition of a previous crime of violence charge for which probable cause has been found;

(III) A crime of violence, as may be defined by the general assembly, alleged to have been committed after two previous felony convictions, or one such previous felony conviction if such conviction was for a crime of violence, upon charges separately brought and tried under the laws of this state or under the laws of any other state, the United States, or any territory subject to the jurisdiction of the United States which, if committed in this state, would be a felony; or

(c) (Deleted by amendment, L. 94, p. 2853, effective upon proclamation of the Governor, L. 95, p. 1434, January 1, 1995.)

(2) Except in the case of a capital offense, if a person is denied bail under this section, the trial of the person shall be commenced not more than ninety days after the date on which bail is denied. If the trial is not commenced within ninety days and the delay is not attributable to the defense, the court shall immediately schedule a bail hearing and shall set the amount of the bail for the person.

(2.5)

(a) The court may grant bail after a person is convicted, pending sentencing or appeal, only as provided by statute as enacted by the general assembly; except that no bail is allowed for persons convicted of:

(I) Murder;

(II) Any felony sexual assault involving the use of a deadly weapon;

(III) Any felony sexual assault committed against a child who is under fifteen years of age;

(IV) A crime of violence, as defined by statute enacted by the general assembly; or

(V) Any felony during the commission of which the person used a firearm.

(b) The court shall not set bail that is otherwise allowed pursuant to this subsection (2.5) unless the court finds that:

(I) The person is unlikely to flee and does not pose a danger to the safety of any person or the community; and

(II) The appeal is not frivolous or is not pursued for the purpose of delay.

(3) This section shall take effect January 1, 1995, and shall apply to offenses committed on or after said date.

The 1876 version was "All persons shall be bailable by sufficient sureties except for capital offenses, when the proof is evident or the presumption great." A 1982 amendment created subsections (1) and (2), denying bail when a defendant poses "a significant peril" of violence. The denial of bail advances the speedy trial date.

A 1994 amendment added subsections (2.5) and (3), restricting post-conviction bail pending appeal.

Bail laws are at C.R.S. §§ 16-4-101 to 115; and Colo. Rules Criminal Pro. 46. The right to bail does not apply to juvenile detention. *L.O.W. v. District Court*, 623 P.2d 125 (Colo. 1981). Nor does it apply to persons being held for extradition to another sovereign. *Johnson v. District Court*, 610 P.2d 1064 (Colo. 1980).

The U.S. Constitution's Eighth Amendment prohibits "excessive" bail (like Colorado's section 20, discussed next), but the Eighth Amendment contains no right to bail *per se*. Although courts have often found a bail right by implication, the absence of a textual guarantee makes it easier for legislatures to create exceptions. Therefore, section 19 provides a protection not found federally.

Art. II, Section 20. Excessive bails, fines or punishments

> Excessive bail shall not be required, nor excessive fines imposed, nor cruel and unusual punishments inflicted.

An exact copy of the federal Eighth Amendment, Section 20 is interpreted the same. Until recently, however, section 20 was quite important, because the U.S. supreme court had not forthrightly incorporated the Excessive Bail Clause or the Excessive Fines Clause.

Excessive bails

The U.S. supreme court has never squarely decided a case on whether the Eighth Amendment ban on excessive bails is incorporated against the states via the Fourteenth Amendment. In a 1971, the court did remark: "Bail, of course, is basic to our system of law [citations omitted], and the Eighth Amendment's proscription of excessive bail has been assumed to have application to the States through the Fourteenth Amendment." *Schilb v. Kuebel*, 404 U.S. 357 (1971). In the 2010 *McDonald v. City of Chicago*, the supreme court held that the Second Amendment is incorporated. Surveying past cases incorporating other parts of the U.S. Bill of Rights, justice Alito's opinion for the court described *Schlib* as having incorporated the Excessive Bail Clause. 561 U.S. 742, 764 n.12 (2010).

Some courts have analyzed particularly egregious high bails as violations of the Due Process Clause of the Fourteenth Amendment.

Further reading: Joshua J. Luna, *Bail Reform in Colorado: A Presumption of Release*, 88 UNIV. OF COLO. L. REVIEW 1067 (2017) (arguing that the general assembly should expand its 2013 statute allowing so that more arrestees could be released without cash bail).

Excessive fines

The federal Excessive Fines Clause was thoroughly examined and unanimously incorporated in *Timbs v. Indiana*, 139 S.Ct. 682 (2019).[51] Previously, the U.S. supreme court had analyzed some excessive fines, including punitive damages, as Due Process violations.

In Colorado courts, a fine is excessive under both the United States and Colorado Constitutions if the amount is so disproportionate to a defendant's circumstances that there can be no realistic expectation that the defendant will be able to pay it. *Boulder County Apartment Ass'n*

[51] For a description of the harsh and unfair operation of civil forfeiture laws nationally *see* the amicus brief of the Drug Policy Alliance, which was joined by many organizations, including the Independence Institute.

v. City of Boulder, 97 P.3d 332 (Colo. App. 2004) (strict liability fine of $2,000 per day on apartment owners for excessive occupancy). Fining a destitute defendant $100,000 fine for $400 of criminal mischief is excessive. *People v. Malone*, 923 P.2d 163 (Colo. App. 1995).

Colorado's most recent excessive fines case involved an immigrant widow who did not speak English. Via a limited liability corporation, she was the sole owner of a motel in a rough neighborhood. Her late husband, the co-owner, had been murdered decades earlier. She was fined $841,200 for a second offense of not having worker's compensation. In her version of events, her insurance agent told her that she did have the required insurance, but he was incorrect. The $841,200 was the sum of daily fines, accumulating over three years, with an aggravated schedule due to previous violation.

At trial, the defendant only raised the U.S. Eighth Amendment, and not Colorado's section 20. The Colorado the attorney general argued that even if the U.S. Eighth Amendment Excessive Fines Clause was incorporated, it did not apply to corporations. As the attorney general pointed out, the Excessive Bail Clause definitely does not apply to corporations.

The Colorado supreme court decided the case post-*Timbs*. The court held that the Eighth Amendment *does* apply to corporations. While it is impossible to put a corporation in jail, it is possible to fine a corporation. As for the excessiveness of fines, the court held that excess for daily fine should be considered only one day at a time, and not by the cumulative amount. If daily fines of $200 to $500 were not excessive, the defendant could not argue that a cumulative fine of $841,200 was unconstitutionally excessive. *Colorado Dept. of Labor & Employment v. Dami Hospitality, LLC*, 442 P.3d 94 (Colo. 2019). The U.S. supreme court denied the attorney general's cert. petition on the corporations issue. 140 S.Ct. 849 (2020).

Cruel and unusual punishments

The parallel federal clause has been definitively incorporated since 1962. *Robinson v. California*, 370 U.S. 660 (1962) (drug use can be criminalized but being a drug addict may not). *Robinson* was among a series of Warren Court decisions that incorporated most of the criminal law and procedure provisions of Amendments IV–VIII.

In general, the U.S. supreme court has been reluctant to address punishments that are disproportionate to the crime, except for capital crimes and (recently) life sentences for juveniles.

Under the Cruel and Unusual Punishments Clause, the defendant's individual characteristics are irrelevant, but such characteristics can be relevant for excessive fines (*e.g.*, ability to pay). Juvenile status does sometimes matter in the Eighth Amendment. *Roper v. Simmons*, 543 U.S. 551 (2005) (no death penalty for crimes committed as a juvenile); *Miller v. Alabama*, 567 U.S. 460 (2012) (juvenile life without parole).

Until recently, Colorado's section 20 jurisprudence had not differed from Eighth Amendment federal precedents. The many cases involving the constitutionality of Colorado's death penalty statutes have followed U.S. supreme court precedent: capital punishment is not unconstitutional, but judicial regulation of procedures is uniquely strict.

In 2019, the Colorado supreme court did what the U.S. supreme court has declined to do and issued detailed standards for proportionality review for criminal sentences. *Wells-Yates v. People*, 2019 CO 90M, 454 P.3d 191 (Colo. 2019) . Overturning or narrowly construing many precedents, the Colorado court brought forth a new system; the court described the new system as mostly congruent with existing Colorado and United States precedents, but the court was being somewhat modest about the breadth of its new handiwork.

Pursuant to *Wells-Yates*, when a sentence is challenged as disproportionate, a court should first conduct an abbreviated proportionality review. The review examines the gravity of the offense (including the defendant's culpability) versus the harshness of the sentence (including whether parole is available). If the court does not find *gross* disproportionality, the defendant loses.

If the abbreviated review creates an inference of gross disproportionality, a court should conduct an extended proportionality review. The extended review includes:

1. Whether the same offense in the same jurisdiction has received similar sentences in other cases. Same-offense review has long been part of proportionality review.
2. The punishments for *different* offenses in the jurisdiction. For example, if selling small quantities of illegal drugs was punished much more severely than a third offense of aggravated sexual assault, the disparity might suggest unconstitutional disproportionality.
3. The punishment for the same offense in *other* jurisdictions. For example, if all the other states imposed a fine of no more than $250 for willfully putting a nonrecyclable bottle in a recycling bin, and Colorado imposed a mandatory minimum sentence of two years in state prison, the disparity might suggest disproportionality.

In the case at bar, the court took into consideration the general assembly's recent significant reduction in penalties for low-level drug sales. Although the general assembly had chosen not to make the reduced penalties retroactive (to the time when Wells-Yates had committed her crimes), the general assembly's prospective statute was still an indication of how seriously, or not, such offenses were now viewed.

Some offenses, such as robbery or drug sales, are "per se grave or serious," which in effect means that a challenge to a sentence is unlikely to get past the abbreviated review stage. The court held possession-with-intent-to-distribute "narcotics" is not automatically grave or serious; whether a particular offense was grave or serious would have to be decided on the circumstances of individual cases.

Under Colorado's habitual offender statutes, a third felony conviction triggers a sentence quadruple the sentence for the same crime by a first-time offender. The *Wells-Yates* decision set forth a system for proportionality review in habitual offender statutes, but the review did Ms. Wells-Yates no good. As with excessive fines, sentences are to be analyzed one at a time, and not for their cumulative effect. Wells-Yates had three prior drug felonies (two for possession, one for possession-with-intent). At her latest trial, she was convicted of burglary (looting homes that had been abandoned due to a fire), conspiracy to commit burglary, theft, possession-with-intent, and four counts of identity theft. She was sentenced to 48 years for the burglary plus 24 years for the drugs, and all the other sentences were concurrent with the 48 years. The 48 year sentence was held not to be disproportionate, and the 24 year sentence was also so held. The fact that 48 + 24 = 72 was irrelevant.

Designation as a sexually violent predator (SVP) leads to a lifetime of restrictions on an individual. The designation, however, has been held not to constitute a form of punishment. Hence, section 20 is inapplicable. *Allen v. People*, 2013 CO 44, 307 P.3d 1102 (2013).

Art. II, Section 21. Suspension of habeas corpus

> The privilege of the writ of habeas corpus shall never be suspended, unless when in case of rebellion or invasion, the public safety may require it.

Also a copy of the U.S. Constitution. Art, I, § 9. Like the U.S. Constitution, section 21 is ambiguous as to *who* may suspend it: the legislature only, or also the executive?

During the Civil War, president Lincoln suspended the right himself. Congress eventually enacted legislation for fairer procedures, reining in secretary of state William Seward's proclivity for incarcerating anti-war Northerners because of their politics.[52]

During a 1904 miners' strike in San Miguel County, governor James Peabody called out the Colorado National Guard, declared that the county was in a state of insurrection, imposed martial law, and had the mine union president arrested and held by the National Guard.[53] The union president filed a petition for a writ of habeas corpus.

The majority asserted, implausibly, 1. that the writ of habeas corpus had not been suspended; and 2. the judiciary had no authority to review the legality of the union president's detention. Even though the purpose of a petition for a writ of habeas corpus is for the judiciary to conduct such a review. Dissenting, justice Steele argued that the governor had no power to suspend habeas corpus unless the legislature had granted him that authority. *In re Moyer*, 35 Colo. 159, 85 P. 190 (1904).

Although habeas corpus is primarily a claim that a person should be set at liberty, Colorado courts have sometimes used it to review a person's conditions of confinement if the conditions "substantially infringe on basic rights." *E.g.*, *Marshall v. Kort*, 690 P.2d 219 (Colo. 1992) (mental inmate who did not assert a right to be released from the institution).

Habeas corpus procedures are at C.R.S. title 13, article 45, part 1.

As discussed in the chapter 10 (Judiciary, art. VI), the Colorado supreme court has original jurisdiction for habeas corpus petitions. The petitioner is not *required* to start in the supreme court. She may instead file in district court or, to the extent allowed by statute, in county court. *Stilley v. Tinsley*, 153 Colo. 66, 385 P.2d 677 (1963) (also noting that the custodian, and not the State of Colorado, is the proper respondent in a habeas petition).

Art. II, Section 22. Military subordinate to civil power, quartering forbidden

> The military shall always be in strict subordination to the civil power; no soldier shall, in time of peace, be quartered in any house without the consent of the owner, nor in time of war except in the manner prescribed by law.

Military subject to civil power

The first provision declares a universally-agreed American principle, expressly stated in many state constitutions and implied in the federal constitution.[54] The second provision copies the federal Third Amendment.

The only case interpreting section 22 was *In re Moyer*, discussed under section 21. The majority held that since the military force imposing martial law in San Miguel County was under the governor's command, section 22 was not violated.

---

[52] *See* WILLIAM REHNQUIST, ALL THE LAWS BUT ONE: CIVIL LIBERTIES IN WARTIME (2000) (title from Lincoln's defense of his actions, which prevented Maryland from seceding: "Are all the laws but one to go unexecuted and the government itself go to pieces lest that one be violated?"); David B. Kopel, *Lyman Trumbull: Author of the Thirteenth Amendment, Author of the Civil Rights Act, and the First Second Amendment Lawyer*, 47 LOYOLA U. CHI. L.J. 1117, 1144–46 (2016) (describing Trumbull's reform statute).

[53] The Western Federation of Miners, a radical socialist labor organization.

[54] U.S. CONST., art. I, § 8 (only Congress had the power to declare war); art. II, § 2, cl. 1 ("The President shall be Commander in Chief of the Army and Navy of the United States, and of the Militia of the several States, when called into the actual Service of the United States . . . .").

The U.S. supreme court later heard the case. According to the unanimous and terse opinion by justice Holmes, the governor had stated that there was an insurrection, Moyer had not challenged the accuracy of the determination, and that was end of the case. *Moyer v. Peabody*, 212 U.S. 78 (1909).

Quartering

The Third Amendment and the Quartering Clause of section 22 arose from notorious abuses of quartering in Europe. For example, France in the 1685 Edict of Fontainebleau revoked the 1598 Edict of Nantes, which had provided some protection to the French Protestants—the Huguenots. With no legal protections, the Huguenots were disarmed, and then their oppressions multiplied.

> [T]he most atrocious—and effective—were the *dragonnades*, or billeting of dragoons [mounted soldiers] on Huguenot families with encouragement to behave as viciously as they wished. Notoriously rough and undisciplined, the enlisted troops of the dragoons spread carnage, beating and robbing the householders, raping the women, smashing and wrecking and leaving filth.[55]

The billeting of soldiers, which had been introduced in 1681, would continue until the family converted to Catholicism.[56]

The first use of billeting (or quartering) to force conversions to Catholicism may have taken place in parts of Germany during the 1620s.[57] In England, kings James I and Charles I used quartering against political opponents in the first part of the 17th century, one of the abuses that eventually led to Charles I being deposed.

After the revocation of the Edict of Nantes, hundreds of thousands of Huguenots fled France, even though they had to be smuggled across the border. Some came to British North America. Paul Revere was among the many Patriots of Huguenot ancestry. The American Founders were acutely aware of the torments to which the French Huguenots were subjected after they were disarmed.[58]

Figure 10. Massacre of a Huguenot congregation in a barn by the Duc de Guise and his men, Vassy, France, 1562.

Art. II, Section 23. Juries and grand juries

> The right of trial by jury shall remain inviolate in criminal cases; but a jury in civil cases in all courts, or in criminal cases in courts not of record, may consist of less than twelve persons, as may be prescribed by law. Hereafter a grand jury shall

---

[55] BARBARA W. TUCHMAN, THE MARCH OF FOLLY: FROM TROY TO VIETNAM 21 (1984).

[56] PHILIP BENEDICT, CHRIST'S CHURCHES PURELY REFORMED: REFORMED: A SOCIAL HISTORY OF CALVINISM 372–74 (2002).

[57] Id. at 379–80.

[58] Don B. Kates Jr., *The Second Amendment and the Ideology of Self-Protection*, 9 CONSTITUTIONAL COMMENTARY 100 (1992).

> consist of twelve persons, any nine of whom concurring may find an indictment; provided, the general assembly may change, regulate or abolish the grand jury system; and provided, further, the right of any person to serve on any jury shall not be denied or abridged on account of sex, and the general assembly may provide by law for the exemption from jury service of persons or classes of persons.

Criminal juries

The first sentence reiterates the criminal jury trial right of section 16.

The jury trial right under the U.S. Sixth Amendment has been partially incorporated by the U.S. supreme court. In federal courts, criminal juries must be twelve, but state criminal juries may be as small as six jurors. *Burch v. Louisiana*, 441 U.S. 130 (1979). Federally, partial incorporation for U.S. Bill of Rights criminal procedure protections was the dominant approach during the 1930s through the 1950s. It was replaced with full-strength incorporation starting in the 1960s. Today, all incorporated rights, other than the Sixth Amendment criminal jury right, apply fully to state and local governments.

Federal criminal juries must be unanimous, but a line of cases from the 1970s had allowed non-unanimous state criminal juries, with at least 10–2 needed to convict. That line was overturned in a 2020 supreme court opinion by justice Gorsuch. Now, all criminal juries must be unanimous, state or federal. *Ramos v. Louisiana*, 140 S.Ct. 1390 (2020).

Colorado has never experimented with non-unanimous criminal juries.

As section 23 states, juries of fewer than twelve are allowed for criminal cases in "courts not of record." The exception has been interpreted broadly, so that the right to a twelve-person jury is only for felonies, not for misdemeanors or petty offenses. *People v. Rodriguez*, 112 P.3d 693 (Colo. 2005). Current law requires a jury of twelve for felonies and six for misdemeanors. C.R.S. § 18-1-406; Colo. R. Crim. Pro. 23.

There is no jury trial right for petty offenses. In Colorado, a petty offense is a step below a misdemeanor, and, technically, is not a "crime."

Juvenile courts need not have juries, under theory that juvenile court proceedings are nonadversarial and are conducted for the benefit of the juvenile. *People in the Interest of T.M.*, 742 P.2d 905 (Colo. 1987).

Grand juries

The Fifth Amendment right to grand jury indictment in federal court is not incorporated. As detailed in the discussion of Colorado's article II, § 8, the general assembly may set up a system that uses a grand jury *or* a criminal information. The latter is essentially a presentation to the judge showing that there is enough evidence to make a plausible case.

The right and duty of women to serve on grand juries was added in 1945.

Civil juries

There is no Colorado analogue to the U.S. Seventh Amendment, which guarantees a right to a jury in civil cases where the amount in controversy is more than $20. By interpretation, the Seventh Amendment right applies to cases where there was a right to civil juries in 1791 (*e.g.*, a case at law for breach of contract), but not to cases where there no jury rights in 1791 (*e.g.*, in admiralty courts, or bankruptcy). For causes of action that were created after 1791, courts look for analogies to the older causes of action.

The Seventh Amendment has not been incorporated against the states, and there is no prospect of incorporation in the foreseeable future.

In Colorado, the only constitutional jury right in civil cases is for eminent domain. Art. II, § 15. In all other civil cases, jury trial is a matter of grace. *Scholz v. Metropolitan Pathologists, P.C.*, 851 P.2d 901 (Colo. 1993). That grace is effectuated for civil cases by Colo. R. Civ. Pro. 38, allowing juries in some civil cases—generally similar to what the Seventh Amendment has been held to require (bottom line: for law, but not equity).

Art. II, Section 24. Rights of assembly and petition

> The people have the right peaceably to assemble for the common good, and to apply to those invested with the powers of government for redress of grievances, by petition or remonstrance.

This parallels the Petition Clause and the Assembly Clause of the U.S. First Amendment. No decisions have interpreted the Colorado and federal provisions differently. All of the First Amendment is fully incorporated against the states.

Starting in the late 1950s, the U.S. supreme court has held that the unwritten right of association is implied by the enumerated rights in the First Amendment. Colorado courts have not taken this step, but of course they do apply the First Amendment associational right. *E.g. Zuments by Zuments v. Colorado High School Activities Ass'n*, 737 P.2d 1113 (Colo. App. 1987) (right of association not violated by rule that athletes who practice with non-school teams may not play on high school teams).

Figure 11. Suffragettes at U.S. Capitol sing "Hymn of the Women," by Ethel Smith. May 9, 1914.

Peaceful picketing and chanting outside the governor's mansion is part of the right to assemble, and participants could not be prosecuted for a violation of a broadly-worded disturbing the peace ordinance. *Flores v. City and County of Denver*, 122 Colo. 71, 220 P.2d 373 (1950).

"Sham litigation" of baseless claims that are brought for the purpose of harassment is not protected by the right to petition, although access to the courts in general is certainly part of the right to petition. *Protect Our Mountain Environment, Inc. v. District Court In and For Jefferson County*, 677 P.2d 1361 (Colo. 1984).

Art. II, Section 25. Due process of law

> No person shall be deprived of life, liberty or property, without due process of law.

This copies one part of section 1 of the U.S. Fourteenth Amendment, which in turn echoed part of the Fifth Amendment.

The Colorado supreme court has sometimes been willing to interpret this clause more broadly than the federal provisions. For example, in Colorado, the prosecution must disprove an affirmative defense (such as insanity) beyond a reasonable doubt. *People ex rel. Juhan v. District Court*, 165 Colo. 253, 439 P.2d 741 (1968). Prosecution under two separate criminal statutes, which are nearly but not perfectly identical, is forbidden. *People v. Marcy*, 628 P.2d 69 (Colo. 1981) (rejecting federal rule that as long as each statute has one distinct fact to be proved, multiple prosecution is permitted).

While much of the Bill of Rights has specific guarantees of fair trial procedures, section 25 serves as an additional basis for appellate courts to address government abuse. *E.g.*, *Wend v. People*, 235 P.3d 1089 (Colo. 2010) (prosecutorial misconduct)

Equal protection

The Colorado Constitution does not have any text paralleling the Fourteenth Amendment's Equal Protection Clause. However, the Colorado supreme court has held that equal protection is implicit in due process. *People v. Marcy*, 628 P.2d 69 (Colo. 1981); *Heninger v. Charnes*, 613 P.2d 884 (Colo. 1980).

This interpretive history has a federal counterpart. The Fourteenth Amendment's Equal Protection Clause is, by its terms, only applicable to states, and not to the federal government. The U.S. supreme court has held that the Fifth Amendment Due Process Clause (which directly applies to the federal government) includes the principle of Equal Protection. *E.g.*, *Bolling v. Sharpe*, 347 U.S. 497 (1954) (striking racial segregation in D.C. public schools; decided on the same day as *Brown v. Board of Education*).

Although the Colorado and federal holdings may seem textually awkward, they are consistent with the Due Process rule that the government is a fiduciary with an obligation to treat all beneficiaries (the people) on a fair and equal basis. Gary Lawson, Guy I. Seidman & Robert G. Natelson, *The Fiduciary Foundations of Federal Equal Protection*, 94 BOSTON U. L. REVIEW 415 (2014).

Economic liberty

In the first seven decades following the ratification of the Fourteenth Amendment in 1868, the U.S. supreme court usually followed some of the original meaning of the Fourteenth Amendment: protecting, *inter alia*, the rights of competent adults to make decisions about what type of contracts they wished to engage.[59]

For example, a Louisville, Kentucky, ordinance required that on blocks where the majority of homeowners were white, any home on the block could only be sold to a white buyer. Conversely, in black majority blocks, homes could only be sold to blacks. This was not a violation of the Equal Protection doctrine of the time, because the law applied equally to both races. The U.S.

---

[59] The 19th century U.S. Court did not follow the original meaning of the Fourteenth Amendment that the Bill of Rights should be enforceable against state and local governments as "privileges or immunities of citizens of the United States." *E.g.*, *United States v. Cruikshank*, 92 U.S. 542 (1876) (First Amendment right of assembly and Second Amendment right to arms are inherent human rights that are found wherever civilization exists. The rights are protected by the U.S. Constitution, but not created by it. Accordingly, they are not "privileges or immunities of citizens of the United States"); *Slaughter-House Cases*, 83 U.S. (16 Wall.) 36 (1873) ("privileges or immunities of citizens of the United States" only includes rights that are created by the Constitution, such as the right to travel interstate, or the right to communicate with the U.S. government about patents, etc.).

Starting in the late 19th century, and continuing to the present, the Court has gradually undone this error one right at a time, using the Fourteenth Amendment's Due Process Clause. Thus, items in the Bill of Rights are said to be "incorporated" by the Due Process Clause. E.g., *McDonald v. City of Chicago*, 561 U.S. 742 (2010) (incorporating Second Amendment; and in a historical review, off-handedly incorporating the Excessive Bail Clause). Justice Thomas's concurrence in McDonald provides an accurate and undisputed (by the other justices) history of the original meaning of the 14th Amendment Privileges or Immunities Clause.

supreme court, however, held that the ordinance violated the Fourteenth Amendment property and contract rights of buyers and sellers. *Buchanan v. Warley*, 245 U.S. 60 (1917). Part of the *Lochner* line of cases, *Buchanan v. Warley* was criticized by the same people who criticized *Lochner*, and for the same reason: judicial interference with economic regulation. *See* David E. Bernstein, *Philip Sober Controlling Philip Drunk:* Buchanan v. Warley *in Historical Perspective*, 51 VANDERBILT L. REVIEW 797 (1998)

Contrary to the caricature that has been taught to generations of law students,[60] the court's decisions never treated liberty of contract as an unlimited right. For example, workplace health and safety regulations were fine, as long as they were not pretexts for favoring some interest group. *Holden v. Hardy*, 169 U.S. 366 (1898) (upholding 8-hour day for Utah miners).

In retrospect, one can second-guess some of those decisions, such as *Lochner* itself.[61] but their overall thrust was to effectuate the Fourteenth Amendment principle that free persons (unlike slaves) have full liberty to make their own economic decisions.

Justice Souter's thoughtful concurrence in *Washington v. Glucksberg*, 521 U.S. 702 (1991) (state may criminalize assisting suicide) surveys the history of "substantive due process." The term "substantive due process" was invented in the mid-20th century to describe use of the 14th Amendment Due Process Clause to protect non-procedural, unenumerated substantive rights (*e.g.*, right to contract, right to send one's children to a nongovernment school, right to use birth control). Justice Souter argued that the supreme court before the 1930s had the right idea, but that some of the court's decisions were too rigid.

Beginning in the early 1930s, the court began moving away from protection of choice in economic matters. A decisive step was the 1938 *Carolene Products* opinion, which greatly reduced judicial review of infringements of the right to contract and to follow a lawful trade or calling. *United States v. Carolene Products*, 304 U.S. 144 (1938) (upholding law to protect dairy producers against competition from alternatives to cows' milk). *Carolene Products* held economic regulations would be presumed constitutional, and only unreasonable regulations were unconstitutional.

Two decades later, the court abandoned even reasonableness review, in *Williamson v. Lee Optical Co*., 348 U.S. 483 (1955). That case invented the "rational basis" standard; it allowed naked wealth transfers for the benefit of powerful special interests (in *Williamson*, ophthalmologists) to the detriment of the less powerful (consumers, opticians).

---

60 Including chief justice Roberts. See his *Lochner*-phobic dissent in *Obergefell v. Hodges*, 576 U.S. 644 (2015).

61 In *Lochner v. New York*, 198 U.S. 45 (1905), various health and safety regulations for bakeshops (*e.g.*, adequate ventilation, no animals except cats in the baking area) were unchallenged. The provision imposing maximum hours on bakery workers received no defense from the State of New York, other than the argument that the New York legislature could do whatever it wanted. Accordingly, a five-justice majority held the maximum baking hours law unconstitutional. In dissent, justice Harlan (joined by two other justices) did his own research and provided evidence showing that baking was in fact an uncommonly dangerous occupation to the baker's long-term health. Dissenting alone, justice Holmes argued that New York could do whatever it wanted; the Holmes dissent was hailed as the epitome of progressive legal thought. According to Holmes, the majority decision was based on the economic theory of Herbert Spencer's book *Social Statics* (1851). Although Holmes was a great stylist, his dissent was nonsense.

Actually, the disagreement between the justice Peckham's majority and justice Harlan's dissent was about who had the burden of proof (the party challenging the law, or the government justifying the law), and how much proof was necessary. Even the *Lochner* majority was willing to uphold maximum hours laws if the government had produced solid proof that the laws were necessary for health or safety. *See* DAVID E. BERNSTEIN, REHABILITATING LOCHNER: DEFENDING INDIVIDUAL RIGHTS AGAINST PROGRESSIVE REFORM (2012).

The Colorado supreme court followed a generally similar path, using the Colorado Due Process Clause in the early twentieth century to find some economic restrictions to be unconstitutional. Again, some of those decisions may have been too hard-edged.

The Colorado court in the 1930s likewise began abandoning protection of economic liberty and stated a devolution towards rational basis review. However, the Colorado court has at times protected citizens' economic liberty from patently obvious government favoritism towards the politically powerful.

In the 1956, the Colorado court held that the Colorado Constitution prohibits price-fixing by government, except in unusual circumstances. So the state Fair Trade Act could not be used to control the price at which a retailer sells ammunition. *Olin Mathieson Chem. Corp. v. Francis*, 301 P.2d 139, 147, 149, 152 (Colo. 1956):

> The General Assembly itself has no power to fix the prices of merchandise sold on the open market, it follows that it cannot lawfully delegate such authority to another . . . Except under the police power in a proper case, no right reposes in the General Assembly to fix prices at which an owner of property shall sell that which he owns and offers to sell . . . Can it be said that the retail sale of Winchester arms or ammunition is different than the sale of milk, meat, bakery goods, shoes and other everyday essentials? We think not . . . We are inclined to the view that while a large segment of our people may use guns and ammunition, and while plaintiff may have a trade-mark on its product, which trade-mark protects plaintiff within the limits of the law under which it was issued, the retail sale of its products is not 'affected with a public interest', and under the police power of this state the General Assembly may not fix prices and so many not confer the power on others to do so, thus taking from the seller and purchaser the right to agree upon a price of their choice, and interfering with their right to freely contract. The right to contract is a property right, protected by the due-process clause of the constitution, Const. art. 2, § 25, and cannot be abridged by legislative enactment. The police power of the state exercisable by the General Assembly, while very broad, is exercisable only within the limits of the constitution. To sustain the price-fixing power attempted by the General Assembly in the statute involved, under a claimed exercise of the police power, would be to place the power of the legislature above the constitution.

In a 1971 case, the Colorado court diverged from the federal *Carolene Products* case, and struck down a law against nondairy alternatives. *People ex. rel. Orcutt v. Instantwhip Denver, Inc.*, 176 Colo. 396, 490 P.2d 940 (1971).[62]

Like *Carolene Products*, the *Instawhip* case grew out of the dairy lobby's long-standing political campaign to protect itself from competition from nondairy alternatives—such as coconut milk, margarine, and powdered milk. The dairy lobby made numerous claims about health, nutrition, and the environment, and these claims were readily accepted by credulous legislators eager to please dairy farmers. The *Carolene Products* opinion cites some of these legislative findings. But on closer examination, the dairy claims were spurious; there was no legitimate reason to prevent consumers from being able to choose dairy substitutes. *See* Geoffrey Miller, *The True Story of Carolene Products*, 1987 SUP. CT. REVIEW 397 (1987).

The *Instawhip* case involved the Colorado statute banning "filled dairy products." These are dairy-like products to which has been added "any fat or oil other than milk fat." The particular product at issue was a sour cream imitation with vegetable oil added.

---

[62] "Defendant in error" or "plaintiff in error" used to be the style for identifying the party who claimed the lower court had erred.

There was no evidence that any consumers had been deceived into thinking that the product was traditional sour cream. Filled milk products were nutritious and wholesome, so there was no public interest in preventing their sale. The Colorado court noted that courts in other states had split on the validity of filled milk laws.

Acknowledging the federal precedent, the Colorado court wrote: "we are not bound to interpret the due process clause of the Constitution of Colorado, art. II, s 25, so narrowly." The filled milk statute was "in excess of the police power of the state and must be declared invalid under the due process clause of the Constitution of Colorado, art. II, s25."

In the modern era, federal courts do occasionally find a statute or government action to be unconstitutionally irrational.[63] The Colorado supreme court when applying the rational basis test often but not always copies the many federal courts that have treated "rational basis" as meaning "the government always wins." *E.g.*, *Rodriguez v. Schutt*, 914 P.2d 921 (Colo. 1996) (different treatment of classes of judgement debtors was irrational).

In sum, since 1876, Colorado courts have mainly interpreted section 25 in harmony with the federal Due Process and Equal Protection doctrines of the given time but have occasionally been willing to go further.

Art. II, Section 26. Slavery prohibited

> There shall never be in this state either slavery or involuntary servitude.

This has the same effect as the federal Thirteenth Amendment. The Thirteenth Amendment and the 1876 Constitution both had exceptions for penal servitude—forced labor by prisoners. A 2018 amendment deleted the Colorado language "except as a punishment for crime, whereof the party shall have been duly convicted."

Only a few cases have interpreted the Colorado provision. They have all involved either penal labor (at the time, expressly allowed by the text) or some form of coerced labor that the court found did not constitute "involuntary servitude." *E.g.*, *People v. McGlotten*, 134 P.3d 487 (Colo. App. 2005) (court reporter forced to create a transcript).

Note that under the federal statute implementing the Thirteenth Amendment, there are today criminal prosecutions for holding people in *de facto* slavery. A typical scenario would be a woman from the Philippines who is brought to the U.S. to be a housekeeper, but then is kept in the house, never permitted to leave the house except with her employer's permission, and not paid.

For almost all of human history, slavery was endemic globally. Some societies developed a practice of not enslaving in-group members. So Muslims enslaved everyone except Muslims; Christians enslaved everyone except Christians; and the Chinese enslaved Koreans and everyone else who was not Chinese. *See, e.g.*, SIMON WEBB, THE FORGOTTEN SLAVE TRADE: THE WHITE EUROPEAN SLAVES OF ISLAM (2021) (enslavement of captured Europeans by North African Muslims); GILES MILTON, WHITE GOLD (2005) (focusing on Morocco); ROBERT DAVIS, CHRISTIAN SLAVES, MUSLIM MASTERS: WHITE SLAVERY IN THE MEDITERRANEAN, THE BARBARY COAST, AND ITALY, 1500–1800 (2003).

In New Spain, which always included most of Colorado, and for a while all of Colorado, a 1680 royal decree prohibited enslaving New World Indians. But enforcement was difficult.

---

[63] But such cases are rare. More usually, the rational basis test is applied as a "'not-insane-therefore-o.k.' imagined basis." Michael Kent Curtis & Shannon Gilreath, *Transforming Teenagers into Oral Sex Felons: The Persistence of the Crime Against Nature after Lawrence v. Texas*, 43 WAKE FOREST L. REVIEW 155, 215 (2008).

Formal slavery was often replaced by *peonage*, a system by which people were bound to labor for a term of years or for life—ostensibly by contractual choice.

Starting in the 1750s, Quakers in Great Britain and in British North America began arguing that slavery was *per se* immoral. In 1772 they got a boost from the King's Bench, the second-highest court. The court held that because slavery is contrary to natural law, slavery in England and Wales could only exist if positively authorized by law. There being no statutory enactment, Somerset, a slave who had been brought to England, was free. *Somerset v Stewart*, 98 Eng. Rep. 499 (1772). The decision did not apply to slavery other than in England and Wales, such as the slavery in England's many overseas colonies, including the treatment of many indentured servants as *de facto* slaves. Nor did it outlaw the trans-Atlantic slave trade by the British. Nor, in practice, did the decision get rid of all slavery in England and Wales.

Even so, the nascent anti-slavery movement continued to grow in strength. By 1799, Pennsylvania, New York, and the New England states had abolished slavery. In all but Massachusetts, abolition was created by statutes for gradual emancipation. The Massachusetts Supreme Judicial Court held that slavery violated the new state's constitution, and so slavery was immediately unlawful for all persons.[64]

In 1807, the British parliament outlawed the trans-Atlantic slave trade and sent the British navy to enforce the ban. The next year, the U.S. Congress outlawed all slave imports. At the Philadelphia Convention, the large majority had favored immediate constitutional prohibition of slave importation; but South Carolina and Georgia balked and threatened not to join the Union. They said that they had lost so many slaves during the American Revolution that they need to bring in new ones. In a compromise, Congress was allowed to ban slave imports, but not until 1808. U.S. CONST., art. I. § 9, cl. 1.

That year, Congress immediately did so. Illegal smuggling continued to some degree, leading Congress into escalating enforcement, and eventually imposing the death penalty for importation.

The British parliament's 1833 Slavery Abolition Act ended legal slavery throughout the British Empire. In the United States, the abolition movement had been originally strongest in the South. But an unintended consequence of gradual abolition in the North was to turn slavery into a sectional issue. Southern governments prohibited abolitionist speech—and even arguments that slavery was economically inefficient—under the pretext that such speech might incite a slave revolt.[65] The polarization eventually led to the American Civil War.

None of the above made much practical difference in Colorado. The eastern part of the Kansas Territory had its own civil war over slavery in the 1850s.[66] The strife in "Bloody Kansas"—over whether the Kansas Territory would allow slavery, and over whether Kansas would join the Union as free or slave, helped cause the American Civil War. With some states already seceded, and war looming, Congress's 1861 Organic Act creating the Territory of Colorado was discretely silent on the slavery issue. Perhaps on both sides in Congress, the legality of slavery in Colorado didn't seem worth a fight, because Colorado was broadly considered unsuitable for slavery. It was a mining territory, dependent for success on individual enterprise and energy, rather than coerced labor. And the Gold Rush settlers were not typically the types of people who could afford a slave, even if they wanted.

---

[64] *Quock Walker v. Jennison,* 13 PROCEEDINGS OF THE MASSACHUSETTS HISTORICAL SOCIETY, 1873-75, at 296 (1st Series, 1875); *Jennison v. Caldwell, id.; Commonwealth v. Jennison, id.* at 293; John D. Cushing, *The Cushing Court and Abolition of Slavery in Massachusetts: More Notes on the "Quock Walker Case,"* 5 AMERICAN JOURNAL OF LEGAL HISTORY 118 (1961).

[65] A retort to the economic efficiency argument came from Virginia political philosopher George Fitzhugh. In *Sociology for the South* (1854) and *Cannibals All* (1857), he argued that slavery was socialist and paternalistic, and therefore the best form of social organization, far superior to the individualistic capitalist competition of man against man in the North.

[66] JAY MONAGHAN, CIVIL WAR ON THE WESTERN BORDER, 1854–1865 (1954).

Unbeknownst to most Americans, slavery already existed in Colorado and had from time immemorial. In the Hobbesian world of the American Southwest, Indian tribes had long been raiding each other to capture humans and horses. Both were kept by the victorious tribe as needed (often being assimilated over time), with the surplus sold to any willing buyer. While many tribes were active in the slave trade, the top of the heap as of the mid-19th century in Colorado were the Utes and Comanches.

The Ute horses thrived in the Rocky Mountain meadows. So the Utes had a big advantage over the Paiutes, who inhabited the deserts of western Utah and environs. Taking and selling Paiutes and other tribes was an important part of the Utes' predatory economy.

The Comanche Empire, based in central Texas, was for many years strong enough to greatly limit expansion by the French, Spanish, Mexican, Americans, and Texans. The Comanche at their height raided deep into Mexico. As opportunities arose, they captured Indians, Mexicans, New Mexicans, and other Americans, and sold them to all buyers, including other Indians, Mexicans, New Mexicans, and other Americans. For centuries New Mexico had a thriving trade in slaves (a/k/a peons), regardless of whether New Mexico was part of New Spain, the United States of Mexico, the Republic of Texas, or the United States of America.

During the American Civil War, the Navajo launched a major offensive against the U.S. in New Mexico. This led to a counteroffensive, in which U.S. military forces, led by Kit Carson, formed an alliance with every tribe neighboring the Navajo. In the combined counteroffensive, the Utes were the tip of spear, sometimes operating in conjunction with U.S. forces, and sometimes independently. The war ended with the Navajo being deported to a miserable reservation in northeastern New Mexico, the Bosque Redondo. In the process of losing a war and then going on the Long Walk to the Bosque Redondo from the Navajo fortress in the Canyon de Chelly, several thousand Navajo were captured and enslaved.[67]

A July 1865 census in Costilla County, Colorado, found 60 Indians held as peons. Fifty of them were Navajo, mostly captured in 1863 or 1864. Next door, in Conejos County, Colorado, there were 88 peons, 63 of them Navajo. About half of the Navajo had been sold by Ute slave traders, and the other half by Mexican traders.

On July 9, 1865, president Andrew Johnson issued a proclamation that holding Indians in peonage was illegal.[68] The Thirteenth Amendment was ratified in December 1865; it has always been interpreted to prohibit peonage, as well as chattel slavery.

Section 2 of the Thirteenth Amendment created a new federal power: "Congress shall have power to enforce this article by appropriate legislation." Exercising section 2 power, Congress passed the Peonage Act of 1867 ("An Act to abolish and forever prohibit the System of Peonage in the Territory of New Mexico and other Parts of the United States"). The Act outlawed "the voluntary or involuntary service of labor of any persons as peons, in liquidation of any debt or obligation, or otherwise." The modern version of the statute, using the same key language, is 42 U.S.C § 1994 ("Peonage abolished").

So by the time the Colorado Convention assembled in December 1875, slavery, including peonage, was unquestionably illegal throughout Colorado. Section 26 makes sure it stays that way, regardless of what the federal government does.

Further reading: ANDRÉS RESÉNDEZ, THE OTHER SLAVERY: THE UNCOVERED STORY OF INDIAN ENSLAVEMENT IN AMERICA (2016); VIRGINIA MCCONNELL SIMMONS, THE UTE INDIANS

---

[67] By 1868, it had become clear the Bosque Redondo could not sustain the Navajo. The U.S. government faced the choice of telling the Navajo to move to Indian County, in Oklahoma—or to let them go back to their homeland in western New Mexico and eastern Arizona. The federal government chose the latter, and the Navajo returned.

[68] President Lincoln's Jan. 1, 1863, Emancipation Proclamation did not by its terms apply to either the Colorado or New Mexico Territories, because neither were in rebellion against the United States.

OF UTAH, COLORADO, AND NEW MEXICO 33, 121 (2000) ; PEKKA HÄMÄLÄINEN, THE COMANCHE EMPIRE 249–59 (2008).

Art. II, Section 27. Property rights of aliens

> Aliens, who are or may hereafter become bona fide residents of this state, may acquire, inherit, possess, enjoy and dispose of property, real and personal, as native born citizens.

Section 27 eliminates various common-law restrictions on alien property rights. Alien property rights for mining claims were fortified by a territorial statute from 1861.[69] An 1887 statute forbade *nonresident* aliens, as well as foreign corporations, from acquiring over 2,000 acres of agricultural or range land.[70] It expressly exempted mining land. *See Billings v. Aspen Min. & Smelting Co.*, 51 F. 338 (8th Cir. 1892) (applying mining exemption).[71]

The one state case interpreting section 27, *People v. Nakamura*, was mostly based on the right to arms (art. II, § 13), but also invoked section 27. *People v. Nakamura*, 62 P.2d 246 (Colo. 1936). The *Nakamura* case struck down a Klan-era law, enacted by the 1921 general assembly, that forbade aliens from possessing firearms.

Ostensibly, the purpose of the statute was to preserve the game for the citizens of Colorado. This was, and remains, an indisputably lawful purpose. However, by prohibiting all gun ownership by aliens, rather than just prohibiting hunting by aliens, the 1921 law violated section 13 (right to arms) and section 27 (property rights of aliens). As noted in the discussion of section 13, the Colorado right to arms is expressly for every "person" and not just for the "citizen."

The two dissenting justices in *Nakamura* agreed with the above analysis, but they would have upheld Nakamura's conviction under the statute, since Nakamura himself had been caught poaching.

The 1876 Colorado Constitution was immigrant-friendly, and not just in sections 13 and 27 of the Bill of Rights. The Constitution required that until 1900, state statutes be published in Spanish and German. COLO. CONST. art. XVIII, § 8 (1876). However, the demand for the non-English published statutes was small.

Art. II, Section 28. Rights reserved not disparaged

> The enumeration in this constitution of certain rights shall not be construed to deny, impair or disparage others retained by the people.

69

> All aliens may take, by deed, will, or otherwise, lands and tenements, and any interest therein, and alienate, sell, assign, and transmit the same to their heirs, or any other persons, whether such heirs or other persons be citizens of the United States or not; and, upon the decease of any alien having title to or interest in any lands or tenements, such land and tenements shall pass and descend in the same manner as if such alien were a citizen of the United States.

Concerning Aliens, 1861 Colo. Laws 57, 57–58.

70 1 Mills' Annotated Stats. of the State of Colo. ch. 3, §§ 99–103, pp. 421–23 (1891).

71 The Tenth Circuit was created in 1929, by removing six states from the Eighth Circuit. Excellent historical information about the federal courts in those states, before and after 1929, is available from the Tenth Circuit Historical Society.

This parallels the Ninth Amendment to the United States Constitution. The major decision interpreting the clause is *Colorado Anti-Discrimination Comm'n v. Case*, 151 Colo. 235, 380 P.2d 34 (1962) (section 28 not violated by law forbidding persons who sell their own home to discriminate on the basis of race).

Section 28 is the final item in the original 1876 Bill of Rights. As described above, there have been post–1876 interpolations in original sections 1–28, such as a massive revision of the right to bail, and the addition of section 16a, crime victim rights.

Like the Ninth and Tenth Amendments in the U.S. Constitution, section 28 should be read as an interpretive guide to everything else. For example, when two interpretations of Bill of Rights language are plausible, section 28 suggests that the broader interpretation should be preferred. *Cf.* ROBERT G. NATELSON, THE ORIGINAL CONSTITUTION: WHAT IT ACTUALLY SAID AND MEANT (2014) (analyzing all clauses of the original U.S. articles and the Bill of Rights).

The right to marry is not enumerated in Colorado. However, it would seem a strong candidate for protection as an unenumerated yet fundamental human right. Consistent with this view, the general assembly in 1957 repealed the statute that had prohibited interracial marriage ("miscegenation"). The leader of the repeal effort was John E. Gorsuch, chair of Domestic Relations Committee of the Colorado Bar Association. *Cf. Jackson v. City & County of Denver*, 124 P.2d 240 (Colo. 1942) (upholding Denver's use of vagrancy statute, which prohibited leading "an immoral course of life," against an inter-racial couple).

Art. II, Section 29. Equality of the sexes

> Equality of rights under the law shall not be denied or abridged by the state of Colorado or any of its political subdivisions on account of sex.

Added by the voters in 1972.[72] As the supreme court stated shortly after enactment, government action that discriminates between the sexes can be upheld only if "reasonably and genuinely based on physical characteristics unique to just one sex." *People v. Salinas*, 551 P.2d 703 (Colo. 1976) (statutory rape).

Salinas provided a bright-line rule. Later decisions are murkier. In U.S. constitutional law, the intermediate scrutiny standard of review was invented for sex discrimination cases under the Equal Protection Clause. *Craig v. Boren*, 429 U.S. 190 (1976).

Cases arising under section 29 have been decided in conjunction with the U.S. Equal Protection Clause. Section 29 does not appear to have changed the result in any case.

However, the Colorado supreme court said that there is a "stricter judicial scrutiny standard" under section 29. *R. McG. v. J.W.*, 615 P.2d 666 (Colo. 1980). Then court said that normal intermediate scrutiny is the standard. *Austin v. Litvak*, 682 P.2d 41 (Colo. 1984); *Lujan v. Colorado St. Bd. of Educ.*, 649 P.2d 1005 (Colo. 1982). Then the court said that sex discrimination requires the "closest judicial scrutiny"—a phrase usually associated with strict scrutiny. *Colorado Civil Rights Comm'n v. Travelers Ins. Co.*, 759 P.2d 1358 (Colo. 1988).

Likewise, the U.S. supreme court once described its intermediate scrutiny standard as "skeptical scrutiny." *United States v. Virginia*, 518 U.S. 515 (1996) (Ginsburg, J.). Some courts applying intermediate scrutiny in other contexts have adopted justice Ginsburg's version of intermediate scrutiny as "skeptical scrutiny." *E.g.*, *State v. DeCiccio*, 105 A.3d 165 (Conn. 2014) (applying skeptical scrutiny to a statute forbidding transporting certain knives when moving from an old residence to a new residence).

---

[72] For the spirit of the times, see Helen Reddy, *I Am Woman* (1972) (officially adopted by the United Nations in 1975 as the theme song for International Women's Year).

However, subsequent U.S. supreme court cases have reverted to the more common, and looser description of intermediate scrutiny, including in sex discrimination cases. The semantic variations in Colorado and the U.S. do not appear to have been decisive in the outcomes of any cases.

Art. II, Section 30. Right to vote or petition on municipal annexation

> (1) No unincorporated area may be annexed to a municipality unless one of the following conditions first has been met:
>
> > (a) The question of annexation has been submitted to the vote of the landowners and the registered electors in the area proposed to be annexed, and the majority of such persons voting on the question have voted for the annexation; or
> >
> > (b) The annexing municipality has received a petition for the annexation of such area signed by persons comprising more than fifty percent of the landowners in the area and owning more than fifty percent of the area, excluding public streets, and alleys and any land owned by the annexing municipality; or
> >
> > (c) The area is entirely surrounded by or is solely owned by the annexing municipality.
>
> (2) The provisions of this section shall not apply to annexations to the city and county of Denver, to the extent that such annexations are governed by other provisions of the constitution.
>
> (3) The general assembly may provide by law for procedures necessary to implement this section. This section shall take effect upon completion of the canvass of votes taken thereon.

Added by voters in 1980, the amendment effectuates the self-government principles of section 1 of the Bill of Rights. A community may not be annexed by a nearby government without that community's consent. (Unless the unwilling annexees live in an enclave surrounded by the annexer.)

Note that section 30 is only about municipal annexations. County annexations are separately covered by article XIV, § 3. Section 30 also does not cover annexations by the City & County of Denver, whose rules are in article XX, § 1. Annexations by the City & County of Broomfield are in article XX, § 10. Denver and Broomfield annexations are regulated by boundary control commissions, which include representatives from adjacent counties.

The statutes for municipal annexations and municipal disconnections are C.R.S. § 31-12-101 et seq.

Landowners who were involuntary annexed have standing to bring a section 30 case. Municipalities do not have standing to challenge an annexation by another municipality unless the plaintiff municipality owned some of the annexed land. *Town of Berthoud v. Town of Johnstown*, 983 P.2d 174 (Colo. App. 1999).

Art. II, Section 30a. Official language

> The English language is the official language of the State of Colorado.
>
> This section is self-executing; however, the general assembly may enact laws to implement this section.

Adopted by citizen initiative in 1988. The general assembly has not exercised its option to enact implementing legislation. Various earlier-enacted statutes do require the use of English, such as: C.R.S. § 13-1-120 (written court proceedings), § 13-71-105(2)(b) (jurors disqualified for "Inability to read, speak, and understand the English language"). The English Language Proficiency Act, C.R.S. § 22-24-101 et. seq., requires public schools to implement programs to help non-native speakers learn English.

The federal Voting Rights Act of 1965 mandates that Colorado supply ballots or other voter services in foreign languages, in certain situations. 52 U.S.C. § 10503.

Contrary to the predictions of opponents of section 30a, the amendment has been applied in a common-sense manner. For example, a government employee who is speaking to an individual (such as a police officer speaking to a crime witness) may choose to use a language other than English, based on the circumstances. *Cf.* C.R.S. § 1-7-111 (assistance in marking ballots or operating voting machines if elector has problem "by reason of disability, inability to read or write, or difficulties with the English language").

Art. II, Section 30b. No protected status based on sexual orientation

> Neither the State of Colorado, through any of its branches or departments, nor any of its agencies, political subdivisions, municipalities or school districts, shall enact, adopt or enforce any statute, regulation, ordinance or policy whereby homosexual, lesbian or bisexual orientation, conduct, practices or relationships shall constitute or otherwise be the basis of or entitle any person or class of persons to have or claim any minority status, quota preferences, protected status or claim of discrimination. This Section of the Constitution shall be in all respects self-executing.

Enacted by the people in 1992. Held to violate the U.S. Constitution's Fourteenth Amendment in *Romer v. Evans*, 517 U.S. 620 (1996).

Further reading: Lynn A. Baker, *The Missing Pages of the Majority Opinion in Romer v. Evans*, 68 U. COLO. L. REVIEW 387 (1997) (arguing for the majority's result, but criticizing its breezy reasoning); Timothy M. Tymkovich, John Daniel Dailey & Paul Farley, *A Tale of Three Theories: Reason and Prejudice in the Battle Over Amendment 2*, 68 U. COLO. L. REVIEW 287 (1997) (the three lawyers for the attorney general who had to defend section 30b examine the three different and inconsistent rationales employed by the state district court, Colorado supreme court, and U.S. supreme court).

Art. II, Section 31. Recognized marriages

> Only a union of one man and one woman shall be valid or recognized as a marriage in this state.

Adopted in 2006. Unconstitutional under *Obergefell v. Hodges*, 576 U.S. 644 (2015). While Justice Kennedy's majority opinion for the court was premised on the court's supreme authority to impose its moral intuitions, the same result could have been reached by a more traditional analysis based on well-established Equal Protection doctrine. *See* Cato Institute amicus brief.

For the argument that there are now few coherent legal arguments (other than deference to tradition) for criminalizing polyamorous relationships, see RONALD C. DEN OTTER, IN DEFENSE OF PLURAL MARRIAGE (Cambridge Univ. Pr., 2015).

CHAPTER 5

Vertical Separation of Powers

Introduction

The phrase "separation of powers" is often used to describe the horizontal separation of powers within a particular level of government. For example, in Colorado, power is expressly divided among the legislative, executive, and judicial branches. COLO. CONST., art. III. A separation of powers also exists in vertical sense, among different levels of government: federal, state, and local. The United States Constitution did something that had heretofore been unimaginable in political thought. It "split the atom of sovereignty" between a federal government that was sovereign on certain enumerated topics, and state governments that retained sovereignty not granted to the United States. *U.S. Term Limits, Inc. v. Thornton*, 514 U.S. 779, 838 (1995) (Kennedy, J., concurring).

Part A of this chapter covers the Federalist Papers' arguments about why the American system of dual sovereignty provided the best protection of Americans' liberty. In short, when either the federal government or the states became oppressive, the people could recur to the one for defense against the other.

The rest of the chapter then examines how the assurances and predictions of James Madison and Alexander Hamilton in *The Federalist* have worked out, from the Early Republic to the present. Federal protection of individuals from state abuse is typically covered in Constitutional Law II classes, especially regarding the Fourteenth Amendment, which creates federal power for courts and Congress to act against state or local violations of individual rights. This chapter examines another side of the Madison-Hamilton system: state defense of individuals against federal abuse.

Part B covers the first crisis that prompted a state response: the censorship of political speech by Congress's 1798 Sedition Act, which resulted in the Kentucky and Virginia Resolutions. The Virginia Resolution was drafted by Madison, and the Kentucky Resolution by Jefferson. The two resolutions had different approaches in how to deal with federal overreach.

Part C addresses state resistance in the first half of the nineteenth century, including the War of 1812, the Tariff of Abominations (during Andrew Jackson's first term), and the Fugitive Slave Act of 1850.

As Part D describes, state resistance was discredited after the Civil War; southern resistance to desegregation in the 1950s and 1960s put resistance in an especially bad light.

But in the last half-century, state sovereignty and resistance to federal over-reach have made a comeback, as Part E explains. One reason was that the Vietnam War, Watergate, and other federal failures ended the era of widespread faith in the federal government.

Starting in the early 1990s, the U.S. supreme court's "New Federalism" began a period of increased respect for state sovereignty, particularly in the operation of state governments. Part F summarizes some of the leading New Federalism cases and doctrine.

Today, state and local governments engage in resistance on all sorts of topics. As has been the case historically, today's resistance spans the political spectrum, and includes issues such as marijuana, firearms, and immigration. Modern Colorado has seen state or local resistance on each of these topics. Part G provides an overview of the vertical separations of powers today, as a tool to resist perceived abuse from above. Finally, Part G briefly discusses jury nullification, a means by which citizens have always participated in the vertical separation of powers, providing protection against abusive prosecutions.

A. The Federalist

This part begins with an essay by Kopel on Madison's Federalist no. 46. It is followed by excerpts from Federalist 28 and Federalist 51.

Federalist 46

***The Influence of the State and Federal Governments Compared.* New York Packet (Madison). David Kopel, for Constituting America, June 30, 2010 (revised for this textbook).**

Federalist 46 continues Madison's arguments that the federal government could never dominate or obliterate the states. He sketches out possible scenarios of federal over-reaching and explains why the states would prevail in every case. Addressing the worst-case scenario, Madison assures his readers that a tyrannical president with a powerful army could never impose his rule on America, because the entire American population possesses firearms.

Madison begins with first principles. The federal and state governments are both servants of the same master—namely the people. Opponents of the Constitution act as if the federal and state governments were uncontrollable entities who would be at war with each other. To the contrary, both governments are mere agents of the people, who are the supreme controlling power. The people choose to use their federal and state agents for different purposes. So there is no reason to think that the people will allow their two agents to fight with each other, or to interfere with each other.

The people, who are the ultimate deciders, will be much more attached to the state governments, Madison predicts. For one thing, there will be many more state employees than federal employees. Not only the individual employees, but their family, friends, social networks, and so on, will therefore inevitably have more affection for their close-at-hand state employer than the distant, small federal government.

Madison's prediction is still true. Beginning with New Deal, the federal government began to grow enormously, but state and local governments also grew rapidly. As of 2008–2009, there were about 3.8 million state government employees, plus 11 million local government employees. This compares to 2.8 million federal civilian employees, plus approximately 1.5 million active duty U.S. military. So today, the number of state/local employees outnumbers federal employees by about 4:1. To the extent that employment promotes loyalty, Madison remains generally right that the states have the advantage.

Then there's practical experience. Madison reminds his readers that even when the Continental Congress was fighting the Revolutionary War, people generally liked their state governments better. Except for a brief period early in the war, the national government was at "no time the idol of popular favor; and that opposition to proposed enlargements of its powers and importance was the side usually taken by the men who wished to build their political consequence on the prepossessions of their fellow-citizens."

But starting with Teddy Roosevelt (1901–09), presidents began to build personality cults. A few presidents in the last century—most notably Calvin Coolidge and Ronald Reagan—led successful political careers by usually resisting proposed enlargements of federal power. But many more politicians have built careers by promising that the federal government be the *de facto* parent over an increasingly childish nation.

Given the advantages currently possessed the by state governments, Madison continues, the people would only transfer their loyalty to the federal government if the federal government were manifestly better and more capable. And if so, there's nothing wrong with the people giving their confidence where it is most due. Even then, the states would have little to fear, "because it is only within a certain sphere that the federal power can, in the nature of things, be advantageously administered."

The early nineteen-sixties were a time when Madison's prediction about a transfer of affections proved prescient. At the time, the federal government was indeed far more competent and vigorous, and far less corrupt, than many state governments. National trust in the federal government rose to levels never since achieved. One reason for post-sixties decline is that as the federal government has tried to do almost everything, it has become less competent at carrying out its core functions. As Madison knew, only with a certain sphere can federal power be advantageously administered.

Suppose one side or the other goes too far? Again, Madison writes, the advantage lies with the states. If a state is inclined to infringe on the federal sphere, the state actions would presumably be popular with the people of the state and would immediately be carried into effect by the state government employees. The federal government would have no practical means to overcome the states, except by use of force, which would always be viewed with reluctance.

Conversely, if the federal government went too far, the state's people and government would refuse to cooperate, and could obstruct federal actions. If a large, resistant state were joined by its neighbors, it would be nearly impossible for the federal government to prevail.

Madison's analysis proved accurate for a long time. Whether in a good cause (such as resisting federal implementation of the Fugitive Slave Act) or in a bad cause (resisting the supreme court's desegregation orders from *Brown v. Board of Education*[1]), state governments with strong popular support have often been able to frustrate locally-unpopular exercises of federal power.

But a major change has upset the Madisonian balance. In the 1936 case *United States v. Butler*,[2] the supreme court said that Congress could use its spending powers for purposes that had nothing to do with the enumerated powers that had been granted to Congress, such as the power to raise armies, establish post offices, and so on. Accordingly, Congress quickly started doling out money to state governments.

The result was to make the state governments into *de facto* wards of their federal sugar daddy. Whenever Congress tugged the purse strings, the states danced.

So Southern state government resistance to school desegregation did not end primarily because of a few instances in which the president sent in federal troops to enforce court orders. As Madison expected, use of military force was still a last resort. Formal southern resistance ended when Congress's Civil Rights Act of 1964 cut off federal education money to segregated schools. A good result, although not all subsequent federal threats of withholding money would be for such benign purposes.

What about a worst-case scenario, in which a federal tyrant attempted to use the federal standing army to impose a national dictatorship? Madison derided the possibility; the people would never consent to the long-term build-up of a powerful military establishment. Here, Madison was correct for about a century and a half. After the Civil War and World War I, the large federal military was quickly demobilized, and the standing army shrunk to a size appropriate for a mid-level European power, or less.

But the aftermath of World War II did not go as planned. The Soviet Union, rather than becoming a global partner in peace and stability, emerged as an aggressive superpower intent on totalitarian expansion wherever possible, ultimately seeking the destruction of the free United States. In the resulting Cold War, the United States by necessity grew used to a large, permanent standing army.

Madison continued his hypothetical: the largest possible federal army could not constitute more than one percent of the total population. This is indeed the size of the current federal military, counting active duty plus reserves. But with conscription, the federal army could be much larger than that. In 1945, the U.S. military constituted 6% of the total population. (8 of 132 million.) Today, that would mean a military of about 18 million.

Against this federal army, Madison said, would be essentially the entire able-bodied male population, with their own guns, and organized into militias directed by the state governments. This huge force could never be conquered by the much smaller federal army.

---

[1] 347 U.S. 483 (1954).

[2] 297 U.S. 1 (1936).

The crucial reason why America was free and Europe was that Americans had guns *and* state governments. The combination of the two would be sufficient to demolish any national tyrant.

Madison's point about Americans being different because they are much better armed, and because they have strong state governments, is an example of *American exceptionalism.* American exceptionalism is a pervasive issue in constitutional understanding. Are practices of Europe relevant to what the Constitution means, as examples to follow? The answer is a resounding "No!" according to liberal justices William Douglas and Hugo Black, and conservatives justices Antonin Scalia and Clarence Thomas. The view that the United States should often look to Europe as a model has been articulated by justices Felix Frankfurter and Stephen Breyer. Justice Anthony Kennedy sometimes supported either position.

Fortunately, we have never had to see whether Madison was right that a federal tyrant with a standing army could be defeated by the people. We do know that in other places (*e.g.*, Israel fighting for independence from Great Britain in 1946–48) armed popular forces have been able to drive out very strong armies. Of course, the modern availability of nuclear weapons would give an American tyrant weapons that armed civilians could never defeat. But the use of nuclear weapons against Americans might cause an outraged U.S. military to depose the tyrant himself.

As Federalist 46 shows, James Madison, the author of the Second Amendment, did not believe that a lone individual could decide that the federal government was tyrannical, and then resort to violence. To the contrary, Madison envisioned that if forcible resistance were necessary, it would be led by the states.

Madison here was following a centuries-old political theory that had first been developed by Catholics and then adopted by Protestants: if resistance to central tyranny is necessary, it should be led by "intermediate magistrates." That is, by officials who were intermediate between the people and the supreme ruler—such as regional governments, or the nobility. Only in the most extreme circumstances, if the tyrant had taken over all the intermediate magistrates (as would happen in Nazi Germany), should individual forcible resistance be contemplated.[3]

Federalist 28

***The Same Subject Continued: The Idea of Restraining the Legislative Authority in Regard to the Common Defense Considered.* The Independent Journal.**
Alexander Hamilton

[Some of the topics in Madison's *Federalist* 46 had also been addressed by Hamilton in Federalist 28, and would be further discussed in *Federalist* 51. Namely: the States would protect the people from any potential central government tyranny. Hamilton's essay was originally meant in a military sense, but it has been later understood to include broadly political senses. The bolding of key phrases below is added by Kopel.]

If the representatives of the people betray their constituents, there is then no resource left but in the exertion of that original right of self-defense which is paramount to all positive forms of government, and which against the usurpations of the national rulers, may be exerted with infinitely better prospect of success than against those of the rulers of an individual state.

In a single state, if the persons intrusted with supreme power become usurpers, the different parcels, subdivisions, or districts of which it consists, having no distinct government in each, can take no regular measures for defense. The citizens must rush tumultuously to arms, without concert, without system, without resource; except in their courage and despair. The usurpers, clothed with the forms of legal authority, can too often crush the opposition in embryo.

The smaller the extent of the territory, the more difficult will it be for the people to form a regular or systematic plan of opposition, and the easier will it be to defeat their early efforts.

---

[3] See DAVID B. KOPEL, THE MORALITY OF SELF-DEFENSE AND MILITARY ACTION: THE JUDEO-CHRISTIAN TRADITION (Praeger 2017).

Intelligence can be more speedily obtained of their preparations and movements, and the military force in the possession of the usurpers can be more rapidly directed against the part where the opposition has begun. In this situation there must be a peculiar coincidence of circumstances to insure success to the popular resistance.

The obstacles to usurpation and the facilities of resistance increase with the increased extent of the state, provided the citizens understand their rights and are disposed to defend them. The natural strength of the people in a large community, in proportion to the artificial strength of the government, is greater than in a small, and of course more competent to a struggle with the attempts of the government to establish a tyranny.

But in a confederacy the people, without exaggeration, may be said to be entirely the masters of their own fate. **Power being almost always the rival of power**, the general government will at all times stand ready to check the usurpations of the state governments, and these will have the same disposition towards the general government.

The people, by throwing themselves into either scale, will infallibly make it preponderate. **If their rights are invaded by either, they can make use of the other as the instrument of redress.** How wise will it be in them by cherishing the union to preserve to themselves an advantage which can never be too highly prized!

It may safely be received as an axiom in our political system, that the State governments will, in all possible contingencies, afford complete security against invasions of the public liberty by the national authority. Projects of usurpation cannot be masked under pretenses so likely to escape the penetration of select bodies of men, as of the people at large. The legislatures will have better means of information. They can **discover the danger at a distance**; and possessing all the organs of civil power, and the confidence of the people, they can at once adopt a regular plan of opposition, in which they can combine all the resources of the community. They can readily communicate with each other in the different States, and unite their common forces for the protection of their common liberty.

The great extent of the country is a further security. We have already experienced its utility against the attacks of a foreign power. And it would have precisely the same effect against the enterprises of ambitious rulers in the national councils. If the federal army should be able to quell the resistance of one State, the distant States would have it in their power to make head with fresh forces. The advantages obtained in one place must be abandoned to subdue the opposition in others; and the moment the part which had been reduced to submission was left to itself, its efforts would be renewed, and its resistance revive.[4]

We should recollect that the extent of the military force must, at all events, be regulated by the resources of the country. For a long time to come, it will not be possible to maintain a large army; and as the means of doing this increase, the population and natural strength of the community will proportionably increase. When will the time arrive that the federal government can raise and maintain an army capable of erecting a despotism over the great body of the people of an immense empire, who are in a situation, through the medium of their State governments, to take measures for their own defense, with all the celerity, regularity, and system of independent nations? The apprehension may be considered as a disease, for which there can be found no cure in the resources of argument and reasoning.

---

[4] This is basically what happened in the American Revolution. The British army and navy could conquer any particular city they wanted. But they could not simultaneously subdue the entire nation.

Federalist 51

***The Structure of the Government Must Furnish the Proper Checks and Balances Between the Different Departments.* New York Packet, Feb. 8, 1788.**
Alexander Hamilton or James Madison.

[T]he great security against a gradual concentration of the several powers in the same department, consists in giving to those who administer each department the necessary constitutional means and personal motives to resist encroachments of the others. The provision for defense must in this, as in all other cases, be made commensurate to the danger of attack. **Ambition must be made to counteract ambition.** The interest of the man must be connected with the constitutional rights of the place. It may be a reflection on human nature, that such devices should be necessary to control the abuses of government.

But what is government itself, but the greatest of all reflections on human nature? **If men were angels, no government would be necessary. If angels were to govern men, neither external nor internal controls on government would be necessary.[5] In framing a government which is to be administered by men over men, the great difficulty lies in this: you must first enable the government to control the governed; and in the next place oblige it to control itself.**

. . .

There are, moreover, two considerations particularly applicable to the federal system of America, which place that system in a very interesting point of view. First. In a single republic, all the power surrendered by the people is submitted to the administration of a single government; and the usurpations are guarded against by a division of the government into distinct and separate departments.

In the compound republic of America, the power surrendered by the people is first divided between two distinct governments, and then the portion allotted to each subdivided among distinct and separate departments. Hence **a double security arises to the rights of the people.** The different governments will control each other, at the same time that each will be controlled by itself.

B. The federal Sedition Act spurs the Kentucky and Virginia Resolutions

In 1798, Great Britain and revolutionary France and were at war. The 1789 French Revolution had degenerated into a radical terrorist dictatorship, which in 1799 would be replaced by the military dictatorship of Napoleon Bonaparte. Neither France nor Great Britain respected the international law rights of neutral ships, including those of the United States.[6]

When an American delegation arrived in France for negotiations, they were told that they must first pay bribes to three French officials. "No, no, not a sixpence, sir!" answered American delegate Charles Cotesworth Pinckney.

---

[5] Alluded to in Ronald Reagan's 1981 inaugural address: "From time to time we've been tempted to believe that society has become too complex to be managed by self-rule, that government by an elite group is superior to government for, by, and of the people. Well, if no one among us is capable of governing himself, then who among us has the capacity to govern someone else? All of us together, in and out of government, must bear the burden. The solutions we seek must be equitable, with no one group singled out to pay a higher price."

[6] This section is partly based on JOHN C. MILLER, CRISIS IN FREEDOM: THE ALIEN AND SEDITION ACTS (1951). *See also* WENDELL BIRD, CRIMINAL DISSENT: PROSECUTIONS UNDER THE ALIEN AND SEDITION ACTS OF 1798 (2020) (examining federal court and secretary of state records and finding that prosecutions under the Act were twice as numerous as had previously been reported by historians).

The administration of president John Adams informed the public about what had happened, but redacted the names of the three French diplomats, referring to them as X, Y, and Z. The XYZ Affair inflamed American opinion against France. Soon the naval Quasi-War between the U.S. and France began. Although it was never an officially declared war, it lasted from 1798 to 1800.

The American mood was well expressed by U.S. rep. Robert Goodloe Harper (S.C.): "Millions for defense, but not a cent for tribute!" (June 18, 1798). There was good reason to fear for the survival of the American republic. By 1798, France had destroyed the republics of Holland, Switzerland, and Venice. These republics had lost their independence because they waited for a declaration of war before acting against French agents in their country. Only the United States and a few other republics remained.

The United States, meanwhile, was full of French visitors who were attempting to influence American policy.

President Adams was part of the Federalist Party, which controlled Congress.[7] The opposition was the Republicans, led by vice-president Thomas Jefferson and U.S. Rep. James Madison (Vir.).

The hardline Federalists in Congress took the opportunity to push through the infamous Alien & Sedition Acts in 1798.

The Alien Act gave the president unilateral power to deport foreigners whom he considered dangerous. Any deported alien who returned would be subject to indefinite detention at the president's whim, with no right of habeas corpus.

President Adams never actually enforced the Alien Act. Its *in terrorem* effect sufficed to convince many French voluntarily to leave the United States.

The Sedition Act created a federal statutory crime based on the common law criminal offense of seditious libel. Seditious libel is a libel that calls the government into disrepute. Notably, the Sedition Act applied to libels against the government of the United States and the president of the United States, but not to libels against the vice-president. Before the ratification of the Twelfth Amendment in 1804, the vice-president was the runner-up in the presidential election, so vice-president Jefferson was president Adams' most important political opponent.

Alexander Hamilton was the lone major Federalist to oppose the Sedition Act—even though he had been attacked in the newspapers more than anyone else.

Of course, the Sedition Act was criticized for violating the First Amendment. It was also criticized for not being within the scope of Congress's enumerated powers, under article I.

This was a fair criticism. When the proposed Constitution was before the people for ratification in 1787–91, proponents had assured skeptics that Congress could never harm the

---

[7] The Federalist party was not the same as the "Federalists" who had promoted ratification of the Constitution. Some of the pro-ratification Federalists were members of the Federalist party (e.g., John Adams, Alexander Hamilton) while other pro-ratification Federalists were members of the opposition Republican party (e.g., James Madison, founder of the party). Neither party existed in the formal sense of modern political parties. Rather, they were informal associations of like-minded people.

The Federalist Party disintegrated in the 1810s, partly because of backlash to their opposition to the War of 1812, which was popular in retrospect, although it had not been popular in New England when the fighting was going on. The Republicans (called "Democratic-Republicans" by their Federalist Party opponents) became the only party on the national stage.

The modern Democratic party was created around Andrew Jackson in the 1820s. The anti-Jackson opposition eventually coalesced into the Whig party. The Whigs later fell apart and were supplanted in the 1850s by a new anti-slavery party comprising former Whigs (*e.g.*, Abraham Lincoln) and anti-slavery former Democrats; the new party called itself the Republican Party. The two-party system that had emerged by 1856 is the one that exists today.

freedom of the press, because Congress had no enumerated power that would be used for such an end.[8]

The 1798 Federalists claimed that the federal government has implicit power over all common law crimes. Further, the federal government has an inherent right of self-defense. Everyone agreed that the government could punish seditious *acts*—attempts to overthrow the federal government by force. Federalists reasoned that because Congress could punish sedition itself, it could punish things that might lead to sedition.

Another Federalist argument was that Sedition Act was justified by the Necessary and Proper Clause—to prevent interference with laws that had been enacted under the enumerated powers.

On paper, the Sedition Act was more speech-protective than its common law counterpart. Under the common law of the time, truth was no defense to a libel charge. The truer the statement, the more injurious the libel—according to the common law. The Sedition Act, however, did allow truth as a defense against the charge of having published "false, scandalous, and malicious" libels.

But the Sedition Act was much worse than it looked on paper. Truth was never successfully asserted as a defense in any Sedition Act trial. Political writing almost always contains a mix of fact and opinion, and opinion was unprotected.

Four of the five leading Republican newspapers were prosecuted. U.S. Rep. Matthew Lyon of Vermont was re-elected in 1798 while in prison for a Sedition Act conviction. There were parallel prosecutions in state courts for common law seditious libel—including for criticizing the Sedition Act.

In the Early Republic, an important responsibility of supreme court justices was *circuit riding*. When the supreme court was not in session, justices would travel to their respective assigned circuits, to preside at trials, or to serve as judges on appellate panels.[9]

The justices were all Federalist sympathizers who had been appointed by presidents Washington or Adams. Their conduct when presiding at Sedition Act trials was extremely biased. The worst was justice Samuel Chase.[10] He instructed U.S. Marshals to keep "democrats" off jury panels. Chase harangued the juries at length, with intemperate speeches essentially ordering convictions.

The Kentucky Resolution: Nullification

In an atmosphere of crisis, two state legislatures took the lead in defending the freedom of the press and the freedom of speech. Even in Great Britain, speeches made on the floor of parliament were absolutely immune from criminal prosecution. This common law freedom was recognized in the United States and fortified by specific guarantees in the federal and state constitutions.[11] So legislatures were the one forum where ideas could be expressed with absolute safety.

Kentucky had been admitted to the Union in 1792, formed from lands ceded by Virginia. The legislature adopted the Kentucky Resolution, which was secretly drafted by Thomas Jefferson.

---

[8] Robert G. Natelson & David B. Kopel, *Commerce in the Commerce Clause*: A Response to Jack Balkin, 109 MICH. L. REVIEW FIRST IMPRESSIONS 55, 60 (2010) (citing James Wilson).

[9] See David R. Stras, *Why Supreme Court Justices Should Ride Circuit Again*, 91 MINN. L. REVIEW 1710 (2007) (Circuit riding declined after a statutory change in 1891 and was formally abolished by Congress in 1911).

[10] Not to be confused with Salmon P. Chase, who was appointed chief justice decades later by President Lincoln.

[11] U.S. CONST., art. I, § 6; English Declaration of Right, item 9 (1689) ("That the freedom of speech and debates or proceedings in Parliament ought not to be impeached or questioned in any court or place out of Parliament."). Colorado's version is in art. V, § 16.

The Resolution explained why the Sedition Act was *ultra vires* to congressional power under the Constitution, why the Act violated the First Amendment, and why it was bad policy.[12]

Further, Jefferson articulated the *compact theory* of the federal government. The federal government had been created by a compact (a multiparty contract) of the states. There was no doubt that the Articles of Confederation has been created by interstate compact, and Jefferson argued that the same was true of the Constitution. Accordingly, parties to the compact (the States) were the final arbiters of whether the federal government was obeying the Constitution:

> [T]hat the several states composing the United States of America, are not united on the principle of unlimited submission to their general government; but that, by a compact under the style and title of a Constitution for the United States, and of amendments thereto, they constituted a general government for special purposes—delegated to that government certain definite powers, reserving, each state to itself, the residuary mass of right to their own self-government; and that whensoever the general government assumes undelegated powers, its acts are unauthoritative, void, and of no force: . . . [and] that, as in all other cases of compact among parties having no common judge, each party has an equal right to judge for itself, as well of infractions, as of the mode and measure of redress.[13]

The Kentucky Resolution is associated with the doctrine of *nullification*: that states can nullify the operation of an allegedly unconstitutional law within their borders. But as we shall see, "nullification" can be used in multiple senses.

While urging nullification, Jefferson also tried to calm his political allies who thought that secession from the Union was a remedy. He wrote to Virginia Senator John Taylor:

> A little patience, and we shall see the reign of witches pass over, their spells dissolve, and the people, recovering their true sight, restore their government to its true principles. It is true that in the meantime we are suffering deeply in spirit, and incurring the horrors of a war and long oppressions of enormous public debt . . . If the game runs sometimes against us at home we must have patience till luck turns, and then we shall have an opportunity of winning back the principles we have lost.[14]

The Virginia Resolution: Interposition

After reading the Kentucky Resolution, James Madison drafted a similar resolution for the Virginia legislature. Like Jefferson, Madison argued for the compact theory, against an excessively broad reading of congressional powers, and for the First Amendment, which he called "the guardian of all other rights."

Madison, however, did not endorse nullification. Instead, he promoted a milder alternative:

> [T]his Assembly . . . doth explicitly . . . declare, that it views the powers of the

[12] *See* WILLIAM J. WATKINS, JR., RECLAIMING THE AMERICAN REVOLUTION: THE KENTUCKY AND VIRGINIA RESOLUTIONS AND THEIR LEGACY 55–75 (2004).

[13] Kentucky Resolution of Nov. 10, 1798, §§ 1, 8, *in* 4 THE DEBATES IN THE SEVERAL STATE CONVENTIONS ON THE ADOPTION OF THE FEDERAL CONSTITUTION 540, 543 (Jonathan Elliot ed., 1891). Elliot's Debates is a five-volume collection of materials on Founding Era. It is available on-line at https://memory.loc.gov/ammem/amlaw/lwed.html.

[14] Letter from Thomas Jefferson to John Taylor (June 4, 1798), *in* 7 THE WRITINGS OF THOMAS JEFFERSON 265–66 (1895).

> federal government, as resulting from the compact, to which the states are parties [*i.e.*, the Constitution]; . . . as no further valid that they are authorized by the grants enumerated in that compact; and that in case of a deliberate, palpable, and dangerous exercise of other powers, not granted by the said compact, the states who are parties thereto, have the right, and are in duty bound, to interpose for arresting the progress of the evil, and for maintaining within their respective limits, the authorities, rights and liberties appertaining to them.[15]

Madison wanted the states to "interpose" themselves to protect the rights of their citizens.

Madison did not fully elaborate the scope of the doctrine of *interposition*, but the Virginia legislature provided an example of it use. The Virginia Resolution was circulated to other state legislatures, along with a further analysis by Madison, inviting them to join Virginia and Kentucky in formally declaring opposition to the unconstitutional Sedition Act.[16]

Madison's *Report* argued that the narrow view of the First Amendment (Blackstone's position that freedom of the press consisted only in freedom from prior restraint) was meaningless if a person could be punished after publication. Punishment afterward would make writers afraid, and thus have the same effect as a prior restraint: preventing the publication from being made in the first place.

More fundamentally, Madison explained, "The people, not the government, possess the absolute sovereignty"—unlike in Great Britain, where parliament was sovereign. The very nature of deciding whether congress and the president deserved to be re-elected required deciding whether elected officials deserved to be held in "contempt or disrepute" or deserved "the hatred of the people of the United States"—yet the Sedition Act forbade creating such sentiments.

Besides, as a practical matter, if the Sedition Act had been in effect before, "might not the United States have been languishing at this day, under the infirmities of a sickly confederation? Might they not possibly be miserable colonies, groaning under a foreign yoke?"

No other legislatures, however, responded affirmatively to Madison's appeal.

Aftermath

The Sedition Act prosecutions had demonstrated that the Federalists were unworthy to govern. They had used national security as pretext to silence political opponents. "They induced hysteria and turned it to party purposes," as historian John C. Miller put it. MILLER, CRISIS IN FREEDOM, at 22.

In the 1800 election, Jefferson and the Republicans ousted the Federalists. Naturalized aliens, many of them voting for the first time, strongly supported Jefferson. Thanks to them, the Republicans narrowly carried New York, and with it, the election.

In 1803, president Jefferson and his congressional allies attempted to impeach justice Chase, and almost succeeded. The attempted impeachment, and its ultimate defeat, established two enduring traditions: 1. Judges should not be impeached for bad rulings. 2. Judges should distance themselves from expressing political opinions.

The Sedition Act expired its own terms in 1801. The question of whether the federal government has common law criminal powers was settled in the negative. In 1812, president Madison's administration, ironically, attempted to prosecute some Federalist newspaper editors for common law seditious libel. Although there was no case law precedent, the supreme court

---

15 Virginia Resolution of Dec. 24, 1798, § 3.

16 James Madison, *Report on the Alien and Sedition Acts* (Jan. 7, 1800).

held that there is no federal common law criminal power, the issue having "been long since settled in public opinion."[17]

As of 1799, it would have been fair to say that there was a split in views of the Freedom of Speech and of the Press. In the orthodox view, expressed by William Blackstone's treatise, those freedoms were an absolute bar to prior restraints, and no impediment at all to subsequent punishment. In the popular view, those freedoms meant no prior restraint and no subsequent punishment for criticizing the government. At least at the federal level, the results of 1798–1800 have been seen forever after as prohibiting the crime of seditious libel.[18]

The supreme court would later write that resistance to the Sedition Act marked the crystallization of a distinctive American conception of the liberty of free speech, one that provided great protection against punishment for expressing opinions about government officials. *See New York Times Co. v. Sullivan*, 376 U.S. 254, 273 (1964);[19] *id.* at 274 ("The people, not the government, possess absolute sovereignty.") (quoting Madison's report).

C. Interposition and Nullification Before the Civil War

The "Principles of '98" had not been vindicated by the courts, but the Sedition Act was retired to the ash heap of history.

Although the Kentucky and Virginia Resolutions have never been recognized as judicially enforceable, they are central documents in the American principles of states' rights. Interposition and nullification would continue to play important roles in America's developing constitutional traditions.

The War of 1812

Interposition and nullification next appeared in opposition to the presidential administration of Thomas Jefferson. While Great Britain and Napoleonic France were fighting each other and seizing American ships, president Jefferson worked to keep the United States out of war. To pressure the European powers to leave American shipping alone, he convinced Congress to impose a complete foreign trade embargo.

The embargo devastated New England's fishing and trading. There was widespread evasion of the embargo, which opponents argued was unconstitutional. The Constitution authorized Congress "To regulate Commerce with foreign nations." U.S. CONST., art. I, § 8. Extinguishing foreign commerce was the opposite of regulating it. The Massachusetts legislature declared the embargo "unconstitutional, and void in divers of its provisions," since Congress had never been granted the power to impose such a thing.[20]

When president Jefferson exercised his constitutional power to call forth the Connecticut militia to help enforce the embargo, Connecticut governor Jonathan Trumbull refused. So did the governors of other New England states. Eventually, the supreme court would hold that state governors may not dispute a federal determination that conditions exist that allow a state militia

---

[17] *United States v. Hudson & Godwin*, 11 U.S. (7 Cranch) 32 (1812) (false article asserting that the president and congress had paid a two-million-dollar bribe to Napoleon Bonaparte).
[18] See LEONARD W. LEVY, EMERGENCE OF A FREE PRESS (rev. ed. 1985).
[19] Holding that the criminal or civil offense of seditious libel does not exist in the United States. Libels of individual government officials may only be punished if the defendant knowingly or reckless uttered a factually false statement.
[20] 2 STATE DOCUMENTS ON FEDERAL RELATIONS 25, 27 (Herman V. Ames ed., 1900) (Feb. 22, 1814).

to be called into federal service.[21] The U.S. Constitution specifically provides that state militias may be called into federal service.[22]

Some historians suggest that the embargo was getting close to making Great Britain come to terms with the U.S.[23] But the unpopular embargo was repealed, and not long after, the U.S. and Great Britain fought the War of 1812.

New England did not like the war very much, and state governments attempted to interfere with the enforcement of a federal statute that allowed males as young as 16 to enlist in the U.S. Army, even without parental consent.

The 1828 Tariff of Abominations

Everyone agrees that Congress has the power to impose tariffs on imported goods. Tariffs are among the "Taxes, Duties, Imposts, and Excises" authorized by article I, § 8. In 1828, Congress enacted what was called the Tariff of Abominations. It was the product of narrow sectional interest. For the protection of incipient industry in the North, the law imposed very high duties on manufactured imports. For 92% of imported goods, the tariff was a staggering 62%. This was sure to provoke retaliatory tariffs from other nations, and the principal victim would be the South, which exported cotton, rice, indigo, and other agricultural goods. The Tariff of Abominations was signed into law by president John Quincy Adams. At the time, the prevailing view was that presidents should not veto congressional bills because of policy disagreement.

In 1832, Congress reformed the tariff a little, but not nearly enough to solve the South's problem. The exclusion of manufactured imports was creating a manufacturing boom in the North, and so the tariff was popular there.

Frustrated, the people of South Carolina assembled in a special convention in 1832 and declared the 1828 and 1832 tariffs to be null and void within the state. South Carolina's John C. Calhoun argued that although tariffs in general were constitutional, the contested tariffs were not really for the purpose of raising federal revenue, but for the purpose of industrial protectionism. Hence, they were *ultra vires* of legitimate congressional power.

One weakness of Calhoun's argument was the historical example of the first federal tariff, drafted by treasury secretary Alexander Hamilton, and enacted under the George Washington administration. Although the purpose of that tariff was revenue, an intended effect of the tariff was protection for certain domestic industries that the tariff was meant to foster.[24]

In retirement, James Madison was appalled by Calhoun's use of Madison's Virginia Resolution arguments.

As the crisis was building in 1830, South Carolina senator Robert Hayne and Massachusetts senator Daniel Webster engaged in a famous debate. Although the debate was partly about tariffs and sectionalism, it delved into profound questions about the nature of the U.S. government under the Constitution. Was the Constitution a compact among the states? Or did the Constitution proceed directly from the American people, with ratification in state conventions simply having

---

[21] *Martin v. Mott*, 25 U.S. 19, 28–33 (1827).

[22] U.S. CONST., art. I, § 8, cl. 15. According to the text, Congress shall have power to "provide for calling forth the Militia to execute the Laws of the Union, suppress Insurrections and repel Invasions." Congress provided (in a sense) for calling forth by delegating the Calling Forth power to the President. First Militia Act of 1792, 1 Stat. 264 (1792).

[23] See, e.g., GORDON S. WOOD, EMPIRE OF LIBERTY: A HISTORY OF THE EARLY REPUBLIC, 1789–1815 (2011).

[24] Calhoun penned his 1830 *South Carolina Exposition and Protest* anonymously, since he was then serving as Vice-President under President Andrew Jackson. Calhoun had previously been vice-president under John Quincy Adams. The only other vice-president to serve under two different Presidents was George Clinton (Thomas Jefferson's second term, and then James Madison's first).

been a convenient means for the American people to express their will? The Webster-Hayne debate was studied by many generations of schoolchildren because there were strong arguments on both sides, eloquently expressed.[25]

President Andrew Jackson had ousted incumbent John Quincy Adams in the 1828 elections. Jackson strongly opposed federal economic centralization, and he was an ardent friend of states' rights. But he would not countenance the purported nullification of federal law. The president sent a pair of warships to Charleston harbor.[26] He warned that "if one drop of blood be shed there in defiance of the laws of the United States, I will hang the first man of them I can get my hands on to the first tree I can find."[27] Notably, eight Southern states condemned South Carolina's actions.[28] Congress passed the Force Bill, 4 Stat. 632 (1833) authorizing military action if South Carolina persisted.

The crisis was averted when Congress enacted the Compromise Tariff of 1833, 4 Stat. 629 (1833), sponsored by South Carolina's new senator John C. Calhoun and by Kentucky's Henry Clay. It provided that tariffs would be gradually reduced over the next ten years, until they returned to the 1816 level of 20%.

The Fugitive Slave Act of 1850

Article I, section 8, of the U.S. Constitution gave Congress certain enumerated powers. Separately, article IV, section 2, required states to return fugitives from other states. This included not only fugitives from criminal justice, but also escaped slaves or indentured servants.

Did the fugitive slave clause (about interstate obligations) create a congressional power to pass a fugitive slave act? Congress thought so and created a fugitive slave act in 1793. Among the most famous supreme court cases in antebellum America was the supreme court test of that act, *Prigg v. Pennsylvania*, 41 U.S. 539 (1842). Justice Joseph Story's opinion for the court read federal powers broadly, as did most of justice Story's opinions. *Prigg* held that article IV had created an implied congressional power.

Runaways were a constant problem for slave-owners, especially in the Upper South, where slave states bordered free states. Most people in free states—such as Pennsylvania, Ohio, or Illinois—were not abolitionists, but they did dislike slavery, and they often refused to allow their state or local government to spend their tax dollars in recapturing fugitive slaves. In Congress, senator Calhoun complained vehemently that Northern states were annulling the section 3 of article IV.[29]

In the Compromise of 1850, Kentucky senator Henry Clay helped lead Congress to a solution that postponed the growing national crisis over slavery. The Compromise averted civil war until 1861.[30]

---

[25] Today, justice Thomas favors the compact theory, without necessarily agreeing with all its possible implications.

[26] Events in Georgia helped fuel South Carolina's boldness. The U.S. Supreme Court had held unconstitutional a Georgia statute that violated the rights of persons in some federal Indian territories claimed by Georgia. *Worcester v. Georgia*, 31 U.S. (6 Pet.) 515 (1832). Significantly, the Court did not order U.S. Marshals to enforce the decision, and so Georgia ignored it. As president Jackson wrote to a friend, "the decision of the Supreme Court has fell still born, and they find that they cannot coerce Georgia to yield to its mandate." Georgia did, after several months, free Mr. Worcester, for whom the Court had granted a writ of habeas corpus.

[27] RICHARD E. ELLIS, THE UNION AT RISK: JACKSONIAN DEMOCRACY, STATES' RIGHTS, AND THE NULLIFICATION CRISIS 78 (1987).

[28] DANIEL WALKER HOWE, WHAT HATH GOD WROUGHT: THE TRANSFORMATION OF AMERICA 1815–1848, at 406–09 (2007).

[29] 27 THE PAPERS OF JOHN C. CALHOUN 201 (1959–2003).

[30] If the Civil War had begun in 1850 instead of 1861, the South probably would have won. Without the rail network that developed in the 1850s, the North would have had a much harder time exploiting its advantage of larger population and industry.

Among the provisions of the Compromise were: the admission of California as a free state; a ban on the slave trade in the District of Columbia; and an amended, much stronger Fugitive Slave Act. Further, the recently admitted State of Texas ceded much of its northern and western lands (including a part of modern Colorado) to the United States, in exchange for the U.S. paying the Republic of Texas's old debts.

Northerners detested the new Fugitive Slave Act. The U.S. Army was deployed to assist slave catchers. Ordinary citizens were ordered to assist U.S. marshals in hunting for fugitive slaves.[31] In a time when identify verification was sketchy at best, legally free blacks in the North were sometimes abducted by Southern slave catchers; when slave catchers could not find the escaped slave, they would sometimes take someone else, and claim that person was the fugitive. Even when alleged fugitives were apprehended by U.S. Marshals, due process protections were nil.

Many states adopted Personal Liberty Laws, to provide due process and trials for captured persons who were alleged to be fugitives.[32] These laws did not expressly contradict the Fugitive Slave Act, but instead constrained the actions of any state or local official who might have custody of an alleged fugitive. Interposition and nullification became buzzwords of anti-slavery advocates, especially in New England and the upper Midwest—homes of the strongest anti-slavery sentiment.

In Wisconsin in 1854, Sherman Booth was arrested by federal law enforcement after his speech incited a mob to rescue a captured slave. A Wisconsin state judge granted Booth a writ of habeas corpus. On appeal, the Wisconsin supreme court affirmed the writ, and held the Fugitive Slave Act of 1850 unconstitutional. U.S. Marshal Stephen Ablemen then turned to the federal courts, but the Wisconsin supreme court said that it did not have to obey federal courts, and its ruling was final. While all this was going on, the slave, Joshua Glover, fled to Canada.

When *Ableman v. Booth* reached the U.S. supreme court, Wisconsin did not bother to argue it side. Unsurprisingly, the unanimous court ruled that a state court cannot annul a federal court conviction.[33] The Wisconsin legislature retorted with a resolution that the *Ableman* decision was "without authority, *void, and of no force*" in Wisconsin.[34]

---

[31] The legal explanation for the above is a little complicated. Ever since the eighth century in Anglo-Saxon England, sheriffs have had the common law power to summon the posse comitatus (the armed, able-bodied male population) whenever needed to assist in law enforcement. This power exists to the present. One of the most notable posse uses in Colorado was in 1977, when a sheriff's posse aided the recapture of serial killer Ted Bundy, who had escaped from the Pitkin County Courthouse. Many Colorado sheriffs presently have permanent posses, composed of citizen volunteers who have received training. These posses are used for everything from county fair security to road management during weather emergencies to hostage situations. *See* Chapter 19 (art. XIV, § 8.5).

As Alexander Hamilton had explained in Federalist 29, the federal government has posse comitatus power as a Necessary and Proper incident of its other powers. Before 1850, U.S. Marshals sometimes summoned posses, and local law enforcement officers often did so. Like jury service, posse service was usually performed with civic pride, as one of the duties of good citizenship. But Northerners hated being called into federal posses to capture fugitive slaves under the 1850 Act. This turned slavery from a distant problem into a personal problem. In effect, they were being forced to do the bidding of the Southern slave-owners.

By tradition, the U.S. army was not supposed to be used for domestic law enforcement. But under a legal fiction known as the Mansfield Doctrine, U.S. army soldiers were claimed to be civilian volunteers who were simply serving as a posse for the U.S. marshals. *See* David B. Kopel, *The Posse Comitatus and the Office of Sheriff: Armed Citizens Summoned to the Aid of Law Enforcement*, 104 JOURNAL OF CRIMINAL L. & CRIMINOLOGY 671 (2015).

[32] See THOMAS D. MORRIS, FREE MEN ALL: THE PERSONAL LIBERTY LAWS OF THE NORTH, 1780–1861 (1974).

[33] *Ableman v. Booth*, 62 U.S. (21 Howell) 506 (1859).

[34] James H. Read & Neal Allen, *Living Dead, and Undead: Nullification Past and Present*, in NULLIFICATION AND SECESSION IN MODERN CONSTITUTIONAL THOUGHT (Sanford Levinson ed., 2016).

In federal courts, the anti-slavery, pro-states' rights nullificationists did not have a leg to stand on. A state court cannot issue a writ of habeas corpus to free a federal prisoner.

In contrast, state interposition was recognized as constitutional. The Maine House of Representatives asked the state's highest court, the Maine Supreme Judicial Court, about the constitutionality of Maine's Personal Liberty Law; the statute had been adopted in 1855, and a slightly revised portion had been added to the state constitution in 1857. Like Colorado, Maine allows its supreme court to answer questions of importance propounded by the legislature.[35] The Maine supreme judicial court answered in February 1861. The court began by explaining that it had not paid any attention to the pro/com policy arguments, emotion, and so on associated with the issue. Instead, the court simply examined whether any provisions of the Maine laws conflicted with the federal Fugitive Slave Acts of 1850 and 1793.

According to the court, there was no conflict in the statute requiring county attorneys to assist the legal defense of fugitive slaves, and for the state to pay witness expenses in defense of fugitives. A good legal defense helped the federal law, by improving the accuracy of enforcement. Even Virginia, a slave state, had a similar law providing indigent defense for persons accused of being fugitive slaves. *See Opinion of Judges Appleton and Kent*, 46 Me. 579, 579–80 (1861).[36]

The statute allowing Maine jailers to keep any U.S. prisoners except fugitive slaves was also constitutional. The State of Maine could decide how its property would be used:

> The jails of the State are the property of the several counties at whose expense they are erected. They are built for State objects. The government of the United States have no more right, without the assent of the State, to use them, than they have to use any other property of the State for purposes of its own. Still less can it claim that they should be used for the safe keeping of the personal chattels of the citizens of other States.

Id. at 580–81. In 1789, Congress had recommended that states pass laws requiring state and local jailers to keep federal prisoners. Ever since, some states had done so, others had refused, and others had varied. *Id.* at 581.

Also constitutional was prohibiting state and local officials *in their official capacities* from assisting in the enforcement of the federal Fugitive Slave Act. The federal act itself said that enforcement would be by U.S. officers. The U.S. supreme court, in *Prigg v. Pennsylvania*, had affirmed that state officials have no duty to help enforce federal law, specifically the Fugitive Slave Act. *Id.* at 582–85.

Importantly, the Maine law did *not* forbid Maine citizens, in their dual capacity as U.S. citizens, from aiding in the enforcement of the federal laws. As the Maine court recognized, prohibiting Maine citizens from serving in a federal posse would have been unconstitutional. *Id.* at 587–93. So a Maine justice of the peace could not use his official powers to assist in fugitive slave capture. But as a U.S. citizen, the man could still be ordered by a federal marshal to join a federal posse.

Northern interposition and nullification aggravated the sectional divisions that eventually caused the Civil War and all its terrible suffering. Still, the states' righters had achieved their objective. When slavery was abolished by the Thirteenth Amendment in 1865, no person and no state government in America could ever be forced to participate in apprehending an individual so that he or she could be enslaved.

---

[35] The Maine House's questions were sent by house speaker James G. Blaine, who would become the Republican presidential nominee in 1884.

[36] Chief justice John Appleton (1852–83) was a leading jurist on evidence law reform and individual rights. He was skeptical of government aid to business and supportive of racial and religious equality. *See* Appleton, John, in 1 GREAT AMERICAN JUDGES: AN ENCYCLOPEDIA (John R. Vile ed., 2003).

D. From the late 19th century to the 1960s: State resistance discredited

The Progressive Era

Between 1890–1920, the situation of people of color became worse. Legally-mandated racial discrimination—Jim Crow laws—flourished in the South. Compared to 1880, there were many more laws forbidding voluntary relations between the races. For example, in some states it was illegal for a black barber to cut a white customer's hair. Many voluntary inter-racial commercial relations were outlawed.

In the early 20th century, Alexander Hamilton's forecast of "double security" via dual sovereignty did not come true for black people. The vast majority of them lived in the South, where they had been stripped of their voting rights.

For example, in Mississippi, a new state constitution in 1890 aimed to prevent blacks, as well as many poor whites, from voting. It required payment of a poll tax two years before election day and imposed a literacy test for voter registration. Anyone whose grandfather had been a registered voter was exempt from the literacy test. In Mississippi in 1890, no black person had a grandfather who had been a registered voter. The literacy test involved explaining a part of the state constitution. A white registrant might be asked to read and explain a simple clause (*e.g.*, the governor serves a two-year term). A black registrant would be asked to explain an intricate provision that only a lawyer would understand. In *Williams v. Mississippi,* 170 U.S. 213 (1898), the court ruled that the Mississippi voting laws did not violate the Fifteenth Amendment; they were facially nonracial, and the plaintiffs had not proven discrimination in administration. Thereafter, similar laws proliferated in other former Confederate states.

Blacks who lived outside the South could vote, but their numbers were too small to have much political power. As a result, Congress failed to exercise its powers under section 2 of the Fifteenth Amendment to act against voting discrimination in the South.

Partly because blacks had little political power, demagogues targeted them. Legal persecution peaked in the early twentieth century. While interracial marriage had been lawful in many states in the 1860s, by the early twentieth century it was banned everywhere, except in Massachusetts.[37] Because of states' rights, lawful inter-racial continued to exist in Massachusetts, alone. If marriage law had been under congressional power, the Massachusetts system could not have survived.

Federal government hostility to people of color reached its apex under the administration of Democratic president Woodrow Wilson. Among other things, he ordered that federal government employees be segregated on the job, for the supposed good of both races.

People of color did get some help from the supreme court. The U.S. supreme court of the period took contract and property rights very seriously, as did the Colorado supreme court.

In *Buchanan v. Warley,* the U.S. supreme court struck down a city law that attempted to impose residential racial segregation by restricting home sales. Home buyers and sellers had the

[37] States varied in what sorts of interracial marriages were prohibited. Western states displayed greater concerns about marriages between whites and various type of Asians. Colorado's law did not apply to former Mexican territories that had been acquired by the United States in the Treaty of Guadalupe-Hidalgo. Further reading: David Kopel, *The original meaning of the 14th Amendment regarding interracial marriage*, VOLOKH.COM, Dec. 5, 2011; PEGGY PASCOE, WHAT COMES NATURALLY: MISCEGENATION LAW AND THE MAKING OF RACE IN AMERICA (2010).

Figure 12. Charles Evans Hughes, U.S. supreme court associate justice 1910-16, chief justice 1920-31.

Fourteenth Amendment liberty to exercise their property and contract rights as they chose, without regard to the color of either party.[38]

An Arizona law required that employers of five or more persons employ at least 80% "qualified electors or native-born citizens of the United States." This was unconstitutional, for, as Chief justice Hughes wrote in *Truax v. Raich*, the law denies "to lawful inhabitants, because of their race or nationality, the ordinary means of earning a livelihood . . . [T]he right to work for a living in the common occupations of the community is of the very essence of the personal freedom and opportunity," guaranteed by the Fourteenth Amendment.[39]

Buchanan and *Truax* were derided by same progressives who derided all judicial enforcement of liberty of contract, property rights, or other constitutional rights.[40]

During World War I and thereafter, many blacks moved North, often to work in the growing factories. The move was facilitated by *Buchanan*, which had quashed the incipient residential segregation laws.

As the black voters grew in number in the North and West, so did their political power, and their broader power to influence public opinion. Slowly, the federal government began to take interest in the problems caused by Jim Crow laws.[41]

Brown v. Board of Education and its aftermath

Starting in the 1930s, the supreme court had begun to issue rulings against racial segregation in higher education. The first case held that because Missouri had no state law school for blacks, blacks could not be forbidden to attend the University of Missouri law school.[42] Later, the court held that even if the racially separate law school in Texas were equal in resources (which it wasn't), racial segregation denied students networking opportunities, and was therefore unconstitutional.[43]

By 1954, the court was ready to take on the far more explosive issues of elementary and secondary education. Southern resistance to *Brown v. Board of Education,* 347 U.S. 483 (1954), was much stronger than the court had anticipated. The intellectual leader of "massive resistance" was James J. Kilpatrick, editorial page editor of the *Richmond News Leader.* His theory was set forth in his 1957 book *The Sovereign States.* Kilpatrick argued that any state could "suspend the operation of a law regarded as unconstitutional pending a decision by all the States in convention assembled."

---

[38] *Buchanan v. Warley*, 245 U.S. 60 (1917).
[39] *Truax v. Raich*, 239 U.S. 33 (1915).
[40] See DAVID E. BERNSTEIN, REHABILITATING LOCHNER: DEFENDING INDIVIDUAL RIGHTS AGAINST PROGRESSIVE REFORM (2012).
[41] See Jack M. Balkin, *How Social Movements Change (Or Fail to Change) the Constitution: The Case of the New Departure*, 39 SUFFOLK U.L. REVIEW 29 (2005).
[42] *Missouri ex rel. Gaines v. Canada*, 305 U.S. 337 (1938). Notwithstanding the state's offer to pay tuition for blacks at an out-of-state school.
[43] *Sweatt v. Painter*, 339 U.S. 629 (1950).

Eight state legislatures resolved that *Brown* was null and void within their borders. Mississippi forbade state employees from obeying federal court desegregation orders.[44]

The supreme court did not directly engage with Kilpatrick's theory, but it did issue a declaration calling itself the supreme and final interpreter of the Constitution, and so everyone must obey the court. *Cooper v. Aaron*, 358 U.S. 1 (1958).[45]

Brown v. Board provided a tremendous morale boost to the Civil Rights Movement. In the long run, the school desegregation battle greatly increased the moral authority, and hence the power, of the U.S. supreme court.

Yet in *Brown's* first decade, the decision made little practical difference to schoolchildren. By 1964, the percentage of schoolchildren who were attending integrated schools in South had barely changed. Only when the federal Civil Rights Act of 1964 threatened to cut off federal education funding to segregated schools did desegregation begin to flourish.[46]

The next year, Congress finally exercised its Fifteenth Amendment powers, and passed the Voting Rights Act. As the voting rights of Southern blacks began to be secured, the political calculus of Southern politicians began to change. Even the notorious segregationist Senator Strom Thurmond of South Carolina eventually became friendly to blacks, once they were voters.

As of 1965, the prestige of the federal government had reached a peak never since seen. Most Americans personally remembered that the federal government had saved civilization in 1941–45 by defeating the genocidal tyrannies of National Socialist Germany and Imperial Japan. The federal government was doing the same in the Cold War, by containing totalitarian Soviet imperialism.

To the neutral observer, the federal government operated with greater efficiency, and better respect for human rights, than did the state governments. When president Lyndon Johnson in 1965 confidently proclaimed a War on Poverty and promised that a beneficent federal government would soon eliminate poverty in the United States, most people believed that the war would be won.

States' rights were discredited, considered mere pretexts for racism. Which was in fact how they had been used in the 1950s and 1960s. In the elite view of the time, states should be administrative arms of the enlightened federal government. To talk about state sovereignty was crazy.

E. Declining confidence in the federal government.

The later 1960s, and thereafter, saw reduced public confidence in the federal government. President Lyndon Johnson had lied to the nation about a naval confrontation between North Vietnam and the United States, the Tonkin Gulf Incident, August 2, 1964. The deceit was not discovered until much later; in the meantime, over half a million American soldiers were deployed in Vietnam. The Johnson administration kept saying that America was winning, but the longer the war dragged on, the fewer who believed.

---

[44] Sanford Levinson, *The 21st Century Rediscovery of Nullification and Secession*, in NULLIFICATION AND SECESSION IN MODERN CONSTITUTIONAL THOUGHT, at 30-31.

[45] "[T]he rhetoric of *Cooper v. Aaron* was the boasting of the weak. The Court's claim of judicial supremacy, where its decisions became the Constitution, was bravado substituting for an inability to do anything." L.A. Powe, Jr., *The Politics of Judicial Review: Reflections on the Marshall, Warren, and Rehnquist Courts*, 38 WAKE FOREST L. REVIEW 697, 713 (2003).

[46] See Nelson Lund, *The Constitution, the Supreme Court, and Racial Politics*, 12 GA. ST. U. L. REVIEW 1129 (1996).

Federal government attempts to manage the economy did not work well. The "misery index" of "inflation + unemployment" crept upward, reaching a peak of 19.72 under Jimmy Carter in 1980.[47]

Civil liberties came under aggressive federal pressure with the Nixon administration's War on Drugs. As later explained by Nixon's Domestic Affairs Advisor John Ehrlichman, the White House decided that its most hardened political opponents were blacks and hippies. So the War on Drugs was invented to disrupt them and put them in prison. Heroin prosecutions were aimed at the blacks, and marijuana prosecutions at the hippies. Enacting and enforcing the Controlled Substances Act of 1970 was the pretext to infiltrate and spy on these groups.[48]

Nixon won a landslide re-election in 1972. In August 1974, he resigned rather than face near-unanimous impeachment and conviction. Tapes that he himself had recorded showed him orchestrating a cover-up of his campaign staff's attempted burglary of Democratic National Committee headquarters, at the Watergate hotel and business complex in D.C. Also, Nixon's re-election campaign was proven to have extorted illegal, secret corporate contributions. Nixon himself had ordered the Internal Revenue Service to target his political opponents.

The Watergate investigations spurred further inquiry into wrongdoing by the Republican Nixon administration. A Senate committee led by Frank Church (D-Idaho) had started out investigating Nixon's misuse of the CIA and had discovered that the abuses had begun in previous administrations. Several reforms were enacted to limit domestic surveillance and other CIA operations.

Nixon's defenders were correct in stating that he hadn't done anything worse than his Democratic predecessor Lyndon Johnson—and that the Kennedy, Eisenhower, Truman, and Franklin Roosevelt administrations did not exactly have clean hands.

It no longer seemed that federal government was the always-reliable defender of the rule of law and civil liberties.

The U.S. supreme court squandered much prestige and goodwill with the *Roe v. Wade* decision. 410 U.S. 113 (1973). No other case in the twentieth century inflicted so much institutional damage on the court. *Roe* held the abortion laws of all 50 states unconstitutional—even the liberal laws such as those written by Colo. state representative (and future governor) Richard Lamm.

The opinion did not stand the test of time. Generations of law professors have written post-hoc alternative rationales for the result, or some of it.[49] Later, *Roe*'s core holding was affirmed on the basis of a generation of practice and continuing expectations.[50]

While many people favored the policy result in *Roe*, the abortion battles at the court have done more than any other issue to create a bipartisan view of the supreme court as a political branch. The supreme court's national answer might be the last word, but that did not make it always right.

By 1980, the American people had decided that president Jimmy Carter, although a good man, was in over his head. They took a chance by electing the most overtly conservative president since Calvin Coolidge in 1924. Ronald Reagan's January 1981 inaugural speech declared "In this present crisis, government is not the solution to our problem; government is the problem."

Reagan had campaigned as a supporter of states' rights, and his administration mostly followed through. States' rights were once again respectable. Meanwhile, as power was being

---

[47] United States Misery Index, *Misery Index by President* .

[48] Dan Baum, *Legalize It All*, HARPER'S (Apr. 2016).

[49] *See, e.g.*, WHAT ROE V. WADE SHOULD HAVE SAID: THE NATION'S TOP LEGAL EXPERTS REWRITE AMERICA'S MOST CONTROVERSIAL DECISION (Jack Balkin ed., 2007).

[50] *Planned Parenthood of Pennsylvania v. Casey*, 505 U.S. 833 (1992).

devolved to state governments, state legislatures were improving in quality. They were no longer the corrupt and lazy backwaters of the 1950s.

During the Reagan years, some states' rights advocates had a solid political base but were unable to achieve their goals. For example, Reagan's 1980 landslide had been built in part on the Sagebrush Rebellion. Western states wanted to exercise more sovereignty over the vast federal lands in Western States. In Nevada, for example, 86% of the land belongs to the federal government. But other Westerners, including many sportsmen, liked federal control of the lands.

Tentatively, the supreme court began to take the first steps towards restoring the state-federal balance—while being careful not to overrule precedents of the New Deal or Warren Courts.[51]

F. The New Federalism

President Nixon in 1969 and President Reagan in the 1980s used the phrase "the New Federalism" to describe their efforts to return power to the states. Reagan's administration was somewhat successful in its objective, Nixon's less so. "The Federalism" is also used to describe the Rehnquist Court's work in enforcing states' rights and limits on federal power. The project begun under chief justice Rehnquist has continued under chief justice Roberts. *See* CHRISTOPHER BANKS & JOHN BLAKEMAN, THE U.S. SUPREME COURT AND NEW FEDERALISM: FROM THE REHNQUIST COURT TO THE ROBERTS COURT (2012).

From the 1940s through the 1960s, the court had been unwilling to find that any exercise of congressional power violated states' rights. One of the first signs of a different approach was the 1976 decision *National League of Cities v. Usery*, 426 U.S. 833 (1976). Congress in 1974 had extended the federal wage and hours law—the Fair Labor Standards Act (FLSA)—to state and local government employees. The 1976 court held that the extension violated the Tenth Amendment,[52] because it interfered with the core operations of state government. But justice Harry Blackmun later changed his mind, and *National League of Cities* was over-ruled. *Garcia v. San Antonio Metropolitan Transit Auth.*, 469 U.S. 528 (1985).

Later, Missouri's constitutional rule that state judges must retire at age 70 was challenged as a violation of the federal Age Discrimination in Employment Act (ADEA).[53] The court pointed out that federal interference with who may serve as a state judge would be an enormous change in the long-standing separation of powers between the federal and state governments. Accordingly, the court would not presume that a congressional statute had intended to intrude deeply on state sovereignty, unless the statute had said so with unmistakable clarity. While the 1974 FLSA had been crystal clear, the ADEA was not. Accordingly, the Missouri retirement rule was not affected by the ADEA. *Gregory v. Ashcroft,* 501 U.S. 452 (1991).

Two issues have been especially important in the New Federalism's state-federal separation of powers: conditional federal grants, and federal commandeering.

---

[51] Reagan's appointees were: Sandra Day O'Connor (the first woman justice, previously an Arizona state judge and state legislator), Antonin Scalia, and William Rehnquist (appointed by Nixon, elevated to chief justice by Reagan). Reagan's successor George H.W. Bush aimed, at least in theory, for appointees favorable to state's rights. He succeeded with Clarence Thomas, and failed spectacularly with New Hampshire attorney general David Souter, a cipher who was appointed at the behest of Bush's chief of staff, former New Hampshire senator John Sununu.

[52] "The powers not delegated to the United States by the Constitution, nor prohibited by it to the States, are reserved to the States respectively, or to the people." U.S. CONST., amend. X.

[53] MO. CONST. art. V, § 26.

Conditional federal grants

The law is clear that conditional federal grants to the states are permissible, and that there are constitutional limits on such grants. The foundational case is *Steward Machine Company v. Davis,* 301 U.S. 548 (1937). By a 5–4 vote, the court upheld the Social Security Act of 1935. The relevant provisions imposed a federal tax on employers. If the state had a federally-approved unemployment compensation program, then up to 90% of the state unemployment tax paid by the employer could be credited against the federal tax. The state tax revenues had to be immediately turned over the federal Unemployment Trust Fund, which would be used for federal grants to the states for unemployment compensation.

Justice Benjamin Cardozo's opinion for the court found that the scheme was within congressional powers and did not violate the Tenth Amendment. A plaintiff raising a successful Tenth Amendment claim would have to show that the tax and credit were "weapons of coercion, destroying or impairing the autonomy of the states." In the *Steward* majority view, the Social Security Act did not cross the line "between duress and inducement." *Id.* at 588. Notably, Alabama (Steward's state of operation) did not claim that it had enacted its unemployment tax system due to federal duress. *Id.* at 589. In general, "the location of the point at which pressure turns into compulsion, and ceases to be inducement, would be a question of degree, at times, perhaps, of fact." *Id.* at 590.

By a 6–3 vote in 1987, the court held that the line had not been crossed by a federal law cutting off 5% of federal highway grants (later raised to 10%) to states that did not enact a 21-year-old minimum drinking age. *South Dakota v. Dole*, 483 U.S. 203 (1987). Championed by President Reagan's secretary of transportation Elizabeth Dole, the law was one of many examples of the Reagan administration not always adhering to its rhetorical support for states' rights.

Steward Machine and *South Dakota v. Dole* had both affirmed that federal conditional grants could be unconstitutional if they were coercive. But no court ever found that any particular grant did go too far.

That changed in the litigation over the 2010 Affordable Care Act. The Act ordered citizens to purchase certain types of health insurance. Further, states were required to double the number of state residents enrolled in Medicaid—a federal medical welfare program, first enacted in 1965, which is funded by federal grants and state appropriations. If states refused to participate in expanded Medicaid, they would lose all funding for traditional Medicaid.

For the first time in history, a majority of states joined together to sue the federal government.[54] Lawsuits by states against the federal government are one form of interposition.

The states and their plaintiff allies won 5–4 on their claims that the Interstate Commerce power, even when augmented by the Necessary and Proper Clause, does not authorize Congress to force individuals to engage in commerce. The plaintiffs won 7–2 on their claim that Congress could not coercively use federal spending to force states to join in massive, novel expansion of the Medicaid program.[55]

While the money at stake in *South Dakota v. Dole* had amounted to less than one percent of a typical state's budget, the Obamacare funding threat was 10% or more of state budgets. That was unconstitutionally coercive, according to the supreme court majority.

---

[54] *See Nat't Fed. of Indep. Business v. Sebelius*, 567 U.S. 519 (2012).

[55] *See* RANDY BARNETT, JONATHAN ADLER, DAVID BERNSTEIN, OREN KERR, DAVID KOPEL, ILYA SOMIN, & TREVOR BURRUS, A CONSPIRACY AGAINST OBAMACARE: THE VOLOKH CONSPIRACY AND THE HEALTH CARE CASE (2013) (intellectual history of the development of the theories for the lawsuits, by the creators of those theories).

Anti-commandeering

Another major front in maintaining vertical separation of powers has been federal commandeering of state governments. To address the national problem of disposal of nuclear waste, Congress enacted a statute requiring state legislatures to enact laws for their state to take title to nuclear waste under certain conditions. But according to a 6–3 supreme court majority, Congress can never commandeer a state legislature by ordering it to pass a law. *New York v. United States*, 505 U.S. 144 (1992).

Pro-leviathan advocates said that the *New York* case was limited solely to federal commandeering of state legislatures. Congress could still commandeer other branches of state governments. Not so, said a 5–4 supreme court majority in *Printz v. United States*, 521 U.S. 898 (1997). In 1993, Congress had passed a statute requiring state or local officials to carry out background checks on retail handgun buyers. The majority held that Congress could order federal employees to carry out the federal check but could not order state or local employees to do so.[56]

G. Vertical separation of powers today

The cases discussed in the previous section set the parameters for today's battles. The ground rules are 1. State employees cannot be ordered to help enforce federal programs.[57] 2. Congress may induce state action by offering conditional grants; the conditions that will trigger a funding cut must be clearly stated in advance, and the amount of money involved may not be so large as to be coercive.

The principles of federalism, including the Tenth Amendment, have been so renormalized that some modern actions to vindicate states' rights are not controversial. For example, in 2016, the Colorado general assembly unanimously passed the Colorado Water Rights Protection Act, C.R.S. § 37-92-310. It orders Colorado's State Engineer to refuse to enforce or administer federal water claims that violate Colorado law. The legislature was concerned the U.S. Forest Service and the Bureau of Land Management (both of which are part of the U.S. Dept. of Agriculture) were coercing holders of Colorado water rights to surrender those rights to the federal government. According to the Act, all water rights in Colorado—including rights claimed by federal entities—are governed by article XVI of the Colorado Constitution, Colorado statutes, and Colorado Water Courts.

More notable in the public eye are states' rights movements closely related to individual liberties. As in previous times, interposition has been more successful than nullification.

While this chapter has concentrated on the state-federal relationship, the past two decades have seen the rise of other actors in the vertical separation of powers: county and municipal governments.

Legally speaking, counties and municipalities are in a weaker position *vis a vis* states, compared to states *vis a vis* the federal government. The states precede U.S. independence by 170

---

[56] The 1993 provisions sunset by their own terms in 1998, replaced by the "National Instant Check System" (NICS). Under NICS, gun stores contact the FBI directly for background checks on buyer of handguns or long guns. States may, if they wish, establish a state agency to take over the FBI's role as stores' point of contact for background checks. Colorado has done so; Colorado firearms dealers contact a unit in the Colorado Bureau of Investigation (CBI). Part of the CBI's background check involves checking the relevant FBI databases.

For more on *Printz*, see David B. Kopel, *The Brady Bill Comes Due: The Supreme Court Saves Federalism*, 9 GEORGE MASON CIVIL RIGHTS & CIVIL LIBERTIES L.J. 189 (1999).

[57] Congress still exercises authority to force state courts to hear certain federal claims. *See, e.g.*, Indian Child Welfare Act (ICWA), 25 U.S.C. §§ 1901 *et seq.*

years, and the ratification of the U.S. Constitution by 182.[58] Constitutionally, states are indestructible. U.S. CONST., art. IV, § 3. States have existed outside the Constitution. The Constitution became effective in June 1788, whereas North Carolina chose not to ratify until November 1789—after the first Congress had sent the Bill of Rights amendments to the states for ratification. Rhode Island stayed out until May 1790 and was threatened with a possible trade embargo from the United States.

In contrast, counties and municipalities are generally held to be mere creations of their state governments and may be abolished by a state at any time, subject to state constitutional or statutory rules. This true even though effective county government in many areas—such as Virginia in the early seventeenth century, or Colorado in the mid-nineteenth—preceded the development of effective state, colonial, or territorial government.

In practice, county and municipal officials have the same advantage over states that states have over the federal government: numerosity of employees. For example, the number of federal law enforcement employees (*e.g.*, FBI, Drug Enforcement Agency, Immigration and Customs Enforcement, etc.) is far smaller than the number of state and local employees. If a state refuses to enforce anti-marijuana laws, the number of available federal employees is too small to take up the slack.

Likewise, the number of municipal county and law enforcement officers far exceeds the number of state officers. If, for example, the Weld County sheriff's office declines to enforce a gun control law, the Colorado State Patrol does not have the resources to take the lead on enforcement.

James Madison's Federalist 46 had discussed the advantage that relative numerosity of employees provided to the state governments against the federal government. The insight can be extended to local governments against state governments.

In the modern political arena, much of the energy for noncooperation with unpopular laws imposed from above has come from the county and municipal level. This has been especially true on immigration issues and has become increasingly so for the right to arms, and sometimes for drug control.

Marijuana

Marijuana had been legal everywhere in America until the 1930s. Then, a national hysteria was engineered by Harry Anslinger, Director of the Federal Bureau of Narcotics under president Franklin Roosevelt. The 1938 Marihuana Tax Act purported to be a revenue law but was intended to eliminate the taxed article. It was modeled on the 1934 National Firearms Act, which had used the tax power to severely restrict machine guns and what the statute called "silencers."[59]

Anslinger's testimony to Congress in support of the "tax" bill included the following letter from the editor of the *Alamosa Daily Courier*:

> I wish I could show you what a small marihuana cigarette can do to one of our degenerate Spanish-speaking residents. That's why our problem is so great; the

[58] The Virginia Colony's charter was granted in 1606. The U.S. Constitution became operative on June 21, 1788, after New Hampshire's ratification. Pursuant to article VII, the proposed Constitution went into effect after ratification by nine of the thirteen states.

[59] *See generally* David B. Kopel & Trevor Burrus, *Sex, Drugs, Alcohol, Gambling, and Guns: The Synergistic Constitutional Effects*, 6 ALBANY GOV'T L. REVIEW 306 (2013). The sound suppressors that the NFA calls "silencers," are more silent in cinema than in real life. They reduce sound levels by up to 30 decibels—still a very loud sound, but less dangerous to hearing. *See* David B. Kopel, *The Hearing Protection Act and 'silencers'*, WASHINGTON POST, June 20, 2017.

> greatest percentage of our population is composed of Spanish-speaking persons, most of who are low mentally, because of social and racial conditions.[60]

All subsequent U.S. administrations have continued the war on drug users. As of 2021, thirty-six states had relegalized the medical use of marijuana. Eighteen have relegalized adult use in general.

Although the first Obama administration had aggressively prosecuted medical marijuana providers in California, the political balance had tipped by 2012. Polls were close, and Colorado might determine the election. Incumbent president Obama (like Bush in 2004) was focusing on base turnout. He campaigned three times at the University of Colorado at Boulder.

Adult marijuana relegalization was on the 2012 Colorado ballot. Governor and former brewer John Hickenlooper opposed the initiative. The Obama campaign urged him to stay on the sidelines, lest his opposition discourage the Obama base, or drive them into the arms of Libertarian candidate Gary Johnson.[61]

After adult use relegalization was approved in the states of Colorado and Washington in 2012, the U.S. Department of Justice mostly backed away from federal enforcement against lawful state businesses and individuals, as long as they were not exporting to other states. Congress passed an appropriations rider to forbid the U.S. Department of Justice from enforcing federal marijuana laws against persons and businesses that were complying with state medical marijuana laws.

Changes in DOJ policy could easily destroy the legal businesses for cultivation and retail sale of marijuana. A threat letter to landlords would usually be sufficient to frighten property owners into evicting marijuana businesses. However, the DOJ lacks the resources to do much about the personal cultivation and use of marijuana pursuant to state law. Possessory or at-home offenses perpetrated by large numbers of people are very difficult to stop, especially without significant enforcement by state and local agencies.

One of Colorado's earlier steps in defying federal marijuana was relegalizing the commercial cultivation of hemp, notwithstanding federal law allowing cultivation only by licensed university researchers. Several other states enacted similar laws. In 2018, the federal Agriculture Improvement Act of 2018, P.L. 115–334, relegalized hemp nationally.

Further reading: MARIJUANA FEDERALISM: UNCLE SAM AND MARY JANE (Jonathan Adler ed., 2020).

Firearms

Some states have imposed limits on state and local law enforcement cooperation with federal gun control. For example, Idaho forbids state or local assistance in enforcement of new federal gun control laws that violate the Idaho Constitution's right to arms.[62] Tennessee, Kansas, and Alaska have similar laws. As with fugitive slaves or marijuana, these laws are straightforward exercises of state choice not to participate in federal law enforcement. Because no major new federal gun control statutes have been enacted subsequent to the passage of the state laws, these laws have not yet been used.

Nine states have enacted Firearms Freedom Acts. These acts declare that firearms made within the state, and that never leave the state, are not subject to federal control under Congress's power to regulate interstate commerce. *See, e.g.,* Montana Firearms Freedom Act, Mont. Code Ann. § 30-20-104 (2009):

---

[60] See David B. Kopel & Michael Krause, *The Drug War on Human Rights and Civil Liberties,* Occasional Paper # 8 from the Liberal Institute of the *Friederich Naumann Foundation* (Potsdam, Germany: 2004).

[61] Former Republican governor of New Mexico, and thereafter a marijuana businessman.

[62] 18 Idaho Code § 3315B (enacted 2014).

> A personal firearm, a firearm accessory, or ammunition that is manufactured commercially or privately in Montana and that remains within the borders of Montana is not subject to federal law or federal regulation, including registration, under the authority of congress to regulate interstate commerce. It is declared by the legislature that those items have not traveled in interstate commerce.

The enacting states are Alaska, Arizona, Idaho, Kansas, Missouri, Montana, South Dakota, Tennessee, Texas, Utah, and Wyoming.

The FFAs are consistent with commerce clause doctrine as it was understood through most of American history. The problem for FFAs, however, is the supreme court's 6–3 decision in *Gonzales v. Raich*, 545 U.S. 1 (2005).[63] According to the *Raich* majority, congress may prohibit cultivating marijuana for personal use within a state where doing is legal. The hyperlocal prohibition was said to be necessary and proper to the regulation of interstate commerce in marijuana. Justices Rehnquist and O'Connor joined justice Thomas's dissent.

Raich's holding was extended to firearms. The Ninth Circuit, while seemingly sympathetic to the Montana FFA, held that it was preempted by federal law, and invalid. *Montana Shooting Sports Ass'n v Holder*, 727 F.3d 975 (9th Cir. 2013).[64]

Since the second Obama administration, the U.S. Department of Justice has mostly forborne enforcing federal marijuana laws against state-sanctioned intrastate marijuana commerce. The policy has *not* been extended to state-sanctioned intrastate firearms commerce. In Kansas, for example, small-time gunsmiths who manufactured and sold firearms compliant with the Kansas FFA were federally prosecuted and convicted. The conviction was upheld by the Tenth Circuit. *United States v. Cox*, 906 F.3d 1170 (10th Cir. 2018).[65]

Vertical separation of powers is also expressed by the Second Amendment sanctuary movement. The immigration sanctuary movement (discussed below) and the marijuana relegalization movement that defied federal law (discussed above) have been noticed by other liberty advocates. The result has been the Second Amendment sanctuary movement.

As of September 2021, of the 3,144 counties in the United States, 1,965 (62.5%) were Second Amendment sanctuaries—either by county action, state action, or both.[66] Many municipalities, too, have declared themselves Second Amendment sanctuaries.

At the least, Second Amendment sanctuaries adopt resolutions against some or all new federal or state gun control laws. Many sanctuary jurisdictions order declare that employees of the county or state may not enforce such laws.

In New Mexico, as in Colorado and other states, many sheriffs stated that they would not enforce gun confiscation orders pursuant to "red flag" laws. In the sheriffs' view, the red flag laws were grossly deficient in due process, and they force law enforcement into unnecessary and dangerous confiscations based on thin evidence. The New Mexico legislative majority retaliated

---

[63] The undisputed record showed that Angel Raich's medical marijuana use was literally a matter of life or death.

[64] *Montana Shooting Sports* noted that plaintiffs did not pursue any argument regarding the Supreme Court's affirmation of the individual right to arms in *District of Columbia v. Heller*, 554 U.S. 570 (2008).

[65] Even if the Tenth Circuit had accepted the defendant's commerce clause arguments, the defendants still would have lost. The arms in question were not just firearms in general (covered by the federal Gun Control Act of 1968, under the interstate commerce power). The arms were short-barreled rifles, which are also regulated by the National Firearms Act of 1934, which is based on the federal tax power; the NFA unquestionably applies to purely intrastate activity, since the federal tax power has never depended on an interstate nexus.

[66] Of these, over 1,100 counties enacted their own resolutions. The rest are in sanctuary states. Noah Davis, *More than 61% of American Counties are Now Second Amendment Sanctuaries*, SANCUTARYCOUNTIES.COM, June 20, 2021.

by authorizing lawsuits against law enforcement officers for injuries resulting from *any* decision not to enforce a statute. In other words, an officer could be sued for not ticketing a driver who is going 46 miles per hour in a 45 M.P.H. zone. Or for using discretion not to attempt to enforce against every observed instance of indecent dancing,[67] personal gambling,[68] and so on.[69]

Further reading: Shawn E. Fields, *Second Amendment Sanctuaries*, 115 NORTHWESTERN U.L. REVIEW 437 (2020); Nicholas J. Johnson, *Defiance, Concealed Carry, and Race*, 83 LAW & CONTEMPORARY PROBLEMS 159 (2020); Stephen Halbrook, *On Target? Assessing Gun Sanctuary Ordinances That Conflict with State Law*, 122 WEST VIRGINIA L. REVIEW 817 (2020); Joyce Lee Malcolm, *The Case for Second Amendment Sanctuaries: The Duty to Defend the Constitution,* George Mason Legal Studies Research Paper No. LS 20-16 (2020).

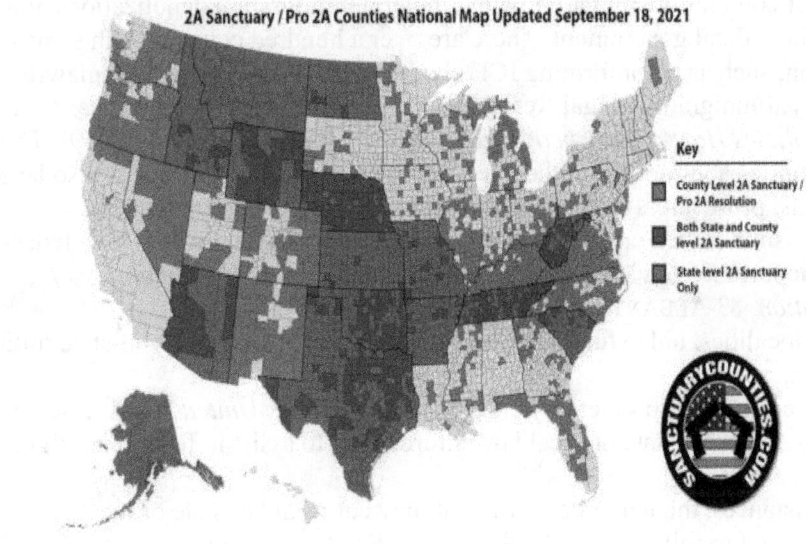

Figure 16. Second Amendment sanctuary counties. SanctuaryCounties.com.

Sanctuary cities and counties for federal immigration law

There are many ways that local law enforcement can choose to cooperate in the enforcement of federal immigration laws. Under the 287(g) program, local law enforcement officials may be federally deputized as immigration agents, so they can enforce immigration laws directly.[70] Jails may contract with federal Immigration & Customs Enforcement (ICE) to be paid to hold detainees pending federal deportation proceedings. ICE sends out alerts that request any law enforcement agency that takes a particular person into custody to notify ICE. Local law enforcement will routinely find out about these alerts during the background checks that are run on arrestees. ICE officials may be given access, without a warrant, to local jails, where they can attempt to speak with persons suspected of being illegally in the United States.

Some state or local governments have forbidden some or all of the above practices. They may also forbid their law enforcement agencies from inquiring about an arrested person's immigration

---

[67] N.M. Stat. § 30-9-14.1.
[68] *Id.*, at § 30-19-2.
[69] For more on New Mexico, see David B. Kopel, *Red Flag Laws: Proceed with Caution*, 45 (Alabama) LAW & PSYCHOLOGY REVIEW 39 (2021).
[70] Section 287(g) of the Immigration and National Act is codified at 8 U.S.C. §1357(g).

status, from participating in joint programs with ICE, or from using any resources to assist with immigration law enforcement.

Many non-cooperating jurisdictions still send the fingerprints of all arrestees to the federal government, under the Priority Enforcement Program. This will identify the fingerprints of any person whose fingerprints are in a federal database (*e.g.*, convicted criminal; previously deported; overstaying a visa).

Cities that refuse to assist in the removal of unlawful aliens have been called "sanctuary cities." In Anglo-American law, "sanctuary" was an English practice (discarded about five hundred years ago) by which criminals who managed to flee to a church could take sanctuary therein; in certain circumstances, the punishment of the criminal might be mitigated or avoided. For example, a person who had committed murder might receive the lesser punishment for manslaughter.[71]

The vast majority of counties do not participate in federal immigration deputizations, nor do they rent jail space to the federal government. There are over a hundred counties with some other form of non-cooperation, such as not informing ICE about the jail release dates for unlawful aliens in county custody. Immigration Legal Resource Center, *Growing the Resistance: How Sanctuary Laws and Policies Have Flourished During the Trump Administration* (2019). The figure for sanctuary counties does not count the number of sanctuary cities, which is also large.

In some jurisdictions, prosecutors have aided the sanctuary movement by refusing to prosecute unlawful aliens for certain crimes, because a criminal conviction would give federal officials the ability to deport the convicted alien swiftly. Zohra Ahmed, *The Sanctuary of Prosecutorial Nullification*, 83 ALBANY L. REVIEW 239 (2020).

In some states and localities, unlawful aliens may serve as civil officers, pay in-state tuition at state colleges, and so on.[72]

Can the federal government curb sanctuary cities? Under *Printz v. United States*, it seems clear that Congress may not order state or local law enforcement to assist in federal immigration law enforcement.

Under some circumstances, the federal government may cut its aid to state or local governments that choose not to follow the federal lead. *NFIB v. Sebelius*, synthesizing precedents such as *Steward Machine*[73] and *South Dakota v. Dole*, held that a cut-off of 10% of a typical state's budget (federal funding for traditional Medicaid) was too much. Compared to federal Medicaid funding in a state budget, federal criminal justice funding in a municipal or state budget is very small—often smaller than the ½ of 1% that was deemed non-coercive in *South Dakota v. Dole*.

The *NFIB/Dole* test also has a qualitative side: is there a link between the federal funds and the policy that the federal government is trying to encourage? This link does not have to be very strong. In *South Dakota v. Dole*, the link between the demanded federal policy (raise the state drinking age from 18 to 21, to reduce drunk driving on federal highways) and the funding (highway construction) was not irrational. But it was not particularly close either. After all, most young adults in Colorado who drank the only form of alcohol allowed to them under state law—weak 3.2 beer—did not drive drunk on federally-funded highways.

---

[71] See Michael J. Davidson, *Sanctuary: A Modern Legal Anachronism*, 42 CAPITAL U. L. REVIEW 583 (2014) (history of sanctuary from ancient times to the present).

[72] Colorado is the among the 20 states that offer in-state tuition. According to a federal statute, any state offering in-state tuition discounts to unlawful aliens must offer the same discount to lawful resident aliens and to citizens of the other 49 states. 8 U.S.C. §1623. California state colleges provided a model, which Colorado has followed, to evade the federal statute. California offers a tuition discount for all persons who have attended California high schools for at least 3 years; this was held not to violate the federal statute. *See Martinez v. Regents of the University of California*, 50 Cal. 4th 1277 (2010).

[73] *Steward Machine Company v. Davis,* 301 U.S. 548 (1937).

A conditional federal grant must specify the conditions up front. The executive branch cannot impose conditions that the appropriating branch (Congress) did not choose to include. Only a small number of congressional grant programs even arguably have statutory conditions involving cooperation with federal law against illegal immigration.

Despite the Trump administration's bluster about cutting off federal funds for sanctuary jurisdictions, funding cuts were only attempted for a few federal programs, most notably the Edward F. Byrne law enforcement grants. Almost all courts ruled against the cuts. Some held that the amount of money was coercive. Instead of looking at the total budget of a jurisdiction (as *Dole* and *NFIB* did), the lower courts looked only at subsections the law enforcement budget. Yet even there, the amount of money at risk is usually smaller than the percentage of highway construction funding that South Dakota lost in *South Dakota v. Dole*.

A stronger basis for the judicial decisions has been that Congress did not expressly make the grants conditional on cooperation in immigration law enforcement. The question comes down to careful parsing of how much discretion the Byrne Grants statute gives to the attorney general. *See City of Providence v. Barr*, 954 F.3d 23 (1st Cir. 2020); *City of Philadelphia v. Attorney Gen.*, 916 F.3d 276 (3rd Cir. 2019); *City of Los Angeles v. Barr*, 941 F.3d 931 (9th Cir. 2019); *City of Chicago v. Sessions*, 888 F.3d 272 (7th Cir. 2018).

Other modern issues in state resistance

The Tenth Amendment Center uses "nullification" in a very broad sense—not solely as declaring a federal law to (supposedly) have no effect within a state. Instead, "nullification" is used in the practical sense: making something ineffectual. For example, local law enforcement refusal to assist enforcement of a federal statute may render the statute ineffectual, even though the statute is not made legally void. Tenth Amendment Center, State of the Nullification Movement: 2021 Tenth Amendment Center Annual Report (2021). Legal philosopher John Austin described "law" as commands given by a sovereign that are habitually obeyed by the bulk of the population.[74] By Austin's definition, a statute that is habitually disobeyed is not really a "law," and has been nullified.

The Tenth Amendment Center extols the historic state and local noncooperation with federal alcohol prohibition. The resistance made prohibition ineffectual in many areas and contributed to the repeal of federal prohibition in 1933.[75]

Two dozen states—Colorado among the first—legalized the "right to try." Persons with fatal diseases must be allowed to try any drug—whether or not the drug is approved by the U.S. Food and Drug Administration.

Some other state laws cited by the Tenth Amendment Center:

- Restricting state and local law enforcement use of drones without warrants. Such warrantless usage is promoted by federal funding. (19 states).
- Restricting state or local enforcement from feeding automated license plate recognition data into the federal databases for tracking all drivers. (6 states).
- Limiting the use of stingrays. Stingrays are a federal government invention, sometimes shared with local law enforcement. They spoof a cell phone tower, thus tricking cell phones into connecting with them, so that their data can be harvested without a warrant. (4 states).

---

[74] JOHN AUSTIN & R. CAMPBELL, LECTURES ON JURISPRUDENCE: OR THE PHILOSOPHY OF POSITIVE LAW (1874).

[75] Federal alcohol prohibition was adopted by the 18th Amendment in 1919 and repealed by the 21st Amendment in 1933. At the time, everyone agreed that the interstate commerce power gave Congress no power regarding intrastate sale, possession, or use of alcohol (except in special situations, such as near federal military bases). Accordingly, federal legislation on the subject required a constitutional amendment.

- Shutting off local supplies of electricity and water to National Security Agency's spay centers for warrantless data-gathering programs on the American people, much of which is used for drug law enforcement, rather than national security. (3 states).
- Creating a state gold reserve, as step towards creating a monetary alternative to Federal Reserve notes (fiat paper currency). (Texas).

Jury powers

The power of nullification is broadly distributed. Under the common law, juries have always had the power to acquit a criminal defendant who is factually guilty, but whose conviction would be unjust, according to the jury. This jury power was celebrated in the Early Republic and is enshrined in four state constitutions for all criminal trials. GA. CONST., art. 1, § 1, ¶ XI ("In criminal cases, the defendant shall have a public and speedy trial by an impartial jury; and the jury shall be the judges of the law and the facts."; IND. CONST., art. 1, §19 ("in all criminal cases whatever the jury shall have the right to determine the law and the facts"); MD. CONST., DECLARATION OF RIGHTS, art. 23 ("In the trial of all criminal cases, the Jury shall be the Judges of Law, as well as of fact, except that the court may pass upon the sufficiency of the evidence to sustain a conviction."); ORE. CONST., art. I, § 16 ("In all criminal cases whatever, the jury shall have the right to determine the law, and the facts under the direction of the Court as to the law, and the right of new trial, as in civil cases.") Twenty other state constitutions, including Colorado's art, II, § 10, specify that in libel cases, the jury shall be the judge of the law.

Today, some judges instruct jurors to the contrary. The judges disqualify jurors from a venire who are aware of their power. Increasingly, juries have been skeptical about convictions for drug offenses with harsh sentences.[76]

The Colorado court of appeals observed:

> Jury nullification occurs in a trial when a jury acquits a defendant even though the members of the jury believe the defendant is guilty of the charges. The doctrine . . . traces its roots to . . . natural rights philosophy; and . . . the shared experience of living under—and then rebelling against—a tyrannical form of government. It is also said to be rooted in the Sixth Amendment's guarantee to a jury trial. The Sixth Amendment provides that "[i]n all criminal prosecutions, the accused shall enjoy the right to a speedy and public trial, by an impartial jury," and this right includes the right to have a jury, rather than a judge, reach "the requisite finding of 'guilty.'" *Sullivan v. Louisiana*, 508 U.S. 275, 279 (1993). Thus, although a judge may direct a verdict in favor of a defendant, a judge may not direct a verdict for the State . . .
>
> Colorado courts "have said little about the issue of jury nullification" and have even stated that "the issue of nullification is best avoided." *People v. Wilson*, 972 P.2d 701, 705–06 (Colo. App. 1998). However, in *Wilson*, a division of this court recognized that because there is a tension between a jury's power to nullify and the jury's duty to follow the court's instructions, a trial court has discretion to preclude counsel from arguing jury nullification. *Id.* at 706. Furthermore, a defendant is not entitled to a jury instruction informing jurors that they have the inherent power to nullify a verdict of guilt. *See id.* While a jury does have the power to nullify, there is no right to jury nullification. *Crease v. McKune*, 189 F.3d 1188, 1194 (10th Cir. 1999).

---

[76] *See generally,* David B. Kopel, *I, The Jury*. book review of Jury Nullification: The Evolution of a Doctrine, by Clay S. Conrad, THE AMERICAN ENTERPRISE, May/June 1999.

People v. Waller, 2016 COA 115, 412 P.3d. 866 (Colo. App. 2016).

The practice of not telling jurors about their powers comes from *Sparf & Hansen v. United States*, 156 U.S. 51 (1895).[77]

Conclusion

States' rights are central to the U.S. Constitution and are firmly declared by the Colorado Constitution. States' rights were defended by James Madison, the father of the Constitution, and by Thomas Jefferson, author of the Declaration of Independence. Their Virginia and Kentucky Resolutions are a foundation of state resistance to national oppression.

Like all rules that divide power, America's divided sovereignty and states' rights sometimes benefit one cause and sometimes another. As the Founders recognized, people tend to favor whatever advances their own ambitions. People are often inconsistent in adhering to constitutional principle. Consistent friends of states' rights are a minority.

Except for the conspicuous failure of efforts to preserve Jim Crow laws, whenever states have considered federal over-reach to be so egregious that the states must resort to interposition or nullification, the states have always won at least partial redress of their grievances in the long run. As Madison predicted in Federalist 46, "The disquietude of the people; their repugnance and, perhaps refusal to cooperate with officers of the Union, the frowns of the executive magistracy of the State; the embarrassment created by legislative devices," have all served as checks on alleged federal over-reach. In this respect, Americans continue to enjoy the constitutional system that the Founders promised.

[77] Dissenting in *Sparf & Hansen*, justice Horace Gray detailed the history of jury nullification in protecting persecuted Quakers in England. The jury power had often been exercised when dissidents were criminally prosecuted for seditious libel. For example, in a case involving the seditious libel against President Thomas Jefferson, Alexander Hamilton had argued: "That in criminal cases, the law and fact being always blended, the jury, for reasons of a political and peculiar nature, for the security of life and liberty, is intrusted with the power of deciding both law and fact." *Id.* at 147 (Gray, J., dissenting) (citing *People v. Croswell*, 3 Johns. Cas. 337, 361–62 (N.Y. Sup. Ct. 1804)).

During the first four decades of the Constitution, the jury's right to criminally acquit, "according to their own judgment and consciences," was repeatedly affirmed by state supreme courts and by federal courts. *E.g.*, *Georgia v. Brailsford*, 3 U.S. (1 Dallas) 1 (1794) (U.S. Supreme Court's only jury trial; jury instructions by chief justice John Jay).

CHAPTER 6

Fighting for Survival

Figure 13. Ute chief Ouray with his wife Chipeta. He is one of 16 people in the Colorado Hall of Fame, at the state Capitol. History Colorado-Denver, Colorado.

Fighting on arrival, fighting for survival . . .
If you know your history
Then you would know where you are coming from
Then you wouldn't have to ask me
Who the heck do I think I am.

Bob Marley, *Buffalo Soldier*.[1]

---

[1] From the album CONFRONTATION (1983).

The buffalo soldiers were the black soldiers in the U.S. Army who fought in the Indian wars after 1866. By the end of the Civil War in 1865, black soldiers comprised 10 percent of Union forces. Their continuing enlistment in the U.S. Army was guaranteed by the 1866 Army Reorganization Act. In Colorado, buffalo soldiers were stationed at Fort Lyon, Fort Garland, and Fort Lewis. They participated in the 1868 Battle of Beecher Island and the 1878 Battle of Milk Creek (both discussed below). *Buffalo Soldiers*, Colorado Encyclopedia.

Colorado's buffalo soldiers are commemorated by the Buffalo Soldier Memorial, erected in 2016 in Colorado Springs. U.S. Highway 24 between Colorado Springs and is the Buffalo Soldiers Memorial Highway. The Buffalo Soldiers Community Memorial Committee educates today's public about the buffalo soldiers.

It would be foolish to study the U.S. Constitution without knowing that the Constitution was preceded by an eight-year revolutionary war and then by the Articles of Confederation. History helps one understand why a constitution was written the way it was—and illuminates the spirit of the Constitution.

Part A of this chapter explores in more depth a topic raised in the chapter 1, "Creation of the State of Colorado." When large scale American settlement of Colorado began in the 1858–59 Gold Rush, the settlements were too remote to be governable by the federal government or the territorial governments of Kansas, Nebraska, Utah, or New Mexico. By necessity, Coloradans established their own governments, beginning a tradition of local sovereignty and self-control.

Part B describes the most dangerous part of the Civil War for Colorado. A Confederate army from west Texas invaded and quickly conquered much of New Mexico. It was on its way to Colorado but was turned back by the audacious and brave volunteers from "Pikes Peak country."

Part C tells the history of the wars of the plains Indians in Colorado. It covers wars between Indian tribes, and war against settlers from "the States." The 1840 peace treaty among the Cheyenne, Arapahoe, Kiowa, and Comanche created great trade and prosperity, but also led to environmental degradation and overuse. The result was disaster for the plains Indians—which led to the Colorado War of 1864–65. During that War, the Indians sliced the Colorado settlers' lifelines to the east, and nearly wiped out the nascent Colorado territory.

The military history of the Colorado plains Indians has previously been told only in scattered episodes, such as descriptions of the infamous Sand Creek Massacre. Part C is the first history of the full scope of plains warfare in Colorado.

Part D covers the Utes, who controlled western Colorado. By the time the Gold Rush began in 1858, Colorado Utes were more or less at peace with Americans. By 1864, that was beginning to change. Part D covers warfare and treaties with the Utes.

Finally, Part E examines the problems of law and order in early Colorado. Even after congressional establishment of the Colorado territory in 1861, government in Colorado often lacked the ability to protect the public from criminals. So the people protected themselves, with people's courts and vigilance committees.

By the time of the 1876 Constitution, however, Colorado did have a functioning judiciary to enforce criminal law. There were now effective governments that could call for collective local self-help only when necessary. As reflected in the text of the Colorado constitutional right to arms, "the civil power" had become sufficiently capable so that it need not to routinely rely on collective citizen bodies to punish criminals.

Everyone should know the history of the place where they live. Persons who want to understand the Colorado Constitution must know Colorado history, especially in the turbulent and dangerous decades preceding 1876. As Cicero observed, "To be ignorant of what occurred before you were born is to remain always a child."[2]

This chapter is based on David B. Kopel, *The Right to Arms in Nineteenth Century Colorado*, 95 DENVER U.L. REVIEW 329 (2018). Readers who prefer footnotes at the end of every sentence may consult that article. Today, all American Indians are American citizens, but in most of the period covered in this chapter, the Colorado tribes were, legally speaking, separate nations, which sometimes had treaty relations with the United States. Therefore, the chapter sometimes uses

---

The nickname "buffalo soldiers" was bestowed by Indians, because of the soldiers' hair. Bob Marley links the Buffalo Soldiers to his own group, the "dreadlock Rasta," a religious movement (Rastafarian) also with notable hair.

The valorous buffalo soldiers were proud to be armed citizens, not disarmed slaves. The buffalo soldiers fought in wars of conquest against foreign nations—namely, the Indian nations. Were the buffalo soldiers admirable exemplars of freedom, or oppressors? Is the answer more complicated than yes/no?

[2] The quote is inscribed above the entrance to the Norlin Library at the University of Colorado, at the suggestion of former university president George Norlin.

"Americans" or "settlers" in distinction from the Indians. The chapter does not refer to the settlers as "whites," because black settlers from "the States" were part of Colorado from the early days. So were Hispanics, mainly from New Mexico.

Key sources

The following sources are oft-cited below. They are collected here for reader convenience, and as a partial bibliography of early Colorado history. Unless otherwise indicated in a footnote, the base cite for short-cited materials in this chapter is here. All of these sources are good starting points for readers of early Colorado history.

JEAN AFTON ET AL., CHEYENNE DOG SOLDIERS: A LEDGERBOOK HISTORY OF COUPS AND COMBAT (1st ed. 1997). Indian ledgerbooks were colored pencil drawings on notepads that had been obtained from Americans. This particular ledgerbook was captured at 1869 Battle of Summit Springs, the last major battle fought by the Cheyenne in Colorado. Most ledgerbooks depicted military encounters. Today, some artists produce modern drawings in the style of the ledgerbooks.

EUGENE H. BERWANGER, THE RISE OF THE CENTENNIAL STATE: COLORADO TERRITORY, 1861–76 (2007). Superb.

BILL BRENNEMAN, MIRACLE ON CHERRY CREEK (1973).

RAY C. COLTON, THE CIVIL WAR IN THE WESTERN TERRITORIES: ARIZONA, COLORADO, NEW MEXICO, AND UTAH (1984).

THE CONSTITUTIONALISM OF AMERICAN STATES (George E. Connor & Christopher W. Hammons eds., 2008). An outstanding source for persons interested in learning about other states. Unfortunately, the Colorado entry suffers from inaccuracies.

DAVID L. ERICKSON, EARLY JUSTICE AND THE FORMATION OF THE COLORADO BAR (2008). The leading study on its subject.

M. MORGAN ESTERGREEN, KIT CARSON: A PORTRAIT IN COURAGE (1962).

T.R. FEHRENBACH, COMANCHES: THE DESTRUCTION OF A PEOPLE (1974).

LOUIS A. GARAVAGLIA & CHARLES G. WORMAN, FIREARMS OF THE AMERICAN WEST 1866–1894 (1985). The leading source on its topic.

JOLIE ANDERSON GALLAGHER, A WILD WEST HISTORY OF FRONTIER COLORADO: PIONEERS, GUNSLINGERS & CATTLE KINGS ON THE EASTERN PLAINS (2011).

GEORGE BIRD GRINNELL, THE FIGHTING CHEYENNES (1915). Written by an author who interviewed many Cheyenne who remembered the early days.

JOHN D.W. GUICE, THE ROCKY MOUNTAIN BENCH: THE TERRITORIAL SUPREME COURTS OF COLORADO, MONTANA, AND WYOMING, 1861–1890 (1972). Argues against the perception that all territorial supreme courts were hapless.

LEROY R. HAFEN, COLORADO: THE STORY OF A WESTERN COMMONWEALTH (1933). By one of Colorado's greatest historians.

1 FRANK HALL, HISTORY OF THE STATE OF COLORADO (1889). The most comprehensive early source of Colorado politics and history, by a former territorial secretary and acting governor.

2 FRANK HALL, HISTORY OF THE STATE OF COLORADO (1890).

3 FRANK HALL, HISTORY OF THE STATE OF COLORADO (1891).

4 FRANK HALL, HISTORY OF THE STATE OF COLORADO (1895).

PEKKA HÄMÄLÄINEN, THE COMANCHE EMPIRE (2008). In much of the nineteenth century, the Comanche's military power and zones of control were formidable to every adjacent power—whether Indian, European, Mexican, Texan, or American.

Donald Wayne Hensel, A History of the Colorado Constitution in the Nineteenth Century (Aug. 9, 1957) (Ph.D. in History thesis, University of Colorado). Still the leading source on its topic. Available in ProQuest's Dissertations library.

2 INDIAN AFFAIRS: LAWS AND TREATIES (Charles J. Kappler ed., 2d ed. 1904). Part of the authoritative multi-volume compilation of treaties. Created by order of the U.S. Senate Interior Committee.

JOSEPH JABLOW, THE CHEYENNE IN PLAINS INDIAN TRADE RELATIONS 1795–1840 (Univ. of Neb. Press 1994) (1950).

NICHOLAS J. JOHNSON ET AL., FIREARMS LAW AND THE SECOND AMENDMENT: REGULATION, RIGHTS, AND POLICY (3d ed. 2021).

HOWARD ROBERTS LAMAR, THE FAR SOUTHWEST 1846–1912: A TERRITORIAL HISTORY (rev. ed. 2000). Wide-ranging and insightful. Masterful history accessibly written for experts and novices alike.

RICHARD D. LAMM & DUANE A. SMITH, PIONEERS & POLITICIANS: COLORADO GOVERNORS IN PROFILE (2d ed. 2008). Survey of some of Colorado's most notable territorial and state governors.

LEGISLATIVE, HISTORICAL AND BIOGRAPHICAL COMPENDIUM OF COLORADO (Denver, C.F. Coleman's Publ'g House 1887) [hereinafter HISTORICAL COMPENDIUM]. Excellent original source of social history.

STEPHEN J. LEONARD & THOMAS J. NOEL, DENVER: MINING CAMP TO METROPOLIS (1st ed. 1990). Superior to the shorter second edition

DORIS MONAHAN, DESTINATION: DENVER CITY: THE SOUTH PLATTE TRAIL (1985).

THOMAS J. NOEL, COLORADO: A HISTORICAL ATLAS (2015). The best book on its subject.

NELL BROWN PROPST, THE SOUTH PLATTE TRAIL: STORY OF COLORADO'S FORGOTTEN PEOPLE (rev. ed. 1984). Heartfelt and poignant coverage of life in early northeast Colorado.

FRANCIS PAUL PRUCHA, AMERICAN INDIAN TREATIES: THE HISTORY OF A POLITICAL ANOMALY (1994). The United States is the only nation that legally recognizes the (partial) sovereignty of interior indigenous nations. The longstanding, anomalous U.S. policy is often determinative of legal rights today.

VIRGINIA MCCONNELL SIMMONS, THE UTE INDIANS OF UTAH, COLORADO, AND NEW MEXICO (2d ed. 2000). The definitive work.

DUANE A. SMITH, THE BIRTH OF COLORADO: A CIVIL WAR PERSPECTIVE (1989).

T.J. STILES, CUSTER'S TRIALS: A LIFE ON THE FRONTIER OF NEW AMERICA (2016).

JOHN TAYLOR, BLOODY VALVERDE: A CIVIL WAR BATTLE ON THE RIO GRANDE, FEBRUARY 21, 1862 (1995).

ELLIOT WEST, THE CONTESTED PLAINS: INDIANS, GOLDSEEKERS, AND THE RUSH TO COLORADO (1998). Superb environmental history. A major advance in understanding the causes of the Colorado War.

J.E. Wharton, *History of the City of Denver: From Its Earliest Settlement to the Present Time to Which is Added a Full and Complete Business Directory of the City by D.O. Wilhelm*, *in* RICHARD A. RONZIO, SILVER IMAGES OF COLORADO: DENVER AND THE 1866 BUSINESS DIRECTORY 10 (1986). Beautiful primary source.

WILLIAM C. WHITFORD, COLORADO VOLUNTEERS IN THE CIVIL WAR: THE NEW MEXICO CAMPAIGN IN 1862 (Rio Grande Press, Inc. 1991) (1906).

RICHENS WOOTTON AS TOLD TO HOWARD LOUIS CONRAD, UNCLE DICK WOOTTON: THE PIONEER FRONTIERSMAN OF THE ROCKY MOUNTAIN REGION (M.M. Quaife ed., Narrative Press 2001) (1890). Memoirs of the one of the most famous of Colorado's mountain men.

A. Making New Governments

1. The far edge of nowhere.

In 1858, the land that would become the State of Colorado was part of four territories:

- Kansas. The capital was Topeka, although that site was contested by pro-slavery forces in the ongoing civil war within the territory.[3]
- Utah. The capital was Salt Lake City, ruled by a theocracy of the Church of Jesus Christ of Latter-day Saints ("Mormon").
- New Mexico. The capital was Santa Fe. Recently acquired by the United States, the territory and its culture bore a strong Spanish influence.
- Nebraska. The capital was Omaha, just across the Missouri River from Iowa.

With the population centers so remote from Colorado, none of the territorial governments could do much to assist Coloradans. The settlers were on their own.

Within future Colorado, the major area of 1858–59 Gold Rush settlement was in the Territory of Kansas: future Denver and Colorado Springs, plus the mining areas to their west, up to the Continental Divide.

The territorial legislature of Kansas in 1855 had divided its Colorado lands into five counties, including Arapahoe County, where the city of Denver would later arise.[4] However, the Colorado portion of Kansas, like much of the rest of western Kansas, was still Indian country by treaty with the U.S. government. The Kansas Territory lacked formal authority to organize county governments in Colorado.[5]

After the reports of 1858 discovery of gold on the Cherry Creek, Kansas governor James W. Denver commissioned men to establish an Arapahoe County government. Among them were Arapahoe County sheriff Edward W. Wynkoop and Treasurer John Larimer.[6] Arapahoe County at

---

[3] The Kansas Territory was created in 1854 by the Kansas-Nebraska Act. Kansas-Nebraska Act, 10 Stat. 277 (1854). The act left the slavery question for the new territory to a vote of the settlers. To try to tip the result, "border ruffians" from the adjacent slave state of Missouri attacked anti-slavery settlers. *See* JAY MONAGHAN, CIVIL WAR ON THE WESTERN BORDER: 1854–1865 (1955). Anti-slavery emigrants defended themselves with "Beecher's Bibles"—Sharps rifles shipped from the Massachusetts Emigrant Aid Society, in boxes of Bibles to conceal the rifles underneath. The famous preacher Henry Ward Beecher organized the shipments. His daughter, Harriet Beecher Stowe wrote the greatest song of the Civil War: *The Battle Hymn of the Republic.*

[4] ERICKSON at 3.

[5] Treaty of Fort Laramie with Sioux etc., 1851, art. 5, Sept. 17, 1851, 11 Stat. 749, *reprinted in* 2 INDIAN AFFAIRS, at 594–96 (granting the Cheyenne and Arapahoe territory between the North Platte and the Arkansas Rivers, between the Rocky Mountains and the Smoky Hill area of Kansas); *see also* 1 HALL, at 209 (the organic act for the Kansas territory expressly excepted any areas where Indians had title). Indeed, in 1863, the U.S. government surveyor general refused to confirm Coloradans' land titles until Indian claims to the area were extinguished. AFTON ET AL., at xv. Such claims were confirmed by Congress in 1864.

The Treaty of Fort Laramie was signed by three Arapaho chiefs and four Cheyenne ones. Other signatories were Sioux, Crows, Assinaboines, Mandans and Gros Ventre, and Arickarees. Treaty of Fort Laramie with Sioux etc., art. 8. Among the terms were that the signatory tribes not war against each other. *Id.* at art. 1.

[6] ERICKSON at 4. Both men are namesakes of streets in lower downtown Denver. Wynkoop's obituary called him "one of the finest pistol shots in the world." CAROL TURNER, FORGOTTEN HEROES & VILLAINS

the time, and until 1902, included Denver. In November 1858, John Larimer and others organized the Denver Town Company.[7] Arapahoe County officers were elected by the people of the county in March 1859, replacing the commissioned officers from Kansas territorial governor James Denver.[8] The newly elected county officers did not wait for consent or orders from Kansas before taking office.[9]

Although the territorial government of Kansas earnestly legislated for Colorado,[10] it had little influence. There was a Kansas judge for Colorado, but he never went there.[11] In one famous case, a Colorado criminal was sent to eastern Kansas for trial, only for the Kansas judge to disavow jurisdiction.

Whatever role Kansas had in the government of the Colorado ended on January 29, 1861, when Kansas was admitted to the Union, with its western boundary the 102nd degree of western longitude.[12] That is, the eastern border of future Colorado.

2. *Self-government when no one else can do it for you*

From Timbuktu to Topeka to anywhere else, there was no government on earth that could govern the settlers of Colorado. They were just too far away.

The settlers' first governments were created by the people themselves, as "miner's districts" in the mining regions, as "claims clubs" in farming areas,[13] and as "town companies."[14] These

OF SAND CREEK 28 (2010) (quoting Wynkoop's obituary published in the *Denver Republican*, and noting his role in exposing the massacre).

[7] 1 HALL at 182. The first settlers had dubbed it "St. Charles." But many of the town founders had gone east for the winter, and those who remained were cajoled or coerced into accepting the new organization of Denver. James Denver was not terribly impressed by the honor of being the city's namesake, and he only visited Denver once in his life. *Id.* Even if he had been flattered, he had no political benefit to confer; unbeknownst to the Denver settlers, he had resigned as Kansas territorial governor on Oct. 10, 1858. 2 HALL at 327.

[8] ERICKSON at 5; 1 HALL at 183.

[9] 1 HALL at 183.

[10] In 1859–60, about third of the Kansas territorial legislation's enactments concerned Colorado. HAFEN at 136. The power to pass laws is not necessarily coextensive with the power to put them into effect.

[11] *See* ERICKSON at 3.

[12] Kansas disclaimed the portion of the Kansas Territory that lay in Colorado. The Kansans had debated between "Big Kansas" or "Little Kansas," and the majority had decided on the latter, partly to keep the state capital in a more easterly location. Also rejected were efforts to claim part of what is now the State of Nebraska. *See* Francis H. Heller & Paul D. Schumaker, *The Kansas Constitution: Conservative Politics through Republican Dominance*, *in* THE CONSTITUTIONALISM OF AMERICAN STATES, at 490, 496–97. The citizens of eastern Kansas wanted to the state capital nearby and feared that a state stretching all the way to Rocky Mountains would need a capital further west than they desired. *Id.*; Calvin W. Gower, *Kansas Territory and Its Boundary Question: "Big Kansas" or "Little Kansas,"* 33 KAN. HISTORICAL. QUARTERLY 1, 3, 8 (1967).

[13] *See, e.g.*, GALLAGHER at 37 (formation of the El Paso Claim Club, whose jurisdiction included Colorado City, which later became Colorado Springs).

[14] The first miners' court was created in the Gregory District of Gilpin County, in 1859. Subsequent courts followed the Gregory model. ERICKSON at 9; 1 HALL at 205 (discussing the Gregory meeting, followed by a July 9th meeting to elect local officers, including Richard Sopris as president and Charles Peck as sheriff). The Gold Hill district was organized by a mass convention on July 23, 1859. 3 HALL at 291. Boulder's town company organized on February 10, 1859. *Id.* at 292.

For an example of early mining town law, see WILLIAM TRAIN MUIR, LAWS OF THE NEVADA MINING DISTRICT 1861 (1962). Nevadaville was 2.5 miles south of Central City, Colorado. Nolie Mumey, *Nevadaville*, *in id.*, at 1 n.1. Its maximum population was about one thousand. *Id.* at 9.

voluntary associations recorded and certified property ownership, provided courts for settling disputes, and organized vigilance committees for law enforcement.[15] Some towns elected their own legislatures.[16] They created "people's courts" for criminal prosecutions.[17]

Ever since Jean-Jacques Rousseau in 1762, many philosophers have written about a hypothetical "social contract." In early Colorado, the social contract was not hypothetical. Colorado's original social contracts were actual contracts of self-government, agreed among equals. "The record of the miner's courts, the people's courts, and the claims clubs in the Pikes Peak region is a praiseworthy one; it exemplifies a high sense of justice and fair dealing."[18]

The decisions of the miner's districts were later ratified in the first session of the territorial legislature.[19] They were also approved by the Colorado Territorial Supreme Court.[20] By accepting and integrating the decisions of the *ad hoc* miners' courts and other early bodies, the developing territorial courts provided continuity of law.[21]

Territorial federal judge Moses Hallett's "recognition of the validity of mining district rules was one of the earliest and most important by a state or territorial court. Since the Colorado miners entered the public domain with no legal authority, the validation of mining district rules was actually a departure from the English common law. Under the common law, some type of permission from the central government would have been prerequisite to valid claims."[22]

Strictly speaking, the entire settlement of Colorado had been of questionable legality. Whatever lands were ceded by Indian treaties belonged to the federal government, which had never enacted any law for transfer of title to settlers. Congress recognized the *fait accompli* in 1864 and gave clear title to all Colorado settlers.[23] "Possession is eleven points in law, and they say there are but twelve."[24]

3. The Jefferson Territory self-organizes

In January 1859, U.S. Representative Alexander Stephens (D-Ga.) introduced a bill in the thirty-fifth Congress to create the Territory of Jefferson, which would comprise most of modern

---

The preamble to the Nevadaville laws explained that they were adopted by we the people in a mass meeting because we "have no civil government extended to us, by the Authorities of the United States, or of the Territory in which we now reside." *Id.* at 26. The laws created the office of sheriff, with the same powers as a Kansas sheriff. *Id.* at 44. Likewise, civil or criminal laws would be based on Kansas, to the extent that they were not changed by the Nevadaville enactments. *Id.* at 50.

A typical mining district provision punished "Any person shooting or threatening to shoot another, or using or threatening to use any deadly weapons, except in self-defense." ERICKSON at 9–10 (quoting laws of the Spanish Bar District, in Clear Creek County). The language should not be read hyperliterally. A butcher's knife is a deadly weapon; the law did not mean to forbid "use" of a butcher knife for cutting meat.

15 ERICKSON at 9; GALLAGHER at 37.

16 *See, e.g.*, 1 HALL at 205.

17 *See, e.g.*, ERICKSON at 9.

18 HAFEN at 137–38.

19 *See* Hensel at 13–18.

20 *Sullivan v. Hense*, 2 Colo. 424, 429 (1874). Similarly, in a water law case, chief judge Moses Hallett explained that the common law must be modified to fit local conditions. *See* chapter 21 (Mining & Irrigation, art. XVI).

21 *See* LAMAR at 257–58.

22 GUICE at 117

23 *See* LEONARD & NOEL at 28.

24 Albert M. Martin, *Answers: To Questions for Further Study in the January Number of "The Chataquan,"* 3 THE CHATAQUAN 355, 355 (Oct. 1882–July 1883) (quoting an old Scottish saying).

Colorado plus much land to the north.[25] Stephens, who would later become vice-president of the Confederate States of America, had been a leading advocate of bringing Kansas into the Union as a slave state, so anti-slavery representatives were wary, and the bill was not enacted.[26]

Since Congress had not organized a territory for Colorado, Coloradans organized one themselves. In response request from mass conventions in Denver and Auraria on September 24, 1859, a convention of eighty-eight delegates assembled in Denver on October 10, 1859, to draft a constitution for a provisional government for the "Territory of Jefferson."[27] The territorial constitution was adopted by popular vote and officers elected on October 24.[28]

At the convention creating the Territory of Jefferson, some citizens had presented a written protest. The protestors said that there was no legal authority to separate from Kansas. Moreover, separation "will abrogate all legal rights, and throw the country upon the results of a gigantic Vigilance Committee."[29]

But "No attention whatsoever was paid to this remonstrance," recalled future Colorado territorial secretary Frank Hall.[30] He continued: "Note the dashing boldness of these resolute pioneers . . . taking measures without precedent, without authority of law, and without the slightest prospect for ratification, for the creation of an independent commonwealth."[31]

When Kansas territorial governor Samuel Medrey found out about what Coloradans had done, he sent them an order instructing them to elect county officers under the laws of Kansas.[32] "This order being disapproved, it was wholly ignored."[33]

Not putting all eggs into the provisional territorial basket, the citizens of Arapahoe County elected Richard Sopris as their delegate to the Kansas legislature on December 9, 1859.[34]

The people of the Jefferson Territory also elected a territorial delegate to the U.S. House of Representatives. United States Territories send nonvoting delegates to the U.S. House of Representatives. Today, the U.S. House of Representatives has delegates from the District of Columbia, the U.S. Virgin Islands, the Commonwealth of Puerto Rico, American Samoa, Guam, and the Commonwealth of the Northern Mariana Islands.

Normally, Congress creates a territory, and then the territory elects a delegate to the U.S. House. But in Colorado ("Jefferson"), the people were the first movers: creating a provisional territory, and then electing their delegate to Congress. Congress did not seat the putative delegate from Jefferson Territory.

---

[25] H.R. 835 sec. 1, 35th Cong. (1859); *see also* CONG. GLOBE, 35th Cong., 2d Sess. 657 (1859) (Committee on Territories had reported the Jefferson Territory bill to the full House, with a favorable recommendation).

A competing bill, to create a Territory of Colona, was introduced by antislavery Republican Schuyler Colfax, of Indiana. BERWANGER at 3. Like the Stephens bill, the Colfax bill was not enacted.

As Speaker of the House (1863–69) and Vice President (1869–73), Schuyler Colfax always took a friendly and helpful interest in Colorado. He visited twice. He is the namesake of Colfax Avenue, in Denver.

[26] *See* H.R. 835 sec. 1, 35th Cong. (1859); *see also* MARK STEIN, HOW THE STATES GOT THEIR SHAPES TOO: THE PEOPLE BEHIND THE BORDERLINES 232 (2011).

[27] Wharton at 17. Auraria (southwest of Cherry Creek) and nearby Denver (northeast of Cherry Creek) had originally been rivals. They were consolidated by a popular vote on Apr. 3, 1860. 4 HALL at 25.

[28] *See* Wharton at 19. The vote was 1,852 in favor of the provisional government, and 280 against. *Id.*

[29] ERICKSON at 12–13 (quoting a written protest filed by H.P.A Smith); *see also* LEONARD & NOEL at 23.

[30] *See* 1 HALL at 209.

[31] *Id.* at 185.

[32] *Id.* at 210.

[33] *Id.*

[34] *Id.* at 170.

Jefferson provisional governor Robert Steele, the "father of Colorado," addressed the opening of the Jefferson legislature on November 7, 1859. He explained that the people had been denied protection of life and property. Being sovereign, they had taken measures for their security.[35]

The provisional legislature created the first legal code for Colorado.[36] While leaving legitimate use of firearms entirely unimpaired, the code imposed additional punishment on burglars who carried a gun.[37] The Jefferson legislature organized a territorial militia, comprising the Jefferson Rangers (from Auraria) and the Denver Guards.[38]

Jefferson Territory claimed future Colorado, plus the Nebraska panhandle, southern Wyoming, and some of eastern Utah.[39] The provisional government did some good, and certainly did not cause a decline in law and order.

However, the provisional government was mostly disregarded outside of Denver, and even in the city "it was powerless to enforce its decrees. The chief reliance of the citizens lay in the Committee of Safety."[40]

The Jefferson legislature granted Denver City a municipal charter, and the city's officers were elected on December 19, 1859.[41] But the officers were desultory about setting up a functioning government, so in September 1860, a series of public meetings adopted a proposed structure of government for Denver; it was submitted to the voters in October 1860, and overwhelmingly adopted.[42] In that same election, city officers were chosen.[43]

---

[35] Governor Steele continued:

> A vigilance committee, the first resource of an isolated and exposed community, was organized, and certain offences occurring during the winter and spring were taken cognizance of. But a more perfect form of government than was afforded by a vigilance committee was needed . . . The only resource left us was in the exercise of that inherent right of self-government which every community of American citizens is held to possess.

Gov. R.W. Steele, Address at the House of Representatives of the Territory of Jefferson (Nov. 7, 1859), quoted in 2 HALL at 516. Steele was remembered in the nineteenth century as a "universally venerated pioneer . . . the first of the great historic figures in the history of Colorado." 4 HALL at 562.

[36] For the history of the first session, see LeRoy R. Hafen, *Colorado's First Legislative Assembly*, 20 COLO. MAG. 41 (no. 2, Mar. 1943).

[37] Provisional Laws and Joint Resolutions, Passed at the First and Called Sessions of the General Assembly of Jefferson Territory, ch. 11, § 37 (1860).

[38] These units disbanded after Congress created the Territory of Colorado. WHITFORD at 38–39. The Denver Guards were mounted and comprised one hundred men. Their First Lieutenant was Edward Wynkoop. Wharton at 33.

[39] *See* STEIN at 230. The provisional boundaries were 37° to 43° of northerly latitude, and 102° to 110° of westerly longitude. *See* H.R. 835 § 1, 35th Cong. (1859). The 1861 boundaries of the Colorado Territory (and later, the state) were 37° to 41° North, and 102° 03' to 109° 03' West. *See* COLO. CONST., art. I (expressing longitude in terms of degrees west of Washington). The sizes of most western states are based on Thomas Jefferson's principle that states should be equals, so that states are approximately equal in height, breadth, or both. *See* chapter 1 (Creation of the State of Colorado).

The Jefferson provisional government, aware of its tenuous status, did not attempt to collect taxes. STEIN at 232. The legislature did pass a one-dollar poll tax, which the miners resolved not to pay. LAMAR at 187.

[40] 1 HALL at 247.

[41] Wharton at 20.

[42] *Id.* at 65–66.

[43] *Id.* at 66. Once a federally authorized territorial legislature was set up, it granted Denver a charter, effective November 8, 1861. *Id.* at 80.

As of 1860, Denver had five competing court systems.[44] Forum shopping was common.[45] Meanwhile, "the mountain counties stood by their Miner's courts, and as much of the Provisional Government as suited them."[46] Other Coloradans created judicial districts for what they called "Idaho Territory."[47] There were multiple governments in Colorado with alleged jurisdiction, and in fact the people of Colorado entirely governed themselves:

> Side by side sat the Idaho "central judicial" officers, the provisional government of Jefferson, the Kansas county officials, the Denver people's government, scores of miners' courts, and local governments and vigilante committees. Never had frontier democracy blossomed so vigorously. With popular sovereignty in the saddle, the northern part of Bent's old empire was already a far cry from the tradition-bound and caste-conscious territory of New Mexico. A new kind of democratic, middle-class, commercial-minded frontier had arrived on the borders of the Spanish Southwest.[48]

On the periphery of the periphery, Coloradans became "a free and radically independent people," in the words of historian Frank Hall.[49]

President Lincoln was inaugurated on March 4, 1861. He appointed William Gilpin to be territorial governor, and Gilpin arrived in May.[50] Gilpin was already familiar with Colorado, having been part of John C. Frémont's second expedition.[51] He loved Colorado and believed the future of civilization lay in the great lands from the Mississippi Valley to the Rocky Mountains.[52]

In 1861, the settlers voted on whether to seek statehood. The vote was 2,007 for territory and 1,649 for statehood. Nebraska in 1860 had also voted to be a territory and not a state, "thereby providing the first indication of a strong desire to limit the cost of government, a theme that

---

[44] ERICKSON at 15. To start, there were the courts of the Jefferson Territory and of Kansas Territory. The Denver legislative council's courts of common pleas and appeals was more influential than either. The people's courts for criminal cases were organized *ad hoc* to hear capital cases brought by vigilance committees. Denver's fifth court was the Arapahoe County Claim Club. 3 HALL at 267–69. "For two years or more the Territorial, county and city affairs were so intermingled it was difficult to draw the distinctions between them." *Id.* at 267.

[45] ERICKSON at 15.

[46] W.B. Vickers, *Territorial Organization, in* LEGISLATIVE, HISTORICAL AND BIOGRAPHICAL COMPENDIUM OF COLORADO 144, 145 (Denver, C.F. Coleman's Publ'g House 1887).

47 *See* LAMAR at 187 (crediting creation of these districts to a convention held in Central City in October 1860).

[48] *Id.* at 187–88. The Colorado pioneers "were as well-versed in self-government as any people in world.". The majority were from Kansas, Nebraska, Iowa, and Missouri. "During the turbulent fifties they had learned much about local self-government, town founding, and territorial organization . . . [B]y 1859 they were all sophisticated practitioners of popular sovereignty." *Id.* at 185.

[49] 1 HALL at 369.

[50] LAMAR at 190.

[51] *Id.* at 191.

[52] *See generally* HUBERT HOWE BANCROFT, HISTORY OF THE LIFE OF WILLIAM GILPIN: A CHARACTER STUDY (San Francisco, The History Co. 1889). "Outside of William Clark [of Lewis & Clark; later, territorial governor of Missouri], Andrew Jackson, and Brigham Young, Gilpin is possibly the most remarkable man ever to be appointed territorial governor." LAMAR at 190. Growing up in Philadelphia and England, he had received an outstanding education from private tutors. Yet he sold his books to head west, where he accidentally ran into, and then joined the Frémont expedition. He traveled as far as Oregon, served as a major in New Mexico during the Mexican War, and made the development of the West his life's mission. He was the "John the Baptist of the West." *Id.* at 191–92.

reemerged in later constitutional debates."[53] Another Colorado vote in 1864 had the same result.[54] In Nebraska and Colorado, territorial government might not be ideal, but the federal government would bear the expense. This was considered acceptable, until territorial government became unbearably corrupt during the Grant Administration, particularly under Grant's appointee territorial governor Edward McCook (1869–73 & 1874–75).

B. The Civil War

Shortly before Gilpin's arrival, the American Civil War began on April 12,1861, when the Confederacy attacked Fort Sumter, South Carolina. "With the federal government otherwise occupied, Colorado was left to save itself, with the governor's aid." Governor Gilpin warned that there was "no place for Coloradans to retreat; they would be compelled to stand and fight."[55]

Yet the new territorial government of Colorado was broke. On August 26, 1861, Gilpin "wrote a desperate but futile letter to Secretary of War Cameron, asking for arms to be sent to the territory." Gilpin stated that the people "are utterly destitute of arms, ammunition, or any weapons for self-preservation." They would fight, if they had the means, for "Energy, loyalty, and bravery preeminently belong to the mountain people. To conquer their enemies appears to them more glorious than to perish."[56]

The first session of the territorial legislature convened on September 9, 1861. Governor Gilpin's address urged prompt creation of a territorial militia.[57] "The citizen must be also a soldier, and armed."[58] An effective military and judiciary, Gilpin told Coloradans, were the "bulwark of their liberties."[59] The legislature, consisting of 13 representatives in the lower house and nine councilmen in the upper house, passed a resolution affirming Colorado's adherence to the Union.[60]

Gilpin's August letter about the complete absence of arms had been hyperbole. There were arms to be had, and Gilpin meant to have them. The territorial government purchased firearms from citizens in exchange for warrants issued the governor. These warrants were supposed to be redeemable by the U.S. Treasury. But there was no law authorizing a territorial governor to issue U.S. debt.[61] "Gilpin's obsession with weapons had resulted in an 'arms race' that summer, as he attempted to purchase as many as possible, lest they fall into the hands of southerners. Inflated prices, if nothing else, were the result."[62] With neither men nor weapons coming from

---

[53] Christopher W. Larimer, *A Self-Righteous and Self-Sufficient Method for Governing: How the Nebraska Constitution Preserves a Way of Life*, *in* THE CONSTITUTIONALISM OF AMERICAN STATES at 529, 531.
[54] SMITH, at 205 (1,520 votes for statehood, and 4,672 against).
[55] LAMM & SMITH at 20.
[56] *Id.* (quoting Gilpin's letter to secretary of war Simon Cameron dated August 26, 1861).
[57] *Id.* at 16–17.
[58] *Id.* (quoting William Gilpin, Governor of Colorado, Address at the First Session of the Colorado Territorial Legislature (Sept. 9, 1861)).
[59] COLTON at 173.
[60] HAFEN at 157–58.
[61] *See* LAMM & SMITH at 19–22; *see also* 1 HALL at 272.
[62] LAMM & SMITH at 20. "As most of the men in the country had either a rifle or a heavy shot gun, a comparatively large number of such arms was soon collected, but as scarcely any two were alike they were poorly adapted for use by organized troops." WHITFORD at 40. Gilpin's team would buy "anything from double-barreled shotguns to ladies' pocket derringers." GALLAGHER at 55.

In 1861, Confederate sympathizers were also attempting to purchase arms and ammunition. They posted notices near Denver City and the mining camps, offering to pay top dollar for firearms, gunpowder, and percussion caps. 1 HALL at 275. A pro-confederate wagon train of guns and other supplies being taken

Washington, Gilpin had to raise a military force on his own. The First, Second, and Third Colorado Volunteers were embodied. "[P]atriotic Coloradans eagerly rallied to the colors. Locating sources of revenue was another matter."[63]

The Colorado Volunteers' guns had been supplied by Colorado's civilian firearms businesses, as well as the businesses in the states from whence Coloradans had come. If there had been no gun businesses, Colorado would have been defenseless.[64]

Gilpin issued drafts for $375,000. When the U.S. Treasury refused to honor them, there was great consternation in Colorado. Eventually, in the spring of 1862, the Treasury agreed to pay the drafts.[65] In the meantime, relentless attacks from the *Rocky Mountain News* and the *Colorado Republican* had made Gilpin so unpopular that president Lincoln had to appoint a new governor in May 1862.[66]

The Third Colorado Volunteers were summoned to "the States" in February 1862, leaving Colorado's defenses weaker.[67] The First Colorado Volunteers might be called out of the territory at any moment. Accordingly, local defense units were created. Denver had its Governors Guards, Black Hawk the Elbert Guards, and Montgomery (in Park County) the Home Guards.[68]

---

to Indian country was intercepted by Coloradans, who turned the Confederates over to federal authorities at Fort Wise. LAMAR at 199.

Pro-"secesh" sentiment was greatest in southern Colorado, where many of the new immigrants were from Georgia, a state "with an important mining heritage." GUICE at 27. Southern Colorado also had a good number of immigrants from Tennessee and Kentucky. For a Southerner, the closest trailhead for Colorado was the Santa Fe trail. It led to southern Colorado.

Early in the Civil War, on April 24, 1861, some men raised a Confederate flag above the downtown Denver merchandise store Wallingford & Murphy. A crowd quickly gathered, with Union men in the majority. Samuel P. Logan mounted the roof and tore down the flag. Logan would later serve as a Captain in the Colorado Volunteers, First Regiment. No such flag was raised again in Colorado. WHITFORD at 39

[63] LAMM & SMITH at 20.

[64] The first federal arms supplied to the Colorado Volunteers were "few in number and inferior in quality." COLTON at 44. As of 1862, the Colorado Volunteers' primary arms were Sharps rifles. *See* OVANDO J. HOLLISTER, COLORADO VOLUNTEERS IN NEW MEXICO 1862, at 112 (Richard Harwell ed., The Lakeside Press 1962) (1863). Hollister's book provides the whole story, from enlistment and the long dull days in a camp in Denver, through the fighting in New Mexico and the return to Colorado. *See* Richard Harwell, *Introduction* to HOLLISTER, at xiii, xix–xxiii. The book was first published in 1863 as HISTORY OF THE FIRST REGIMENT OF COLORADO VOLUNTEERS, and republished in 1949 as BOLDLY THEY RODE: A HISTORY OF THE FIRST COLORADO REGIMENT OF VOLUNTEERS (The Golden Press 1949) (1863). Hollister had a long career as a journalist and married the sister of vice president Schuyler Colfax. *Id.* at xiii, xx–xxi. He also served a U.S. Collector of Internal Revenue for Utah. *Id.* at xxi–xxii.

[65] LAMM & SMITH at 21–23. The federal government paid only the drafts that were still in the hands of their original holders. Anyone who had bought a draft was out of luck unless the original holder could be persuaded to submit a claim. WHITFORD at 55.

[66] LAMM & SMITH at 21–22.

[67] SMITH at 111.

[68] *Id.*; *see also* WHITFORD at 44.

1. *The Confederate invasion*

In March 1861, New Mexican secessionists declared that the portion of the New Mexico Territory below the 34th parallel was now part of "Confederate Territory of Arizona."[69] Confederate lieutenant colonel John Baylor was appointed Confederate territorial governor.[70]

Texans, led by general Henry Hopkins Sibley, invaded New Mexico in January 1862.[71] His plan was to capture Fort Craig (in southern New Mexico) and Fort Union (farther north), and then march into Colorado. There, he would raise Confederate volunteers from what was hoped to the quarter or third of sympathetic Coloradan population; they would capture the gold fields.[72] Once Colorado was secured, the next step would be to head west. Utah was expected to be neutral, or perhaps even sympathetic to the Confederacy.[73] Next, the Confederate forces would aim for Nevada, southern California (where there was plenty of Confederate sympathy), and maybe northern California.[74] The final objectives were the northern Mexican states of Chihuahua, Sonora, and Baja California.[75] Mexico was busy fighting a French invasion that had begun in 1861, so perhaps it might yield its lightly populated north, which was semiautonomous.[76]

Even partial success for Sibley's Army of New Mexico would have been a catastrophe for the Union.[77] First of all, Colorado and California gold bullion were absolutely essential for the federal government being able to borrow money to finance the war. President Lincoln called the gold "the life-blood of our financial credit."[78] Besides obtaining the gold, the Confederacy would also impede the federal government's communications with the Pacific West.

Even worse, Sibley's success could change the attitude of neutral powers, who might overtly support the Confederacy if the secessionists could prove they were winning. Near Colorado, in present-day Oklahoma, were the Five Tribes, who had been removed from the Southeast in the 1830s. They formally allied with the Confederacy, which had offered them very favorable terms, including perpetual control of their lands and affirmation of their power to own slaves. Soon, other tribes in Oklahoma joined the Confederacy. The Comanche (who were present in southeastern Colorado) and the Wichita did not promise to fight the Union, but they did sign a treaty recognizing the Confederacy, not the Union, as sovereign where they lived.[79]

---

[69] JOHN TAYLOR, BLOODY VALVERDE: A CIVIL WAR BATTLE ON THE RIO GRANDE, FEBRUARY 21, 1862, at 5 (1st ed. 1995). At the time, Arizona was part of the New Mexico Territory. The 34th parallel is just below Socorro, New Mexico, so the Confederate Territory was about forty percent of the modern states of New Mexico and Arizona.

[70] He proclaimed the Confederate government on August 1, 1861, and later claimed most of the rest of the New Mexico Territory for the Confederacy. WHITFORD at 30.

[71] *See* ROBERT LEE KERBY, THE CONFEDERATE INVASION OF NEW MEXICO AND ARIZONA 1861–1862, at 63 (1958).

[72] *See* COLTON at 9, 40–41.

[73] TAYLOR at 12.

[74] Jerome C. Smiley, *Preface* to WHITFORD at 10, 13; TAYLOR at 12. Most American settlers in the Southwest had come from the South, so there was some reason for the Confederacy to expect sympathy for a Confederate conquest. KERBY, *supra* note 71, at 50.

[75] *See* Smiley at 11–12 (reporting plans that we were disclosed after the war by Major Trevanian T. Teel, one of Sibley's officers).

[76] *See generally* ALFRED JACKSON HANNA & KATHRYN ABBEY HANNA, NAPOLEON III AND MEXICO: AMERICAN TRIUMPH OVER MONARCHY (1971); STUART F. VOSS, ON THE PERIPHERY OF NINETEENTH-CENTURY MEXICO: SONORA AND SINALOA, 1810–1877 (1982).

77. It was also known as Sibley's Brigade. "No volunteers more hardy, courageous and efficient ever entered the service of the Confederacy." WHITFORD at 33.

[78] Smiley, *supra* note 74, at 12.

[79] PRUCHA at 261–63.

Confederate diplomats were attempting to woo other tribes who were remaining neutral for the time being. But even if the tribes stayed neutral, the Civil War might be a good time to drive out the whites.[80] Indeed, in August through December 1862, the massive Santee Uprising of the Sioux in Minnesota would force 40,000 white settlers to flee.[81] In Texas, Indians took advantage of the Civil War to push back the frontier of white settlement by 150 miles to the southeast.[82]

To the west, Brigham Young's theocracy in Utah, which the Mormons called "Deseret," was almost entirely free of federal influence.[83] Young offered some platitudes in support of the Union, but the Latter-day Saints were keeping a keen eye on the possibility of their own secession.[84]

Most dangerous of all, the news that vast western territories had been taken by the Confederacy might affect the attitudes of neutral France and Great Britain.[85] Both nations saw strategic interests in weakening the United States, and they inherently had a more economically harmonious relation with the South, whose economy was based on agriculture exports and manufactured goods imports. The core Confederate strategy was based on winning diplomatic recognition from at least one of these great powers.[86] French recognition of the independent United States in 1778 had been a *sine qua non* for the success of the American War of Independence;[87] the Confederate States of America aimed to emulate that example.

---

[80] *See* GRINNELL at 129.

[81] FEHRENBACH at 458–59. "In Colorado, then the greatest center of population of all the plains country, a like fear was felt that the Indians generally would follow the example of the Minnesota Sioux." GRINNELL at 129. "Intelligent Indians saw in the Civil War the opportunity, while the whites were killing one another, to drive the intruders out of the land of their fathers or exterminate them." COLTON at 121. Governor Gilpin reported in October 1861 that the Indian population west of the Arkansas River were supportive of the Georgians in southern Colorado who favored secession. However, some Indians there enlisted in the Union army. *Id.* at 148. In May 1862, it was learned that the Confederates were negotiating with the Comanche and other tribes to gain Indian support (or at least neutrality) for Confederate attacks on Union forts on the Arkansas River, namely Fort Wise (in southeastern Colorado) and Fort Larned (in Kansas). GRINNELL at 127–28.

[82] JAMES L. HALEY, THE BUFFALO WAR: THE HISTORY OF THE RED RIVER INDIAN UPRISING OF 1874, at 85 (1976).

[83] "Mormon" is an informal name for members of the Church of Jesus Christ of Latter-day Saints. In the LDS scripture, "deseret" is said to be an ancient name for the honeybee. *See Ether* 2:3 (Book of Mormon) ("And they did also carry with them deseret, which, by interpretation, is a honey bee"). It represents the cooperative and hardworking spirit of the Mormon pioneers. The official symbol of Utah is the beehive. Kevin L. Barney, *On the Etymology of Deseret*, BY COMMON CONSENT (Nov. 3, 2006).

[84] *See* LAMAR at 285–302. Indeed, in 1862, the Mormons proclaimed statehood and warned that they were prepared to remove "the federal yoke" and forcefully to assert their rights of self-government. Although the Utah Territory was nominally governed by federal appointees, the Mormons set up a "Ghost State" government, with Brigham Young as governor, and this ghost government had far more effective power than did the federal territorial government. JOHN ALTON PETERSON, UTAH'S BLACK HAWK WAR 13, 32 (1998).

The 1847 Mormon Migration to the Great Salt Lake had intentionally moved the Mormons outside the United States, into Mexican territory over which the government in Mexico City exerted very little influence. Because of the U.S. 1848 victory in the Mexican War, Utah and much of the rest of the southwest was sold by Mexico to the United States, in the Treaty of Guadalupe-Hidalgo. *See* chapter 1 (Creation of the State of Colorado).

[85] Smiley, *supra* note 74, at 13; SMITH at 25.

[86] *See generally* AMANDA FOREMAN, A WORLD ON FIRE: BRITAIN'S CRUCIAL ROLE IN THE AMERICAN CIVIL WAR (2d ed. 2012); HOWARD JONES, BLUE & GRAY DIPLOMACY: A HISTORY OF UNION AND CONFEDERATE FOREIGN RELATIONS (Gary W. Gallagher & T. Michael Parrish eds., 2010).

[87] *See generally* TOM SHACHTMAN, HOW THE FRENCH SAVED AMERICA: SOLDIERS, SAILORS, DIPLOMATS, LOUIS XVI, AND THE SUCCESS OF A REVOLUTION (2017).

Finally, both sides of the 1860 federal election had agreed that if Southern slavery could not expand, it would inevitably die for economic reasons. Hence, the Confederates viewed New Mexico as essential for their long-term viability.[88]

Marching north from El Paso along the Rio Grande, General Sibley's Texans met Union forces on Feb. 21, 1862, at Valverde, New Mexico, near Fort Craig. The federals included the regular army, the New Mexico militia, New Mexico volunteers (some of them commanded by Kit Carson), and part of the Second Colorado Infantry, who had marched south in December 1861, from Cañon City.[89]

The Coloradans were responsible for the far-left side of the Union line. Their first taste of battle was a cavalry charge by Texas lancers, who carried nine-foot poles with one-foot blades. When the Texan horsemen closed within 100 feet, the Coloradans opened fire. The Texans took heavy casualties and fell back.[90]

But the day belonged to the Texans and the Union army was forced to retreat.[91] The seventy-one Colorado Volunteers suffered a fifty-six percent casualty rate of dead, wounded, or missing.[92] The Confederates then waltzed into Albuquerque and Santa Fe without opposition.[93]

2. *Coloradans to the rescue: The Gettysburg of the West*

The Union commander, Colonel Edward Canby, knew that without reinforcements, Sibley's Texans would soon take Fort Union, and New Mexico would be lost. He dispatched a message to governor Gilpin asking for aid. The message reached Denver on March 1.[94]

As soon as permission was obtained from the federal commander at Fort Leavenworth, Kansas, the Coloradans hurried south. The First Regiment of Colorado Volunteers left from Camp Weld in Denver, where they had spent a dull winter with poor rations.[95] They were soon

---

[88] MARTIN HARDWICK HALL, SIBLEY'S NEW MEXICO CAMPAIGN 151 (Univ. N.M. Press 2000) (1960) (Southern concern that if the Confederate States of America were hemmed in by free Union territory, then slavery would "sting itself to death"); JONES, *supra* note 86 (Republicans and Democrats agreed with Lincoln's view that preventing the territorial expansion of slavery would lead to its "ultimate extinction," because cotton depletes the soil of nitrogen). *See generally* JAMES OAKES, THE SCORPION'S STING: ANTISLAVERY AND THE COMING OF THE CIVIL WAR (2014) (abolitionist theory that if slave states were surrounded by a "cordon of freedom" consisting of free states, free federal territories, and a free high seas with no slave trade, then slavery would eventually collapse).

[89] *See* JOHN TAYLOR, BLOODY VALVERDE: A CIVIL WAR BATTLE ON THE RIO GRANDE, FEBRUARY 21, 1862, at 26 (1st ed. 1995); WHITFORD at 35, 43.

[90] TAYLOR at 67–70.

[91] *See id.* at 85–96 (chronicling the ending of the Battle of Valverde); COLTON at 33–34. The New Mexicans did not fight well because of their "traditional fear of Texans." They surrendered quickly, giving the Texans their arms in exchange for being allowed to go home. HALL, *supra* note 88, at 87.

The Texans brought their own arms, supplemented by what Sibley bought for them in the open market. They were "armed with practically every type of small arm in existence: squirrel guns, bear guns, sportsman's guns, single and double-barreled shotguns, navy revolvers, six-shooters, Minié muskets, common rifles, and many others." Plus several howitzers. *Id.* at 27–28. These were augmented with about 250 firearms, mainly rifles, captured after the victory at Valverde. *See id.* at 77.

[92] TAYLOR at 104.

[93] LAMAR at 103.

[94] TAYLOR at 106.

[95] *See* COLTON at 42–44; LAMAR at 200–01. Camp Weld was named for Lewis Ledyard Weld, the first secretary of the Colorado territory, appointed by president Lincoln. Besides being the namesake of Weld County, he designed Colorado's great seal, and used his family motto as the Colorado motto: *Nil Sine Numine* (Nothing Without Providence). PROPST at 43; Wharton at 34. He was a nephew of Theodore Dwight Weld, a leading abolitionist. BERWANGER at 9.

joined by other forces from Fort Wise in southeastern Colorado.[96] They completed a 400-mile forced march from Denver in just thirteen days, including a thirty-six-hour march covering ninety-two miles.[97]

Everyone reconnoitered at Fort Union by March 10. There, they were finally given proper equipment, with standardized rifles, ammunition, and uniforms.[98] Soon, on March 26–28, 1862, the Battle of Glorieta Pass was fought in the Sangre de Cristo Mountains southeast of Santa Fe.[99]

> Having cowed the Southern sympathizers in Denver and elsewhere and having chased off several Texas raiding parties, the Colorado volunteers were a far more formidable body than their New Mexico counterparts. Made up of miners and frontiersmen and a sprinkling of former Kansas free-soilers, the companies possessed officers who seemed not to know the meaning of caution or fear.[100]

"The men were uncommonly hardy and well seasoned, and not in the habit of being afraid."[101]

The men of the Texas Mounted Rifles fought well. So did the New Mexico militia and the Colorado infantry. While the fighting on the front lines was mostly a draw, if one had to declare a winner, it would be Sibley and the Texans.

But the fighting in the rear changed everything. On the third day of battle, New Mexicans spotted the Confederate baggage train. Five companies of Colorado infantry and cavalry, plus two federal companies, descended steep mountainsides for a surprise attack on the supply train. "They crawled, slid and were lowered by ropes and leather straps while carrying their guns." They lit the supply wagons on fire, spiked the cannons, and killed or ran off hundreds of horses and mules.[102] "This was the irreparable blow that compelled the Texans to evacuate the Territory. Its audacity was the principle cause of its success."[103] Without food or supplies, the Confederates limped to Santa Fe and eventually back to Texas.[104]

A Texan soldier morosely wrote to his wife, "Instead of Mexicans and regulars, [the Coloradans] were regular demons, that iron and lead had no effect upon, in the shape of Pike's Peakers from the Denver City Gold mines . . . Had it not been for the devils from Pike's Peak,

---

[96] *See* COLTON at 45. The trading post of "Bent's New Fort" had been turned into a military post, named for Virginia governor Henry A. Wise. Charles C. Post, *Diary*, *in* OVERLAND ROUTES TO THE GOLD FIELDS, 1859: FROM CONTEMPORARY DIARIES 25, 46 n.25 (LeRoy R. Hafen ed., 1942). Owing to Virginia's 1861 secession, the name was changed in 1862 to "Fort Lyon," for major general Nathaniel Lyon, who gave his life fighting for the Union at Wilson's Creek, Missouri, on August 10, 1861. Because of floods, the fort was moved in 1867 to a location near Las Animas, Colorado. *See* STEPHEN B. OATS, CONFEDERATE CAVALRY WEST OF THE RIVER 16–17 (1961); Post at 46 n.25. The facility later became a state prison, and later a rehabilitation center for homeless people with substance abuse problems. Fort Lyon, COLO. DEP'T LOC. AFFAIRS.

[97] SMITH at 26. In New Mexico, the Coloradans had to make their way through "a bitterly cold and furious windstorm, a mountain hurricane, which showered and blinded them with driven snow, dust, and sand." WHITFORD at 78.

[98] *Id.* at 78–79.

[99] *See* SMITH at 26–27.

[100] LAMAR at 104.

[101] WHITFORD at 50.

[102] COLTON at 70–73; *see also* Leo Oliva, *Chivington and the Mules at Johnson's Ranch*, WAGON TRACKS, Aug. 1992, at 16, 16–17 (stating that most mules were run off).

[103] HOLLISTER, *supra* note 64, at 117.

[104] *See* COLTON at 75–76, 81–99.

Figure 14. One of nine cannons used at the Battle of Glorieta Pass. History Colorado-Denver, Colorado.

this country would have been ours."[105] The Battle of Glorieta Pass, "the Gettysburg of the West," had saved Colorado and New Mexico for the Union.[106]

The Colorado Volunteers then consolidated with the federal army and harried the Texans back to Texas.[107] Along the way, they almost mutinied because the federal commander, colonel Edward Canby, was not as aggressive as they wanted to be.[108] The Colorado Volunteers spent the rest of the year in New Mexico fighting Indians. They arrived back in Denver for a victory parade in January 1863.[109] Some of them were demobilized, and others chose to be sent to "the States," where they fought in Kansas, Missouri, and Arkansas, including against "bushwhackers" and "jayhawkers"—Confederate guerillas.[110]

These guerillas were turning into robbery gangs who would remain active even after the war ended. One of these gangs preyed on the South Park in July 1864 and declared its intention to pillage Denver. They were apprehended by a local posse.[111] Among the group that hunted down the marauders was Wilbur Fiske Stone, future justice of the Colorado supreme court.[112]

"Quite a number of small bands of guerillas and bandits were operating at this time in southern Colorado."[113] Not all of them were affiliated with the Confederacy. The most notorious and cruel were the Espinosa brothers, racist serial killers who murdered over thirty victims in the area between Pueblo and Park counties. One brother was killed by a posse; the other escaped but was later tracked and killed by a group of miners.[114]

C. Plains Indian Wars

The Confederate danger was diminished by the summer of 1862, but the Indian problem was getting much worse. There were three trails leading to the Colorado settlements: in the southeast,

---

[105] HOLLISTER, *supra* note 64, at 262–65 (quoting Letter from George M. Brown to his wife (Apr. 30, 1862) (originally published in *Denver News*)). Brown had been captured and paroled (allowed his freedom, based on his promise not to fight any more). While his letter was being carried through New Mexico, a Union officer discovered it, which led to its newspaper publication. COLTON at 54 n.10.

[106] *See* Robert McCoy, *Forward* to WHITFORD at 1; P.G. NAGLE, GLORIETA PASS inside front jacket (1999).

The Colorado Volunteers were nicknamed "Gilpin's Pet Lambs." The Texans were "Baylor's Babes," named for the Texan lieutenant colonel who had authorized Sibley to raise an army for a western offensive, and who claimed to rule as Confederate governor over New Mexico and Arizona. *See* Harwell, *supra* note 64, at xxiv. After three days of fighting at Glorieta Pass:

> Night fell upon the scene and the Babes and the Lambs each sought their own corner. The Lambs found theirs all right, but the Babes did not. It appeared that a part of the Lambs had been there during the fight and destroyed their commissary and transportation, totally. There being no grub in New Mexico in general way, there certainly was none now since armies had been sustained by her during the Winter, so the Babes had to go home to get something to eat. The Lambs accompanied them to the door, and wished them a safe journey. And so ended the war of the Babes and the Lambs in the Rocky Mountains.

Id. at xxiv–xxv.

[107] ESTERGREEN at 233.

[108] LAMAR at 105. Canby could have destroyed the retreating Confederates, but he would have taken major losses in his own forces, thus leaving New Mexico vulnerable to a second invasion. KERBY, *supra* note 71, at 114–16. Canby and Sibley were brothers-in-law. *Id.* at 52.

[109] *See* HOLLISTER, *supra* note 64, at 256.

[110] 1 HALL at 295–99; *see also* SMITH at 239.

[111] Wharton at 54; WHITFORD at 141; *see also* GALLAGHER at 68–73.

[112] 1 HALL at 315–16.

[113] Wharton at 54.

[114] GALLAGHER at 63–67; 1 HALL at 378–81; Wharton at 54.

a branch of the Santa Fe Trail; in the center, the Smoky Hill Trail, from Fort Leavenworth, Kansas, to Denver; and in the north, the South Platte Trail, which traversed Nebraska and then dropped down to Denver. Goods were transported in wagons drawn by oxen or mules.[115] The greatest share of immigrants, imported goods, and Colorado exports moved via the South Platte Trail.[116]

On February 18, 1861, the Treaty of Fort Wise granted the United States most of the Cheyenne and Arapahoe territory in northeastern Colorado, including Denver.[117] But not all chiefs had signed it.[118] Neither side made much effort to obey it.[119]

The white and black settlers, clustered along the Front Range and in mining towns, could not survive a cutoff of their trade routes with the states. The territory was not self-sufficient in food, and imports were essential for survival. Irrigation was just beginning to be developed in semiarid Colorado, so nearly all agriculture was near the rivers.[120] This was not enough to feed the population. The mountain mining towns were even more precarious because snow might close the wagon trails to the mines for extended periods. In January and February 1862, Gilpin County mining had to stop due to a shortage of gunpowder.[121]

---

[115] 3 HISTORICAL COMPENDIUM at 70.

[116] *See* PROPST at 34.

The Smoky Hill Trail was the shortest, but in the western portion, there was little water, and it was easy to get lost in the rolling hills.

The Arkansas River Trail was an extension of the Sante Fe Trail, and thus required traveling through Missouri and Kansas.

To get to the South Platte Trail, a person would follow the Overland Trail west from Ft. Kearney, Nebraska, and then branch off to the southwest when the person arrived at the South Platte River. The large majority of emigrants to Colorado came via the South Platte Trail. There was always water, and the trail was easy to follow. The main difficulty was the sandy stretches that made wagon movement arduous.

The Overland Trail was used by settlers traveling to California and Oregon in the late 1840s and early 1850s. *See* JOHN PHILLIP REID, POLICING THE ELEPHANT: CRIME, PUNISHMENT, AND SOCIAL BEHAVIOR ON THE OVERLAND TRAIL 1, 21, 73–76, 91–93 (1997) (explaining how Overland Trail migrants successfully maintained law and order among themselves; homicides were few, but firearms accidents were common, as many of the migrants had just purchased firearms but had not taken the time to learn how to use them safely).

[117] Treaty with the Arapaho and Cheyenne 1861 art. 1, Feb. 18, 1861, 12 Stat. 1163, *reprinted in* 2 INDIAN AFFAIRS 807.

[118] LEONARD & NOEL at 16–17. Indeed, the Cheyenne signatories, such as Black Kettle, said that they were signing for themselves, and not on behalf of non-participating Cheyenne. AFTON ET AL. at xv. The Arapaho chief Little Raven did sign, but later said that he did not understand what the treaty meant. GRINNELL at 126 n.6. The treaty had been signed in February 1861 but was not ratified by the U.S. Senate until August, nor proclaimed by the President until December. 2 INDIAN AFFAIRS at 807. "So, for some time even after the treaty, the town lots carried titles that were maintained with guns." BRENNEMAN at 27. Which was similar to how things had always been in Colorado.

[119] TURNER, *supra* note 6, at 107.

[120] *See* HISTORICAL COMPENDIUM at 105; Wharton at 58 (in 1866, 136 miles of irrigating ditches were constructed, at a cost of $1,000 per mile); *see also id.* at 60 ("There is no certainty in any crop without the land to be irrigated"); BERWANGER at 11 (stating that in the early days, irrigation extended no further than half a mile from watercourses).

According to the *Rocky Mountain News*, which was always a Colorado booster, the territory could have been self-sufficient in food by 1865 if a locust plague had not wiped out most of the crops that year and the year before. *Id.*; 1 HALL at 449; 2 HALL at 216 (locusts came Aug. 26, 1864, "destroying all late crops").

[121] SMITH at 33 (also noting that the shortage ended in mid-March, when the trails re-opened).

Not long after the Civil War began, the Smoky Hill Trail and the Santa Fe Trail became too dangerous to use. Federal troops there were sent east, leaving travelers vulnerable to Confederate guerillas and to Indians in the river valleys.[122] The South Platte Trail was the only lifeline connecting Denver to the States.

There had always been occasional Indian raids on wagon trains, stagecoaches, station stops, homes, and farms.[123] By May 1862, "it became apparent that Arapaho, Cheyenne, and other Indian tribes were stealthily preparing for war." In June, a show of force by the Second Colorado Volunteers halted Indian raids along the South Platte River.[124]

Figure 15. Jim Beckwourth.

One cause of Indian attacks on the white settlers was inter-Indian wars. War parties on their way to combat often harassed whites. Whoever lost the battle would be straggling home, and inclined to replenish their loss of horses by taking some from the whites, and forcing the settlers to give them supplies.[125] For example, in 1862, 600 Arapahoe and Sioux, returning home after a battle against the Utes, took everything movable from a ranch at Hartsell Hot Springs.[126] Colorado territorial governor John Evans attempted, without much success, to stop the Ute versus Cheyenne/Arapaho wars.[127]

A more direct cause of increased bellicosity was a change in the Indian agent. Indian treaties typically provided for annual federal delivery of goods and food to the signatory tribes. The tools, food, and other items were intended, in part, to provide a starting point for the Indians to be less dependent on hunting, and to take up agriculture. Albert Gallatin Boone (a grandson of Daniel) had treated the Indians fairly when he was agent, as had his predecessor, Acting Indian Agent Jim Beckwourth, a mountain man.[128] But Boone was replaced by Samuel Colley, who along with his wife stole much of the annuity, and sold it for

---

[122] *See* BERWANGER at 12–13. So, even more traffic went via the South Platte Trail. *See id.*

[123] *See, e.g.*, SMITH at 114 (discussing crimes in Boulder County during a "time of apparent peace").

[124] COLTON at 149.

[125] GRINNELL at 130–31.

[126] 4 HALL at 464.

[127] GRINNELL at 131.

[128] *See* GALLAGHER at 104; *see also* ELINOR WILSON, JIM BECKWOURTH: BLACK MOUNTAIN MAN AND CHIEF OF THE CROWS, 167–68 (1972); W. Sherman Savage, *James Beckwourth-Negro Fur Trader*, 17 NEGRO HIST. BULL. 123 (1954).

Boone had first come to Colorado in 1824–25, as part of a hunting and trapping expedition in Middle Park. He had "a pretty thorough knowledge of most of the Indian tongues," and founded the town of Booneville, twenty miles south of Pueblo. He passed away in Denver in 1884, "the last of a noble race, and a fit descendant of famous ancestors."

On the last day of Beckwourth's life, he was visited by fellow mountain man Jim Baker. 2 HALL at 249–50. Baker is memorialized in the Colorado Hall of Fame in the State Capitol. *See* ch. 12 (State Institutions, art. VIII).

their own profit, putting the Cheyenne and Arapaho close to starvation.[129] Even when Indian agents were honest, Congress sometimes cut the annuities from what the treaties had provided, or neglected to appropriate funds for the annuities.[130]

1. Environmental catastrophe

As historian Elliott West explains, even if distribution of Indian annuities had been perfect, war was inevitable for environmental reasons. To begin with, the annuities provided only a modest amount of food. More importantly, the acquisition of horses and firearms had dramatically changed the Cheyenne way of life in a manner that was ultimately unsustainable.

Pre-horse and pre-gun, the Cheyenne has been agriculturalists in the upper Midwest. Their main service animal was the dog, which needed the same food resources that the Cheyenne did. The horse, in contrast, fed on prairie grass. Thus, the horse amounted to major new source of energy, and brought with it a tremendous increase in standard of living. Instead of walking from place to place, with dogs pulling loads on travois, Indians with horses for personal transportation and for pack animals were much more mobile.[131]

However, once the Cheyenne adopted a full-time life of hunting and warfare, they needed a minimum of six horses per person, and ten per person was preferable.[132] From 1800 to 1830, when the plains enjoyed unusually good rainfall, Indian life was prosperous. The Indian population on the high plains skyrocketed from the late eighteenth century to 1850.[133] But the late 1840s and thereafter had less rain and several droughts.[134] In the summer, when grass was abundant, there was not a problem, but it was in the winter.[135] Winter survival on the open plains was impossible, so in the cold months the Cheyenne would break into small groups, and spend the winters in river valleys, cliff sides, and other areas with natural shelters and trees. At the end

---

[129] GALLAGHER at 104–05. Theft by Indian agents was a constant problem in the nineteenth century. The honest agents, like Boone and Beckwourth, were the minority. In 1865, major Edward Wynkoop was appointed Indian agent for the Cheyenne and Arapaho, who respected him for fair dealing. He had previously tried to persuade colonel Chivington not to perpetrate the Sand Creek Massacre. *See* PROPST at 100.

The enduring, fatal problem in white-Indian relations was racial generalizations on both sides:

> The hostility that was thus growing up between Indians and white men was racial. To the white man an Indian was an Indian, and the white man who had been robbed or threatened by an Indian felt himself justified in taking vengeance on the next Indian he saw, without regard to whether he had been injured by that man or by men of that tribe. In the same way if an Indian had been killed by a white man the members of his tribes were ready to revenge the injury on the next white man that came along. Thus it came about that persons innocent of any fault were constantly punished for the harm done by one of their race. The guilty never suffered. As a result of this feeling neither the Indians nor white men felt they could trust one of the opposite race, and each held the other always in suspicion.

GRINNELL at 100.

[130] *See, e.g.*, WEST at 282 (discussing Indian complaints in 1861 about failure to deliver the annuities promised in the Treaty of Fort Laramie).

[131] *See id.* at 49–52.

[132] Indian horses, often called "ponies," were smaller than the settlers' horses. Unlike the settler horses, the Indian ponies could survive on a diet solely of prairie grass. However, the hard demands of long-distance hunting, fast riding on a chase, and hauling villages from place to place was too much for any single pony on a continuous basis, so the ponies had to be rotated in service.

[133] WEST at 67–69.

[134] *Id.* at 89–90.

[135] *Id.* at 84.

of the winter, the Indian horses that had survived the winter would be scrawny and near starvation. In the spring, there would again be enough food for them, and they would be ready for hunting in the summer.[136]

By the 1850s, the once-abundant cottonwood trees in the winter areas were being consumed for firewood faster than they could regrow, while the grass there was eaten so low it could not regrow.[137] Even before the Americans started migrating, hunting pressure thinned the buffalo herds and made them ever more difficult to locate.[138] The problem was aggravated by the harvesting of buffalo robes for trade with the Americans.

Americans travelers made the problem even worse; river trails were denuded of trees, and grass was eaten up for a mile or more in both directions.[139] Heavy traffic along the trails frightened away the buffalo herds.[140] As of 1859, there were four U.S. Army forts on the high plains, but by 1865 there were fifteen—all of them located near critical rivers and all of them consuming the wood, grass, and other resources in the area on a permanent basis.[141]

Ironically, the 1840 Plains Indian peace agreement made things even worse. The Cheyenne-Arapahoe alliance agreed with the Comanche-Kiowa alliance to make Colorado a noncombat zone for trade and hunting.[142] This resulted in so much buffalo hunting that, by the 1850s, it was difficult to find buffalo within a hundred miles of the Rocky Mountains.[143] This led to a decline in the Indian–American trade in buffalo robes that had been the main economic tie between them.[144]

Kansas was not covered by the peace agreement. This was good for the buffalo population there, some of which had fled Colorado.[145] But the wars were taking a toll on the Indians.[146] The intertribal warfare was fierce. Participants included many tribes with no connection to Colorado, some of whom came from further east after having been forced out of their previous lands.[147] Of course the Cheyenne also continued to fight the Utes, whose main territory was the western Rocky Mountains.[148]

By 1855, there were only two adult Arapaho, Southern Cheyenne, and Comanche males for every three adult females.[149] On a per-capita basis, the inter-Indian wars were three or four times deadlier than the U.S. Civil War, the deadliest war, by far, in U.S. history.[150]

All of the Indian population was being devastated by the depletion of the food supply and by epidemics resulting from contact with Americans, who carried diseases originally from Europe or Africa, for which Indians had no immunity.[151] The Americans urged them to take up agriculture,

---

136 *See id.* at 84–87.

137 *See id.* at 229–30.

138 *See id.* at 193; *see also* AFTON ET AL. at xv (discussing Yellow Wolf's observation of the declining buffalo population in 1846).

139 WEST at 230, 233.

140 STILES at 271–72.

141 WEST at 275, 291 ("Indians were furious precisely because the army sat in places that could support the soldiers and nobody else.").

142 *Id.* at 77.

143 *Id.* at 192.

144 *See id.* at 260.

145 *See id.* at 192.

146 *Id.* at 78.

147 *See id.* at 255 (including Sac and Fox, Osage, Potawatomies).

148 *Id.* at 286. The Utes also lived in northwestern New Mexico, far northeastern Arizona, a little bit of southern Wyoming, and, of course, in eastern Utah. The Utah territory and state were named for them, and federal officials did not want Mormon name, "Deseret."

149 *Id.* at 256. Southern Cheyenne were those below the Platte River. JABLOW at 63. Most of the Cheyenne activity in this chapter involves the Southern Cheyenne. The division of the Cheyenne took place around 1830. *Id.* at 60–65.

150 WEST at 256.

151 *Id.* at 87–91.

but this was not a viable option. For Indian agriculture to succeed in Colorado, the settlers would have had to give the Indians extensive lands near the rivers, and these were precisely the lands that the settlers were taking for themselves.[152] Almost every major settler–Indian battle in Colorado took place near one of the environmentally crucial river areas.[153]

2. *The path to the Colorado War*

Some Indians, such as the Cheyenne chief Black Kettle or the Ute chief Ouray, recognized that overwhelming American numerical superiority made the settlers unstoppable in the long run. The only thing to do was to try to survive on the basis of whatever unequal terms the Americans would impose.

Yet many Indians wanted something better. As one historian writes:

> Armed resistance was a rational policy option . . . Their existence was based on war. They had won their lands in fierce aggression against other peoples . . . Signing treaties had only brought more pressure on the critical river valleys. It was natural to think that force—a familiar tool—might work where diplomacy has failed.[154]

Many of the fighters agreed with Black Kettle's assessment of the situation, that in the long run, no amount of military success against the Americans would permanently drive them out of the plains or stop their growing encroachments. Still, many Indians decided that it was better to die fighting than to submit.[155] "Live free or die" is the New Hampshire state motto.[156] It expresses a widely shared attitude of many peoples, certainly including many Plains Indians.

Raiding increased in 1863, apparently for obtaining arms. Additionally, "Many of the Indians in Colorado obtained firearms and ammunition from Mexican traders of New Mexico and from corrupt, mercenary Americans, and probably encouragement and material aid from Confederate officials."[157] Indians raids on freighting, combined with a drought in the summer of 1863, drove food and provision prices in the mountain towns "to famine prices, and it was but little better in Denver."[158]

Governor John Evans tried to arrange a September meeting with the Cheyenne, Arapaho, and Sioux to buy peace by supplying provisions, but no one came.[159] There was a meeting between Elbridge Gerry (an emissary from Evans) and Bull Bear, a Cheyenne.[160] When Gerry acknowledged that the settlers wanted Indians to live like them (that is, as farmers), Bull Bear replied, "Well, you can just go back to the Governor and tell him we are not reduced that low yet."[161] In November, governor Evans ordered a halt in firearms and ammunition sales to Indians;

---

[152] *Id.* at 260–62.
[153] *See id.* at 274 (map with the battle locations between Indians and settlers).
[154] STILES at 285.
[155] BERWANGER at 27.
[156] N.H. REV. STAT. § 3:8 (2017).
[157] COLTON at 150; *see also* 1 HALL at 324–26.
[158] 1 HALL at 306.
[159] COLTON at 151; LEONARD & NOEL at 17.
[160] PROPST at 50; *see* COLTON at 151. Gerry was a relative of the famous Founder of the same name (signer of the Declaration of Independence; U.S. vice-president under James Madison). He was married to an Indian woman, the sister of Chief Red Cloud. Augusta Hauck Block, *Lower Boulder and St. Vrain Valley Home Guards and Fort Junction*, 16 COLO. MAGAZINE 186, 188 (1939); *see also* PROPST at 63–64 (discussing Gerry's prior marriages).
[161] LEONARD & NOEL at 17. Bull Bear would continue fighting until 1874, only surrendering in Texas when he and his warriors were surrounded and ran out of ammunition. HALEY, *supra* note 82, at 193.

since the order was indiscriminate, even friendly Indians had a harder time obtaining food that winter.[162]

3. *The Colorado War begins*

The Colorado War began on April 12, 1864, with a clash between federal troops and Cheyenne Dog Soldiers who were accused of stealing mules.[163] The Dog Soldiers were the leading Cheyenne military society.[164] Large-scale attacks by the Cheyenne and Arapaho soon followed.[165] Meanwhile, the small number of federal troops guarding the South Platte route were moved down to Fort Lyon (the new name for Fort Wise), on the Arkansas River in southeastern Colorado, because of fears of imminent Confederate attack.[166] In May, much of Denver and Auraria were destroyed by a flood of the Cherry Creek, making settlers' survival all the more perilous.

For many young Indian men who were wondering whether to fight, an answer was soon provided by an incident in western Kansas. In 1863, Cheyenne Chief Starving Bear had been part of an Indian delegation that traveled to Washington and met with president Lincoln. After amicable discussion, Lincoln had given Starving Bear a peace medal. The next May, back in Kansas, Starving Bear's camp was approached by the U.S. Army. Wearing his peace medal, Starving Bear and a companion slowly rode out to parlay with the soldiers. The army opened fire and killed both of them.[167] Both sides claimed victory in the ensuing battle.

At a nearby camp was Starving Bear's brother Bull Bear, a leader of the Dog Soldiers. The death of his brother convinced Bull Bear that it was time for all-out war with the whites, and many young men agreed, joining the Dog Soldiers. "At least the Dog Soldiers were independent for the moment. And if death waited on everyone, there were better ways to find it than Starving Bear's."[168]

On June 11, 1864, the young Hungate family, who had a ranch near the future town of Elizabeth near Denver, was attacked, raped, murdered, and brutally mutilated, including the small children. A general panic in the Denver area ensued. In July, the stage stops along the South

---

[162] PROPST at 50–51.

[163] WEST at 287.

[164] The other Cheyenne warrior societies were the Kit Foxes, Crazy Dogs, Elk Scrapers, Red Shields, and Wolf Soldiers. STILES at 271.

The Dog Soldiers lived separately from other Cheyenne, favoring the Kansas area between the Republican and Smoky Hill Rivers; they developed a close friendship with the Sioux. BERWANGER at 27; WEST at 198. The Dog Soldiers were so named because during battle, their best fighters might tie themselves to a rope that attached to a stake in the ground. Immobile, the warrior provided a fixed spot to which other warriors could rally—to stand and fight—or die trying. *See* JOHN H. MONNETT, THE BATTLE OF BEECHER ISLAND AND THE INDIAN WAR OF 1867–1869, at 41 (1992). Lieutenant colonel George A. Custer wrote that they were "fine-looking braves of magnificent physique, and in appearance and demeanor more nearly conformed to the ideal warrior than those of any other tribe." GEORGE ARMSTRONG CUSTER, MY LIFE ON THE PLAINS OR, PERSONAL EXPERIENCES WITH INDIANS 125 (Univ. of Okla. Press 1962) (1874).

Although the Dog Soldiers were originally a group of warriors, they later became a band, traveling with their families. AFTON ET AL. at xvii. The Arapaho had a similar warrior society, the Dog Men, who also staked themselves to a fixed spot on the battlefield, from which they could not retreat unless released by another warrior. *See* VIRGINIA COLE TRENHOLM, THE ARAPAHOES: OUR PEOPLE 79 (1st ed. 1970).

[165] *See* COLTON at 151–52; *see also* MONAHAN at 147–65.

[166] LAMAR at 211.

[167] *See* 1 HALL at 309.

[168] WEST at 289–90.

Platte were hit hard.[169] On the South Platte Trail, "[f]or the next four years it would not be safe to travel in groups of less than fifty to one hundred."[170] The Santa Fe Trail was also attacked.[171]

On August 11, 1864, Territorial governor John Evans issued a proclamation: "All citizens of Colorado, whether organized or individually," were "empowered to go in pursuit of the hostiles . . . and kill and destroy them wherever found, and to capture and hold to their own private use and benefit all the property they could take."[172] Declaring martial law, the governor initiated recruiting for the Third Colorado, with an enlistment term of 100 days.[173] In Denver, the entire militia—every able-bodied male of at least sixteen years—was called into service; many were put to work building a chain of block houses on the city's perimeter.[174] Likewise in Boulder, the townspeople dug defensive trenches and constructed the adobe Fort Chambers near Boulder Creek.[175] Citizens also erected forts in Huntsville (today, Larkspur), Pueblo, and Colorado City (now, Colorado Springs).[176] In the St. Vrain area, the settlers built Fort Junction, organized the Lower Boulder and St. Vrain Valley Home Guard, and were given handguns and rifles by the federal government.[177] Pueblans temporarily safeguarded their women and children in a former saloon while the men constructed an adobe fort.[178]

Elbridge Gerry brought news that massive and coordinated Indian attacks were planned.[179] But when the Indians found out that their plan had been discovered, the attacks were called off.[180]

Mail service from the States was blocked by the Indians on August 15, and could not be reopened until September 29.[181] "The halting of supply trains caused prices to soar, and starvation threatened."[182] When the governors of Kansas and Colorado asked for federal troops, they were told by the federal commander of the Trans-Mississippi Theater, General Samuel R. Curtis, "We have none to spare, you must protect yourselves."[183]

As of August 1864, Indian raids on thoroughfares were in progress from Texas to British Columbia and from the Missouri River to the Rocky Mountains.[184]

Cheyenne chief Black Kettle, who blamed the conflicts on a minority of bad men on both sides, traveled to Denver to attempt to arrange a truce in September 1864, but the Camp Weld Council accomplished nothing.[185] As Black Kettle admitted to governor Evans, the chiefs who

---

[169] COLTON at 153. One author suggests that the Hungate perpetrators were four Arapaho, one of whom was angry at having been required to return some stolen animals. TRENHOLM, *supra* note 164, at 180.

[170] PROPST at 60.

[171] COLTON at 145.

[172] "The conflict is upon us," said Evans, "and all good citizens are called upon to do their duty for the defense of their homes and their families." The Governor also emphasized the importance of *not* molesting friendly Indians. 1 HALL at 326–27; TRENHOLM, *supra* note 164, at 183; COLTON at 154.

[173] SMITH at 213. At least initially, their arms were "old guns that had been bought in Europe, and men were short of even such basics as blankets and food." PROPST at 67.

[174] Wharton at 54.

[175] MONAHAN at 171.

[176] GALLAGHER at 102–03.

[177] Block, *supra* note 160, at 188.

[178] *See* 3 HALL at 453.

[179] Block, *supra* note 160, at 188.

[180] *Id.* HAFEN at 169. Gerry was therefore dubbed "the Paul Revere of Colorado." PROPST at 64.

[181] During this period, outbound mail from Denver was sent to San Francisco by stagecoach, thence by ship to Panama, and from Panama to New York City, for distribution to the States. TRENHOLM, *supra* note 164, at 184–186.

[182] COLTON at 156.

[183] 1 HALL at 328. Likewise, Secretary of War Edwin M. Stanton told Colorado, "in effect, 'Fight it out among ourselves; we are too busy with more weighty affairs to give you any attention or assistance.'" *Id.* at 330–31.

[184] *Id.*

[185] 1 HALL at 339–40; *see also* MONAHAN at 175–76.

wanted peace could not control the many warriors who wanted to fight.[186] Evans told them to go to Fort Lyon, which they did; there, they received mixed signals about whether they were under U.S. Army protection.[187] According to some settlers, the Cheyenne were playing a double game; while some of them fought, others feigned friendliness with the whites, the better to procure more arms and ammunition.[188]

Raids on the South Platte Trail and the Santa Fe Trail continued. The telegraph line along the South Platte Trail—Colorado's means of communication to the outside—was sliced repeatedly.[189] "Cut off, the Colorado mining camps were almost starving."[190] Colorado was not the only territory in deep trouble. "During 1864, virtually every wagon train proceeding down the Canadian River to New Mexico was attacked."[191]

4. *The Sand Creek massacre*

The Plains Indians custom was not to war during the winter because their ponies lacked sufficient grass. Some warriors took winter quarters at the Sand Creek camp, where Black Kettle had earlier led a group. On November 29, 1864, Sand Creek was attacked by the Third Colorado Volunteers. Most officers made no effort to discriminate between friendly Indians and hostiles. The commander, colonel John Chivington, ordered the deliberate killing of women and children, which was contrary to U.S. Army practice and law. America vs. Indian warfare and inter-Indian warfare had often been characterized by the killing of noncombatants, but even in this context, the scale of slaughter at Sand Creek was atrocious.[192] Among the victims was Left Hand, an Arapaho chief who had advocated peace with the whites.[193]

There is no doubt that the Sand Creek encampment included warriors who were taking a break.[194] White scalps—including those of children and the elderly—were discovered in some teepees and brought back to Denver.[195]

Militarily speaking, the Sand Creek Massacre was close to useless. Shortly before the massacre, Fort Lyon commander Edward Wynkoop, who had a very positive relationship with the Indians, had been replaced by the much harsher major Scott Anthony.[196] Anthony had no

---

186 MONAHAN at 178–79; *see also* MONNETT, *supra* note 164, at 42 (Cheyenne chiefs had no authority to prevent warriors from fighting).

The problem was endemic during the Plains Wars. White negotiators suffered from the "fallacious but pervasive notion . . . that the signatory chiefs held strict command authority over the entirety of their tribes." Likewise, "many times the federal government exercised little control over its citizens or military forces on the distant prairie." STAN HOIG, WHITE MAN'S PAPER TRAIL: GRAND COUNCILS AND TREATY-MAKING ON THE CENTRAL PLAINS 12 (2008).

187 1 HALL at 341–44.

188 *See id.* at 327–30; WOOTTON at 265.

189 The telegraph line to Denver had been opened in October 1863. 1 HALL at 303. Starting in 1861, Denver had begun to receive overland mail deliveries, via the Pony Express. MONAHAN at 165.

190 FEHRENBACH at 460. Flour went from nine dollars per hundred pounds to forty-five. PROPST at 62. "Sugar, tea, and many other items were simply unobtainable." *Id.*

191 FEHRENBACH at 463.

192 "It will not do, as some have done, to fall back to the atrocities of the Indians upon our people as a justification." By such reasoning, president Lincoln would have been justified in mistreating Confederate prisoners of war, as the Confederates had done to Union prisoners at the notorious Andersonville camp. 1 HALL at 351.

193 Left Hand was wounded at Sand Creek, and later died from the wounds. MARGARET COEL, CHIEF LEFT HAND: SOUTHERN ARAPAHO 292–93 (1st ed. 1981).

194 WEST at 296, 299.

195 1 HALL at 355; WOOTTON at 266; HAFEN at 171.

196 *See* WEST at 297–99.

objection to Sand Creek per se, but he thought that Chivington should have followed up by heading into western Kansas to fight the Dog Soldiers. In the winter, the Indians' grass-fed ponies were malnourished at best, and so the Indian warriors were at their weakest. Meanwhile, Fort Lyon had been provided with many large U.S. horses. These horses needed grain fodder, and the army had brought in plentiful supplies, precisely so that American cavalry could advance deep into the plains.

Instead of attempting a decisive stroke against the Dog Soldiers, Chivington led his Third Cavalry on a search for Little Raven's peaceful band of Arapaho.[197] Not finding them after a few days, he took the Colorado Third back to Denver, and proclaimed that he had won a great victory at Sand Creek. Immediately, several other officers of the Third Cavalry denounced the massacre. A U.S. Army investigation and congressional hearings soon followed. Captain Silas Soule, one of the officers who testified against Chivington, was assassinated on a dark street in Denver, and the perpetrator escaped.[198]

Sand Creek was the most counterproductive act in the history of the Colorado territorial government. The perpetrators had ignored warnings about radicalizing and uniting the Indians. Those warnings immediately came true. Some Cheyenne, led by Black Kettle, headed south of the Arkansas River, to live with some Kiowa and Comanche, and get away from the war.[199] But many others began planning a counterstrike. Messengers bearing war pipes were sent to the Sioux. At Solomon Fork, Kansas, "the Sioux smoked the war pipe."[200]

The old mountain man Jim Beckwourth visited the Indians to urge them to call off the war, because the whites were as "numerous as leaves on the trees." He later testified to Congress:

> "We know it," was the general response of the council. But what do we want to live for? The white man has taken our country, killed all our game; was not satisfied with that, but killed our wives and children. Now no peace. We want to go and meet our families in the spirit land . . . We have raised the battle-axe until death.[201]

The hundred-day enlistments of the Colorado Volunteers from the past September expired in late December 1864.[202] The federal army, namely the Eleventh Kansas Volunteer Cavalry, was all that was left.[203]

5. The Indian counter-offensive of 1865

Just days after Sand Creek, raids began along the Platte.[204] They massively escalated starting January 6, 1865. At Bulen's Ranch, a stagecoach station near Julesburg, a war party of at least

---

[197] *Id.* at 306–07.
[198] TURNER, *supra* note 6, at 92–95.
[199] MONAHAN at 199; PROPST at 74.
[200] MONAHAN at 198. "The tribes were united and committed as they had never been before, and it would not be long before the frontiersmen of the Platte would feel their wrath." PROPST at 71.
[201] WILSON, *supra* note 128, at 179–80 (quoting S. EXEC. DOC. NO. 39-26, at 68–74).

The mixed-race son of a Virginia white man and a slave, Beckwourth was the most famous non-Indian person of color in early Colorado. He "was an expert shot and could handle dagger, lance, and bow." *Id.* at 5. As a fur trader, he lived with the Crow Indians for eight years, and his valor in battle made him one of their chiefs. Beckwourth served as a guide for the Third Colorado on the expedition that led to the Sand Creek Massacre. He later testified under oath that he had done so only because colonel Chivington had threatened to hang him if he refused. *Id.* at 175.
[202] *See* MONAHAN at 200.
[203] *See id.*
[204] *See* WEST at 307.

500 Indians attacked a stage coach, and sacked the station.[205] After the station had been restocked, they attacked it again on February 2, and this time burned it to the ground.[206] In January through February, large and coordinated war parties of Cheyenne, Arapaho, and Sioux ravaged the South Platte Trail. Most surviving settlers in the area fled, and almost every building along the trail was burned to the ground. Two hundred miles of settlements were wiped out.[207]

While governor John Evans was in Washington, acting governor S.H. Elbert telegraphed him to urge him to send 5,000 federal troops, or else the settlers would have to leave Colorado.[208]

With the supply trains halted, "the cost of several food items" soared "to almost starvation prices."[209] A huge convoy of 105 wagons and 300 men was able to leave Denver on January 14.[210] But a concentrated force like this could not protect all the supply stations.[211]

In the wake of Sand Creek, Coloradans had been reluctant to volunteer for the militia.[212] So the federal army commander, colonel Thomas Moonlight, declared martial law on February 6. One consequence was many new volunteers for territorial militia, some of whom did not want to be drafted by the U.S. army.[213] Some were teenage boys.[214] Martial law was lifted on February 20.[215] The militia defended the South Platte Trail from February through April, and well-guarded commerce resumed.[216]

Meanwhile, the Indian warriors headed north to fight the Crow.[217] They returned for another series of raids in April 1865. But this time, they encountered larger bodies of federal troops. Back in the States, the Civil War was ending. Some Confederate prisoners were given their freedom in exchange for Western service in the U.S. army. There were enough of these "galvanized rebs" to deter major attacks; there were a few raids in the summer, although the telegraph line was cut most of the time.[218]

The U.S. Army had also learned the importance of Pawnee scouts, who were happy to help fight the Sioux and Cheyenne, always their mortal enemies.[219] In August, an entrepreneur opened up the Smoky Hill Trail from Denver east through central Kansas for reliable travel and

---

[205] *See* MONAHAN at 201–05.

[206] AFTON ET AL. at 234.

[207] *See* MONAHAN at 208–22. The notable exception was the Godfrey Ranch. It has been built like a fortress and had loopholes in the walls through which the defenders could shoot rifles. It also had a well on the inside, so that flaming arrows from the Indians could be extinguished. GALLAGHER at 113–14.

[208] COLTON at 159 (telegram of Jan. 7, 1865).

[209] *Id. See also* Wharton at 56 ("Supplies and provisions raised to famine prices, and the poor of Denver were reduced to such a strait, that an idea of a descent upon the provision stores of the city was seriously entertained.").

[210] COLTON at 160; *see also* GALLAGHER at 112 ("With every man armed and seventy-five soldiers guarding them, the big train slowly crawled east").

[211] COLTON at 160.

[212] 1 HALL at 359–60.

[213] MONAHAN at 225. The volunteers "were poorly supplied with arms, ammunition and clothing, which articles, many were required to supply themselves with, in addition to the horses they rode." Wharton at 56.

[214] MONAHAN at 227.

[215] COLTON at 160.

[216] *See* MONAHAN at 225–28.

[217] AFTON ET AL. at 246. They were joined in the anti-Crow campaign by Arapaho and Lakota Sioux. *Id.*

[218] MONAHAN at 228, 232–36.

[219] *See* GEORGE E. HYDE, THE PAWNEE INDIANS 269 (Univ. of Okla. Press 2d. ed. 1974) (1951); PROPST at 95. The first Pawnee scouts were recruited in 1864. They initially used muzzleloading Springfield rifled muskets and were issued Spencer repeating carbines in 1866. AFTON ET AL. at 258. Some of the displaced tribes from the east, such as the Delaware, also served as army scouts. *Id.* at 104. Other Indians who helped the Army fight the Cheyenne were the Osage and Kansas (Kaw). *Id.* at 55.

commerce by digging wells for station stops.[220] But the new Butterfield Overland Despatch route cut through the heart of the remaining buffalo country and inflamed the Indians even further.[221] Indian activity drove freight prices so high "that it came near to bankrupting the country."[222]

Governor Evans was ordered to resign in July 1865 by secretary of state William Seward, due to Evans's responsibility for the Sand Creek Massacre.[223]

Some Cheyenne and Arapaho signed the Treaty of Upper Arkansas on October 14, 1865. It included a U.S. government condemnation of the "gross and wanton outrages" at Sand Creek and also provided reparations.[224] Three days later, the Apache joined the treaty.[225] The next day, the Comanche and Kiowa signed a similar treaty.[226]

6. Fighting in 1866 and thereafter

While some Cheyenne were accepting the U.S. offer for new, smaller reservations, others were conducting more attacks along the South Platte. Because of imminent danger, federal soldiers trained the armed citizens of Julesburg.[227] The Colorado War is usually said to have ended in 1865; and 1866 was relatively quiet.[228] Still, attacks continued along the South Platte Trail, mostly the part east of Julesburg, in Nebraska.[229] In the 1866 Fetterman Fight, near Fort Kearney, Nebraska, all eighty-one U.S. soldiers present were killed.[230]

Starting in May 1867 and continuing all summer, Cheyenne, Arapahoe, Kiowa, and Sioux "struck hard both along the Smoky Hill route and the Platte River road."[231] An October 19, 1867, treaty at Medicine Lodge, Kansas, provided for the Kiowa and Southern Cheyenne to give up their 1865 treaty right to a reservation in Kansas, to move to reservations in Indian Territory

---

220 PROPST at 96.

The Smoky Hill Trail was not new, but it had been hard to use because of its long western stretch with no water and difficult navigation.

221 WEST at 308–09.

222 1 HALL at 305.

223 TURNER, *supra* note 6, at 36 (quoting letter from William H. Seward, U.S. sec'y of state, to John Evans, governor of the territory of Colo. (July 18, 1865)).

224 Treaty with the Cheyenne and Arapaho, 1865, art. 6, Oct. 17, 1865, 14 Stat. 703, *reprinted in* 2 INDIAN AFFAIRS at 889–90 ("The United States being desirous to express its condemnation of, and, as far as may be, repudiate the gross and wanton outrages perpetrated against certain bands of Cheyenne and Arrapahoe Indians, on the twenty-ninth day of November, A.D. 1864, at Sand Creek, in the Colorado Territory."). The treaty made various land grants, free of taxation, to named chiefs, widows, or persons who had lost a parent. The October 14, 1865, treaty is known as the Treaty of the Little Arkansas. MONAHAN at 239. Signed in Kansas, it provided for reservations. Treaty with the Cheyenne and Arapaho, arts. 2–3. However, the Kansas state government did not allow a reservation. PRUCHA at 271.

225 Treaty with the Apache, Cheyenne, and Arapaho, 1865, Oct. 17, 1865, 14 Stat. 713, *reprinted in* 2 INDIAN AFFAIRS at 891–92.

226 *See* Treaty with the Comanche and Kiowa, 1865, Oct. 18, 1865, 14 Stat. 717, *reprinted in* 2 INDIAN AFFAIRS at 892–95. The terms included a reservation in Texas, but the federal government owned no Texas land, and the state of Texas declined to accept a reservation. PRUCHA at 271.

227 *See* MONAHAN at 239.

228 *See* AFTON ET AL. at 286–321 (listing all known Cheyenne military actions from April 1864 to July 1869).

229 *See* MONAHAN at 239–40.

230 *Introduction* to EYEWITNESS TO THE FETTERMAN FIGHT: INDIAN VIEWS 3, 3–4 (John H. Monnet ed., 2017).

231 MONNETT, *supra* note 164, at 75.

(today, the State of Oklahoma), and forbade them to hunt north of the Arkansas River.[232] But many Cheyenne did not accept another round of surrendering their homeland. There were more battles in Colorado with the Cheyenne (occasionally with Sioux allies) in 1867–1869.[233] "Hundreds of whites were killed in the post-Civil War years north of the Arkansas River."[234]

While the Cheyenne Dog Soldiers were warring against the settlers in the 1860s, they did not neglect enemy tribes. They also fought the Pawnee, Kaw (Kansas), Osage, Shawnee, Delaware, Omaha, Ponca, Crow, Shoshoni, and (most relevantly for Colorado) the Ute.[235]

"[T]he years of 1868 and 1869 were, statistically, the worst two years, from the white man's point of view, experienced on the plains."[236] When Colorado hay was being harvested in 1868, Indians "began to be very active and sniped off white people here and there. This caused all homesteaders to keep their guns primed . . . ."[237]

Things looked gloomy. The new transcontinental railroad was going to go through Cheyenne, Wyoming, not Denver (a sensible decision, given the comparative difficulty of the mountain passes to the west of those cities). Grasshopper plagues were wiping out the crops. The easiest gold to find was "placer" gold (derived from the Spanish word of pleasure), such as loose gold in a creek that could be found by panning, but the placer gold had mostly been played out. The more plentiful form of gold was in "refractory ore"—that is, gold mingled in other rocks. At the time, smelting was too primitive to profitably extract gold from refractory ore. Congress had approved a statehood bill for Colorado, but president Andrew Johnson had vetoed it. For one thing, Colorado did not really have the minimum population required by statute. And president Johnson was not interested in adding a pair of Colorado Republicans to the U.S. Senate to vote against him. As the economy slid downward, so did immigration. "These years in the sixties were

---

[232] As a result, the buffalo tended to stay north of the Arkansas, so Indians who abided by the treaty were unable to hunt. *Id.* At 65. The American negotiators orally promised that guns and ammunition for winter hunting would be provided, but only a few defective revolvers were supplied. *See* HOIG, *supra* note 186, at 11.

[233] *See* PROPST at 102–25. Indian battles with settlers in Colorado include Fisher's Creek (Trinidad, June 4, 1854, Jicarilla Apache), Pueblo (Dec. 25, 1854, Ute and Apache), Saguache Creek (March 19, 1855, Ute and Apache), Chicosa Arroyo (Trinidad, April 25, 1855, Ute and Apache), Poncha Pass (April 29, 1855, Ute), Blackwater Spring (Eads, July 11, 1860, Kiowa and Comanche), Fremont's Orchard (Orchard, April 12, 1864, Cheyenne), Eayre's Fight (Flagler, Apr. 15, 1864, Cheyenne), Cedar Canyon (Sterling, May 3, 1864, Cheyenne), Hungate Massacre (Parker, June 11, 1864, Arapaho), Sand Creek (August 11, 1864, Arapaho), White Butte Creek (Sterling, October 10, 1864, Cheyenne), Sand Creek Massacre (Chivington, November 29, 1864, Cheyenne and Arapaho), Julesburg (January 7, 1865, Cheyenne and Lakota Sioux), Valley Station (Sterling, January 7, 1865, Cheyenne and Lakota Sioux), American Ranch (Merino, January 14, 1865, Cheyenne and Lakota Sioux), Godfrey's Ranch (Merino, January 14–15, 1865, Cheyenne and Lakota Sioux), Julesburg (February 2, 1865, Cheyenne and Lakota Sioux), Spring Canyon (Campo, June 14, 1865, Kiowa and Comanche), Big Timber (Arapahoe, June 11, 1867, likely involving Cheyenne), Rule Creek (Toonerville, September 10, 1868, Cheyenne), Big Sandy Creek (Aroya, September 15, 1868, Cheyenne), Beecher's Island (Wray, Sept. 17–21, 1868, Cheyenne), Dog Creek (Laird, July 8, 1869, Cheyenne), Summit Springs (Sterling, July 11, 1869, Cheyenne and Lakota Sioux), Milk Creek (Meeker, September 29–October 5, 1879, Ute), and the Meeker Massacre (September 29, 1879, Ute). *See* GREGORY F. MICHNO, ENCYCLOPEDIA OF INDIAN WARS: WESTERN BATTLES AND SKIRMISHES 1850–1890, at 26–27, 30, 32–33, 77–78, 134–37, 141–42, 149–50, 154, 157–65, 173–74, 197, 220, 222–24, 234–36, 327–28 (2003). This listing does not include inter-tribal battles, and it does not purport to be a complete list of settler-Indian battles. *Id.* at 1.

[234] FEHRENBACH at 483.

[235] Indeed, fighting Indians was preferable to the Cheyenne, for Indians readily engaged in hand-to-hand combat, which offered the greatest opportunity for individual valor, whereas settlers preferred to fight behind fortified positions, or with long-range weapons. AFTON ET AL. at 200.

[236] TRENHOLM, *supra* note 164, at 225.

[237] Block, *supra* note 160, at 189.

probably the gloomiest ones in Colorado history, but 'the darkest hours are just before the dawn,' and so it proved to be for Colorado."[238]

In August 1868, Arapaho and Cheyenne raided up and down the Arkansas River and also in Larimer County. U.S. House speaker and Republican vice-presidential nominee Schuyler Colfax was touring the Colorado mountains on the day that the attacks began. A friendly group of Utes escorted Colfax and his party back to Colorado Springs safely.[239] In Colorado Springs, "the gunsmiths' shops were jam-full. The Springs was arming itself in haste."[240] Arapaho roamed through the town, but having "looked over the town's military preparedness," they "promptly announced that they were after their traditional enemies, the Utes."[241] They helped themselves to 150 horses when they left.[242] Near Bijou Basin in El Paso County, fifty white scouts were surrounded by 500 Indians. After "Texas Bill" rode through Indian lines to escape and summon aid, the Indians departed, shortly before the arrival of a settler force from Denver.[243]

After seventy-nine Colorado settlers had been killed, acting Colorado governor Frank Hall asked U.S. general Philip Sheridan for assistance.[244] Militias were embodied throughout Colorado. Sheridan raised a special cavalry force of fifty Kansans, designating them as U.S. Army scouts. [245] In mid-September the scouts were ambushed at Beecher Island, a sandbar on the Arikaree River (near the modern town of Wray, Colorado), and nearly destroyed.[246] Although difficult, the situation in Colorado was considerably milder than in western Kansas.[247]

During September, the Indians continued raids against isolated settlers in El Paso County, killing about twenty persons, taking scalps and driving off 500 head of cattle. The Indians had long range rifles, giving them an advantage over many settlers.[248]

To the southeast, U.S. lieutenant colonel George Armstrong Custer attacked the Cheyenne at Washita in Indian Territory in November 1868 and killed peaceful Indians, including Black Kettle, as well as warriors who were encamped with them.[249] But many Cheyenne kept fighting.[250]

---

[238] HAFEN at 180.
[239] *See* 1 HALL at 457.
[240] R.B. TOWNSHEND, A TENDERFOOT IN COLORADO 217 (Stephen J. Leonard & Thomas J. Noel eds., Univ. Press of Colo. 2008) (1923).
[241] MONNETT, *supra* note 164, at 70.
[242] BERWANGER at 31.
[243] 3 HALL at 344.
[244] *See* 1 HALL at 457–58.
[245] *See* MONNETT, *supra* note 164, at 70–72 (noting that Colorado lacked arms to supply the militias).
[246] *Id.* at 1. The sandbar, which has since been washed away, was named "Beecher Island" in honor of the scouts' second-in-command, who was killed in the battle. STILES at 2, 317–18. He was a nephew of the abolitionist Massachusetts preacher Henry Ward Beecher. *Id.* At 81. The federal army also sent a "train of guns and ammunition" to Denver, "for use in arming the citizens." It arrived on October 29, 1868. 1 HALL at 462.
[247] *See* MONNETT, *supra* note 164, at 70.
[248] 3 HALL at 344–45 ("The settlers were not provided with long range rifles as were the Indians.").
[249] The battle was fought on November 27. Custer's forces killed all adult males. Unlike at Sand Creek, the women and children were taken prisoner, rather than killed. STILES at 317–18. During the battle, the Cheyenne executed their two white prisoners: a woman and her child. MONNETT, *supra* note 164, at 61.
[250] STILES at 321 (the army estimated 1,400 Cheyenne at large after Washita). Black Kettle had been "instrumental in saving countless lives," both Indian and other. THOM HATCH, BLACK KETTLE: THE CHEYENNE CHIEF WHO SOUGHT PEACE BUT FOUND WAR Kindle pos. 3362, Conclusion (2004). He is honored as the namesake of the Black Kettle National Grasslands, near Washita.

Guided by Pawnee scouts and also by a young tracker named William Cody, the U.S. Fifth Cavalry defeated Cheyenne led by Tall Bull at Summit Springs, Colorado, in July 1869.[251] The commander of the military Department of the Missouri wrote in his 1869 annual report that "It is believed . . . that there are no hostile Indians on the Plains of Kansas or Colorado."[252] Yet in 1870, as the Kansas Pacific Railroad was laying tracks toward Denver, the construction crews were attacked at ten locations in far east-central Colorado, near the present town of Kit Carson. Eleven workers were killed, nineteen wounded, and 400 head of livestock were taken. [253] U.S. General John Pope attempted, with limited success, to protect the construction crews, and the line was eventually completed.[254]

Douglas County, Colorado, originally extended to the Kansas border.[255] During the pre-statehood days, the pioneers of Douglas County had been the most "frequently exposed to Indian depredations, horse and cattle thieves." "Widely scattered, they became an easy prey to both. They built forts and stockades to protect women and children, "and with trusty rifles themselves drove their enemies across the border. As for the white desperadoes, they were pursued and shot, or if captured, hanged to the nearest tree." [256]

The removal of Colorado's Plains Indians from Colorado did not mean the end of their warfare in Colorado. The U.S. Army did nothing to stop white hunters who, starting in 1873, were illegally shooting the buffalo to extermination in Indian lands in Oklahoma and Texas.[257] Combined with the typical federal government failure to supply adequate provisions, the destruction of the buffalo brought the Indians near starvation.[258] So in 1874, the Cheyenne, Comanche, Arapaho, and Kiowa rose up in the Red River War. The main theaters of battle were Texas, Oklahoma, and Kansas, but Cheyenne warriors also attacked southeastern Colorado.[259] Among the notable incidents of the war were the Short Massacre (in Kansas) and the Hennessey Massacre (in Oklahoma).[260] The uprising was so serious that U.S. Army central command was moved from Washington to St. Louis.[261]

On June 25–26, 1876, a few days before Coloradans would vote on ratification of their proposed new constitution, lieutenant col. Custer attacked a camp of Sioux and Northern Cheyenne at Little Big Horn, in the future state of Montana. The federal forces were wiped out in

---

[251] JAMES T. KING, WAR EAGLE: A LIFE OF GENERAL EUGENE A. CARR 101–13 (1963); GALLAGHER at 120–24; STILES at 323. When Cody later became a professional entertainer in Buffalo Bill's Wild West show, the Battle of Summit Springs was the climax of the spectacle. MONNETT, *supra* note 164, at 192. The Dog Soldiers may have been defeated, but they were not eliminated as a military force. For example, they were active in the Red River War of 1874–75. HALEY, *supra* note 81, at 96.

[252] KING, *supra* note 250, at 118 (second alteration in original) (citing maj. Gen. J.M. Schofield to brevet maj. Gen. G.L. Hartsuff (Oct. 23, 1869), National Archives Records Service, Record Group 94, Adjutant General's Office).

[253] BRENNEMAN at 53–54.

[254] 1 HALL at 490–91.

[255] It thus included most of modern Elbert County" , the northern part of Lincoln County, and all of Kit Carson County. NOEL at 68–73.

[256] 3 HALL at 337.

[257] HALEY, *supra* note 26, at 24–31.

[258] Among their other grievances was that the federal government was not supplying them with enough firearms and ammunition. *Id.* At 10–11.

[259] *See id.* At 78, 95. In response, Las Animas County summoned its posse comitatus. Arapaho participation in the war was small-scale, compared to the activities of the other tribes. TRENHOLM, *supra* note 164, at 248–49.

[260] HALEY, *supra* note 81, at xx–xxi, 97–98, 139–46. One of the perpetrators of the Short Massacre (a/k/a Lone Tree Massacre) was Buffalo Calf Woman, whose family had been murdered at Sand Creek. *Id.* At 139.

[261] *See id.* At 183.

one of the worst defeats in U.S. military history.[262] Then in 1878, Dull Knife and Little Wolf led Cheyenne who left the Oklahoma reservations and raided as far north as Nebraska, although not in Colorado.[263]

By the time that Coloradans were drafting and voting on their proposed constitution, including its right to arms, the Plains Indian wars had shown that firearms can be used for mass killing. Sand Creek was the most notorious example, and there were many other examples, including those perpetrated by Indians. It might have been understandable for the Colorado Constitution to omit a right to arms, or to limit the types of firearms that might be possessed, or to exclude Indians, who at the time were not citizens, yet Coloradans adopted a different approach. When the right to arms section was being debated by the Colorado Convention, the draft (copied from Missouri) had guaranteed the right of every "citizen." Colorado expanded to the guarantee to encompass every "person." The wording was the basis for the Colorado supreme court in 1936 holding unconstitutional a state statute banning resident aliens from possessing long guns. *People v. Nakamura,* 62 P.2d 246 (Colo. 1936). Chapter 4 (Bill of Rights, art. II, § 13).

D. The Utes

During the 1860s, the Utes were mostly at peace with the Colorado settlers.[264] Instances of Utes killing or harassing them were hardly unknown, but there was no general warfare. The Utes were, however, at war with the Cheyenne, Sioux, and Arapaho in the 1860s and 1870s.[265] Indeed, after 1873 victories against the Arapaho, and in 1874 against the Cheyenne and Sioux, the returning Ute warriors celebrated with scalp dances in Denver.[266]

In the 1863 Treaty of Conejos, a thousand Utes led by chief Ouray agreed to leave the lower San Luis Valley and move to the Uncompahgre region, in exchange for annuities.[267] The standard Indian treaties of the era promised annual deliveries of supplies to the signing tribe and also promised certain tradesmen to live with the tribe. Usually this included a blacksmith, who at the

---

[262] In the Indian Wars, Custer's loss of 260 troops was eclipsed only by St. Clair's Defeat, in 1791 in western Ohio, with the loss of 600 soldiers—at the time, two-thirds of the U.S. Army.

[263] *See generally* STAN HOIG, PERILOUS PURSUIT: THE U.S. CAVALRY AND THE NORTHERN CHEYENNES (2002). The 1878 raids were by Northern Cheyenne who hated living on the reservation on Oklahoma. The raids helped lead to the establishment of a separate Northern Cheyenne reservation in Montana in 1884. THE GALE ENCYCLOPEDIA OF NATIVE AMERICAN TRIBES 222 (1998).

In modern times, Colorado's most famous Cheyenne is former U.S. Senator Ben Nighthorse Campbell. *See generally* HERMAN J. VIOLA, BEN NIGHTHORSE CAMPBELL: AN AMERICAN WARRIOR (1993).

[264] Some Utes had been in a usually friendly treaty relationship with the United States since the late 1840s, following defeats at the hands of federal soldiers led by Kit Carson. LAMAR at 208–09; Treaty with the Utah, 1849, Dec. 30, 1849, 9 Stat. 984; 2 INDIAN AFFAIRS at 585–87. As was typical of treaties at this time and in the subsequent two decades, the Indians agreed to stop being nomads, and to settle down; "to cease the roving and rambling habits which have hitherto marked them as a people." *Id.* at 586. The provision was completely ignored, and the U.S. made virtually no effort to enforce it. It was not until the 1870s that the U.S. government began a serious effort to confine the Utes to reservation land.

[265] SIMMONS at 120–21 (1868 war with Cheyenne and Arapaho); *id.* at 139 (1870 war with Sioux in the Upper Arkansas Valley).

[266] *Id.* at 141.

[267] Treaty with the Utah–Tabeguache Band, 1863, Oct. 7, 1863, 13 Stat. 673; 2 INDIAN AFFAIRS at 856–59; MONAHAN at 132 (number of Utes); COLTON at 151; SIMMONS at 117. As was common in the nineteenth century, the Ute annuity was not fully and regularly delivered. GALLAGHER at 120.

time often had some gunsmithing skills.[268] The Ute treaty specifically provided that the blacksmith must repair guns.[269] This was similar to an 1857 treaty with the Pawnee.[270]

Tensions increased in 1864–65. The rations promised by the treaty did not come, and game was scarce in the winter. Some Utes went to southern Colorado homes and intimidated settlers into giving them food.[271]

Then in April 1865, the Black Hawk War commenced in the Utah Territory, pitting the Utes against Mormon settlers. The most intense part of the war ended in 1867 but fighting continued until 1872.[272] The Black Hawk War made the Utes of southwestern Colorado much more hostile to settlers, and the area was a fertile recruiting ground for Utes to join the Black Hawk War. Southwestern Colorado was a transit zone for the enormous quantities of livestock that the Utes captured during the war, to be sold in Santa Fe.[273] One side effect of the war was greatly increased Ute raids of Colorado livestock.[274]

The Utes were also unhappy with an 1865 proclamation by president Johnson shortly after the end of the Civil War that outlawed Indian slavery and the Indian slave trade. This was a serious economic blow to the Utes, who had long been selling captives from other tribes as slaves. Until the ratification of the Thirteenth Amendment in December 1865, slavery was legal in the New Mexico Territory, and the Ute's slave trade continued in the San Luis Valley after 1861,

---

[268] STANLEY VESTAL, JIM BRIDGER: MOUNTAIN MAN 152 (1946) (describing the mountain man's blacksmithing skills).

[269] 2 INDIAN AFFAIRS at 858 ("The Government also agrees to establish and maintain a blacksmith-shop, and employ a competent blacksmith, for the purpose of repairing the guns and agricultural implements which may be used by said band of Indians."). The Ute in turn agreed not to furnish arms to any tribe "not in amity with the United States." *Id.* at 857.

[270] Treaty with the Pawnee, 1857, art. 4, Sept. 24, 1857, 11 Stat. 729; 2 INDIAN AFFAIRS at 765 ("two complete sets of blacksmith, gunsmith, and tinsmith tools . . . two blacksmiths, one of whom shall be a gunsmith and tinsmith; but the Pawnees agree to furnish one or two young men of their tribe to work constantly in each shop as strikers or apprentices, who shall be paid a fair compensation"). For a list of gunsmiths employed by the War Department in 1832 to aid friendly Indians, see CARL P. RUSSELL, FIREARMS, TRAPS AND TOOLS OF THE MOUNTAIN MEN 365–66 (2011).

[271] SIMMONS at 120–21; PETERSON, *supra* note 84, at 211 (1863 Conejos Treaty mostly ignored by Americans). This happened again in the winter of 1866–67. SIMMONS at 125.

[272] PETERSON, *supra* note 84, at 121–22, 340–42, 368–71. As the Utes well knew, the Mormons were fearful of calling for federal military assistance, because once the troops had dispatched the Indians, they might crack down on the Mormon theocracy, and impose federal control. To prevent federal intervention, deceptive Mormon reports to Washington downplayed the intensity of the Black Hawk War. The federal government did not appear to mind leaving the Mormons to fight alone. *Id.* at 3–5. The Mormon militia that was raised for the war was known as the Nauvoo Legion. *Id.* at 13–14. Finally, in 1872, the federal army did intervene. The army not only suppressed the Indians, it outlawed the Nauvoo Legion. *Id.* at 374.

Previously, Indian relations with Mormons had been much better than with any other group of settlers, partly because of Mormon scripture that Indians (the Lamanites) were descendants of a lost tribe of Israel, and would eventually become Latter-day Saints. *Id.* at 5–7, 22–23.

Black Hawk, a Ute, assembled a large pan-Indian coalition for the war. The main theater of operations was Sanpete and Sevier Counties, in central and eastern Utah, where Utes were angry at their treatment by Mormon settlers; the Black Hawk warriors did not consider themselves to be at war with the Mormons as a whole. *Id.* at 10–12.

[273] *Id.* at 184–87, 198–200. Some of the livestock captured in Utah were brought to southern Colorado. SIMMONS at 128. Arms and ammunition sales by Coloradans were an important supply for the Black Hawk warriors. So were Mexican traders in the San Luis Valley. All such trade was contrary to federal law prohibiting unlicensed trading with Indians. PETERSON, *supra* note 84, at 187, 193–94, 198.

[274] *Id.* at 198–99.

when northern New Mexico became part of the new Colorado Territory.[275] *See* Ch. 4 (Bill of Rights, art. II, § 26).

Overt hostilities broke out in 1866 when chief Kaneatche led Ute raids in Las Animas County in 1866, until forced to retreat by a U.S. Cavalry force.[276] Farther west, Kit Carson reported that the Utes in the Four Corners area were "a powder magazine" ready for "a spark."[277]

In 1868, territorial governor Alexander Cameron Hunt and Kit Carson negotiated a new agreement with the Utes that was "the most generous treaty ever made between the U.S. government and any Native American group."[278] The Hunt Treaty was generous partly because the governor wanted to keep the Utes from allying with the Arapaho and Cheyenne, leaving Colorado completely surrounded by hostiles.[279]

The new Consolidated Ute Reservation was for Utes in Colorado and New Mexico. It encompassed the western thirty percent of Colorado.[280] However, the Indian agents appointed to deliver annuities to the Utes were especially bad, and much of what the Utes had been promised was filched before delivery.[281] The problem was even worse because governor Hunt, who was much respected by the Utes, was replaced by Edward M. McCook, whose main interest in the governorship was stealing the annuities. Territorial secretary Frank Hall later described McCook's annuity thefts as "a scheme of rascality and plunder without a parallel in our annals."[282]

---

[275] SIMMONS at 33, 121. The New Mexico Territory had hardly any black slaves, but several thousand Indian ones. MARTIN HARDWICK HALL, SIBLEY'S NEW MEXICO CAMPAIGN 6 (Univ. of N.M. Press 2000) (1960); PETERSON, *supra* note 84, at 65 (estimating about 4,000 slaves in New Mexico as of the mid-1860s).

The Jan. 1, 1863, Emancipation Proclamation did not by its terms apply to either the Colorado or New Mexico Territories, because neither were in rebellion against the United States. The Thirteenth Amendment was ratified on Dec. 6, 1865, outlawing all slavery throughout the U.S.

The Apaches were also active slave traders. WEST at 45. The Comanche Empire, which dominated the region from Arizona to Texas until about 1850, also carried on a thriving slave trade. PEKKA HÄMÄLÄINEN, THE COMANCHE EMPIRE 2 (2008).

[276] 4 HALL at 93.

[277] PETERSON, *supra* note 84, at 211. An attempt was made in 1866 to get the Utes to agree to settle down and take up ranching and agriculture, which they had first promised to do in the 1849 treaty. 2 INDIAN AFFAIRS at 586. But the Utes explained that if they were sedentary, their enemies would know where they were and be able to find them and kill them. The Utes would not consent to stop roaming until their enemy tribes were on reservations. P. DAVID SMITH, OURAY: CHIEF OF THE UTES 68 (1986).

[278] BERWANGER at 38–39; ESTERGREEN at 272–73; Treaty with the Ute, 1868, Mar. 2, 1868, 15 Stat. 619; 2 INDIAN AFFAIRS at 990–96. Hunt served as Governor from May 1867 to June 1869. He had come to Colorado in 1858. BERWANGER at 55–56.

[279] *Id.* at 38–39.

[280] Not including land fifteen miles or farther north of the fortieth parallel. In other words, the northern border was mostly in-between the Yampa and White Rivers. The eastern border was about ten miles west of Aspen. SIMMONS at 131–33. The Utes gave up claims to North Park, Middle Park, the San Luis Valley, and the Yampa River Valley, all of which had mostly been taken by the settlers already. P. DAVID SMITH, *supra* note 279, at 72–73 (1986).

[281] SIMMONS at 137–38.

[282] 3 HALL at 18; *see also* LAMAR at 247–48; 2 HALL at 166–69. McCook complained that the Hunt Treaty treated Indians better than whites. Under the federal Homestead Act, a settler could acquire 160 acres of land, which was fine in eastern Kansas, but insufficient to make a living in semiarid Colorado. In contrast, the Ute Reservation amounted to over 2,000 acres per Ute, who at the time numbered no more than 6,000. P. DAVID SMITH, *supra* note 280, at 85, 91, 108 (the reservation was over fourteen million acres).

Ulysses Grant was personally an honest man, but he was willfully blind to the thievery of his friends. 3 VERNON LOUIS PARRINGTON, MAIN CURRENTS IN AMERICAN THOUGHT: THE BEGINNINGS OF CRITICAL REALISM IN AMERICA, 1860–1920, at 30 (Univ. of Okla. Press 1987) (1930). The vast corruption that Grant tolerated was described as "The Great Barbecue." *See id.* at 23–31.

McCook's kleptocracy eventually convinced many Coloradans that territorial government had become a problem and statehood was the solution. "It is interesting to note that virtually every new state that had undergone the territorial experience had reacted in a similar way by clipping gubernatorial wings."[283] Thus, article IV of the 1876 Colorado Constitution would divide executive power among seven elected officers,[284] require biannual reports from executive departments on expenditures,[285] forbid pay raises during a constitutional officer's term,[286] and mandate legislative participation in executive pardons.[287]

The boundaries of the Ute reservation, based on straight lines of latitude and longitude, were incomprehensible to the Ute. Many refused to move to the reservation. The Utes who were already inside the reservation had no compunction about leaving—sometimes for hunting and sometimes for raids on isolated settlements.[288] Nor did the Americans have much respect for reservation boundaries, whose borders they violated by settling or prospecting.[289]

After the discovery of silver and gold in the San Juan Mountains in 1871, settlers began to flood in. During 1872 negotiations, chief Ouray and other Utes refused to cede more territory. The federal government issued orders that the U.S. army remove illegal immigrants in the San Juans, but the orders were quickly rescinded.[290]

The Utes did sign the 1873 Brunot Agreement, ceding the mining regions, which constituted about a quarter of the reservation, while reserving hunting rights in the ceded areas.[291] The 1873 document was styled as an "agreement" rather than a "treaty" due to an 1871 federal statute that forbade treating Indian nations as sovereigns.[292] A key motive for the statute was the desire of the House of Representatives to be able to vote on agreements with Indians, since treaties need ratification only from the Senate. Courts in the twentieth century were unwilling to cast aside the pre-1871 treaties; instead, they remain an important component of the rule of law, by which the United States defines itself.[293]

Notwithstanding the Brunot Agreement, illegal immigration into the remaining reservation could not be contained. Nor could Utes be contained to the reservation; for example, in 1878, a large band of hunters led by chief Shavano killed Joseph McClane, a resident of Cheyenne County, on the far eastern plains.[294]

In the September 29, 1879, Meeker Massacre, White River Utes killed Indian agent Nathan Meeker and nine other men and took their wives and children hostage. Governor Pitkin called out

---

283 LAMAR at 254.

284 COLO. CONST. art. IV, § 1 (amended 1956).

285 Art. IV, § 16.

286 Art. IV, § 19.

287 Art. IV, § 7.

288 SIMMONS at 140–42; *see also* 3 HALL at 345 (noting the 1878 Ute summer encampment at Garden of the Gods).

289 SIMMONS at 138.

290 P. DAVID SMITH, *supra* note 280, at 91–92, 104–06.

291 Brunot Agreement with the Ute Indians, ch. 136, art. 1–2, 18 Stat. 36, 37 (1874); BERWANGER at 39; 2 HALL at 189–92. The ceded area was most of the modern counties of Archuleta, Hinsdale, Dolores, La Plata, Montezuma, Ouray, San Juan, and San Miguel. P. DAVID SMITH, *supra* note 280, at 114. Initial attempts to settle in the Animas River and San Juan region had begun in 1860, but had ended in failure, as no valuable finds of minerals were made, and the settlers were forced out by the Utes. 2 HALL at 192–97.

292 Indian Appropriations Act of 1871, 16 Stat. 544, 566 (codified at 25 U.S.C. § 71) ("No Indian nation or tribe within the territory of the United States shall be acknowledged or recognized as an independent nation, tribe, or power with whom the United States may contract by treaty").

293 *See* PRUCHA at 386–88. The fight between the House and Senate over the issue delayed the passage of appropriations for Indian annuities until the final days of the forty-first Congress and prevented the passage of any Indian appropriation bill in the fortieth Congress (1867–69). *Id.* at 295–305.

294 4 HALL at 89.

the state militia, who joined federal forces from Wyoming in war against the Utes.[295] The ultimate result was congressional passage of the 1880 Ute Removal Act, drastically reducing the Colorado reservation and ordering many Utes to go to the Uintah Reservation in Utah.[296] Through the 1910s, some Utes, including those led by chief Colorow, ventured off the reservation to hunt in Colorado, which sometimes resulted in violent skirmishes with settlers.[297] Indeed by 1895, off-reservation hunting by Utes was so extensive as to raise concerns about the extermination of elk, deer, and other game.[298]

Like the Cheyenne's Black Kettle, the Ute chief Ouray had been a great warrior in earlier days. Like Black Kettle, he recognized the settlers' overwhelming demographic advantage and pragmatically tried to make the best deals possible for his people, although he knew he was dealing from a position of weakness.[299] But among the Utes, as among the Cheyenne, the authority of a single chief, or even several chiefs, was limited to whoever chose to follow them, and many young men chose to stand and fight.[300]

The Ute reservations in Colorado were greatly reduced by the 1880 Removal Act, and then whittled thereafter.[301] What remains today are the Ute Mountain Ute Reservation and the Southern Ute Indian Reservation, both in far southwestern Colorado.[302]

In the twenty-first century, Utes have asserted their Brunot Agreement hunting rights, which provided that the "United States shall permit the Ute Indians to hunt upon said lands so long as the game lasts and the Indians are at peace with the white people."[303] The Colorado Division of Parks and Wildlife has negotiated agreements with Utes allowing them to hunt in Brunot areas outside the normal hunting seasons, at levels consistent with wildlife sustainability.[304]

---

[295] SIMMONS at 186–89. "Like most difficulties with this and other Indian nations, it was directly ascribable to the neglect and indifference of the Indian Bureau at Washington." 2 HALL at 494. *See generally* ROBERT SILBERNAGEL, TROUBLED TRAILS: THE MEEKER AFFAIR AND THE EXPULSION OF UTES FROM COLORADO (2011) (detailed account of the events of 1879–1881).

[296] SIMMONS at 191.

Ouray died in 1880, at age 47. *Id.* at 192. He is the namesake of Ouray County. The Uintah Reservation, in Utah, is now the Uintah and Ouray Reservation.

Ouray's widow, Chipeta, outlived him by half a century. Although the Utes were ill-treated in the late nineteenth century, Chipeta was celebrated in southern Colorado during the early twentieth century. *See* CYNTHIA S. BECKER & P. DAVID SMITH, CHIPETA: QUEEN OF THE UTES 202–03 (2003) (Chipeta's meeting with president Taft). Today, she is remembered by several place names in Colorado and Utah. *Id.* at 253–54.

[297] SIMMONS at 204–06. In a 1914 incident, about a hundred Utes hunting off-reservation near Rangely were rounded up by civilians and returned to Utah. *Id.* at 228.

[298] 4 HALL at 66. Until 1914, the federal Commissioner of Indian Affairs was willing to ignore Ute off-reservation hunting. The crackdown in 1914 seems to have been provoked by the Utah Utes asking for more rations during a particularly hungry time. BECKER & SMITH, *supra* note 296, at 221–22.

[299] *See* SIMMONS at 193.

[300] *See id.* at 179 (White River Utes in 1875–1878).

[301] Act of June 15, 1880, ch. 223, 21 Stat. 199; SIMMONS at 217 (discussing the 1895 Hunter Act).

[302] *See generally* RICHARD K. YOUNG, THE UTE INDIANS OF COLORADO IN THE TWENTIETH CENTURY (1997) (development of differing cultural and political views between the two reservations, starting in the 1890s).

[303] Brunot Agreement with the Ute Indians, ch. 136, art. 2, 18 Stat. 36, 37 (1874).

[304] MEMORANDUM OF UNDERSTANDING BETWEEN UTE MOUNTAIN UTE TRIBE AND THE STATE OF COLORADO CONCERNING WILDLIFE MANAGEMENT AND ENFORCEMENT IN THE BRUNOT AREA (2013); BRAD WEINMEISTER, COLO. PARKS & WILDLIFE, BIGHORN SHEEP MANAGEMENT PLAN, DATA ANALYSIS UNIT RBS-20 18 (2012); SOUTHERN UTE INDIAN TRIBE, 2017–2018 BRUNOT AREA HUNTING & FISHING PROCLAMATION FOR BRUNOT AREA HUNTING & FISHING BY SOUTHERN UTE TRIBAL MEMBERS (tribal hunting regulations for Southern Utes in Brunot area).

E. Law and Order

Meanwhile in the towns, law and order issues had to be addressed. Although Colorado would later become a great agriculture and ranching state, we should not think of gold rush Colorado as rural. Except for Indians, the large majority of people lived in towns that were either base camps for miners (*e.g.*, Gold Hill, in Boulder County) or commercial centers for supplying the miners and other inhabitants (*e.g.*, Denver, Golden).[305] The core criminal problem was that among the people who had moved to Colorado were "roughs" from Kansas, Missouri and elsewhere, leaving areas where they already had a criminal record and seeking new opportunities for predation.[306]

Individual self-defense was a necessity. In 1859, "All carried deadly weapons, to protect themselves from the lawless."[307] One new arrival in June 1864 wrote, "I do not enjoy living in a country where every man you meet, thinks it is safe to carry a loaded pistol. The practice is universal in all parts of Colorado."[308]

Although individual self-defense was necessary, it was not sufficient in the eyes of Coloradans. Communities had to organize for collective self-defense. As described in Section A of this chapter, this collective community organization had to be *ad hoc*, by the pioneers themselves. Neither the federal government, the Kansas territorial government, nor any other external organization had more than a minor capacity to construct functioning government in Colorado.

Early Colorado never devolved into the anarchy that had characterized California in its own early gold rush years, a decade before. Because about thirty percent of Colorado's miners had experience in California, they understood the importance of creating effective local self-government immediately. Thus, the miners' districts were quickly established. Experienced code writers traveled from town to town, helping to create local law.[309]

The early informal courts were not contrary to law and order. Instead, they were the foundation of the Colorado judiciary. Gilpin County's first sheriff recalled how the first judge of the miners' court was selected:

> [A young prospector] was in partnership with a bunch of the boys that were sluicing some ground up in Russell Gulch. He never did take kindly to the hard work around the sluice boxes, so the boys told him off to be the camp cook. Now that didn't work out very well, either, for [he] was always reading Blackstone or some law book, and forgetting about his cooking, and there was many a dish of beans scorched because he was too much interested in a book.

During the latter decades of the twentieth century, Indian tribes had success in reasserting treaty right for hunting and fishing. PRUCHA at 385; *Washington v. Wash. State Commercial Passenger Fishing Vessel Ass'n,* 443. U.S. 658 (1979); *Puyallup Tribe v. Dep't of Game of Wash.*, 391 U.S. 392 (1968) (generating two follow-up cases of the same name).

305 *See* DUANE A SMITH, ROCKY MOUNTAIN MINING CAMPS: THE URBAN FRONTIER (Indiana Univ. Pr. 1967). Subsequent cites to "Smith" in this chapter are to Smith's book *The Birth of Colorado*, which is cited in full in the Key Sources section at the beginning of this chapter).

306 HISTORICAL COMPENDIUM at 144; LAMAR at 184.

307 1 HALL at 207; *see also* ALBERT D. RICHARDSON, BEYOND THE MISSISSIPPI: FROM THE GREAT RIVER TO THE GREAT OCEAN: LIFE AND ADVENTURE ON THE PRAIRIES, MOUNTAINS, AND PACIFIC COAST 305 (1867) ("fully half the citizens wore sixshooters") (famed travelogue by Boston journalist).

308 SMITH, BIRTH OF COLORADO, at 234; LEONARD & NOEL at 27. The man was Nathaniel Hill, who had been a professor of chemistry at Brown University. He discovered an improved method of smelting, which made him rich and contributed greatly to Colorado's prosperity. He was later elected to the U.S. Senate. SMITH at 201, 249. He is honored in the Colorado Hall of Fame, in the State Capitol. *See* chapter 12 (State Institutions).

309 LAMAR at 186.

> Well, as I say, he wasn't much of a cook, and completely no good as a placer miner, so the boys made him into a Judge. (Here the Old sheriff chuckled). I must say that as the years have piled up, he has made a damn good one. [310]

The miner's court judge was Moses Hallett.[311] He later served in the Territorial Council (the upper body of the legislature) 1863–1866,[312] as Denver city attorney,[313] and as chief judge of the federal territorial court 1866–1877.[314] There, he created the foundation of Colorado water law.[315] In 1877, he was appointed U.S. district judge for the District of Colorado and served until 1906.[316]

Wilbur Fiske Stone came to Colorado as a miner in 1860.[317] He was elected to the territorial legislature in 1862 and 1864 and was an assistant U.S. attorney in 1862–1866.[318] In 1877, he

---

[310] LAFAYETTE HANCHETT, THE OLD SHERIFF AND OTHER TRUE TALES 8–9 (1937).

[311] *Id.* at 8.

[312] He served on the Council of the third Territorial Assembly in 1864 and in the fourth Assembly in 1865. 2 HALL at 537, 539.

[313] As city attorney: April 1, 1863, to April 1, 1864, and April 1, 1865, to April 1, 1866. *Id.* at 524.

[314] *Hallett, Moses*, FED. JUD. CTR.

[315] Judge Hallett explained that the common law doctrine in favor of riparian rights, which had developed in Great Britain and the eastern U.S., where water is plentiful, could not be applied in semiarid Colorado, where beneficial use of water is essential to the survival of the community:

> [R]ules respecting the tenure of property must yield to the physical laws of nature, whenever such laws exert a controlling influence.
>
> . . . .
>
> When the lands of this territory were derived from the general government, they were subject to the law of nature, which holds them barren until awakened to fertility by nourishing streams of water, and the purchasers could have no benefit from the grant without the right to irrigate them.

Yunker v. Nichols, 1 Colo. 551, 553, 555 (1871). Colorado constitutional water law is further discussed in chapter 21 (Mining & Irrigation, art. XVI).

[316] The court was created by the Act of June 26, 1876, ch. 147, 19 Stat. 61. During and after service on the district court, judge Hallett taught at the University of Colorado Law School and became dean emeritus. Hallett, Moses, *supra* note 314. He is the namesake of Hallett Hall at the University.

The 1876 Republican State Convention was about to nominate Hallett as its candidate for Colorado supreme court, until it was pointed out that Hallett would likely be named to the federal bench. 2 HALL at 331. He was appointed on Jan. 9, 1877, by president Grant. *Id.* at 361. Unlike most judges, Hallett did not allow "smoking, card playing, hats, or guns" in his courtroom. ERICKSON at 48.

[317] ERICKSON *Id.* at 86.

[318] 2 HALL at 539–40 (representative from Park County); 4 HALL at 565–66.

Figure 16. Future Colorado supreme court justice Wilbur Fiske Stone, in his Fremont County days. History Colorado-Denver, Colorado.

became a justice of the Colorado supreme court.[319] During the early days of Cañon City, he helped organize the people's court there.[320] Fremont County in 1860–1863 was beset by "a gang of horse and cattle thieves." Because of danger from these "roughs," people usually wore pistols and bowie knives. Justice Stone later recalled, "As to the character and results of these people's courts I can sum it all up by declaring that, if their administration was not always strictly law, it was rarely ever anything else than acknowledged justice." [321]

On the whole, the mining districts were successfully self-sufficient in criminal justice. The miner's courts and people's courts hanged murderers; lesser criminals were whipped, had half their heads shaved, and were banished.[322] The result was public safety: "No miner locked the doors to his cabin, though there might be hundreds or thousands of gold dust within, and wholly unguarded."[323] The mining districts did not feel much need for additional government.

Denver, however, with its larger population, had a much worse crime problem, and it wanted a regular territorial government to be established.[324] During the city's first two years, it had fifteen murders.[325] The frequent shootings in saloons and gambling dens were usually ignored as a problem that voluntary combatants brought on themselves. But the

---

[319] Stone had been a Democratic nominee for the supreme court in 1876 but had lost in what was a mostly Republican year statewide. One of the winners, justice E.T. Wells, resigned after serving for one year. A special meeting of Colorado lawyers nominated Stone for the vacancy, and both political parties acceded to the result. Stone served as a justice until 1886. *Id.*

In 1891, president Benjamin Harrison appointed Stone to a commission to investigate the Spanish land grants in the southwest, which had wrapped up huge amounts of land in continuing disputes over title. Stone spoke Spanish, French, and German, and he went to Madrid to investigate the origin of claims to 12 million acres, the 1748 Peralta grant from the king of Spain. Stone's investigation revealed that the Peralta claim was a fraud. Towards the end of his life, Stone edited a four-volume *History of Colorado*, published in 1918. ERICKSON at 86–88. The first volume is the best. Latter volumes consist mainly of short biographies of notable Coloradans of the early twentieth century.

[320] ERICKSON at 86. Stone's co-author of the code for the people's court was George Hinsdale. 4 HALL at 566. In 1868, Hinsdale and Stone co-founded the *Colorado Chieftain* newspaper, now known as the *Pueblo Chieftain. Id.*; 1 HALL at 477.

[321] ERICKSON at 10.

[322] Townspeople were authorized to shoot the offender on sight if he returned. SMITH at 74.

[323] 1 HALL at 481 (describing Spanish Bar mining settlement, near Clear Creek).

[324] *Id.* at 219–21.

[325] BRENNEMAN at 15.

bad men did not always confine themselves to fighting each other. For one thing, "the community was infested with horse thieves, whose depredations were of almost daily occurrence."[326] There were many "lawless characters" who "rejoiced in being denominated 'holy terrors.' . . . [T]hese desperadoes conceived the idea that they ought to and would run the town."[327] Vigilance committees, informal people's courts, and a formal People's Tribunal in Denver did their best to maintain public safety.[328]

"Uncle Dick" Wootton was an experienced mountain man who had been induced to open a merchandise store in Denver in exchange for a grant of 160 acres of land.[329] It was the first Denver building constructed of hewn logs, and, for a time, was the only two-story building in Denver City.[330] Wootton recalled, "The scoundrels and thieves came pretty near running the country until the vigilantes organized." The first instance involved a Hungarian who murdered his brother-in-law to take his gold dust. [331] When the *corpus delecti* was discovered by some Mexican[332] boys, the man was apprehended, and confessed. A jury of twelve was quickly assembled; the defendant had good counsel, but the confession settled the matter, and the jury voted for him to be hanged that day. According to Wootton, the execution "was the first of a series which revolutionized Denver society." Over the next few months, several notorious criminals were hanged, and others decided to leave town.[333]

In next-door Auraria, the "Bummers"—a gang of thieves—had been stealing property in December 1859 and January 1860. Things came to a head when they filched a bunch of turkeys from a Mexican's wagon. A citizens committee was appointed, and they gathered testimony that various Bummers, including William Todd ("Chuck-a-luck") and William Karl ("Buckskin Bill") were guilty. In response, the Bummers paraded in the streets with their arms and threatened to burn the city—no small threat for a city built of flimsy wood, which would in fact suffer a disastrous fire in 1863. They were faced down by the Jefferson Rangers, a militia unit that had embodied on January 18, 1860. After some nonlethal violence between the two sides, the Bummers decided to accept the offer to leave town within five hours, never to return, under penalty of hanging. "A few nights of vigilant guard was maintained, and thus ended the famous 'Turkey War.'"[334]

---

[326] RONZIO, SILVER IMAGES OF COLORADO at 62 (cited in full as part of the Wharton entry in "Key Sources."

[327] 1 HALL at 183.

[328] Another problem arose on January 30, 1860, when some claim jumpers began erecting buildings on unimproved land that was owned by others. Both sides were heavily armed, and some shots were fired, almost killing the Denver sheriff. However, attorney Edward Wynkoop, representing the jumpers, worked out a compromise by which the jumpers would abandon their claims, in return for compensation for the expenses they had incurred. The "War against the Jumpers" ended peacefully. BRENNEMAN at 17; RONZIO, *supra* note 326, at 21–23.

[329] WOOTTON at 244. Wootton lived in Denver for four years, moving to southern Colorado in 1862. *Id.* at 251–52. Mountain men tended to shorten the appellations of their fellows, so Richens Wootton was known as "Dick" to his fellow trappers, and as "Uncle Dick" to the younger generation. *Id.* at 17–18.

[330] *Id.* at 244. The April 11, 1859, public assembly that began the effort to seek statehood was held in Wootton's second story. *Id.* at 249 n.103.

[331] *Id.* at 247.

[332] As in described in chapter 1, "Creation of the State of Colorado," parts of early Colorado and all of New Mexico had once been part of the United States of Mexico. In the 1848 Treaty of Guadalupe Hidalgo, the United States of America purchased New Mexico, part of Colorado, and other Southwestern land. The treaty allowed all Mexican inhabitants to remain, and offered them American citizenship if they wanted it. Some but not all Mexicans accepted. Early Colorado writers used "Mexican" to encompass all persons of Mexican ancestry, regardless of whether they citizens of the U.S. or of Mexico.

[333] WOOTTON at 247–48.

[334] RONZIO, *supra* note 326, at 23–24; 1 HALL at 222.

The jurisdiction of the popular courts was questionable, but there was nobody else to exercise jurisdiction. Indeed, in one case a murder defendant had been transported to eastern Kansas at great expense, only to have the state judge declare that he had no jurisdiction over the defendant, and no other court did either. The case was eventually heard by a Colorado people's court.[335] These courts were effective and fair:

> The country was, in fact, peaceable and law-abiding, with the exception of that dangerous class common to the border . . . [T]hese roughs were kept in check by the fear of summary punishment. Miners' courts in the mountains had been supplemented by people's courts in the valleys. The proceeding of the latter were as open and orderly as those of the former; indeed, they approached the dignity of a regularly constituted tribunal.
>
> They were always presided over by a magistrate, either a Probate Judge or a Justice of the Peace. The prisoner had counsel and could call witnesses, if the latter were within reach.[336]

According to William Byers, who moved to Denver in 1859 and founded the *Rocky Mountain News*, "We never hanged on circumstantial evidence. I have known a great many such executions, but I don't believe one of them was unjust."[337] Byers and his employees, by the way, were always armed for defense against persons irate about their articles.[338] One of the most

---

[335] STEPHEN J. LEONARD, LYNCHING IN COLORADO 1859–1919, at 24–25 (2002); RICHARDSON, *supra* note 307, at 292 (noting that defendant James Gordon's Colorado custodians saved him from a lynch mob in Kansas).

[336] HISTORICAL COMPENDIUM at 146.

[337] ERICKSON at 183. Frank Hall, who served as territorial secretary from 1866–74 and acting governor in 1868, concurred: "There is not an instance upon our records where an innocent person, nor one whose guilt was not clearly established, suffered injury at their [vigilante] hands." 1 HALL at 473; *see also id.* at 220 (there was not known "a single instance wherein any man was unfairly tried or punished"); 2 HALL at 533, 541 (noting Hall's service; also noting that he was a Black Hawk representative to the territorial House, elected in 1865). Hall credited the 1868 vigilante executions of two notorious Denver outlaws with "a salutary and enduring effect . . . [T]here was no more orderly community on the frontier than Denver in the succeeding two years." 1 HALL at 472–73.

[338] *See* LAMAR at 186–87. The *News* had criticized Charley Harrison for what it called the "cold-blooded murder" of a black man known as Professor Stark. Harrison's friends kidnapped *News* publisher William Byers, but Harrison told them to let Byers go. Harrison advised Byers to "arm yourself for protection against those sonsofbitches." BRENNEMAN at 18. After Byers was released, two ruffians went back to the *News* building and started shooting at it. They were driven off by return fire from the *News*, and from a crowd of citizens, which captured them. WHARTON at 179–80. Thereafter, Byers and his staff were constantly armed at work. BRENNEMAN at 18.

> About the first question Byers asked of an employee in those days was whether he could handle a gun to good advantage, and a printer who was handy in this respect stood well with the proprietors of the paper, even though he had a multitude of shortcomings as a compositor.

WOOTTON at 245. "The establishment was always in a state of armed neutrality. Printers and editors were moving arsenals, with revolvers at their belts and shot-guns standing beside their cases and desks." RICHARDSON, *supra* note 307, at 293. The offending *News* article was printed on July 25, 1860, and the attack on the *News* took place on July 31. WHARTON at 177–79. *See generally* GALLAGHER at 46–50 (accounting the complete incident).

Denver soon had three daily newspapers, and their employees were also well-armed, for "no journalist who aims to tell the truth is wise to step into these streets without some display of fire-arms, unless partial to having his nose pulled or being made a target." RICHARDSON, *supra* note 307, at 297.

notable men to serve as a judge of a people's court was Alexander C. Hunt, who later served as territorial governor.[339]

Outside of the popular courts, there were instances in which vigilantes took it upon themselves to inflict summary punishment (hanging, whipping, or banishment) with no legal process provided to the accused. One motive was that the people's courts were supposedly too lenient.[340]

Pueblo County's vigilantes were "a respectable and earnest body of men."[341] In Colorado, as was typical in the West, vigilantes were not a spontaneous rabble, but were organized by the middle- and upper-class men of the area.

In an exhaustive study of lynching in Colorado, historian Stephen Leonard defines lynching very broadly; he includes the people's courts and even posses (which by definition were led by sheriffs or similar officials).[342] With this definition, he counts 175 "lynchings" in Colorado history.[343] Of these, he finds only three lynchings based on "weak evidence" before the 1870s[344]—by which time the practice was on its way out, as will be explained below.

Leonard offers several reasons why lynching existed. First, he says it was legitimated by the people's courts.[345] But this is questionable, as there is a difference between an immediate hanging and a process that involves trials, witnesses, cross-examination, juries, and sometimes acquittals. Second, the jails in Colorado were of poor quality. Often, they were converted buildings from which escape was easy. It was possible for lynch mobs to break into jails and extract their target. Third, some law enforcement officers were in fact leaders of undercover criminal gangs.[346] Fourth, the formal court system in the early days was not very good. Unfortunately, this did not change when the territory of Colorado was established in 1861, and three federal territorial judges were appointed. One was a Confederate sympathizer who fled the territory after his efforts to promote secession failed. Another did virtually no work, and the third was conscientious.[347]

The quality of the federal judiciary did improve after 1866 as Coloradans succeeded in pressuring presidents to appoint well-qualified locals, such as Moses Hallett and E.T. Wells, rather than easterners in search of sinecures.[348] But the federal court had a huge backlog of cases, and the appeals process (to the three district judges, sitting en banc as territorial supreme court justices) took many years.

The third judicial district comprised the southern half of the state, and it was something of a moveable feast with the judge, court officers, lawyers, parties, and witnesses traveling through the south, camping out along the way, and holding a mobile court in small adobe houses or

---

[339] He served a judge in Denver in 1860 and was later appointed territorial governor by president Grant. Hunt had previously been a California gold miner. FORBES PARKHILL, THE LAW GOES WEST 17, 98, 139–40 (1956).

[340] LEONARD, *supra* note 335, at 156.

[341] 3 HALL at 453.

[342] LEONARD, *supra* note 335, at 6, 15–29, 119–20.

[343] *Id.* at 6.

[344] *Id.* at 165–72 tbl. A.1.

[345] *Id.* at 28.

[346] *Id.* at 106–07. A secure territorial prison was opened in 1871. BERWANGER at 124.

[347] GUICE at 27–32, 63–66, 79; PARKHILL, *supra* note 339, at 19–24; LEONARD, *supra* note 334, at 41–42 (all discussing the poor quality of the territorial bench pre-Hallett).

[348] President Andrew Johnson appointed Hallett in response to a memorial from the territorial legislature, which wanted Hallett because he was a local man who understood local issues, such a mining law, and because of "his eminence as a lawyer, and his identification with the higher interests of the people." 4 HALL at 463.

whatever facility could be found.[349] Allen Brandford was its first judge and Moses Hallett the second.[350]

Colorado supreme court justice Wilbur Fiske Stone later recalled that the traveling lawyers and judges had "more fun, legal and unlegal, than the Bench and Bar have ever seen since in the effeminate days of railroads and fine court houses."[351] It may have been interesting, but one itinerant judge was hardly enough to bring law and order to southern Colorado. If effective justice were to be established, the people of Colorado would have to tax themselves to create a criminal justice system much larger than what the federal government was willing to provide. That would happen eventually, but not in the 1860s.

R.B. Townshend, a professor from England who lived in Colorado for a decade as a traveler and rancher, had a keen understanding of early vigilantism, and why it became a problem. In December 1869, Townshend was in the brand-new small town of Evans in Weld County. The town had sprung up at the terminus of the first railroad line into Colorado, from Cheyenne, Wyoming, which was along the route of the transcontinental railroad.[352] Evans was dominated and terrorized by "toughs from Cheyenne."[353]

One day, a tough shot and killed in cold blood an old man who ran a boarding house. The killer tried to flee on horseback, but was quickly apprehended by the townspeople, who had armed and organized themselves beforehand for such an occasion. There being "no building in the town that could resist a determined assault for five minutes," jailing the perpetrator was impossible. For the moment, the murderer was surrounded by ten men with cocked revolvers.[354] But what if the toughs attempted a rescue?

Richard Sopris had served as a judge in people's courts in Denver.[355] In 1878, he would be elected Denver mayor, and re-elected in 1879.[356] He happened to be in Evans and was chosen by acclamation to convene a people's court, starting with all the townspeople, who were now in the streets. After receiving popular assent, he selected a jury.[357]

A young lawyer was found, and he was ordered to represent the defendant. Witnesses were summoned, sworn, and examined. The perpetrator did not have much to say in his defense, except that he had not meant to hurt the decedent—which was not credible, since he had shot the decedent in the head at close range. The jury convicted, and when judge Sopris asked the crowd

---

349 ERICKSON at 43–44.

350 TAYLOR at 78.

351 ERICKSON at 44 (quoting Wilbur Fiske Stone, *Pioneer Bench and Bar in Colorado*, Rep., Colo. B. Ass'n, Eleventh Ann. Meeting at Fort Collins, July 23, 1908, at 110).

352 The railroad to Evans was completed on Dec. 13, 1869. 1 HALL at 436.

353 R.B. TOWNSHEND, A TENDERFOOT IN COLORADO 110 (Stephen J. Leonard & Thomas J. Noel eds., Univ. Press of Colo. 2008) (1923).

354 *Id.* at 110–12, 119–20. The murderer was being held by a deputy sheriff, but the townspeople knew that the county jail could not withstand an attack by the toughs. The deputy surrendered custody when a vigilante pointed a handgun at him, thus providing a face-saving excuse for him to yield. *Id.* at 114–16.

355 *See id.* at 113.

356 4 HALL at 569. Sopris had also been elected as the first President of a miner's district in Gilpin County, and as Colorado's delegate to the Kansas territorial legislature. *See supra* Section A.2. He had served as captain in the First Colorado, the volunteer regiment that won the Battle of Glorieta Pass. WHITFORD at 48, 123–24. Sopris was a leader in creating Denver city government during the pre-territorial days and was later elected sheriff of Arapahoe County in 1865 and 1867. 4 HALL at 569. He "was one of the most conspicuous of the Colorado pioneers. His name appears at every stage of our early annals" including the "organization of numerous mining camps, the formation of local governments, in Denver, Auraria, Central City, Gregory, Jackson, in the San Juan country, and in the gallant record made by the First Regiment of Colorado Volunteers" at Glorieta Pass. 1 HALL at 523. He arrived in Colorado on March 15, 1859, age 45, from Indiana. 2 HALL at 563.

357 TOWNSHEND, *supra* note 353, at 112–14.

for the punishment, they chose hanging. It was carried out immediately. The leader of the vigilance committee gave a short speech urging the rest of the toughs to leave town.[358]

They did, "some in their haste walking all the way to Denver to get clear of a spot so ominous to them. The rowdyism, the displaying of revolvers and shooting at lamps out of bravado, stopped instanter." Evans immediately became a peaceful town.[359]

Townshend's initial impression of actions like those in Evans was favorable, but after five years of living in the Colorado territory, he changed his mind. "Whenever atrocious murderers are hanged as soon as caught, there arises at once a strong presumption that a manslayer, who is left to be dealt with by an ordinary jury, has probably much to excuse him. This feeling vastly increased the difficulty of getting juries to convict." Moreover, horse thieves and cattle thieves, knowing that if caught they would be hanged, "never hesitate to shoot, thinking they may as well be hanged for killing a man as for killing a calf . . . The remedy is worse than the disease."[360]

This was not universally true. Townshend wrote favorably about "a cowmen's vigilance committee" that enforced laws against cattle thievery. This included upholding the law that unbranded stray cattle became the property of the trustees of the public school fund.[361]

The remedy was, for a time, the only one available; but once the superior remedy of formal criminal courts had begun to function well, continuing resort to the first remedy harmed the second remedy. We can see the development in Wilbur Fiske Stone; at one time he was the well-armed creator of the people's court in Canon City, which dispensed justice to the violent criminals of Fremont County. In 1877, he became associate justice of the Colorado Supreme court. At all times he was upholding law and public safety; the means of doing so had changed by 1877, because Colorado now had a good formal court system.

Stephen Leonard writes that people's courts or lynching (which he conflates) were abandoned in the larger and wealthier towns (starting with Denver) as those towns developed connections with the rest of the nation and sought to project a peaceable and respectable image.[362] Thus, in the 1870s lynching was mostly in small and isolated towns.[363] The exception was Leadville, which was new and booming in the 1870s, thanks to silver, and going through growing pains not unlike Denver two decades earlier.[364]

Everywhere in Colorado lynching was falling out of favor by the end of the 1870s. Vigilantes had previously operated in daylight, with no effort to disguise themselves. By the end of the decade, they wore masks, and did their business in the dark.[365] Lynching was much rarer after 1880 and nearly extinct by the early twentieth century.[366] This was in great contrast to the American Southeast, where lynching soared in the latter two decades of the nineteenth century. While the Southeast had a long history of lynching, it was not until the 1886 that the majority of persons lynched there annually were black.[367]

---

[358] *Id.* at 116–19, 122–28.

[359] *Id.* at 129.

[360] *Id.* at 129–30.

[361] *Id.* at 225–26.

[362] LEONARD, *supra* note 334, at 70–71. Lynching "fell into disrepute" in Pueblo County after the construction of a solid new jail in the early 1870s. 3 HALL at 458.

[363] LEONARD, *supra* note 334, at 54.

[364] *Id.* at 48 ("Leadville's skimpy police force was either unable or unwilling to protect citizens."). When Leadville boomed as a silver city, the usual collection of ruffians had moved in, to the terror of the good citizens. A vigilance committee in 1879 hanged several of them and persuaded the rest to leave. 2 HALL at 454–55. Atrociously, in 1875 a Leadville judge was murdered after he attempted to crack down on vigilante activities. LEONARD, *supra* note 334, at 54.

[365] LEONARD, *supra* note 335, at 67.

[366] *See id.* at 53.

[367] *Lynchings: By Year and Race*, UMKC (University of Missouri at Kansas City).

Although Colorado's court system had its early problems, it eventually overcame them. As the territory had grown, "Colorado's judicial system, unlike New Mexico's, was generally competent and professional." This made vigilantism relatively uncommon, compared to the rest of the Southwest.[368]

For whatever reason, "every visitor after 1870 commented that Colorado was tame."[369] By the early 1870s, Colorado Springs "was the most quiet, orderly little town in those days you ever saw, at least for anyone who didn't deliberately run his head into mischief."[370] Many people thought that Colorado had much less crime than in the early days; they attributed the improvement to the salutary effects of the early people's courts, and to the increasing numbers of women and children, who induced men to behave better.[371] Other than an oft-ignored law against carrying concealed weapons in towns, peaceful Colorado had little gun control.[372]

The 1876 Colorado Constitution right to arms reflects the challenges of territorial days and the vision for the future: the right to arms for self-defense may not be questioned; there is a separate, second right to arms "in aid of the civil power *when thereto legally summoned*."[373] This includes answering a summons to serve in the militia, or in a sheriff's posse. The right to arms "in aid of the civil power" does *not* include participating in a lynching. Whatever the necessities of territorial and pre-territorial days had been, the new state of Colorado expected that exercise of the right to bear arms "in aid of the civil power" would be orderly and regularized. Perhaps the 1876 constitution's implicit rebuke to lynching helped delegitimize the practice.

---

[368] LAMAR at 257.

[369] *Id.* at 246.

[370] TOWNSHEND, *supra* note 353, at 215. Mischief-seekers went to the bars in the old part of town (Colorado City), where they "might easily come in for a shooting scrape." *Id.*

[371] BERWANGER at 103–04.

[372] David B. Kopel, *The Right to Arms in Nineteenth Century Colorado*, 95 DENVER U L. REVIEW 329, 448–55 (2018).

[373] COLO. CONST. art. II, § 13 (emphasis added).

Part II
State Government Departments and Institutions

Chapter 7

Executive Powers and Departments, article IV

Introduction

Under the United States Constitution, the executive power is centralized in the president. He appoints the attorney general, the secretary of the treasury, the secretary of state, the U.S. attorneys, and so on. The same is true in New Jersey, where the governor appoints everyone.

The constitutional system in the other 49 states is very different. The executive power is not centralized in the governors. Rather, key executive officers are elected by the people. The governor of Colorado can be of one political party, and the attorney general of Colorado of a different party.

Coloradans have always reserved to themselves the right to elect their constitutional officers. Over time, the officers who are elected has changed. For example, the state auditor was once elected, but no longer. Art. V, § 49. The lieutenant governor was once elected on a separate ballot from the governor and could be of a different party. The last such split was in 1967–71, when Republican John Love was governor and Democrat Mark Hogan with lieutenant governor. Then the two offices were put on a single ticket. And later, the separate primary for lieutenant governor was eliminated; today, as with the vice-presidency of the United States, the choice of Colorado lieutenant governor is the fiat of a party's nominee for governor.

Like other U.S. territories, the Colorado territory had suffered under corrupt territorial governors appointed from Washington. Colorado's worst was Edward McCook (1869–73, 1874–75). He was notorious for stealing the Indian allotments—federal grants of food and other goods and services to Indians in treaty relations with the United States. Indeed, McCook's terrible governance eventually convinced many Coloradans that territorial government had become a problem and statehood was the solution. "It is interesting to note that virtually every new state that had undergone the territorial experience had reacted in a similar way by clipping gubernatorial wings."[1] Thus, article IV of the 1876 Colorado Constitution would divide executive power among seven elected officers,[2] require biannual reports from executive departments on expenditures,[3] forbid pay raises during a constitutional officer's term,[4] and mandate legislative participation in executive pardons.[5]

Most of article IV concerns the governor, with other constitutional offices receiving more cursory treatment. A list of all Colorado governors—starting with Jefferson Territory provisional governor Robert Steele in 1859—is provided in section 2.

The sixteen cabinet departments that are headed by gubernatorial appointees are the departments of:

- Agriculture
- Corrections
- Health Care Policy and Financing
- Human Services
- Labor & Employment
- Local Affairs
- Military & Veterans Affairs
- Natural Resources

[1] HOWARD ROBERTS LAMAR, THE FAR SOUTHWEST 1846–1912: A TERRITORIAL HISTORY 254 (rev. ed. 2000).
[2] COLO. CONST. art. IV, § 1 (amended 1956).
[3] *Id.* art. IV, § 16.
[4] *Id.* art. IV, § 19.
[5] *Id.* art. IV, § 7.

- Personnel & Administration
- Public Health & Environment
- Public Safety
- Regulatory Agencies
- Revenue
- Transportation
- Education
- Higher Education

The departments of Education and Higher Education are not as directly under gubernatorial control as the other departments.[6] In general, as described in chapter 17 (Officers, art. XII), the governor's appointing authority for state personnel is shallow. The governor can appoint department heads, and the department heads can appoint division heads. Below that, almost everyone is covered by civil service, and difficult to remove.

However, the governor does have broad power to appoint the members of numerous boards and commissions.

Art. IV, Section 1. Officers, terms

> (1) The executive department shall include the governor, lieutenant governor, secretary of state, state treasurer, and attorney general, each of whom shall hold his office for the term of four years, commencing on the second Tuesday of January in the year 1957, and each fourth year thereafter. They shall perform such duties as are prescribed by this constitution or by law.
>
> (2) In order to broaden the opportunities for public service and to guard against excessive concentrations of power, no governor, lieutenant governor, secretary of state, state treasurer, or attorney general shall serve more than two consecutive terms in such office. This limitation on the number of terms shall apply to terms of office beginning on or after January 1, 1991. Any person who succeeds to the office of governor or is appointed or elected to fill a vacancy in one of the other offices named in this section, and who serves at least one-half of a term of office, shall be considered to have served a term in that office for purposes of this subsection (2). Terms are considered consecutive unless they are at least four years apart.

Until a 1956 amendment, state constitutional officers were elected for two-year terms. The limit of two consecutive four-year terms was added by the voters in 1990. Terms are consecutive unless there is a four-year gap.

The first governor elected to a four-year term was Democrat Steve McNichols in 1958. Five governors have been elected to three terms: William "Billy" Adams, Edwin Johnson, John Love, Richard Lamm, and Roy Romer. *See* Table of Governors, in section 2, below.

Statutory provisions for constitutional officers are:

- Governor, C.R.S. § 24-20-101 et seq.
- Lieutenant governor, § 24-20-105.
- Secretary of state, § 24-21-101 et seq.

---

[6] An organizational chart of Colorado state government, mainly the executive branch, is available online, https://www.colorado.gov/pacific/sites/default/files/State%20Org%20Chart%20112916.pdf.

- State treasurer, § 24-22-101 et seq.
- Attorney general, § 24-31-101 et seq.

Art. IV, Section 2. Governor is supreme executive

> The supreme executive power of the state shall be vested in the governor, who shall take care that the laws be faithfully executed.

The governor is the supreme executive, but he does not hold all the executive power. The secretary of state, state treasurer, and attorney general are elected separately, and they are beholden to the people, not to the governor.

As the personification of the state, the governor is the proper defendant in a lawsuit alleging that a state law is unconstitutional. *Developmental Pathways v. Ritter*, 178 P.3d 524 (Colo. 2008) (First Amendment challenge to article XXIX gift ban; plaintiffs held to lack standing, because the law had not been enforced against them).

by Jerry Kopel
There have been 37 individuals who held the office of governor from 1876 to 2020. Seventeen were Republicans, 19 were Democrats, and one, Davis Waite, was a Populist.

Most governors left office while still in their fifties (14 governors) or their forties (nine governors). One governor, James Grant, was only 37 when he left office. Three governors left in their 70s: Billy Adams, Ed Johnson, and Roy Romer.

The first elected governor to be born in the 20th century was Dan Thornton, born in 1911 and elected in 1950. No lieutenant governor who took over the governor's office by succession has been later elected as governor. There are three in that category: Jesse McDonald, 1905-07; Walter Johnson, 1950-51; and John Vanderhoof, 1973–75.

Only three Colorado governors have been elected to the U.S. Senate. First was Charles S. Thomas, governor from 1899 to 1901, and U.S. senator 1913–21.

Second was John F. Shafroth, governor from 1909–13, and senator 1913–19. He was the first to move directly from one office to the other.

The third is Edwin C. Johnson, who never passed a farmhouse without stopping in to say hello. "Big Ed" served as Colorado governor from 1933 through 1937, went to the U.S. Senate in 1937–55, and then was elected to two more years as governor. The Democrat from Craig had begun his career with four consecutive terms in the Colorado House starting in 1923, and then became Democrat lieutenant governor (and therefore president of the Senate) in 1931–32. He is the only Coloradan elected governor three terms and U.S. senator three terms.

In the table on the next page are our state's governors, along with their birthdays. For biographies of some of the most notable, see RICHARD D. LAMM & DUANE A. SMITH, PIONEERS AND POLITICIANS: COLORADO GOVERNORS IN PROFILE (2d ed. 2008).[7]

[7] Territorial Governors are from FRANK HALL, 2 HISTORY OF COLORADO 533 (2008) (1890). An appendix to volume 2 of HALL also contains dates of service for other territorial officers, including justices. Governor Alva Adams was the father of U.S. senator Alva Adams, who served 1923–24 and 1933–41.

Table 1. Governors

First name	Last name	Party	Served	Birthday
William	Gilpin	R	Appointed by Abraham Lincoln. July 8, 1861	
John	Evans	R	Appointed by Lincoln. Apr. 19, 1862	
Alexander	Cummings	R	Appointed by Andrew Johnson. Oct. 17, 1865	
A.C.	Hunt	R	Appointed by Johnson. May 27, 1867	
Edward	McCook	R	Appointed by Ulysses Grant. June 15, 1869	
Edward	McCook	R	Appointed by Grant. Jan. 27, 1874	
John	Routt	R	Appointed by Grant. Mar. 29, 1875. Elected Oct. 1876. Served until Jan. 1879.	4/25/1826
Frederick	Pitkin	R	1879–83	8/31/1837
James	Grant	D	1883–85	1/2/1848
Benjamin	Eaton	R	1885–87	12/15/1833
Alva	Adams	D	1887–89	5/14/1850
Job	Cooper	R	1889–91	11/6/1843
John	Routt	R	1891–93	4/25/1826
Davis	Waite	Pop.	1893–95	4/9/1825
Albert	McIntire	R	1895–97	1/15/1853
Alva	Adams	D	1897–99	5/14/1850
Charles	Thomas	D	1899–01. Also U.S. Senator 1913–21	12/6/1849
James	Orman	D	1901–03	11/4/1849
James	Peabody	R	1903–05	8/21/1852
Alva	Adams	D	Jan–Mar 1905	5/14/1850
Jesse	McDonald	R	1905–07. Lt. Gov. who succeeded to office	6/30/1858
Henry	Buchtel	R	1907–09	9/30/1847
John	Shafroth	D	1909–13	6/9/1854
Elias	Ammons	D	1913–15. Father of Gov. Teller Ammons	7/28/1860
George	Carlson	R	1915–17	10/23/1876
Julius	Gunter	D	1917–19	10/31/1858
Oliver	Shoup	R	1919–23	12/13/1869
William	Sweet	D	1923–25	1/27/1869
Clarence	Morley	R	1925–27	2/9/1869
William	Adams	D	1927–33. First to be elected to 3 consecutive terms	2/15/1862
Edwin	Johnson	D	1933–37, 1955–57	1/1/1884
Teller	Ammons	D	1937–39	12/3/1896
Ralph	Carr	R	1939–43	12/11/1887
John	Vivian	R	1943–47	6/30/1887
William	Knous	D	1947–50. Resigned upon appointment as U.S. Dist. Judge	2/2/1887
Walter	Johnson	D	1950–51. Succeeded to office	4/16/1904
Dan	Thornton	R	1951–55	1/31/1911
Stephen	McNichols	D	1957–63. First to be elected to a 4-year term, in 1958	3/7/1914
John	Love	R	1963–73. Resigned to be federal "Energy Czar"	11/29/1916
John	Vanderhoof	R	1973–75. Succeeded to office	5/27/1922
Richard	Lamm	D	1975–87	8/3/1935
Roy	Romer	D	1987–99	10/31/1928

William	Owens	R	1999–2007	10/22/1950
William	Ritter	D	2007–11	2/26/1950
John	Hickenlooper	D	2011–19	2/7/1952
Jared	Polis	D	2019–	5/12/1975

Omitted from above list: James Peabody, who served one day in 1905; Ray Talbot, who served 9 days in 1937, when Gov. Edwin Johnson resigned to serve in the U.S. Senate.

Art. IV, Section 3. State officers

> The officers named in section one of this article shall be chosen on the day of the general election, by the registered electors of the state. The governor and the lieutenant governor shall be chosen jointly by the casting by each voter of a single vote applicable to both offices. The returns of every election for said officers shall be sealed up and transmitted to the secretary of state, directed to the speaker of the house of representatives, who shall immediately, upon the organization of the house, and before proceeding to other business, open and publish the same in the presence of a majority of the members of both houses of the general assembly, who shall for that purpose assemble in the house of representatives. The joint candidates having the highest number of votes cast for governor and lieutenant governor, and the person having the highest number of votes for any other office, shall be declared duly elected, but if two or more have an equal and the highest number of votes for the same office or offices, one of them, or any two for whom joint votes were cast for governor and lieutenant governor respectively, shall be chosen thereto by the two houses, on joint ballot. Contested elections for the said offices shall be determined by the two houses, on joint ballot, in such manner as may be prescribed by law.

Three governors in 25 hours

by Jerry Kopel
In 1904, Colorado had just gone through a bitter election for governor. Both Republican and Democratic cemeteries had voted. While the Democrat, Alva Adams, began serving as governor, the House and Senate were meeting in a joint session of the 15th general assembly to decide who had really been elected.

On the afternoon of March 3, 1905, John Waldron, counsel for James Peabody, the Republican candidate, made the following comment:

> My attention has just been called to the fact that owing either to gross carelessness or unbridled license of the reporter of one of the newspapers in this city, I have been reported in the paper, which has just been published, as denominating (the opposing speaker) as a 'liar.' I did not call him a "liar." I plainly said "lawyer." (Applause.)

Journal of the Fifteenth General Assembly 35 (Mar. 3, 1905) (joint session).

The general assembly determined that election fraud on both sides was so pervasive that it was impossible to say who had won the election. But the supreme court held that this was not an acceptable resolution of the legislature's duty to decide gubernatorial election contests. *In re Senate Resolution No. 10*, 33 Colo. 307, 79 P. 1009 (1905).

Accordingly, an unusual compromise was worked out. Alva Adams, the Democrat, had served 65 days. He was to resign. James Peabody, the Republican, was sworn in to serve one day. He was to resign, and Jesse McDonald, the Republican lieutenant governor, was to serve the rest of the term. In a period of 25 hours, Colorado had three governors.

Art. IV, Section 4. Qualifications of state officers

> No person shall be eligible to the office of governor or lieutenant governor unless he shall have attained the age of thirty years, nor to the office of secretary of state or state treasurer unless he shall have attained the age of twenty-five years, nor to the office of attorney general unless he shall have attained the age of twenty-five years and be a licensed attorney of the supreme court of the state in good standing, and no person shall be eligible to any one of said offices unless, in addition to the qualifications above prescribed therefor, he shall be a citizen of the United States, and have resided within the limits of the state two years next preceding his election.

Article V forbids dual office-holding, so that a member of the general assembly cannot hold any of the section 4 offices, or other executive or judicial offices. But a legislator may be nominated for one of the above offices and resign prior to assuming the new office. Colo. Att'y Gen. File No. CLS/AGBDX/KL, Feb. 24, 1977.

Art. IV, Section 5. Governor commander-in-chief of militia

> The governor shall be commander-in-chief of the military forces of the state, except when they shall be called into actual service of the United States. He shall have power to call out the militia to execute the laws, suppress insurrection or repel invasion.

The state militia is established in article XVII. Today, the Colorado National Guard is the "active" component of the militia. All able-bodied males 18–44 are the inactive component and are subject to being summoned to militia service. Chapter 21 (Militia).

In 1894, Populist governor David Waite went to "War with City Hall" in Denver. He exercised his statutory authority to remove allegedly corrupt members of the Denver Police and Fire Board. Denver was tolerant of illegal gambling and prostitution, much to the annoyance of the rest of the state. Two of the three board members gathered sympathetic public employees, who armed themselves, and took over City Hall and adjacent buildings, refusing to yield their offices.

The governor then called forth the militia, which surrounded the insurrectionists. The matter ended peacefully when a district court injunction recognized the governor's full control of the board. Eventually, the Colorado supreme court affirmed that the governor's calling forth of the militia had been lawful, although the court added that the governor had been reckless, and he should have waited for the legal process to solve the problem. *People ex rel. Engley v. Martin*, 19 Colo. 565, 36 P. 543 (1894).

The governor's decision that an insurrection exists is not subject to judicial review. *In re Moyer,* 35 Colo. 159, 85 P. 190 (1904)*; Ex Parte Moyer*, 35 Colo. 154, 91 P. 738 (1905); *Moyer v. Peabody,* 212 U.S. 78 (1909) (Holmes, J.) (upholding governor's martial law imprisonment of the president of the Western Federation of Miners for 10 weeks, as not being a due process violation) (all three cases involving use of National Guard to put down a miners' strike in San Miguel County).

During the Great Depression in 1936, Democratic governor Edwin Johnson deployed the militia at the New Mexico border, to thwart the immigration of indigents. After several months of protests by New Mexico, he withdrew the militia. In 1941, the U.S. supreme court ruled that the right to migrate from one state to another is an implicit right of U.S. citizenship. Accordingly, California's anti-Okie law, which prohibited bringing a non-resident indigent into the state, was void. *Edwards v. People of State of California*, 314 U.S. 160 (1941).

Art. IV, Section 6. Vacancy appointment of officers

> (1) The governor shall nominate, and, by and with the consent of the senate, appoint all officers whose offices are established by this constitution, or which may be created by law, and whose appointment or election is not otherwise provided for, and may remove any such officer for incompetency, neglect of duty, or malfeasance in office. If the vacancy occurs in any such office while the senate is not in session, the governor shall appoint some fit person to discharge the duties thereof until the next meeting of the senate when he shall nominate and, by and with the consent of the senate, appoint some fit person to fill such office.
>
> (2) If the office of state treasurer, secretary of state, or attorney general shall be vacated by death, resignation, or otherwise, the governor shall nominate and, by and with the consent of the senate, appoint a successor. The appointee shall hold the office until his successor shall be elected and qualified in such manner as may be provided by law. If the vacancy occurs in any such office while the senate is not in session, the governor shall appoint some fit person to discharge the duties thereof until the next meeting of the senate, when he shall nominate and, by and with the consent of the senate, appoint some fit person to fill such office.
>
> (3) The senate in deliberating upon executive nominations may sit with closed doors, but in acting upon nominations they shall sit with open doors, and the vote shall be taken by ayes and noes, which shall be entered upon the journal.

This covers appointment and removal of officers who are named in the Constitution. Procedures for other officers are governed by statute.

Art. IV, Section 7. Governor may grant reprieves and pardons

> The governor shall have power to grant reprieves, commutations and pardons after conviction, for all offenses except treason, and except in case of impeachment, subject to such regulations as may be prescribed by law relative to the manner of applying for pardons, but he shall in every case where he may exercise this power, send to the general assembly at its first session thereafter, a transcript of the petition, all proceedings, and the reasons for his action.

The statutory procedures related to this provision are in C.R.S. § 16-17-101 to 103. The Colorado governor's pardon power is narrower than the U.S. president's pardon power; the latter may be exercised for all federal crimes, even treason, and does not require any legislative consultation.

U.S. CONST. art. II, § 2, clause 1. In no case does governor's or president's pardon power extend to impeachments.

A statute allowed prisoners to petition the courts for a post-conviction reduction in their sentences, when they had been sentenced under the old criminal code and the new criminal code provided for a lesser sentence. The statute was held to violate the governor's exclusive power to grant commutations. *People v. Herrera*, 183 Colo. 155, 516 P.2d 626 (1973), *People v. Simms*, 186 Colo. 447, 528 P.2d 228 (1974) (declining to reconsider *Herrera*).

Art. IV, Section 8. Governor may require information from officers, must issue message

> The governor may require information in writing from the officers of the executive department upon any subject relating to the duties of their respective offices, which information shall be given upon oath whenever so required; he may also require information in writing at any time, under oath, from all officers and managers of state institutions, upon any subject relating to the condition, management and expenses of their respective offices and institutions. The governor shall, at the commencement of each session, and from time to time, by message, give to the general assembly information of the condition of the state, and shall recommend such measures as he shall deem expedient. He shall also send to the general assembly a statement, with vouchers, of the expenditures of all moneys belonging to the state and paid out by him. He shall, also, at the commencement of each session, present estimates of the amount of money required to be raised by taxation for all purposes of the state.

The governor can require executive department heads to provide written reports. By statute, these reports must be shared with the general assembly. C.R.S. § 24-20-104.

At the beginning of each session of the general assembly, the governor must report on the condition of the state and make recommendations for revision of laws. The address is known as the State of the State.

Art. IV, Section 9. Governor may convene legislature

> The governor may, on extraordinary occasions convene the general assembly, by proclamation, stating therein the purpose for which it is to assemble; but at such special session no business shall be transacted other than that specially named in the proclamation. He may by proclamation, convene the senate in extraordinary session for the transaction of executive business.

The governor can call a special session of the general assembly. The legislature may not pass legislation outside the scope of the purpose for which the special session was called. The governor's discretion to call a special session is absolute. *In re State Census*, 9 Colo. 642, 21 P. 477 (1886). But the call must be specific; otherwise, the special session's legislation is void. *Denver & Rio Grande Railroad v. Moss*, 50 Colo. 282, 115 P. 696 (1911) (Gov. Shafroth called special session for "any and all legislating relating to or in any wise affecting corporations"; statute governed railroad liability for killing livestock).

The general assembly may enact laws that have a "rational nexus" to the content of the governor's call. *Empire Sav., Bldg. and Loan Ass'n v. Otero Sav. and Loan Ass'n*, 640 P.2d 1151 (Colo. 1982); *see also In re Opinion of the Justices*, 94 Colo. 215, 29 P.2d 705 (1934) (detailed liquor code not within scope of proclamation for special session called for poor relief, even though liquor taxes were earmarked for old age pension fund).

Note that under Article V, two-thirds of the general assembly can call the body into special session. Special sessions have no time limit—in contrast to the 120 Calendar Day limit for regular sessions. Art. V, § 7.

Art. IV, Section 10. Governor may adjourn legislature

> The governor, in case of a disagreement between the two houses as to the time of adjournment, may upon the same being certified to him by the house last moving adjournment, adjourn the general assembly to a day not later than the first day of the next regular session.

If the House and Senate cannot agree on when to adjourn, the governor can adjourn them. Ever since the 1988 GAVEL amendment limited the length of legislative sessions, sessions have always adjourned on the last day allowed by GAVEL, or even later. *See* art. V, § 8 (chapter 8, Legislative Power).

Also note art. V, § 15, which prevents either chamber from adjourning for more than three days without the consent of the other.

Art. IV, Section 11. Presentment of bills to governor for signature or veto

> Every bill passed by the general assembly shall, before it becomes a law, be presented to the governor. If he approve, he shall sign it, and thereupon it shall become a law; but if he do not approve, he shall return it, with his objections, to the house in which it originated, which house shall enter the objections at large upon its journal, and proceed to reconsider the bill. If then two-thirds of the members elected agree to pass the same, it shall be sent, together with the objections, to the other house, by which it shall likewise be reconsidered, and if approved by two-thirds of the members elected to that house, it shall become a law, notwithstanding the objections of the governor. In all such cases the vote of each house shall be determined by ayes and noes, to be entered upon the journal. If any bill shall not be returned by the governor within ten days after it shall have been presented to him, the same shall be a law in like manner as if he had signed it, unless the general assembly shall by their adjournment prevent its return, in which case it shall be filed with his objections in the office of the secretary of state, within thirty days after such adjournment, or else become a law.

The governor can sign a bill, veto a bill, or allow it to become law without his signature—if he does not veto within 10 days of when the bill is presented to him. The House and Senate may override a veto by a 2/3 vote. But if the governor times the 10-day presentment window, he can veto legislation enacted in the last 10 days of a session, since the House and Senate will have adjourned, and thus cannot override a veto.

In calculating the 10-day limit, count either the day the governor receives a bill, or the day he returns it with a veto, but not both. There are no fractional days. Something that happens at 7 A.M. or 11 P.M. counts as one day. If the return day is a Sunday, when the legislature is not in session and so the governor cannot communicate with it, the governor can deliver the veto on Monday. *In re Senate Resolution Relating to Senate Bill No. 56*, 9 Colo. 632, 21 P. 475 (1886).

The governor's rationale for a veto is not subject to judicial review. *Colorado General Assembly v. Lamm*, 704 P.2d 1371 (Colo. 1985).

What if a bill specifies that it will take effect at 12:01 A.M. on a certain date, but the governor does not sign the bill until 3:50 P.M. on that date? The bill does not go into effect until the minute of the governor's signature. *People v. Glenn*, 200 Colo. 416, 615 P.2d 700 (1980).

Art. IV, Section 12. Governor may veto items in appropriation bills

> The governor shall have power to disapprove of any item or items of any bill making appropriations of money, embracing distinct items, and the part or parts of the bill approved shall be law, and the item or items disapproved shall be void, unless enacted in manner following: If the general assembly be in session, he shall transmit to the house in which the bill originated a copy of the item or items thereof disapproved, together with his objections thereto, and the items objected to shall be separately reconsidered, and each item shall then take the same course as is prescribed for the passage of bills over the executive veto.

Unlike the U.S. president, the governor may veto line items in appropriation bills. *Clinton v. City of New York*, 524 U.S. 417 (1998) (federal statute for line-item veto is unconstitutional).

While the governor can *veto* a line item, he cannot diminish the size of the line-item appropriation.

Unlike section 11 (general vetoes), section 12 does not have an express 10-day time limit for a veto. But the 10-day rule has been held applicable to line-item vetoes. *In re Interrogatories of Governor Regarding Certain Bills of Fifty-First General Assembly*, 195 Colo. 198, 578 P.2d 200 (1978).

The general assembly cannot use definitional headnotes to legislate in the long bill. (The long bill provides the general appropriations for operation of the state government.) For bills that contain legislation and an appropriation, the governor can veto the entire bill but cannot veto the appropriation only. *Colorado General Assembly v. Owens*, 136 P.3d 262 (Colo. 2006).

Art. IV, Section 13. Succession to the offices of governor and lieutenant governor

> (1) In the case of the death, impeachment, conviction of a felony, or resignation of the governor, the office of governor shall be vacant and the lieutenant governor shall take the oath of office and shall become governor.
>
> (2) Whenever there is a vacancy in the office of the lieutenant governor, because of death, impeachment, conviction of a felony, or resignation, the governor shall nominate a lieutenant governor who shall take office upon confirmation by a majority vote of both houses of the general assembly. If the person nominated is a member of the general assembly, he may take the oath of office of lieutenant governor, and the legislative seat to which he was elected shall be vacant and filled in the manner prescribed by law pursuant to section 2 of article V of this constitution.

(3) In the event that the governor-elect fails to assume the office of governor because of death, resignation, or conviction of a felony, or refuses to take the oath of office, the lieutenant governor-elect shall take the oath of office and shall become governor on the second Tuesday in January in accordance with the provisions of section 1 of article IV of this constitution. In the event the lieutenant governor-elect fails to assume the office of lieutenant governor because of death, resignation, or conviction of a felony, or refuses to take the oath of office, the governor-elect upon taking office shall nominate a lieutenant governor who shall take the oath of office upon confirmation by a majority vote of both houses of the general assembly. If the person nominated is a member of the general assembly, he may take the oath of office of lieutenant governor, and the legislative seat to which he was elected shall be vacant and filled in the manner prescribed by law pursuant to section 2 of article V of this constitution.

(4) In the event the lieutenant governor or lieutenant governor-elect accedes to the office of governor because of a vacancy in said office for any of the causes enumerated in subsections (1) and (3) of this section, the office of lieutenant governor shall be vacant. Upon taking office, the new governor shall nominate a lieutenant governor who shall take the oath of office upon confirmation by a majority vote of both houses of the general assembly. If the person nominated is a member of the general assembly, he may take the oath of office of lieutenant governor, and the legislative seat to which he was elected shall be vacant and filled in the manner prescribed by law pursuant to section 2 of article V of this constitution.

(5) In the event the governor or lieutenant governor, or governor-elect or lieutenant governor-elect, at the time either of the latter is to take the oath of office, is absent from the state or is suffering from a physical or mental disability, the powers and duties of the office of governor and the office of lieutenant governor shall, until the absence or disability ceases, temporarily devolve upon the lieutenant governor, in the case of the governor, and, in the case of the lieutenant governor, upon the first named member of the general assembly listed in subsection (7) of this section who is affiliated with the same political party as the lieutenant governor; except that if the lieutenant governor and none of said members of the general assembly are affiliated with the same political party, the temporary vacancy in the office of lieutenant governor shall be filled by the first named member in said subsection (7). In the event that the offices of both the governor and lieutenant governor are vacant at the same time for any of the reasons enumerated in this subsection (5), the successors to fill the vacancy in the office of governor and in the office of lieutenant governor shall be, respectively, the first and second named members of the general assembly listed in subsection (7) of this section who are affiliated with the same political party as the governor; except that if the governor and none of said members of the general assembly are affiliated with the same political party, the vacancy in the office of governor and the vacancy in the office of lieutenant governor, respectively, shall be filled by the first and second named members in said subsection (7). The pro rata salary of the governor or lieutenant governor shall be paid to his successor for as long as he serves in such capacity, during which time he shall receive no other salary from the state.

(6) The governor or governor-elect, lieutenant governor or lieutenant governor-elect, or person acting as governor or lieutenant governor may transmit to the

> president of the senate and the speaker of the house of representatives his written declaration that he suffers from a physical or mental disability and he is unable to properly discharge the powers and duties of the office of governor or lieutenant governor. In the event no such written declaration has been made, his physical or mental disability shall be determined by a majority of the supreme court after a hearing held pursuant to a joint request submitted by joint resolution adopted by two-thirds of all members of each house of the general assembly. Such determination shall be final and conclusive. The supreme court, upon its own initiative, shall determine if and when such disability ceases.
>
> (7) In the event that the offices of both the governor and lieutenant governor are vacant at the same time for any of the reasons enumerated in subsections (1), (2), and (3) of this section, the successor to fill the vacancy in the office of governor shall be the first named of the following members of the general assembly who is affiliated with the same political party as the governor: president of the senate, speaker of the house of representatives, minority leader of the senate, or minority leader of the house of representatives; except that if the governor and none of said members of the general assembly are affiliated with the same political party, the vacancy shall be filled by one such member in the order of precedence listed in this subsection (7). The member filling the vacancy pursuant to this subsection (7) shall take the oath of office of governor and shall become governor. The office of lieutenant governor shall be filled in the same manner as prescribed in subsection (3) of this section when the lieutenant governor-elect fails to assume the office of lieutenant governor.

When the office of governor is vacated (*e.g.*, by felony conviction, resignation, or by impeachment), the lieutenant governor takes over. This is also the case when the governor is outside the state, or is temporarily incapacitated, such as by illness.

If there is no lieutenant governor, the chain of succession is the Senate and House leadership, with the proviso that the successor must be of the same political party as the governor.

This is different from the federal system. The U.S. Constitution (art. II, § 1, cl. 6), specifies that the vice-president succeeds the president, and that Congress can provide by law for additional successors. Details of vice-presidential succession are specified by the 20th and 25th Amendments. Under the Presidential Succession Act of 1947, 3 U.S.C. § 19, the line of succession after vice-president is speaker of the House, president of the Senate, and then the cabinet officers, in order of seniority for when their department was created. (So secretary of state is first, and the secretary of homeland security is last.)

Subsection (5) of Colorado's section 13 covers the same ground as does the U.S. 25th Amendment, allowing for the lieutenant governor to temporarily assume the office of governor if the governor is unable to perform the job because of mental or physical disability.

Subsection (5) also puts the lieutenant governor in charge whenever the governor is outside the state. During territorial days, the secretary of state was often called up to act as governor, such as while the governor was in Washington, there being no office of lieutenant governor at the time. In 1978, lieutenant gov. George Brown took advantage of governor Lamm's travel outside of Colorado and issued a spree of pardons. Governor Lamm quickly rescinded the pardons, which were invalid because they had not complied with the statute (C.R.S. § 16-17-102) that required a pardon applicant to produce a certificate of good conduct from the superintendent of the correctional facility, plus notice to and comment from the district attorney and sentencing judge. *People ex rel. Garrison v. Lamm*, 622 P.2d 87 (Colo. 1980).

The last Colorado governor to permanently leave office was John Love, whom president Nixon appointed as "Energy Czar" in 1973, to address the energy crisis that had begun with the Arab oil embargo against the United States.

Art. IV, Section 14. Lieutenant governor is president of the senate (repealed)

The Lieutenant governor's authority to preside over the Senate was eliminated by the voters in 1974.

By Jerry Kopel
In 1966, Democrat Mark Hogan was elected lieutenant governor, defeating Joe Shoemaker by about 17,000 votes. At the time, the constitution provided for separate elections for that office and the office of governor. Republican John Love was elected to his second term as governor over Bob Knous.

The Democrats lost 15 seats in the Colorado House and every executive office election except lieutenant governor. Attorney general Duke Dunbar defeated Bill Chisholm; secretary of state Byron Anderson defeated Arch Decker (he was a Democrat at the time),[8] and Virginia Blue defeated Homer Bedford for state treasurer.[9] In the other major race, Republican Gordon Allott won a third term in the U.S. Senate defeating Roy Romer by 100,000 votes.

The 1966 election made Hogan the focus of the Democratic party, and the holder of that office had much more power than it does now.

Hogan was, by law, president of the state senate and in charge of assigning bills to committees, even though the Senate had 20 Republicans and 15 Democrats. In the event of a tie in a recorded senate vote, Hogan could break the tie.

The Republicans were not happy to have Hogan around. They began the 1967 term by assigning Evelyn Davidson, Hogan's administrative assistant, a desk in the same office as Republicans, which meant she could not expect privacy as she discussed items either in person or on the phone. Mrs. Davidson had been chief clerk of the House in 1965 when the House was under Democratic control.

Hogan went public. He had Davidson's desk moved into the corridor outside the office, where the general public, the lobbyists, and the legislators would have to pass by. If there weren't going to be privacy, then the world would know about it. The picture of Mrs. Davidson sitting out in the corridor made good copy for the newspapers, and enough pressure for the Senate Republicans to eventually provide Davidson and Hogan with privacy.

---

[8] Decker served as a Democratic Colorado state legislator from 1963 to 1979, including as senate minority leader. In the 1972 Democratic primary for Denver's U.S. House seat, Decker lost to Patricia Schroeder. Schroeder went on to unseat one-term incumbent Republican Mike McKevitt. She continued to win re-election until retiring in 1996. In 1982, Decker switched parties, ran as the Republican nominee against Schroeder, and was defeated 62% to 38%.

[9] You will find Bedford's name in many reported Colorado cases. From 1933 through 1967, he alternated between serving as state treasurer and state auditor, winning a two-year term in every race. The only time he was out of office as 1943–45, because he had been the Democratic nominee for governor in 1942 and was defeated by Republican John Vivian.

Art. IV, Section 15. Who to act as governor if lieutenant governor cannot (repealed)

This used to govern succession in situations when there was no lieutenant governor.

Art. IV, Section 16. Accounts and report of moneys

> An account shall be kept by the officers of the executive department and of all public institutions of the state, of all moneys received by them severally from all sources, and for every service performed, and of all moneys disbursed by them severally, and a semi-annual report thereof shall be made to the governor, under oath.

A good government provision requiring two reports per year by executive departments of their income and spending.

Art. IV, Section 17. Executive officers to make reports (repealed)

Repealed 1974. Originally:

> The officers of the Executive Department, and of all public institutions of the State, shall, at least twenty days preceding each regular session of the General Assembly, make full and complete report of their actions to the Governor, who shall transmit the same to the General Assembly.

Art. IV, Section 18, State Seal

> There shall be a seal of the state, which shall be kept by the secretary of state, shall be called the "Great Seal of the State of Colorado", and shall be in the form prescribed by the general assembly

Frank Hall, who served as a territorial secretary of Colorado, recalled territorial governor Cummings as "perhaps the most unpopular because wholly unfitted by the peculiar bent of his disposition to govern a free and radically independent people . . . He came not as the servant of the people, but as their master, and believing that the entire scheme of government should be under his personal control." FRANK HALL, 2 HISTORY OF COLORADO 369–70 (2008) (1890). Fearing the clear legal independence of territorial secretary Samuel Elbert, governor Cummings "surreptitiously entered the Secretary's office during the temporary absence of that official, and carried the seal to his own quarters." Elbert sent a note demanding the return of the seal, but Cummings refused. *Id.* at 372–73.[10]

---

[10] Frank Hall succeeded Elbert as Territorial Secretary, and his relationship with governor Cummings was even more conflict-ridden than Elbert's had been. EUGENE H. BERWANGER, THE RISE OF THE CENTENNIAL STATE: COLORADO TERRITORY, 1861–76, at 48 (2007).

History and meaning of the Great Seal

by Jerry Kopel

On Nov. 6, 1861, the first territorial assembly of Colorado passed a law creating Colorado's Territorial Great Seal. With few changes, it became the model for Colorado's State Seal, adopted in 1877. It had been proposed by territorial secretary Lewis Ledyard Weld.

The Latin motto is *Nil Sine Numine*, in black letters on a white background. The words have two possible interpretations: "Nothing Without Providence" or "Nothing Without Deity."[11]

In 1861, as today, at the very top of the Great Seal is "the eye of God" enclosed within golden rays thrusting into the lines of an outer triangle. On the back of a $1 bill, you will find the same "eye of God," on the left side.

Directly below the triangle is the Roman fasces, a bundle of sticks tied together by a band of red, white and blue, with the words "Union and Constitution." The Territory of Colorado was showing where it stood in the Civil War.

During the Roman Republic and Empire, the fasces were a bundle of wooden rods, wrapped around an ax. The fasces are a visual metaphor for the idea that a stick by itself can easily be snapped, but a bundle of sticks tied together (by Union and Constitution) is hard to break.

Below the fasces is a heraldic shield. At the top of the shield are three snow-capped mountains, as high as the clouds, against a red background of Colorado soil.

Below the clouds, separated by a thin line, are the pickaxe and sledgehammer of a miner. Mining was the foundation of the Colorado economy.

On March 15, 1877, the general assembly adopted the and the Great Seal of Colorado, with little change from the territorial seal. C.R.S. § 24-80-901. In the new seal, there is "1876" where "1861" once appeared. The Latin phrase *Sigillum Territorii Coloradenesis* ("Seal of the Territory of Colorado") became the English words "State of Colorado."

Today, at the bottom are six stars, three on each side of the numerals "1876." But our state statute doesn't mention the six stars, and nobody today has identified what they represent. So if you want, you can create your own meanings for the six stars of Colorado seal.

Figure 21. Great Seal of Colorado.

[11] The territorial motto proposed by Weld happened to be his family motto. He was the nephew of famed abolitionist Theodore Dwight Weld. He went east to fight in the Civil War, rose to the rank of major, and commanded some of the early units of black troops, the U.S. Colored Infantry. He died at the siege of Petersburg, Virginia, in 1864. EUGENE H. BERWANGER, THE RISE OF THE CENTENNIAL STATE: COLORADO TERRITORY, 1861–76, at 9 (2007).

Other Colorado emblems

The information below is from the pamphlet *Emblems of the State of Colorado* (no date).

Figure 17. State flag.

Adopted June 5, 1911. It uses "the colors of the national flag, the blue of Colorado skies, the gold of her metal, the white of mountain snows, and the red of her soil."

Figure 18. State flower, the Columbine.

Aquilegia caerules. White and lavender-blue Rocky Mountain Columbine. Adopted Apr. 4, 1889. "Chosen because of blue for skies, white for snow and yellow for gold."

Figure 19. State animal, Rocky Mountain Big Horn Sheep.

Adopted May 1, 1961. “Is peculiar to the Rocky Mountains. Shows much bravery and tremendous endurance.”

Figure 20. State bird, Lark Bunting.

Calmospiza malanocorys Stejneger. Adopted Apr. 29, 1931. “While in flight sings varied and pleasant songs.”

Figure 21. State tree, Colorado Blue Spruce.

Picea pungens. Adopted 1939. Grows at elevations of 5,000 to 9,000 feet. "Color ranges from green to blue to true silver."

Art. IV, Section 19. Officer salaries

> The officers named in section one of this article shall receive for their services a salary to be established by law, which shall not be increased or diminished during their official terms. It shall be the duty of all such officers to collect in advance all fees prescribed by law for services rendered by them severally, and pay the same into the state treasury.

By prohibiting changes in an officer's salary during a term, section 19 prevents the general assembly from threatening or cajoling an officer to perform his or her job in a certain manner.

Section 19 has been interpreted broadly to prohibit a special appropriation for "expenses" that seemed to be a compensation increase—as when the lieutenant governor was given money for "expenses" equal to half his salary:

> The claim is made that it was for his expenses. But what expenses? He has no office, books, records, or papers to keep or care for. In his official capacity as Lieutenant Governor, he has no acts to perform for the public except to go to the Capitol, preside over the Senate, and return home, and, when it adjourns sine die, his duties with the public service cease. He has no expenses which are made a charge against the state. While the Legislature is in session, an office is furnished him free at the Capitol, and the appropriation of $38,000 to pay for printing, stationery, stamps, supplies, and miscellaneous expenses, include him while presiding over the Senate, with the officers and members of the Legislature; and when acting as Governor he is entitled to the pay and emoluments of the Governor. As Lieutenant Governor, he has no official or semiofficial duties to perform other than to preside over the Senate.

Leckenby v. Post Printing & Publishing Co., 65 Colo. 443, 446-47, 176 P. 490, 491-92 (1918).[12]

Constitutional officer salaries are provided by C.R.S. § 24-9-101. Formerly, salaries were enumerated amounts, such as $90,000 for the governor. But starting in 2019, salaries were set as a percentage of other salaries.

- Governor: 66% of the chief justice's salary.
- Lt. gov. 58% of the salary for county court judges in Class B counties. If the lieutenant gov. is also appointed to head a department, the lieutenant gov. gets the higher salary of the department head.
- Attorney general, 60% of the chief judge of the court of appeals.
- Secretary of state, same at lt. governor.
- State treasurer, same at lt. governor.

Salary revisions are quadrennial, so that no-one's salary is increased during a term. The new system makes it easy for the legislator to raise executive branch salaries via a bill that only mentions judicial salaries—a much less controversial issue than overtly raising salaries of the executive branch.

Art. IV, Section 20. State librarian (repealed)

Thanks to repeal in 2004, the office of state librarian is no longer constitutionalized. Formerly, the state superintendent of education was the ex officio state librarian.

The State Library is currently part of the Department of Education.

Art. IV, Section 21. Elected state auditor (repealed)

The requirement that the state auditor be elected was removed in 1974. In contrast, Denver requires that the city auditor be elected. Being independent, the Denver city auditor has often served as a check on financial shenanigans at city hall.

For more on the state auditor, see art. V, § 49.

Art. IV, Section 22. Principal departments

> All executive and administrative offices, agencies, and instrumentalities of the executive department of state government and their respective functions, powers, and duties, except for the office of governor and lieutenant governor, shall be allocated by law among and within not more than twenty departments. Subsequently, all new powers or functions shall be assigned to departments, divisions, sections, or units in such manner as will tend to provide an orderly arrangement in the administrative organization of state government. Temporary commissions may be established by law and need not be allocated within a principal department. Nothing in this section shall supersede the provisions of section 13, article XII, of this constitution, except that the classified civil service of the state shall not extend to heads of principal departments established pursuant to this section.

[12] The court also rejected the argument that the "expenses" appropriation could be for "mileage," and that the legislature's supposed determination thereon could not be questioned. The court pointed out that there was no statute authorizing the lieutenant governor to take mileage.

By this 1966 amendment, there be no more than 20 principal departments in the executive branch. This includes departments whose heads are elected by the people. For example, the attorney general is the head of the Department of Law.

The organizational hierarchy in the executive branch is departments, divisions within departments, sections within divisions, and units within sections.

As the last sentence of section 22 indicates, the civil service provisions in article XII do not apply to department heads, but they do apply for everyone below them. Accordingly, the Colorado governor's appointment power is unusually weak. A new governor can appoint the members of his office, and the heads of 17 departments. (Since three department heads are elected by the people: treasurer, attorney general, secretary of state). The department heads usually can appoint their own division heads. (Or the division heads suggested by the governor.) Beyond division heads, the governor is stuck with the other employees of his 17 departments; they are in civil service positions for which removal is very difficult.

Outside the civil service system, the governor does enjoy very broad appointive powers for boards and commissions, many of which have extensive legal authority.

Art. IV, Section 23. Commissioner of insurance appointed by governor

> The governor shall nominate and, by and with the consent of the senate, appoint the commissioner of insurance to serve at his pleasure, and the state personnel system shall not extend to the commissioner of insurance.

The commissioner is the head of the division of insurance, which is part of the department of regulatory agencies (DORA). C.R.S. § 10-1-104. Normally, division heads are appointed by department heads. The 1984 addition of section 23 allows the governor to choose the commissioner.

CHAPTER 8

Legislative Power, art. V

Introduction

This chapter covers most of article V of the Colorado Constitution. Article V address three main topics:

First, the legislative power itself. Section 1 describes the legislative power, including the people's reserved powers of referendum and initiative. Those powers are covered in chapter 9. This chapter 8 covers the parts of section 1 that apply to the general assembly.

The second major topic of article V is the operation of the general assembly—the state legislature. Most of sections 2 through 43 are about the structure of the general assembly, its procedures, spending, appropriations, ethical rules, and the like. Gifts for legislators and other government employees are also regulated by article XXIX, added by initiative in 2006.

The third major topic of article V is legislative apportionment:1 How to create boundaries for Colorado House of Representatives and Colorado Senate districts. 2. How to create boundaries for U.S. House of Representatives districts. Apportionment comprises most of sections 44 through 50.[1]

Apportionment was comprehensively revised by constitutional amendment in 2018. The general assembly voted unanimously to refer the amendment to the people. The people approved by over 80%.

Article V rules of legislative operation have many analogues for counties, municipalities, and other local bodies that exercise legislative power. Such rules are contained in charters and other governing laws. Knowing article V is a good step towards understanding local government legislative powers.

The remainder of this Introduction covers several topics useful to understanding Colorado legislation:

- Why Colorado Constitution rules on legislative operation are so detailed.
- Compilations of historical Colorado statutes, and where to find them.
- Colorado's statutory rules of statutory interpretation.
- A brief introduction to the House Rules and Senate Rules.
- The 1988 GAVEL Amendment, the most important reform of legislative process in Colorado constitutional history.

[1] Section 49, as amended, replaces the elected state auditor with an appointee. Section 50 restricts the legislature's ability to spend taxpayer dollars on abortion.

This chapter contains two tables, as the end. Table 2 details the partisan composition of every general assembly from 1901 to the present. Table 3 lists every Colorado U.S. Senator from 1876 statehood to the present.

Why Colorado Constitution rules on legislative operation are so detailed

The first American state constitutions were usually terse. Starting in the 1830s, state constitutions became increasingly specific. Specificity was considered necessary to prevent special interest misuse of government. G. ALAN TARR, UNDERSTANDING STATE CONSTITUTIONS 118 (1998). Many provisions in article V are typical of post-1830 state constitutions.

The first phase of state constitution making had been under the wartime conditions of the American Revolution. The next phase had been with a nation getting on its feet. The early state constitutions declared important and enduring principles. Those who propounded such constitutions were sometimes short on time, and necessarily limited in experience in American state constitutional law.

By the 1830s, there was a consensus that the initial state constitutions had been insufficient to prevent abuses. Constitutions began becoming longer. Colorado's 1876 Constitution was the longest to date.

The U.S. Constitution could be terse because it involved only limited powers. The U.S. Constitution gives Congress a specific list of enumerated powers; most of them are listed in article I, section 8. In the eighteenth and nineteenth centuries, everyone accepted the constitutional rules that Congress could only legislate pursuant to enumerated powers. (Much later, in the mid-twentieth century, the Interstate Commerce Clause and the Spending Power began to be treated like general powers over almost everything.)

Unlike the U.S. Congress, state legislatures were not confined to enumerated powers. "Because state legislatures possessed plenary legislative power, successful restriction required prohibitions and limitations that were specific and detailed. Much of the constitutional legislation that swelled state constitutions . . . reflected . . . a determined attempt to restrict state legislative forays into economic boosterism and favoritism." TARR at 112-13.

The people had seen how easily state legislators were seduced into diverting the taxpayer's earnings into the hands of special interests that could procure legislative influence. The Colorado Territory (1861–76) had seen similar problems. Railroads had made big promises to procure government subsidies. When the railroads went bust, the taxpayers were stuck.

State legislatures were not confining themselves to general rules for society; they were often passing bills to give special benefits to someone or the other. The reform movement that had begun in the1830s was stronger than ever in the 1870s. In long-established states, the people enacted new constitutions to crack down on state legislatures. For example, Missouri's new 1875 constitution had 56 subject matter restrictions on the state legislature. Illinois (1870) had 20, Pennsylvania (1873) had 40, and California (1879) had 33.[2]

In Colorado, section 25 of article V contains 23 subject matter prohibitions. Of these, only one (benefits for particular corporations) is routinely disobeyed. Besides the section 25 prohibitions, various other provisions of the Colorado Constitution include restrictions or prohibitions of legislative action on particular subjects.

Many of the Colorado Constitution's rules for the legislature are based on common sense. For example, the bill title should express what the bill is about; unrelated subjects should not be hidden under a deceptive title. While such rules are always salutary, experience by 1876 had

---

[2] In the nineteenth century, many states held new constitutional conventions to replace their older state constitutions. See Donald Marritz, *Making Equality Matter (Again): The Prohibition against Special Laws in the Pennsylvania Constitution*, 3 WIDENER J. PUBLIC L. 161 (1993).

shown that the rules were necessary was to prevent government economic favoritism to special economic interests.

The rules were indeed necessary, but they were not always sufficient. Post-1876 amendments have attempted to keep government neutral, neither favoring one interest nor the other.

Colorado statutory compilations

Colorado's statutes are officially complied in Colorado Revised Statutes. The Legislative Council, a research arm of the state legislature, suggests the following cite forms for earlier editions of Colorado statutes:

Revised Statutes of Colorado. Begun in 1868. Cite as: R.S. P.____, § ____.
General Laws of Colorado 1877. G.L. § ____.
General Statutes of Colorado. 1883. G.S. § ____.
Revised Statutes of Colorado. 1908. R.S. 08, § _____.
Compiled Laws of Colorado. 1921. C.L. § ___.
Colorado Revised Statutes 1953. C.R.S. 53, § ____.
Colorado Revised Statutes 1963. C.R.S. 1963, § ___.
Colorado Revised Statutes. 1973. C.R.S. § ____.[3]

All of the above, and many other early editions of Colorado statutes are available in the State Statutes libraries in HeinOnline.com. All the territorial statutes are there, including the 1859 Provisional Territory of Jefferson.

Legislative resolutions

Unlike statutes, legislative resolutions do not have force of law. They express the opinion of the House, the Senate, or the joint bodies on a particular matter. For resolution research tips, see Chris Hudson, *Researching Colorado Resolutions and Memorials*, 46 COLO. LAWYER 14 (Aug./Sept. 2017).

Statutory rules of statutory interpretation

Colorado Revised Statutes, title II, articles 4 & 5, contains statutory rules for statutory interpretation. If you are ever involved in a dispute about Colorado statutory interpretation, make sure to read these articles. All the rules below can be altered in a given statute if the statute so provides. Among the general rules:

- "Words and phrases shall be read in context and construed according to the rules of grammar and common usage. Words and phrases that have acquired a technical or particular meaning, whether by legislative definition or otherwise, shall be construed accordingly." C.R.S. § 2-4-102.
- "The singular includes the plural, and the plural includes the singular." C.R.S. § 2-4-102.
- "Words in the present tense include the future tense." C.R.S. § 2-4-104.
- "In computing a period of days, the first day is excluded and the last day is included." C.R.S. § 2-4-108(1). "If the last day of any period is a Saturday, Sunday, or legal holiday,

[3] This was originally cited as "Colorado Revised Statutes 1973," but the number was dropped in 1983. See 1983 Session Laws 377.

the period is extended to include the next day which is not a Saturday, Sunday, or legal holiday." *Id.* at (2).

- "(1) In enacting a statute, it is presumed that: (a) Compliance with the constitutions of the state of Colorado and the United States is intended; (b) The entire statute is intended to be effective; (c) A just and reasonable result is intended; (d) A result feasible of execution is intended; (e) Public interest is favored over any private interest." C.R.S. § 2-4-201.
- "A statute is presumed to be prospective in its operation." C.R.S. § 2-4-202. This provides another layer of protection against ex post facto law.
- "(1) If a statute is ambiguous, the court, in determining the intention of the general assembly, may consider among other matters: (a) The object sought to be attained; (b) The circumstances under which the statute was enacted; (c) The legislative history, if any; (d) The common law or former statutory provisions, including laws upon the same or similar subjects; (e) The consequences of a particular construction; (f) The administrative construction of the statute; (g) The legislative declaration or purpose." C.R.S. § 2-4-203.
- "If statutes enacted at the same or different sessions of the general assembly are irreconcilable, the statute prevails which is latest in its effective date. If the irreconcilable statutes have the same effective date, the statute prevails which is latest in its date of passage." C.R.S. § 2-4-206.
- "The common law of England so far as the same is applicable and of a general nature, and all acts and statutes of the British parliament, made in aid of or to supply the defects of the common law prior to the fourth year of James the First [1607, the year of the establishment of the Virginia Colony], excepting the second section of the sixth chapter of forty-third Elizabeth, the eighth chapter of thirteenth Elizabeth, and the ninth chapter of thirty-seventh Henry the Eighth,[4] and which are of a general nature, and not local to that kingdom, shall be the rule of decision, and shall be considered as of full force until repealed by legislative authority." C.R.S. § 2-4-206.
- "All general provisions, terms, phrases, and expressions, used in any statute, shall be liberally construed, in order that the true intent and meaning of the general assembly may be fully carried out." C.R.S. § 2-4-212.
- "The general assembly hereby finds and declares that the rule of statutory construction expressed in the Colorado supreme court decision entitled *People v. McPherson,* 200 Colo. 429, 619 P.2d 38 (1980), which holds that '. . . relative and qualifying words and phrases, where no contrary intention appears, are construed to refer solely to the last antecedent with which they are closely connected . . .' has not been adopted by the general assembly and does not create any presumption of statutory intent." C.R.S. § 2-4-214.
- Because each general assembly is a separate entity, "no legislation passed by one general assembly requiring an appropriation shall bind future general assemblies." C.R.S. § 2-4-215.
- The general assembly's creation of a program does not create any obligation for future funding of that program. C.R.S. § 2-4-216.
- "The repeal of a repealing statute does not revive the statute originally repealed." C.R.S. § 2-4-302.

---

[4] The statute means that English common law from before 1607 is part of the common law of Colorado. However, a few English laws are expressly not the law in Colorado: 43 Elizabeth, ch. 6, § 2 (1601) (temporary statute forbidding plaintiffs to recover attorneys fees in certain cases involving less than 40 shillings); 13 Elizabeth, ch. 8 (1571) ("An Acte against Userie); 37 Henry VIII 9 (1545) ("An Acte against Userys").

- Statutory repeals do not terminate any liability or punishment that has already been incurred, unless the repeal statute expressly says so. C.R.S. § 2-4-303.
- Definitions of various terms. For example, "child" includes child by adoption. "Minor" means anyone under 21 unless a statute expressly says otherwise. "Registered mail" includes certified mail. "Must" does not create a duty. C.R.S. § 2-4-401.[5]

House and Senate Rules

The Colorado House and Senate have each created rules for their operation. There are also Joint Rules, such as about transmission of information from one chamber to another. Colorado's legislative rules are based on Robert's Rules of Order. They were written by U.S. Army General Henry Martin Robert, and first published in 1876. His rules were based on English parliamentary procedure, later imported to America.

Useful summaries are available in Colorado House of Representatives Selected Rules at a Glance and Colorado Senate Selected Rules at a Glance.

Anyone involved in bill drafting may usefully consult the 662 page Colorado Legislative Drafting Manual, from the Office of Legislative Legal Services.

Further reading: Herrick K. Lidstone & Jeremy Schupbach, *How the Colorado General Assembly Works*, 45 COLO. LAWYER 33 (Dec. 2016).

The 1988 GAVEL Amendment

In 1988, State Representative Wayne Knox (D-Denver) teamed up with Common Cause to pass the Constitution's most significant reform of general assembly operations. "[N]ever . . . known as either a conservative or a maverick," Knox would become the most experienced state representative in Colorado history (32 years in the State House, 1961–96, continuously after 1975). Since Republicans controlled both houses, GAVEL proponents wisely had a Republican as chief sponsor in each house. After the Amendment was enacted, Knox bucked Democratic governor Romer and Democratic colleagues who tried to evade the new rules on caucuses.[6]

GAVEL stood for "give a vote to every legislator." GAVEL's provisions were:

- 120 calendar day limit on regular legislative sessions. Art. V, § 7.
- Reforming procedures for hearings and votes on bills—such as preventing committee chairs from refusing to hold a vote on a bill. Art. V. § 20.
- Prohibition on binding caucus positions. Art. V, §§ 22a.
- All actions in violations of sections 20 or 22a are "null and void." Art. V, § 22b.

As in all chapters of this textbook, <u>underlining of constitutional text indicates text that has been entirely or mostly nullified in practice</u>. Nullification is often a result of judicial decisions not to enforce textual prohibitions on legislative or executive misbehavior.

The people's powers of initiative and referendum are discussed in chapter 9. In the text of section 1 below, subsections only about initiative and referendum are summarized in brackets.

---

[5] However, in this book, when I write "must" in the narrative, I am referring to actions that are mandatory, not optional.

[6] Peter Blake, *House Dems Deny Caucus Conspiracy*, ROCKY MOUNTAIN NEWS, May 11, 1990, 1990 WLNR 414421.

Art. V, Section 1. General Assembly. Initiative and Referendum

(1) The legislative power of the state shall be vested in the general assembly consisting of a senate and house of representatives, both to be elected by the people, but the people reserve to themselves the power to propose laws and amendments to the constitution and to enact or reject the same at the polls independent of the general assembly and also reserve power at their own option to approve or reject at the polls any act or item, section, or part of any act of the general assembly.

(2) [Power of initiative.]

(2.5) [2016 amendment on signature gathering for initiative petitions.]

(3) The second power hereby reserved is the referendum, and it may be ordered, <u>except as to laws necessary for the immediate preservation of the public peace, health, or safety</u>, and appropriations for the support and maintenance of the departments of state and state institutions, against any act or item, section, or part of any act of the general assembly, either by a petition signed by registered electors in an amount equal to at least five percent of the total number of votes cast for all candidates for the office of the secretary of state at the previous general election or by the general assembly. Referendum petitions, in such form as may be prescribed pursuant to law, shall be addressed to and filed with the secretary of state not more than ninety days after the final adjournment of the session of the general assembly that passed the bill on which the referendum is demanded. The filing of a referendum petition against any item, section, or part of any act shall not delay the remainder of the act from becoming operative.

(4) [Governor cannot veto measures enacted by initiative or referendum.]

(5) [Process for creating ballot titles for initiatives.]

(5.5) [Petition measures may contain only a single subject. Added 1995]

(6) [Petition forms]

(7) [Secretary of state processes the petitions.]

(7.3) [Nonpartisan research staff of the general assembly shall publish the text and title of every measure in a legal publication of general circulation.]

(7.5) [Nonpartisan research staff shall create a "blue book" containing the pro/con arguments in measures. The blue book will be sent to all voters before the election.]

(8) The style of all laws adopted by the people through the initiative shall be, "Be it Enacted by the People of the State of Colorado".

(9) [The initiative and referendum powers reserved to the people by this section are hereby further reserved to the registered electors for all forms of local government.].

(10) This section of the constitution shall be in all respects self-executing; except that the form of the initiative or referendum petition may be prescribed pursuant to law.

Safety and Emergency Clauses

The checks and balances in the Colorado Constitution include provisions that apply after a bill has been enacted. The first of these, in effect from 1876 until 1950, provided that no bill could take effect until 90 after enactment. The 90-day rule did not apply to appropriations. The rule could be avoided "in case of emergency," based on a finding of emergency by two-thirds of each house.

In 1910, the long campaign to secure the people's rights of initiative and referendum succeeded. The legislature voted to send a proposed constitutional amendment to the people, and the people adopted it in the 1910 general election. Article V, section 1, was substantially revised. The new subsection (3), on referendum, provided that the operation of a new law may be suspended if five percent of the voters sign a petition against it. Then, the new law will be put to a public vote in the next general election. The five percent figure is calculated based on the total number of persons who voted in the most recent election for secretary of state.

A new bill can be immunized from the petition and referendum if the legislature declares that the bill is immediately necessary for public safety.

Early abuse of the Emergency Clause

The 1876 Constitution had provided that bills could not take effect for 90 days unless they were for an "emergency." In the early years of statehood, about one third of bills were labeled "emergency" measures. Sometimes, there was good reason. For example, laws about irrigation, fishing, or cattle roundups might need immediate effect because of seasonal conditions. By the early 1890s, almost every bill was supposedly an "emergency."[7]

Safety Clause abuse

Under the 1910 amendment on the right of referendum, general assembly bills could be shielded from referendum if they were "necessary for the immediate preservation of the public peace, health, or safety, and appropriations for the support and maintenance of the departments of state and state institutions." Art. V, § 1 (3). So legislators began adding a Safety Clause to their bills. The standard wording is: "The General Assembly hereby finds, determine and declares that this act is necessary for the immediate preservation of the public peace, health, and safety."

With a Safety Clause, the bill was protected from the possibility of referendum by the people. Further, the Safety Clause exempted the bill from the rule that the bills cannot take effect until 90 days after enactment.

According to the 1876 constitutional text, putting an Emergency Clause in a bill required a two-thirds vote in both the House and Senate. But a Safety Clause only needed a simple majority in each house. And the Safety Clause could be used to thwart the 90-day rule.

---

[7] Donald Wayne Hensel, A History of the Colorado Constitution in the Nineteenth Century (Ph.D. thesis in History, Univ. of Colo. 1957) (available in ProQuest Dissertations and Theses). The Hensel thesis remains the leading work on its subject. Unfortunately, the ProQuest version is a scan, without optical character recognition, so the reader cannot search by key words.

Safety clauses were routinely inserted in almost all bills. No one paid the slightest attention to whether a given bill was genuinely "necessary for the immediate preservation of the public peace, health, and safety." Even a 1911 bill to provide for printing the records of the 1876 Colorado Constitutional Convention was an "emergency." Although the convention's records had gone 35 years without being published, a further delay of 90 days was an "emergency."

Accordingly, the constitutional 90-day waiting period, and the provision for an emergency exception, were repealed in 1950.

In practice, most general assembly bills are enacted to take effect on July 1. This will normally be at least 45 days after the end of a general assembly regular session, which is required to conclude by mid-May. (The session limits are specified in article V, § 7.)

The 1910 referendum amendment's obvious purpose was to make a referendum possible on almost all legislation if the legislation were so controversial that the requisite number of signatures could be gathered. After voters in 1932 used the referendum to have a popular vote about a bill that imposed a new tax on margarine, the general assembly began attaching a safety clause to every single bill.

During the 1990s, Safety Clause abuse was criticized by retired state representative Jerry Kopel in his columns in the *Colorado Statesman*—a weekly newspaper now known as *Colorado Politics*. Then and now, the weekly is much read by persons involved in state politics.

In 1995, three Senators managed to get five bills passed without a safety clause. Three bills were by minority leader Mike Feeley (D), and one each by Sen. Bob Schaffer (R) and Rep. Martha Kreutz (R).

In 1997, automatic insertion of the Safety Clause in every bill ended; legislative drafters were instructed to ask the sponsor whether to include a Safety Clause.[8] Yet even today, "Nearly half of all bills in the last three years have come with a safety clause. 2019: 46% of 460 bills. 2018: 44% of 432 bills. 2017: 45% of 423 bills."[9]

According to the Colorado supreme court, legislative use of the Safety Clause is "conclusive and not subject to judicial review." *Cavanaugh v. State*, 644 P.2d 1, 4 (Colo. 1982). In the foundational case for non-review, the court's majority stated:

> It is a question of which the Legislature alone is the judge, and when it determines the fact to exist, its action is final . . . Power may be abused, but that is not a valid reason for one coordinate branch of the government to assign for limiting the power and authority of another department.

Van-Kleeck v. Ramer, 62 Colo. 4, 10–12, 156 P. 1108 (1916). The *Van-Kleeck* dissent criticized the majority for holding:

> that the ipse dixit of the assembly is paramount to the Constitution; that it can, if it pleases, declare that to be constitutional, which the Constitution prohibits in unmistakable terms. Such is the logic of the majority opinion . . . I think no sane person will insist that a civil service law can be "immediately necessary for the preservation of the public peace, health or safety," under any sort of meaning to be applied to such terms.

Id. at 26–28 (Scott, J., dissenting).

---

[8] See Office of Legislative Legal Services, *Safety Clauses and Effective Date Clauses* (2018) (discussing history of Safety Clause.

[9] Marshall Zelinger, *Safety clauses: This is how state legislators get new laws on the book quickly*, 9NEWS.COM, Feb. 17, 2020.

A Safety Clause blocks a referendum petition, which would suspend the operation of the new statute until the general election. But a Safety Clause cannot block a citizen initiative to repeal the law. If sufficient initiative petitions were gathered, the law would remain in effect until the general election results were certified.

Big little lies

Routine overuse of the Safety Clause is harmful to the legislature and the Constitution. Every use of the Safety Clause for bills that having nothing to do with immediate preservation of public safety makes the bill a lie and makes its sponsors liars. When people get accustomed to routinely telling small lies, it becomes easier for them to tell bigger lies.

When the final section of most bills introduced by most legislators is a lie, a legislative culture of respect for honesty, the Constitution, and the law-making rights of the people is degraded. If every bill a legislator introduces includes a clause that treats the Constitution as a pesky technicality to be evaded, the legislator is moving in the direction of treating the oath to uphold the Constitution as having no meaningful effect.

Art. V, Section 2. Election of Members, Vacancies, Oath

> (1) A general election for members of the general assembly shall be held on the first Tuesday after the first Monday in November in each even-numbered year, at such places in each county as now are or hereafter may be provided by law.
>
> (2) Each member of the general assembly, before he enters upon his official duties, shall take an oath or affirmation to support the constitution of the United States and of the state of Colorado and to faithfully perform the duties of his office according to the best of his ability. This oath or affirmation shall be administered in the chamber of the house to which the member has been elected.
>
> (3) Any vacancy occurring in either house by death, resignation, or otherwise shall be filled in the manner prescribed by law. The person appointed to fill the vacancy shall be a member of the same political party, if any, as the person whose termination of membership in the general assembly created the vacancy.

This aligns general assembly elections with federal congressional elections, which by an 1872 statute must take place on the above date. 2 U.S.C. § 7 (also specifying that new Congress will convene on the following Jan. 3). The same date is federally required for the presidential election. 3 U.S.C. § 1. The dates were set by Colorado statute until 1950, and then constitutionalized that year.

Art. V, Section 3. Terms and term limits of senators and representatives

> (1) Senators shall be elected for the term of four years and representatives for the term of two years.
>
> (2) In order to broaden the opportunities for public service and to assure that the general assembly is representative of Colorado citizens, no senator shall serve more than two consecutive terms in the senate, and no representative shall serve more than four consecutive terms in the house of representatives. This limitation

> on the number of terms shall apply to terms of office beginning on or after January 1, 1991. Any person appointed or elected to fill a vacancy in the general assembly and who serves at least one-half of a term of office shall be considered to have served a term in that office for purposes of this subsection (2). Terms are considered consecutive unless they are at least four years apart.

Starting with Oklahoma in 1990, term limits initiatives swept the nation; by 1994, 20 more states had adopted state legislative term limits. Colorado's first term limits amendments were part of the 1990 wave.

In 1995, the U.S. supreme court held 5–4 that states may not impose term limits on members of the U.S. House or Senate. *U.S. Term Limits, Inc. v. Thornton*, 514 U.S. 779 (1995). The majority ruled that states may not create qualifications for congresspersons beyond those contained in the U.S. Constitution, article I, §§ 2–3 (U.S Representatives must be at least 25 years old; a citizen for at least 7 years; and an inhabitant of the state from which elected; Senators must be at least 30, a citizen for 9 years, and a state inhabitant).

The U.S. Constitution does not prohibit states from creating term limits for state government officers. Of the states whose voters enacted term limits for state legislators, the limits are in effect in 15 states. In four states, the limits were nullified by the courts (Massachusetts, Oregon, Washington, Wyoming). In two they were repealed by the state legislature (Idaho, Utah).

In Colorado, Attorney General Opinions are *not* binding law, but courts may consider them to be persuasive. A 2000 Colorado Attorney General Opinion said that elected officials may not evade term limits by running in a different district. Colo. Atty' Gen. Op. No. 00-05, July 10, 2000.

There are many good arguments pro and con about term limits. Below is the perspective of an experienced legislator. He served 1965–66, lost the 1966 election, then won in 1970, 1972, and 1974. He was defeated in 1976, won in 1978 and served until 1992, when he retired. His successor in his northeast Denver district was his campaign treasurer, Diana DeGette. She was elected to the U.S. House from Denver in 1996 and has served ever since.

By Jerry Kopel

What's the impact of term limits? Loss of experience, mostly in the House. There are one hundred legislators in Colorado, 65 in the House and 35 in the Senate. When I entered the legislature in 1965, more than half of the House had never served one day in the legislature. But we had experienced legislators to guide the new members with some historical perspective and with a decade or more of experience.

I keep hearing about how the only way you open up the legislature to new blood is through term limits. So I decided to see if that was true.

I went to the 1991 roster to discover which legislators were no longer around even though they could have technically stayed through 1998 under the term limit law. Then I checked the 1993, 1995, and 1997 rosters.

A few had died in office, some had run for other offices, but the vast majority had simply decided enough was enough. Between 1991 through 1998, 81 legislators left the legislature, 55 in the House and 26 in the Senate.

With 100 legislators and an eight-year term limit, we should see an average of 25 removed from office every two years. But without term limits, during the past eight years, an average of 20 legislators have been removed every two years.

The lack of experience is bad news for House members and good news for lobbyists. There are no term limits for lobbyists. At least 30 are former legislators with a wealth of experience. And at least another 30 have been lobbyists in Colorado for 20 or more years. Lobbyists will be more than happy to provide information to inexperienced House members.

Often in a House committee, when the good and bad points of a bill are discussed, some experienced House member of the committee will say "we had that same bill before the committee 10 years ago, and here is one of the problems that resulted in its defeat." That sort of response is no longer possible. And you can't run to the Senate to find someone who was in the House ten years ago if you don't know there was a bill on the topic ten years ago.

Art. V, Section 4. Qualification of Members

> No person shall be a representative or senator who shall not have attained the age of twenty-five years, who shall not be a citizen of the United States, and who shall not for at least twelve months next preceding his election, have resided within the territory included in the limits of the district in which he shall be chosen.

In 2008, the people rejected a referendum that would have reduced the minimum age from 25 years to 21. Minimum ages in other states range for 18 to 30, with many states having different ages for the upper and lower chambers.

The U.S. Constitution sets minimum ages of for 25 for the House, and 30 for the Senate. U.S. CONST., art. I, §§ 2–3.

Art. V, Section 5. Classification of senators

> The senate shall be divided so that one-half of the senators, as nearly as practicable, may be chosen biennially.

Art V, Section 6. Salary and expenses of members

> Each member of the general assembly shall receive such salary and expenses as are prescribed by law. No general assembly shall fix its own salary. Members of the general assembly shall receive the same mileage rate permitted for travel as other state employees.

The provision is similar to the U.S. Twenty-seventh Amendment, which was proposed in 1791 (as part of the Bill of Rights) and finally ratified in 1992. A legislative salary increase may not take effect until there has been an intervening biennial election.

The same is true for the *per diem* funds that the legislature provides for the daily expenses of members while the legislature is in session, or while legislators are participating in work that takes place outside of a legislative session. Such funding may include travel and lodging expenses for legislators who do not live near the Capitol. The current per diem is $45 daily for legislators who live within 50 miles of the Capitol, and $219 for those further away. Marianne Goodland & Pat Poblete, *Legislature shells out for its members' expenses in 2021*, COLO. POLITICS, Sept. 10, 2021.

The rule "No general assembly shall fix its own salary" allows one general assembly to set the salary for the next general assembly. Because state senators serve four-year terms, a senator who was elected in 1964 and voted for a salary raise in 1966 could enjoy the raise in 1967—without the senator having had to face an intervening election. The Colorado supreme court held that the salary increase was permissible, because the 1965–66 general assembly was not the 1967–68 general assembly. *In re Interrogatories by Governor*, 163 Colo. 113 (1967). In contrast, a similar case from 1947 had said that holdover senators from the 36th general assembly could not receive a per diem increase in the 37th general assembly. *In re Interrogatories by the Governor as to Senate Bill No. 26*, 116 Colo. 318 (1947).

A 1969 case held that that the legislature's determination of what travel expenses are necessary is conclusive. The rule for "same mileage rate" does not limit the frequency or the total miles of the legislature's spending on its travel. *In re Interrogatories by the Colorado State Senate, Forty-Sixth General Assembly*, 168 Colo. 558 (1969).

As the captions of the above cases indicate, the governor or the general assembly may propound questions to the Colorado supreme court. The procedures for interrogatories are in art. VI, § 3.

Art. V, Section 7. General assembly meetings and committees

> The general assembly shall meet in regular session at 10 a.m. no later than the second Wednesday of January of each year. The general assembly shall meet at other times when convened in special session by the governor pursuant to section 9 of article IV of this constitution or by written request by two-thirds of the members of each house to the presiding officer of each house to consider only those subjects specified in such request. The term of service of the members of the general assembly shall begin on the convening of the first regular session of the general assembly next after their election. The committees of the general assembly, unless otherwise provided by the general assembly, shall expire on the convening of the first regular session after a general election. <u>Regular sessions of the general assembly shall not exceed one hundred twenty calendar days.</u>

Subjects of special sessions

The language allowing the general assembly to call itself into special session was added by a referred amendment in 1974. This power is broader than the governor's power to call a special session. Under article IV, § 9, the governor may call a special session only "on extraordinary occasions" and only for topics which are "specially named." In contrast, a special session initiated by the legislature is not limited to "extraordinary occasions."

The subject matter of the legislatively initiated special session is also broader: whatever subjects are "specified" by the legislature. In drafting the referred amendment, the 1974 general assembly deliberately chose language broader than the language applicable to governor-initiated special sessions.

Time limits of legislative sessions

Nineteenth century constitutions often limited the length of legislative sessions, to reduce the quantity of lawmaking. G. ALAN TARR, UNDERSTANDING STATE CONSTITUTIONS 120-21 (1998).[10] A popular saying was that "No man's life, liberty, or property are safe while the legislature is in

---

[10] For early examples, Tarr cites North Carolina (1835) (legislature may only meet biennially) and Virginia (biennially "and not oftener," with session of no more than 90 days). By 1900, 33 state constitutions limited the length of sessions, and only six allowed annual meetings. "Although limiting legislative sessions served the reformers' goal of economy in government, equally important was their assumption that shorter sessions gave legislators less opportunity to do harm." TARR at 121.

session." *Final Accounting in the Estate of A.B.*, 1 Tucker 247, 249 (N.Y. Surr. 1866) (Judge Gideon J. Tucker).

Under the 1876 Constitution, legislative sessions were limited to 40 days.[11] Because the first session of the legislature would have to create an entire legal code for the state and establish the departments of state government, it was exempt from the time limit. The first general assembly sat for 140 days.[12]

Regular sessions of the Colorado legislature were held only in odd-numbered years.[13] This is still the practice in Texas.

A 1950 constitutional amendment allowed for regular sessions in even-numbered years. The "short session" could only address topics that were enumerated in the "Governor's call," plus appropriations and revenue.[14]

The "Governor's call" limit on the topics of even-year sessions was eliminated by amendment in 1982. The short session could be up to 140 calendar days, and there was no limit on the odd-year session. The 140 days that had once been sufficient to create an entire state government from scratch were now labeled a "short" session.

The Colorado ideal has always to have a citizen legislature. The view was, and is, that full-time professional legislatures were part of the cause of excessive and bad government in such states as New York and California. During the 1980s, Colorado general assembly sessions in both odd and even years began to stretch longer and longer. The longer a session runs, the less the ability of a legislator to earn an independent living. Thus the greater the legislator's dependence on powerful interests to promote re-election. In a vicious cycle, powerful interests become more powerful, as legislators protect them from competition and subsidize them with tax dollars.

The corrective was the 1988 GAVEL Amendment's Calendar Days Clause, which limits regular legislative sessions to 120 calendar days. As the *Colorado Springs Gazette* editorialized that year:

> The Legislature can currently stay in session as long as it wants on odd-numbered years and 140 days on even-numbered years. There has been a growing perception, inside and outside the capitol, that Colorado's legislative sessions have been dragging on too long. Since 1967, the Legislature has stayed in session as many as 185 days (more than half the year), with an average in the unrestricted odd years of 162.4 days and 128.2 days in even years.
>
> The result has been tired lawmakers who find it difficult to balance their duties as elected officials with their private lives outside government. In recent years, a number of legislators have retired from the public arena, citing the long sessions and the conflicts with their obligations to family and career.
>
> Since becoming a state, Colorado has aspired to maintain a "citizens' legislature." We have never wanted our elected representatives to be professional politicians. We'd rather they be business people, professionals and other productive members of society who are willing to take time from their private lives to serve the public. A true citizens' legislature allows elected representatives to spend more time working and living in the communities that elected them, rather

---

[11] COLO. CONST., art. V, § 6 (1876) ("No session of the General Assembly, after the first, shall exceed forty days").

[12] 2 FRANK HALL, HISTORY OF THE STATE OF COLORADO 362 (1890).

[13] COLO. CONST., art. V, § 7 (1876) (alternate year sessions only, except when the Governor calls a special session)

[14] If the general assembly during a short session enacted legislation that went beyond the scope of the Governor's call, the law was void. *Burciaga v. Shea*, 187 Colo. 78, 530 P.2d 508 (1974) (changes in welfare program); *People v. Larkin*, 183 Colo. 363, 517 P.2d 389 (1973) (criminal law about explosives).

> than in the closed world of the capitol dome, with its lobbyists and its heady games of political wheeling and dealing.[15]

Accordingly, the time limit of "one hundred and twenty calendar days" was added by the GAVEL Amendment in 1988.

The Calendar Days Clause imposes no restriction on the ability of the governor or the general assembly to call special sessions.

In the English language, "one hundred twenty calendar days" has only one possible meaning. There is no such thing as "non-calendar day."[16] Every day that exists is on the calendar. "[O]ne hundred twenty calendar days" does not mean "any 120 of the 365 days on the calendar." It means one hundred twenty days in a row. In *People v. Zhuk*, 239 P.3d 437, 437–38 (Colo. 2010), the Colorado supreme court stated that the time from December 3 to December 17 is "fourteen calendar days." This was contrasted with a criminal procedure filing limit of "ten days"; the procedural rule was interpreted as skipping weekends and legal holidays. So the defendant's motion filed on December 17 was timely. The day-skipping "ten days" criminal procedure rule was the same amount of time as "fourteen calendar days." *Id.* at 438-39.

Given the widespread prior abuse of the Safety Clause and the Emergency Clause, the Calendar Days Clause did not authorize an exception for emergencies, or for anything else.

Nevertheless, the general assembly in 2009 adopted Joint Rule 44(g) stating that counting of days for the 120 Calendar Days Clause would be suspended is the legislature adjourned pursuant to an emergency declared by the governor.

In March 2020, the legislature did do adjourn, because of the COVID-19 pandemic. The Colorado supreme court accepted an interrogatory about whether the suspended period was exempt from the 120 Calendar Days Clause. By a 4–3 vote, the court held that "calendar days" is ambiguous, and the legislature's rule was a reasonable interpretation of the ambiguity. *In re Interrogatory on House Joint Resolution 20-1006*, 2020 CO 23 (Colo. 2020). In the 2021 legislative session, the Democratic leadership immediately exploited the court's nullification of the 120 Calendar Day Clause and orchestrated a legislative session that began in early January and ended in June, far longer than the 120 calendar days constitutional limit.

The 2009 adoption of a Joint Rule to exempt the legislature from the Constitution was wrong. The proper approach would have been to refer a constitutional amendment to the voters. That is what the legislature did the next year, when it asked the voters for an amendment to article VIII, § 3, allowing the seat of government to be moved during emergencies.

Art. V, Section 8. Members may not hold other office

> No senator or representative shall, while serving as such, be appointed to any civil office under this state; and no member of congress, or other person holding any office (except of attorney-at-law, notary public, or in the militia) under the United States or this state, shall be a member of either house during his continuance in office.

[15] Editorial, *Assure citizens' legislature*, THE GAZETTE (Colo. Springs), Nov. 5, 1988. Nevertheless, the editorial urged a vote against GAVEL, because of concerns that GAVEL's rule against binding caucuses and pocket vetoes in committee or on the floor could cause "chaos . . . The result could be longer sessions and endless hearings, which would run directly counter to the worthwhile benefits of a shorter session embodied in Amendment 3." *Id.* Happily, the editorial's fears that requiring a vote on every bill would thwart the 120 Calendar Days Clause did not come to pass.

[16] Except perhaps on other planets. Since a "day" is one revolution of a planet, a day on earth is not the same length of time as a day on planets that rotate at different speeds. "Calendar days" exist in places where calendars are kept.

Members of the Colorado legislature may not hold a state "civil office." This does not encompass some low-ranking positions in the executive branch, which have been held not be civil offices. *Hudson v. Annear*, 101 Colo. 551, 555, 75 P.2d 587 (1938) (low position in tax department; "A position, the duties of which are undefined, and which can be changed at the will of the superior; . . . is not an office but a mere employment, and the incumbent is not an officer but a mere employee.") (internal quote omitted). Nor does it preclude service in an elected executive branch position, such as state treasurer. *Carpenter v. People ex rel. Tilford*, 8 Colo. 116, 5 P. 828 (1885) (ban on being "appointed" does not preclude being "elected").

The Colorado Constitution is broader than the U.S. Constitution's Sinecure Clause, which prohibits members of Congress being appointed to any federal office "which shall have been created, or the Emoluments whereof shall have been increased" during the legislator's term. U.S. CONST., art. I, § 6, cl. 2. The prohibition on sinecures was created after England's Glorious Revolution, in order to preserve parliament's independence; it ended the practice of monarch being able to bribe members of parliament by offering them a lucrative position under the king's control. Act of Settlement, 12 & 13 William III, ch. 2 (1700).[17]

Art. V, Section 9. (repealed)

Formerly, a control on legislative salary increases. Now covered by other provisions of the Constitution.

Art. V, Section 10. Each house chooses its officers

> At the beginning of the first regular session after a general election, and at such other times as may be necessary, the senate shall elect one of its members president, and the house of representatives shall elect one of its members as speaker. The president and speaker shall serve as such until the election and installation of their respective successors. Each house shall choose its other officers and shall judge the election and qualification of its members.

As in the U.S. Constitution, the House and Senate choose their own officers, and are the conclusive judges of elections to their bodies. U.S. CONST., art I, §§ 2, 3, 5.

Colorado courts *may* hear cases involving election recounts or other election procedures. *Meyer v. Lamm,* 846 P.2d 862 (Colo. 1993) (write-in candidate's challenge to counting of votes). But once the secretary of state has transmitted election certificates to the general assembly, and the general assembly has decided who shall be seated, the general assembly's determination is conclusive, and not subject to judicial review. *Hughes v. Felton*, 11 Colo. 489, 19 P. 444 (1888).

Any elector in a state house or senate district may file a contest over the correctness of the secretary of state's election certificates. The relevant house shall transmit the contest to an administrative law judge for factual determinations. After the ALJ has issued findings, the relevant house may declare a particular candidate to have been the winner, may hold a trial on the matter, or may order a special legislative election. C.R.S. §§ 1-11-208 to 210.

[17] The Act of Settlement, as amended over the centuries, is one of the key documents of the British Constitution. Most notably, it provided the terms and conditions for succession of the Crown. It also provided that judges could be removed only by Parliament, not by the monarch.

Art. V, Section 11. Quorum

> A majority of each house shall constitute a quorum, but a smaller number may adjourn from day to day, and compel the attendance of absent members.

By Jerry Kopel

The House or the Senate may compel the attendance of absent members in order to form a quorum, or for any other purpose. The formal compulsion comes through a Call of the House or a Call of the Senate. You may have been excused, but that doesn't mean a thing if the house speaker or senate president decides your presence is needed. Perhaps once every couple years there is a call of monumental proportions.

When I first came to the House, the story that was used to frighten freshman was about the call in which state patrolman entered the synagogue to remove Ben Klein and return him to the House for a vote.

There was a time, late at night, when an ill Walt Hinman was forced to leave his bed, dress, and return for the call. To get even, he voted the opposite of what the callers wanted.

It is sometimes hard to separate fact from fiction. I cannot honestly report that someone was forced to fly home from Hawaii. I do know the House has left messages at airports to catch legislators before they board flights.

But I was there, watching, when the senate required Vince Massari to return from Pueblo in a state patrol car. In the meantime, the divergent forces had compromised and taken the necessary vote without him.

As senator Massari walked up the steps of the Capitol, he was met and told his presence was no longer needed. This being a family publication, I cannot print his response.

Art. V, Section 12. Each house makes and enforces its rules

> Each house shall have power to determine the rules of its proceedings and adopt rules providing punishment of its members or other persons for contempt or disorderly behavior in its presence; to enforce obedience to its process; to protect its members against violence, or offers of bribes or private solicitation, and, with the concurrence of two-thirds, to expel a member, but not a second time for the same cause, and shall have all other powers necessary for the legislature of a free state. A member expelled for corruption shall not thereafter be eligible to either house of the same general assembly, and punishment for contempt or disorderly behavior shall not bar a prosecution for the same offense.

The Open Meeting Law (also known as the Sunshine Law), enacted by citizen initiative, is broad statute requiring that most meetings of state or local government officials be open to the public. C.R.S. 24-6-401 to 402. Further, notice of the meeting must be published in advance. The statute prevents party caucuses of the House and Senate from having private meetings. This was held not to conflict with the constitutional powers of the houses to make their own rules. *Cole v. State*, 673 P.2d 345 (Colo. 1983).

Art. V, Section 13. Journal of each house, recording of ayes and noes

> Each house shall keep a journal of its proceedings and publish the same, except such parts as require secrecy, and the ayes and noes on any question shall, at the desire of any two members, be entered on the journal.

A typical American provision, section 13 prevents a revival of the old practice of the English parliament that forbade publication of which members of parliament voted for or against a measure.

Art. V, Section 14. Open sessions

> The sessions of each house, and of the committees of the whole, shall be open, unless when the business is such as ought to be kept secret.

Early meetings of the U.S. Senate were closed to the public. This was consistent with English practice, which, at the time, closed meetings of the House of Lords.[18] Meetings of the House of Commons had been closed until the middle of the 18th century.

The House and Senate rules on closed meetings are not the same. The House rule is No. 17: "When in the opinion of any member, the business before the House requires that the discussion thereof be carried on in secret, such member may move the House proceed in executive session when such motion shall have been adopted by the affirmative vote of a majority of all members elected."

Under Senate Rule 27, to go into secret or executive session, the motion has to be made and seconded to discuss "any business which may, in the opinion of any senator require secrecy." Unlike the House Rule, the Senate Rule does not require any vote.

The Senate Rule is contrary to the Sunshine Law, an open government statute enacted by voter initiative in 1972. The Sunshine law requires a vote, and a public announcement of the general reason for the secret session. C.R.S. § 24-6-402. In the Senate's view, the Senate's constitutional power to make its own rules trumps the initiated statute.

Art. V, Section 15. Adjournment for more than three days

> Neither house shall, without the consent of the other, adjourn for more than three days, nor to any other place than that in which the two houses shall be sitting.

This is an exact parallel of U.S. CONST., art. I, § 5 (Adjournment Clause) (to prevent one house from being unilaterally able to shut down congressional operation).

[18] The lower house in the United Kingdom is the House of Commons, which is elected. The upper house is the House of Lords. Its members are appointed for life, and some seats are hereditary. Since the early twentieth century, the House of Lords has lost most of its once-mighty power.

Art. V, Section 16. Privileges of members for speech and debate, and against arrest

> The members of the general assembly shall, in all cases except treason or felony, be privileged from arrest during their attendance at the sessions of their respective houses, or any committees thereof, and in going to and returning from the same; and for any speech or debate in either house, or any committees thereof, they shall not be questioned in any other place.

The Speech or Debate guarantee for members of the legislature parallels the U.S. Constitution, art. I, § 6. The same is true for the Privilege from Arrest Clause.

Even when the 1798 federal Sedition Act (in effect until 1801) criminalized much criticism of the president or the U.S. government, the established tradition of Speech or Debate immunity provided a shield for state legislators to denounce president John Adams from the floors of the state legislatures.

The U.S. Speech or Debate Clause was based on the 1689 English Bill of Rights: "That the freedom of speech, and debates in proceedings in Parliament, ought not to be impeached or questioned in any Court or place out of Parliament." 1 Wm. & Mary, sess. 2, ch. 2, art. 9 (1689).[19] In England, the Speech or Debate immunity was essential for members of parliament to criticize the monarch, when such words spoken outside of parliament would have led to prosecution for seditious libel or for treason.

The "going to and returning" immunity was found necessary because of the behavior of monarchs such as Charles I, who in 1641 arrested opposition members of parliament in their offices minutes after parliament had adjourned.

Art. V, Section 17. Laws may passed only by original purpose bills

> No law shall be passed except by bill, and no bill shall be so altered or amended on its passage through either house as to change its original purpose.

There is no comparable provision in the U.S. Constitution. In Congress, bills sometimes are altered from their original purpose. For example, the bill that in the U.S. Senate became the

---

[19] English statutes have historically been cited by the regnal name and year. The above statute was enacted in the first year of the joint reign of King William III and Queen Mary II. After King James II was ousted in the Glorious Revolution of 1688, Parliament offered the crown to Queen Mary (James's daughter by his first marriage) and her husband King William (a Dutchman).

The statute was enacted in early 1689. At the time, the English considered the year to be 1688; under their "Old Style" calendar, the new year began on March 25, the date that the Virgin Mary was believed to have conceived Jesus. The English calendar was changed from Old Style (Julian) to New Style (Gregorian) in 1752. So some English or colonial American statutory citations may be written in dual form, such as 1703/04. If something was enacted on Feb. 1, 1704 (New Style), the dual cite reminds readers that the enactors considered the year to be 1703 (Old Style).

Readers using Western European date citations between 1582 (when France adopted the New Style calendar) and 1752 should be aware that the days between January 1 and March 24 may be assigned to a different year, depending on the country. The shift can also move the calendar date as far forward as 11 days. For example, July 1 Old Style can become July 12 New Style. The shift occurs because Old Style had an incorrect number of leap year days. New Style omits leap year day every 100 years, except for every 400th year. So, under New Style, there was no leap year day in 1800 or 1900, but there was one in 2000.

"Affordable Care Act," began by being passed by the U.S. House as a minor bill involving veterans' affairs. The Senate then gutted and replaced the bill's original text.

Section 17 reinforces the Single Subject requirement of Section 21. As the supreme court explained: "The trick denounced by the learned writer and expounder of constitutional law[20] is where a member, entertaining an idea that he may at some future date desire legislation upon some subject not thought of within the time limited for the introduction of bills, introduces one or more sham bills, for the purpose of using the same as stocks to graft upon, as occasion may arise, without reference to the character or contents of the parent bill." *In re Amend. Legis. Bills*, 19 Colo. 356, 359, 35 P. 917 (1894). *See also Gronert v. People*, 95 Colo. 508, 37 P.2d 396 (1934) (introduced bill's purpose was to regulate businesses loaning money at more than 12% interest, but enacted bill prohibited loans at more than 1%).

Art. V, Section 18. Enacting Clause

> The style of the laws of this state shall be: "Be it enacted by the General Assembly of the State of Colorado".

This language is mandatory. Those words are always the first line in every bill. If a bill creating a law does not contain the above words, it has no validity

How to kill a bill

by Jerry Kopel

Because a bill without an enacting clause is a nullity, a motion often made during House or Senate debate is to "strike the enacting clause."

Under the House and Senate rules, there are several other ways to kill a bill. There is the motion to "Postpone Indefinitely," referred to by legislators as "Pee-Eyed." As *Robert's Rules of Order* explains, "Its effect is to entirely remove the question from before the assembly for that session."

Another way to get rid of a bill is to ask that "the bill be laid over until [one day after the end of the legislative session]." So if the 120-day legislative term ends on May 9, the bill is laid over until May 10.

Then there is a motion "to lay the bill on the table." This motion is usually made by the sponsor of the bill who has determined he or she lacks the votes to pass a controversial measure and doesn't want to put fellow legislators on the spot by voting the bill up or down.

Of course, the cleanest way to kill a bill is to vote on its merits. A bill is "lost" after debate and a vote on the floor of the House or Senate in the sense that a baseball game is lost because the other side got more runs.

---

[20] Namely, Thomas Cooley—Michigan Supreme Court justice, Dean of the University of Michigan Law School, and the leading constitutional treatise author of the latter 19th century. In 1868 he wrote *A Treatise on the Constitutional Limitations Which Rest Upon the Legislative Power of the States of the American Union*, examining state constitutional law. The second edition, from 1871, is available at https://repository.law.umich.edu/books/10/.

In 1880, Cooley wrote *The General Principles of Constitutional Law in the United States of America*. New editions of Cooley's treatises continued to be published even after Cooley's death in 1898, but these are unreliable, and sometimes contrary to Cooley's own views.

Art. V, Section 19. Effective date of laws, time limits on introduction of bills

> An act of the general assembly shall take effect on the date stated in the act, or, if no date is stated in the act, then on its passage. A bill may be introduced at any time during the session unless limited by action of the general assembly. No bill shall be introduced by title only.

The current provision allowing the introduction of a bill at any time during the legislative session is a major change from the 1876 Constitution, which forbade the introduction of bills after the first 25 days of a legislative session. Subsequent amendment raised this to 30 days (1884) and then lowered it to 15 days (1918).

The protection against late bills was based on the experience of other states; late bills were often rushed through the legislature without sufficient public consideration, and often involved major enactments that the sponsors hoped to shield from public scrutiny.

The constitutional protection against late bills was removed in 1950, with the matter left up the rules of each house. The present rules limit each legislator to five introduced bills per session. Joint Rule 23 sets up a schedule requiring the last bills be introduced by the 17th day (Senate) or 22nd day (House). There are exceptions for some appropriations bills.

However, the bill limits on quantity and lateness can be waived, on a bill-by-bill basis, with the permission of two of the three top officers in the relevant house (house speaker or senate president, majority leader, minority leader). Since the 1990s, waivers have been granted on a massive basis, so that every year there are many dozens of late bills

In conjunction with the 120 calendar days limit on legislative sessions (art. V, § 7), the proliferation of the late bills means that the last two weeks of the legislative session are chaotic, as legislators attempt hasty work on bills that have not been considered under the ordinary schedule.

In a typical session, the number of late bills that truly involve new circumstances and could not have been introduced on a timely basis is zero.

Art. V, Section 20. Bills must be printed and referred to a committee

> No bill shall be considered or become a law unless referred to a committee, returned therefrom, and printed for the use of the members. Every measure referred to a committee of reference of either house shall be considered by the committee upon its merits, and no rule of either house shall deny the opportunity for consideration and vote by a committee of reference upon such a measure within appropriate deadlines. A motion that the committee report the measure favorably to the committee of the whole, with or without amendments, shall always be in order within appropriate deadlines. Each measure reported to the committee of the whole shall appear on the appropriate house calendar in the order in which it was reported out of the committee of reference and within appropriate deadlines.

The first sentence was part of the 1876 Constitution. The rest was added by the 1988 GAVEL amendment.

How bills move through the legislature

The "committee of the whole" means the entire legislative body. For example, a representative introduces a bill to change how plumbers are licensed. The bill receives an immediate "first reading." (The reading requirements for bills are in section 22.) The Speaker of the House assigns the bill to the House Business Affairs & Labor Committee. Pursuant to section 20, and implementing legislative rules, the committee chair will have to bring up the bill for a vote by a certain date.

If the bill passes the first committee, it then goes to the floor of House. On "second reading" of the bill, the House acts as a "committee of the whole." This committee of the whole may propose amendments to the bill. After amendments, the committee of the whole votes on the bill. If the bill passes on second reading, then there is a final, "third reading" vote on another day. On third reading, the House is just the House, and not a committee of the whole. If the bill passes third reading, it crosses over to the Senate, and the same process begins.

The House majority leader controls the calendar and chooses which post-committee bills to bring up on which days—subject to the constitutional requirement that everything must get a vote, and further subject to legislative rules specifying deadlines for each chamber to complete its work.

Since a session must end after 120 calendar days, time runs out for votes on various bills. For example, when there are only two days left in a legislative session, the House might have dozens of bills that originated in the Senate, passed there, and have passed House committee. Given the finite amount of time available, the majority leader selects which bills to bring up for second or third readings, and which bills will die by inaction.

The above scenario described a bill that only needed approval by a single committee in each chamber. However, rather than sending an approved bill to the "committee of the whole," a committee can instead send the bill to another committee. For example, a complicated bill might benefit from review by two committees, each of while has expertise relevant to the bill's subject.

If a bill has a *fiscal impact* (that is, increasing spending, or affecting taxes), the bill will be so identified by legislative staff when the bill is introduced. Suppose that a bingo regulation bill will require the secretary of state to hire additional employees to monitor bingo halls. After the bill passes the Business Affairs & Labor Committee, the bill must go the Appropriations Committee. Any bill with a fiscal impact must be approved by the Appropriations Committee or the Finance Committee in each chamber.

Consequently, legislators who want to increase the prospects that their bill will be enacted may work carefully to ensure that their bill will be scored as NFI: "no fiscal impact."

Art. V, Section 21. Bills must contain a single subject, clearly expressed in the title

> <u>No bill, except general appropriation bills, shall be passed containing more than one subject, which shall be clearly expressed in its title</u>; but if any subject shall be embraced in any act which shall not be expressed in the title, such act shall be void only as to so much thereof as shall not be so expressed.

There is no single subject rule in the U.S. Constitution. Congressional bills often contain multiple subjects and inaccurate titles. The purpose of Colorado's Single Subject and Clear Title Clauses is to prevent controversial legislation from being hidden under an innocuous or unrelated title.

In first quarter-century of statehood, courts took the Clear Title Clause seriously. Of the 30 laws that were struck down because of improper enactment, 11 were found to have violated the Clear Title Clause.[21]

As the court pointed out, Section 21, unlike the similar provisions in other state constitutions, required that the subject be "clearly" expressed in the title. *In re Breene*, 14 Colo. 401, 406, 24 P. 3 (1890).

Under modern doctrine, every bill passed by the legislature is presumed constitutional. The burden of proving otherwise beyond a reasonable doubt is on the opponents. That burden was met in a major decision on "single subject" legislation. *In re H.B. 1353*, 738 P.2d 371 (Colo. 1987).

The title of HB 1353 set the stage: "Concerning an Increase in the Availability of Moneys to Fund Expenditure Priorities for the 1987 Regular Session of the General Assembly Through Reallocation of Funds, Program Cuts, Expenditure Reductions, Use of Revenue from Unclaimed Property, and Increases of Fees."

Aware there could be problems, a legislative declaration in section 1 of the bill said the bill comported with the single subject requirement of the Colorado Constitution, article V, § 21, and decisions of the Colorado supreme court interpreting that requirement.

The bill was 44 pages long and included such disparate subjects as reducing contributions to state employee retirement funds, charging prison inmates for each medical visit, eliminating the comparable salary survey for state employees, ending winter payment to old age pensioners for increased heating expenses, transferring severance tax funds to the general fund, and revising the formula for Medicaid reimbursement to nursing homes. All told, twenty different subjects. The bill became law on June 1, 1987, without the signature of the governor. (The governor may sign a bill, veto a bill, or let it become law without his signature.)

Republican attorney general Duane Woodard took on his own political party in a display of integrity and bravery, filing an amicus brief to the Colorado supreme court in support of the interrogatory by Democratic governor Romer. Woodard argued that the bill violated the single subject clause of the Constitution.

The court agreed, and laid down some guidelines:

1. The purpose served by limiting a bill to a single subject is to make each legislative proposal depend upon its own merits for passage.

2. It enables the governor to determine whether to exercise veto power related to a single subject.

3. The fact that there is a "single common feature" in the sense of finding additional moneys, or reducing expenses, to fund certain priorities, doesn't qualify as "one subject."

4. Numerous and diverse subjects, each of significance, transcends any common characteristic of financial impact.

5. For subjects to be necessarily or properly connected, the connection must be logical.

Once the court declared the bill unconstitutional, the legislative leadership responded quickly. Separate bills on each subject were introduced. None reached the House floor until the House Republican Caucus had 33 binding votes to pass each one and to reject any Democratic amendments. Nearly all the substitute bills passed. (This was before the 1988 GAVEL Amendment to the state constitution outlawed binding caucus votes.)

---

[21] Thomas P. Fry, *Constitutional Regulation of Legislative Procedure in Colorado*, 3 ROCKY MOUNTAIN L. REVIEW 50 (Nov. 1930). The periodical is now known as the University of Colorado Law Review.

And of course, there was retaliation against attorney general Woodward, with huge cuts to his office budget, resulting in him switching parties, running as a Democrat for re-election in 1990, and being defeated by Republican Gale Norton. Woodard returned to the Republican fold in 1994.

In the best of all worlds a bill should not leave the legislative drafting office (part of the Office of Legislative Legal Services) unless it meets the single subject requirement. However, the drafting office doesn't have control over spur-of-the-moment amendments offered to bills in the House and Senate. There are many laws presently on the statute books that didn't meet the single subject requirement.

For example, every year, the District Attorney's Council drafts omnibus bills with the titles "Concerning Criminal Law" and "Concerning Criminal Procedure." Notwithstanding the obvious violation of the Single Subject Clause, these bills are never challenged on a point of order, and no court has ever declared these multi-subject bills to be unconstitutional.

In contrast, the single-subject rule for citizen initiatives has sometimes been enforced quite aggressively on matters that conflict with the Colorado supreme court's policy views. COLO. CONST., art. V, § 1(5.5) (added 1995). The matter is discussed in chapter 9 ("Initiative and Referendum").

Art. V, Section 22. Readings for passage of bills must be on three separate days

> Every bill shall be read by title when introduced, and at length on two different days in each house; provided, however, any reading at length may be dispensed with upon unanimous consent of the members present. All substantial amendments made thereto shall be printed for the use of the members before the final vote is taken on the bill, and no bill shall become a law except by a vote of the majority of all members elected to each house taken on two separate days in each house, nor unless upon its final passage the vote be taken by ayes and noes and the names of those voting be entered on the journal.

Thirty-three other states have similar provisions. Because the first, second, and third readings must be on different days, a bill cannot be rushed through the legislature in fewer than three days.

The first reading, upon introduction, is by title only. Thereafter, the second reading (after the bill has passed a committee and is on the floor of the House or Senate for amendment) and the third reading (for final passage in the chamber) must be at length. Reading at length may be dispensed by unanimous consent.

The requirement for reading at length was not because legislators were illiterate. Rather, Coloradans of 1876 instituted the requirement "To afford protection from hasty legislation." Colorado Convention, *Address to the People*, reprinted in chapter 1. *See also* WILBUR FISKE STONE, 1 HISTORY OF COLORADO 186 (1918) (Convention's aim to prevent hasty legislation).

Increasing the time needed to pass legislation allows more time for public scrutiny, and encourages rigor in public debate about the costs and benefits of legislation.

Current practices in the legislature are to dispense with reading at length. However, one of the few tools available to the minority party is to request such readings, and thereby slow the process.

In response, senate presidents and house speakers have been known to resort to chicanery—such as having four readers each read different parts of the bill simultaneously. In 2019 Senate president Leroy Garcia had a bill read by computer at incomprehensibly high speed. A Denver district court ruled that computer reading did not comply with section 22. With much difficulty, the Colorado supreme court agreed 4–3. The dissenters would have held that the legislature's decision that its "reading" format complied with the Constitution was conclusive and nonjusticiable. *Markwell v. Cooke*, 2021 CO 17, 483 P.3d 422 (Colo. 2021).

Art. V, Section 22a. Caucus positions prohibited, with exceptions

> (1) No member or members of the general assembly shall require or commit themselves or any other member or members, through a vote in a party caucus or any other similar procedure, to vote in favor of or against any bill, appointment, veto, or other measure or issue pending or proposed to be introduced in the general assembly.
>
> (2) Notwithstanding the provisions of subsection (1) of this section, a member or members of the general assembly may vote in party caucus on matters directly relating to the selection of officers of a party caucus and the selection of the leadership of the general assembly.

Pursuant to the 1988 GAVEL amendment, party caucuses may not bind the votes of caucus members, except in elections for legislative offices, such as speaker of the house or caucus chair.

After the enactment of GAVEL, Common Cause (the lobby that had been leading advocate for GAVEL) sued the House Republican caucus, because the caucus had adopted binding positions on the Long Bill. (The bill for general appropriations for the state government. *See* art. V, § 32.) The caucus had also adopted a binding position on a transportation bill.

Because of constitutional Speech and Debate immunity (art. V, § 16), the Colorado supreme court held that no injunction could be issued against the Republican representatives. However, a court could provide declaratory relief, stating that the representatives had violated Section 22a. The declaratory relief did not violate the Speech or Debate Clause, because it compelled no action and inflicted no punishment. *Colorado Common Cause v. Bledsoe*, 810 P.2d 201 (Colo. 1991).

By Jerry Kopel

Steve Durham (a lobbyist and former Republican state senator) and I entered a capitol elevator one day while the Democrat and Republican House legislators were in caucus discussing the long bill (the major appropriations bill for state government).

Durham: "What's the difference between a cactus and a caucus?"

Kopel: "I don't know, what is the difference?"

Durham: "With a cactus, the pricks are on the outside."

Art. V, Section 22b. Actions in violation of sections 20 and 22a are void

> Any action taken in violation of section 20 or 22a of this constitution shall be null and void.

Also part of the 1988 GAVEL amendment.

Art. V, Section 23. House or Senate votes to concur with other body must be by recorded ayes and noes of each member

> No amendment to any bill by one house shall be concurred in by the other nor shall the report of any committee of conference be adopted in either house except by a vote of a majority of the members elected thereto, taken by ayes and noes, and the names of those voting recorded upon the journal thereof.

Section 23 covers the resolution of differences between House and Senate versions of a bill. Suppose that the House passes a bill. The bill then goes to the Senate, which amends the bill, and then passes the amended version. The amended version then returns to the House. Pursuant to Section 23, the House may only concur in the Senate amendments if a majority of House members do so, and the individual votes are recorded in the House Journal.

Instead of concurring with the Senate amendment(s), the House could simply vote down the Senate version of the bill. Alternatively, the House could request a conference committee. Each body appoints three members to the conference committee for the bill. Conferees typically are two members from the majority party in a house, and one from the minority. The conference committee can revise the bill. If two of the three members from each body agree with the revisions, the revised bill returns to the House and Senate. If both the House and the Senate accept the revised version, the bill is passed.

Section 23 requires that votes to accept a conference report be by majority vote, with the individual votes recorded in each chamber's journal.

Art. V, Section 24. No revival or revision of law by reference to title only

> No law shall be revived, or amended, or the provisions thereof extended or conferred by reference to its title only, but so much thereof as is revived, amended, extended or conferred, shall be re-enacted and published at length.

Colorado legislative drafting generally complies with this requirement. The evil it prevents is substantive changes in the law that cannot be readily discerned from reading a bill. For example: "remove the word 'not' and change '90' to '10'." A person who simply read this bill would have no idea what was happening.

So instead, the bill text would include all of a changed subsection, using strikethroughs and ALL CAPS to indicate the language that was being deleted or added.

Art. V, Section 25. No special legislation

> The general assembly shall not pass local or special laws in any of the following enumerated cases, that is to say; for granting divorces; laying out, opening, altering or working roads or highways; vacating roads, town plats, streets, alleys and public grounds; locating or changing county seats; regulating county or township affairs; regulating the practice in courts of justice; regulating the jurisdiction and duties of police magistrates; changing the rules of evidence in any trial or inquiry; providing for changes of venue in civil or criminal cases;

> declaring any person of age; for limitation of civil actions or giving effect to informal or invalid deeds; summoning or impaneling grand or petit juries; providing for the management of common schools; regulating the rate of interest on money; the opening or conducting of any election, or designating the place of voting; the sale or mortgage of real estate belonging to minors or others under disability; the protection of game or fish; chartering or licensing ferries or toll bridges; remitting fines, penalties or forfeitures; creating, increasing or decreasing fees, percentage or allowances of public officers; changing the law of descent; granting to any corporation, association or individual the right to lay down railroad tracks; granting to any corporation, association or individual any special or exclusive privilege, immunity or franchise whatever. In all other cases, where a general law can be made applicable no special law shall be enacted.

Part of the 1876 Constitution. Slightly amended in 2000 to eliminate references to "justices of the peace" and "constables," which no longer exist in Colorado.

Special legislation was widely perceived as a legislative evil. In the sense of section 25, the main objective is to avoid legislative determinations of the legal status or rights of particular individuals. For example, a husband sues in court for divorce; under the restrictive laws of the time, the judge rejects the suit, since the husband has not proven proper cause (such as abandonment or adultery by the wife). So the well-connected husband goes to the legislature, which enacts a bill granting him a divorce.

Jefferson territory provisional governor R.W. Steele, in his Nov. 7, 1859, address to the provisional legislature stated:

> [I]t would be well to avoid, as much as possible, special legislation: but provide by general laws for the incorporation of all bodies, whether corporations for pecuniary profit or municipal governments.
>
> The evil of too much special legislation is one which Western legislators are very prone to run into, thereby neglecting important laws of a general character; when once the door is thrown open to this abuse of legislative power, it is very difficult to check it. It is therefore hoped, that your course on this subject will be a conservative one.

FRANK HALL, 2 HISTORY OF COLORADO 518 (2008) (1890) (appendix reprinting speech).

Bans on special legislation, including corporate welfare, were "undoubtedly beneficial and probably constitute the most important achievements of American public policy in dealing with private enterprise." ERNST FREUND, STANDARDS OF AMERICAN LEGISLATION 174 (1917). *See also* Robert F. Williams, *Equality Guarantees in State Constitutional Law*, 63 TEXAS L. REVIEW 1195 (1985).

Except in regard to special benefits for particular businesses, section 25 has generally been successful in keeping the legislature from making determinations about the rights or status of particular individuals. As will be discussed in chapters 14–16 on taxes and debt (arts. X & XI), constitutional restrictions on legislation for the direct financial benefit of a favored corporation have been nullified by the Colorado supreme court.

Art. V, Section 25a. General assembly shall enact eight-hour day for mining and smelting

> (1) The general assembly shall provide by law, and shall prescribe suitable penalties for the violation thereof, for a period of employment not to exceed eight (8) hours within any twenty-four (24) hours (except in cases of emergency where life or property is in imminent danger) for persons employed in underground mines or other underground workings, blast furnaces, smelters; and any ore reduction works or other branch of industry or labor that the general assembly may consider injurious or dangerous to health, life or limb.
>
> (2) The provisions of subsection (1) of this section to the contrary notwithstanding, the general assembly may establish whatever exceptions it deems appropriate to the eight-hour workday.

Adopted in 1902, this provision made it clear that the legislature could limit the workday to no more than 8 hours in dangerous occupations. The amendment overturned a Colorado supreme court opinion that had held the 8-hour workday to be unconstitutional, as violating the rights of persons to contract for their own labor as they chose. *In re Morgan*, 26 Colo. 415, 58 P. 1071 (1899).

Although the constitutional amendment was added in 1902, it took several years for the legislature to enact an eight-hour law. Anger at the legislature's blatant defiance of the Constitution led to bitter and sometimes violent labor strikes in the succeeding years. Most mines had already adopted an eight-hour policy by 1902, but 10- or 12-hour days were common in smelting.[22]

Subsection (2) was added in 1988.

Art. V, Section 26. Presiding officers of each house shall sign bills

> The presiding officer of each house shall sign all bills and joint resolutions passed by the general assembly, and the fact of signing shall be entered on or appended to the journal thereof.

In 1893, governor Davis H. Waite vetoed 20 bills for failure to comply with this section. The negligent and impatient state Senate had forgotten to obtain the signature of its presiding officer. At the time, this was the lieutenant governor (who was elected separately from the governor). Governor Davis H. Waite, *Proclamation for Special Session*, HOUSE JOURNAL, 9th General Assembly, Special Session 22 (Dec. 27, 1893). Waite, a Populist, was Colorado's only third-party governor.

---

[22] JAMES EDWARD RIGHT, THE POLITICS OF POPULISM: DISSENT IN COLORADO 226–36 (1974).

Art. V, Section 27. General assembly employees may be paid only according to law or joint resolution

> The general assembly shall prescribe by law or by joint resolution the number, duties, and compensation of the appointed officers and employees of each house and of the two houses, and no payment shall be made from the state treasury, or be in any way authorized to any person except to an officer or employee appointed and acting pursuant to law or joint resolution.

The general assembly soon began evading section 27, with 175 employees who were being paid and given raises outside the constitutional system. Attorney general Theodore H. Thomas told the state auditor that the warrants for salary payments were unlawful and should not be paid by the state treasury. After a fierce interbranch battle, the attorney general's position was enforced in *People ex rel. Clement v. Spuance*, 8 Colo. 307, 6 P. 831 (1885); FRANK HALL, 4 HISTORY OF COLORADO 597 (1895). Since then, legislative compliance has been impeccable.

Art. V, Section 28. No extra compensation to officers, employees, or contractors

> <u>No bill shall be passed giving any extra compensation to any public officer or employee, agent, or contractor after services have been rendered</u> or contract made nor providing for the payment of any claim made against the state without previous authority of law.

Although this section was enforced for decades, judicial enforcement ceased after 1940, when the supreme court 4–3 upheld a statute increasing judicial pensions. The most troublesome aspect was the increase of pensions for judges who had retired before the 1939 pension increase law was enacted. *Bedford v. White,* 106 Colo. 439, 106 P.2d 469 (1940).

In dissent, justice Burke wrote: "My position is that there must be some reasonable theory of public benefits. If there be such the soundness of it rests with the Legislature. If, as here, there is no such theory, the grant is purely private and the constitutional inhibition stands . . . [The retired judges] could neither have come into the service, stayed in it, nor left it, because of the Act of 1939. Hence I think they are not permitted by the constitution to take under that Act and the judgment of the court should be reversed." 106 Colo. at 461–62.

Art. V, Section 29. Contracts for certain services must be given to the lowest responsible bidder

> All stationery, printing, paper, and fuel used in the legislative and other departments of government shall be furnished; and the printing and binding and distributing of the laws, journals, department reports, and other printing and binding; and the repairing and furnishing the halls and rooms used for the meeting of the general assembly and its committees, shall be performed under contract, to be given to the lowest responsible bidder, below such maximum price and under such regulations as may be prescribed by law. No member or officer of any department of the government shall be in any way interested in any such

> contract; and all such contracts shall be subject to the approval of the governor or his designee.

By section 29, government printing projects must be given to the lowest bidder. Government employees may not have a financial interest in the contract.

Thus, a stationary contract had not been put out for bid was unlawful. *Mulnix v. Mutual Ben. Life Ins. Co.*, 23 Colo. 71, 46 P. 123 (1896).

But it was held that section 29 does not apply to the printing of appellate court opinions. *Gillette v. Peabody*, 19 Colo. App. 356, 75 P. 18 (1904). The court applied the rule of *ejusdem generis*, by which "general words must be construed as having reference only to matters of the same kind as those enumerated." *Id.* at 363–64. Appellate opinions are not "laws, journals, department reports." Nor can they be considered "other printing and binding," because appellate opinions are not "of the same kind" as the enumerated items.

Art. V, Section 30. (repealed)

This provision on salaries for the governor and judges is now covered by other sections.

Art. V, Section 31. Revenue bills must originate in the house of representatives

> <u>All bills for raising revenue shall originate in the house of representatives</u>; but the senate may propose amendments, as in the case of other bills.

Similar to the Origination Clause of the U.S. Constitution, art. I, § 7. According to dubious judicial interpretation, this applies only to bills whose primary purpose is revenue. For example, a bill about public schools that included a tax increase did not have to originate in the House. *Chicago, Burlington & Quincy R.R. Co. v. School Dist. No. 1 in Yuma County*, 63 Colo. 159, 165 P. 260 (1917).

Art. V, Section 32. Appropriation bills

> The general appropriation bill shall embrace nothing but appropriations for the expense of the executive, legislative and judicial departments of the state, state institutions, interest on the public debt and for public schools. All other appropriations shall be made by separate bills, each embracing but one subject.

The general appropriations bill is commonly known as "the Long Bill." It is drafted by the Joint Budget Committee. The six-member JBC consists of three members from each house. The majority party supplies two members, and the minority party one.

The JBC is a very hard-working committee. Members assigned to the committee are known to be diligent, intelligent, and detail oriented.

The "nothing but" language prohibits substantive riders on the long bill and has been strictly enforced. *Anderson v. Lamm*, 579 P.2d 620 (Colo. 1978) (Repub. sen. president vs. Democratic gov.).

A special appropriations bill that made appropriations to four state institutions and did not contain the word "appropriations" in the title was void. *In re House Bill no. 168*, 21 Colo. 46, 38 P. 1096 (1895).

Art. V, Section 33. Disbursement of public money only on appropriations made by law

> No moneys in the state treasury shall be disbursed therefrom by the treasurer except upon appropriations made by law, or otherwise authorized by law, and any amount disbursed shall be substantiated by vouchers signed and approved in the manner prescribed by law.

Similar to the Appropriations Clause of the U.S. Constitution: "No Money shall be drawn from the Treasury, but in Consequence of Appropriations made by Law; and a regular Statement and Account of the Receipts and Expenditures of all public Money shall be published from time to time." U.S. CONST., art. I, § 9.

Appropriations Clauses aim to ensure that the power of the purse will be in the hands of the people, through the legislative branch. Part of the background was the seventeenth-century conflict between the English parliament and the despotic kings from the House of Stuart, who attempted to rule unilaterally. Parliament had the sole power to tax, and it wanted to make sure that it could also control spending of tax revenue.

Legislative control of government spending is presently evaded by direct federal grants, private grants, or legal settlements that go to particular executive branch offices. Because the money does not come from the state treasury, section 33 does not apply. So the executive branch can raise its own money, and spend it as it wishes—as the Stuarts did. For example, the governor, not the legislature, can decide how to spend congressional grants for emergencies, such as the Sept. 11 terrorist attacks or the CoVid-19 pandemic. Governor Hickenlooper used interest accrued on September 11 grants to pay for his legal defense on ethics charges. When attorney general Phil Weiser sued opioid manufacturers, the nearly $400 million that the manufacturers agreed to pay was distributed not to victims, and not by the general assembly, but by attorney general Weiser.

Art. V, Section 34. No appropriations to private institutions

> No appropriation shall be made for charitable, industrial, educational or benevolent purposes to any person, corporation or community not under the absolute control of the state, nor to any denominational or sectarian institution or association.

Enforced for decades, then nullified by the courts starting in 1940. *Bedford v. White*, 106 Colo. 439, 106 P.2d 469 (1940). As we shall see for similar provisions prohibiting the government from contracting debt on behalf of corporations (art. XI), the courts have invented an exception that destroys the rule. Whenever the government asserts that the money given to a special interest is intended to have a "public purpose" (*e.g.*, helping the economy), the courts accept the legislative declaration as conclusive.

The special restriction against aid to "sectarian" institutions will be discussed in chapter 13 ("Education," art. IX).

Art. V, Section 35. No delegation of power to perform any municipal function to any special commission, private corporation or association

> The general assembly shall not delegate to any special commission, private corporation or association, any power to make, supervise or interfere with any municipal improvement, money, property or effects, whether held in trust or otherwise, or to levy taxes or perform any municipal function whatever.

Because of section 35, the statewide Public Utilities Commission may not regulate municipal utilities within the municipality. The supreme court oddly defined "municipal" to include counties, not just cities and towns. *E.g., City of Durango v. Durango Transp., Inc.*, 807 P.2d 1152 (Colo. 1991) (PUC may not regulate bus service operated by La Plata County and the City of Durango).

However, to the extent that a municipal utility serves customers outside the municipality, the extra-territorial service may be regulated. *E.g., City of Loveland v. PUC*, 195 Colo. 298, 580 P.2d 381 (1978) (electrical utility).

The Public Utilities Commission is created by article XXV of the Colorado Constitution.

Art. V, Section 36. General assembly makes laws on investment of trust funds

> The general assembly shall, from time to time, enact laws prescribing types or classes of investments for the investment of funds held by executors, administrators, guardians, conservators and other trustees, whose power of investment is not set out in the instrument creating the trust.

Enacted in 1949, the present language was a long overdue reform of trustee powers. Previously, trustees were prohibited from investing in stocks or bonds of private corporations.

Art. V, Section 37. (repealed)

The section formerly had given courts the authority to determine when changes of venue would be granted. Repealed because it is duplicative of art. VI, § 21.

Art. V, Section 38. General assembly may not release debt owed to government

> No obligation or liability of any person, association, or corporation, held or owned by the state, or any municipal corporation therein, shall ever be exchanged, transferred, remitted, released, or postponed or in any way diminished by the general assembly, nor shall such liability or obligation be extinguished except by payment thereof into the proper treasury. This section shall not prohibit the write-off or release of uncollectible accounts as provided by general law.

Among other things, Section 38 prevents the state and municipalities from loaning money to a corporation, and then forgiving all or part of the debt.

Art. V, Section 39. Legislative acts shall be presented to governor for signature or veto

> Every order, resolution or vote to which the concurrence of both houses may be necessary, except on the question of adjournment, or relating solely to the transaction of business of the two houses, shall be presented to the governor, and before it shall take effect, be approved by him, or being disapproved, shall be re-passed by two-thirds of both houses, according to the rules and limitations prescribed in case of a bill.

Similar to the Presentment Clause of article I, § 7, of the U.S. Constitution, requiring legislative actions to be presented to the president for signature or veto.

Regardless of how something is labeled, if its effect is "regulating norms of public conduct," presentment is required. *Colo. General Assembly v. Lamm*, 700 P.2d 508, 515 (Colo. 1985).

This does not apply House Resolutions, Senate Resolutions, or Joint Resolutions, which are simply expressions of opinion on a topic. These resolutions have no legal effect.

The Colorado Presentment Clause likewise does not apply to state legislative ratification of a proposed U.S. constitutional amendment. The power to ratify, or not, is given to the state legislature by U.S. Constitution article V, and not by the Colorado Constitution. The U.S. Constitution does not allow governors to have a role in the ratification of a proposed amendment. *Prior v. Noland*, 68 Colo. 263, 188 P. 729 (1920) (also holding that the people of Colorado may not use a referendum to over-ride the general assembly's ratification of the national alcohol prohibition amendment).

Nor does the Presentment Clause apply to the decision of the general assembly to refer a ballot question to the voters to hold a state constitutional convention, pursuant to COLO. CONST., art. XIX, § 1. *People ex rel. Stewart v. Ramer*, 62 Colo. 128, 160 P.1032 (1916).

Art. V, Section 40. Bribery and vote-trading

> If any person elected to either house of the general assembly shall offer or promise to give his vote or influence in favor of or against any measure or proposition pending or proposed to be introduced in the general assembly in consideration or upon condition that any other person elected to the same general assembly will give or will promise or assent to give his vote or influence in favor of or against any other measure or proposition pending or proposed to be introduced in such general assembly, the person making such offer or promise, shall be deemed guilty of solicitation of bribery. If any member of the general assembly shall give his vote or influence for or against any measure or proposition pending in such general assembly, or offer, promise or assent so to do, upon condition that any other member will give or will promise or assent to give his vote or influence in favor of or against any other measure or proposition pending or proposed to be introduced in such general assembly, or in consideration that any other member hath given his vote or influence for or against any other measure or proposition in such general assembly, he shall be deemed guilty of bribery; and any member of the general assembly, or person elected thereto, who shall be guilty of either of such offenses shall be expelled, and shall not be thereafter eligible to the same general assembly;

> and, on conviction thereof in the civil courts, shall be liable to such further penalty as may be prescribed by law.

Note that this provision applies *only* to legislators. The last vote-trading investigation in the legislature was in the middle 1980s, when the attorney general found that a legislator had traded votes. He was not expelled, but he did not seek re-election.

There is no counterpart in the U.S. Constitution, and vote-trading in Congress is common.

Art. V, Section 41. (repealed). Section 42. (repealed)

Dealing with bribery. Moved to article XII (Officers) in 1974.

Art. V, Section 43. Member with private interest shall not vote

> A member who has a personal or private interest in any measure or bill proposed or pending before the general assembly, shall disclose the fact to the house of which he is a member, and shall not vote thereon.

In general, this is left up the good judgment of individual legislators. The goodness of individual judgment has varied. House Rule 21 and Senate Rule 41 add some specifics for when legislators should recuse themselves.

Art. V, Section 44. Representatives in congress

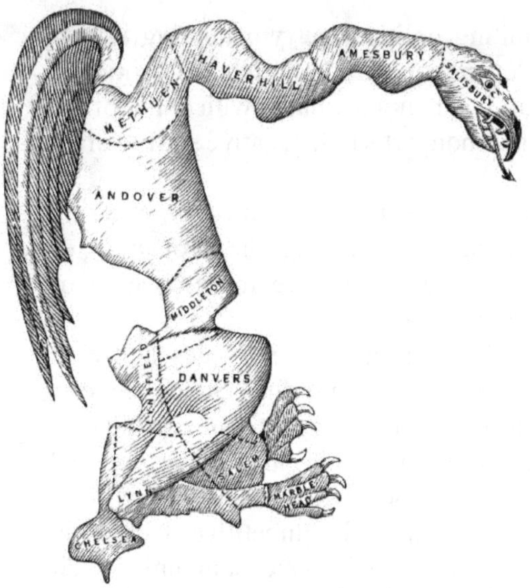

Figure 22. The Massachusetts political cartoon that coined "gerrymander."

Most of the subsequent provisions of article V deal with legislative reapportionment. "Gerrymandering" is the practice of drawing legislative districts with odd shapes, so as to obtain electoral advantage for one's political allies. The word "gerrymander" was created to criticize an 1812 Massachusetts redistricting bill that has been signed by Massachusetts governor Elbridge Gerry.[23] The cartoon made the district look like a salamander. "Gerrymander" is a portmanteau of Gerry + salamander. (A portmanteau combines parts of two words to make a new word. *E.g.* smoke + fog = smog.) In 1974, a constitutional amendment attempted to eliminate gerrymandering by creating a bipartisan special commission. The decisive vote went to an appointee of the chief justice

[23] His name is pronounced "Gary." But "gerrymander" is pronounced like "Jerry." One of Gerry's eponymous descendants played a heroic role warning Coloradans about an impending Indian attack in 1863. See chapter 6 (Fighting for Survival).

of the Colorado supreme court. Commission decisions could be appealed to the Colorado supreme court.

Since 1974, all Colorado governors have been Democrats, except for Bill Owens, 2001–09. Accordingly, the supreme court has been run by Democratic appointees. In disputes, the commission and the supreme court always found that the Democratic redistricting proposal is superior to the Republican one.

So gerrymandering continued, albeit subject to some constraints. The 2011 redistricting made the Colorado House of Representatives the second-most gerrymandered state legislative body in the United States. In the 2014 state house elections, Republicans received many more votes than Democrats. Despite losing the popular vote for state House, Democrats retained control by a 34-31 margin. Republican voters had been segregated into Republican-heavy districts, while Democratic voters had been strategically dispersed to as to create a large number of districts with a small Democratic advantage.

In 2018, the legislature unanimously referred an entirely new system to the voters, who overwhelming approved it. The new system conduct the 2021 redistricting based on the 2020 census.

Because the text of these sections in long and dense, the text is preceded by short summaries written by Kopel.

Section 44 summary: An independent congressional redistricting commission is created. It shall create congressional districts to try to keep together communities that share a common interest. Such communities include race, urban, rural, agricultural, industrial, trade areas, education, employment, environment, public health, transportation, water needs and supplies, and issues of demonstrable regional significance.

(1) The people of the state of Colorado find and declare that:

(a) The practice of political gerrymandering, whereby congressional districts are purposefully drawn to favor one political party or incumbent politician over another, must end;

(b) The public's interest in prohibiting political gerrymandering is best achieved by creating a new and independent commission that is politically balanced, provides representation to voters not affiliated with either of the state's two largest parties, and utilizes nonpartisan legislative staff to draw maps;

(c) The redistricting commission should set district lines by ensuring constitutionally guaranteed voting rights, including the protection of minority group voting, as well as fair and effective representation of constituents using politically neutral criteria;

(d) Competitive elections for members of the United States house of representatives provide voters with a meaningful choice among candidates, promote a healthy democracy, help ensure that constituents receive fair and effective representation, and contribute to the political well-being of key communities of interest and political subdivisions;

(e) For years certain political interests opposed competitive districts in Colorado because they are primarily concerned about maintaining their own political power at the expense of fair and effective representation; and

(f) Citizens want and deserve an inclusive and meaningful congressional redistricting process that provides the public with the ability to be heard as redistricting maps are drawn, to be able to watch the witnesses who deliver testimony and the redistricting commission's deliberations, and to have their written comments considered before any proposed map is voted upon by the commission as the final map.

(2) There is hereby created the independent congressional redistricting commission. The commission shall divide the state into as many congressional districts as there are representatives in congress apportioned to this state by the congress of the United States for the election of one representative to congress from each district. When a new apportionment is made by congress, the commission shall divide the state into congressional districts accordingly.

(3) As used in this section and in sections 44.1 through 44.6 of this article V, unless the context otherwise requires:

(a) "Commission" means the independent congressional redistricting commission created in subsection (2) of this section.

(b)

(I) "Community of interest" means any group in Colorado that shares one or more substantial interests that may be the subject of federal legislative action, is composed of a reasonably proximate population, and thus should be considered for inclusion within a single district for purposes of ensuring its fair and effective representation.

(II) Such interests include but are not limited to matters reflecting:

(A) Shared public policy concerns of urban, rural, agricultural, industrial, or trade areas; and

(B) Shared public policy concerns such as education, employment, environment, public health, transportation, water needs and supplies, and issues of demonstrable regional significance.

(III) Groups that may comprise a community of interest include racial, ethnic, and language minority groups, subject to compliance with subsections (1)(b) and (4)(b) of section 44.3 of this article V, which subsections protect against the denial or abridgement of the right to vote due to a person's race or language minority group.

(IV) "Community of interest" does not include relationships with political parties, incumbents, or political candidates.

(c) "Race" or "racial" means a category of race or ethnic origin documented in the federal decennial census.

(d) "Redistricting year" means the year following the year in which the federal decennial census is taken.

(e) "Staff" or "nonpartisan staff" means the staff of the general assembly's legislative council and office of legislative legal services, or their successor offices, who are assigned to assist the commission by the directors of those offices in accordance with section 44.2 of this article V.

(4) If any date prescribed in sections 44.1 through 44.5 of this article V falls on a Saturday, Sunday, or legal holiday, then the date is extended to the next day that is not a Saturday, Sunday, or legal holiday.

Under the U.S. Constitution, it is lawful for a state legislature to specify that all U.S. Representatives would be elected at large. The 1974 amendment of section 44 required that U.S.

Representatives be elected by individual district. The requirement was retained in the 2018 amendment. Previously, the legislature had sometimes provided that part of Colorado's U.S. House delegation would be elected at large.

§ 44.1. Congressional redistricting commission composition

Summary: Commission members may not be current or recent elected officials. The commission shall hold public hearings. The chief justice will appoint a panel to review the qualifications of applicants. The panel will identify the best applicants who are Democrats, the best Republicans, and the best unaffiliateds. Third parties, such as Libertarians or Greens, are excluded. The majority and minority leaders in the state House and Senate may propose applicants.

Through a process that includes random selections and personal interviews, the panel will choose a commission of four Democrats, four Republicans, and four unaffiliateds. The twelve-member commission must include commissioners from each current congressional district and must reflect Colorado diversity to the extent possible.

Whether the commission is actually balanced, in a partisan sense, depends on the four unaffiliated commissioners. The panel might choose four genuinely neutral ones. Or it might choose commissioners who are nominally unaffiliated, but who lean to one major party or the other.

> (1) After each federal decennial census of the United States, the members of the commission shall be appointed and convened as prescribed in this section.
>
> (2) The commission consists of twelve members who have the following qualifications:
>
> (a) Commissioners must be registered electors who voted in both of the previous two general elections in Colorado;
>
> (b) Commissioners must either have been unaffiliated with any political party or have been affiliated with the same political party for a consecutive period of no less than five years at the time of the application; and
>
> (c) No person may be appointed to or serve on the commission if he or she:
>
> (I) Is or has been a candidate for federal elective office within the last five years preceding the date on which applications for appointment to the commission are due under subsection (4) of this section;
>
> (II) Is or has been, within the last three years preceding the date on which applications for appointment to the commission are due under subsection (4) of this section, compensated by a member of, or a campaign committee advocating the election of a candidate to, the United States house of representatives or the United States senate;
>
> (III) Is or has been, within the last three years preceding the date on which applications for appointment to the commission are due under subsection (4) of this section, an elected public official at the federal, state, county, or municipal level in Colorado;
>
> (IV) Is or has been, within the last three years preceding the date on which applications for appointment to the commission are due under subsection (4) of this section, an elected political party

official above the precinct level in Colorado or an employee of a political party;
(V) Is a member of the commission responsible for dividing the state into senatorial and representative districts of the general assembly; or
(VI) Is or has been a professional lobbyist registered to lobby with the state of Colorado, with any municipality in Colorado, or at the federal level within the last three years preceding the date on which applications for appointment to the commission are due under subsection (4) of this section.

(3)

(a) By August 10 of the year prior to the redistricting year, nonpartisan staff shall, after holding one or more public hearings, prepare an application form that will allow appointing authorities to evaluate a person's experience and qualifications and make such application available on the general assembly's website or comparable means of communicating with the public.
(b) The application form must clearly state the legal obligations and expectations of potential appointees. Information required of applicants must include, but is not necessarily limited to, professional background, party affiliation, a description of past political activity, a list of all political and civic organizations to which the applicant has belonged within the previous five years, and whether the applicant meets the qualifications stated in subsection (2) of this section. In addition, the application form must require the applicant to explain why they want to serve on the commission and afford the applicant an opportunity to make a statement about how they will promote consensus among commissioners if appointed to the commission. Applicants may also choose to include up to four letters of recommendation with their application.

(4) By November 10 of the year prior to the redistricting year, any person who seeks to serve on the commission must submit a completed application to nonpartisan staff. All applications are public records and must be posted promptly after receipt on the general assembly's website or comparable means of communicating with the public.

(5)

(a) No later than January 5 of the redistricting year, the chief justice of the Colorado supreme court shall designate a panel to review the applications. The panel must consist of the three justices or judges who most recently retired from the Colorado supreme court or the Colorado court of appeals, appointed sequentially starting with the most recent justice or judge to retire who has been affiliated with the same political party or unaffiliated with any political party for the two years prior to appointment; except that no appointee, within two years prior to appointment, shall have been affiliated with the same political party as a justice or judge already appointed to the panel. If any of the three justices or judges who most recently retired from the Colorado supreme court or the Colorado court of appeals is unable or unwilling to serve on the panel or has been affiliated within two years prior to appointment with a political party already represented on the panel, then the chief justice shall appoint the next justice or judge who most recently retired from the Colorado supreme court or the Colorado court of appeals and who has not been affiliated within two years prior to appointment with the same political party as any justice or judge already appointed to the panel. If, after considering all justices and judges who have retired from the Colorado supreme court and the Colorado court of appeals, fewer than three eligible participants for the panel have been identified who are able and willing to serve, the chief justice shall appoint the most recently retired district court judge who has not been affiliated within two years prior to appointment with the same political party as any previous appointee to the panel and who accepts such appointment. No justice or judge shall serve both on this panel and the panel assisting in the process of choosing members of the commission responsible for dividing the state into state senate and state house of representatives districts.

(b) All decisions of the panel regarding the selection of applicants pursuant to this section require the affirmative approval of all three members of the panel.

(c) The general assembly shall prescribe by law the compensation of members of the panel. Nonpartisan staff shall assist the panel in carrying out its duties.

(6) After applications are submitted, nonpartisan staff, with the cooperation and assistance of the secretary of state, shall make an objective and factual finding based on, to the extent possible, publicly available information, including information contained in the application and information contained within the records maintained by the secretary of state, whether each applicant meets the qualifications specified in subsection (2) of this section. No later than January 11 of the redistricting year, nonpartisan staff shall make its findings publicly available and notify the applicants of the staff's finding. If the staff finds that an applicant is not eligible, then the staff shall include the reasons in its finding.

(7) By January 18 of the redistricting year, the panel, in a public meeting, shall randomly select by lot from all of the applicants who were found to meet the qualifications specified in subsection (2) of this section the names of three hundred applicants who are affiliated with the state's largest political party, three hundred applicants who are affiliated with the state's second largest political party, and four hundred fifty applicants who are not affiliated with any political party, or such lesser number as there are total applicants who meet the qualifications specified in subsection (2) of this section for each of those groups.

(8)

(a) In one or more public hearings conducted on or before February 1 of the redistricting year, after reviewing the applications of the applicants selected in accordance with subsection (7) of this section, the panel shall identify fifty applicants who are affiliated with the state's largest political party, fifty applicants who are affiliated with the state's second largest political party, and fifty applicants who are unaffiliated with any political party and who best demonstrate:

(I) Experience in organizing, representing, advocating for, adjudicating the interests of, or actively participating in groups, organizations, or associations in Colorado; and

(II) Relevant analytical skills, the ability to be impartial, and the ability to promote consensus on the commission.

(b) No later than February 1 of the redistricting year, from the applicants identified in subsection (8)(a) of this section, the panel shall choose by lot six applicants to serve on the commission as follows:

(I) Two commissioners who are not affiliated with any political party;

(II) Two commissioners who are affiliated with the state's largest political party; and

(III) Two commissioners who are affiliated with the state's second largest political party.

(c) In the process of choosing applicants by lot for appointment to the commission, no applicant whose name is chosen may be appointed if he or she is registered to vote in a congressional district that is already represented on the commission; except that, when all then-existing congressional districts in Colorado are represented on the commission, a congressional district may be represented by a second commissioner. No congressional district may be represented by more than two commissioners. Any persons whose names are chosen but duplicate a congressional district's representation on the commission and are not appointed to the commission shall be eligible for appointment pursuant to subsections (9) and (10) of this section.

(9)

(a) By February 16 of the redistricting year, the majority leader of the state senate, the minority leader of the state senate, the majority leader of the state house of representatives, and the minority leader of the state house of representatives shall each select a pool of ten applicants who are affiliated with one of the state's two largest political parties from all applications submitted to nonpartisan staff and notify the panel of their selections.

(b) As determined by the legislative leaders in selecting their respective pools, the applicants selected for each pool must meet the qualifications set forth in subsection (2) of this section and demonstrate the qualities listed in subsection (8)(a) of this section.

(c) For each congressional district not represented by a commissioner appointed pursuant to subsections (8)(b) and (8)(c) of this section, each pool must consist of at least one applicant who is registered to vote in that congressional district.

(d) If there is an insufficient number of available applicants that meet the requirements of subsection (9)(b) of this section to select any complete pool, then the pool must consist of only those applicants who meet those requirements.

(10) By March 1 of the redistricting year, the panel of judges shall select, in such order as the panel determines, one commissioner from each legislative leader's pool of applicants and two commissioners from those applicants who are not affiliated with any political party and whose names were randomly selected by lot

pursuant to subsection (7) of this section. The panel of judges must ensure that the commission includes four commissioners who are not affiliated with any political party, four commissioners who are affiliated with the state's largest political party, and four commissioners who are affiliated with the state's second largest political party. The panel of judges may interview applicants before making the appointments. In selecting applicants, the panel shall, in addition to considering applicants' other qualifications:

(a) To the extent possible, ensure that the commission reflects Colorado's racial, ethnic, gender, and geographic diversity;

(b) Ensure that at least one commissioner is registered to vote in each congressional district but no more than two commissioners are registered to vote in any single congressional district;

(c) Ensure that at least one commissioner resides west of the continental divide; and

(d) Ensure that all commissioners meet the qualifications set forth in subsection (2) of this section and demonstrate the qualities listed in subsection (8)(a) of this section.

(11)

(a) A commissioner's position on the commission will be deemed vacant if he or she, having been appointed as a registered elector who is not affiliated with a political party, affiliates with a political party before the supreme court has approved a plan pursuant to section 44.5 of this article V. A commissioner's position on the commission will also be deemed vacant if he or she, having been affiliated with one of the state's two largest political parties at the time of appointment, affiliates with a different political party or becomes unaffiliated with any political party before the supreme court has approved a plan pursuant to section 44.5 of this article V.

(b) Any vacancy on the commission, including one that occurs due to death, resignation, removal, failure to meet the qualifications of appointment, refusal or inability to accept an appointment, or otherwise, must be filled as soon as possible by the designated appointing authority from the designated pool of eligible applicants for that commissioner's position and in the same manner as the originally chosen commissioner; except that no commissioner chosen to fill a vacancy will be bypassed for appointment if all congressional districts are already represented on the commission.

(12) For purposes of this section, the state's two largest political parties shall be determined by the number of registered electors affiliated with each political party in the state according to voter registration data published by the secretary of state for the earliest day in January of the redistricting year for which such data is published.

§ 44.2. Redistricting commission organization and procedures

Summary: The commission must follow specified procedures for transparency, public hearings, and record-keeping.

(1)

(a) The governor shall convene the commission no later than March 15 of the redistricting year and appoint a temporary chairperson from the commission's members. Upon convening, the commission shall elect a chair and a vice-chair, who are not members of the same political party, and other such officers as it determines.

(b) The director of research of the legislative council and the director of the office of legislative legal services, or the directors of successor nonpartisan offices of the general assembly, shall appoint nonpartisan staff from their respective offices as needed to assist the commission and the panel of judges as described in section 44.1 of this article V. Nonpartisan staff shall acquire and prepare all necessary resources, including computer hardware, software, and demographic, geographic, and political databases, as far in advance as necessary to enable the commission to begin its work immediately upon convening.

(c) The commission may retain legal counsel in all actions and proceedings in connection with the performance of its powers, duties, and functions, including representation of the commission before any court.

(d) The general assembly shall appropriate sufficient funds for the payment of the expenses of the commission, the compensation and expenses of nonpartisan staff, and the compensation and expenses of the panel of judges as described in section 44.1 of this article V. Members of the commission shall be reimbursed for their reasonable and necessary expenses and may also receive such per diem allowance as may be established by the general assembly. Subject to available appropriations, hardware and software necessary for the development of plans may, at the request of any commissioner, be provided to the commissioner. The commission and its staff must have access to statistical information compiled by the state and its political subdivisions as necessary for its duties. State agencies and political subdivisions shall comply with requests from the commission and its staff for such statistical information.

(e) The commission shall adopt rules to govern its administration and operation. The commission must provide at least seventy-two hours of advance public notice of all proposed rules prior to consideration for adoption; except that proposed rules may be amended during commission deliberations without such advance notice of specific, related amendments. Neither the commission's procedural rules nor its mapping decisions are subject to the "State Administrative Procedure Act", article 4 of title 24, C.R.S., or any successor statute. Rules must include but need not be limited to the following:

(I) The hearing process and review of maps submitted for its consideration;

(II) Maintenance of a record of the commission's activities and proceedings, including a record of written and oral testimony received, and of the commission's directions to nonpartisan staff on proposed changes to any plan and the commission's rationale for such changes;

(III) The process for removing commissioners for participating in communications prohibited under this section;

(IV) The process for recommending changes to plans submitted to the commission by nonpartisan staff; and

(V) The adoption of a statewide meeting and hearing schedule, including the necessary elements of electronic attendance at a commission hearing.

(2) A simple majority of the appointed commissioners may approve rules and procedural decisions. The election of the commission's chair and vice-chair requires the affirmative vote of at least eight commissioners, including the affirmative vote of at least one commissioner who is unaffiliated with any political party. Removal of any commissioner as provided in this

section requires the affirmative vote of at least eight commissioners, including the affirmative vote of at least two commissioners who are unaffiliated with any political party. Adoption of the final plan for submission to the supreme court and the adoption of a revised plan after a plan is returned to the commission from the supreme court requires the affirmative vote of at least eight commissioners, including the affirmative vote of at least two commissioners who are unaffiliated with any political party. The commission shall not vote upon a final plan until at least seventy-two hours after it has been proposed to the commission in a public meeting or at least seventy-two hours after it has been amended by the commission in a public meeting, whichever occurs later; except that commissioners may unanimously waive the seventy-two hour requirement.

(3)

(a) All Colorado residents, including individual commissioners, may present proposed redistricting maps or written comments, or both, for the commission's consideration.
(b) The commission must, to the maximum extent practicable, provide opportunities for Colorado residents to present testimony at hearings held throughout the state. The commission shall not approve a redistricting map until at least three hearings have been held in each congressional district, including at least one hearing that is held in a location west of the continental divide and at least one hearing that is held in a location east of the continental divide and either south of El Paso county's southern boundary or east of Arapahoe county's eastern boundary. No gathering of commissioners can be considered a hearing for this purpose unless it is attended, in person or electronically, by at least ten commissioners. The commission shall establish by rule the necessary elements of electronic attendance at a commission hearing.
(c) The commission shall maintain a website or comparable means of communicating with the public through which any Colorado resident may submit proposed maps or written comments, or both, without attending a hearing of the commission.
(d) The commission shall publish all written comments pertaining to redistricting on its website or comparable means of communicating with the public as well as the name of the Colorado resident submitting such comments. If the commission or nonpartisan staff have a substantial basis to believe that the person submitting such comments has not truthfully or accurately identified himself or herself, the commission need not consider and need not publish such comments but must notify the commenter in writing of this fact. The commission may withhold comments, in whole or in part, from the website or comparable means of communicating with the public that do not relate to redistricting maps, policies, or communities of interest.
(e) The commission shall provide simultaneous access to the regional hearings by broadcasting them via its website or comparable means of communicating with the public and maintain an archive of such hearings for online public review.

(4)

(a) Commissioners are guardians of the public trust and are subject to antibribery and abuse of public office requirements as provided in parts 3 and 4 of article 8 of title 18, C.R.S., as amended, or any successor statute.
(b) To ensure transparency in the redistricting process:

(I)

(A) The commission and the commissioners are subject to open meetings requirements as provided in part 4 of article 6 of title 24, C.R.S., as amended, or any successor statute.
(B) Except as provided in subsection (4)(b)(I)(D) of this section, a commissioner shall not communicate with nonpartisan staff on the mapping of congressional

districts unless the communication is during a public meeting or hearing of the commission.

(C) Except for public input and comment, nonpartisan staff shall not have any communications about the content or development of any plan outside of public hearings with anyone except other staff members. Nonpartisan staff shall report to the commission any attempt by anyone to exert influence over the staff's role in the drafting of plans.

(D) One or more nonpartisan staff may be designated to communicate with commissioners regarding administrative matters, the definition and scope of which shall be determined by the commission.

(E) Any commissioner who participates in a communication prohibited in this section must be removed from the commission, and such vacancy must be filled within seven days.

(II) The commission, each commissioner, and nonpartisan staff are subject to open records requirements as provided in part 1 of article 72 of title 24, C.R.S., as amended, or any successor statute; except that maps in draft form and not submitted to the commission are not public records subject to disclosure. Work product and communications among nonpartisan staff are subject to disclosure once a plan is submitted to the supreme court.

(III) Persons who contract for or receive compensation for advocating to the commission, to one or more commissioners, or to the nonpartisan staff for the adoption or rejection of any map, amendment to a map, mapping approach, or manner of compliance with any of the mapping criteria specified in section 44.3 of this article V are lobbyists who must disclose to the secretary of state any compensation contracted for, compensation received, and the person or entity contracting or paying for their lobbying services. Such disclosure must be made no later than seventy-two hours after the earlier of each instance of such lobbying or any payment of such compensation. The secretary of state shall publish on the secretary of state's website or comparable means of communicating with the public the names of such lobbyists as well as the compensation received and the persons or entities for whom they work within twenty-four hours of receiving such information. The secretary of state shall adopt rules to facilitate the complete and prompt reporting required by this subsection (4)(b)(III) as well as a complaint process to address any lobbyist's failure to report a full and accurate disclosure, which complaint must be heard by an administrative law judge, whose decision may be appealed to the court of appeals.

§ 44.3. Rules for drawing congressional districts

Summary: The commission has very little discretion to deviate from perfect equality of population among the districts. The districts should keep communities of interest together. It should likewise keep together political subdivisions, such as counties and municipalities. Then, to the extent possible, the commission should make the districts politically competitive.

(1) In adopting a congressional redistricting plan, the commission shall:

(a) Make a good-faith effort to achieve precise mathematical population equality between districts, justifying each variance, no matter how small, as required by the constitution of the United States. Districts must be composed of contiguous geographic areas;

(b) Comply with the federal "Voting Rights Act of 1965", 52 U.S.C. sec. 50301, as amended.

(2)

(a) As much as is reasonably possible, the commission's plan must preserve whole communities of interest and whole political subdivisions, such as counties, cities, and towns.
(b) Districts must be as compact as is reasonably possible.

(3)

(a) Thereafter, the commission shall, to the extent possible, maximize the number of politically competitive districts.
(b) In its hearings in various locations in the state, the commission shall solicit evidence relevant to competitiveness of elections in Colorado and shall assess such evidence in evaluating proposed maps.
(c) When the commission approves a plan, or when nonpartisan staff submits a plan in the absence of the commission's approval of a plan as provided in section 44.4 of this article V, the nonpartisan staff shall, within seventy-two hours of such action, make publicly available, and include in the commission's record, a report to demonstrate how the plan reflects the evidence presented to, and the findings concerning, the extent to which competitiveness in district elections is fostered consistent with the other criteria set forth in this section.
(d) For purposes of this subsection (3), "competitive" means having a reasonable potential for the party affiliation of the district's representative to change at least once between federal decennial censuses. Competitiveness may be measured by factors such as a proposed district's past election results, a proposed district's political party registration data, and evidence-based analyses of proposed districts.

(4) No map may be approved by the commission or given effect by the supreme court if:

(a) It has been drawn for the purpose of protecting one or more incumbent members, or one or more declared candidates, of the United States house of representatives or any political party; or
(b) It has been drawn for the purpose of or results in the denial or abridgement of the right of any citizen to vote on account of that person's race or membership in a language minority group, including diluting the impact of that racial or language minority group's electoral influence.

§ 44.4. Public hearings and participation

Summary: The commission, relying on nonpartisan staff, will draw up a preliminary plan. After public hearings and comment, the commission will create a final plan. If the commission cannot agree, a map drawn by legislative staff will be used.

(1) The commission shall begin by considering a plan, created by nonpartisan staff alone, to be known as the "preliminary plan". The preliminary plan must be presented and published no earlier than thirty days and no later than forty-five days after the commission has convened or the necessary census data are available,

whichever is later. Within the first twenty days after the commission has convened, any member of the public and any member of the commission may submit written comments to nonpartisan staff on the creation of the preliminary plan and on communities of interest that require representation in one or more specific areas of the state. Nonpartisan staff shall consider such comments in creating the preliminary plan and such comments must be part of the record of the commission's activities and proceedings. At the first public hearing at which the preliminary plan is presented, nonpartisan staff shall explain how the plan was created, how the plan addresses the categories of public comments received, and how the plan complies with the criteria prescribed in section 44.3 of this article V.

(2) By July 7 of the redistricting year, the commission shall complete public hearings on the preliminary plan in several places throughout the state in accordance with section 44.2 of this article V.

(3) Subsequent to hearings on the preliminary plan, nonpartisan staff shall prepare, publish online, and present to the commission no fewer than three plans, except as provided in subsection (5) of this section. These plans will be known as the "staff plans" and must be named and numbered sequentially for purposes of subsection (6) of this section. Staff plans must be prepared, published online, and presented in accordance with a timetable established by the commission; except that each staff plan must be presented to the commission no fewer than ten days after the presentation of any previous staff plan and no fewer than twenty-four hours after it has been published online. If the commission fails to establish a timetable for the presentation of staff plans within ten days after the completion of hearings on the preliminary plan, nonpartisan staff shall establish such timetable. Nonpartisan staff shall keep each plan confidential until it is published online or by a comparable means of communicating with the public using generally available technologies. The commission may provide direction, if approved by at least eight commissioners including at least one commissioner unaffiliated with any political party, for the development of staff plans through the adoption of standards, guidelines, or methodologies to which nonpartisan staff shall adhere, including standards, guidelines, or methodologies to be used to evaluate a plan's competitiveness, consistent with section 44.3(3)(d) of this article V. In preparing all staff plans, nonpartisan staff shall also consider public testimony and public comments received by the commission that are consistent with the criteria specified in section 44.3 of this article V.

(4) Any commissioner or group of commissioners may request nonpartisan staff to prepare additional plans or amendments to plans. Any such request must be made in a public hearing of the commission but does not require commission approval. Plans or amendments developed in response to such requests are separate from staff plans for purposes of subsection (6) of this section.

(5)

(a) The commission may adopt a final plan at any time after presentation of the first staff plan, in which case nonpartisan staff does not need to prepare or present additional staff plans.

(b) No later than September 1 of the redistricting year, the commission shall adopt a final plan, which must then be submitted to the supreme court

for its review and determination in accordance with section 44.5 of this article V.
(c) The commission may adjust the deadlines specified in this section if conditions outside of the commission's control require such an adjustment to ensure adopting a final plan as required by this subsection (5).
(d) The commission may grant nonpartisan staff the authority to make technical de minimis adjustments to the adopted plan prior to its submission to the supreme court.

(6) If for any reason the commission does not adopt a final plan by the date specified in subsection (5) of this section, then nonpartisan staff shall submit the unamended third staff plan to the supreme court.

§ 44.5. Supreme court review

Summary: The supreme court will review the final plan for abuse of discretion.

(1) The supreme court shall review the submitted plan and determine whether the plan complies with the criteria listed in section 44.3 of this article V. The court's review and determination shall take precedence over other matters before the court. The supreme court shall adopt rules for such proceedings and for the production and presentation of supportive evidence for such plan. Any legal arguments concerning such plan must be submitted to the supreme court pursuant to the schedule established by the court.

(2) The supreme court shall approve the plan submitted unless it finds that the commission or nonpartisan staff, in the case of a staff plan submitted in the absence of a commission-approved plan, abused its discretion in applying or failing to apply the criteria listed in section 44.3 of this article V, in light of the record before the commission. The supreme court may consider any maps submitted to the commission in assessing whether the commission or nonpartisan staff, in the case of a staff plan submitted in the absence of a commission-approved plan, abused its discretion.

(3) If the supreme court determines that the submitted plan constitutes an abuse of discretion in applying or failing to apply the criteria listed in section 44.3 of this article V, in light of the record before the commission, the supreme court shall return the plan to the commission with the court's reasons for disapproval.

(4)

(a) By November 1 of the redistricting year, the supreme court shall approve the plan submitted or return the plan to the commission.
(b) If the court returns the plan to the commission, the commission shall have twelve days to hold a commission hearing that includes public testimony and to return an adopted plan that resolves the court's reasons for disapproval.
(c) If the commission fails to adopt and return a plan to the court within twelve days, nonpartisan staff shall have an additional three days to prepare a plan that resolves the court's reasons for disapproval and return it to the court for approval.

> (d) The supreme court shall review the revised plan in accordance with subsections (1), (2), and (3) of this section.
>
> (5) The supreme court shall approve a plan for the redrawing of congressional districts no later than December 15 of the redistricting year. The court shall order that such plan be filed with the secretary of state no later than such date.

§ 44.6. Severability

Summary: The Colorado Constitution contains a severability clause that is applicable to everything in the Constitution. COLO. CONST. art. XVIII, § 10. The severability clause in article V, § 44.6 is therefore redundant and is inserted in abundance of caution. Which is usually a good idea in legal drafting. Never underestimate the power of willful misreading.

> If any provision of sections 44.1 through 44.5 of this article V is found by a court of competent jurisdiction to be unconstitutional, or if any application of these sections is found by such a court to be unconstitutional, such invalidity shall not affect other provisions or applications of the remaining provisions of these sections that can be given effect without the invalid provision or application. The provisions of sections 44.1 through 44.5 of this article V are deemed and declared severable.

The first case involving the new congressional redistricting rules in sections 44 to 44.6, and the parallel rules for state legislature redistricting in sections 46 to 48.4, involved an effort by the majority party in the 2021 state legislature to control the commission. The constitutional amendments impose strict deadlines on the redistricting commissions' work. But final results for the 2020 census had been delayed. A Senate bill purported to order the commissions to use preliminary census data when drawing districts. The Colorado supreme court held that the commissions had the authority to choose to use preliminary data, but the general assembly could not order them to do so.

As the 5–2 supreme court majority emphasized, the purpose of the 2018 amendments was to remove the general assembly from the redistricting process. "Put differently, any power that the General Assembly asserts over a constitutionally created independent commission that was expressly designed to divest the legislature of authority must derive from the amendment that created the commission, not the constitution's general grant of legislative authority."

The bill also said that courts should review commission compliance with the Constitution based on a "substantial compliance" standard for technical, nonsubstantive requirements. The supreme court held that determining constitutional compliance of commission acts was the job of the courts, not the general assembly, and the general assembly could not mandate any particular standard of review.

Dissenting, justice Hood, joined by justice Gabriel, agreed with the majority about the legislature's attempt to control the standard of review. He argued, however, that the general assembly had the inherent power to enact legislation about the redistricting amendments, except to the extent that the amendments forbade general assembly action. *In Re: Interrogatories on Senate Bill 21-247 Submitted by the Colorado General Assembly*, 2021 CO 37 (Colo. 2021).

After the first congressional redistricting commission had completed its work in 2021, the supreme court unanimously upheld the plan, applying the constitutionally required standard of abuse of discretion. The court rejected claims that the commission's decision not to draw lines so as to maximize Hispanic concentration was unconstitutional. *In re Colo. Indep. Cong. Redistricting Comm'n*, 2021 CO 73.

Art. V, Section 45. General assembly composed of 35 senators and 65 representatives

> The general assembly shall consist of not more than thirty-five members of the senate and of not more than sixty-five members of the house of representatives, one to be elected from each senatorial and each representative district, respectively.

The 1876 Constitution had 26 Senators and 39 Representatives. The increase to the current number was enacted in 1891.

Art. V, Section 46. General assembly redistricting commission

Summary: The current versions of sections 46 through 48.4 create a separate commission for reapportionment of the state House and state Senate. The system is similar to the congressional apportionment process described above.

The earlier and oft-revised versions of sections 46–48 also addressed legislative apportionment.

> (1) The people of the state of Colorado find and declare that:
>
> (a) The practice of political gerrymandering, whereby legislative districts are purposefully drawn to favor one political party or incumbent politician over another, must end;
>
> (b) The public's interest in prohibiting political gerrymandering is best achieved by creating a new and independent commission that is politically balanced, provides representation to voters not affiliated with either of the state's two largest parties, and utilizes nonpartisan legislative staff to draw maps;
>
> (c) The redistricting commission should set district lines by ensuring constitutionally guaranteed voting rights, including the protection of minority group voting, as well as fair and effective representation of constituents using politically neutral criteria;
>
> (d) Competitive elections for members of the general assembly provide voters with a meaningful choice among candidates, promote a healthy democracy, help ensure that constituents receive fair and effective representation, and contribute to the political well-being of key communities of interest and political subdivisions;
>
> (e) For years certain political interests opposed competitive districts in Colorado because they are primarily concerned about maintaining their own political power at the expense of fair and effective representation; and
>
> (f) Citizens want and deserve an inclusive and meaningful legislative redistricting process that provides the public with the ability to be heard as redistricting maps are drawn, to be able to watch the witnesses who deliver testimony and the redistricting commission's deliberations, and to have their written comments considered before any proposed map is voted upon by the commission as the final map.

(2) There is hereby created the independent legislative redistricting commission. The commission shall divide the state into as many senatorial and representative districts as there are members of the senate and house of representatives respectively. After each federal decennial census, the senatorial districts and representative districts shall be established, revised, or altered, and the members of the senate and the house of representatives apportioned among them, by the independent legislative redistricting commission.

(3) As used in this section and in sections 47 through 48.4 of this article V, unless the context otherwise requires:

(a) "Commission" means the independent legislative redistricting commission created in subsection (2) of this section.

(b)

(I) "Community of interest" means any group in Colorado that shares one or more substantial interests that may be the subject of state legislative action, is composed of a reasonably proximate population, and thus should be considered for inclusion within a single district for purposes of ensuring its fair and effective representation.

(II) Such interests include but are not limited to matters reflecting:

(A) Shared public policy concerns of urban, rural, agricultural, industrial, or trade areas; and

(B) Shared public policy concerns such as education, employment, environment, public health, transportation, water needs and supplies, and issues of demonstrable regional significance.

(III) Groups that may comprise a community of interest include racial, ethnic, and language minority groups, subject to compliance with subsections (1)(b) and (4)(b) of section 48.1 of this article V, which subsections protect against the denial or abridgement of the right to vote due to a person's race or language minority group.

(IV) "Community of interest" does not include relationships with political parties, incumbents, or political candidates.

(c) "Race" or "racial" means a category of race or ethnic origin documented in the federal decennial census.

(d) "Redistricting year" means the year following the year in which the federal decennial census is taken.

(e) "Staff" or "nonpartisan staff" means the staff of the general assembly's legislative council and office of legislative legal services, or their successor offices, who are assigned to assist the commission by the directors of those offices in accordance with section 48 of this article V.

(4) If any date prescribed in sections 47 through 48.3 of this article V falls on a Saturday, Sunday, or legal holiday, then the date is extended to the next day that is not a Saturday, Sunday, or legal holiday.

Under Colorado's 1876 system each county had at least one state representative. Further, counties could not be divided, so counties with larger populations would elect several members at large. Giving each county its own state representative was typical in state constitutions. G. ALAN TARR, UNDERSTANDING STATE CONSTITUTIONS 104–05 (1998).

Senate districts were created by joining contiguous counties. High population counties, with more than one senator or representative, elected them at large. Denver at its peak had 18 representatives and 9 senators, all elected at large.

Under the 1876 Colorado system, voters in low-population counties had proportionately greater weight than voters in high-population counties.

In some states, legislatures refused for decades to reapportion based on new census data. They excessively over-weighted rural voters; rural districts might have comprised half of a state's population in 1900, but only a fifth in 1950.

However, it is not true that county-based representation was always the result of a small rural minority tenaciously clinging to unjust power. In 1952–62, the *voters* of Michigan, California, Washington, and Colorado all rejected initiatives to make population a greater factor in the reapportionment of their upper houses. TARR at 146.

In a series of cases in the 1960s, the U.S. supreme court ruled that state legislative districts must have equal populations, because of the Fourteenth Amendment's Equal Protection Clause. The first of the cases was *Baker v. Carr*, 369 U.S. 186 (1962), which held that the question is justiciable, and set up the inevitable future cases holding that the Equal Protection Clause was violated. Ultimately, the legislative apportionment in 46 of the 50 states was declared unconstitutional.

As the dissenters pointed out, the court's novel principle had no basis in the original meaning of the Fourteenth Amendment. In the U.S. Senate, each state has two senators, even though some states have much larger populations than other states. This is part of the checks and balances that protect lower density areas from being politically dominated and oppressed by large metropolitan areas. The United States Constitution is not purely democratic. Rather, the objective is enduring liberty and independence, national and individual. Checks and balances work to prevent majorities from abusing minorities.

It is difficult to see why the U.S. supreme court should be able to force states to abandon representation systems that are based on the model of the federal Constitution.

A 1964 U.S. supreme court decision held that the new rule about equal population districts applies to state legislative upper houses, not just the lower houses. *Lucas v. 44th General Assembly*, 377 U.S. 713 (1964) (Colorado Senate).

Art. V, Section 47. Commission composition

> (1) After each federal decennial census of the United States, the members of the commission shall be appointed and convened as prescribed in this section.
>
> (2) The commission consists of twelve members who have the following qualifications:
>
> > (a) Commissioners must be registered electors who voted in both of the previous two general elections in Colorado;
> > (b) Commissioners must either have been unaffiliated with any political party or have been affiliated with the same political party for a consecutive period of no less than five years at the time of the application; and
> > (c) No person may be appointed to or serve on the commission if he or she:
> >
> > > (I) Is or has been a candidate for the general assembly within the last five years preceding the date on which applications for appointment to the commission are due under subsection (4) of this section;

(II) Is or has been, within the last three years preceding the date on which applications for appointment to the commission are due under subsection (4) of this section, compensated by a member of, or a campaign committee advocating the election of a candidate to, the general assembly;

(III) Is or has been, within the last three years preceding the date on which applications for appointment to the commission are due under subsection (4) of this section, an elected public official at the federal, state, county, or municipal level in Colorado;

(IV) Is or has been, within the last three years preceding the date on which applications for appointment to the commission are due under subsection (4) of this section, an elected political party official above the precinct level in Colorado or an employee of a political party;

(V) Is a member of the commission responsible for dividing the state into congressional districts; or

(VI) Is or has been a professional lobbyist registered to lobby with the state of Colorado, with any municipality in Colorado, or at the federal level within the last three years preceding the date on which applications for appointment to the commission are due under subsection (4) of this section.

(3)

(a) By August 10 of the year prior to the redistricting year, nonpartisan staff shall, after holding one or more public hearings, prepare an application form that will allow appointing authorities to evaluate a person's experience and qualifications and make such application available on the general assembly's website or comparable means of communicating with the public.

(b) The application form must clearly state the legal obligations and expectations of potential appointees. Information required of applicants must include, but is not necessarily limited to, professional background, party affiliation, a description of past political activity, a list of all political and civic organizations to which the applicant has belonged within the previous five years, and whether the applicant meets the qualifications stated in subsection (2) of this section. In addition, the application form must require the applicant to explain why they want to serve on the commission and afford the applicant an opportunity to make a statement about how they will promote consensus among commissioners if appointed to the commission. Applicants may also choose to include up to four letters of recommendation with their application.

(4) By November 10 of the year prior to the redistricting year, any person who seeks to serve on the commission must submit a completed application to nonpartisan staff. All applications are public records and must be posted promptly after receipt on the general assembly's website or comparable means of communicating with the public.

(5)

(a) No later than January 5 of the redistricting year, the chief justice of the Colorado supreme court shall designate a panel to review the applications.

The panel must consist of the three justices or judges who most recently retired from the Colorado supreme court or the Colorado court of appeals, appointed sequentially starting with the most recent justice or judge to retire who has been affiliated with the same political party or unaffiliated with any political party for the two years prior to appointment; except that no appointee, within two years prior to appointment, shall have been affiliated with the same political party as a justice or judge already appointed to the panel. If any of the three justices or judges who most recently retired from the Colorado supreme court or the Colorado court of appeals is unable or unwilling to serve on the panel or has been affiliated within two years prior to appointment with a political party already represented on the panel, then the chief justice shall appoint the next justice or judge who most recently retired from the Colorado supreme court or the Colorado court of appeals and who has not been affiliated within two years prior to appointment with the same political party as any justice or judge already appointed to the panel. If, after considering all justices and judges who have retired from the Colorado supreme court and the Colorado court of appeals, fewer than three eligible participants for the panel have been identified who are able and willing to serve, the chief justice shall appoint the most recently retired district court judge who has not been affiliated within two years prior to appointment with the same political party as any previous appointee to the panel and who accepts such appointment. No justice or judge shall serve both on this panel and the panel assisting in the process of choosing members of the commission responsible for dividing the state into congressional districts.
(b) All decisions of the panel regarding the selection of applicants pursuant to this section require the affirmative approval of all three members of the panel.
(c) The general assembly shall prescribe by law the compensation of members of the panel. Nonpartisan staff shall assist the panel in carrying out its duties.

(6) After applications are submitted, nonpartisan staff, with the cooperation and assistance of the secretary of state, shall make an objective and factual finding based on, to the extent possible, publicly available information, including information contained in the application and information contained within the records maintained by the secretary of state, whether each applicant meets the qualifications specified in subsection (2) of this section. No later than January 11 of the redistricting year, nonpartisan staff shall make its findings publicly available, and notify the applicants of the staff's finding. If the staff finds that an applicant is not eligible, then the staff shall include the reasons in its finding.

(7) By January 25 of the redistricting year, the panel, in a public meeting, shall randomly select by lot from all of the applicants who were found to meet the qualifications specified in subsection (2) of this section the names of three hundred applicants who are affiliated with the state's largest political party, three hundred applicants who are affiliated with the state's second largest political party, and four hundred fifty applicants who are not affiliated with any political party, or such lesser number as there are total applicants who meet the qualifications specified in subsection (2) of this section for each of those groups.

(8)

(a) In one or more public hearings conducted on or before February 15 of the redistricting year, after reviewing the applications of the applicants selected in accordance with subsection (7) of this section, the panel shall identify fifty applicants who are affiliated with the state's largest political party, fifty applicants who are identified with the state's second largest political party, and fifty applicants who are unaffiliated with any political party and who best demonstrate:

(I) Experience in organizing, representing, advocating for, adjudicating the interests of, or actively participating in groups, organizations, or associations in Colorado; and

(II) Relevant analytical skills, the ability to be impartial, and the ability to promote consensus on the commission.

(b) No later than February 15 of the redistricting year, from the applicants identified in subsection (8)(a) of this section, the panel shall choose by lot six applicants to serve on the commission as follows:

(I) Two commissioners who are not affiliated with any political party;

(II) Two commissioners who are affiliated with the state's largest political party; and

(III) Two commissioners who are affiliated with the state's second largest political party.

(c) In the process of choosing applicants by lot for appointment to the commission, no applicant whose name is chosen may be appointed if he or she is registered to vote in a congressional district that is already represented on the commission; except that, when all then-existing congressional districts in Colorado are represented on the commission, a congressional district may be represented by a second commissioner. No congressional district may be represented by more than two commissioners. Any persons whose names are chosen but duplicate a congressional district's representation on the commission and are not appointed to the commission shall be eligible for appointment pursuant to subsections (9) and (10) of this section.

(9)

(a) By February 16 of the redistricting year, the majority leader of the state senate, the minority leader of the state senate, the majority leader of the state house of representatives, and the minority leader of the state house of representatives shall each select a pool of ten applicants who are affiliated with one of the state's two largest political parties from all applications submitted to nonpartisan staff and notify the panel of their selections.

(b) As determined by the legislative leaders in selecting their respective pools, the applicants selected for each pool must meet the qualifications set forth in subsection (2) of this section and demonstrate the qualities listed in subsection (8)(a) of this section.

(c) For each congressional district not represented by a commissioner appointed pursuant to subsections (8)(b) and (8)(c) of this section, each pool must consist of at least one applicant who is registered to vote in that congressional district.

(d) If there is an insufficient number of available applicants that meet the requirements of subsection (9)(b) of this section to select any complete pool, then the pool must consist of only those applicants who meet those requirements.

(10) By March 16 of the redistricting year, the panel of judges shall select, in such order as the panel determines, one commissioner from each legislative leader's pool of applicants and two commissioners from those applicants who are not affiliated with any political party and whose names were randomly selected by lot pursuant to subsection (7) of this section. The panel of judges must ensure that the commission includes four commissioners who are not affiliated with any political party, four commissioners who are affiliated with the state's largest political party, and four commissioners who are affiliated with the state's second largest political party. The panel of judges may interview applicants before making the appointments. In selecting applicants, the panel shall, in addition to considering applicants' other qualifications:

(a) To the extent possible, ensure that the commission reflects Colorado's racial, ethnic, gender, and geographic diversity;
(b) Ensure that at least one commissioner is registered to vote in each congressional district but no more than two commissioners are registered to vote in any single congressional district;
(c) Ensure that at least one commissioner resides west of the continental divide; and
(d) Ensure that all commissioners meet the qualifications set forth in subsection (2) of this section and demonstrate the qualities listed in subsection (8)(a) of this section.

(11)

(a) A commissioner's position on the commission will be deemed vacant if he or she, having been appointed as a registered elector who is not affiliated with a political party, affiliates with a political party before the supreme court has approved a plan pursuant to section 48.3 of this article V. A commissioner's position on the commission will also be deemed vacant if he or she, having been affiliated with one of the state's two largest political parties at the time of appointment, affiliates with a different political party or becomes unaffiliated with any political party before the supreme court has approved a plan pursuant to section 48.3 of this article V.
(b) Any vacancy on the commission, including one that occurs due to death, resignation, removal, failure to meet the qualifications of appointment, refusal or inability to accept an appointment, or otherwise, must be filled as soon as possible by the designated appointing authority from the designated pool of eligible applicants for that commissioner's position and in the same manner as the originally chosen commissioner; except that no commissioner chosen to fill a vacancy will be bypassed for appointment if all congressional districts are already represented on the commission.

(12) For purposes of this section, the state's two largest political parties shall be determined by the number of registered electors affiliated with each political party

in the state according to voter registration data published by the secretary of state for the earliest day in January of the redistricting year for which such data is published.

Art. V, Section 48. Commission procedures

(1)

(a) The governor shall convene the commission no later than March 30 of the redistricting year and appoint a temporary chairperson from the commission's members. Upon convening, the commission shall elect a chair and a vice-chair, who are not members of the same political party, and other such officers as it determines.

(b) The director of research of the legislative council and the director of the office of legislative legal services, or the directors of successor nonpartisan offices of the general assembly, shall appoint nonpartisan staff from their respective offices as needed to assist the commission and the panel of judges as described in section 47 of this article V. Nonpartisan staff shall acquire and prepare all necessary resources, including computer hardware, software, and demographic, geographic, and political databases, as far in advance as necessary to enable the commission to begin its work immediately upon convening.

(c) The commission may retain legal counsel in all actions and proceedings in connection with the performance of its powers, duties, and functions, including representation of the commission before any court.

(d) The general assembly shall appropriate sufficient funds for the payment of the expenses of the commission, the compensation and expenses of nonpartisan staff, and the compensation and expenses of the panel of judges as described in section 47 of this article V. Members of the commission shall be reimbursed for their reasonable and necessary expenses and may also receive such per diem allowance as may be established by the general assembly. Subject to available appropriations, hardware and software necessary for the development of plans may, at the request of any commissioner, be provided to the commissioner. The commission and its staff must have access to statistical information compiled by the state and its political subdivisions as necessary for its duties. State agencies and political subdivisions shall comply with requests from the commission and its staff for such statistical information.

(e) The commission shall adopt rules to govern its administration and operation. The commission must provide at least seventy-two hours of advance public notice of all proposed rules prior to consideration for adoption; except that proposed rules may be amended during commission deliberations without such advance notice of specific, related amendments. Neither the commission's procedural rules nor its mapping decisions are subject to the "State Administrative Procedure Act", article 4 of title 24, C.R.S., or any successor statute. Rules must include but need not be limited to the following:

(I) The hearing process and review of maps submitted for its consideration;

(II) Maintenance of a record of the commission's activities and proceedings, including a record of written and oral testimony received, and of the commission's directions to nonpartisan staff on proposed changes to any plan and the commission's rationale for such changes;

(III) The process for removing commissioners for participating in communications prohibited under this section;

(IV) The process for recommending changes to plans submitted to the commission by nonpartisan staff; and

(V) The adoption of a statewide meeting and hearing schedule, including the necessary elements of electronic attendance at a commission hearing.

(2) A simple majority of the appointed commissioners may approve rules and procedural decisions. The election of the commission's chair and vice-chair requires the affirmative vote of at least eight commissioners, including the affirmative vote of at least one commissioner who is unaffiliated with any political party. Removal of any commissioner as provided in this section requires the affirmative vote of at least eight commissioners, including the affirmative vote of at least two commissioners who are unaffiliated with any political party. Adoption of the final plan for submission to the supreme court and the adoption of a revised plan after a plan is returned to the commission from the supreme court requires the affirmative vote of at least eight commissioners, including the affirmative vote of at least two commissioners who are unaffiliated with any political party. The commission shall not vote upon a final plan until at least seventy-two hours after it has been proposed to the commission in a public meeting or at least seventy-two hours after it has been amended by the commission in a public meeting, whichever occurs later; except that commissioners may unanimously waive the seventy-two hour requirement.

(3)

(a) All Colorado residents, including individual commissioners, may present proposed redistricting maps or written comments, or both, for the commission's consideration.

(b) The commission must, to the maximum extent practicable, provide opportunities for Colorado residents to present testimony at hearings held throughout the state. The commission shall not approve a redistricting map until at least three hearings have been held in each congressional district, including at least one hearing that is held in a location west of the continental divide and at least one hearing that is held in a location east of the continental divide and either south of El Paso county's southern boundary or east of Arapahoe county's eastern boundary. No gathering of commissioners can be considered a hearing for this purpose unless it is attended, in person or electronically, by at least ten commissioners. The commission shall establish by rule the necessary elements of electronic attendance at a commission hearing.

(c) The commission shall maintain a website or comparable means of communicating with the public through which any Colorado resident may submit proposed maps or written comments, or both, without attending a hearing of the commission.

(d) The commission shall publish all written comments pertaining to redistricting on its website or comparable means of communicating with the public as well as the name of the Colorado resident submitting such comments. If the commission or nonpartisan staff have a substantial basis to believe that the person submitting such comments has not truthfully or accurately identified himself or herself, the commission need not consider and need not publish such comments but must notify the commenter in writing of this fact. The commission may withhold comments, in whole or in part, from the website or comparable means of communicating with the public that do not relate to redistricting maps, policies, or communities of interest.

(e) The commission shall provide simultaneous access to the regional hearings by broadcasting them via its website or comparable means of communicating with the public and maintain an archive of such hearings for online public review.

(4)

(a) Commissioners are guardians of the public trust and are subject to antibribery and abuse of public office requirements as provided in parts 3 and 4 of article 8 of title 18, C.R.S., as amended, or any successor statute.

(b) To ensure transparency in the redistricting process:

(I)

(A) The commission and the commissioners are subject to open meetings requirements as provided in part 4 of article 6 of title 24, C.R.S., as amended, or any successor statute.

(B) Except as provided in subsection (4)(b)(I)(D) of this section, a commissioner shall not communicate with nonpartisan staff on the mapping of legislative districts unless the communication is during a public meeting or hearing of the commission.

(C) Except for public input and comment, nonpartisan staff shall not have any communications about the content or development of any plan outside of public hearings with anyone except other staff members. Nonpartisan staff shall report to the commission any attempt by anyone to exert influence over the staff's role in the drafting of plans.

(D) One or more nonpartisan staff may be designated to communicate with commissioners regarding administrative matters, the definition and scope of which shall be determined by the commission.

(E) Any commissioner who participates in a communication prohibited in this section must be removed from the commission, and such vacancy must be filled within seven days.

(II) The commission, each commissioner, and nonpartisan staff are subject to open records requirements as provided in part 1 of article 72 of title 24, C.R.S., as amended, or any successor statute; except that maps in draft form and not submitted to the commission are not public records subject to disclosure. Work product and communications among nonpartisan staff are subject to disclosure once a plan is submitted to the supreme court.

(III) Persons who contract for or receive compensation for advocating to the commission, to one or more commissioners, or to nonpartisan staff for the adoption or rejection of any map, amendment to a map, mapping approach, or manner of compliance with any of the mapping criteria specified in section 48.1 of this article V are lobbyists who must disclose to the secretary of state any compensation contracted for, compensation received, and the person or entity contracting or paying for their lobbying services. Such disclosure must be made no later than seventy-two hours after the earlier of each instance of such lobbying or any payment of such compensation. The secretary of state shall publish on the secretary of state's website or comparable means of communicating with the public the names of such lobbyists, as well as the compensation received and the persons or entities for whom they work within twenty-four hours of receiving such information. The secretary of state shall adopt rules to facilitate the complete and prompt reporting required by this subsection (4)(b)(III) as well as a complaint process to address any lobbyist's failure to report a full and accurate disclosure, which complaint must be heard by an administrative law judge, whose decision may be appealed to the court of appeals.

§ 48.1. Rules for drawing general assembly districts

(1) In adopting a legislative redistricting plan, the commission shall:

(a) Make a good-faith effort to achieve mathematical population equality between districts, as required by the constitution of the United States, but in no event shall there be more than five percent deviation between the

most populous and the least populous district in each house. Districts must be composed of contiguous geographic areas.
(b) Comply with the federal "Voting Rights Act of 1965", 52 U.S.C. sec. 50301, as amended.[24]

(2)

(a) As much as is reasonably possible, the commission's plan must preserve whole communities of interest and whole political subdivisions, such as counties, cities, and towns. To facilitate the efficient and effective provision of governmental services, with regard to any county, city, city and county, or town whose population is less than a district's permitted population, the commission shall presume that such county, city, city and county, or town should be wholly contained within a district; except that a division of such county, city, city and county, or town is permitted where, based on a preponderance of the evidence in the record, a community of interest's legislative issues are more essential to the fair and effective representation of residents of the district. When the commission divides a county, city, city and county, or town, it shall minimize the number of divisions of that county, city, city and county, or town.
(b) Districts must be as compact as is reasonably possible.

(3)

(a) Thereafter, the commission shall, to the extent possible, maximize the number of politically competitive districts.
(b) In its hearings in various locations in the state, the commission shall solicit evidence relevant to competitiveness of elections in Colorado and shall assess such evidence in evaluating proposed maps.
(c) When the commission approves a plan, or when nonpartisan staff submits a plan in the absence of the commission's approval of a plan as provided in section 48.2 of this article V, the nonpartisan staff shall, within seventy-two hours of such action, make publicly available, and include in the commission's record, a report to demonstrate how the plan reflects the evidence presented to, and the findings concerning, the extent to which competitiveness in district elections is fostered consistent with the other criteria set forth in this section.
(d) For purposes of this subsection (3), "competitive" means having a reasonable potential for the party affiliation of the district's representative to change at least once between federal decennial censuses. Competitiveness may be measured by factors such as a proposed district's past election results, a proposed district's political party registration data, and evidence-based analyses of proposed districts.

---

[24] The citation is incorrect. As a statute explains, "(3) Because of a misprint in the measures referring these constitutional amendments to the voters, the federal statute was . . . incorrectly cited as '52 U.S.C. sec. 50301, as amended' when the proper citation is '52 U.S.C. sec. 10301 et seq., as amended.' (4) The general assembly finds and declares that voter intent was clear and should not be frustrated by a clerical error in referring to a federal law that has long been applied by federal courts and the Colorado courts in the redistricting context and was intended to be applied based on the measures' context and legislative analyses provided to voter households in advance of the 2018 general election." C.R.S. § 2-1-103.

(4) No map may be approved by the commission or given effect by the supreme court if:

(a) It has been drawn for the purpose of protecting one or more incumbent members, or one or more declared candidates, of the senate or house of representatives, or any political party; or

(b) It has been drawn for the purpose of or results in the denial or abridgement of the right of any citizen to vote on account of that person's race or membership in a language minority group, including diluting the impact of that racial or language minority group's electoral influence.

§ 48.2. Public hearings and participation

(1) The commission shall begin by considering a plan for the state senate and a plan for the state house of representatives, created by its nonpartisan staff alone, to be known as the "preliminary senate plan" and the "preliminary house plan". Such plans must be presented and published no earlier than thirty days and no later than forty-five days after the commission has convened or the necessary census data are available, whichever is later. Within the first twenty days after the commission has convened, any member of the public and any member of the commission may submit written comments to nonpartisan staff on the creation of the preliminary plans and on communities of interest that require representation in one or more specific areas of the state. Nonpartisan staff shall consider such comments in creating the preliminary plans, and such comments shall be part of the record of the commission's activities and proceedings. At the first public hearing at which the preliminary plans are presented, nonpartisan staff shall explain how the plans were created, how the plans address the categories of public comments received, and how the plans comply with the criteria prescribed in section 48.1 of this article V.

(2) By July 21 of the redistricting year, the commission shall complete public hearings on the preliminary senate plan and the preliminary house plan in several places throughout the state in accordance with section 48 of this article V.

(3) Subsequent to hearings on the preliminary senate plan and the preliminary house plan, nonpartisan staff shall prepare, publish online, and present to the commission no fewer than three plans for the state senate and three plans for the state house of representatives, except as provided in subsection (5) of this section. These plans will be known as the "staff plans" and must be named and numbered sequentially for purposes of subsection (6) of this section. Staff plans must be prepared, published online, and presented in accordance with a timetable established by the commission; except that each staff plan must be presented to the commission no fewer than ten days after the presentation of any previous staff plan, and no fewer than twenty-four hours after it has been published online. If the commission fails to establish a timetable for the presentation of staff plans within ten days after the completion of hearings on the preliminary plan, nonpartisan staff shall establish such timetable. Nonpartisan staff shall keep each plan confidential until it is published online or by a comparable means of communicating with the public using generally available technologies. The commission may provide direction, if approved by at least eight commissioners including at least one commissioner unaffiliated with any political party, for the development of staff

plans through the adoption of standards, guidelines, or methodologies to which nonpartisan staff shall adhere, including standards, guidelines, or methodologies to be used to evaluate a plan's competitiveness, consistent with subsection (3)(d) of section 48.1 of this article V. In preparing all staff plans, nonpartisan staff shall also consider public testimony and public comments received by the commission that are consistent with the criteria specified in section 48.1 of this article V.

(4) Any commissioner or group of commissioners may request nonpartisan staff to prepare additional plans or amendments to plans. Any such request must be made in a public hearing of the commission but does not require commission approval. Plans or amendments developed in response to such requests are separate from staff plans, for purposes of subsection (6) of this section.

(5)

(a) The commission may adopt a final senate or house plan at any time after presentation of the first staff plans, in which case nonpartisan staff does not need to prepare or present additional staff plans for the house for which a map has been adopted.

(b) No later than September 15 of the redistricting year, the commission shall adopt final senate and house plans, which must then be submitted to the supreme court for its review and determination in accordance with section 48.3 of this article V.

(c) The commission may adjust the deadlines specified in this section if conditions outside of the commission's control require such an adjustment to ensure adopting a final plan as required by this subsection (5).

(d) The commission may grant its nonpartisan staff the authority to make technical de minimis adjustments to the adopted senate and house plans prior to their submission to the supreme court.

(6) If, for any reason, the commission does not adopt a final plan for both houses of the general assembly by the date specified in subsection (5) of this section, then nonpartisan staff shall submit the unamended third staff plan to the supreme court for review pursuant to section 48.3 of this article V. If the commission approves a plan for one house of the general assembly but not the other house, then the plan for the approved house shall be submitted to the supreme court as the final plan for that house, and the unamended third staff plan shall be submitted to the supreme court as the final plan for the house for which the commission did not approve a plan.

§ 48.3. Supreme court review

(1) The supreme court shall review the submitted plans and determine whether the plans comply with the criteria listed in section 48.1 of this article V. The court's review and determination shall take precedence over other matters before the court. The supreme court shall adopt rules for such proceedings and for the production and presentation of supportive evidence for such plans. Any legal arguments concerning such plans shall be submitted to the supreme court pursuant to the schedule established by the court.

(2) The supreme court shall approve the plans submitted unless it finds that the commission or nonpartisan staff, in the case of a staff plan submitted in the absence of a commission-approved plan, abused its discretion in applying or failing to apply the criteria listed in section 48.1 of this article V, in light of the record before the commission. The supreme court may consider any maps submitted to the commission in assessing whether the commission or nonpartisan staff, in the case of a staff plan submitted in the absence of a commission-approved plan, abused its discretion.

(3) If the supreme court determines that the submitted state senate plan or the submitted state house of representatives plan constitutes an abuse of discretion in applying or failing to apply the criteria listed in section 48.1 of this article V, in light of the record before the commission, the supreme court shall return the respective plan to the commission with the court's reasons for disapproval.

(4)

(a) By November 15 of the redistricting year, the supreme court shall approve or return to the commission the submitted state senate plan and the submitted state house of representatives plan.
(b) If the court returns a plan to the commission, the commission shall have twelve days to hold a commission hearing that includes public testimony and to return an adopted plan that resolves the court's reasons for disapproval.
(c) If the commission fails to adopt and return a plan to the court within twelve days, nonpartisan staff shall have an additional three days to prepare a plan that resolves the court's reasons for disapproval and return it to the court for approval.
(d) The supreme court shall review the revised plan in accordance with subsections (1), (2), and (3) of this section.

(5) The supreme court shall approve plans for the redrawing of state senate districts and state house of representative districts no later than December 29 of the redistricting year. The court shall order that such plans be filed with the secretary of state no later than such date.

§ 48.4. Severability

If any provision of sections 46 through 48.3 of this article V is found by a court of competent jurisdiction to be unconstitutional, or if any application of these sections is found by such a court to be unconstitutional, such invalidity shall not affect other provisions or applications of the remaining provisions of these sections that can be given effect without the invalid provision or application. The provisions of sections 46 through 48.3 of this article V are deemed and declared severable.

Art. V, Section 49. State auditor

(1) The general assembly, by a majority vote of the members elected to and serving in each house, shall appoint, without regard to political affiliation, a state auditor, who shall be a certified public accountant licensed to practice in this state, to serve for a term of five years and until his successor is appointed and

> qualified. Except as provided by law, he shall be ineligible for appointment to any other public office in this state from which compensation is derived while serving as state auditor. He may be removed for cause at any time by a two-thirds vote of the members elected to and serving in each house.
>
> (2) It shall be the duty of the state auditor to conduct post audits of all financial transactions and accounts kept by or for all departments, offices, agencies, and institutions of the state government, including educational institutions notwithstanding the provisions of section 14 of article IX of this constitution [University of Colorado autonomy, later repealed], and to perform similar or related duties with respect to such political subdivisions of the state as shall from time to time be required of him by law.
>
> (3) Not more than three members of the staff of the state auditor shall be exempt from the personnel system of this state.

Adopted by referendum in 1964. Modified by referendum in 1974. Previously, the state auditor was directly elected by the people. In Denver, the City Auditor is independently elected and continues to serve as an effective watchdog on the rest of the city government.

Art. V, Section 50. No public funding of abortion

> No public funds shall be used by the State of Colorado, its agencies or political subdivisions to pay or otherwise reimburse, either directly or indirectly, any person, agency or facility for the performance of any induced abortion, PROVIDED HOWEVER, that the General Assembly, by specific bill, may authorize and appropriate funds to be used for those medical services necessary to prevent the death of either a pregnant woman or her unborn child under circumstances where every reasonable effort is made to preserve the life of each.

Enacted by initiative in 1984. Section 50 was held to violate the federal Medicaid statutes (medical welfare for low-income people) to the extent that it denies funding to Medicaid-eligible women who seek to terminate pregnancies that resulted from rape or incest. *In re Hern v. Beye,* 57 F.3d 906 (10th Cir. 1995). *Cf. Urbish v. Lamm*, 761 P.2d 756 (Colo. 1988) (upholding some but not all state regulations as consistent with Section 50, following U.S. supreme court precedent upholding the federal law—"the Hyde Amendment"—banning most uses for federal funds for abortions).

Under the U.S. Constitution, the Fourteenth Amendment right to choose abortion, first articulated in *Roe v. Wade*, 410 U.S. 113 (1973), does not create any right to force taxpayers to pay for abortions. *Beal v. Doe*, 432 U.S. 438 (1977); *Maher v. Roe*, 432 U.S. 464 (1977).

However, state courts, interpreting state constitutions, have held that abortion funding is mandatory in Alaska, Arizona, California, Connecticut, Illinois, Massachusetts, Minnesota, Montana, New Jersey, New Mexico, Oregon, Vermont, and West Virginia. Courts in Florida, Idaho, Kentucky, Michigan, North Carolina, Pennsylvania, and Texas have rejected claims that state constitutions compel abortion funding.

Table 2. Historical partisan make-up of Colorado legislature

Bold = Majority party.
Bold italic = Veto-proof majority in both houses.

Year	Senate D	Senate R	Senate other	House D	House R	House other
1901	**19**	2	7 Silver R; 6 Populist; 1 Single Tax	**37**	7	8 Silver R; 13 Populist
1903	**23**	12		31	**34**	
1905	15	**20**		18	**47**	
1907	12	**23**		18	**47**	
1909	**20**	15		**53**	12	
1911	**26**	9		**41**	24	
1913	***24***	11		***48***	17	
1915	17	**18**		26	**39**	
1917	**18**	17		**40**	25	
1919	**21**	14		24	**41**	
1921	11	***24***		7	***58***	
1923	12	**23**		32	**33**	
1925	14	**21**		12	**52**	
1927	16	**19**		22	**43**	
1929	12	**23**		18	**47**	
1931	13	**22**		**34**	31	
1933	***26***	9		***54***	11	
1935	***29***	6		***50***	15	
1937	***29***	6		***50***	15	
1939	**23**	12		28	**37**	
1941	**18**	17		28	**37**	
1943	11	***24***		10	***55***	
1945	8	***27***		19	***46***	
1947	8	***27***		19	***46***	
1949	14	**21**		**41**	24	
1951	15	**20**		18	**47**	
1953	12	**23**		20	**45**	
1955	15	**20**		29	**36**	
1957	**21**	14		**38**	27	
1959	**22**	13		**44**	21	
1961	**19**	16		**33**	32	
1963	15	**20**		24	**41**	
1965	15	**20**		**42**	23	
1967	15	**20**		27	**38**	
1969	11	**24**		27	**38**	
1971	14	**21**		27	**38**	
1973	13	**22**		28	**37**	
1975	16	**19**		**39**	26	
1977	17	**18**		30	**35**	
1979	13	**22**		27	**38**	

1981	13	**22**		25	**40**	Reflects 1 D defection post-election
1983	14	**21**		24	**41**	Reflects 1 D defection post-election
1985	11	***24***		18	***47***	
1987	10	**27**		24	**41**	Reflects 1 D defection post-election
1989	11	**24**		26	**39**	
1991	12	**23**		27	**38**	
1993	16	**19**		31	**34**	
1995	16	**19**		24	**41**	
1997	15	**20**		24	**41**	
1999	15	**20**		25	**40**	
2001	**18**	17		27	**38**	
2003	17	**18**		28	**37**	
2005	**18**	17		**35**	30	
2007	**20**	15		**39**	26	
2009	**21**	14		**38**	27	
2011	**20**	15		32	**33**	
2013	**20**	15		**37**	28	
2015	17	**18**		**34**	31	
2017	16	**18**	1 Dem. to Ind. 12/17	**37**	28	
2019	**19**	16		**41**	24	
2021	**20**	15		**41**	24	

The *People's Party* (known as the *Populists*) won a substantial following starting in the late 1880s, and for a little over a decade thereafter. *Silver Republicans* left the national Republican party in the 1890s because the national party adhered to the gold standard, whereas Silver Republicans favored bimetallism (gold *and* silver as legal tender). The *Single Tax party* was based on the ideas of writer Henry George, who argued that taxes on the appreciation of real estate could replace all other taxes.

Table 3. Colorado U.S. Senators

Name	Party	Years served
Henry Teller	R, Silver R, D	1876–82, 1885–1909
Jerome Chaffee	R	1876–79
Nathaniel Hill	R	1879–85
George Chilcott	R	1882–83
Horace Tabor	R	1883
Thomas Bowen	R	1883–89
Edward Wolcott	R	1889–1901
Thomas Patterson	D	1901–07
Simon Guggenheim	R	1907–13
Charles Hughes Jr.	D	1909–11
Charles Thomas	D	1913–21
John Shafroth	D	1913–19
Lawrence Phipps	R	1919–31
Samuel Nicholson	R	1921–23
Alva Adams	D	1923–24, 1933–41
Rice Means	R	1924–27
Charles Waterman	R	1927–32
Edward Costigan	D	1931–37
Walter Walker	D	1932
Karl Schuyler	R	1932–33
Edwin Johnson	D	1937–55
Eugene Milikin	R	1941–57
Gordon Allott	R	1955–73
John Carroll	D	1957–63
Peter Dominick	R	1963–75
Floyd Haskell	D	1973–79
Gary Hart	D	1975–87
Bill Armstrong	R	1979–91
Tim Wirth	D	1987–93
Hank Brown	R	1991–97
Ben Nighthorse Campbell	D, R	1993–2005
Wayne Allard	R	1997–2009
Ken Salazar	D	2005–2009
Michael Bennet	D	2009–present
Mark Udall	D	2009–2015
Cory Gardner	R	2015–2021
John Hickenlooper	D	2021–present

Source for up to 2008: Ed Sealover, *Not a Lifelong Job*, ROCKY MOUNTAIN NEWS, Nov. 2, 2008, at 22.

Notes on some U.S. Senators

Henry Teller and Jerome Chaffee were chosen by the Colorado general assembly as the state's first U.S. Senators, in 1876.

Teller was the most significant political figure of Colorado's early decades. He was the first Coloradan appointed to the presidential cabinet, and the first to become a national political figure. Teller left the Senate 30 days before the end of his first term, in 1883, because president Chester

Arthur had appointed him secretary of the interior. Silver magnate Horace Tabor was appointed to finish Teller's 30 days. During that period, Tabor, who had divorced his first wife, scandalously married a young woman who was nicknamed "Baby Doe" Tabor.

At the 1896 Republican Convention, Teller, now back in the Senate, pushed for a platform in favor of bimetallism. That is, the U.S. dollar would be backed by gold *and* silver, as had been under U.S. policy initiated by treasury secretary Alexander Hamilton, but ended by the Grant administration in 1873. Defeated on the platform vote, Teller bolted the regular Republican party to help form the Silver Republicans. He later became a Democrat. The Democrat party adopted bimetallism in its 1896 platform, thanks in part to nominee William Jennings Bryan's powerful "Cross of Gold" speech at the Convention. (Here is a recording of Bryan reenacting the speech: https://youtu.be/9SafTrjVY9o.) Further reading: DUANE A. SMITH: HENRY M. TELLER: COLORADO'S GRAND OLD MAN (2002).

Alva Adams served a partial term in 1925–26, a full term 1933–39, and then died in office during a third term of 1939–41.

Eugene Miliken finished Alva Adams' final term, and then was elected to two full terms.

Lawrence Phipps was a leading industrialist and philanthropist. His sons Gerald and Allan Phipps were early owners of the Denver Broncos.

Ed Johnson served two two-year terms as governor in 1933–37, then three terms in the U.S. Senate, then again as governor in 1955–57. He is the most significant political figure of twentieth century Colorado.

Gordon Allott's staff included the writer George Will (1970–72).

Peter Dominick was one of the first associates at Holland & Hart. Among his accomplishments was legislation relegalizing the ownership of gold by U.S. citizens.

Floyd Haskell was a Republican when he served in the Colorado Senate. After retiring from politics, he married National Public Radio correspondent Nina Totenberg.

Bill Armstrong later served as president of Colorado Christian University.

Ben Nighthorse Campbell was first elected as a Democrat, switched parties in 1995, and was then re-elected as a Republican.

Ken Salazar was appointed secretary of the interior by president Barack Obama in 2009.

Michael Bennet was appointed to serve the remainder of the Salazar term, slightly less than two years. Thereafter, he was elected to full terms in 2010 and 2016.

Other interior secretaries from Colorado have been James Watt and Donald Hodel (under Ronald Reagan) and Gale Norton (under George W. Bush).

CHAPTER 9

Initiative and Referendum, article V, Section 1

Introduction

The sections below are introduced by bolded subheadings. These are written by Kopel, and are not part of the constitutional text.

> (1) **Reservation of people's legislative power.** The legislative power of the state shall be vested in the general assembly consisting of a senate and house of representatives, both to be elected by the people, but the people reserve to themselves the power to propose laws and amendments to the constitution and to enact or reject the same at the polls independent of the general assembly and also reserve power at their own option to approve or reject at the polls any act or item, section, or part of any act of the general assembly.
>
> (2) **Power of initiative.** The first power hereby reserved by the people is the initiative, and signatures by registered electors in an amount equal to at least five percent of the total number of votes cast for all candidates for the office of secretary of state at the previous general election shall be required to propose any measure by petition, and every such petition shall include the full text of the measure so proposed. Initiative petitions for state legislation and amendments to the constitution, in such form as may be prescribed pursuant to law, shall be addressed to and filed with the secretary of state at least three months before the general election at which they are to be voted upon.
>
> (2.5) **Stricter petition rules for constitutional initiatives compared to statutory initiatives.** In order to make it more difficult to amend this constitution, a petition

for an initiated constitutional amendment shall be signed by registered electors who reside in each state senate district in Colorado in an amount equal to at least two percent of the total registered electors in the senate district provided that the total number of signatures of registered electors on the petition shall at least equal the number of signatures required by subsection (2) of this section. For purposes of this subsection (2.5), the number and boundaries of the senate districts and the number of registered electors in the senate districts shall be those in effect at the time the form of the petition has been approved for circulation as provided by law. [Added 2016]

(3) **Power of referendum.** The second power hereby reserved is the referendum, and it may be ordered, except as to laws necessary for the immediate preservation of the public peace, health, or safety, and appropriations for the support and maintenance of the departments of state and state institutions, against any act or item, section, or part of any act of the general assembly, either by a petition signed by registered electors in an amount equal to at least five percent of the total number of votes cast for all candidates for the office of the secretary of state at the previous general election or by the general assembly. Referendum petitions, in such form as may be prescribed pursuant to law, shall be addressed to and filed with the secretary of state not more than ninety days after the final adjournment of the session of the general assembly that passed the bill on which the referendum is demanded. The filing of a referendum petition against any item, section, or part of any act shall not delay the remainder of the act from becoming operative.

(4)

(a) **Initiatives and referenda not subject to governor's veto.** The veto power of the governor shall not extend to measures initiated by or referred to the people. All elections on measures initiated by or referred to the people of the state shall be held at the biennial regular general election, and all such measures shall become the law or a part of the constitution, when approved by a majority of the votes cast thereon or, if applicable the number of votes required pursuant to paragraph (b) of this subsection (4), and not otherwise, and shall take effect from and after the date of the official declaration of the vote thereon by proclamation of the governor, but not later than thirty days after the vote has been canvassed. This section shall not be construed to deprive the general assembly of the power to enact any measure.

(b) **Constitutional initiatives need at least 55%.** In order to make it more difficult to amend this constitution, an initiated constitutional amendment shall not become part of this constitution unless the amendment is approved by at least fiftyfive percent of the votes cast thereon; except that this paragraph (b) shall not apply to an initiated constitutional amendment that is limited to repealing, in whole or in part, any provision of this constitution. [Added 2016.]

(5) **Process of submitting initiative drafts for review by the legislature's staff.** The original draft of the text of proposed initiated constitutional amendments and initiated laws shall be submitted to the legislative research and drafting offices of the general assembly for review and comment. No later than two weeks after submission of the original draft, unless withdrawn by the proponents, the legislative research and drafting offices of the general assembly shall render their

comments to the proponents of the proposed measure at a meeting open to the public, which shall be held only after full and timely notice to the public. Such meeting shall be held prior to the fixing of a ballot title. Neither the general assembly nor its committees or agencies shall have any power to require the amendment, modification, or other alteration of the text of any such proposed measure or to establish deadlines for the submission of the original draft of the text of any proposed measure.

(5.5) **Single subject rule for initiatives and referenda**. No measure shall be proposed by petition containing more than one subject, which shall be clearly expressed in its title; but if any subject shall be embraced in any measure which shall not be expressed in the title, such measure shall be void only as to so much thereof as shall not be so expressed. If a measure contains more than one subject, such that a ballot title cannot be fixed that clearly expresses a single subject, no title shall be set and the measure shall not be submitted to the people for adoption or rejection at the polls. In such circumstance, however, the measure may be revised and resubmitted for the fixing of a proper title without the necessity of review and comment on the revised measure in accordance with subsection (5) of this section, unless the revisions involve more than the elimination of provisions to achieve a single subject, or unless the official or officials responsible for the fixing of a title determine that the revisions are so substantial that such review and comment is in the public interest. The revision and resubmission of a measure in accordance with this subsection (5.5) shall not operate to alter or extend any filing deadline applicable to the measure. [Added 1994, partly in response to the 1992 adoption of the Taxpayer's Bill of Rights.]

(6) **Petition forms and procedures.** The petition shall consist of sheets having such general form printed or written at the top thereof as shall be designated or prescribed by the secretary of state; such petition shall be signed by registered electors in their own proper persons only, to which shall be attached the residence address of such person and the date of signing the same. To each of such petitions, which may consist of one or more sheets, shall be attached an affidavit of some registered elector that each signature thereon is the signature of the person whose name it purports to be and that, to the best of the knowledge and belief of the affiant, each of the persons signing said petition was, at the time of signing, a registered elector. Such petition so verified shall be prima facie evidence that the signatures thereon are genuine and true and that the persons signing the same are registered electors.

(7) **Secretary of state shall submit measures to a vote of the people.** The secretary of state shall submit all measures initiated by or referred to the people for adoption or rejection at the polls, in compliance with this section. In submitting the same and in all matters pertaining to the form of all petitions, the secretary of state and all other officers shall be guided by the general laws.

(7.3) **Legislative staff shall publish the text and title of all ballot measures in publications of general circulation in each county and the state.** Before any election at which the voters of the entire state will vote on any initiated or referred constitutional amendment or legislation, the nonpartisan research staff of the general assembly shall cause to be published the text and title of every such measure. Such publication shall be made at least one time in at least one legal publication of general circulation in each county of the state and shall be made at least fifteen days prior to the final date of voter registration for the election. The form and manner of publication shall be as prescribed by law and shall ensure a reasonable opportunity for the voters statewide to become informed about the text and title of each measure.

(7.5) **Legislative staff must create the blue book of pro/con information on statewide initiatives and referenda. It will be distributed at no cost to active registered voters.**

(a) Before any election at which the voters of the entire state will vote on any initiated or referred constitutional amendment or legislation, the nonpartisan research staff of the general assembly shall prepare and make available to the public the following information in the form of a ballot information booklet:

(I) The text and title of each measure to be voted on;

(II) A fair and impartial analysis of each measure, which shall include a summary and the major arguments both for and against the measure, and which may include any other information that would assist understanding the purpose and effect of the measure. Any person may file written comments for consideration by the research staff during the preparation of such analysis.

(b) At least thirty days before the election, the research staff shall cause the ballot information booklet to be distributed to active registered voters statewide.

(c) If any measure to be voted on by the voters of the entire state includes matters arising under section 20 of article X of this constitution, the ballot information booklet shall include the information and the titled notice required by section 20(3)(b) of article X, and the mailing of such information pursuant to section 20(3)(b) of article X is not required.

(d) The general assembly shall provide sufficient appropriations for the preparation and distribution of the ballot information booklet pursuant to this subsection (7.5) at no charge to recipients.

(8) The style of all laws adopted by the people through the initiatives shall be, "Be it Enacted by the People of the State of Colorado".

(9) The initiative and referendum powers reserved to the people by this section are hereby further reserved to the registered electors of every city, town, and municipality as to all local, special, and municipal legislation of every character in or for their respective municipalities. The manner of exercising said powers shall be prescribed by general laws; except that cities, towns, and municipalities may provide for the manner of exercising the initiative and referendum powers as to their municipal legislation. Not more than ten percent of the registered electors may be required to order the referendum, nor more than fifteen percent to propose any measure by the initiative in any city, town, or municipality.

(10) This section of the constitution shall be in all respects self-executing; except that the form of the initiative or referendum petition may be prescribed pursuant to law. [A "self-executing" constitutional provision or treaty does not need any implementing statute; many constitutional provisions are self-executing, and some declare themselves so, to avoid any ambiguity.]

Colorado election statutes are in title 1 of C.R.S. The statutes for initiative and referendum are in article 40 of title 1.

A popular vote on an "initiative" is initiated by a petition from the people to change a constitution or state statutes. A "referendum" is the English adoption of the Latin word for "that which must be returned" or "that which must be carried back." In a referendum, a legislative body votes to "refer" a proposed constitutional or statutory change to the people, who will vote on whether to adopt it.

The campaign to add initiative and referendum to the Constitution was begun in 1893, when Populist governor Davis Waite called a special session of the legislature, for that purpose and others. The legislature ignored the proposal. The next year, the attorney general endorsed the idea. In the 1895 legislative session, four Populist legislators introduced I&R bills; the furthest that any got was passing the Senate 18–14, which was short of the necessary two-thirds for a proposed constitutional amendment. Donald Wayne Hensel, *A History of the Colorado Constitution in the Nineteenth Century* 263–64 (Ph.D. thesis in History, Univ. of Colo. 1957).

By the early twentieth century, Colorado had, despite the work and the hopes of the 1876 Convention and the people, become known as "the worst governed state in the Union." RICHARD D. LAMM & DUANE A. SMITH, PIONEERS & POLITICIANS: COLORADO GOVERNORS IN PROFILE 90 (2d ed. 2008). The first step in fixing the problem was securing the rights of initiative and referendum. Once those rights were secured, much reform would proceed from them.

The state legislature's website contains a list of all referenda and initiatives measures since 1880. The list includes the percentage vote for and against, and links to the full ballot titles.

On a general election ballot, a citizen-initiated constitutional amendment will have a number from 1 to 99. A citizen-initiated statute will be 100 to 199. A legislatively-referred constitutional amendment will have a letter from A to Z. Legislatively-referred statutes are from AA to ZZ. C.R.S. § 1-5-407(5.3) & (5.4).

From 1876 to 1910, the legislature could refer measures of citizen approval, but there was no provision for citizen initiative. Overall, from 1880 to 2020, the voters of Colorado voted on 492 ballot measures. They adopted 223 and rejected 269. Erin Reynolds, Matt Bishop, & Katie Ruedebusch, Legislative Council Staff, *Overview and History of Statewide Ballot Measures in Colorado* 3, table 2, Aug. 2021 (also detailing wins and losses in various categories).

A fundamental power and right

- The power of initiative "is not a grant to the people but a reservation by them for themselves." *Board of County Com'rs of County of Archuleta v. County Road Users Ass'n,* 11 P.3d 432 (Colo. 2000).
- "Like the right to vote, power of initiative is a fundamental right at very core of our republican form of government." *McKee v. City of Louisville,* 200 Colo. 525, 616 P.2d 969 (1980).
- "[T]he right to initiative adopted by a state is fundamental right, to be tested by application of standard of strict scrutiny." *Committee for Better Health Care for All Colorado Citizens v. Meyer,* 830 P.2d 884, 890 n.7 (Colo. 1992).
- "[T]he initiative provisions of the constitution must not be narrowly construed, but rather that they must be liberally construed to effectuate their purpose and to facilitate the exercise by electors of this most important right reserved to them by the constitution." Because the "initiative provisions are expressly declared to be self-executing . . . only legislation which will further the purpose of the constitutional provision or facilitate its operation, is permitted." "[T]he Legislature may not impose restrictions which limit in any way the right of the people of initiate proposed laws and amendments except as those

> limitations are provided in the constitution itself." *Colorado Project-Common Cause v. Anderson,* 178 Colo. 1, 495 P.2d 220 (1972).

Not for counties

Subsection (1) provides for the power of initiative for statewide matters. Subsection (9) provides for initiatives for "every city, town, and municipality." Counties are notably absent from this list. There is no constitutional right of initiative for county law. The general assembly has enacted the County Sales Tax Act, which allows county initiatives for the sole purpose of raising a county's sale tax. C.R.S. § 29-2-104.

No use of public resources on initiative campaigns

Public resources may not be used to propagandize for or against an initiative. Such use of resources violates state law, as well as the First Amendment rights of freedom of speech and of petition for redress of grievances. *Mountain States Legal Foundation v. Denver School Dist. No. 1*, 459 F. Supp. 357 (D. Colo. 1978). A preliminary injunction was issued against the Denver Public Schools Board ordering it not to contribute taxpayer money to a campaign against a proposed state constitutional amendment.

The same principle applies to use of government resources, such as employee office mailboxes or the office email system, to distribute propaganda. When government officials, such as governors, strictly adhere to this rule, they do not campaign for or against initiatives during the 9–5 M–F working day. Not everyone is always scrupulous.

Title Board review

The screener of the text of proposed initiatives is "a title board consisting of the secretary of state, the attorney general, and the director of the office of legislative legal services or their designees." By majority vote, the title board shall "designate and fix a proper fair title for each proposed law or constitutional amendment." The title board shall set titles to avoid public confusion and to make clear the effect of a yes/no vote. The board also approves the abstract of the initiative, which will appear on the ballot. The board may not set titles that violate the single subject rule, nor may it consider the policy merits of a proposed initiative. C.R.S. § 1-40-106 et seq.

Challenges to Title Board decisions go straight to the supreme court. The court claims to "employ all legitimate presumptions in favor of the propriety of the Board's actions." A Title Board decision about single subject or the abstract will be overturned only in "a clear case." *In the Matter of the Title, Ballot Title and Submission Clause for 2017–2018 #4*, 395 P.3d 318 (Colo. 2017).

Limits on pre-election review

For initiatives that are provided for in the Constitution (subsection 1 for statewide, subsection 9 for municipal), government officials may not keep an initiative off the ballot because they believe that it is unconstitutional or meritless. Judicial review of constitutionality will only take place *after* an initiative passes, assuming that there is a case. *McKee v. Louisville, supra.*

However, there are two important exceptions. First, because county sales tax initiatives are created by statute, not by the Constitution, a court may pre-review a proposed sales tax initiative, to determine conformity to the County Sales Tax Act. *Board of County Com'rs of County of Archuleta, supra.*

Second, initiatives must be of a legislative character, not an administrative character. The distinction is discussed below. A court may conduct limited pre-election review of an initiative to determine whether it is legislative or administrative. *City of Idaho Springs v. Blackwell,* 731 P.2d 1250 (Colo. 1987); *City of Colorado Springs v. Bull*, 143 P.3d 1127 (Colo. App. 2006).

Initiatives must be legislative in nature, not administrative

Ballot measures for initiated ordinances must involve legislative, not administrative matters. The tests for a legislative matter:

- First, actions that relate "to subjects of a permanent or general character are legislative, while those that are temporary in operation and effect are not."
- Second, "acts that are necessary to carry out existing legislative policies and purposes" are administrative, "while acts constituting a declaration of public policy are deemed to be legislative."
- There is also, the "legislative amendment test." If the initiative amends something that was originally a legislative act, then the initiative is also legislative.

Vagneur v. City of Aspen, 295 P.3d 493 (Colo. 2013); *City of Aurora v. Zwerdlinger*, 194 Colo. 192, 571 P.2d 1074 (1977).

Under the legislative/administrative test, some of the initiatives that have been held to be improper include those changing municipality utility rates (*e.g.*, water, electricity), or controlling the disposition or acquisition of government property, usually real estate.

Addresses on petition forms

The signer's address must be written on the petition at the time the petition is signed. Filling in addresses afterwards is not allowed. *Elkins v. Milliken*, 80 Colo. 135, 249 P. 655 (1926).

A municipal ordinance stated that the city clerk must reject signatures if the address did not include the full street name. E.g., "727 16th" would be disqualified, but "727 E. 16th Ave." would be sufficient. The ordinance also required apartment numbers, where applicable. Use of ditto marks (*e.g.*, because the signer was from the same city as the previous signer) also voided a signature. All this was held not to be a facial violation of article V, § 1. Two dissenting justices disagreed on the issue of ditto marks. *Clark v. City of Aurora*, 782 P.2d 771 (Colo. 1989).

Signatures

Requiring a printed name after the signature facilitates the right of referendum, since a signature may be illegible. *Clark, supra.*

A married woman may sign her husband's name preceded by "Mrs." For example, "Mrs. John W. Hickenlooper" or "Mrs. J.W. Hickenlooper." This "is quite universally recognized and constitutes a social custom, which so largely prevails that it may be called a general one." If there were a specific statute requiring married women to use their given names, the result would be different. *Case v. Morrison*, 118 Colo. 517, 197 P.2d 621 (1948) (citations and internal quotation marks omitted).

Petition gathering

The new rule in section 2.5 (constitutional initiatives must have signatures of at least 2% of registered voters in every state senate district) does not violate the U.S. Constitution's Fourteenth Amendment Equal Protection Clause. Although Colorado senate districts may vary by up to 60% in the number of registered voters, the districts are approximately equal in population. *Semple v. Griswold*, 934 F.3d 1134 (10th Cir. 2019) (reversing district court).

Colorado's statutory ban on paying petition circulators in any form violated the First Amendment. *Meyer v. Grant*, 486 U.S. 414 (1988).

A state statute forbidding signature collectors to be paid on a per-signature basis violated the First Amendment, because plaintiffs proved the rule made it much more difficult to collect signatures. *Independence Institute v. Gessler*, 936 F. Supp. 2d 1256 (D. Colo. 2013).

In *Buckley v. Am. Constitutional Law Found.*, 525 U.S. 182 (1999), the majority opinion by justice Ginsburg affirmed the Tenth Circuit's determination that several Colorado statutory rules for petition gatherers were constitutional:

- Circulators must be at least 18 years old. C.R.S. § 1-40-112 (1);
- A six-month limit on the petition circulation period. § 1-40-108;
- Circulators must sign an affidavit containing the circulator's name and address and a statement that "he or she has read and understands the laws governing the circulation of petitions," § 1-40-111(2).

The court also affirmed the Tenth Circuit's finding that the following provisions were unconstitutional:

- Circulators must be registered voters;
- Circulators must wear badges stating their names, whether they are "VOLUNTEER" or "PAID." If paid, also containing the name and phone number of their employer;
- When the petitions are turned in initiative proponents disclose the name, address, and county of voter registration of all paid circulators, the amount of money proponents paid per petition signature, and the total amount paid to each circulator;
- Every month, proponents must disclose the names of the proponents and the names and addresses of all paid circulators.

The statute that circulators must be state residents was not challenged. However, the statute is often evaded by itinerant circulators who establish a "residence" for several weeks in a Colorado motel, and then move on the next state to gather petitions there.

Justice Thomas concurred in the judgment. He wrote that the badge, registration, and reporting requirements should be reviewed under strict scrutiny, and they failed that standard.

Justice O'Connor, joined by Justice Breyer agreed that the badge requirement failed strict scrutiny, but would have upheld the rest.

Single subject

Pursuant to a 1994 amendment, constitutional amendments may be about only a single subject. Disputes go directly from the title board to the supreme court. The court is sometimes fair in its analysis of single subject, but not always.

One initiative proposed gradual reductions in certain local taxes. The general assembly would be required to give local governments money to make up for the local taxes. The tax cuts would take place only in years when state revenues grew by at least $200 million. This was held to violate the single subject rule. *Matter of Title, Ballot Title and Submission Clause, Summary for 1997-98 No. 84*, 961 P.2d 456 (Colo. 1998).[1]

Another case overturned a Title Board decision that the following was a single subject: "any ballot issue that raises a tax rate, continues a tax that would otherwise expire, creates a new tax, or increases public indebtedness" shall "sunset, expire, and end within ten years of its passage." The court explained:

> In short, rather than presenting the single subject of "time limits for ballot issues authorized by article X, Section 20," Initiative # 74 presents multiple subjects: (1) time limits for tax measures; (2) time limits for public debt authorizations; and (3) time limits for voter-authorized relief from spending limits. While voters may well be receptive to a broadly applicable ten-year limitation upon the duration of tax increases, they may not realize that they will be simultaneously limiting their ability to incur multiple-fiscal year district debt obligation to fund public projects. While either or both tax or debt limitations may be attractive, the voters would also be limiting prospectively the duration of all future ballot issues designed to provide relief from Amendment l's wholly independent spending caps. Certainly, the voters are entitled to have each of these separate subjects considered upon its own merits.

In the Matter of the Title, Ballot Title and Submission Clause for 2005-2006 # 74, 136 P.3d 237, 242 (Colo. 2006).

A proposed new section of the Bill of Rights had eight subsections. The ballot language was:

> An amendment to the Colorado constitution concerning a public right to Colorado's environment, and, in connection therewith, declaring that Colorado's environment is the common property of all Coloradans; specifying that the environment includes clean air, pure water, and natural and scenic values and that state and local governments are trustees of this resource; requiring state and local governments to conserve the environment; and declaring that if state or local Iaws conflict the more restrictive law or regulation governs.

It was held to contain only a single subject. *Matter of Title, Ballot Title, and Submission Clause for 2013-2014, No. 89*, 328 P.3d 172 (Colo. 2014).

---

[1] The ballot question was:

> AN AMENDMENT TO THE COLORADO CONSTITUTION ESTABLISHING A $25 TAX CUT TO LOWER EACH 1999 STATE AND LOCAL TAX BILL FOR EACH UTILITY CUSTOMER TAX AND FRANCHISE CHARGE, VEHICLE OWNERSHIP TAX, YEARLY INCOME TAX, AND SPECIFIED PROPERTY TAX, AND, IN CONNECTION THEREWITH, INCREASING THE TAX CUT $25 THE NEXT YEAR AND $50 YEARLY THEREAFTER; REQUIRING MONTHLY STATE REPLACEMENT OF AFFECTED LOCAL REVENUE WITHIN TAX AND SPENDING LIMITS AND YEARLY STATE AUDITS OF SUCH LIMITS; AWARDING MANDATORY LEGAL FEES AND COSTS TO SUCCESSFUL PLAINTIFFS ONLY; AND ALLOWING A DELAY IN YEARLY INCREASES IN ONE OR- MORE TAX CUTS IF REMAINING YEARLY STATE REVENUE FROM ALL SOURCES WILL GROW LESS THAN $200 MILLION.

CHAPTER 10

Judiciary, article VI

Introduction

Article VI was comprehensively revised and reenacted in 1962. The revisions removed the constitutional status of low-level criminal courts, justices of the peace, and police magistrates—none of which exist in present-day Colorado.

A 1966 initiative changed the system for choosing judges. Previously, they were elected in partisan elections. Now, under the "Missouri system," judges are appointed by the governor or home rule executives. The appointer must choose from a list presented by a nominating commission. Thereafter, judges are subject to yes/no retention elections, after certain periods of years.

The right to judicial review of constitutionality

A flaw of the progressive movement of the late 19th and early 20th centuries was hostility to judicial protection of individual rights. Rights-protective decisions were derided for thwarting the will of the majority.

A 1912 amendment forbade any Colorado court except the supreme court from ruling on the state or federal constitutionality of state or local laws. Further, any law that was held unconstitutional by the Colorado supreme court could be revived by referendum. The Colorado supreme court eventually held that this provision violated the Due Process Clause of the federal Fourteenth Amendment and the Supremacy Clause.

> When a federal constitutional question is raised in any of the trial courts of Colorado the right is given, and the duty is imposed upon these courts, by that instrument itself, to adjudicate and determine it. That right so given can neither be taken away nor that duty abrogated by the state of Colorado, by constitutional provision or otherwise, and any attempt to do so is null and void. Such pretended constitutional inhibition is no part of the Constitution of the state of Colorado, and the judge's oath binding him to the support and enforcement of that instrument has no relation to such void provisions. The question may be brought by writ of error to this court for review, and from our judgment the cause may be taken for final determination to the Supreme Court of the United States itself. It cannot be reviewed by popular vote of the citizens of Colorado, or one of its municipalities, and any pretended constitutional provision of this state, assuming to provide such method of review, is null and void. To hold otherwise is not only to vest in the people of Colorado the power to nullify the United States Constitution, but is likewise to vest that tremendous power in every municipality of this state, having a population of 2,000 or more, which sees fit to bring itself within the terms of the home rule amendment to our Constitution.

People v. Western Union Tel. Co., 70 Colo. 90, 98–99, 198 P. 146 (1921).

> Morever, said section is invalid because it deprives the defendant of 'due process of law.' That such a result ensues when one is prosecuted under an unconstitutional statute, and all the courts are deprived of authority to entertain his defenses, is too clear to admit of discussion. If the prohibition of this section, so far as it relates to trial courts construing the state Constitution, be upheld, where may the defense of the unconstitutionality of the statute be adjudicated? Not in the trial court, for that is prohibited. Not in the Supreme Court under its appellate jurisdiction, if the trial court was without jurisdiction, for there is then nothing to be reviewed . . . If an unconstitutional statute, creating a crime unknown to the common law, may be passed by the Legislature; if a citizen may be put upon trial thereunder; if the trial court may be prohibited from hearing his plea that the statute violates the constitutional guaranties of his state; if, when this court has so held, that statute may be reenacted by a bare majority of those voting thereon and the severest penalties be thereupon inflicted—then law has become a phantom and justice a dream, and constitutional guaranties of the sacredness of life, liberty and property. "A tale Told by an idiot, full of sound and fury, Signifying nothing."[1]

People v. Max, 70 Colo. 100, 198 P. 150 (1921).

The progressives were sure that their criticisms of judicial review were on the right side of history. A century later, some of the cases that the progressives hated so much do not seem so bad.

According to *Buchanan v. Warley*, 245 U.S. 60 (1917), home buyers and home sellers have the constitutional right to buy and sell with a person of any race. The government cannot restrict sales according to race, even when the law applies the same to all races.

In 1908, the U.S. supreme court had held that maximum hours laws for women only were constitutional. Women were the weaker sex and more in need of protection from making unwise choices. *Muller v. Oregon*, 208 U.S. 412 (1908). But in 1920, the Nineteenth Amendment was adopted: "The right of citizens of the United States to vote shall not be denied or abridged by the United States or by any State on account of sex."

The next year, a sex discrimination employment case came to the U.S. supreme court. Can a government forbid women employment choices that are allowed for men? In particular, can legislation allow a man to work at a certain job for any agreeable salary, whereas women must be paid a minimum wage? In *Adkins v. Children's Hospital*, 261 U.S. 525 (1923), the court stated that the Nineteenth Amendment had changed more than just voting. The amendment expressed the broader social truth that women and men are now considered equal in many ways—including their ability to decide their own conditions of employment. Paternalistic legislation limiting women's choices for their own supposed good had become harder to justify after the Nineteenth Amendment. So said a 5–3 majority scorned by progressives for interfering with the legislative will.

Justice George Sutherland wrote the majority opinion in *Adkins.* Before justice Ruth Bader Ginsburg, he was the justice most known for public advocacy for women's rights.

Today, one can look back the decisions from a century ago, agree with some, and disagree with others. The progressive critique was not on a case-by-case basis. The progressives opposed almost all judicial review of the constitutionality of statutes. The right side of history developed in a different direction, however. After World War II, as the free world began to rebuild itself from the ashes, new constitutions in France, West Germany, Italy, South Korea, India, Japan, and Pakistan created courts with the authority to enforce the constitution. C. Neal Tate, *Judicial review*, ENCYCLOPEDIA BRITANNICA.

---

[1] *Macbeth,* act. V, scene 5.

Judicial review is by its nature undemocratic. Yet in the long run, a judicial branch with the authority and the nerve to enforce a constitution can help to preserve a well-functioning democracy, where the other branches of government operate within the constitution's limits on their power, and the rights of everyone are secure even against the will of the majority.

Art. VI, Sec. 1. Vestment of judicial power

> The judicial power of the state shall be vested in a supreme court, district courts, a probate court in the city and county of Denver, a juvenile court in the city and county of Denver, county courts, and such other courts or judicial officers with jurisdiction inferior to the supreme court, as the general assembly may, from time to time establish; provided, however, that nothing herein contained shall be construed to restrict or diminish the powers of home rule cities and towns granted under article XX, section 6 of this constitution to create municipal and police courts.

The courts with constitutional status are the supreme court, district courts, county courts, and two specialized Denver courts: juvenile and probate. Additional courts may be established by the general assembly or home rule municipalities.[2] The Colorado court of appeals and the water courts are among those that have been established by the general assembly.

Colorado Court of Appeals

The court of appeals is covered in C.R.S. § 13-4-101 et seq. The court of appeals has existed by statute since 1969. There was also a court of appeals in 1891–1905 and 1911–1915.

The original Colorado supreme court had three members. As the only appellate court, it developed a huge backlog of cases. An attempted solution was the creation of a "Supreme Court Commission." Based on a similar commission in North Dakota, it took a first cut at cases before the court, including by writing proposed findings of fact. In practice, the system did not work well. The supreme court had to review the appellate record anyway, to check the commission's work, and the court often wrote its own factual findings.

Today, the court of appeals is a respected system for managing the mass of appeals from trial courts, while leaving the supreme court with the time to concentrate on the most important cases, by granting discretionary writs of certiorari. But at the turn of the 20th century, the court of appeals was not highly regarded, and was considered by some to be a time-wasting step on the way to the supreme court.

Statutes narrowing jurisdiction should be express

By *clear statement rule*, certain results will be allowed only if the relevant statute makes a clear statement. For example, statutes are presumed to *not* be retroactive, unless a statute clearly says that it is. (Which in Colorado, would raise problems with the Constitution's broad ban on Ex Post Facto legislation. Art. II, § 11.)

Similarly, federal statutes are presumed *not* to limit state sovereign immunity, unless the statute clearly says so. *Atascadero State Hospital v. Scanlon*, 473 U.S. 234, 242 (1985).

In Colorado the general assembly has broad power to limit the jurisdiction of courts. But no statute will be construed to narrow jurisdiction, unless the statute expressly says so, or the

---

[2] Weld County and Pitkin County are home rule counties. They do not have the power to establish courts.

limitation is a necessary implication of the statute. *Colorow Health Care, LLC v. Fischer*, 420 P.3d 259 (Colo. 2018).

Art. VI, Section 2. Appellate jurisdiction

> (1) The supreme court, except as otherwise provided in this constitution, shall have appellate jurisdiction only, which shall be coextensive with the state, and shall have a general superintending control over all inferior courts, under such regulations and limitations as may be prescribed by law.
>
> (2) Appellate review by the supreme court of every final judgment of the district courts, the probate court of the city and county of Denver, and the juvenile court of the city and county of Denver shall be allowed, and the supreme court shall have such other appellate review as may be provided by law. There shall be no appellate review by the district court of any final judgment of the probate court of the city and county of Denver or of the juvenile court of the city and county of Denver.

This covers the supreme court's appellate jurisdiction. Its original jurisdiction is in section 3. Supreme court certiorari rules are in Colorado Rules of Appellate Procedure, rule 49. Supreme court review of court of appeals cases is covered by C.R.S. § 13-4-108 et seq. Statutes governing the supreme court are at C.R.S. § 13-2-101 et seq.

Under subsection (2), the supreme court has "such other appellate review as may be provided by law." This means that the general assembly can expand supreme court appellate review; it does not mean that the supreme court can do so itself. *People ex rel. City of Aurora v. Smith*, 162 Colo. 72, 424 P.2d 772 (1967) (finding a Colo. supreme court rule of procedure unconstitutional).

By statute, the Colorado court of appeals has initial jurisdiction over all appeals from the district courts, and from many administrative boards, commissions, such as the State Personnel Board, Civil Rights Commission, Board of Pharmacy, Commissioner of Insurance). C.R.S. § 13-4-102. This is similar to the federal system, in which many administrative agency decisions may be appealed to the U.S. circuit courts of appeal.

The supreme court, however, is a court of immediate appellate resort for:

- "Cases in which a statute, a municipal charter provision, or an ordinance has been declared unconstitutional."
- Cases involving Public Utilities Commission acts
- Water cases
- Writs of habeas corpus
- Many election law cases. Anything involving title 1, articles 1-13.5 (state election laws), or title 31, article 10 (Municipal Election Code).
- Post-conviction relief cases involving a party under a capital sentence.

Id.

A disappointed litigant has the option of appealing first to the Colorado court of appeals, even if the litigant could proceed immediately to the supreme court. For example, if you lose a constitutional case in district court, you may hope that a win in the court of appeals may make your case more credible when it eventually gets to the supreme court. Even if you lose in the court of appeals, you might get a good dissenting opinion that could persuade the supreme court.

Appeals from county courts go to district courts. Thereafter, the only appeal is to the supreme court by writ of certiorari. C.R.S. § 13-6-130.

Further reading: Barbara Bintliff, *Jurisdictional History of the Colorado Courts*, 65 COLO. L. REVIEW 577 (1994); Mary J. Mullarkey, *Brief History of Women of the Colorado Supreme Court*, 41 COLO. LAWYER 27 (Oct. 2012).

Art. VI, Sec. 3. Supreme court original jurisdiction

> The supreme court shall have power to issue writs of habeas corpus, mandamus, quo warranto, certiorari, injunction, and such other original and remedial writs as may be provided by rule of court with authority to hear and determine the same; and each judge of the supreme court shall have like power and authority as to writs of habeas corpus. The supreme court shall give its opinion upon important questions upon solemn occasions when required by the governor, the senate, or the house of representatives; and all such opinions shall be published in connection with the reported decision of said court.

Supreme court original jurisdiction is in Colo. Rules App. Pro. Rule 21. An article by chief justice Boatright explains the procedures for Rule 21 petitions. The supreme court receives about 250 Rule 21 petitions annually; the court takes action on about a dozen, with the petitioner receiving some relief in about three-quarters of those. *See* Brian D. Boatright & Will Hauptman, *Practical Considerations for Rule 21 Proceedings in the Colorado Supreme Court*, 96 DENVER U. L REVIEW 203 (2019).

Writs in general are in C.R.S. § 13-1-115, and Colo. Rules Civ. Pro. Rule 106. *See also* CATHY STRICKLIN KRENDL, 1B COLORADO PRACTICE § 35.9.[3]

Writs

Section 3 specifically mentions five writs:

• habeas corpus,
• mandamus,
• quo warranto,
• certiorari,
• injunction.

Certiorari. The well-known modern vehicle for discretionary review by a supreme court.

Habeas corpus. A writ of *habeas corpus* may be issued by a single justice. So a writ of habeas corpus could be issued even when the supreme court is not in term.

Statutes for habeas corpus are at C.R.S. § 13-45-101 et seq. "Habeas corpus" is a shorthand for several different writs. The "great writ of liberty" is the one that compels the custodian of a prisoner to produce the body of a person who is being detained, and to justify the detention. The full name is *habeas corpus ad subjuciendum.*

Like the Great Writ, the other *habeas corpus* writs involve moving a person's body from one place to another for a judicial proceeding.

For example, there is the writ of *habeas corpus ad prosequendum.*[4] It is to remove a prisoner to a jurisdiction that is proper for the prosecution of the prisoner on a particular charge. Example: Maryland is imprisoning X in a Maryland state penitentiary because X was convicted for perpetrating a robbery in Maryland. Thanks to improved DNA evidence, a Colorado district

[3] The must-have multi-volume treatise for Colorado procedure.

[4] Plus a similar writ of *ad deliberandum et recipiendum*, for county-to-county transfers for criminal trials.

attorney determines that X should be prosecuted for an alleged rape in Colorado. But Colorado cannot prosecute X unless X is present in a Colorado courtroom.

Normally, the Colorado D.A. would file a request with Maryland for custody of X pursuant to the Interstate Agreement on Detainers Act—a federal statute ratifying an interstate and state-federal compact for prisoner transfers.[5]

But what if a state refuses to yield custody of its prisoner? A recent case: Jason Pleau robbed and murdered a gas station proprietor, who was transporting his day's receipts to a bank for deposit. After pleading guilty to first-degree homicide and robbery, Pleau was sentenced by Rhode Island to life in prison without parole.

Pleau's acts also violated federal bank robbery laws. The U.S. Attorney wanted to prosecute Pleau and filed the statutorily required announcement that the government might seek a capital sentence. Rhode Island has no death penalty, and R.I. governor John Chafee refused to yield his prisoner, so the U.S. attorney filed a federal court petition for a writ of *habeas corpus ad prosequendum.* The district court granted the writ, and the First Circuit affirmed.

Governor Chafee's petition for a writ of certiorari got a serious look from the supreme court, being thrice relisted for conference. But the court finally denied *certiorari.*[6]

A variety of other *habeas corpus* writs (all in *Black's Law Dictionary*) bring persons currently in custody into a court for civil cases, via inter-county transfers, to testify, etc.

Mandamus. To compel a person to perform a non-discretionary duty. *Marbury v. Madison,* 5 U.S. (1 Cranch) 137 (1803) was a petition for a writ of mandamus. James Madison, the new secretary of state, was refusing to deliver a commission of office to Marbury, who had been a "midnight appointment" to a federal office by outgoing president John Adams. The U.S. supreme court held that the federal statute conferring original jurisdiction on the court for this type of mandamus action violated article III.

Mandamus can be used as an interlocutory appeal mechanism for pre-judgement decisions of a trial court. For example, regarding the scope of allowed discovery. But such a petition for a writ of mandamus is appropriate, at most, only for the most compelling cases in extreme circumstances. Appeals courts are busy enough dealing with final judgments, and do not want to get into the business of trial or discovery supervision.

Quo warranto. Latin for "by what authority?" It claims that a person has usurped an office, franchise, or liberty. *Quo warranto* can also be used for neglect of office, or for revocation of corporate charters.

Injunction. That you *can* directly ask the supreme court for an injunction does not mean that you *should,* unless you have a supremely compelling case. The supreme court did grant an original jurisdiction injunction against election fraud by election officials in *People v. Tool,* 35 Colo. 225, 86 P. 224 (1905). The decision came on the heels of the 1904 gubernatorial election that was pervaded by fraud on all sides.

> According to the averments of the bill [the petition for the injunction], a wide-spread conspiracy exists, which, if not frustrated, will deprive the people of the constitutional right to an open, fair, and honest election; that officials upon whom devolves the duty of conducting the election are engaged in this conspiracy; and that part of the nefarious scheme has already been consummated, in that thousands of fictitious names have been placed upon the registration lists which it is the

---

[5] 18 U.S.C. App. III; Pub.L. No. 91-538, 84 Stat. 1397 (1970) (as amended).

[6] For the Cato Institute and Independence Institute, I submitted an amicus brief in support of the cert. petition. It argued that the Supreme Court's early ad prosequendum case law, the federal statute, the leading Supreme Court opinion on the interstate detainers agreement, and principles of federalism all supported "the sovereign right of Governors to refuse a writ of habeas corpus ad prosequendum." *Chafee v. United States*, 2012 WL 4481320.

> purpose of the conspirators to have voted by repeaters and personators [repeat voters, and voters pretending to be someone else] with the connivance of judges and clerks of election.
>
> ...
>
> The cardinal principle of our government is that it shall be controlled by the people through the medium of the ballot box. Destroy this right, and the government itself is destroyed.
>
> ...
>
> If these frauds are perpetrated, if they cannot be prevented, then the entire state, so far as the election is concerned, is practically at the mercy of those who control the election machinery in the city and county of Denver.
>
> ...
>
> [The supreme court's original jurisdiction for writs] was...conferred ...for the purpose of protecting the sovereignty of the state, its prerogatives, and the liberties of its citizens.
>
> ...
>
> [These writs] are the very armor of sovereignty. Because they are designed for the very purpose of protecting the sovereignty and its ordained offices from invasion or intrusion, and also to nerve its arm to protect its citizens in their liberties, and to guard its prerogatives and franchises against usurpation. [Citations and quote marks omitted.]

Therefore, the supreme court will "specifically direct that the election officials comply with the law in the conduct of elections, and that two watchers in each of the several precincts be appointed by this court for the purpose of observing how the election in these precincts is conducted."

In modern practice, the supreme court grants original jurisdiction writs only in cases where the facts are compelling, and the petitioner has no other adequate remedy. RICHARD COLLINS & DALE A. OESTERLE, THE COLORADO STATE CONSTITUTION 175–76 (2d ed. 2020). The exception is the writ of certiorari, whose issuance is routine.

Opinions upon important questions upon solemn occasions

The duty to issue advisory opinions was added by amendment in 1886, since the supreme court had been dutiful in striking unconstitutional enactments. By the amendment, the court "shall give" its opinions under certain circumstances. The first sessions after 1886 produced a dozen or more interrogatories per session.

The court grew annoyed with so many questions and set some limits. First, the court decides for itself whether a question is "important" and whether an occasion is "solemn." *See, e.g.*, *In re Opinion of the Justices*, 94 Colo. 215, 29 P.2d 705 (1934).

Proposed questions must be specific. *In re H.B. 1503*, 163 Colo. 45, 428 P.2d 75 (1967) (refusing to answer questions about an economic development bill that involved 11 sections of the Constitution).

Usually, but not always, the court will not answer a question about a bill that has not yet passed both houses. COLLINS & OSTERLE at 176 (listing cases).

By the plain language of Section 3, the questions must be propounded by the governor, house, or senate. *Cameron v. Carroll & Co.*, 138 Colo. 432, 334 P.2d 748 (1959) (rejecting statutory interpretation question from securities commissioner).

Opinions on advisory questions have the same precedential force as opinions in contested cases. *In re Senate Bill No. 65*, 12 Colo. 466, 21 P. 478 (1889).

The U.S. Constitution's article III is interpreted to prohibit advisory opinions. Article III courts only have jurisdiction for "Cases" and "Controversies." By long-standing interpretation, if a party lacks standing (a specific, concrete interest that could protected by a judicial decision), then there is no case or controversy. Hence, the federal court has no jurisdiction to issue an opinion.

The Colorado Constitution consciously diverges from the U.S. Constitution by compelling advisory opinions from the supreme court. An advantage to the Colorado system is prompt resolution of important issues. In 2020, could the legislature exempt itself from constitutional "120 calendar days" limit on general legislative sessions? In 1992, could the state proceed with offering the new corporate welfare package to United Airlines? Why not resolve such questions expeditiously, rather than trying to find a plaintiff with standing, filing a case in district court, and waiting months or years before the supreme court announces the final result?

The downside of advisory opinions is that when there is no involved party with something at stake that is concrete and particular (standing), the court may not hear a strong presentation from the non-government side. Yet the court's opinion could affect the rights of many people. So there is good reason for state courts to be cautious about issuing advisory opinions, even when they have the power to do so.

Further reading: William H. Robinson, Jr., *Limitations upon Legislative Opinions under Colorado Advisory Opinions Clause*, 4 ROCKY MTN. L. REVIEW 237 (1932) (predecessor to U. COLO. L. REV.); Edwin Philip Banks, *The Colorado Advisory Opinion* (Univ. of Colo. Master's thesis, 1952).

Two other types of original jurisdiction

The supreme court also uses the term "original jurisdiction" for its review of two types of decisions by other bodies: attorney discipline by the disciplinary panel, *In re Sather*, 3 P.3d 403 (Colo. 2000),[7] and decisions by the general assembly's title board on proposed ballot issues. *In re Title, etc., to Branch Banking Initiative*, 612 P.2d 96 (Colo. 1980).

The review of title board decisions is pursuant to statute. C.R.S. § 1-40-107 (enacted 1941). The statute ensures speedy and final resolution of disputes about proposed ballot questions.

Art. VI, Sec. 4. Supreme court must hold at least two terms

> At least two terms of the supreme court shall be held each year, at the seat of government.

By statute, the supreme court has three terms. They begin: the second Monday in September, the second Monday in January, and the second Monday in April. C.R.S. § 13-2-101. The court may set its own rules for special terms. C.R.S. § 13-2-102.

By practice, the court holds all its terms in Denver, with occasional days of argument held elsewhere, for educational purposes.

The court recesses for July and August and sits for the other 10 months.

[7] The Presiding Disciplinary Judge, plus two volunteer attorneys. Appeals to the supreme court are Rule 251.27.

Art. VI, Section 5. Supreme court justices

(1) The supreme court shall consist of not less than seven justices, who may sit en banc or in departments. In case said court shall sit in departments, each of said departments shall have full power and authority of said court in the determination of causes, the issuing of writs and the exercise of all powers authorized by this constitution, or provided by law, subject to the general control of the court sitting en banc, and such rules and regulations as the court may make, but no decision of any department shall become judgment of the court unless concurred in by at least three justices, and no case involving construction of the constitution of this state or of the United States shall be decided except by the court en banc. Upon request of the supreme court, the number of justices may be increased to no more than nine members whenever two-thirds of the members of each house of the general assembly concur therein.

(2) The supreme court shall select a chief justice from its own membership to serve at the pleasure of a majority of the court, who shall be the executive head of the judicial system.

(3) The supreme court shall appoint a court administrator and such other personnel as the court may deem necessary to aid the administration of the courts. Whenever the chief justice deems assignment of a judge necessary to the prompt disposition of judicial business, he may: (a) Assign any county judge, or retired county judge who consents, temporarily to perform judicial duties in any county court if otherwise qualified under section 18 of this article, or assign, as hereafter may be authorized by law, said judge to any other court; or (b) assign any district, probate, or juvenile judge, or retired justice or district, probate, or juvenile judge who consents, temporarily to perform judicial duties in any court. For each day of such temporary service a retired justice or judge shall receive compensation in an amount equal to 1/20 of the monthly salary then currently applicable to the judicial position in which the temporary service is rendered.

(4) The chief justice shall appoint from the district judges of each judicial district a chief judge to serve at the pleasure of the chief justice. A chief judge shall receive no additional salary by reason of holding such position. Each chief judge shall have and exercise such administrative powers over all judges of all courts within his district as may be delegated to him by the chief justice.

The size of the supreme court was expanded to "at least seven" justices, to help share the workload.

Although the supreme court is authorized to hear non-constitutional cases in three-justice panels rather than *en banc*, the court has never chosen to do so. Since the constitution requires a panel decision to be supported by at least three justices, a panel would have to comprise at least five justices.

The chief justice is elected by the court and is the chief executive of the judicial branch.

Chief judges in each judicial district are chosen by the chief justice and can administrate according to whatever powers the chief justice gives them.

In situations when there is a shortage of judges, a county judge or a retired county judge may be assigned to a county court anywhere in the state. Similarly, retired or active district, probate, or juvenile judges may be assigned to any court, including the court of appeals or the supreme court.

The supreme court must appoint a state court administrator. C.R.S. § 13-3-101. The court may appoint subordinate administrators. C.R.S. § 13-2-111 (supreme court clerks, librarian, reporters, bailiffs, and other necessary assistants).

Pursuant to statute, the chief justice appoints the five-member Public Defender Commission (3 attorneys, 2 lay), which supervises the office of state public defender. This has been held not to violate the separation of powers. C.R.S. § 21-1-101; *People v. Mullins*, 188 Colo. 29, 532 P.2d 736 (1975). In Colorado, all public defenders work for one statewide employer.

Art. VI, Section 6. (repealed)

Repealed in 1967. Section 6 had required that supreme court justices be elected at large. Now, pursuant to section 20, they are appointed, and face retention elections that they always win.

Art. VI, Section 7. Terms of office of supreme court justices

> The full term of office of justices of the supreme court shall be ten years.

A 1904 change from the 9-year term in the original Constitution, which had necessitated many odd-year general elections.

Art. VI, Section 8. Qualification of justices

> No person shall be eligible to the office of justice of the supreme court unless he shall be a qualified elector of the state of Colorado and shall have been licensed to practice law in this state for at least five years.

This section has never been violated. In section 8 and elsewhere, the original requirement that judges be "learned in the law" has been replaced with the more objective standard of admission to practice in Colorado for a certain period. The original language represents an ideal, whereas the present language has the advantage of being specific and readily enforceable.

Art. VI, Section 9. District courts

> (1) The district courts shall be trial courts of record with general jurisdiction, and shall have original jurisdiction in all civil, probate, and criminal cases, except as otherwise provided herein, and shall have such appellate jurisdiction as may be prescribed by law.
>
> (2) Deleted by S.C.R. 02-006, § 1, eff. Dec. 20, 2002.
>
> (3) In the city and county of Denver, exclusive original jurisdiction in all matters of probate, settlements of estates of deceased persons, appointment of guardians, conservators and administrators, and settlement of their accounts, the adjudication of the mentally ill, and such other jurisdiction as may be provided by law shall be vested in a probate court, created by section 1 of this article.

Jurisdiction

District courts are governed by C.R.S. § 13-5-101 et seq. *See also* Colo. Rules Civ. Pro. rule 121 (local rules). District courts have general jurisdiction, except when there is a specific exception. *Emmons v. Colorado Department of Revenue by and through Cordova*, 459 P.3d 784 (Colo. App. 2020). Before 1962, county courts were the courts of general jurisdiction. Municipal courts only have jurisdiction as specifically granted by a charter or ordinance. *Burger Investments Family Limited Partnership v. City of Littleton*, 2019 COA 127, 463 P.3d 303 (Colo. App. 2019).

By statute, district courts have appellate jurisdiction for county court cases. Thereafter, the only appeal is by certiorari to the supreme court. C.R.S. § 13-6-311. By statute, some final administrative agency actions may be appealed directly to the court of appeals. C.R.S. § 24-4-106.

Writs

District courts have the power to issue all the common law remedial writs, including habeas corpus, mandamus, quo warranto, certiorari, prohibition, scire facias (a family of writs used to enforce judgements), and ne exeat (a person or thing may not be removed from the geographic area of the court's jurisdiction). The common law special forms for these writs have been abolished, and they have all been consolidated under a single rule. Colo. R. Civ. Pro. 106. Nevertheless, common law precedents governing particular writs are still applicable. *Ahern v. Baker*, 366 P.2d 366 (Colo. 1961). *See also* C.R.S. § 13-1-114 (powers of all Colorado courts to enforce order in the immediate presence of the court and to enforce its judgments); -115 (authorizing all courts to issue writs).

Elections

Colorado courts have jurisdiction over cases involving election recounts or other election procedures. *Meyer v. Lamm*, 846 P.2d 862 (Colo. 1993) (write-in candidate's challenge to counting of votes). But once the secretary of state has transmitted election certificates to the general assembly, and the general assembly has decided who shall be seated, the general assembly's determination is conclusive, and not subject to judicial review. *Hughes v. Felton*, 11 Colo. 489, 19 P. 444 (1888).

Art. VI, Section 10. Judicial districts

> (1) The state shall be divided into judicial districts. Such districts shall be formed of compact territory and be bounded by county lines. The judicial districts as provided by law on the effective date of this amendment shall constitute the judicial districts of the state until changed. The general assembly may by law, whenever two-thirds of the members of each house concur therein, change the boundaries of any district or increase or diminish the number of judicial districts.
>
> (2) In each judicial district there shall be one or more judges of the district court. The full term of office of a district judge shall be six years.
>
> (3) The number of district judges provided by law for each district on the effective date of this amendment shall constitute the number of judges for the district until changed. The general assembly may by law, whenever two-thirds of the members

> of each house concur therein, increase or diminish the number of district judges, except that the office of a district judge may not be abolished until completion of the term for which he was elected or appointed, but he may be required to serve in a judicial district other than the one for which elected, as long as such district encompasses his county of residence.
>
> (4) Separate divisions of district courts may be established in districts by law, or in the absence of any such law, by rule of court.

Currently, there are 22 judicial districts in Colorado. C.R.S. Title 13, article 5, Part 1. The districts may not split counties. By Denver's home rule amendment (article XX), Denver must be a single judicial district.

Pursuant to section 24(3), a judicial district may comprise no more than seven counties. This is because a judicial district's nominating commission consists of seven people, and the commission must include at least one member from every county in the district.

Art. VI, Section 11. Qualifications of district judges

> No person shall be eligible to the office of district judge unless he shall be a qualified elector of the judicial district at the time of his election or selection and shall have been licensed to practice law in this state for five years. Each judge of the district court shall be a resident of his district during his term of office.

District judges must live in their districts. This means actual residence, not legal or constructive residence. *People v. Owers*, 29 Colo. 535, 69 P. 515 (1902) (but refusing to do anything about a Lake County judge who was living in Denver and practicing law there, in violation of section 18; supposedly the move was temporary and for health reasons). If a non-resident district judge gets caught, his previous decisions are still valid. *Relative Value Studies, Inc. v. McGraw-Hill Companies*, 981 P.2d 687 (Colo. App. 1999).

Art. VI, Section 12. District courts must hold at least one term annually in each county

> The time of holding courts within the judicial districts shall be as provided by rule of court, but at least one term of the district court shall be held annually in each county.

The implementing statute provides that at least one term must be held in each county within a district and must be held at the county seat. C.R.S. § 13-5-101. Even when a court is in recess between terms, it must always remain open for filings. Colo. Rules Civ. Pro. 77(a).

Art. VI, Section 13. District attorneys

> In each judicial district there shall be a district attorney elected by the electors thereof, whose term of office shall be four years. District attorneys shall receive such salaries and perform such duties as provided by law. No person shall be eligible to the office of district attorney who shall not, at the time of his election possess all the qualifications of district court judges as provided in this article. All

> district attorneys holding office on the effective date of this amendment shall continue in office for the remainder of the respective terms for which they were elected or appointed.

Notwithstanding the placement of district attorneys in article VI, they are part of the executive branch, not the judicial branch. *Beacom in and for Seventeenth Judicial Dist., Adams County v. Board of County Commissioners of Adams County*, 657 P.2d 440 (Colo. 1983).

As in most states, district attorneys are elected by the people, by judicial district, for four-year terms. In New Jersey, district attorneys are appointed by the governor, with the predictably deleterious consequence of prosecutors who are gung-ho for the governor's pet peeves, and lackadaisical about prosecuting the governor's friends.

District attorneys are subject to the same term limits as other local officials. *Davidson v. Sandstrom*, 83 P.3d 648 (Colo. 2004).

Art. VI, Section 14. Probate courts

> The probate court of the city and county of Denver shall have such jurisdiction as provided by section 9, subsection (3) of this article. The judge of the probate court of the city and county of Denver shall have the same qualifications and term of office as provided in this article for district judges. Vacancies shall be filled as provided in section 20 of this article. The number of judges of the probate court of the city and county of Denver may be increased as provided by law.

Denver's probate court is established by C.R.S. §§ 13-9-101 to 124.

Further reading: Paula Constantakis Young, *The Expanded Jurisdiction of the Probate Court Under in re J.C.T.*, 37 COLO. LAWYER 83 (Nov. 2008).

Art. VI, Section 15. Juvenile courts

> The juvenile court of the city and county of Denver shall have such jurisdiction as shall be provided by law. The judge of the juvenile court of the city and county of Denver shall have the same qualifications and term of office as provided in this article for district judges. Vacancies shall be filled as provided in section 20 of this article. The number of judges of the juvenile court of the city and county of Denver may be increased as provided by law.

Denver's juvenile court is established by C.R.S. § 13-8-101 et seq. One of the few judges to have lost a retention election was Denver juvenile judge Ted Rubin, who was rejected for what voters saw as excessive leniency.

Further reading: BENJAMIN B. LINDSEY, THE BEAST (Univ. Pr. of Colo. 2009) (1911) (a judge's best-selling expose of juvenile justice in Denver).

Art. VI, Section 16. County judges

> In each county there shall be one or more judges of the county court as may be provided by law, whose full term of office shall be four years, and whose qualifications shall be prescribed by law. County judges shall be qualified electors of their counties at the time of their election or appointment.

Unlike district judges, county judges do not need to be admitted to the practice of law. However, statute requires a law degree for judges in the larger counties. C.R.S. § 13-6-203 (in A and B counties, judge must be admitted to the practice of law in Colorado; in C and D counties, high school graduation or a GED is required; the latter group of judges must take a training course supervised by the supreme court).

For county court purposes, counties are classified as follows:

- Class A. City and county of Denver.
- Class B. Adams, Arapahoe, Boulder, Douglas, Eagle, El Paso, Fremont, Jefferson, La Plata, Larimer, Mesa, Montrose, Pueblo, Summit, Weld, and the city and county of Broomfield.
- Class C. Alamosa, Delta, Garfield, Las Animas, Logan, Montezuma, Morgan, Otero, Prowers, and Rio Grande.
- Class D. Archuleta, Baca, Bent, Chaffee, Cheyenne, Clear Creek, Conejos, Costilla, Crowley, Custer, Dolores, Elbert, Gilpin, Grand, Gunnison, Jackson, Hinsdale, Huerfano, Kiowa, Kit Carson, Lake, Lincoln, Mineral, Moffat, Ouray, Park, Phillips, Pitkin, Saguache, San Juan, San Miguel, Sedgwick, Rio Blanco, Routt, Teller, Washington, and Yuma.

C.R.S. § 13-6-201.

County court judges may be designated to sit as district court judges, pursuant to section 5 of article VI. As temporary district judges, they can hear all the types of cases appropriate in district court, including felonies. *People v. Johnson*, 77 P.3d 845 (Colo. App. 2003).

Art. VI, Section 17. County courts

> County courts shall have such civil, criminal, and appellate jurisdiction as may be provided by law, provided such courts shall not have jurisdiction of felonies or in civil cases where the boundaries or title to real property shall be in question. Appellate review by the supreme court or the district courts of every final judgment of the county courts shall be as provided by law.

County courts cannot hear criminal felony cases, or civil cases involving real property boundaries or title. Other than that, their jurisdiction may be established by statute.

County courts are established by C.R.S. § 13-6-101 et seq. Their current jurisdiction is: civil actions involving $15,000 or less; lien foreclosures; name changes (concurrent with district courts); civil restraining orders (concurrent jurisdiction); and motor vehicle impoundment (original jurisdiction). C.R.S. § 13-6-104.

Art. VI, Section 18. Compensation of judges

> Justices and judges of courts of record shall receive such compensation as may be provided by law, which may be increased but may not be decreased during their term of office and shall receive such pension or retirement benefits as may be provided by law. No justice or judge of a court of record shall accept designation or nomination for any public office other than judicial without first resigning from his judicial office, nor shall he hold at any other time any other public office during his term of office, nor hold office in any political party organization, nor contribute to or campaign for any political party or candidate for political office. No supreme

> court justice, judge of any intermediate appellate court, district court judge, probate judge, or juvenile judge shall engage in the practice of law. Justices, district judges, probate judges, and juvenile judges when called upon to do so, may serve in any state court with full authority as provided by law. Any county judge may serve in any other county court, or serve, as hereinafter may be authorized by law, in any other court, if possessing the qualifications prescribed by law for a judge of such county court, or other court, or as a municipal judge or police magistrate as provided by law, or in the case of home rule cities as provided by charter and ordinances.

Judicial compensation is set by C.R.S. § 13-30-101 et seq.

A 1952 amendment authorized the legislature to provide judicial pensions as it wishes. Unfortunately, the amendment was not in effect in 1940, when the supreme court began the process of destroying article V's limits on special legislation in order to uphold a statute raising pensions for retired judges. *Bedford v. White*, 106 Colo. 439, 106 P.2d 469 (1940).

Section 18 forbids most judges, except county judges, to practice law. *See also* C.R.S. § 13-6-204 (County court judges in C and D counties may practice if the matter will not come before the county court).

Judge may not hold non-judicial public office or participate in candidate campaigns, other than their own retention elections.

Judge in one court may serve by designation on other courts.

Art. VI, Section 19. Court laws must be uniform

> All laws relating to state courts shall be general and of uniform operation throughout the state, and except as hereafter in this section specified the organization, jurisdiction, powers, proceedings, and practice of all courts of the same class, and the force and effect of the proceedings, judgments and decrees of such courts severally shall be uniform. County courts may be classified or graded as may be provided by law, and the organization, jurisdiction, powers, proceedings, and practice of county courts within the same class or grade, and the force and effect of the proceedings, judgments and decrees of county courts in the same class or grade shall be uniform; provided, however, that the organization and administration of the county court of the city and county of Denver shall be as provided in the charter and ordinances of the city and county of Denver.

Although court laws must be uniform, section 19 allows for the creation of county courts of different classes, with uniformity within the class. But the diversity of classes in county courts does not permit different rights for jury trials in counties of different classes. *Board of County Commissioners v. First National Bank*, 24 Colo. 124, 48 P. 1043 (1897).

In situations where a municipal court rule conflicts with state law, "Section 19 often influences the interpretation in favor of state law." RICHARD COLLINS & DALE A. OESTERLE, THE COLORADO STATE CONSTITUTION 187 (2d ed. 2020). For example, a home rule city charter that eliminated jury trials for petty offenses was trumped by a state statute requiring jury trials. *Hardamon v. Municipal Court*, 497 P.2d 1000 (Colo. 1972).

Art. VI, Section 20. Vacancies in judicial offices

> (1) A vacancy in any judicial office in any court of record shall be filled by appointment of the governor, from a list of three nominees for the supreme court and any intermediate appellate court, and from a list of two or three nominees for all other courts of record, such list to be certified to him by the supreme court nominating commission for a vacancy in the supreme court or a vacancy in any intermediate appellate court, and by the judicial district nominating commission for a vacancy in any other court in that district. In case of more than one vacancy in any such court, the list shall contain not less than two more nominees than there are vacancies to be filled. The list shall be submitted by the nominating commission not later than thirty days after the death, retirement, tender of resignation, removal under section 23, failure of an incumbent to file a declaration under section 25, or certification of a negative majority vote on the question of retention in office under section 25 hereof. If the governor shall fail to make the appointment (or all of the appointments in case of multiple vacancies) from such list within fifteen days from the day it is submitted to him, the appointment (or the remaining appointments in case of multiple vacancies) shall be made by the chief justice of the supreme court from the same list within the next fifteen days. A justice or judge appointed under the provisions of this section shall hold office for a provisional term of two years and then until the second Tuesday in January following the next general election. A nominee shall be under the age of seventy-two years at the time his name is submitted to the governor.
>
> (2) Repealed by S.C.R. 02-006, §1, eff. Dec. 20, 2002.
>
> (3) Other vacancies occurring in judicial offices shall be filled as now or hereafter provided by law.
>
> (4) Vacancies occurring in the office of district attorney shall be filled by appointment of the governor. District attorneys appointed under the provisions of this section shall hold office until the next general election and until their successors elected thereat shall be duly qualified. Such successors shall be elected for the remainder of the unexpired term in which the vacancy was created.

Until 1966, judges were chosen by the people in contested partisan elections. Now, when there is a judicial vacancy, the governor makes an appointment from a list provided by a judicial nominating commission. At the appellate level, the list must include three names. For trial courts, two or three names.

Appointed judges serve for two years *plus* however long until the next general election, when they are subject to a retention vote. If the people vote to retain the judge, then the judge's new term is a full term (*e.g.*, 10 years for supreme court).

The commission nominating system is for "any court of record"—that is, courts whose proceedings are recorded. The category includes all state courts, and some municipal courts. C.R.S. § 13-10-102.

For district attorney vacancies, the governor appoints whomever he wishes, with no need for a list. The newly appointed D.A. holds office until the next general election.

Art. VI, Section 21. Supreme court shall make court rules

> The supreme court shall make and promulgate rules governing the administration of all courts and shall make and promulgate rules governing practice and procedure in civil and criminal cases, except that the general assembly shall have the power to provide simplified procedures in county courts for the trial of misdemeanors.

The supreme court makes the rules of procedure, except that the legislature can make procedural rules for county court misdemeanors. The supreme court's authority over "procedure" is "exclusive." *Blue Mountain Credit Alternatives Master Fund L.P. v. Regal Entertainment Group*, 2020 COA 6, 465 P.3d 122 (Colo. App. 2020).

The unauthorized practice of law is a matter exclusively for the supreme court. *People v. Adams*, 243 P.3d 256 (Colo. 2010).

Both the supreme court and the general assembly can make rules of evidence. If there is a conflict, the question is whether the rule is substantive (legislature wins) or procedural (court wins). *People v. Hollis*, 670 P.2d 441 (Colo. App. 1983) (number of peremptory challenges is substantive). If possible, the judicial rule and the legislature's rule will be construed so as not to conflict. COLLINS & OESTERLE at 189.

Art. VI, Section 22. Prosecutions shall run in the name of "The People of the State of Colorado"

> In all prosecutions for violations of the laws of Colorado, process shall run in the name of "The People of the State of Colorado"; all prosecutions shall be carried on in the name and by the authority of "The People of the State of Colorado," and conclude, "against the peace and dignity of the same"

Small deviations from the required words do not void an indictment. *E.g.*, *People v. Hunter*, 666 P.2d 570 (Colo. 1983).

Note that when a plaintiff seeks a writ of habeas corpus, the proper defendant is the person who is holding the plaintiff in custody, not "the People." *Stilley v. Tinsley*, 153 Colo. 66, 385 P.2d 677 (1963) ("he could get himself into a heap of trouble in turning the prisoner loose").

Art. VI, Section 23. Retirement, discipline, and removal of justices and judges

> (1) On attaining the age of seventy-two a justice or judge of a court of record shall retire and his judicial office shall be vacant, except as otherwise provided in section 20(2).
>
> (2) Whenever a justice or judge of any court of this state has been convicted in any court of this state or of the United States or of any state, of a felony or other offense involving moral turpitude, the supreme court shall, of its own motion or upon petition filed by any person, and upon finding that such a conviction was had, enter its order suspending said justice or judge from office until such time as said judgment of conviction becomes final, and the payment of salary of said justice or judge shall also be suspended from the date of such order. If said judgment of

conviction becomes final, the supreme court shall enter its order removing said justice or judge from office and declaring his office vacant and his right to salary shall cease from the date of the order of suspension. If said judgment of conviction is reversed with directions to enter a judgment of acquittal or if reversed for a new trial which subsequently results in a judgment of dismissal or acquittal, the supreme court shall enter its order terminating the suspension of said justice or judge and said justice or judge shall be entitled to his salary for the period of suspension. A plea of guilty or nolo contendere to such a charge shall be equivalent to a final conviction for the purpose of this section.

(3)

(a) There shall be a commission on judicial discipline. It shall consist of: Two judges of district courts and two judges of county courts, each selected by the supreme court; two citizens admitted to practice law in the courts of this state, neither of whom shall be a justice or judge, who shall have practiced in this state for at least ten years and who shall be appointed by the governor, with the consent of the senate; and four citizens, none of whom shall be a justice or judge, active or retired, nor admitted to practice law in the courts of this state, who shall be appointed by the governor, with the consent of the senate.

(b) Each member shall be appointed to a four-year term; except that one-half of the initial membership in each category shall be appointed to two-year terms, for the purpose of staggering terms. Whenever a commission membership prematurely terminates or a member no longer possesses the specific qualifications for the category from which he was selected, his position shall be deemed vacant, and his successor shall be appointed in the same manner as the original appointment for the remainder of his term. A member shall be deemed to have resigned if that member is absent from three consecutive commission meetings without the commission having entered an approval for additional absences upon its minutes. If any member of the commission is disqualified to act in any matter pending before the commission, the commission may appoint a special member to sit on the commission solely for the purpose of deciding that matter.

(c) No member of the commission shall receive any compensation for his services but shall be allowed his necessary expenses for travel, board, and lodging and any other expenses incurred in the performance of his duties, to be paid by the supreme court from its budget to be appropriated by the general assembly.

(d) A justice or judge of any court of record of this state, in accordance with the procedure set forth in this subsection (3), may be removed or disciplined for willful misconduct in office, willful or persistent failure to perform his duties, intemperance, or violation of any canon of the Colorado code of judicial conduct, or he may be retired for disability interfering with the performance of his duties which is, or is likely to become, of a permanent character.

(e) The commission may, after such investigation as it deems necessary, order informal remedial action; order a formal hearing to be held before it concerning the removal, retirement, suspension, censure, reprimand, or other discipline of a justice or a judge; or request the supreme court to appoint three special masters, who shall be justices or judges of courts of record, to hear and take evidence in any such matter and to report thereon to the commission. After a formal hearing or after considering the record and report of the masters, if the commission finds good cause therefor, it may take informal remedial action, or it may recommend to the supreme court the removal, retirement, suspension, censure, reprimand, or discipline, as the case may be, of the justice or judge. The commission may also recommend that the costs of its investigation and hearing be assessed against such justice or judge.

(f) Following receipt of a recommendation from the commission, the supreme court shall review the record of the proceedings on the law and facts and in its discretion may permit the introduction of additional evidence and shall order removal, retirement, suspension, censure, reprimand, or discipline, as it finds just and proper, or wholly reject the recommendation. Upon an order for retirement, the justice or judge shall thereby be retired with the same rights and privileges as if he retired pursuant to statute. Upon an order for removal, the justice or judge shall thereby be removed from office, and his salary shall cease from the date of such order. On the entry of an order for retirement or for removal of a judge, his office shall be deemed vacant.

(g) Prior to the filing of a recommendation to the supreme court by the commission against any justice or judge, all papers filed with and proceedings before the commission on judicial discipline or masters appointed by the supreme court, pursuant to this subsection (3), shall be confidential, and the filing of papers with and the giving of testimony before the commission or the masters shall be privileged; but no other publication of such papers or proceedings shall be privileged in any action for defamation; except that the record filed by the commission in the supreme court continues privileged and a writing which was privileged prior to its filing with the commission or the masters does not lose such privilege by such filing.

(h) The supreme court shall by rule provide for procedures before the commission on judicial discipline, the masters, and the supreme court. The rules shall also provide the standards and degree of proof to be applied by the commission in its proceedings. A justice or judge who is a member of the commission or supreme court shall not participate in any proceedings involving his own removal or retirement.

(i) Nothing contained in this subsection (3) shall be construed to have any effect on article XIII of this constitution.

(j) Repealed by S.C.R. 02-006, §1, eff. Dec. 20, 2002.

Judges must retire when they turn 72. Judges must resign (or be removed) if convicted of a felony or a crime of moral turpitude. The Colorado Commission on Judicial Discipline is in charge of initial investigations, which are confidential until the commission makes a public recommendation to the supreme court. The supreme court decides what, if any, discipline to impose, up to involuntary retirement. *Higgins v. Owens*, 13 P.3d 837 (Colo. App. 2000).

Two county judges and two district judges are appointed to the commission by the supreme court. Six other members are appointed by the governor and confirmed by the senate; two of these members must be lawyers, and four must not be.

Art. VI, Section 24. Judicial nominating commissions

(1) There shall be one judicial nominating commission for the supreme court and any intermediate appellate court to be called the supreme court nominating commission and one judicial nominating commission for each judicial district in the state.

(2) The supreme court nominating commission shall consist of the chief justice or acting chief justice of the supreme court, ex officio, who shall act as chairman and shall have no vote, one citizen admitted to practice law before the courts of this state and one other citizen not admitted to practice law in the courts of this state residing in each congressional district in the state, and one additional citizen not admitted to practice law in the courts of this state. No more than one-half of the commission members plus one, exclusive of the chief justice, shall be members of the same political party. Three voting members shall serve until December 31, 1967, three until December 31, 1969, and three until December 31, 1971. Thereafter each voting member appointed shall serve until the 31st of December of the 6th year following the date of his appointment.

(3) Each judicial district nominating commission shall consist of a justice of the supreme court designated by the chief justice, to serve at the will of the chief justice who shall act as chairman ex officio, and shall have no vote, and seven citizens residing in that judicial district, no more than four of whom shall be members of the same political party and there shall be at least one voting member from each county in the district. In all judicial districts having a population of more than 35,000 inhabitants as determined by the last preceding census taken under the authority of the United States, the voting members shall consist of three persons admitted to practice law in the courts of this state and four persons not admitted to practice law in the courts of this state. In judicial districts having a population of 35,000 inhabitants or less as determined above, at least four voting members shall be persons not admitted to practice law in the courts of this state; and it shall be determined by majority vote of the governor, the attorney general and the chief justice, how many, if any, of the remaining three members shall be persons admitted to practice law in the courts of this state. Two voting members shall serve until December 31, 1967, two until December 31, 1969, and three until December 31, 1971. Thereafter each voting member appointed shall serve until the 31st of December of the 6th year following the date of his appointment.

(4) Members of each judicial nominating commission selected by reason of their being citizens admitted to practice law in the courts of this state shall be appointed by majority action of the governor, the attorney general and the chief justice. All other members shall be appointed by the governor. No voting member of a judicial nominating commission shall hold any elective and salaried United States or state public office or any elective political party office and he shall not be eligible for reappointment to succeed himself on a commission. No voting member of the supreme court nominating commission shall be eligible for appointment as a justice of the supreme court or any intermediate appellate court so long as he is a member of that commission and for a period of three years thereafter; and no voting member of a judicial district nominating commission shall be eligible for

> appointment to judicial office in that district while a member of that commission and for a period of one year thereafter.

For the appellate courts, there is a single statewide judicial nominating commission. Each of the 22 judicial districts has its own nominating commission for district and county judges.

The supreme court nominating commission (which also nominates for the court of appeals) is chaired by the chief justice, who cannot vote. There are two members from each congressional district, plus one at-large. Of the two members from each congressional district, one must be admitted to the practice of law, and one must not be admitted.

The judicial district nominating commissions are chaired by an associate justice, who does not vote. They consist of seven members, including at least one member from each county in the district. Of the seven, four must *not* be admitted to the practice of law. In large counties, the other three members *must* be lawyers.

Because the district commissions comprise seven members, and a commission must include at least one member from every county in the district, a judicial district may include a maximum of seven counties. *In re Interrogatories Propounded by the Senate*, 452 P.2d 382 (Colo. 1969).

No more than a bare majority of any commission may belong to a same political party.

Lawyer members of the commissions are appointed by majority vote of the chief justice, governor, and attorney general. The non-lawyer members are appointed by the governor.

Appointments are for staggered six-year terms. A member may not serve consecutive terms. Members cannot hold "any elective and salaried United States or state public office." According to an attorney general opinion, members may hold local or municipal offices. AG File No. CLS/AGBAM/ED Oct. 12, 1979. They may not hold "an elective political party office." The attorney general interprets the text to apply to state or local party chairs, vice-chairs, secretaries, central committee members, or precinct committeepersons. Colo. Att'y Gen. Op. No. 04-03, Apr. 12, 2004. In Colorado, attorney general opinions can be persuasive but they do not bind courts.

Commissioners may not nominate their own members for judgeships. Or former members (three years for statewide judges; one year for district judges).

Section 24 has been reasonably successful in limiting judicial nominations to people who meet general standards of resume-worthiness. So the governor cannot appoint his best friend from law school to the state's highest court, as N.Y. governor Mario Cuomo once did.

By design, section 24 does not remove politics from judicial selection. It simply transfers political power from the people to the governor (for the non-lawyer appointments) and a troika (for the lawyer appointments).

Water judges are a type of district court judge, but they are appointed by the supreme court. They are divided geographically into divisions based on the seven major drainages of Colorado's rivers.

Art. VI, Section 25. Retention elections for justices and judges

> A justice of the supreme court or a judge of any other court of record, who shall desire to retain his judicial office for another term after the expiration of his then term of office shall file with the secretary of state, not more than six months nor less than three months prior to the general election next prior to the expiration of his then term of office, a declaration of his intent to run for another term. Failure to file such a declaration within the time specified shall create a vacancy in that office at the end of his then term of office. Upon the filing of such a declaration, a

> question shall be placed on the appropriate ballot at such general election, as follows:
>
> "Shall Justice (Judge) . . . of the Supreme (or other) Court be retained in office? YES/ . . . /NO/ . . . /." If a majority of those voting on the question vote "Yes," the justice or judge is thereupon elected to a succeeding full term. If a majority of those voting on the question vote "No," this will cause a vacancy to exist in that office at the end of his then present term of office.
>
> In the case of a justice of the supreme court or any intermediate appellate court, the electors of the state at large; in the case of a judge of a district court, the electors of that judicial district; and in the case of a judge of the county court or other court of record, the electors of that county; shall vote on the question of retention in office of the justice or judge.

Judges are subject to periodic retention elections. This is a common system in many states, although far from universal. In some states, judicial appointments are for life, as in federal courts established under the U.S. Constitution's article III. In some states, judges are elected in ordinary partisan elections. In still others, several candidates may contest an election, but the candidates are not nominated by parties (similar to Denver mayor and city council elections.)

In practice, the retention election system in Colorado is a failure. The Colorado Commissions on Judicial Performance do a conscientious job of collecting information about judges and identifying deficiencies in performance. But only the most egregious problems lead to a recommendation that a judge not be retained. "The judge says he is trying to improve" is almost always sufficient for a retention recommendation.

In the rare situation of a non-retention recommendation, the defective judge usually still wins the retention election.

By interpretation, retention elections are not "ballot questions," and therefore advocacy groups for or against a judge's retention do not have to comply with Colorado's Fair Campaign Practices Act. *Colorado Ethics Watch v. Clear the Bench Colorado*, 277 P.3d 931 (Colo. App. 2012).

Further reading: David L. Masters, *A Closer Look at Colorado's Judicial Selection and Retention Systems*, 41 COLO. LAWYER 5 (Jan. 2012); Elizabeth A. Larkin, *Judicial Selection Methods: Judicial Independence and Popular Democracy*, 79 DENVER U.L. REVIEW 65 (2001).

Art. VI, Section 26. Denver county judges

> The provisions of sections 16, 20, 23, 24 and 25 hereof shall not be applicable to judges of the county court of the City and County of Denver. The number, manner of selection, qualifications, term of office, tenure, and removal of such judges shall be as provided in the charter and ordinances of the City and County of Denver.

Denver does not have to follow the constitutional rules for appointment and retention of Denver county court judges. Denver has adopted a system for a nominating commission to give the mayor a choice of names to appoint to the county court, and for retention elections for those appointees. DENVER REV. MUNI. CODE, §§ 4.1.4 to .5.

Further reading: THE FEDERAL COURTS OF THE TENTH CIRCUIT (James K. Logan ed., 1992); JOHN D.W. GUICE, THE ROCKY MOUNTAIN BENCH (1972) (nineteenth century courts).

CHAPTER 11

Suffrage and Elections, article VII

Figure 23. Minnie J. Reynolds, founder Denver Women's Press Club. 1895. Reynolds was Press Secretary for the successful 1893 women's suffrage referendum. History Colorado-Denver, Colorado.

Art. VII, Section 1. Voter qualifications

> Only a citizen of the United States who has attained the age of eighteen years, has resided in this state for such time as may be prescribed by law, and has been duly registered as a voter if required by law shall be qualified to vote at all elections.

In the 1876 Constitution, the franchise was for males over 21. This was an improvement over the territorial law, which had excluded blacks. Revised Statutes of Colorado, R.S. P. ch. 28, § 1 ("not being a negro or mulatto"[1]).

Section 1 was amended in 1901, to reflect the 1893 referendum in favor of female suffrage. In 1971, the Twenty-Sixth Amendment extended suffrage to persons aged 18–20; a 1988 Colorado amendment brought section 1 into alignment.

A 2020 amendment changed the opening words from "Every citizen" to "Only a citizen." The effect is to prevent legal resident aliens from voting. While federal law has always prohibited noncitizens from voting in federal elections, in the nineteenth century many states, Colorado included, allowed immigrants who had declared an intent to naturalize to vote in state and local elections. Today, San Francisco and some other cities allow noncitizens to vote in local elections. The 2020 amendment forecloses that possibility in Colorado.

Statutes for suffrage are in C.R.S. §§ 1-2-101 et seq. Some notable provisions: allowing pre-registration by 16-year-olds who will be 18 by election day (§ 101); rules of determining residence, including for homeless people (§ 102); rules of persons in military service, students living away from home, jail and prison inmates, and persons in mental institutions (§ 103); registration process (§ 201); county clerk and recorder duties (§ 202); online registration or changes in voter information, such as changing party (§ 202.5); Indian reservations (§ 203); information to be provided by the person registering (§ 204, including "The elector's gender identity, if the elector wishes to state it"); requiring affirmation, and criminal penalty for false registration (§ 205); persons in youth correctional facilities (§ 210.5); registration at driver's license facilities (§ 213);

[1] Mixed-race, including some black.

registration via course registration at state colleges (§ 213.5); change of address (§ 216); allowing registration on election day or shortly before (§ 217.7); allowing unaffiliated voters to vote in presidential primaries (§ 218.5, added by a 2016 statutory initiative); party change (§ 219); penalty for false statement of residence (§ 228).

Art. VII, Section 1a. Residents on federal land may vote

> Any person who otherwise meets the requirements of law for voting in this state shall not be denied the right to vote in an election because of residence on land situated within this state that is under the jurisdiction of the United States.

Added by the voters in 1970. This rectified a blatant violation of the Enabling Act. Pre-1970, persons residing on federal land (including military bases and Indian reservations) were not considered Colorado residents for voting purposes. *See Cuthair v. Montezuma-Cortez, Colo. Sch. Dist. No. RE-1*, 7 F. Supp. 2d 1152, 1161–62 (D. Colo. 1998) (describing the effect of 1970 amendment on reservation Indians).

The discussion of section 4, below, cites the U.S. supreme court Equal Protection decisions that impelled Colorado to fix the problem.

Art. VII, Section 2. Suffrage for women (repealed)

The 1876 Constitution provided that women could vote in school board elections, and that there would a statewide referendum on female suffrage for other elections. That referendum was defeated in 1877.

In 1892, the Populists had a great election.[2] In the 1893 House there were 27 Populists, 5 Democrats, and 33 Republicans. In the Senate, 13 Populists, 7 Democrats and 15 Republicans. Populist David Nichol was president of the Senate. Republican Elias Ammons (a future Democratic governor) was speaker of the House. Rep. J.T. Heath, a Populist from Montrose and Delta counties, sponsored HB 118, amending section 2 by deleting the word "male." It was duly put on the general election ballot, and on Nov. 7, 1893, was passed with 35,798 votes for, 29,451 votes against.

Section 2 was repealed in 1988, as obsolete. Federally the Nineteenth Amendment, prohibiting abridgement of the right to vote on account of sex, was ratified in 1920.[3]

---

[2] Formed in the early 1890s, the People's Party was commonly known as the "Populists." When William Jennings Bryan won the Democratic presidential nomination in 1896, the Populists gained ascendency within the Democratic party, so the separate party faded away. See JOHN D. HICKS, THE POPULIST REVOLT: A HISTORY OF THE FARMERS' ALLIANCE AND THE PEOPLE'S PARTY (1931). The party's first national platform, written in 1892 by former Republican senator Lyman Trumbull (author of the Thirteenth Amendment), denounced use of the federal militia against strikers, called for limits on the amount of property that could be transmitted by inheritance, no government issuance of bonds during peacetime, silver coinage at a 16:1 ratio to gold, and government ownership of all monopolies affecting the public interest, with employees to be protected by civil service rules.

In conclusion: "Resolved, That we inscribe on our banner, 'Down with monopolies and millionaire control! Up with the rights of man and the masses!' And under this banner we march to the polls and to victory." See David B. Kopel, *Lyman Trumbull: Author of the Thirteenth Amendment, Author of the Civil Rights Act, and the First Second Amendment Lawyer*, 47 LOYOLA U. OF CHICAGO LAW JOURNAL 1117 (2016).

[3] The ratification that made the Nineteenth Amendment the law of the land was accomplished in Tennessee in August 1920, by a single vote. Rep. Harry Burns represented an "anti" constituency, but his mother

In 1874, the U.S. supreme court held that Equal Protection Clause does not grant the elective franchise to women, nor is male-only suffrage a violation of the U.S. Constitution's Republican Form of Government guarantee, in article IV. *Minor v. Harpesett*, 88 U.S. 162 (1874).

Until California passed female suffrage in 1911, Denver was the largest U.S. city with women voters. Tom I. Romero, II, *Law and Equity in Colorado's 19th Century Suffrage Movement*, COLO. LAWYER, May 2003.

Further reading: Billie Barnes Jensen, *Let the Women Vote*, COLO. MAG. 42, Winter 1964; *Colorado Women's Suffrage Campaigns of the 1870s*, JOURNAL OF THE WEST, Apr. 1973; Marcia T. Goldstein & Rebecca A. Hunt, *From Suffrage to Centennial: A Research Guide to Colorado and National Women's Suffrage Sources*, COLO. HERITAGE, Spring 1993.

Amos Steck

by Jerry Kopel

There is an unknown hero in the Colorado battle to give women the right to vote. His name is Amos Steck. He served in the first, second, seventh and eighth territorial legislatures, and was a member of the state Senate from 1891 through 1894.

On Nov. 7, 1893, Colorado male voters recognized women should have the right to vote. But Steck knew it was the right thing to do back in 1870 during the eighth session of the Legislative Assembly of the Territory of Colorado.

On Jan. 4, 1870, territorial governor Edward M. McCook addressed the 13-member Council (now called the Senate) and the 26 member House. One portion of his message to "Fellow Citizens of the Council and House of Representatives" covered female suffrage:

> Our higher civilization has recognized woman's equality with man in all respects save one—suffrage...It rests with you to say whether Colorado will accept this reform...as our sister territory of Wyoming has done;[4] whether Colorado will be a leader in the movement or a follower; for the logic of a progressive civilization leads to the inevitable result of a universal suffrage.

Amos Steck, a Republican from Denver/Arapahoe, was appointed chairman of the council committee to consider this part of the governor's message.[5] On Jan. 19, 1870, he presented a nine-page report to the council.

If anyone thinks of early Colorado legislators as buffoons or drunken gold miners, they should read this extremely literate, well-written argument for women's suffrage.

Steck knew he had to find a way to make the male population of Colorado recognize it was to their interests to make the change. His report starts with a history of another disenfranchised group: Free "colored" males in 12 of the 13 original states were allowed to vote, as presently could the male "colored" population of the "several states lately in insurrection."

Steck then got to the issue at hand:

> We do not see how it can be made to appear that the proper sphere of woman is exclusively the social circle and the precincts of the fireside. We think it a matter

persuaded him to vote for ratification. See Jerry Kopel, *Woman's Suffrage becomes part of U.S. constitution thanks to Tennessee State Rep. Harry Burn*, COLO. STATESMAN, Aug. 20, 2001.

[4] In 1869. Wyoming was the first territory to enfranchise women for all elections. During the Early Republic, women had been allowed to vote in New Jersey, but female suffrage was abolished at the same time the state abolished the minimum property requirement for voters.

[5] Until the adoption of Denver Home Rule (art. XX) in 1902, Denver was part of Arapahoe County.

of much regret that the women of our country have been heretofore so little educated in the business concerns of life.

Scarcely any of them have made themselves at all familiar with the laws which govern the transfer of property, or regulate its distribution to themselves or their children, in case of the demise of fathers and husbands . . . Oftentimes they fall into the hands of sharpers through this neglect in their education . . .

Your committee, in the examination of this question, are not without hope that in the adoption of this new policy, the avenues of profitable employment to females will be widely extended in those lines of industry which are suitable to her sex and which are now almost exclusively filled by males. . . .

We have great hope that by making women electors, causing them to be more familiar with the laws, the manner of transacting business, putting them fully on an equality with men before the law, stimulating them to inquiring into the everyday affairs of life, they will gradually but surely remove the prejudice now existing against their employment as clerks, bookkeepers, saleswomen, and in all lighter but necessary labor now exclusively performed by males.

Its effect will be, if such results shall be attained, largely to contribute to remove from communities that class of unfortunates who live their brief existence upon the wages of sin. For it is undeniable that the want of proper employment, by means of which they may be enabled to live respectably . . . is the real cause of filling the haunts of infamy everywhere . . .

Give to women employment, put into her hand the ballot as a means by and through which she may demand and enforce her claims to such employment, for which she is as well fitted as her brother, and you remove the incentive which causes the fall . . .

The integrity of the opinion of women, the desire to be right and to do justice, whatever the results, we believe, as a rule, to be stronger in women than in men. Familiarize her with political questions, with all the details which men habitually examine as political partisans, and women in that respect becomes fully equal to the man.

Why should man and women quarrel any more when both vote, than when the husband votes alone? What is there in the relation of mother, sister, or daughter, that is incompatible with the relation of elector? Is there anything of the lovely and beautiful in woman in her social sphere, that would be destroyed by the right to vote?

What man has ever made the political views of a sweetheart the cause of declining a conjugal alliance, when beauty, grace, and loveliness had wooed her to his heart? And what is there after the consummation of their union, in an honest difference of views on political measures or men, that would excite discord between "two hearts that beat as one?" We repudiate the imputation as grossly unjust . . .

It is believed that all that is wanting to produce amongst women the number of distinguished characters equal with men, is opportunity. We cannot and do not anticipate that women will distinguish themselves in the barbarous art of war, which has made so many names immortal, nor in the rough or coarser labors of life, where the brawny, muscular strength of man is only equal to their accomplishment.

What we insist upon is OPPORTUNITY for women, to choose for themselves what they are best fitted to perform. And to that end we insist that women be clothed with the ballot, to enforce their claims to enter upon any of the labors of life for which they may deem themselves qualified equally well with men . . .

> We see no cause to shut out women from any of the civil offices necessary to be filled, however high and important they may be. We think that in places where integrity and high moral purpose is requisite, we may with great safety commit such trusts to women . . .
>
> With respectful deference to the opinions of that respectable class, who may differ with us, we may be permitted to say that the moral, intelligent, progressive, just, and conscientious portion of the community, who see in woman more than a subordinate, who see in her their equal, nay, their superior in many things, are hopefully anxious for her redemption from the thralldom into which ages of uniform legislation have unjustly condemned her . . .
>
> Your committee therefore recommends the repeal of so much of section one of chapter twenty-eight of the Revised Statutes as inhibits females from voting, and the enactment of such laws as will permit them to stand equal in all respects with men before the law.

Well, the 1870 bill for suffrage for women did not pass the legislature.

The Colorado Constitution, adopted by the people on July 1, 1876, gave the general assembly the option of authorizing women suffrage, if the expansion of suffrage was thereafter approved by a vote of the people in a general election.

When the question was put on the ballot in 1877, it lost 14,053 to 6,612. National suffragists blamed the 1877 result on "the Mexican vote." ELIZABETH CADY STANTON, SUSAN B. ANTHONY, ET AL., 4 THE HISTORY OF WOMEN'S SUFFRAGE 317 (1887). However, the margin of the 1877 was far too large to be ascribed to any one ethnic group.

The first women legislators

By Jerry Kopel

In the 1894 election, six women ran as state legislative candidates—three Republicans and three Populists (running on a fusion ticket with the Democrats). It was good year for Republicans. They swept Populist governor Davis E. Waite out of power, kept the House and took over the Senate. The three Republican women won, and in 1895 became the first women elected to serve in a state legislature anywhere in the United States. Each of them would serve a single term.

Five of the six women contestants were from Arapahoe County, which at that time included Denver. The sixth woman, Republican Carrie Clyde Holly, was from Pueblo.

Clara Cressingham (age 32 when elected) and Frances Klock were the other two successful Republican candidates. Even though newcomers, were awarded power positions. Klock chaired the Indian and Veterans Affairs Committee, sponsored successful legislation to create a home for delinquent girls, and later served as director of the home. Cressingham was elected secretary of the Republican house caucus.

Pueblo's Holly often stood up to the Republican leadership and passed bills by gaining votes from Democrats and Populists. She was born in 1857 and was an attorney from New York who came to Colorado in 1889. She married Charles F. Holly, who had been speaker of the house in the territorial legislature's first session, begun Sept. 9, 1861, in Denver. Charles Holly later served on the Colorado supreme court. In 1895 she was 38, with two children, and he was 74 Carrie Clyde Holly focused on suffrage, sex discrimination, and crimes. She introduced 14 bills. Klock had seven bills, and Cressingham four. Each of them passed two bills into law.

Historian Elizabeth Cox's article *The Three Who Came First*, STATE LEGISLATURES, Nov. 1994, explained that during the 1894 campaign, Republican Holly charged Populist gov. Waite with "misrule" and "anarchy." Holly claimed Waite "was not a true friend of women," because in his inaugural address he had only called for female suffrage in municipal elections.

Rep. Holly introduced the first state legislative bill by a woman, HB 24, a proposed Equal Rights Amendment to the state constitution. It did not pass. In 1972, the people added an amendment for "Equality of the Sexes" to the Bill of Rights. Art. II, § 29.

Rep. Holly's age of consent bill, HB 59, passed, and drew the largest applause and criticism. HB 59 did not mention prostitution, but that was the real subject. It defined as statutory rape any sex by a male over 14 with a female under 18, regardless of consent.

HB 59 did not interfere with the 1876 statute allowing females under 18 and males under 21 to be married with the consent of their parents or guardians.

Figure 24. Clara Cressingham. History Colorado-Denver, Colorado.

Because HB 59 had to go through a conference committee, it did not have the honor of being the first law sponsored by a female legislator. That honor went to HB 391 by Rep. Cressingham, "Encouraging the Sugar Beet Industry." It set a bounty of $3 per ton on sugar beets raised in the state and sold to a factory within the state borders.

All three House women played an important role in the passage of Senate Bill 89, which provided that a married woman is the joint guardian of the children, with equal powers, rights, and duties as the husband.

Art. VII, Section 3. Educational qualification of voters (repealed)

The 1876 Constitution had allowed the general assembly to set educational qualifications for voters. The idea was based on an 1857 Massachusetts statute. No such legislation was ever enacted in Colorado.

In the former Confederate states, literacy tests for voters were applied with extreme racial bias. The bias could have been avoided by an objective test, such as a short multiple-choice exam, but the objective in those states was a malleable test that was able to be administered by county clerks in an arbitrary manner.

In 1965, the federal Voting Rights Act outlawed literacy tests for voting. 52 U.S.C. § 10303. Section 3 of the Colorado Constitution was repealed in 1990.

Colorado in the nineteenth century did have a serious problem with voter illiteracy. The ballot form that is familiar today was adopted in Colorado in 1891 and was known as the "Australian Ballot." *See Peter Brent, The Australian ballot: Not the secret ballot*, 41 AUSTRALIAN J. OF

POLITICAL SCIENCE 39 (2006). The voter is given a single ballot, which contains the names of all candidates from all parties. Before that, parties would distribute ballots containing only the names of their candidates, and voters could simply deposit the single-party ballot in the ballot box.

After 1891, only ballots containing all candidates were acceptable. But instead of voting for candidates one by one, a voter could choose all the candidates of a single party, by marking an X at the top of the ballot. For example, for "Democratic ticket."

Parties catered to illiterate voters by placing emblems for the party next to the party's name. In Colorado, Democrats had the rooster, the Republicans an eagle, the Miner's Party a miner, the People's Party a cottage home, and the Prohibitionists an American flag. Ballot emblems were prohibited in 1899. 1899 Colo. Sess. Laws ch. 94, at 177; currently codified at C.R.S. § 1-5-409. *See* Frank Gibbard, *Of Roosters and Eagles: Colorado's Voting Emblem Cases*, COLO. LAWYER (Jan. 2006), *reprinted in* Frank Gibbard et al., STEAM, STEEL & STATUTES: TRUE TALES FROM COLORADO LEGAL HISTORY (2010) (reprints of legal history articles from *Colorado Lawyer*, 2002–2010).

Art. VII, Section 4. Voting residence not changed by military service, schooling, or confinement

> For the purpose of voting and eligibility to office, no person shall be deemed to have gained a residence by reason of his or her presence, or lost it by reason of his or her absence, while in the civil or military service of the state, or of the United States, nor while a student at any institution of learning, nor while kept at public expense in any asylum, nor while confined in public prison.

This ensures that military personnel, other government employees, or students who are outside the state can still vote. It is effectuated by C.R.S. §§ 2-3-102 & 103.

If a state denied the vote to persons living in federal enclaves, such as military bases, that would violate the Equal Protection clause of the Fourteenth Amendment. *Evans v. Cornman*, 398 U.S. 419 (1970). This is also true for military personnel, including those who live off the base. *Carrington v. Rash*, 380 U.S. 89 (1965).

Art. VII, Section 5. Voters may not be arrested while voting, or going to and from

> Voters shall in all cases, except treason, felony or breach of the peace, be privileged from arrest during their attendance at elections, and in going to and returning therefrom.

This parallels the Speech and Debate Clause that protects legislators. Art. V, § 16.

Art. VII, Section 6. Only qualified electors may hold civil or military office

> No person except a qualified elector shall be elected or appointed to any civil or military office in the state.

This reserves the government of Colorado to adult citizens who are eligible to vote. Persons who do not bear allegiance to Colorado may not be part of the higher levels of government. Section 6 is effectuated by statute. Persons who are ineligible for an office for any reason (including minimum age for certain offices, or admission to the Colorado bar for attorney general) may not appear on the ballot. No one may run for two offices at once, but this limit does not apply to special district boards (*e.g.*, RTD). C.R.S. § 1-4-501.

Under modern Equal Protection doctrine, state discrimination based on alienage is subject to strict scrutiny, whereas congressional discrimination need only pass the rational basis test. *See, e.g.*, *Mathews v. Diaz*, 426 U.S. 67 (1976) (no Medicare eligibility if you have lived in U.S. for fewer than five years).

This is an example of the Plenary Power Doctrine, which grants nearly unfettered, unreviewable power to certain government actors. Leading examples are the presidential pardon power and congressional immigration law. *See, e.g.*, David A. Martin, *Why Immigration's Plenary Power Doctrine Endures*, 68 OKLA. L. REVIEW 29 (2015).

Although strictly limited in many respects, states may reserve a "governmental function" or "political function" for citizens if the functions are part of democratic self-government, such as voting, serving in elected office, and government jobs that exercise discretion. *See Ambach v. Norwick*, 441 U.S. 68 (1979) (upholding application to public school teachers; "a State need show only some rational relationship between the interest sought to be protected and the limiting classification"); *Cabell v. Chavez-Salido*, 454 U.S. 432 (1982) (peace officers). The *Cabell* test is:

> First, the specificity of the classification will be examined: a classification that is substantially overinclusive or underinclusive tends to undercut the governmental claim that the classification serves legitimate political ends . . . Second, even if the classification is sufficiently tailored, it may be applied in the particular case only to "persons holding state elective or important nonelective executive, legislative, and judicial positions," those officers who "participate directly in the formulation, execution, or review of broad public policy" and hence "perform functions that go to the heart of representative government."

Id. at 440.

A state cannot bar a legal resident alien from being a notary public. *Bernal v. Fainter*, 467 U.S. 216 (1984). Or an attorney. *Cf. In re Thomas,* 16 Colo. 441, 27 P. 707 (1891) (attorneys are not civil officers, and hence women may be admitted to the bar, even though they cannot vote).

Unlawful aliens are not a suspect class under the Equal Protection Clause. But states may not bar them from public schools. *Plyler v. Doe*, 457 U.S. 202 (1982). Except for public schools, a state may deny any other form of state aid to unlawful aliens. Because of federal preemption (not because of Equal Protection), states can, at most, enforce other laws aimed at unlawful aliens (*e.g.*, barring the knowing employment of an unlawful alien) to the extent that they mirror federal laws.

Art. VII, Section 7. General election shall be held on days prescribed by law

> The general election shall be held on such day as may be prescribed by law.

The legislature has prescribed that general elections be held on the first Tuesday after the first Monday in November, in even-numbered years. C.R.S. § 1-4-201. This is the same date that Congress has set for federal elections, since 1872. 2 U.S.C. § 7. *Cf.* U.S. CONST., art. I, § 4 (States shall set time, place, and manner of electing congresspersons, "but the Congress may at any time by Law make or alter such Regulations").

Under the Colorado Constitution, state house and state senate elections must be held on the same day as the federal general election. Art. V, § 2(1). Like Colorado, most states hold their state offices general election on the same day as the federal election. New Jersey and Virginia hold state general elections in odd-numbered years.

In Colorado, general elections in odd-numbered years are sometimes held for proposed tax or spending increases, pursuant to the Taxpayer's Bill of Rights, art. X, § 20(3)(a).[6]

The 1876 Constitution had provided for general elections annually. The odd-year elections were necessary because county commissioners had three-year terms, and supreme court justices had nine-year terms. Today, the commissioners have four-year terms, and the justices ten. Art. VI, § 7 (justices), art. XIV § 6 (counties).

A *general* election in the sense of section 7 is for service in the state or county government, or for related initiatives or referenda. The Constitution does not specify a date for other elections, such as for municipalities or school districts. By statute, school district elections are to be held on the first Tuesday in November in odd-numbered years. C.R.S. §§ 22-31-104, 22-31-131. The odd-year elections have relatively lower turnout, and thus provide an advantage for school employee unions, whose members vote reliably, and whose skills at turning out supporters make a bigger difference in a smaller electorate.

Although the Denver Public Schools Board is chosen in the usual odd-year elections, by statute the board could have a different election day. The DPS board must consist of five members elected in districts, and two elected at large. C.R.S. § 22-31-131.

As for municipal elections such as mayor or city council, the majority of voters in a municipality may set municipal elections for any day they choose. C.R.S. § 31-1-101(10).

Art. VII, Section 8. Rules for paper ballots and voting machines

> All elections by the people shall be by ballot, and in case paper ballots are required to be used, no ballots shall be marked in any way whereby the ballot can be identified as the ballot of the person casting it. The election officers shall be sworn or affirmed not to inquire or disclose how any elector shall have voted. In all cases of contested election in which paper ballots are required to be used, the ballots cast may be counted and compared with the list of voters, and examined under such safeguards and regulations as may be provided by law. Nothing in this section, however, shall be construed to prevent the use of any machine or mechanical contrivance for the purpose of receiving and registering the votes cast at any election, provided that secrecy in voting is preserved.
>
> When the governing body of any county, city, city and county or town, including the city and county of Denver, and any city, city and county or town which may be governed by the provisions of special charter, shall adopt and purchase a voting machine, or voting machines, such governing body may provide for the payment therefor by the issuance of interest-bearing bonds, certificates of indebtedness or other obligations, which shall be a charge upon such city, city and county, or town; such bonds, certificates or other obligations may be made payable at such time or

---

[6] Under TABOR, the odd-year elections shall be on the first Tuesday in November. So Tuesday, November 1, could be an-odd year election date. Under the even-year rule (first Tuesday after the first Monday), a general election could not be held on Nov. 1.

> times, not exceeding ten years from date of issue, as may be determined, but shall not be issued or sold at less than par.

The secret ballot is comprehensively protected by section 8. The current language dates from 1946.

The secret ballot was a reform of the nineteenth century. It protects the autonomy of the individual's vote.

The rules for voting machines are set by C.R.S. § 1-7-401 et. seq.; *see also* C.R.S. § 31-10-701 et seq. (voting machines in municipal elections).

Art. VII, Section 9. Limits on protection against self-incrimination in election cases

> In trials of contested elections, and for offenses arising under the election law, no person shall be permitted to withhold his testimony on the ground that it may criminate himself, or subject him to public infamy; but such testimony shall not be used against him in any judicial proceeding, except for perjury in giving such testimony.

In other words, illegal voters may be compelled to testify in election contests—even though their truthful testimony would incriminate them. Accordingly, truthful testimony in an election contest may not be used against the witness in a separate criminal proceeding. The Colorado Bill of Rights provides that a person may not be compelled to self-incriminate in a criminal case. Art. II, § 18.

For purposes of section 9, "trials of contested elections" means only a post-voting challenge. It does not include disputes over pre-election issues. *People v. Onesimo Romero*, 746 P.2d 534 (Colo. 1987) (does not include petition to be on primary election ballot; defendant's testimony in a civil case involving the petition may be used against him in a criminal prosecution).

For election contest process, see arts. IV, § 3; V, § 10; VII, § 12.

Art. VII, Section 10. Prisoners may not vote

> No person while confined in any public prison shall be entitled to vote; but every such person who was a qualified elector prior to such imprisonment, and who is released therefrom by virtue of a pardon, or by virtue of having served out his full term of imprisonment, shall without further action, be invested with all the rights of citizenship, except as otherwise provided in this constitution.

Some states bar convicted felons from voting for lifetime. These laws are compliant with the U.S. Constitution. *See, e.g.*, *Richardson v. Ramirez*, 418 U.S. 24 (1974) (lifetime bans do not violate Fourteenth Amendment, although some voting restrictions are subject to strict scrutiny). Indeed, section 2 of the Fourteenth Amendment authorizes disenfranchisement "for participation in rebellion, or other crime."

Colorado, however, restores voting rights when the convict has finished his or her sentence. A statute specifies that post-confinement parole must be completed. C.R.S. § 1-2-103(4).

Pretrial detainees are allowed to vote. *In re Interrog. of U.S. Dist. Ct.*, 642 P.2d 496 (Colo. 1982). So are persons on probation. *Sterling v. Archambault*, 138 Colo. 222, 332 P.2d 994 (1958).

Art. VII, Section 11. General assembly shall pass laws to secure the purity of elections

> The general assembly shall pass laws to secure the purity of elections, and guard against abuses of the elective franchise.

A statute to purge inactive voters—those who did not vote in last biennial election—from the voting rolls is a proper exercise of the duty of the general assembly. *Duprey v. Anderson*, 184 Colo. 70, 518 P.2d 807 (1974).

The necessity of purity of elections means that home rule cities must still obey state election laws. *Mauff v. People*, 52 Colo. 562, 123 P. 101 (1912).

A ballot form that had no room for write-in votes for undeclared candidates violated section 11, as well as the Bill of Rights guarantee that "All elections shall be free and open; and no power, civil or military, shall at any time interfere to prevent the free exercise of the right of suffrage." (art. II, §5). *Littlejohn v. People ex rel. Desch*, 52 Colo. 217, 121 P. 159 (1912).

Art. VII, Section 12. Election contests

> The general assembly shall, by general law, designate the courts and judges by whom the several classes of election contests, not herein provided for, shall be tried, and regulate the manner of trial, and all matters incident thereto, but no such law shall apply to any contest arising out of an election held before its passage.

When the Constitution says, "courts and judges," does this include city councils? The Colorado courts have said "yes," upholding laws making city councils the judges in municipal election contests. *Booth v. County Court*, 18 Colo. 561, 33 P. 581 (1893) (applying state statute giving judgement power to city council); *People ex rel. Barton v. Londoner*, 22 P. 764 (Colo. 1889) (Denver charter); *City Council of Cripple Creek v. Hanley*, 19 Colo. App. 390, 390, 75 P. 600 (1904).

The statutes for election contests are in C.R.S. §§ 1-11-201 et seq.

CHAPTER 12

State Institutions, article VIII

Art. VIII, Section 1. Established and supported by state

> Educational, reformatory and penal institutions, and those for the benefit of insane, blind, deaf and mute, and such other institutions as the public good may require, shall be established and supported by the state, in such manner as may be prescribed by law.

This is one of many Colorado provisions requiring the state government to provide for social welfare. In contrast, the U.S. Constitution is mostly silent on the subject, and the enumerated powers have almost nothing to do with social welfare—a topic that the U.S. Constitution leaves to the states.

Since the 1930s, U.S. supreme court decisions have allowed Congress to exercise the spending power for things unrelated to carrying out the enumerated powers. Today, the largest portion the Colorado budget is federal grants and state matches for federal welfare programs, especially Medicaid.

For the state institutions mentioned in section 1, the implementing statutes are:

Educational

University of Colorado. Colo. Rev. Stats. § 23-20-101 et seq.
State university. § 23-31-101 et seq.
Colorado State University-Pueblo. § 23-31.5-101 et seq.

State colleges. §§ 23-31.5-101 et seq., 23-51-101 et seq., 23-52-101 et seq., 23-53-101 et seq., 23-54-101 et seq., 23-56-101 et seq.
University of Northern Colorado. § 23-40-101 et seq.
Colorado School of Mines. § 23-41-101 et seq.
Community colleges. § 23-60-101 et seq.
Junior colleges. § 23-71-101 et seq.

Reformatory and penal

Correctional facilities. § 17-19-101 et seq.
Children's diagnostic center. § 23-23-101 et seq.

Insane

Colorado mental health institute of Pueblo. § 27-93-101 et seq.
Fort Logan mental health center. § 27-94-101 et seq.
Psychopathic hospital. § 23-22-101 et seq.

Blind, deaf, and mute

School for the deaf and the blind. § 22-80-101.5 et seq.

Priority for the involuntarily confined, with much discretion otherwise

The Panic of 1893 was second-worst economic downtown in U.S. history, exceeded only the Great Depression. It hit Colorado hard. In the view of most Coloradans, the Panic occurred because the Congress had repealed a statutory mandate that the federal government buy certain quantities of silver every year, to mint. The economies of Colorado and other Rocky Mountain states depended on silver mining. The majority of the U.S., however, felt that too much silver coinage was the root cause of the bad economy; in presidential elections, most states chose a candidate favoring a gold standard, not bimetallism (silver & gold).

Regardless of what was at fault, state tax revenues plunged. When state revenues are inadequate to support all of the section 1 institutions, what does the Constitution require? In 1894, the Colorado supreme court held that the spending preference should be for people are involuntarily confined. *Goodykoontz v. People ex rel. Sawyer*, 20 Colo. 374, 38 P. 473 (1894).

The constitutional mandate to establish particular institutions does not require the State to assume the full burden care for everyone. *See Wicks v. City and County of Denver*, 61 Colo. 266, 156 P. 1100 (1916) (refusing to issue mandamus to transfer county's insane prisoners to the state institution for the insane, when the state institution was already full).

The general assembly has great discretion whether to establish "other institutions." *Hessick v. Moynihan,* 83 Colo. 43, 262 P. 907 (1927).

Art. VIII, Section 2. General assembly may not change seat of government

> The general assembly shall have no power to change or to locate the seat of government of the state, which shall remain at the city and county of Denver.

The 1876 Constitution had provided that voters would choose a permanent seat of government by election in 1881. Denver won a solid majority, far outpolling all other contenders.

Table 4. Seat of government 1881 election results. WILBUR FISKE STONE, 1 HISTORY OF COLORADO 195 (1918).

Denver	30,248
Pueblo	6,047
Colorado Springs	4,790
Canon City	2,788
Others	1,600
Total	45,473

The current text, adopted in 1988, removes obsolete language.

The State Capitol building

Henry C. Brown was an early homesteader in Denver. Pursuant to the 1862 federal Homestead Act, he acquired title to unoccupied federal land by occupying and improving it. Brown apparently had a knack for real estate; in 1892 he would build the Brown Palace Hotel, then and now the most iconic in Denver. Back in 1868, he donated 10 acres to the Colorado Territory for construction of a capitol building for the future state.

Statehood was achieved in 1876, but the following years saw no start on constructing a capitol. Exasperated, Brown sued for return of the land. He lost, but the suit forced state officials finally to get to work.

The official dedication—the laying of the cornerstone—was held on July 4, 1890. The cornerstone is 20 tons of hollowed stone, with a 5-ton cap. Inside the cornerstone is a copper box of patriotic memorabilia.[1] The cornerstone is integral part to the building, so its contents will only be seen again if the Capitol is destroyed. The final construction for full occupation of the Capitol was completed in 1896.

The cornerstone was rededicated August 4, 1990, with burial of a time capsule to be opened in July 2090.

---

[1] Including: a 43-star American flag, a copy of Zebulon Pike's journal, speeches from the ceremony, gold and silver coins, and autographs of leading Colorado citizens. Other items in the cornerstone include a Bible, the U.S. and Colorado Constitutions, state records, and state historical data.

There was one notable item not connected to Colorado: "a walking stick made from a piece of the keel of Old Ironsides." 1959–61 COLORADO YEARBOOK (the yearbooks recorded facts and developments in state government). Old Ironsides is the nickname for the most honored ship in U.S. naval history. Commissioned as the USS Constitution 1794, she protected American merchant ships in the 1798–1800 Quasi-War with France. Then she fought and defeated the Barbary pirates the First Barbary War—against North African raiders who seized American ships and enslaved the passengers and crew. In the War of 1812, the USS Constitution defeated five warships of the British Navy, the greatest in the world. Her victory over HMS Guerriere won her the nickname "Old Ironsides." Too beloved to ever be scrapped, she sailed to the Paris Exposition of 1878. She most recently sailed under her own power in 2012, celebrating the 200th anniversary of victory over the Guerriere.

The Colorado Hall of Fame

Adorning the inner dome of the Colorado State Capitol are the sixteen images of the "Colorado Hall of Fame."[2]

Jim Baker. Starting in the 1820s, the mountain men were the middlemen in trade between Indians and Americans. Baker was among the most notable in Colorado. In 1858, after his itinerant days were over, he built a cabin and toll bridge north of Denver.[3]

Casimero Barela. Territorial legislator, sheriff, Colorado Convention delegate, and then Colorado's longest-serving state senator, 1876–1916. In the territorial legislature, Barela sponsored the bill to publish state statutes in Spanish. At the Convention, he proposed the provisions that published the proposed Constitution in Spanish and German.[4]

William Byers. Founder of the *Rocky Mountain News*, Colorado's first newspaper, which published until 2009.[5]

Dr. Richard Buckingham. Helped establish the School of Deaf and Blind, one of the state institutions described in article VIII, § 1.

Kit Carson. Based mainly in Taos, Colonel Carson "ranged the Great Plains, the Colorado Rockies, and the Uinta Basin."[6] He guided John C. Frémont's 1842–1846 expeditions.[7] He led New Mexico troops who fought alongside Colorado militia in New Mexico during the Civil War.[8] Future Colorado supreme court justice Wilbur Fiske Stone called Carson

> pre-eminent among the pathfinders . . . [H]is long career, ennobled by hardship and danger, is unsullied by the record of a littleness or meanness. He was nature's model of a gentlemen, kindly of heart, tolerant to all men . . . leaving behind him a name and memory to be cherished by his countrymen so long as modesty, valor, unobtrusive worth, charity and true chivalry survive among men.[9]

He is the namesake of Kit Carson County, Colorado, as well as Carson City, the capital city of Nevada. The Kit Carson Highway takes travelers through southeastern Colorado into New Mexico.[10]

Sometimes an Indian fighter, Carson was also a mediator. After he defeated the Utes, he became their trusted intermediary and advocate. In the 1860s, Utes joined U.S. Army forces led by Carson in war against the Navajo. *See* chapter 4 (art. II, § 26).

In 1868, Colorado Territorial governor Alexander Cameron Hunt and Kit Carson negotiated with the Utes "the most generous treaty ever made between the U.S. government and any Native

---

[2] This section relies in part on DEREK R. EVERETT, THE COLORADO STATE CAPITOL: HISTORY, POLITICS, PRESERVATION (2005).

[3] STEPHEN J. LEONARD & THOMAS J. NOEL, DENVER: MINING CAMP TO METROPOLIS 29 (1st ed. 1990); RICHENS WOOTTON AS TOLD TO HOWARD LOUIS CONRAD, UNCLE DICK WOOTTON: THE PIONEER FRONTIERSMAN OF THE ROCKY MOUNTAIN REGION 103 n.37 (M.M. Quaife ed., Narrative Press 2001) (1890).

[4] JOSÉ E. FERNÁNDEZ, THE BIOGRAPHY OF CASIMIRO BARELA 16–18, 38–42 (A. Gabriel Meléndez trans., 2003) (1911). Originally a Democrat, Barela switched to Republican in the twentieth century because he disagreed with the Democrats' move to the left. *Id.* at xviii–xxix.

[5] ROBERT L. PERKIN, THE FIRST HUNDRED YEARS 1859–1959: AN INFORMAL HISTORY OF DENVER AND THE ROCKY MOUNTAIN NEWS (1959).

[6] JOHN D. BAIRD, HAWKEN RIFLES: THE MOUNTAIN MAN'S CHOICE 7 (1968).

[7] M. MORGAN ESTERGREEN, KIT CARSON: A PORTRAIT IN COURAGE 89, 103, 106, 126 (1962).

[8] *Id.* at 230–31.

[9] 1 FRANK HALL, HISTORY OF THE STATE OF COLORADO 161 (1889) (quoting Wilbur Fiske Stone, *Death of Kit Carson*, COLO. CHIEFTAIN, June 1, 1868 at 1).

[10] ESTERGREEN at 279. Carson passed away at Ft. Lyon, Colorado, in 1868. Id. at 275–78.

American group."[11] The new Consolidated Ute Reservation for Utes in Colorado and New Mexico included most of the western third of Colorado—over 2,000 acres per Ute.[12]

In the Denver Civic Center, the Pioneer Monument marks the end of the Smoky Hill Trail, an Indian trail from central Kansas that was used by pioneers in the Gold Rush and thereafter. At the top of the fountain, rising on horseback from the basin, is the bronze figure of Kit Carson wearing buckskin, carrying a rifle, and pointing westward. The monument also features a prospector, a trapper, and a pioneer mother. She cradles a baby in one arm and holds a rifle in the other.

After vandals toppled a nearby Colorado State Capitol statue honoring Colorado soldiers who died in the Civil War, the Denver city government "proactively" removed the Carson statue in June 2020.

Figure 25. Kit Carson.

Another equestrian statue of Carson is in Kit Carson Park, in Trinidad, Colorado, next to a Santa Fe Trail route.[13]

James Denver. Governor of Kansas Territory, which included part of future Colorado during the first phase of the Gold Rush.

John Lewis Dyer. Methodist-Episcopal preacher in the mining camps, known for pointing his gun at drunks who tried to interrupt his services.[14]

Benjamin Eaton. Developer of irrigation near Greeley, which was a cooperative agricultural colony.[15] Eaton helped Colorado become self-sufficient in food. He served as governor 1885–87.

John Evans. Colorado territorial governor. Conscientious and serious, but with a fatal misjudgment. Due to his conduct that allowed the Sand Creek Massacre to take place, he was ordered to resign in July 1865 by U.S. secretary of state William Seward.[16] Aware that a political career was over, Evans put his energy into civic and educational projects, such as co-founding the University of Denver.

William Gilpin. First governor of the Colorado Territory. With bold action, he saved Colorado from Confederate invasion.[17]

Nathaniel Hill. Formerly a professor of chemistry at Brown University, Hill discovered how to efficiently smelt gold from refractory ore. Without Hill's innovation, Colorado might have

---

[11] EUGENE H. BERWANGER, THE RISE OF THE CENTENNIAL STATE: COLORADO TERRITORY, 1861–76, at 38–39 (2007); ESTERGREEN at 272–73; Treaty with the Ute, 1868, Mar. 2, 1868, 15 Stat. 619; 2 INDIAN AFFAIRS: LAWS AND TREATIES 990–96 (CHARLES J. KAPPLER ed., 2d ed. 1904). Hunt served as Governor from May 1867 to June 1869. He had come to Colorado in 1858. BERWANGER at 55–56.

[12] Discussed further in chapter 6.E.

[13] The Sante Fe Trail led from southern Missouri to Sante Fe, New Mexico. A spur led to southern Colorado.

[14] JOHN L. DYER, THE SNOW-SHOE ITINERANT: AN AUTOBIOGRAPHY OF THE REV. JOHN L. DYER (Andesite Press 2015) (1890).

[15] Named for Horace Greeley, famed New York newspaperman who advocated westward migration and the founding of cooperative colonies.

[16] CAROL TURNER, FORGOTTEN HEROES & VILLAINS OF SAND CREEK 36 (2010) (quoting Letter from William H. Seward, U.S. Sec'y of State, to John Evans, Governor of the Territory of Colo., July 18, 1865). The 1864–65 Colorado War and the Sand Creek Massacre are discussed in chapter 6, "Fighting for Survival."

[17] Discussed in chapter 6.B.

collapsed economically in the late 1860s. Hill's Boston & Denver Smelting Company may be the most important corporation in Colorado history. Professor Hill served as mayor of Black Hawk, territorial legislator, and U.S. senator.

Bela Metcalf Hughes. Co-founder of the Overland Stage Company, which traveled between central Kansas and Denver, on the old Smoky Hill trail. President of the first Denver-Cheyenne railroad.

Figure 26. 100th anniversary of the Pony Express.

Frances Jacobs. Organizer of help for the destitute, a program that later became Community Chest. Started free kindergartens. Founder of the National Jewish Hospital, which today is the leading respiratory hospital in the United States. From territorial days to the present, persons suffering from tuberculosis or other respiratory ailments have found relief in Colorado's thin and pure air.

Alexander Majors. Carried supplies to forts and stations in the West. Helped start the Pony Express, which beginning in 1861 delivered mail to Denver.

Chief Ouray. A leader of the Southern Utes, the tribe with the longest inhabitation of Colorado. Adroitly negotiated the best deals he could.[18]

William Jackson Palmer. Founder of Colorado Springs, and of the Denver & Rio Grande Railroad.

Art. VIII, Section 3. Governor may change seat of government during disaster emergencies

> (1) When the seat of government shall have been located in the city and county of Denver as provided in section 2 of this article, the location thereof shall not thereafter be changed, except by a vote of two-thirds of all the qualified electors of the state voting on that question, at a general election, at which the question of location of the seat of government shall have been submitted by the general assembly.
>
> (2) Notwithstanding the provisions of subsection (1) of this section, if the governor determines that a disaster emergency exists that substantially affects the ability of the state government to operate in the city and county of Denver, the governor may issue an executive order declaring a disaster emergency. After declaring the disaster emergency and after consulting with the chief justice of the supreme court, the president of the senate, and the speaker of the house of representatives, the governor may designate a temporary meeting location for the general assembly.
>
> (3) After the declaration of a disaster emergency by the governor, the general assembly shall convene at the temporary meeting location, whether during regular session or in a special session convened by the governor or by written request by two-thirds of the members of each house. The general assembly, acting by bill, may then designate a temporary location for the seat of government. The bill shall

[18] Discussed in chapter 6.E.

contain a date on which the temporary location of the seat of government shall expire.

(4) As used in this section:

(a) "Disaster emergency" means the occurrence or imminent threat of widespread or severe damage, injury, illness, or loss of life or property resulting from an epidemic or a natural, man-made, or technological cause.

(b) "Seat of government" means the location of the legislative, executive, and judicial branches of the state of Colorado.

Once the seat of government was established by vote, section 3 was revised to make Denver the permanent seat of government. So permanent that it is harder to change than anything else in the Colorado Constitution. To move the seat of government away from Denver 1: the general assembly must refer the question to the people; 2: two-thirds of the people must approve.

Nothing else in the Constitution requires a two-thirds vote of the people. Nothing else in the Constitution requires that a change be made only if the general assembly has referred the question; all other constitutional changes may be made by initiative of the people alone, with no prerequisite for general assembly action.

The amendment allowing a temporary move of the seat of the government during a disaster emergency was added in 2010. The previous year, the legislature passed a Joint Rule exempting itself during declared emergencies from the constitutional 120 calendar days limit on regular legislative sessions. *See* chapter 8 (art. V, § 7). The 2010 constitutional amendment for moving the seat of government during emergencies was properly presented to the people for adoption. The legislature should have followed a similar course in requesting an exemption from the session limits.

Art. VIII, Section 4. (repealed)

Section 4 of the 1876 Constitution had provided that state money could not be spent on the capitol building and grounds until a permanent site was chosen. It was repealed in 1988.

Art. VIII, Section 5. State higher education institutions

(1) The following educational institutions are declared to be state institutions of higher education: The university at Boulder, Colorado Springs, and Denver; the university at Fort Collins; the school of mines at Golden; and such other institutions of higher education as now exist or may hereafter be established by law if they are designated by law as state institutions. The establishment, management, and abolition of the state institutions shall be subject to the control of the state, under the provisions of the constitution and such laws and regulations as the general assembly may provide; except that the regents of the university at Boulder, Colorado Springs, and Denver may, whenever in their judgment the needs of that institution demand such action, establish, maintain, and conduct all or any part of the schools of medicine, dentistry, nursing, and pharmacy of the university, together with hospitals and supporting facilities and programs related to health, at Denver; and further, that nothing in this section shall be construed to prevent state educational institutions from giving temporary lecture courses in any part of the state, or conducting class excursions for the purpose of investigation and study; and provided further, that subject to prior approval by the general assembly,

> nothing in this section shall be construed to prevent the state institutions of higher education from hereafter establishing, maintaining, and conducting or discontinuing centers, medical centers, or branches of such institutions in any part of the state.
>
> (2) The governing boards of the state institutions of higher education, whether established by this constitution or by law, shall have the general supervision of their respective institutions and the exclusive control and direction of all funds of and appropriations to their respective institutions, unless otherwise provided by law.

The original five institutions were the "university at Boulder," the Colorado School of Mines (Golden), the Colorado Agricultural College (Fort Collins) (in 1935 renamed Colorado State Coll. of Agricultural & Mechanic Arts; in 1957 re-renamed Colo. State U.); and the Institute for the Education of Mutes (Colo. Springs) (later, Colo. Sch. for the Deaf and Blind). For more on the University of Colorado, see Art. IX, §§ 12–13

The cities that hosted the above institutions were proud and jealous. They were not inclined to allow satellite campuses. Yet over time, the Constitution was amended to allow the core educational institutions to establish branches. The first step was a 1909 amendment (revised 1922) allowing CU to conduct part of its graduate education in Denver.

The biggest step was the final sentence of subsection (1). Adopted in 1972, it allowed state higher education institutions to create branches anywhere, subject to prior approval by the general assembly. CU-Denver, CU-Colorado Springs, and CSU-Pueblo are among the fruits.

Exactly how special is the University of Colorado?

Only three institutions of higher education are specifically referenced in the Colorado Constitution: the university of Boulder, the one in Fort Collins, and the school of mines in Golden.

The University of Colorado has sometimes argued that being specifically mentioned in the Constitution—plus having an elected Board of Regents (art. IX, § 12)—means that the University does not have to comply with general statewide laws. The University is compelled only if the legislature expressly states, "Mother may I make this law applicable to the University of Colorado?" *See Associated Students of University of Colorado v. Regents of University of Colorado,* 189 Colo. 482. 543 P.2d 59 (1975) (Regents need not comply with Open Meeting Law); *Uberoi v. University of Colorado*, 686 P.2d 785 (Colo. 1984) (Open Records Act, same).

Figure 27. Old Main, first building at the University of Colorado.

The doctrine has not been read broadly by subsequent decisions. *Colorado Civil Rights Com'n ex rel. Ramos v. Regents of the University of Colorado*, 759 P.2d 726 (1988) (State Civil Rights Commission has jurisdiction over tenure denial allegedly based on professor's national origin or ancestry, even though state statute did not expressly name CU); *Students for Concealed Carry on Campus, LLC v. Regents of University of Colorado*, 271 P.3d 496 (Colo. 2012) (CU not exempt from Concealed Carry Act; the CCA's intent for a uniform statewide system was clear and unmistakable).

Lectures, concerts, and theater are educational, but watching football isn't

The City of Boulder may not charge an admission tax on public events related to CU's educational mission, such as lectures, concerts, or theater. Boulder may tax football games, because they are not part of the constitutional educational function. Even then, the University may not be forced to collect the tax for the city. *City of Boulder v. Regents of the Univ. of Colorado*, 179 Colo. 420, 501 P.2d 123 (1972).

CHAPTER 13

Education, article IX

Introduction to Colorado education law

In Colorado, governance of public schools is divided between the elected State Board of Education (art. IX, § 1) and school district elected boards (§ 15). The general assembly is also central to education. In the Colorado Revised Statutes, education is Title 22, and postsecondary education is title 23.

State vs. local control is an enduring contest in Colorado constitutional education law. This is as it should be. The Constitution gives voters several mechanisms to control education governance. Voters elect a local board and a state board. They also elect legislators who appropriate funds and write school laws. As *Federalists* 28, 46, and 51 argued, divided sovereignty provides the people with more than one remedy.

Before 1935, legislative funding for public schools consisted of distribution from the Public School Fund, arising from the federal land grants in the 1875 Enabling Act. *See* chapter 1. In 1935, the legislature also began providing general fund revenue to the public schools.

In the past half-century, the legislature has tremendously increased funding. In constant dollars (adjusted for inflation) per pupil funding has approximately doubled in Colorado since the early 1970s, with very little to show in terms of improved student learning.[1] The legislature has also imposed numerous mandates on the public schools, such as anti-drug education, civics education, and so on. Further, there is now a statewide system of annual standardized testing for most public school students, now known as CMAS (Colorado Measures of Academic Success). Thus, parents and the community have a measure of some education outcomes.

A brief overview of school finance

Colorado public school finance is a complicated subject. In part, the funding is controlled by the Constitution. As will detailed below, section 17, enacted by the people in 2000, requires state per-pupil funding for public schools always to increase by at the least the rate of inflation.

Section 2 orders the legislature to establish "a thorough and uniform system of free public schools throughout the state." Three cases have argued that section 2 requires the legislature to increase education funding (beyond what section 17 already requires). No case has succeeded. *Marshall v. School Dist. RE 3*, 191 Colo. 451, 553 P. 2d 784 (1976) (free textbooks for non-indigent students not mandatory); *Lujan v. Colorado State Board of Education*, 649 P.2d 1005 (1982) (expenditures need not be equal among every district), and *Lobato v. State*, 2013 CO 30, 304 P.3d 1132 (Colo. 2013) (current spending levels are not unconstitutionally low). The *Lobato*

[1] Although Colorado public students often perform better than the national average, in neither Colorado nor the nation do the majority of fourth grade or eighth grade students achieve grade-level proficiency in Mathematics or Reading. Annual student test scores on various metrics from the 1970s to the present are available from the National Assessment of Educational Progress, *Explore Assessment Data*, https://nces.ed.gov/nationsreportcard/data/.

case, a 4–3 decision, is excerpted at the end of this chapter. Overall, Colorado's level of K-12 funding is in the middle, compared to other states.[2]

The School Finance Act is article 54 of title 22, C.R.S. It was enacted in 1994 and has been substantially revised ever since. The basic system of Colorado public school finance is as follows:

For annual operating expenses (*e.g.*, teacher and administrator salaries, building maintenance), school districts receive revenue from property taxes and motor vehicle ownership taxes in their district. The revenues are collected by the county treasurer (along with all other property taxes) and distributed to the school districts and other tax recipients. Of course, some districts collect more revenue than others because the property in some districts is more valuable.

On top of local property taxes, the state legislature provides additional money to public schools. Some of the extra money comes from the School Land Trust: the millions of acres of property that the federal government donated to Colorado in 1875, for the "common schools." The state legislature provides additional money from the general fund. General fund revenue comes mainly from the state income tax and state sales tax. Pursuant to art. IX, § 17, described below, some annual state revenue must be set aside in a State Public School Fund, which is used to pay some state education expenses.

Every school district receives a baseline minimum of per-pupil funding. Under section 17 (adopted 2000), per-pupil base funding must always increase annually by at least the rate of inflation.

Above the per-pupil baseline, the general assembly's extra funding is calculated with a complicated formula. Here is a basic version:

- Count the number of K-12 students in the district. Instead of counting the number of students enrolled in the given academic year, some districts with declining enrollment can use average enrollment that includes the preceding two to five years.
- Multiply the number of students in the district by the statewide base per-pupil funding. This is the basic amount of district funding.
- Add cost of living adjustments to reflect the need to pay higher salaries in areas where the cost of living is higher, such as the Front Range and most of the ski communities. Reduce the cost of living bonus by the *nonpersonnel costs factor*—the percentage of district annual spending that does not go to salaries. This factor is typically 10–20% of a district's annual budget, with small districts being at the higher end.
- Give districts a per-pupil bonus based on their *size factor*. Every district gets at least 3% more, but districts with total enrollments under 5,000 students get much more, because they cannot use economies of scale.

---

[2] This is true in absolute dollars spent. Because Coloradans are, in general, better educated and more prosperous than the people of many other states, they have average higher incomes. Since school spending is average, and personal income is high, the percentage of Coloradans' income that is taken for school funding is relatively low. The low percentage of income taken is why Colorado is sometimes claimed to rank "49th" (or some similar number) in education funding.

Many people who hear the "49th" claim think that Colorado schools receive very little funding. To the contrary, per-pupil Colorado spending on education is in the middle, in relation to other states.

The 49th factoid presumes that whenever income rises, government education spending should automatically increase. Coloradans have voted three times on statewide education taxation and spending. The people twice rejected tax increases for education—in 2013 and 1992. In 2000 they voted to make some education spending increases automatic. As a result, the general assembly must provide some priority to public schools (traditional and charter) compared to other spending.

While Colorado voters have often supported tax or spending increases of their own school district, they have rejected blanket statewide tax increases. On the whole, Coloradans seem to trust local government higher taxes than state government higher taxes.

- For every at-risk student, add 12% to the per-pupil funding. For districts that have a high percentage of at-risk students, add up to 18% more, depending how much the district's at-risk enrollment exceeds the state average. "At-risk" means either low income (eligible for free lunch under the National School Lunch Act), or English language learner (not proficient in English, and from a home where English is not the predominant language, as defined by the state's English Language Proficiency Act).
- We now have the total funding for each district. From this total, subtract the amount of school funding raised locally by the district, through property and motor vehicle taxes. The amount left is the starting point for how much state aid to give to the school district.
- Now apply the *budget stabilization factor* (formerly known as the *negative factor*). This 2010 statute, as amended, caps growth of total state K-12 spending. HB 10-1369; SB 11-230; SB 17-296. The statute limits the total level of state aid to schools, but not the baseline per-pupil amount. Proportionately reduce the state aid to all school districts to comply with the budget stabilization factor—provided that no district may ever have less than the statewide base per-pupil funding. Pursuant to art. IX, § 17, the base per-pupil funding must always increase by the rate of inflation.
- Add grants to school districts for *categorical funding*. According to section 17, these programs too must increase by at least the annual rate of inflation. Categorical programs are: special education, gifted and talented children, public school transportation, vocational education, English language proficiency, small attendance centers (schools under 200 enrollment not located near any other school for the same grades), comprehensive health education, and expelled and at-risk student services. Most of these grants pay for some but not all of a district's costs for the programs.

Additionally, there is a Colorado Preschool Program, which makes per-pupil grants to school districts for children ages 3–5 who lack learning readiness, need language development, or are in programs for neglected or dependent children. Districts may provide preschool programs themselves, or may contract with local providers, such as a Head Start agency. The number of students in program is capped at 29,360 statewide. These preschool students, typically in half-day programs, count as .5 of a student in the above formula. Similarly, kindergarten students in a half-day program count at .58 of a full-time student. However, *all* of the preschool grants are subject to reduction via the budget stabilization factor.

There are additional complexities to the funding formula, such as for students who are formally enrolled in a school district but who do not receive education directly from the district. These include students in ASCENT (Accelerating Students through Concurrent Enrollment), which pays tuition via high schools for certain post-secondary classes by some high school graduates. Students enrolled in multidistrict online schools are another example.

Some districts raise all they need through local property and motor vehicle taxes. They may receive no state funding and may even have to give money to the state, via a forced "buy-out" of categorical programs. School district mill levies for annual operations are capped at 27 mills. HB 20-1148. Most school districts in the Denver metro and Pueblo areas are at the maximum. Mill levies are explained in chapter 14 (art. X, § 3, property taxes).

The above description is based on Legislative Council Staff, *School Finance in Colorado*, Research Pub. No. 758 (2021). *See also* Brenda Bautsch Dickhoner, *Dollars and Data 2021: A Look at K-12 Education Funding in Colorado*, COMMON SENSE INSTITUTE (Sept. 2021).

Capital spending

Construction, renovation, or expansion of school buildings has its own, separate funding system. Capital spending is partly financed by bond issues that are approved by voters in a school district, to increase their property taxes. The state provides matching grants via the Public School Capital Construction Assistance Fund. The fund receives revenue from: the School Land Trust, sales of certificates of participation (discussed in chapter 16), some lottery revenue (chapters 23 and 32), and a 15% excise tax on retail marijuana (chapter 31).

Expanding choices

As of 1970, Colorado had no school choice. A child could attend a public school to which he or she was assigned based on geography. If that school did not meet the student's needs, the only alternative was for the family to pay tuition at an independent school. Things are very different today.

First, homeschooling has been relegalized.[3]

Second, students may choose to attend any public school within a district, or even in another district. To exercise the choice, there must be available space at the target school, and the family is responsible for transportation to and from the school.

Third, charter schools are a type of public school that enjoy greater autonomy and flexibility than traditional neighborhood public schools. Charter schools often offer special programs (*e.g.*, arts, focus on disadvantaged students, academic rigor, on-line education) that better meet the needs of some students.

Charter schools usually receive their charters from the school district in which they are located. They may also be chartered by the state board of education. Charter school enrollment is typically by lottery, with many more applicants than available spaces—as is common for charter schools nationwide.

The original charter school law, enacted in 1993, allowed school districts to rake off a substantial amount of the charter school's per-pupil funding. For capital construction, allowable discrimination was even worse. Subsequent legislation has reduced but not eliminated funding discrimination. *See*, *e.g.*, House Bill 17-1375 (for per-pupil school construction or repair funded by mill levy overrides, public charter schools receive 95% of what other schools receive).

---

[3] In the Early Republic and before, home schooling was generally regarded as a fundamental right, including by advocates of public schools. S. Ernie Walton, *A Fundamental Right to Homeschool: A Historical Response to Professor Bartholet*, 25 TEX. REV. OF LAW & POLITICS 377 (2021). It has been argued that courts should require legislatures to impose a "presumption against homeschooling," allowing it only in exceptional cases. Elizabeth Bartholet, *Homeschooling: Parent Rights Absolutism vs. Child Rights to Education & Protection*, 62 ARIZ. LAW REV. 1, 72–76 (2020). The U.S. supreme court addressed a related issue in 1925, when Oregon outlawed nongovernment elementary and secondary education. Holding that the law violated the "liberty" guaranteed by the Fourteenth Amendment, the court stated:

> The fundamental theory of liberty upon which all governments in this Union repose excludes any general power of the State to standardize its children by forcing them to accept instruction from public teachers only. The child is not the mere creature of the State; those who nurture him and direct his destiny have the right, coupled with the high duty, to recognize and prepare him for additional obligations.

Pierce v. Society of Sisters, 268 U.S. 510, 535 (1925).

For data on outcomes of various types of education, see Ying Chen, Christina Hinton, & Tyler J. VanderWeele, *School types in adolescence and subsequent health and well-being in young adulthood: An outcome-wide analysis*, 16 PLOS ONE (issue 11, 2021).

Higher education

Colorado's higher education funding is now very different from the original system. The Taxpayer's Bill of Rights (TABOR, Art. X, § 20, enacted 1992) requires voter approval for some government tax, revenue, or spending increases. TABOR does not apply to a "government-sponsored enterprise" (GSE). A GSE is an entity that is controlled by government but receives less than 10 percent of its revenue from the government.

Accordingly, almost all public institutions of higher education have been converted into GSEs. The state's College Opportunity Fund (COF) partially pays tuition costs for Colorado residents who attend colleges within Colorado. The COF currently pays $94 per credit hour at public colleges, and $47 per credit hour at private colleges. This state support is not counted against the 10% government funding limit for TABOR-exempt government-supported enterprises.

Art. IX, Section 1. State board of education

> (1) The general supervision of the public schools of the state shall be vested in a board of education whose powers and duties shall be as now or hereafter prescribed by law. Said board shall consist of a member from each congressional district of the state and, if the total number of such congressional districts is an even number, one additional member, and said members shall be elected as hereinafter provided. The members of said board shall be elected by the registered electors of the state, voting at general elections, in such manner and for such terms as may be by law prescribed; provided, that provisions may be made by law for election of a member from each congressional district of the state by the electors of such district; and provided, further, that each member from a congressional district of the state shall be a qualified elector of such district. If the total number of congressional districts of the state is an even number, the additional member of said board shall be elected from the state at large. The members of said board shall serve without compensation, but they shall be reimbursed for any necessary expenses incurred by them in performing their duties as members of said board.
>
> (2) The commissioner of education shall be appointed by the board of education and shall not be included in the classified civil service of the state.
>
> (3) The qualifications, tenure, compensation, powers, and duties of said commissioner shall be as prescribed by law, subject to the supervision of said board.

The state board of education has general supervisory authority over K-12 public schools. It consists of members elected by congressional district, plus one at large if the number of congressional districts is even. The Board appoints a Commissioner of Education, who is a full-time salaried employee.

The state board of education is covered in C.R.S. § 22-2-106 -109. The Commissioner of Education is C.R.S. § 22-2-112 & 113.

Art. IX, Section 2. Thorough, uniform, and free public schools

> The general assembly shall, as soon as practicable, provide for the establishment and maintenance of a thorough and uniform system of free public schools throughout the state, wherein all residents of the state, between the ages of six and twenty-one years, may be educated gratuitously. One or more public schools shall be maintained in each school district within the state, at least three months in each year; any school district failing to have such school shall not be entitled to receive any portion of the school fund for that year.

"Uniform" does not mean that all public schools must be the same. Colorado does not favor a highly centralized education system, with a unitary curriculum forcing every school to teach the same thing on the same day.

"Thorough and uniform" is the subject of the *Lobato* case, below, which alleged that Colorado's school spending was unconstitutionally low.

The leading scholarly examination of the original meaning of section 2 is Thomas I. Romero, II, *"Of Greater Value than the Gold of Our Mountains": The Right to Education in Colorado's Nineteenth-Century Constitution*, 83 U. COLO. L. REVIEW 781 (2012).

Kindergarten is legal

Section 2 orders the legislature to establish a public-school system for Coloradans "between the ages of six and twenty-one years." Does this forbid the legislature to establish kindergartens, where most students are under 6 years of age? No. Section 2 is the minimum that the legislature must do, not a maximum on what it may do. This is so even though kindergartens would be paid for in part by the Public School Fund, which, arguably, is exclusively for use in the public schools that are required by the Constitution. *In re Kindergarten Schools*, 18 Colo. 234, 32 P. 422 (1893).

Tuition is free, but textbooks are not

School districts do not have to furnish free textbooks to non-indigent students. A statute enacted in 1883, and continued with some wording changes ever since, ordered school districts to supply free textbooks to *indigent* students. This suggests that the original meaning of the 1876 Constitution did not require public schools to provide free textbooks to all students. Otherwise, the 1883 statute would have been pointless and incomplete. *Marshall v. School Dist. RE No. 3 Morgan County*, 191 Colo. 451, 553 P.2d 784 (1976).

What is a child's school district?

A child's parent or parents live in school district X. The child lives with someone else, such as an uncle, in school district Y. Because the child's residence is in Y, the child is entitled to attend Y district public schools. This does not apply if the child adopted residence in Y for the purpose of attending Y district schools. *Cline v. Knight*, 111 Colo. 8, 137 P.2d 680 (1943).

Charter schools

A charter school may receive a charter from a school district *or* from the state board of education, via the Charter School Institute established by the board. If a school district rejects a charter application, the applicants may file an appeal with the state board of education. If the state board rejects the charter, the applicant may file a suit in district court for review under the Colorado Administrative Procedure Act. *Brannberg v. Colo. State Board of Education*, 2021 COA 132 (Colo. App. 2021). Alternatively, the state board could remand the application to the local school board. If the local board rejects the application again, and the state board affirms the denial, there is no further appeal. The same rules apply if a charter application is granted, but the applicants believe that the local board has imposed unfair conditions on the charter school.

The vast majority of charter schools receive local charters. However, the potential availability of a state charter provides an incentive for anti-charter school district administrations to negotiate in good faith with charter school applicants.

Charters are for a term of years, not perpetual, so they must be renewed from time to time by the school district or the charter school institute. To charter advocates, nonperpetual charters are an advantage. If the school fails to attract families who want to enroll, it will have to close. Unlike traditional public schools, charter public schools have a built-in protection so that the ones that are badly operated will cease operations. Charter school statutes are at C.R.S. § 22-30.5-101 to 120.

If the state board determines that a school district has been fair in general to charter applicants, the board must grant the district exclusive authority for chartering. If a district has previously had a moratorium on charters (as the Boulder Valley School District once did), the district is per se disqualified from exclusive chartering power. School districts with enrollments of fewer than 3,000 students automatically have exclusive chartering authority.

When the charter school institute granted a charter within the boundaries of the Boulder Valley School District, the district argued that the charter was unconstitutional, because it violated section 2 and section 15. Under section 15, school district boards have control of instruction in the district's schools. The court of appeals disagreed. The state's granting a charter does not force a school district to do anything, nor to spend any money. Nor does the existence of a charter school affect the district's ability to control instruction in its own schools. In *Boulder Valley School Dist. RE-2 v. Colorado State Bd. of Educ.*, 217 P.3d 918 (Colo. App. 2009),

Moreover, by precedent the general assembly has almost unlimited power to abolish, divide, or alter school districts. The BVSD had no right to absolute control over every public school within its geographical area. There is nothing in the Constitution that forbids the existence of geographically overlapping school districts. A charter institute school can exist within the geographic boundaries of the Boulder Valley School District. *Id.*

For data on charter school performance in Colorado, see Brenda Bautsch Dickhoner, *Digging Into the Data on Colorado Charter Schools: An In-Depth Look at Graduation Rates for Students of Color*, COMMON SENSE INSTITUTE, July 2020.

Art. IX, Section 3. School fund inviolate

> The public school fund of the state shall, except as provided in this article IX, forever remain inviolate and intact and the interest and other income thereon, only, shall be expended in the maintenance of the schools of the state, and shall be distributed amongst the several counties and school districts of the state, in such manner as may be prescribed by law. No part of this fund, principal, interest, or other income shall ever be transferred to any other fund, or used or appropriated, except as provided in this article IX. The state treasurer shall be the custodian of

> this fund, and the same shall be securely and profitably invested as may be by law directed. The state shall supply all losses thereof that may in any manner occur. In order to assist public schools in the state in providing necessary buildings, land, and equipment, the general assembly may adopt laws establishing the terms and conditions upon which the state treasurer may (1) invest the fund in bonds of school districts, (2) use all or any portion of the fund or the interest or other income thereon to guaranty bonds issued by school districts, or (3) make loans to school districts. Distributions of interest and other income for the benefit of public schools provided for in this article IX shall be in addition to and not a substitute for other moneys appropriated by the general assembly for such purposes.

Congress's 1875 Enabling Act granted Colorado federal lands, constituting over 5% of the state's area, for a perpetual fund for public schools. Section 3 establishes that fund. The fund's interest and income are given to the public schools. The principal is inviolate.

In 2017–18, the fund contributed about $130 million towards the 9.32 billion of public school spending that year. RICHARD A. COLLINS & DALE OESTERLE, THE COLORADO STATE CONSTITUTION 213 (2d ed. 2020).

No loans to the state

The Colorado legislature in the late 19th century often flagrantly violated constitutional restrictions. The legislature ordered the public-school fund to loan $650,000 to the state for general revenue to be expended in 1887–89. The legislature said that it would start paying the loan back in 1892, but provided no schedule for repayment, no particular revenue stream for repayment, and no security for the forced loan.

Unlike federal courts, the Colorado supreme court may answer interrogatories on questions of public importance. The court can answer such questions without the existence of a "case or controversy." Art. VI, § 3. In 1893, after the Populist Party won control of the Senate, the Senate asked the supreme court if the forced loan was constitutional.

The court answered that the forced loan violated art. IX, § 3. The court also urged that questions submitted to it should be specific and should not just ask about constitutionality in general. *In re Loan of School Fund*, 18 Colo. 195, 32 P. 273 (1893).

No using the money for non-school infrastructure

The legislature could not finance an irrigation canal from Cañon City to Pueblo by selling some sections of school land that the canal would traverse. The legislature has no authority to force the sale of school lands. Revenue from school lands is to be used only for schools, and not for non-school infrastructure projects. *In re Canal Certificates*, 19 Colo. 63, 34 P. 274 (1893).

Local infrastructure fees may be imposed

The state land board owns Arapahoe Community College, located in Littleton. The city charged fees to the college for connection with the city's storm water and flood management system. The fees were the same that would be assessed to any owner of a comparable amount of land in the city. The fees did not violate the constitutional requirement that state land board funds must be spent only for educational school purposes. *City of Littleton v. State*, 855 P.2d 448 (Colo. 1993). The result is different when a special fee, unique to a particular property, is assessed. *People ex rel. Dunbar v. City of Littleton*, 183 Colo. 195, 515 P.2d 1121 (1973).

Art. IX, Section 4. County treasurer to collect and disburse school funds

> Each county treasurer shall collect all school funds belonging to his county, and the several school districts therein, and disburse the same to the proper districts upon warrants drawn by the county superintendent, or by the proper district authorities, as may be provided by law.

The county treasurer disburses funds to school districts.

Art. IX, Section 5. School fund composition

> The public school fund of the state shall consist of the proceeds of such land as have heretofore been, or may hereafter, be granted to the state by the general government for educational purposes; all estates that may escheat to the state; also all other grants, gifts or devises that may be made to this state for educational purpose.

Besides the U.S. land grants, the school fund includes the estates of people who die intestate and without heirs. When the state takes the decedent's property, the money must go to the school fund. Also, people may make gifts to the school fund.

Art. IX, Section 6. County superintendent of schools

Stop! Don't read the block quote. There are no more county superintendents in Colorado. The people in every county have exercised their choice under section 6 to abolish the office.

> There may be a county superintendent of schools in each county, whose term of office shall be four years, and whose duties, qualifications, and compensation shall be prescribed by law.
>
> The provisions of section 8 of article XIV of this constitution to the contrary notwithstanding, the office of county superintendent of schools may be abolished by any county if the question of the abolishment of said office is first submitted, at a general election, to a vote of the qualified electors of said county and approved by a majority of the votes cast thereon. In any county so voting in favor of such abolishment, the office of county superintendent of schools and the term of office of any incumbent in said county shall terminate on June 30 following.

Art. IX, Section 7. No aid to sectarian institutions

> Neither the general assembly, nor any county, city, town, township, school district or other public corporation, shall ever make any appropriation, or pay from any public fund or moneys whatever, anything in aid of any church or sectarian society, or for any sectarian purpose, or to help support or sustain any school, academy, seminary, college, university or other literary or scientific institution, controlled by any church or sectarian denomination whatsoever; nor shall any grant or

> donation of land, money or other personal property, ever be made by the state, or any such public corporation to any church, or for any sectarian purpose.

Section 7 is a specific application of the general prohibition on all appropriations to private institutions, expressed in art. V, § 34. However, section 34 has been judicially nullified. As long as the legislature can rationally claim that the grant to a private institution serves some public purpose, private appropriations are allowed. Section 7's separate, specific prohibition does remain in effect.

Douglas County decision vacated by U.S. supreme court

The Colorado supreme court's interpretation of section 7 has run into trouble from the U.S. supreme court's interpretation of the First Amendment. State or local government discrimination against religion violates the First Amendment right of free exercise of religion, which has been made applicable to the states by the Fourteenth Amendment.

Some states or districts have enacted choice programs that allow some government funding to be used to help students who attend an independent school. There is no constitutional requirement for government schools to have choice programs. But if they do, may they exclude religious schools? According to the 5–4 decision in *Espinoza v. Montana Dept. of Revenue*, 140 S.Ct. 2246 (2020), religious schools may not be singled out for exclusion.

Previously, the court had ruled 7–2 that a state's program to provide rubber mats, made from recycled tires, for school playgrounds cannot exclude a school solely because it is religious. *Trinity Lutheran Church of Columbia, Inc. v. Comer*, 137 S.Ct. 2012 (2017).

After announcing the decision in *Trinity Lutheran*, the U.S. supreme court vacated a Colorado decision for which a cert. petition had been filed. The Douglas County School District had proposed a limited voucher program with a group of cooperating independent schools. Some of the schools were religious and some were not.

The Colorado supreme court ruled that the program's non-exclusion of religious schools violated article IX, § 7, of the Colorado Constitution. Thirty-seven states have constitutional provisions similar to section 7. One of them is Missouri, which was on the losing side of *Trinity Lutheran*. The U.S. supreme court did not hold section 7 and its brethren unconstitutional. Rather, the court found the Missouri and Colorado applications of the clauses to be incompatible with the First Amendment. *Taxpayers for Public Education v. Douglas County School District*, 2015 CO 50, 351 P.3d 461 (Colo. 2015) (plurality op.), vacated sub nom. *Colorado State Board of Education v. Taxpayers for Public Education*, 137 S.Ct. 2327 (2017).

Section 7's text prohibits aid to "sectarian" institutions. In nineteenth century (and often still today), "sectarian" was a term of disapproval—for heretical, bigoted, or fanatical religions. Catholics and Mormons were often considered "sectarian." *See Espinoza*, 140 S.Ct. at 2268, 2270 (Alito, J., concurring) (citing, inter alia, Independence Inst. amicus brief, and scholarship of Ind. Inst.'s prof. Rob Natelson).

Further reading: David B. Kopel, *The Colorado Constitution's No Aid to Sectarian Institutions Clause and Its Impact on Civil Rights*, Colorado State Advisory Committee to the United States Commission on Civil Rights, Sept. 2018; Alexandra J. Berger, *Lessons to Be Learned: Taxpayers for Public Education v. Douglas County School District and the Flaws of the Douglas County Choice Scholarship Program*, 96 DENVER L. REVIEW 145 (2018).

Fair exchanges with sectarian institutions are lawful

A school district informally allowed its custodian to spend some of his work hours in helping to construct a church. In exchange, some boys from the church would perform the custodian's tasks at school. This did not violate section 7, because it was a fair, arms-length exchange of services, and not a payment to the church. *School Dist. No. 97 in Weld County v. Schmidt*, 128 Colo. 495, 263 P.2d 581 (1953).

Art. IX, Section 8. No religious tests, sectarian tenets, or race discrimination

> No religious test or qualification shall ever be required of any person as a condition of admission into any public educational institution of the state, either as a teacher or student; and no teacher or student of any such institution shall ever be required to attend or participate in any religious service whatsoever. No sectarian tenets or doctrines shall ever be taught in the public school, nor shall any distinction or classification of pupils be made on account of race or color, nor shall any pupil be assigned or transported to any public educational institution for the purpose of achieving racial balance.

Section 8 provides additional protection to the general guarantee of religious freedom in the Bill of Rights. Art. 2, § 4.

Colorado's 1876 prohibition on racial discrimination in the public schools made it different from many other states of the time.

Racial segregation in schools

Because of "certain unpleasant incidents which have occurred within the past two or three years between the colored and white pupils," the Denver Public Schools in 1924 adopted a policy of having separate social events for white and non-white students. This also included separate swimming classes. The Denver policy was held to be a plain violation of section 8. *Jones v. Newlon*, 81 Colo. 25, 253 P. 386 (1927). The year 1924 was a peak of influence in Colorado for the second Ku Klux Klan.

The original KKK, America's first domestic terrorist organization, was founded after the Civil War, and destroyed by vigorous federal action under president Ulysses S. Grant (1869–77). Grant's policy included prosecutions by the new Department of Justice, and declarations of martial law in some areas.

After 1915 film *Birth of a Nation* extolled the original Klan, the "second Ku Klux Klan" arose. During the first part of the 1920s, it was very powerful. Colorado and Oregon were some of its strongest states. Klan power reached a peak in the 1925–26 legislature. The DPS 1924 policy reflected its time. Unlike Southern Klans, the Colorado KKK was not violent, but it was hostile to people of color, immigrants, and non-Protestants. Governor Clarence J. Morley won a single term in 1924 and was a puppet of the Klan. RICHARD D. LAMM & DUANE A. SMITH, PIONEERS AND POLITICIANS: COLORADO GOVERNORS IN PROFILE (2d ed. 2008).

Notwithstanding the plain language of section 8, the University of Colorado at Boulder makes certain dormitory housing only available by race. Elizabeth Hernandez, *CU Boulder creating Social Justice Living Environment program in campus dorm*, BOULDER DAILY CAMERA, May 16, 2017; Peter Appenzeller, *CU Boulder pursuing diversity through segregation*, COMPLETE COLORADO, Dec. 4, 2017.

Bible reading

For many decades, some public-school districts had a daily reading from the King James Version of the Bible (KJV). The reading stood on its own, without commentary. The practice matched the "Protestant-lite" ethos that governed many American public schools. The KJV was acceptable to all Protestants, and the mere text, without further instruction, did not offend the sensibilities of any Protestant denomination.

Obviously the KJV was not inclusive for Jewish students (who do not consider the New Testament to be scripture), for Japanese or Chinese immigrant families who were non-Christian, and for others. Especially Catholics. The Roman Catholic Church does not consider the KJV to be an authoritative translation, and, as of 1927, discouraged individual Bible reading not under the guidance of a church instructor.

In 1927, the Colorado supreme court heard a Catholic student's challenge to the Denver Public Schools Bible-reading. As the court noted, the DPS allowed any student to opt out of participation in the daily readings. The court then explained why the King James Bible is not "sectarian" within the meaning of section 8. The court followed the standard definition of "sectarian": "Religious and sectarian are not synonymous." *People ex rel. Vollmar v. Stanley*, 81 Colo. 276, 290, 255 P. 610, 616 (1927):

> The ultimate answer to the question 'sectarian or not?' whether with reference to the Bible or any other book or doctrine, must be by the courts. *Hackett v. Brooksville School Dist.*, [120 Ky. 608 (1905)]. We are now answering it with reference to the Bible. The Bible is a compilation of many books. Even an atheist could find nothing sectarian in the book of Esther. [The only book of the Bible in which the word "God" or synonyms do not appear.] Is it not as practicable to say that that book is not sectarian as to say that the whole Bible is? Can we not separate the sectarian teachings of the Bible as practically as those of any other book? What right have we to say that the whole is when we know that part is not?
>
> It is argued that, because some sects regard the whole Bible as sacred and inspired and others not, it is therefore sectarian. Non sequitur. Sectarian or not cannot be determined of a book by how sects regard it. The decisive question is whether it teaches some doctrine peculiar to a sect. That part which does not is not sectarian. The eloquence of Amos and Isaiah and the wisdom of the parables is sectarian or not, whether read from King James version, the English Revised, the American Revised, the Douai, or any of the many other translations, or from any other book.
>
> It is said that King James Bible is proscribed by Roman Catholic authority; but proscription cannot make that sectarian which is not actually so. *Hackett v. Brooksville,* etc., 120 Ky. 608, 617, 618. If it could, the atheists could proscribe the Star Spangled Banner, the Calvinists Whittier [John Greenleaf Whittier, Quaker poet], and the fundamentalists half of modern science. Neither can the fact that it is authorized by a sect make it sectarian.
>
> True, the address of the Constitutional Convention to the people stated that the Constitution provided 'that no religious or sectarian dogmas' shall ever be taught in any of the schools under the patronage of the state, but 'dogma' here has its ordinary meaning when used in connection with religion, which is 'arbitrary dictum.' Webster. It has no reference to the Bible or its teaching, but to arbitrary propositions of religion or theology.

Id. at 81 Colo. 291–92.

In 1963, the U.S. supreme court ruled that daily Bible readings in public schools violated the Establishment Clause of the First Amendment. *Abington School District v. Schempp*, 374 U.S. 203 (1963). Accordingly, *Vollmar* was later partially overruled by the Colorado supreme court, to the extent that it conflicted with *Abington. Conrad v. City and County of Denver, Colo.*, 656 P.2d 662, 670 n.6 (Colo. 1982).

Pledge of Allegiance

Jehovah's Witnesses do not believe in taking oaths. A JW student may not be punished for refusing to recite the Pledge of Allegiance. The Colorado supreme court reversed the student's expulsion:

> Judicial authority is not lacking for the proposition that a law that restricts the freedom of the individual in matters of his purely personal concern either by prohibiting action under penalty or enjoining upon him action for an avowed objective, cannot be sustained unless there is some appropriate relation between the legislative command and the prescribed punishment on the one hand, and the avowed objective on the other . . . [C]ompelling the expression of a sentiment not felt or the doing of an act that it is feared will subject the actor to punishment hereafter, will not only fail to create and foster respect for the compelling authority, but will endanger a sentiment of rebellion against it.

Zavilla v. Masse, 112 Colo. 183, 147 P.2d 823 (1944).

Bussing

For attendance, Denver Public Schools were never been formally racially segregated. However, a federal court found that the DPS had engaged in quasi-segregation in the drawing of attendance boundaries, and in decisions about where to locate new schools. The U.S. supreme court decision affirming the lower court decision was the first time that a non-Southern school district with no express policy of segregation had been found to be unconstitutionally segregated. *Keyes v. School District No. 1*, 413 U.S. 189 (1973).

In Denver, as in other districts found to be unconstitutionally segregated, the standard remedy was forced bussing. Rather than attending schools in their own neighborhood, many black students and white students would be bussed to a much more distant school, so that each school building would mirror the racial composition of the district as a whole. Bussing worked for some people, but was enormously unpopular for many, who did not want their children spending 75 minutes on a bus twice a day rather than being able to walk to a nearby school.

In 1974, the voters added section 8's final clause, against assigning students to schools based on race. However, the Colorado Constitution could not negate a federal court order based on the Fourteenth Amendment. In 1995, the federal district court ruled that Denver had achieved a "unitary" school system, and so federal court control was lifted, and governing authority returned to the school board. *Keyes v. Congress of Hispanic Educators*, 902 F. Supp. 1274 (D. Colo. 1995).

Art. IX, Section 9. State board of land commissioners

Summary: The school lands will be managed by 5 appointed commissioners. They shall hire a director and staff.

(1) The state board of land commissioners shall be composed of five persons to be appointed by the governor, with the consent of the senate, one of whom shall be elected by the board as its president.

(2) The governor shall endeavor to appoint members of the board who reside in different geographic regions of the state. The board shall be composed of one person with substantial experience in production agriculture, one person with substantial experience in public primary or secondary education, one person with substantial experience in local government and land use planning, one person with substantial experience in natural resource conservation, and one citizen at large.

(3) The governor shall appoint a new board of land commissioners on or before May 1, 1997. The term of each member shall be for four years; except that of the first board members appointed under this subsection (3), two members shall be appointed for terms that expire June 30, 1999, and three members shall be appointed for terms that expire June 30, 2001. No member shall serve more than two consecutive terms. Members of the board shall be subject to removal, and vacancies on the board shall be filled, as provided in article IV, section 6 of this constitution.

(4) The board shall, pursuant to section 13 of article XII of this constitution, hire a director with the consent of the governor, and, through the director, a staff, and may contract for office space, acquire equipment and supplies, and enter into contracts as necessary to accomplish its duties. Payment for goods, services, and personnel shall be made from the income from the trust lands. The general assembly shall annually appropriate from the income from the trust lands, sufficient moneys to enable the board to perform its duties and in that regard shall give deference to the board's assessment of its budgetary needs. The members of the board shall not, by virtue of their appointment, be employees of the state; they may be reimbursed for their reasonable and necessary expenses and may, in addition, receive such per diem as may be established by the general assembly, from the income from the trust lands.

(5) The individual members of the board shall have no personal liability for any action or failure to act as long as such action or failure to act does not involve willful or intentional malfeasance or gross negligence.

(6) The board shall serve as the trustee for the lands granted to the state in public trust by the federal government, lands acquired in lieu thereof, and additional lands held by the board in public trust. It shall have the duty to manage, control, and dispose of such lands in accordance with the purposes for which said grants of land were made and section 10 of this article IX, and subject to such terms and conditions consistent therewith as may be prescribed by law.

(7) The board shall have the authority to undertake nonsimultaneous exchanges of land, by directing that the proceeds from a particular sale or other disposition be deposited into a separate account to be established by the state treasurer with the interest thereon to accrue to such account, and withdrawing therefrom an equal or lesser amount to be used as the purchase price for other land to be held and managed as provided in this article, provided that the purchase of lands to complete such an exchange shall be made within two years of the initial sale or disposition.

> Any proceeds, and the interest thereon, from a sale or other disposition which are not expended in completing the exchange shall be transferred by the state treasurer to the public school fund or such other trust fund maintained by the treasurer for the proceeds of the trust lands disposed of or sold. Moneys held in the separate account shall not be used for the operating expenses of the board or for expenses incident to the disposition or acquisition of lands.

Subsections (2) through (7) were added by amendment in 1996, in conjunction with the amendments to section 10. Statutes for the state board of land commissioners are the subject of title 36, article 1, C.R.S.

The board of land commissioners has some constitutional autonomy, while the general assembly retains some power to direct their activities. For cases on the conflict, *see, e.g.*, *Colorado State Bd. of Land Com'rs v. Colorado Mined Land Reclamation Bd.*, 809 P.2d 974 (Colo. 1991) (state statue could compel state land board to comply with county zoning law for mining); *Evans v. Simpson*, 190 Colo. 426, 547 P.2d 931 (1976) (inquiring whether a term in a state land board lease was forbidden by a statute).

Further reading: Charles E. Bedford, *The "New" Colorado State Land Board*, 78 DENVER U.L. REVIEW 347 (2001).

Art. IX, Section 10. Public trust lands

Summary: Imposes fiduciary standards for management of all public trust lands, including school lands. As always, boldface headings are by Kopel.

> (1) **State school lands should be managed for open space, wildlife habitat, and so on.** The people of the state of Colorado recognize (a) that the state school lands are an endowment of land assets held in a perpetual, inter-generational public trust for the support of public schools, which should not be significantly diminished, (b) that the disposition and use of such lands should therefore benefit public schools including local school districts, and (c) that the economic productivity of all lands held in public trust is dependent on sound stewardship, including protecting and enhancing the beauty, natural values, open space and wildlife habitat thereof, for this and future generations. In recognition of these principles, the board shall be governed by the standards set forth in this section 10 in the discharge of its fiduciary obligations, in addition to other laws generally applicable to trustees.
>
> It shall be the duty of the state board of land commissioners to provide for the prudent management, location, protection, sale, exchange, or other disposition of all the lands heretofore, or which may hereafter be, held by the board as trustee pursuant to section 9(6) of this article IX, in order to produce reasonable and consistent income over time. In furtherance thereof, the board shall:
>
> > (a) **Before selling, exchanging, or leasing school lands for development, the board should find out whether the financial benefits of the deal will be exceeded by impacts on school districts. *E.g.*, if the board sells land for apartment buildings, how much more money will the school district have to spend to educate children of families who move into the apartments?** Prior to the lease, sale, or exchange of any lands for commercial, residential or industrial development, determine that the income from the lease, sale, or exchange can reasonably be anticipated

to exceed the fiscal impact of such development on local school districts and state funding of education from increased school enrollment associated with such development;

(b) Protect and enhance the long-term productivity and sound stewardship of the trust lands held by the board, by, among other activities:

(I) **Set aside up to 300,000 acres to be managed primarily for environmental benefit.** Establishing and maintaining a long-term stewardship trust of up to 300,000 acres of land that the board determines through a statewide public nomination process to be valuable primarily to preserve long-term benefits and returns to the state; which trust shall be held and managed to maximize options for continued stewardship, public use, or future disposition, by permitting only those uses, not necessarily precluding existing uses or management practices, that will protect and enhance the beauty, natural values, open space, and wildlife habitat thereof; at least 200,000 acres of which land shall be designated on or before January 1, 1999, and at least an additional 95,000 acres of which land shall be designated on or before January 1, 2001; specific parcels of land held in the stewardship trust may be removed from the trust only upon the affirmative vote of four members of the board and upon the designation or exchange of an equal or greater amount of additional land into said trust.

(II) **Have sound stewardship in agricultural leases.** Including in agricultural leases terms, incentives, and lease rates that will promote sound stewardship and land management practices, long-term agricultural productivity, and community stability;

(III) **Develop natural resources to conserve long-term value.** Managing the development and utilization of natural resources in a manner which will conserve the long-term value of such resources, as well as existing and future uses, and in accordance with state and local laws and regulations; and

(IV) **Sell conservation easements (easements that prohibit all future development or use of the land).** Selling or leasing conservation easements, licenses and other similar interests in land.

(c) Comply with valid local land use regulations and land use plans.

(d) **Let public schools use the land for outdoor education.** Allow access by public schools without charge for outdoor educational purposes so long as such access does not conflict with uses previously approved by the board on such lands.

(e) **Let public schools buy local lands for building sites.** Provide opportunities for the public school districts within which such lands are located to lease, purchase, or otherwise use such lands or portions thereof as are necessary for school building sites, at an amount to be determined by the board, which shall not exceed the appraised fair market value, which amount may be paid over time.

> (2) **If you settle on school lands notwithstanding a survey, don't expect any money when the land is sold.** No law shall ever be passed by the general assembly granting any privileges to persons who may have settled upon any such public trust lands subsequent to the survey thereof by the general government, by which the amount to be derived by the sale, or other disposition of such lands, shall be diminished, directly or indirectly.

Section 10, originally consisting of a single paragraph, was rewritten by 1996 amendment.

The 1996 amendments appeared to violate the terms of the federal land grants in the 1875 Enabling Act. However, the Tenth Circuit held that the (old) fiduciary duty to maximize income might not be inconsistent with the (new) fiduciary to provide "reasonable" income. *Branson School District RE–82 v. Romer*, 161 F.3d 619 (10th Cir. 1998) (discussed in chapter 1). At least so far, the Tenth Circuit was correct. Oil and gas leases on state lands currently provide a great deal of income, and do not necessitate sale of any lands. RICHARD A. COLLINS & DALE OESTERLE, THE COLORADO STATE CONSTITUTION 219 (2d ed. 2020) .

Further reading: Charles E. Bedford, *The "New" Colorado State Land Board*, 78 DENVER U.L. REVIEW 347 (2001).

Art. IX, Section 11. Compulsory education

> The general assembly may require, by law, that every child of sufficient mental and physical ability, shall attend the public school during the period between the ages of six and eighteen years, for a time equivalent to three years, unless educated by other means.

If a child has attended the public schools "for a time equivalent to three years," may the general assembly "require" even more? The supreme court said "yes." *People v. In re Interest of Y.D.M.*, 197 Colo. 403, 593 P.2d 1356 (1979).

Current law compels public school attendance from ages 6 to 16. Alternatively, children may attend an independent school or home school. C.R.S. § 22-33-104.

Art. IX, Section 12. Regents of university of Colorado

> There shall be nine regents of the university of Colorado who shall be elected in the manner prescribed by law for terms of six years each. Said regents shall constitute a body corporate to be known by the name and style of "The Regents of the University of Colorado." The board of regents shall select from among its members a chairman who shall conduct the meetings of the board and a vice-chairman who shall assume the duties of the chairman in case of his absence.

The University of Colorado is governed by nine elected regents.

Originally, the University could offer instruction only in Boulder. The restriction was removed in stages. Art. VIII, § 5. Statutes for the University and its regents are in C.R.S. § 23-20-101 et seq.

Art. IX, Section 13. President of university of Colorado

> The regents of the university shall elect a president of the university who shall hold his office until removed by the board of regents. He shall be the principal executive officer of the university, a member of the faculty thereof, and shall carry out the policies and programs established by the board of regents.

The president of the University must be an employee at will. C.R.S. § 23-20-106. The president must make an annual report to the regents on September 1. C.R.S. § 23-20-107.

Art. IX, Section 14. (repealed)

Before this was repealed, the board of regents had "exclusive control" of all University funds and appropriations.

Art. IX, Section 15. School districts

> The general assembly shall, by law, provide for organization of school districts of convenient size, in each of which shall be established a board of education, to consist of three or more directors to be elected by the qualified electors of the district. Said directors shall have control of instruction in the public schools of their respective districts.

Local school board duties and organization are specified in great detail in C.R.S. § 22-32-101 et seq.

A major supreme court case on local vs. state control of schools stated:

> [T]he constitution requires balancing the local board's interest in exercising control over instruction with the State Board's interest in asserting its general supervisory authority . . . That balance will rarely be rigid. Indeed, it cannot be. . . [W]here the General Assembly has allocated authority between the State Board and local boards in order to further a legitimate educational purpose, we will give deference to the balance that it sought to maintain between the two entities. That is, we will presume the allocation is valid unless it clearly impedes the capacity of either the State Board or a local board to exercise its independent constitutional authority.

Board of Educ. of School Dist. No. 1 in City and County of Denver v. Booth, 984 P.2d 639 (Colo. 1999).

In Colorado, after three years in one district, a teacher becomes "nonprobationary" and is a nearly impossible to fire without great effort. An education reform statute requires a public school's principal to consent to the assignment of a teacher to the school. Likewise, a teacher can only be assigned to a school if he or she consents. Teacher Employment, Compensation, and Dismissal Act (TECDA), C.R.S. § 22-63-202. The purpose was to end the practice of shuffling incompetent teachers from one school to another. Pursuant to TECDA, if no principal within a district is willing to take a teacher, the teacher is placed on unpaid leave. The Colorado supreme court held that the statute violated no contractual or property rights of the teachers. *Johnson v. School District No. 1 in the County of Denver*, 2018 CO 17, 413 P.3d 711 (2018) (certified question from 10th Cir.); *School District No. 1 in City and County of Denver v. Masters*, 2018 CO 18, 413 P.3d 723 (Colo. 2018).

The above cases did not raise claims under article IX, Section 15. But after the teacher plaintiffs lost, a new suit was brought, based on taxpayer standing. It argued that TECDA, by requiring a principal's consent, violated section 15's standard that school boards "have control" of education in their districts. Since TECDA neither increased nor decreased school funding and taxes, the supreme court held that plaintiff's status as a taxpayer was not a basis for standing. *Reeves-Toney v. School District No. 1 in City and County of Denver*, 442 P.3d 81 (Colo. 2019).

Art. IX, Section 16. Textbooks

> Neither the general assembly nor the state board of education shall have power to prescribe textbooks to be used in the public schools.

Section 16 appears to have been obeyed from 1876 to the present.

The Midwest is the region with the strongest state constitutional tradition in favor of local decision-making, rather than statewide uniformity. Of the four state constitutions most influential to the Colorado framers, three were from the Midwest: Illinois (1870), Missouri (1875), Nebraska (1875), plus Pennsylvania (1873). (All of these states were replacing older constitutions.)

Section 16 is thoroughly Midwestern in spirit. Contrast Colorado's textbook policy with that of California and Texas. There, state boards create lists of textbooks that are authorized for use in the public schools.

Art. IX, Section 17. Automatic funding for K-12

In 2000, a citizen initiative championed by Jared Polis, among others, required extraordinary increases in state per-pupil education funding for the next decade. Thereafter (now), per-pupil funding must increase by at least the inflation rate. The general assembly can spend more if it chooses.

Section 17 is often said to be in tension with the Taxpayer's Bill of Rights (art. X, § 20). The former requires spending increases, while the latter limits spending increases. I suggest that there is no conflict. TABOR requires voter approval if the general assembly wants to increase overall state government spending beyond inflation plus population growth. Section 17 requires base per-pupil funding to increase at the inflation rate. If the pupil population goes up, then total per pupil must also rise. Accordingly, section 17 and TABOR are harmonious. Both are based on automatic spending increases at the inflation rate plus population growth.

The Colorado Constitution demands solid state support for public education, and the Constitution also demands voter control of extraordinary increases in state spending. Synthesizing section 17 and TABOR, here are some constitutional rules for public education spending:

- No matter what else is going on in the state budget, K-12 base per-pupil spending will always increase at the rate of inflation. Total per pupil spending will also in step with increased enrollment.
- Such spending may increase even further if:

  The legislature economizes on some other spending and devotes the savings to education. OR

  The legislature asks the voters to increase taxes for education, and the voters agree. OR

A school district asks the voters to increase taxes for education, and the voters agree.

Since TABOR was enacted in 1992, statewide voters have rejected a proposed state tax increase for education funding and a proposed increase of the state's revenue limits that was promised to be used for school funding. There are 179 school districts in Colorado. Almost all of them have made requests pursuant to TABOR to increases taxes or spending. Most such requests have been granted by the district's voters. *See* chapter 15.G. The voters likewise approved section 17, which did not raise taxes or total state spending, but did require the legislature to give greater priority to K-12 education funding.

(1) **Purpose.** In state fiscal year 2001-2002 through state fiscal year 2010-2011, the statewide base per pupil funding, as defined by the Public School Finance Act of 1994, article 54 of title 22, Colorado Revised Statutes on the effective date of this section, for public education from preschool through the twelfth grade and total state funding for all categorical programs [defined below] shall grow annually at least by the rate of inflation plus an additional one percentage point. In state fiscal year 2011-2012, and each fiscal year thereafter, the statewide base per pupil funding for public education from preschool through the twelfth grade and total state funding for all categorical programs shall grow annually at a rate set by the general assembly that is at least equal to the rate of inflation.

(2) **Definitions.** For purposes of this section:

(a) "Categorical programs" include transportation programs, English language proficiency programs, expelled and at-risk student programs, special education programs (including gifted and talented programs), suspended student programs, vocational education programs, small attendance centers, comprehensive health education programs, and other current and future accountable programs specifically identified in statute as a categorical program.

(b) "Inflation" has the same meaning as defined in article X, section 20, subsection (2), paragraph (f) of the Colorado constitution.

(3) **Implementation.** In state fiscal year 2001-2002 and each fiscal year thereafter, the general assembly may annually appropriate, and school districts may annually expend, monies from the state education fund created in subsection (4) of this section. Such appropriations and expenditures shall not be subject to the statutory limitation on general fund appropriations growth, the limitation on fiscal year spending set forth in article X, section 20 of the Colorado constitution, or any other spending limitation existing in law.

(4) **State Education Fund Created.**

(a) There is hereby created in the department of the treasury the state education fund. Beginning on the effective date of this measure, all state revenues collected from a tax of one third of one percent on federal taxable income, as modified by law, of every individual, estate, trust and corporation, as defined in law, shall be deposited in the state education fund. Revenues generated from a tax of one third of one percent on federal taxable income, as modified by law, of every individual, estate, trust and corporation, as defined in law, shall not be subject to the limitation on fiscal year spending set forth in article X, section 20 of the Colorado

> constitution. All interest earned on monies in the state education fund shall be deposited in the state education fund and shall be used before any principal is depleted. Monies remaining in the state education fund at the end of any fiscal year shall remain in the fund and not revert to the general fund.
>
> (b) In state fiscal year 2001-2002, and each fiscal year thereafter, the general assembly may annually appropriate monies from the state education fund. Monies in the state education fund may only be used to comply with subsection (1) of this section and for accountable education reform, for accountable programs to meet state academic standards, for class size reduction, for expanding technology education, for improving student safety, for expanding the availability of preschool and kindergarten programs, for performance incentives for teachers, for accountability reporting, or for public school building capital construction.
>
> (5) **Maintenance of Effort.** Monies appropriated from the state education fund shall not be used to supplant the level of general fund appropriations existing on the effective date of this section for total program education funding under the Public School Finance Act of 1994, article 54 of title 22, Colorado Revised Statutes, and for categorical programs as defined in subsection (2) of this section. In state fiscal year 2001-2002 through state fiscal year 2010-2011, the general assembly shall, at a minimum, annually increase the general fund appropriation for total program under the "Public School Finance Act of 1994," or any successor act, by an amount not below five percent of the prior year general fund appropriation for total program under the "Public School Finance Act of 1994," or any successor act. This general fund growth requirement shall not apply in any fiscal year in which Colorado personal income grows less than four and one half percent between the two previous calendar years. (Brackets added, parentheses in original).

Section 17 applies to "statewide base per pupil funding." The *base* funding per pupil is not the same as the *total* funding per pupil.

Base funding is the same for every pupil statewide. Pursuant to section 17, it always increases by the rate of inflation. Additional spending is not covered by section 17. The additional spending is calculated by first adding *factor funding* to the base funding.

Factor funding is a formula that gives varying additional amounts of money to districts based on: personnel costs, nonpersonnel costs, cost of living, district size, and the "at-risk factor." The single largest element in factor funding is the higher cost of living in most of the Front Range.

Once the formula has been applied to each school district, the next step is to add all the state funding together, to calculate the total amount of spending. Pursuant to a statute enacted in 2010, the total school spending in any given year is capped. If the initial calculation of total spending would exceed the cap, then the total spending must be reduced.

To reduce total spending, the factor funding is automatically cut as much as necessary. The base per pupil funding is never reduced. The cut in factor funding is the *budget stabilization factor* or the *negative factor*.

The supreme court, in an opinion by chief justice Rice, ruled that the negative factor does not violate the language of section 17. Three dissenters, led by justice Marquez, argued that since there was no negative factor in 2000, when section 17 was enacted, the voters must have expected that no future reduction in factor funding would be allowed. *Dwyer v. State*, 357 P.3d 185 (Colo. 2015).

The case below challenged state education funding as constitutionally inadequate. In *Lobato I*, the court held that the issue was justiciable. Then, following discovery and a district court decision, the court considered the merits in *Lobato II.*

Lobato v. State

304 P.3d 1132 (Colo. 2013) ("Lobato II")

[Background: A lawsuit argued that Colorado education spending was too low to create "a thorough and uniform" public school system, as required by section 2. In the *Lobato I* case, cited below, the court held that the question was justiciable. Thereafter, a district court agreed and stated that additional spending of $1.35 to 4.15 billion annually was constitutionally required. RICHARD B. COLLINS & DALE A. OESTERLE, THE COLORADO STATE CONSTITUTION 212 (2d ed. 2020). In *Lobato* II, the supreme court reversed 4–2. Recently appointed justice Marquez did not participate, since she had previously worked for the attorney general's office, which represented the defendants. Excerpts of the majority opinion and a dissent are below.]

JUSTICE RICE delivered the Opinion of the Court.

¶ 1 The public school financing system enacted by the General Assembly complies with the Colorado Constitution. It is rationally related to the constitutional mandate that the General Assembly provide a "thorough and uniform" system of public education. COLO. CONST. art. IX, § 2 (the "Education Clause"). It also affords local school districts control over locally-raised funds and therefore over "instruction in the public schools." COLO. CONST. art. IX, § 15 (the "Local Control Clause"). As such, the trial court erred when it declared the public school financing system unconstitutional. We accordingly reverse.

I. Facts and Procedural History

¶ 2 Respondent Plaintiffs, Anthony Lobato, et al. (the "Plaintiffs"), initiated this action for declaratory and injunctive relief in 2005. They claimed that the current public school financing system violates the Education Clause because the system fails to provide sufficient funding to support a "thorough and uniform" system of free public schools. Plaintiffs also claimed that local school districts' lack of sufficient financial resources, coupled with the public school financing system's restrictions on spending, prevents the districts from exerting meaningful control over educational instruction and quality in violation of the Local Control Clause.

[Discussion of earlier decision in the case, *Lobato I*, which held the funding question is justiciable.]

¶ 6 The case proceeded to trial. Plaintiffs and Defendants presented extensive evidence addressing the constitutionality of the public school financing system. Adopting the Plaintiffs' proposed findings of fact and conclusions of law almost verbatim, the trial court held that Colorado's current public school financing system is not rationally related to the General Assembly's constitutional mandate to provide a "thorough and uniform" system of free public schools. The trial court also held that the "irrational" public school financing system violates the Local Control Clause because it deprives individual school districts of the opportunity to implement the Education Clause's "thorough and uniform" mandate. Accordingly, the trial court enjoined Defendants from continuing to execute the current public school financing system. The trial court stayed enforcement of this injunction to provide the state reasonable time to create and implement a system of public school financing that complies with the Colorado Constitution.

¶ 7 Defendants appealed the trial court's order directly to this Court pursuant to section 13-4-102(1)(b), C.R.S. (2012). [Which allows the option of direct appeal to the Colorado supreme court if a state statute or local ordinance is held unconstitutional.]

. . .

C. The Public School Financing System is Rationally Related to the "Thorough and Uniform" Mandate

¶ 14 The Education Clause of the Colorado Constitution directs the General Assembly to "provide for the establishment and maintenance of a thorough and uniform system of free public schools throughout the state." COLO. CONST. art. IX, § 2. This mandate requires the General Assembly to enact education policy that furnishes a "thorough and uniform" free education to "all residents of the state, between the ages of six and twenty-one years." *Id.* We held in *Lobato I* that the legislative scheme that makes up Colorado's public school financing system must be "rationally related to the constitutional mandate that the General Assembly provide a 'thorough and uniform' system of public education" to comply with the Education Clause. 218 P.3d at 363.

¶ 15 Despite articulating this custom-tailored rational basis test, this Court did not expressly interpret the Education Clause or define the phrase "thorough and uniform" in *Lobato I.* Therefore, before addressing the public school financing system, we interpret the plain meaning of "thorough and uniform" as it appears in the Education Clause. We then briefly discuss the unique type of rational basis review set out in *Lobato I* in light of our definition of "thorough and uniform." Finally, we apply the *Lobato I* test and conclude that the public school financing system is "rationally related to the constitutional mandate that the General Assembly provide a 'thorough and uniform' system of public education." *See id.*

1. Thorough and Uniform

¶ 16 We hold that the phrase "thorough and uniform" in the Education Clause describes a free public school system that is of a quality marked by completeness, is comprehensive, and is consistent across the state.

¶ 17 The Colorado Constitution tasks the judicial branch with construing the meaning of constitutional language. *See* Colo. Const. art. VI, § 1. "In giving effect to a constitutional provision, we employ the same set of construction rules applicable to statutes." *Danielson v. Dennis*, 139 P.3d 688, 691 (Colo. 2006). We begin by giving the relevant constitutional terms "their plain and commonsense meaning." *Id.* (citing *Bd. of Cnty. Comm'rs v. Vail Assocs., Inc.*, 19 P.3d 1263, 1273 (Colo. 2001)). We also read the applicable constitutional provisions as a whole. *Id.*

¶ 18 . . . The adjective "thorough" commonly refers to something of a quality that is "marked by completeness." WEBSTER'S THIRD NEW INTERNATIONAL DICTIONARY 2380 (1971). It also refers to something that is "marked by attention to many details," or is, in other words, comprehensive. *Id.* The term "uniform" connotes something that is characterized "by a lack of variation, diversity, [or] change in form" or that is "consistent . . . in character." *Id.* at 2498. Thus, a "thorough and uniform" system of public education is of a quality marked by completeness, is comprehensive, and is consistent across the state.

¶ 19 Reading the "thorough and uniform" mandate in context supports our plain language construction. First, the Education Clause requires the state to provide public school opportunities to "all residents of the state, between the ages of six and twenty-one years." Colo. Const. art. IX, § 2. This language supports our interpretation of "thorough and uniform" because a public school system that serves all Colorado residents between the ages of six and twenty-one is of a quality marked by completeness, is comprehensive, and is consistent across the state by providing educational opportunities to all Colorado residents within a broad age-range. In addition, the Education Clause provides that "[o]ne or more public schools" be open "at least three months in each year" in each school district to receive state funding. Id. This minimal requirement also supports our interpretation of the phrase "thorough and uniform" because it, together with the "thorough and uniform" mandate, simply establishes the constitutional floor upon which the General Assembly must build its education policy.

¶ 20 Our interpretation of "thorough and uniform" is consistent with this Court's previous treatment of the "thorough and uniform" mandate. For example, instead of affirmatively defining "through and uniform" in *Lujan*, this Court described what a "thorough and uniform" system of public schools does not require. 649 P.2d at 1024–25. The Court held that the "thorough and uniform" mandate does not necessitate "absolute equality in educational services or expenditures," nor does it direct "the General Assembly [to] establish a central public school finance system restricting each school district to equal expenditures per student." *Id.* at 1017-18. Furthermore, the Lujan Court noted that "'thorough and uniform' does not require complete equality in the sense of providing free textbooks to all students." *Id.* (citing *Marshall v. Sch. Dist. RE # 3 Morgan Cnty.*, 191 Colo. 451, 553 P.2d 784 (1976)). Our interpretation of "thorough and uniform" is consistent with the exclusions described in Lujan because providing a public school system that is of a quality marked by completeness, is comprehensive, and is consistent across the state does not demand absolute equality in the state's provision of educational services, supplies, or expenditures.

. . .

2. The *Lobato I* Rational Basis Test

¶ 22 This Court held in *Lobato I* that the judiciary must "determine whether the state's public school financing system is rationally related to the constitutional mandate that the General Assembly provide a 'thorough and uniform' system of public education." 218 P.3d at 363. Inserting our interpretation of "thorough and uniform" into this test and clarifying the meaning of "rationally related" in this unique context, we hold that Colorado's public school financing system is rationally related to the "thorough and uniform" mandate of the Education Clause if it funds a public school system that is of a quality marked by completeness, is comprehensive, and is consistent across the state.

¶ 23 As this Court stated in *Lobato I*, our custom-tailored form of rational basis review "satisfies the judiciary's obligation to evaluate the constitutionality of the state's public school financing system without unduly infringing on the legislature's policymaking authority." *Id.* In applying this test to the public school financing system, our task is not to determine "'whether a better financing system could be devised,'" but rather to determine "whether the system passes constitutional muster." Id. (quoting *Lujan*, 649 P.2d at 1025). We presume that the statutes that make up the public school financing system are constitutional, and we will uphold the legislation unless the Plaintiffs have proven beyond a reasonable doubt that the statutes fail to pass the *Lobato I* rational basis test, and are therefore unconstitutional. *See Owens v. Colo. Cong. of Parents, Teachers & Students*, 92 P.3d 933, 942 (Colo.2004).

3. Application

¶ 24 The current public school financing system is rationally related to the "thorough and uniform" mandate because it funds a system of free public schools that is of a quality marked by completeness, is comprehensive, and is consistent across the state. Therefore, the financing system satisfies the *Lobato I* rational basis test and complies with the Education Clause. We describe the basic components of the public school financing system and then analyze its rational relationship to the "thorough and uniform" mandate in the following subsections.

a. Colorado's Public School Financing System

¶ 25 The public school financing system combines local taxes, state appropriations, and federal monies to fund the statewide standards-based public education system. The Public School Financing Act of 1994 ("PSFA") governs the majority of state and local funding for education. §§ 22-54-101 to -135, C.R.S. (2012). The PSFA sets out a uniform per-pupil formula that the state uses to calculate the amount of education funding each school district shall receive in a given year. § 22-54-104(1)(a); *see, e.g.,* § 22-54-104(5) (XIX). This formula requires the state to multiply a statutory per-pupil base level of funding by the number of students enrolled in the subject school district. § 22-54-104(1)(a). The state then adjusts the resulting product to account for district-specific "factors" such as personnel costs, cost of living, concentrations of at-risk students, online education enrollment, and the number of fifth-year high school pupils enrolled in the district. § 22-54-104(2) -(4). The money each school district receives as a result of these calculations is called the district's "total program." § 22-54-104(1)(a). In response to the reality of statewide budget reductions in recent years, the state now uniformly reduces each district's total program by a "negative factor" that reflects statewide funding cuts. § 22-54-104(5)(g)(1).

¶ 26 The PSFA also defines the contours of the dual-funded public school financing system by describing the sources of revenue needed to ensure that each school district receives its total program. The "local share" of a school district's total program consists of proceeds from a mill levy upon the assessed valuation of the taxable property within a school district's boundaries and, to a lesser degree, a "specific ownership tax." *See* § 22-54-106(1)(a)(I). Although the statutes restrict the amount of money school districts may raise using mill levies, *see* § 22-54-106(2)(a), the PSFA permits school districts to supplement their total programs with additional local revenues by asking their electorates to approve additional mill levies for education purposes, *see* § 22-54-108. This supplemental form of local revenue for education is known as a "mill levy override." *See id.*

¶ 27 The "state share" of a school district's allocated funding is derived by subtracting the district's "local share" from its total program. § 22-54-106(1)(b)(I). The money for each school district's "state share" comes from the state general fund, the Education Fund, and from a portion of the rents generated by state school lands and federal mineral leases. *See* § 22-55-105, C.R.S. (2012) (general fund appropriation requirements for education).

¶ 28 In addition to the total program funding provided by the PSFA, the public school financing system provides "categorical" funding to serve particular groups of students and particular student needs. § 22-5-102(4), C.R.S. (2012) (defining "categorical programs"); § 22-55-107, C.R.S. (2012) (describing funding for categorical programs). For example, categorical funding is available for English language learners, at-risk students, and disabled children. § 22-55-102(4). The system also permits school districts to contract bonded indebtedness for education-related capital improvements or construction with voter approval. § 22-42-102(2)(a), C.R.S. (2012).

b. The System is Rationally Related to the "Thorough and Uniform" Mandate

¶ 29 The public school financing system is rationally related to the "thorough and uniform" mandate because it funds a system of free public schools that is of a quality marked by completeness, is comprehensive, and is consistent across the state. It does so using a multi-faceted statutory approach that applies uniformly to all of the school districts in Colorado.

¶ 30 The primary component of the public school finance system, the PSFA, uses a standard formula that incorporates enrollment numbers, a per-pupil base amount of money, and applicable statutory factors to calculate an amount of money each district will receive in a given year from a combination of state and local sources. By supplying the single statutory framework whereby the state may calculate every district's total program, and by describing the sources of state and local revenue that make up the calculated amounts, the PSFA applies uniformly to all of Colorado's school districts and serves as the cornerstone of a public school financing system that funds a public education system that is of a quality marked by completeness, is comprehensive, and is consistent across the state.

¶ 31 In addition, the public school financing system's "categorical" funding for particular groups of students—for example, English language learners, at-risk students, and children with disabilities—also contributes to the public school financing system's rational relationship to the "thorough and uniform" mandate. Categorical funding allocates money beyond the base PSFA amount for children that require supplemental resources. It therefore assists in providing every child in Colorado, including children with greater needs than the general student population, with educational opportunities. Thus, categorical funding contributes to the public school financing system's rational relationship to the "thorough and uniform" mandate by helping fund a statewide public school system that is more complete and comprehensive.

¶ 32 Furthermore, the public school financing system provides a mechanism—contracting for bonded indebtedness—whereby individual school districts may ask their constituents to fund capital improvements or the construction of new school facilities. This mechanism contributes to the rational relationship between the public school financing system and the "thorough and uniform" mandate because bonded indebtedness gives local school districts the authority to generate funding for capital improvements that help facilitate the implementation of a public school system that is of a quality marked by completeness, is comprehensive, and is consistent across the state.

¶ 33 In sum, our de novo review of the relevant legislation reveals that the public school financing system is rationally related to the "thorough and uniform" mandate. The Plaintiffs did not establish beyond a reasonable doubt that the system fails to pass constitutional muster under the Lobato I rational basis test. While we sympathize with the Plaintiffs and recognize that the public school financing system might not provide an optimal amount of money to the public schools, the statutory public school financing system itself is constitutional. Accordingly, we reverse the trial court's holding that "the entire system of public school financing is not rationally related to the mandate of the Education Clause."

D. Local Control

¶ 34 The dual-funded public school financing system complies with the Local Control Clause because it affords local school districts control over locally-raised funds and therefore over "instruction in the public schools."

¶ 35 We presume that the statutes that make up the public school financing system are constitutional, and we will uphold the legislation unless the Plaintiffs have proven the statutes are unconstitutional beyond a reasonable doubt. *See Owens*, 92 P.3d at 942. The Local Control Clause limits the state's power over instruction in each district's public schools. To determine whether the dual-funded public school financing system complies with the Local Control Clause, we analyze whether that system affords local school districts control over locally-raised funds and therefore over "instruction in the public schools." *Id.* at 935.

. . .

1. Local Control Principles and Precedent

¶ 37 The Local Control Clause of the Colorado Constitution provides:

> The general assembly shall, by law, provide for organization of school districts of convenient size, in each of which shall be established a board of education, to consist of three or more directors to be elected by the qualified electors of the district. *Said directors shall have control of instruction in the public schools of their respective districts.*

Colo. Const. art. IX, § 15 (emphasis added).

¶ 38 "'[T]he historical development of public education in Colorado has been centered on the philosophy of local control'" due to the freedom and flexibility local control provides. *Owens*, 92 P.3d at 941 (quoting *Lujan*, 649 P.2d at 1021). "The use of local taxes affords a school district the freedom to devote more money toward educating its children than is otherwise available in the state-guaranteed minimum amount." *Lujan*, 649 P.2d at 1023. Prioritizing local control "also enables the local citizenry greater influence and participation in the decision making process as to how the[ir] local tax dollars are spent. Some communities might place heavy emphasis on schools, while others may desire greater police or fire protection, or improved streets or public transportation." *Id.*; *see Owens*, 92 P.3d at 941 ("Allowing a district to raise and disburse its own funds enables the district to determine its own education policy, free from restrictions imposed by the state or any other entity."). Furthermore, "local control provides each district with the opportunity for experimentation, innovation, and a healthy competition for educational excellence." *Lujan*, 649 P.2d at 1023. Thus, the question of whether the General Assembly has afforded school districts local control over instruction in the public schools plays a crucial role in this Court's constitutionality analysis of public school financing legislation.

. . .

2. Application

¶ 42 The dual-funded public school financing system at issue in this case complies with the Local Control Clause because it affords local school districts control over locally-raised funds and therefore over instruction in the public schools. As it did when this Court decided *Lujan* and Mesa County, the PSFA permissibly requires that the money comprising the total program for each school district in a given year come from a combination of state and local revenues, with the local districts retaining responsibility for imposing, collecting, and expending local property taxes collected for education purposes. *See* § 22-54-106.

¶ 43 Unlike the unconstitutional pilot program in *Owens*, however, the public school financing system does not affirmatively require school districts to use their locally-raised revenue in any particular manner. Even if school districts use a substantial portion of their locally-raised funds to help their students achieve state standards—as the trial court found they do—nothing in the public school financing system itself requires a particular allocation of local funds.

¶ 44 The system also provides mill levy override and bonded indebtedness mechanisms which authorize school districts to raise additional revenue beyond their total programs. These mechanisms afford school districts the opportunity to exert additional local control over instruction by generating and using supplemental local funds. While we recognize that "disparities in wealth" may impair a low-wealth district's ability to pass mill levy overrides and bonded indebtedness, such a "result, by itself, does not strike down the entire school finance system" on Local Control grounds, just as the same result did not strike down the entire school finance system for equal protection purposes in *Lujan.* 649 P.2d at 1023 (citations omitted). Therefore, the public school financing system does not unconstitutionally usurp local control over instruction in the public schools. Instead, it affords local school districts control over locally raised funds, and therefore over "instruction in the public schools," by providing a dual-funded financing regime that refrains from affirmatively directing school districts to use their locally raised revenues in any particular fashion. *See Mesa Cnty*., 203 P.3d at 530; *Owens*, 92 P.3d at 943. While we do not dispute that public education in Colorado would benefit from additional funding, the local control built into the public school financing system "provides each district with the opportunity for experimentation [and] innovation" in using limited resources to achieve educational excellence. Lujan, 649 P.2d at 1023. The public school financing system is therefore constitutional under the Local Control Clause.

III. Conclusion

¶ 45 We have held that "courts must avoid making decisions that are intrinsically legislative. It is not up to the court to make policy or to weigh policy." *Town of Telluride v. Lot Thirty–Four Venture, L.L.C.*, 3 P.3d 30, 38 (Colo. 2000); *see also Lobato I*, 218 P.3d at 381 (Rice, J., dissenting). While the trial court's detailed findings of fact demonstrate that the current public school financing system might not be ideal policy, this Court's task is not to determine "'whether a better financing system could be devised, but rather to determine whether the system passes constitutional muster.'" *Lobato I*, 218 P.3d at 374 (quoting *Lujan*, 649 P.2d at 1025) (internal citation omitted).

¶ 46 Our holding today that the current public school financing system complies with the Education and Local Control Clauses of the Colorado Constitution satisfies this Court's duty "to say what the law is," *see Marbury v. Madison*, 5 U.S. 137, 177, 1 Cranch 137, 2 L.Ed. 60 (1803), without unduly infringing upon the policy-making power of the General Assembly. It thereby affords the General Assembly an opportunity to reform Colorado's education policy, including the public school financing system, consistent with this opinion.

¶ 47CHIEF JUSTICE BENDER dissents, and JUSTICE HOBBS joins in the dissent.
¶ 48 JUSTICE HOBBS dissents, and CHIEF JUSTICE BENDER joins in the dissent.
JUSTICE MÁRQUEZ does not participate.
CHIEF JUSTICE BENDER, dissenting.

¶ 49 Today, the majority abdicates this court's responsibility to give meaningful effect to the Education Clause's guarantee that all Colorado students receive a thorough and uniform education. In my view, a thorough and uniform system of education must include the availability of qualified teachers, up-to-date textbooks, access to modern technology, and safe and healthy facilities in which to learn. The record, however, reveals an education system that is fundamentally broken. It is plagued by underfunding and marked by gross funding disparities among districts. Colorado's school-age population has exploded, with dramatic increases in the number of Hispanic students, low-income students, English language learners, and students with special needs. The General Assembly has failed to recognize these changes and to fund the increased costs necessary to educate these children. Colorado's education system is, beyond any reasonable doubt, neither thorough nor uniform. I would hold that Colorado's method for financing public education is not rationally related to the General Assembly's affirmative duty to provide and to maintain a thorough and uniform system of free public schools. This affirmative obligation requires the General Assembly to implement a finance system that provides Colorado's students the education system to which they are constitutionally entitled. Hence, I respectfully dissent.

I.

. . .

¶ 54 Colorado is one of the wealthiest states in the nation, but it ranks 49th in the country in per-pupil spending per $1,000 of personal income. Colorado ranks 45th in the country for the amount of taxable resources dedicated to public education. In one national study, Colorado received an "F" for funding "effort"—a measure of whether a state takes advantage of its fiscal capacity to fund public education—because Colorado spends such a small percentage of its gross state product on public schools. By almost any measure, Colorado ranks in the bottom third nationally in education spending.

¶ 55 And the cost of educating Colorado's changing population continues to increase. Colorado's population of students requiring more expensive education services—such as English language learners (ELL), low-income children, and special education students—has exploded. Since 1995, Colorado's ELL population has grown 250%. In some districts, the ELL population has grown by as much as 800% in the last decade. Colorado has the fastest growing rate of childhood poverty in the nation. Across the state, 30% of students are eligible for the federal free lunch program . . . .

¶ 56 Meanwhile, the General Assembly continues to promulgate new education standards. These standards require all Colorado students to attain proficiency in a broad range of subjects and be ready for postsecondary education or entry into the "twenty-first-century workforce" by graduation. They stress "information technology application" and other modern skills. To conform to these new standards, school districts must develop updated curricula, buy new instructional materials, train teachers, and have access to modern technology . . . .

¶ 57 These historical developments have not occurred in a vacuum. Student performance rates continue to decline. Colorado ranks 46th in the nation in the rate of high school completion. For those students who do graduate high school, 29% are not college-ready, meaning they must take remedial classes before taking college-level courses. In some districts, over 50% of students are not college-ready by graduation . . . . Despite these gaps, Colorado boasts one of the most college-educated populations in the country, but most of Colorado's college graduates are from other states. According to former state Senator Keith King, this "Colorado Paradox" shows that Colorado has not prepared its own students for college . . . .

II.

. . .

¶ 61 Many of Colorado's students lack safe and healthy school buildings . . . The average school building is nearly 40 years old, and many have architectural problems and inadequate heating, lighting, and plumbing systems. Several witnesses testified to leaking roofs and falling ceiling tiles. . . . Some schools are infested with mice, bats, or rattlesnakes.

¶ 62 Many schools do not comply with the Americans with Disabilities Act and are largely inaccessible to students with special needs. [The ADA applies to new construction and to remodels of old construction; it does not require that old construction, which is not remodeled, be brought into conformity with modern standards.] . . .

¶ 63 Students lack books and basic supplies. Schools in Adams County, Boulder, Colorado Springs, Greeley, Pueblo, and rural areas do not have enough textbooks for each student to have one. Some schools allow students to take books home only on a first-come, first-served basis. Other schools employ strict no-take-home policies because if a student loses or damages a book, they do not have money to replace it . . . In the Boulder Valley School District, Fairview High School has to, in the words of principal Donald L. Stensrud, "choose desks or choose books."[4]

¶ 64 The textbooks that districts do have are often out of date. Kevin Edgar, the superintendent of Sanford, testified that a high school student approached him with a physics book and said, "I'm using the same book you did." . . .[5]

. . . .

¶ 66 Students who require additional support, such as ELL students, special education students, and gifted and talented students, do not receive it. At best, Colorado funds two years of English-language instruction despite expert testimony that ELL students need between four and seven years of instruction to become proficient. Several parents testified that their children, who did not speak English when they began school, received only one or two years of English-language instruction and still struggle to speak English in high school.[6]

. . .

¶ 68 Colorado's director for gifted and talented programs, Jacquelin Medina, testified to a lack of funding for gifted and talented programs. Two Boulder elementary schools rely on parent volunteers to help with gifted and talented programming because the schools do not have money to hire enough teachers. Many rural districts do not offer advanced placement classes because they do not have the teachers to teach them. At one rural school, 8th graders identified as gifted and talented in math were given a CD and sent to the library to teach themselves algebra. Taylor Lobato, the named plaintiff in this case, graduated first in her class and was, according to Superintendent George Welsh, one of the best students he had ever seen. Still, as a freshman at the University of Denver, her professors sent her to the grammar center because she lacked grammar skills. Whereas her college roommate received 45 college credits for advanced placement classes she took in high school, Lobato took no advanced placement classes because her district, like many others, could not afford to offer them.

---

[4] [As everyone in Boulder knows, Fairview is not a school on the knife edge of poverty. If Fairview could not, at the time, afford both desks and books, the dilemma suggests mismanagement.]

[5] [Discoveries in physics since 1980 have not really changed the necessary content of high school physics textbooks.]

[6] [Instead of keeping immigrant children in ELL, a different approach would be a year of education dedicated full-time to learning English, after which students could join regular classes.]

III.

. . .

A. Thorough

¶ 71 Since the inception of the PSFA, the base amount of per-pupil funding has never been determined in relation to the costs necessary to educate Colorado's students. It was born out of political compromise and budgetary wrangling. The PSFA has never been significantly revised. No adjustments have been made to account for Colorado's changing demographics, the increased costs associated with educating Colorado's changing student population, or the increased funds necessary to implement the new state-mandated education standards. The funding provided by the PSFA bears no rational relationship to the actual cost of providing a thorough and uniform education.

. . .

¶ 80 For the reasons stated, I respectfully dissent.

I am authorized to state that Justice HOBBS joins in this dissent.

JUSTICE HOBBS, dissenting.

[Historical exposition of the importance of education, in the 1876 Constitution.]

I am authorized to state that Chief Justice BENDER joins in the dissent.

Further reading: Molly A. Hunter & Kathleen J. Gebhardt, *Legal Precedent and the Opportunity for Educational Equity: Where to Now, Colorado?* 50 U. RICHMOND L. REVIEW 893 (2016) (Gebhardt was lead counsel for plaintiffs in the *Lobato* cases).

Part III

Taxes and Spending

CHAPTER 14

Taxes and Revenue, article X

Taxation without consent is illegitimate, and it provides good cause to replace the nonconsensual government with a consensual one. At least that is the theory of government upon which the United States is based. Article X is the mechanism by which the people of Colorado consent to some taxation, prohibit some taxation, and reserve their options to give or withhold consent.

Property taxes are imposed by state, county, and other local governments. They are governed by Art. X, § 3. The state income tax was created by section 17. Other Colorado taxes include sales taxes, severance taxes, excise taxes, and many "fees" and "special assessments"—for example, a "transfer fee" on real property sales, or special assessments for hook-ups to water or sewer lines.

This chapter does not cover the Taxpayer's Bill of Rights (art. X, § 20), or tobacco taxes (art. X, § 21). The Taxpayer's Bill of Rights is covered in the next chapter. Tobacco taxes are discussed in chapter 31 (Vices?).

The statutes for property taxes are in title 39, articles 1-14 of C.R.S. Other taxes (*e.g.*, income, gasoline) are covered in articles 15-35 of the same title.

Art. X, Section 1. Fiscal Year

> The fiscal year shall commence on the first day of October in each year, unless otherwise provided by law.

The fiscal year may be changed, "as provided by law." By statute, the Colorado state government fiscal year commences on July 1. C.R.S. § 24-30-204.

Art. X, Section 2. Every fiscal year of spending must be paid by annual sufficient taxes

> The general assembly shall provide by law for an annual tax sufficient, with other resources, to defray the estimated expenses of the state government for each fiscal year.

In other words, the legislature must raise enough revenue every year to pay for the year's spending. No deficit spending. *E.g., People ex rel. Regents of State University v. State Bd. of Equalization of Colorado*, 20 Colo. 220, 37 P. 964 (1894). See also section 16, which requires that appropriations not exceed revenue.

Art. X, Section 3. Uniform property taxation, and exceptions

This is the main section for property taxes. One of the Constitution's many anti-special interest provisions, it requires property taxes must be uniform within the relevant taxable jurisdiction. Property taxes can include real property and other property. Bolded headings are by Kopel.

> (1) **Property tax shall be uniform within the levying authority's territory. Agricultural land is taxed based on its agricultural value, not its potential value for development. Residential property is taxed based on its cost and market value—not upon how much income might be earned if it were converted to rental.**
>
> (a) <u>Each property tax levy shall be uniform upon all real and personal property</u> not exempt from taxation under this article located within the territorial limits of the authority levying the tax. The actual value of all real and personal property not exempt from taxation under this article shall be determined under general laws, which shall prescribe such methods and regulations as shall secure just and equalized valuations for assessments of all real and personal property not exempt from taxation under this article. Valuations for assessment shall be based on appraisals by assessing officers to determine the actual value of property in accordance with provisions of law, which laws shall provide that actual value be determined by appropriate consideration of cost approach, market approach, and income approach to appraisal. However, the actual value of residential real property shall be

determined solely by consideration of cost approach and market approach to appraisal; and, however, the actual value of agricultural lands, as defined by law, shall be determined solely by consideration of the earning or productive capacity of such lands capitalized at a rate as prescribed by law.

(b) Residential real property, which shall include all residential dwelling units and the land, as defined by law, on which such units are located, and mobile home parks, but shall not include hotels and motels, shall be valued for assessment. All other taxable property shall be valued for assessment. The valuation for assessment for producing mines, as defined by law, and lands or leaseholds producing oil or gas, as defined by law, shall be a portion of the actual annual or actual average annual production therefrom, based upon the value of the unprocessed material, according to procedures prescribed by law for different types of minerals. Non-producing unpatented mining claims, which are possessory interests in real property by virtue of leases from the United States of America, shall be exempt from property taxation.

(c) **Household furnishings, business inventory, livestock, and agricultural equipment are exempt from property taxes.** The following classes of personal property, as defined by law, shall be exempt from property taxation: Household furnishings and personal effects which are not used for the production of income at any time; inventories of merchandise and materials and supplies which are held for consumption by a business or are held primarily for sale; livestock; agricultural and livestock products; and agricultural equipment which is used on the farm or ranch in the production of agricultural products.

(d) **Irrigation channels may not be separately taxed.** Ditches, canals, and flumes owned and used by individuals or corporations for irrigating land owned by such individuals or corporations, or the individual members thereof, shall not be separately taxed so long as they shall be owned and used exclusively for such purposes.

(2) **The general assembly must provide for studies to ensure that all county assessors are assessing property according to law. If the county assessors are seriously undervaluing property, the state board of equalization will conduct a reassessment.**

(a) During each property tax year beginning with the property tax year which commences January 1, 1983, the general assembly shall cause a valuation for assessment study to be conducted. Such study shall determine whether or not the assessor of each county has complied with the property tax provisions of this constitution and of the statutes in valuing property and has determined the actual value and valuation for assessment of each and every class of taxable real and personal property consistent with such provisions. Such study shall sample at least one percent of each and every class of taxable real and personal property in the county.

(b)

(I) If the study conducted during the property tax year which commences January 1, 1983, shows that a county assessor did not comply with the property tax provisions of this constitution or the statutes or did not determine the actual value or the valuation for assessment of any class or classes of taxable real and personal property consistent with such provisions, the state board of equalization shall, during such year, order such county assessor to reappraise during the property tax year which commences January 1, 1984, such class or classes for such year. Such reappraisal shall be performed at the expense of the county.

(II) If the study performed during the property tax year which commences January 1, 1984, shows that the county assessor failed to reappraise such class or classes as ordered or failed in his reappraisal to meet the objections of the state board of equalization, the state board of equalization shall cause a reappraisal of such class or classes to be performed in the property tax year which commences January 1, 1985. The cost of such reappraisal shall be paid by the state by an appropriation authorized by law. However, if such reappraisal shows that the county assessor did not value or assess taxable property as prescribed by the provisions of this constitution or of the statutes, upon certification to the board of county commissioners by the state board of equalization of the cost thereof, the board of county commissioners shall pay to the state the cost of such reappraisal.

(III) The reappraisal performed in the property tax year which commences January 1, 1985, shall become the county's abstract for assessment with regard to such reappraised class or classes for such year. The state board of equalization shall order the county's board of county commissioners to levy, and the board of county commissioners shall levy, in 1985 an additional property tax on all taxable property in the county in an amount sufficient to repay, and the board of county commissioners shall repay, the state for any excess payment made by the state to school districts within the county during the property tax year which commences January 1, 1985.

(c)

(I) Beginning with the property tax year which commences January 1, 1985, and applicable to each property tax year thereafter, the annual study conducted pursuant to paragraph (a) of this subsection (2) shall, in addition to the requirements set forth in paragraph (a) of this subsection (2), set forth the aggregate valuation for assessment of each county for the year in which the study is conducted.

(II) If the valuation for assessment of a county as reflected in its abstract for assessment is more than five percent below the valuation for assessment for such county as determined by the study, during the next following year, the state board of

> equalization shall cause to be performed, at the expense of the county, a reappraisal of any class or classes of taxable property which the study shows were not appraised consistent with the property tax provisions of this constitution or the statutes. The state board of equalization shall cause to be performed during the next following year, at the expense of the county, a reappraisal of any class or classes of taxable property which the study shows were not appraised consistent with the property tax provisions of this constitution or the statutes even though the county's aggregate valuation for assessment as reflected in the county's abstract for assessment was not more than five percent below the county's aggregate valuation for assessment as determined by the study. The reappraisal shall become the county's valuation for assessment with regard to such reappraised class or classes for the year in which the reappraisal was performed.
> (III) In any case in which a reappraisal is ordered, state equalization payments to school districts within the county during the year in which the reappraisal is performed shall be based upon the valuation for assessment as reflected in the county's abstract for assessment. The state board of equalization shall also order the board of county commissioners of the county to impose, and the board of county commissioners shall impose, at the time of imposition of property taxes during such year an additional property tax on all taxable property within the county in an amount sufficient to repay, and the board of county commissioners shall repay, the state for any excess payments made by the state to school districts within the county during the year in which such reappraisal was performed plus interest thereon at a rate and for such time as are prescribed by law.
> (IV) If the valuation for assessment of a county as reflected in its abstract for assessment is more than five percent below the valuation for assessment for such county as determined by the study and if the state board of equalization fails to order a reappraisal, state equalization payments to school districts within the county during the year following the year in which the study was conducted shall be based upon the valuation for assessment for the county as reflected in the county's abstract for assessment. The board of county commissioners of such county shall impose in the year in which such school payments are made an additional property tax on all taxable property in the county in an amount sufficient to repay, and the board of county commissioners shall repay, the state for the difference between the amount the state actually paid in state equalization payments during such year and what the state would have paid during such year had such state payments been based on the valuation for assessment as determined by the study.

Original section 3 was one paragraph, requiring:

- "All taxes shall be uniform on the same class of subjects" within the taxing authority's jurisdiction.

- Taxes "shall be levied and collected under general laws."
- The general laws "shall secure a just valuation for the taxation for taxation of all property."

While the Constitution favored uniformity of taxation as the standard rule, the Constitution made a special rule for mining: mines and claims for precious metals would not be taxed for the first 10 years. Mining surface improvements would be taxed under the normal rules. To encourage irrigation, "[d]itches, canals, and flumes" used for irrigating one's own land could be "separately taxed."

As of 1876, mining was the *sine qua non* of the Colorado economy. Irrigation was essential for survival of most of the population. While the Constitution laid down the worthy principle of uniformity of taxation, it also allowed for exceptions based upon the practical needs of the time—mining and irrigation. The constitutional amendment process allows for continuing adjustment of the rules, based on consent of the voters. Section 3 has been amended 13 times.

Additional constitutional rules against tax favoritism are in article X, sections 8 and 9, below.

"The general assembly has been resourceful and has narrowed considerably Section 3's limitations on its discretion. It has created exceptions by defining 'real and personal property,' has creatively defined the section's explicit exemptions, and has liberally used its power to define and apply separate rates to the classes of property." RICHARD COLLINS & DALE A. OESTERLE, THE COLORADO STATE CONSTITUTION 232 (2d ed. 2020).

The assessment of property values is done by the county assessor. Section (2) requires the state board of equalization to audit the county assessors, to ensure that the county assessors are valuing property pursuant to the constitutional rules. In particular, to be sure that assessors are not undervaluing property in the county.

Agricultural and irrigation

Pursuant to subsection (1), agricultural land is to be taxed based on its agricultural value. Consider a family farm that might be twice as valuable if sold to a shopping mall developer rather than used for agriculture. Subsection (1) protects farm or ranch land from having to be sold for development because of a crushing tax burden.

The original 1876 generous treatment of irrigation continues in today's subsection (2)(d). Before the introduction of irrigation in Colorado in 1870, there was hardly any agriculture in the territory, except near rivers. The Colorado Constitution is strongly pro-irrigation. This can also be seen in article XVI (Mining and Irrigation). Breaking with water law doctrine of states to the east, semiarid Colorado gives water use priority based on the doctrine of *prior appropriation*. The first person to put the water to beneficial use has the highest priority for use of the water. As article XVI specifies, the ownership of a water right includes a right to whatever easements are necessary for ditches or other channels. Again, this is a constitutional change from the common law system of property rights.

The irrigation exemption does not apply to the owner of an irrigation system who does not own the land where the system is located. *San Luis Power & Water Co. v. Trujillo*, 93 Colo. 385, 26 P.2d 537 (1933). The exemption *does* apply to "headgates, dams, reservoirs, reservoir beds, the earth upon which a dam stands, and the lands surrounding the reservoirs with the improvements thereon that are an integral part of the irrigation system as a whole and necessary for its proper maintenance and operation." *Jacobucci v. District Court In and For Jefferson County*, 189 Colo. 380, 386-87, 541 P.2d 667 (1975). The tax exemption does not apply to horses, machinery, or tools used for maintenance or repair. *Koenig v. Jewish Consumptives' Relief Soc'y*, 98 Colo. 253, 55 P.2d 325 (1936) ("Said section 3 exempts from separate taxation certain ditches, canals, and flumes. These are worthless unless cleaned and repaired. But the exemption does not reach the horses, machinery, and tools with which the cleaning and repairing is done.").

Related to section 3, the Taxpayer's Bill of Rights, art. X, § 20, forbids any new state tax on real property. It also requires that residential property taxes be based on the market value of the home. Chapter 15.

The Gallagher Amendment

From enactment in 1982 until repeal in 2020, section 3 contained the Gallagher Amendment.[1] It specified that residential property taxes must comprise 45% of a county's real property tax revenue. The long-term effect was to shift property tax burdens from residences to businesses. Although a 1998 effort to repeal Gallagher failed by 3:1 margin, a well-organized repeal effort succeeded in 2020. Proponents pointed out that the Gallagher formula caused difficulties in some counties where residential property values have risen much faster than business property. Opponents pointed out that the repeal of Gallagher opens the gates for huge increases in property taxes, with no guarantee that businesses will be partially relieved from their own heavy tax burdens. The proponents and opponents were both accurate.[2]

Art. X, Section 3.5. Homestead exemption for senior citizens and disabled veterans

If a person has owned and occupied a home for at least 10 years, and the person is either over 65 years old, or is a disabled veteran, then 50% of the value of the home is exempt from property taxes. The exemption is capped at 50% of the first $200,000 in value. The general assembly can raise or lower the limit. During tight fiscal years, the legislature does reduce or eliminate the exemption. Section 3.5 was added by citizen initiative in 2000 and expanded to disabled veterans in 2006.

Because property tax exemptions reduce revenues for local governments, the state government must provide local governments with make-up funds. State spending to provide backfills for local government is exempt from the spending limits in the Taxpayer's Bill of Rights. Bolded headings are by Kopel.

> (1) **50% exemption for the first $200,000 of a primary residence.** For property tax years commencing on or after January 1, 2002, fifty percent of the first two hundred thousand dollars of actual value of residential real property, as defined by law, that, as of the assessment date, is owner-occupied and is used as the primary residence of the owner-occupier shall be exempt from property taxation if:
>
> > (a) **Owner is 65 or more and has lived there for at least 10 years.** The owner-occupier is sixty-five years of age or older as of the assessment date and has owned and occupied such residential real property as his or her primary residence for the ten years immediately preceding the assessment date;
> >
> > (b) **Or the spouse of such a person.** The owner-occupier is the spouse or surviving spouse of an owner- occupier who previously qualified for a property tax exemption for the same residential real property under paragraph (a) of this subsection (1); or

---

[1] The Gallagher Amendment was sponsored by Dennis Gallagher, a Democrat of northwest Denver. After a long career in the state legislature, he served as a Denver city councilman and then as Denver's elected city auditor. His admirable career is told in the film *Gallagher: One of a Kind.*

[2]Amendment 32, Ballotpedia, https://ballotpedia.org/Colorado_2003_ballot_measures.

(c) **Or a disabled veteran.** For property tax years commencing on or after January 1, 2007, only, the owner-occupier, as of the assessment date, is a disabled veteran.

(1.3) An owner-occupier may claim only one exemption per property tax year even if the owner-occupier qualifies for an exemption under both paragraph (c) of subsection (1) of this section and either paragraph (a) or paragraph (b) of subsection (1) of this section.

(1.5) For purposes of this section, "disabled veteran" means an individual who has served on active duty in the United States armed forces, including a member of the Colorado national guard who has been ordered into the active military service of the United States, has been separated therefrom under honorable conditions, and has established a service-connected disability that has been rated by the federal department of veterans affairs as one hundred percent permanent disability through disability retirement benefits or a pension pursuant to a law or regulation administered by the department, the department of homeland security, or the department of the army, navy, or air force.

(2) **General assembly can raise or lower the $200,000 maximum exemption amount.** Notwithstanding the provisions of subsection (1) of this section, section 20 of this article, or any other constitutional provision, for any property tax year commencing on or after January 1, 2003, the general assembly may raise or lower by law the maximum amount of actual value of residential real property of which fifty percent shall be exempt under subsection (1) of this section.

(3) **Compensation for local governments.** For any property tax year commencing on or after January 1, 2002, the general assembly shall compensate each local governmental entity that receives property tax revenues for the net amount of property tax revenues lost as a result of the property tax exemption provided for in this section. For purposes of section 20 of article X of this constitution, such compensation shall not be included in local government fiscal year spending and approval of this section by the voters statewide shall constitute a voter-approved revenue change to allow the maximum amount of state fiscal year spending for the 2001-02 state fiscal year to be increased by forty-four million one hundred twenty-three thousand six hundred four dollars and to include said amount in state fiscal year spending for said state fiscal year for the purpose of calculating subsequent state fiscal year spending limits. Payments made from the state general fund to compensate local governmental entities for property tax revenues lost as a result of the property tax exemption provided for in this section shall not be subject to any statutory limitation on general fund appropriations because the enactment of this section by the people of Colorado constitutes voter approval of a weakening of any such limitation.

The statutes effectuating section 3.5 are C.R.S. § 39-3-201 to 208. The rationale for section 3.5 is that many old people have low fixed incomes, yet their property taxes continue to rise as home values increase.

Art. X, Section 4. Government property is exempt from property taxes

> The property, real and personal, of the state, counties, cities, towns and other municipal corporations and public libraries, shall be exempt from taxation.

Government property is exempt from taxation. The state cannot assess a property tax on the Denver City and County Building, nor on the business personal property therein. The city of Denver cannot assess a property tax on state government buildings located in the city.

> The logic of Section 4 is straightforward: governmental units levy taxes to raised revenue for government services. Taxes on governmental property would be circular; the tax costs to government unit would have to be paid by taxes on private property. The only real effect would be to redistribute revenue among the various government units if one unit could tax the property holdings of another.

COLLINS & OESTERLE at 235.

The exemption applies whether or not a city's property is located within its municipal boundaries. *Stewart v. City and County of Denver*, 70 Colo. 514, 202 P. 1085 (1921). Thus exempt is Denver's Winter Park Ski Resort; located in Grand County, the area was acquired as part of Denver's construction of the Moffat Tunnel, and is currently operated by lessors. *City and County of Denver v. Board of Assessment Appeals of State of Colo.*, 782 P.2d 817 (Colo. App. 1989).

According to statute, the exemption is not lost when a government unit engages in sham transactions—such as certificates of participation—that purport to convey a government building to a private party who will rent the building to the government in year-to-year leases. C.R.S. § 39-3-124.

If a political subdivision does *not* have its own taxing authority, the constitutional exemption does not apply. However, the legislature may enact a specific exemption. *City and County of Denver v. Board of Assessment Appeals*, 30 P.3d 177 (Colo. 2001).

Textually, the exemption is for property taxes only. So when the Denver city government buys gasoline for its automobiles, it must pay the state excise tax on gas, just like everyone else. *People v. City & County of Denver*, 84 Colo. 576, 272 P. 629 (1928).

Based on judicial interpretation of the U.S. Constitution, states and localities cannot tax federal government property within their jurisdiction. *See, e.g., McCulloch v. Maryland*, 17 U.S. (4 Wheat.) 316 (1819). Voluntarily, the federal government appropriates Payments in Lieu of Taxes (PILT or PILOT) to some local governments where the federal government has large landholdings. 31 U.S.C. ch. 69.

Art. X, Section 5. Property used for worship, schools, or charity is exempt

> Property, real and personal, that is used solely and exclusively for religious worship, for schools or for strictly charitable purposes, also cemeteries not used or held for private or corporate profit, shall be exempt from taxation, unless otherwise provided by general law.

This is part of the church and state compromise created by the 1876 Constitution. On the one hand, religious schools cannot receive state aid. (Art. IX, § 7). On the other hand, religious institutions are immune from taxation. Unless the general assembly decides that it wants to tax them. So far, the general assembly has never chosen to do so.

The exemption is based on use, not ownership. If a church leases a building and the building is used only for church purposes, the exemption applies. *United Presbyterian Ass'n v. Board of County Comm'rs of Jefferson Cnty.*, 167 Colo. 485, 448 P.2d 967 (1968) (but here, the church's residential home for seniors was not exempt, since its fee structure was similar to commercial residences).

Also exempted is land used for youth camps and lodges for religious retreats. *Maurer v. Young Life*, 779 P.2d 1317 (Colo. 1989) (camping activities integrated into religious education and discussion). C.R.S. § 39-2-117 sets for the procedures for applying for the religious or charitable exemption.

Note that section 5's text applies to property "used solely and exclusively for religious worship, for schools or for strictly charitable purposes." The Young Men's Christian Association (YMCA) operates the Snow Mountain Ranch in Grand County, and the Estes Park Center (YMCA of the Rockies) in Larimer County, where guests hike, fish, and so on. The organization benefited from a statute declaring that:

> [R]eligious worship has different meanings to different religious organizations; . . . many activities of religious organizations are in the furtherance of the religious purposes of such organizations; that such religious activities are an integral part of the religious worship of religious organizations; and that activities of religious organizations which are in furtherance of their religious purposes constitute religious worship for purposes of section 5 of article X of the Colorado constitution. This legislative finding and declaration shall be entitled to great weight in any and every court.

C.R.S. § 39-3-106(2).

Accordingly, the YMCA could use the section 5 property tax exemption, even though its religious philosophy discouraged proselytization. *Grand Cnty. Bd. of Comm'rs v. Colo. Prop. Tax Adm'r*, 2016 COA 2, 401 P.3d 561 (Colo. App. 2016). The court of appeals rejected Larimer County's efforts to tax the Estes Park Center's recreational buildings (*e.g.* swimming pool, skating rink) while not taxing the chapel. *Larimer County Bd. of Comm'rs v. Colo. Prop. Tax. Adm'r*, 2013 COA 49M, 316 P.3d 60 (Colo. App. 2013).

The exemption was extended to personal business property (not just real property) in 1936.

Art. X, Section 6. General assembly shall enact specific property taxes for motor vehicles

> The general assembly shall enact laws classifying motor vehicles and also wheeled trailers, semi-trailers, trailer coaches, and mobile and self-propelled construction equipment, prescribing methods of determining the taxable value of such property, and requiring payment of a graduated annual specific ownership tax thereon, which tax shall be in lieu of all ad valorem taxes upon such property; except that such laws shall not exempt from ad valorem taxation any such property in process of manufacture or held in storage, or which constitutes the inventory of manufacturers or distributors thereof or dealers therein; and further except that the general assembly shall provide by law for the taxation of mobile homes.

> Such graduated annual specific ownership tax shall be in addition to any state registration or license fees imposed on such property, shall be payable to a designated county officer at the same time as any such registration or license fees are payable, and shall be apportioned, distributed, and paid over to the political subdivisions of the state in such manner as may be prescribed by law.
>
> All laws exempting from taxation property other than that specified in this article shall be void.

The original section 6 was the final sentence. The Taxpayer's Bill of Rights (art. X, § 20(8)(b)) enacted in 1992 allows state or local exemptions for the business personal property tax.

Most of section 6 is from a 1936 amendment, allowing motor vehicles to be taxed on a unique schedule, not on their resale value. An *ad valorem* tax is based on the property's assessed value; it is the standard method for taxing real or personal property.

The 1936 system applies to trailers, such as a teardrop camper that is towed by an automobile. In 1966, the legislature recognized that "mobile homes" (which are transportable, but not ever mobile) were more like houses than like camping trailers. A referred amendment allowed the general assembly to tax mobile homes under a separate schedule, and today they are taxed *ad valorem*, just like homes that are built on a site.

Motor vehicle taxes are detailed in C.R.S. title 42, article 3, part 1.

Part 2 of the motor vehicle tax statute provides for the government to raise extra revenue by selling special licenses plates on many themes. For some of these, the extra revenue goes to a dedicated fund (*e.g.*, state parks). For others, the plate allows the owner to express a viewpoint, but the money simply goes to the general fund (*e.g.*, Colorado Rockies, adopt a shelter pet, Italian–American heritage). If you consider buying such a plate, remember that none of your money will go to benefit baseball players, pets, or Italian-Americans. The forms provided by the county offices for license plates do not, unfortunately, inform consumers about which plates will or will not benefit a particular cause.

Art. X, Section 7. General assembly may not tax for county or municipal purposes

> The general assembly shall not impose taxes for the purposes of any county, city, town or other municipal corporation, but may by law, vest in the corporate authorities thereof respectively, the power to assess and collect taxes for all purposes of such corporation.

By the text of section 7, counties and local governments must raise their own tax revenue. The state cannot do it for them. The theory is that the people of each county or municipality know best what they want from county or municipal government and can tax themselves accordingly. Thus, it would be unconstitutional for a state statute to provide: "All operations of county government shall be funded by a 1% state sales tax, to be distributed to county governments based on population."

However, article XI, § 7, added in 1970, expressly allows state grants to local governments. Further, the state income tax, added by amendment in 1936 (art. X, § 17) expressly authorizes its revenues to be distributed to local governments.

Aside from the permission granted in 1970, judicial application of section 7 allows the general assembly to give state tax revenues to county or local governments for *state* purposes, or for joint state-county purposes, but not purely county purposes.

In 1935 the Colorado supreme court allowed part of the state inheritance tax to be distributed to counties for a statutory old-age pension fund. Opponents argued that poor relief had always been a county matter. The court upheld the statute. *In re Hunter's Estate*, 97 Colo. 279, 949 P.2d 1009 (1935). The voters settled the issue the next year by constitutionally establishing the Colorado Old Age Pension fund (COAP). Art. XXIV (chapter 27). Thereafter, the COAP was absolutely a state purpose.

School finance, by constitutional text, has always involved both the state and the school districts. *Mesa County Bd. of County Com'rs v. State*, 203 P.3d 519 (Colo. 2009). Welfare programs as a joint state and county matter were approved in *Colo. Dept. of Social Services v. Board of County Commissioners*, 697 P.2d 1 (Colo. 1985).

Although the scope of joint state-county spending has expanded, it would be unconstitutional for the legislature to impose a specific tax with revenues earmarked for a "purely local purpose." *Mesa County*, at Colo. 528. An obvious example would be paying the salaries of the county commissioners.

Art. X, Section 8. No county, city, town shall be released from its share of state taxes

> No county, city, town or other municipal corporation, the inhabitants thereof, nor the property therein, shall be released or discharged from their or its proportionate share of taxes to be levied for state purposes.

Another provision based on Colorado's general principle of uniform taxation, with no special exemptions.

Art. X, Section 9. Power to tax corporations may never be suspended or relinquished

> The power to tax corporations and corporate property, real and personal, shall never be relinquished or suspended.

A common feature of state constitutions in the last two-thirds of the nineteenth century. Some corporations, especially railroads, demanded special tax exemptions before they would operate in a state. Desperate and credulous, territorial, state, and local governments acceded. Often, the exemptions turned into privatization of the corporation's profits, and socialization of the corporation's losses. The 1876 Constitution contains many strong provisions to prevent favoritism to powerful corporations. *See, e.g.*, chapters 11, 15 (Debt, art. XI; Corporations, art. XV).

Unfortunately, such provisions have been nullified in practice. For example, in 1991, United Airlines demanded tax exemptions and other welfare for building a maintenance facility in Denver. The attorney general opined that the courts would probably not hold the exemptions unconstitutional, because the legislature had the power to repeal them. Colo. Att'y Gen. Op. No. 91-04, ORL9102269.ASK, June 3, 1991. This might be a plausible interpretation of the word "relinquished," but not of the word "suspended."

The United Airlines welfare law was upheld by the supreme court, explaining that the special aid to United was not a violation of art. II, § 11 (irrevocable grant of special privileges), art. V, § 34 (appropriations to private institutions), art. V, § 25 (special legislation), art. XI, § 2 (aid to corporations), and art. XI, § 3 (state debt). Dissenting in part, justice Kirshbaum would have found a violation of art. V, § 34. Justice Quinn's dissent agreed about the violation of art. V, § 34, and criticized the majority for only using rational basis review. He also argued that art. XI, § 2 had been contravened. *In re Interrog. by Gov. Romer*, 814 P.2d 875 (Colo. 1991). The United Airlines welfare law is detailed in Dale A. Oesterle, *Lessons on the Limits of Constitutional Language from Colorado: The Erosion of the Constitution's Ban on Business Subsidies*, 73 U. COLO. L. REVIEW 587 (2002)

Today, most big businesses that are considering relocating hold an auction among several states, who compete in who can offer the most welfare, including special tax abatements. In the Colorado executive branch, there is a Colorado Office of Economic Development and International Trade, which specializes in creating corporate welfare packages. This is the opposite of the system of government created by the Colorado Constitution.

Art. X, Section 10. Corporations doing business in Colorado are taxable

> All corporations in this state, or doing business therein, shall be subject to taxation for state, county, school, municipal and other purposes, on the real and personal property owned or used by them within the territorial limits of the authority levying the tax.

Except for the special corporate pets that move to Colorado so that they can immediately go on welfare, enjoying suspended or rebated taxes. In today's theory of "economic development," a vibrant economy is based on the cost of government being paid by individual taxpayers, small business, and native Colorado big business, whereas immigrant big businesses that refuse to pay their own way are to be supported by everyone else.

Art. X, Section 11. Maximum rate of state property taxation

> The rate of taxation on property, for state purposes, shall never exceed four mills on each dollar of valuation; provided, however, that in the discretion of the general assembly an additional levy of not to exceed one mill on each dollar of valuation may from time to time be authorized for the erection of additional buildings at, and for the use, benefit, maintenance, and support of the state educational institutions; provided, further, that the rate of taxation on property for all state purposes, including the additional levy herein provided for, shall never exceed five mills on each dollar of valuation, unless otherwise provided in the constitution.

One *mill* is 1/1,000th of a property's value. If property is worth $1,000, then an annual property tax of one mill would be $1. If you home is worth $300,000, then a tax of one mill = $300. A tax of 4 mills = $1,200.

Limiting taxes has always been a principle of the Colorado Constitution. The 1876 Constitution created a 6-mill cap on state property taxes, which would decline to 2 mills as the taxable value of property in the state increased. By an 1891 amendment, state property taxes were capped at 4 mills. A 1920 vote allowed an additional mill for spending for capital construction at state education institutions. (The state institutions are created by article VIII.)

So the *state* property tax (*not* local property taxes) is capped at 4 mills for general purposes, plus one additional mill for state education.

The 5-mill cap does not apply to excise or severance taxes (*e.g.*, per barrel of oil extracted), or to occupational taxes (*e.g.*, for retail sale of liquor), or to inheritance taxes. *California Co. v. State*, 141 Colo. 288, 348 P.2d 382 (1959) (excise tax on gross income from oil or natural gas extraction); *Parsons v. People*, 32 Colo. 221, 76 P. 666 (1904) (liquor retailer); *Brown v. Elder*, 32 Colo. 527, 77 P. 853 (1904) (inheritance tax; giving the fruits of your life's labor to your family is a mere "privilege" and does not involve the ownership of property).

After the legislature in 1882 raised taxes above the 4-mill constitutional limit, attorney general Theodore H. Thomas stated that they were illegal. His position was upheld by the Colorado supreme court. FRANK HALL, 4 HISTORY OF COLORADO 597 (1895).

As of 1873, assessed valuation of all property in Colorado was $35,582,438.50. Counties with over one million dollars in assessed value were Arapahoe (which included Denver) 11.9 million; Pueblo 3.1; Gilpin 2.5; Jefferson 2.2; El Paso 2.1; Boulder 2.1; Weld 2.1; Douglas 1.9 (at the time, stretching to the Kansas border); Clear Creek 1.4, and Fremont 1.2. These assessments reflected less than 50 percent of the actual property value. FRANK HALL, 2 HISTORY OF COLORADO 207 (2008) (1890). By the next year, the statewide assessment had risen to $44,393,806.

None of the figures include mines, which were not subject to property taxes. HALL, 2 HISTORY OF COLORADO at 213–14. Instead mines paid severance taxes, based on the value of minerals that they extracted.

Today, thanks to the state income tax (section 17, added 1936) and the state sales tax, the state is much less dependent on the state property tax than it used to be.

Art. X, Section 12. State treasurer shall keep accounts and make reports

> (1) The general assembly may provide by law for the safekeeping and management of the public funds in the custody of the state treasurer, but, notwithstanding any such provision, the state treasurer and his sureties shall be responsible therefor.
>
> (2) The state treasurer shall keep adequate records of all moneys coming into his custody and shall at the end of each quarter of the fiscal year submit a written report to the governor, signed under oath, showing the condition of the state treasury, the amount of money in the several funds, and where such money is kept or deposited. Swearing falsely to any such report shall be deemed perjury.
>
> (3) The governor shall cause every such quarterly report to be promptly published in at least one newspaper printed at the seat of government, and otherwise as the general assembly may require.

This does not apply to funds within the control and direction of the University of Colorado regents. Pursuant to statute, the regents have their own treasurer. Colo. Att'y Gen. Op. No. 94-2, Feb. 9, 1994.

A *Comprehensive Annual Financial Report* (CAFR) is produced annually by the State Controller, which is part of the Department of Personnel & Administration. If you enjoy reading this, you might consider a career with general assembly staff, or another state entity that produces tax and spending reports. Indeed, you may be well suited not only for election to the general assembly, but for service on the Joint Budget Committee.

For an earlier report from simpler times, see the *1966 Report of State Treasurer Homer Bedford.*

Art. X, Section 13. Making a profit on public money is a felony

> The making of profit, directly or indirectly, out of state, county, city, town or school district money, or using the same for any purpose not authorized by law, by any public officer, shall be deemed a felony, and shall be punished as provided by law.

Notwithstanding this provision, starting in 1876, when the state treasurer deposited public funds in private banks, the bank would keep the interest on the account, and give the treasurer a kickback. The people were deprived of the interest revenue. The practice was not suppressed until 1892.

Part of the problem was that section 13 was not self-executing. The treasurer keeping the interest for himself was not a crime at common law, and the legislature had not enacted a statute felonizing interest retention. *In re Breene*, 14 Colo. 401, 24 P. 3 (1890).

Many constitutional amendments include a clause specifying that they are self-executing. Today, the execution of non-self-executing section 13 is in C.R.S. § 24-22-110.

Art. X, Section 14. Private property not taken for government debt

> Private property shall not be taken or sold for the payment of the corporate debt of municipal corporations.

Suppose the City of Pueblo, a municipal corporation, owes money to a creditor. Pueblo is insolvent and cannot pay. Can the creditor levy the private property of people who live in Pueblo, since they are members (like shareholders) in the municipal corporation? Definitely not, according to section 14, which constitutionalizes the common law.

Section 14 has been interpreted to allow municipal corporations to give welfare to private corporations, and make the municipal taxpayers pay for it, pursuant to the Economic Development Revenue Bond Act, currently codified at C.R.S. § 29-3-101 et seq. Thus, Adams County issued revenue bonds to buy a Ralston Purina Company agricultural feed plant for two million dollars, and then lease the plant back to the company. The court held there was no section 14 problem, since if Ralston Purina did not pay and the revenue bonds defaulted, bondholders would have no recourse against the private property of citizens of Adams County. *Allardice v. Adams County*, 173 Colo. 133, 476 P.2d 982 (1970)

Art. X, Section 15. Boards of equalization

Summary: The county boards of equalization adjust the assessments of taxable real property in their counties. They are supervised by a state board of equalization. The boards can change the assessment of property, but they cannot change the mill levy tax rate for a given jurisdiction. The main purpose of the boards of equalization is to make sure the county assessors, who are elected by the people, do not assess property too low.

> (1)
>
> > (a) There shall be in each county of the state a county board of equalization, consisting of the board of county commissioners of said

> county. As may be prescribed by law, the county boards of equalization shall raise, lower, adjust, and equalize valuations for assessment of taxes upon real and personal property located within their respective counties, subject to review and revision by the state board of equalization.
> (b) There shall be a state board of equalization, consisting of the governor or his designee, the speaker of the house of representatives or his designee, the president of the senate or his designee, and two members appointed by the governor with the consent of the senate. Each of such appointed members shall be a qualified appraiser or a former county assessor or a person who has knowledge and experience in property taxation. The general assembly shall provide by law for the political composition of such board and for the compensation of its members and, with regard to the appointed members, for terms of office, the filling of vacancies, and removal from office. As may be prescribed by law, the state board of equalization shall review the valuations determined for assessment of taxes upon the various classes of real and personal property located in the several counties of the state and shall, upon a majority vote, raise, lower, and adjust the same to the end that all valuations for assessment of taxes shall be just and equalized; except that said state board of equalization shall have no power of original assessment. Whenever a majority vote of the state board of equalization is prescribed by this constitution or by statute, "majority vote" means an affirmative vote of the majority of the entire membership of such board.
> (c) The state board of equalization and the county boards of equalization shall perform such other duties as may be prescribed by law.

> (2) The state board of equalization shall appoint, by a majority vote, a property tax administrator who shall serve for a term of five years and until his successor is appointed and qualified unless removed for cause by a majority vote of the state board of equalization. The property tax administrator shall have the duty, as provided by law, of administering the property tax laws and such other duties as may be prescribed by law and shall be subject to the supervision and control of the state board of equalization. The position of property tax administrator shall be exempt from the personnel system of this state.

The county boards of equalization are at C.R.S. Title 39, article 8. The state board of equalization is at article 9.

Until a 1982 amendment, the equalization system was a mess. County assessors are elected by the people, and so had an incentive to undervalue the property of the voters in their county. County or municipal governments could make up for the underassessment by simply raising the mill levy rate. Until the Taxpayer's Bill of Rights was enacted in 1992, mill levy increases did not require a vote of the people.

But the state government's mill levy rate was capped at 5 mills, pursuant to section 11. Before the introduction of the state income tax in 1936 (section 17), the state government was underfunded in relation to the true value of taxable property in Colorado. The state partially made up the difference with new taxes that did not run into any of the constitutional limits on property taxes—such as excise taxes, inheritance taxes, and so on. COLLINS & OESTERLE (2d ed.) at 243–45.

Art. X, Section 16. No appropriations that exceed tax revenues

> No appropriation shall be made, nor any expenditure authorized by the general assembly, whereby the expenditure of the state, during any fiscal year, shall exceed the total tax then provided for by law and applicable for such appropriation or expenditure, unless the general assembly making such appropriation shall provide for levying a sufficient tax, not exceeding the rates allowed in section eleven of this article, to pay such appropriation or expenditure within such fiscal year. This provision shall not apply to appropriations or expenditures to suppress insurrection, defend the state, or assist in defending the United States in time of war.

Like many other states, Colorado has an exception to its balanced budget constitutional rule. In some states, the exception applies any time the legislature declares an "emergency." For example, in some states, the routine declaration of "emergency" is simply the affirmation that the legislature is so irresponsible that it will not control its appetite for spending, and the legislature is also so cowardly that it will not require that taxpayers pay for the full cost of operating the bloated government desired by the legislature. This is similar to the "emergency" of a glutton wanting to eat even more and promising that one day he will eventually pay for his fifth trip today through the buffet line.[3]

Colorado's balanced budget exception is only "to suppress insurrection, defend the state, or assist in defending the United States in time of war." During the American Revolution, the three major military forces were the Continental Army (a national army, created by the Continental Congress), state armies, and the state militias. Under the U.S. Constitution, states can always have militias, but they can raise and employ state armies only in certain circumstances. *See* U.S. CONST., art. I, § 10, cl. 3 ("No State shall, without the Consent of Congress, . . . keep Troops, or Ships of War in time of Peace . . . or engage in War, unless actually invaded, or in such imminent Danger as will not admit of delay.")

Pursuant to the text, bonds to pay off Colorado's expenses resulting from the Civil War, the "Insurrection Bonds," were held to be exempt from section 16. *In re State Bd. of Equalizations*, 24 Colo. 446, 51 P. 493 (1897).

Section 16 was the last section of the 1876 Constitution's article X. The following sections were added by amendment.

Art. X, Section 17. Income tax enacted

> The general assembly may levy income taxes, either graduated or proportional, or both graduated and proportional, for the support of the state, or any political subdivision thereof, or for public schools, and may, in the administration of an income tax law, provide for special classified or limited taxation or the exemption of tangible and intangible personal property.

Added by a vote of the people in 1934. The state income tax is at C.R.S. title 39, article 22.

Section 17 substantially modifies several provisions of the 1876 Constitution. Under section 7, the state is not allowed to levy taxes for the benefit of municipal corporations. But section 17

---

[3] In the Popeye comics of the 1930s, Popeye's friend J. Wellington Wimpy ("Wimpy") was famous for promising "I'll gladly pay you Tuesday for a hamburger today."

allows state income tax revenue to be given to local governments. While several constitutional provisions demand uniformity of taxation for property, section 17 authorizes special exemptions from income taxes. This is one reason the legislature could not simply impose an income tax by statute, without a constitutional amendment. Because section 3 only provides for property taxes, there was doubt about whether the legislature could levy an income tax, absent a constitutional amendment. *See* Note, *Would an Income Tax in Colorado be Constitutional?* 7 ROCKY MTN. L. REVIEW 147 (1935).[4]

Only the state, and not localities may impose an income tax. Nevertheless, Denver's "occupation tax" (the more income you earn in Denver, the more you pay) was held not to be an "income tax" for purposes of section 17. *See Rountree v. City & County of Denver*, 197 Colo. 497, 596 P.2d 739 (1979); *see also* art. X, § 20 (TABOR, forbidding any new local income tax). A gross receipts tax on businesses was held to be a local income tax, and therefore void. *Johnson v. City & County of Denver*, 527 P.2d 883 (Colo. 1974).

According to TABOR (Art. X, § 20(8), enacted in 1992), the income tax rate must be uniform, not graduated. Any increase in the income tax rate requires a vote of the people. Colorado's current rate is 4.55%.

Art. X, Section 18. Vehicle and gas taxes must be used for public highways

> On and after July 1, 1935, the proceeds from the imposition of any license, registration fee, or other charge with respect to the operation of any motor vehicle upon any public highway in this state and the proceeds from the imposition of any excise tax on gasoline or other liquid motor fuel except aviation fuel used for aviation purposes shall, except costs of administration, be used exclusively for the construction, maintenance, and supervision of the public highways of this state. Any taxes imposed upon aviation fuel shall be used exclusively for aviation purposes.

Adopted by citizen initiative in 1934, section 18 forced a recalcitrant legislature to appropriate funds for state highway construction and maintenance. Motor vehicle fees and gasoline excise taxes must be deposited in the Highway User's Tax Fund. The aviation fuel provision was added in 1974.

By forcing spending on highways, section 18 of article X is in the spirit of section 17 of article IX, which orders that state base per-pupil spending may never be cut and must always increase by at least the rate of inflation.

Notwithstanding the express language of section 18, the Regional Transportation District, which does not construct, maintain, or supervise public highways, is subsidized by motor vehicle taxes. C.R.S., § 43-4-605.

Art. X, Section 19. State income taxes may be based on United States income taxes

> The general assembly may by law define the income upon which income taxes may be levied under section 17 of this article by reference to provisions of the laws of the United States in effect from time to time, whether retrospective or

[4] The University of Colorado law school's law review had this name from 1929 to 1962.

> prospective in their operation, and shall in any such law provide the dollar amount of personal exemptions to be allowed to the taxpayer as a deduction. The general assembly may in any such law provide for other exceptions or modifications to any of such provisions of the laws of the United States and for retrospective exceptions or modifications to those provisions which are retrospective.

Adopted by the voters in 1962, section 19 makes state income taxes track the federal income tax system. By the text, section 19 is merely suggestive. It does not say that the Colorado income tax *must* track the federal income tax system. Further, the legislature may deviate from the federal model as much as it wishes.

In Colorado, state taxable income begins with federal taxable income, as shown on the relevant year's federal form 1040. After that, Colorado taxable income is adjusted by removing some items that are federal deductions but not state deductions (*e.g.*, Colorado income tax paid during the previous year), and adding some deductions that exist at the Colorado level but not the federal level (*e.g.*, contributions to a qualified College Educational Savings Account).

The time and productivity savings for Colorado taxpayers are enormous. This gives Colorado an economic advantage over states such as New York that have a completely separate state income tax system. If you have ever earned income in New York, you may have discovered that filling out the New York income tax form is much more difficult than is the federal form 1040.

Section 19 produced an inadvertent windfall for the Colorado state government as a result of the 2017 federal tax reform bill, the *Tax Cuts and Jobs Act* (TCJA). The federal law removed many federal tax deductions, so that for many people, their federal taxable income for 2018 and future years was *greater* than under the old federal tax code. At the same time, the new federal law widened tax brackets, and lowered tax rates. So even though many taxpayers have a higher federal taxable income, they paid less in federal taxes. In Colorado, because net federal taxable income rose, so did Colorado taxable income, increasing state tax revenue by $400 million.

Art. X, Section 20. Taxpayer's Bill of Rights

Covered in the next chapter.

Art. X, Section 21. Tobacco taxes

Covered in chapter 31 (Vices?).

CHAPTER 15

Taxpayer's Bill of Rights, article X, section 20

As in other chapters, constitutional text that has been nullified by the judiciary and other branches is underlined. Bolded headings and text are in the original.

> **(1) General provisions.** This section takes effect December 31, 1992 or as stated. Its preferred interpretation shall reasonably restrain most the growth of government. All provisions are self-executing and severable and supersede conflicting state constitutional, state statutory, charter, or other state or local provisions. Other limits on district revenue, spending, and debt may be weakened only by future voter approval. Individual or class action enforcement suits may be filed and shall have the highest civil priority of resolution. Successful plaintiffs are allowed costs and reasonable attorney fees, but a district is not unless a suit against it be ruled frivolous. Revenue collected, kept, or spent illegally since four full fiscal years before a suit is filed shall be refunded with 10% annual simple interest from the initial conduct. Subject to judicial review, districts may use any reasonable method for refunds under this section, including temporary tax credits or rate reductions. Refunds need not be proportional when prior payments are impractical to identify or return. When annual district revenue is less than annual payments on general obligation bonds, pensions, and final court judgments, (4)(a) and (7) shall be suspended to provide for the deficiency.
>
> **(2) Term definitions.** Within this section:
>
> (a) "Ballot issue" means a non-recall petition or referred measure in an election.
>
> (b) "District" means the state or any local government, excluding enterprises.
>
> (c) "Emergency" excludes economic conditions, revenue shortfalls, or district salary or fringe benefit increases.
>
> (d) "Enterprise" means a government-owned business authorized to issue its own revenue bonds and receiving under 10% of annual revenue in grants from all Colorado state and local governments combined.
>
> (e) "Fiscal year spending" means all district expenditures and reserve increases except, as to both, those for refunds made in the current or next fiscal year or those from gifts, federal funds, collections for another government, pension contributions by employees and pension fund earnings, reserve transfers or expenditures, damage awards, or property sales.
>
> (f) "Inflation" means the percentage change in the United States Bureau of Labor Statistics Consumer Price Index for Denver-Boulder, all items, all urban consumers, or its successor index.
>
> (g) "Local growth" for a non-school district means a net percentage change in actual value of all real property in a district from construction of taxable real property improvements, minus destruction of similar improvements, and additions to, minus deletions from, taxable real property. For a school district, it means the percentage change in its student enrollment.

(3) Election provisions.

(a) Ballot issues shall be decided in a state general election, biennial local district election, or on the first Tuesday in November of odd-numbered years. Except for petitions, bonded debt, or charter or constitutional provisions, districts may consolidate ballot issues and voters may approve a delay of up to four years in voting on ballot issues. District actions taken during such a delay shall not extend beyond that period.

(b) At least 30 days before a ballot issue election, districts shall mail at the least cost, and as a package where districts with ballot issues overlap, a titled notice or set of notices addressed to "All Registered Voters" at each address of one or more active registered electors. The districts may coordinate the mailing required by this paragraph (b) with the distribution of the ballot information booklet required by section 1(7.5) of article V of this constitution in order to save mailing costs. Titles shall have this order of preference: **"NOTICE OF ELECTION TO INCREASE TAXES/TO INCREASE DEBT/ON A CITIZEN PETITION/ON A REFERRED MEASURE."** <u>Except for district voter-approved additions, notices shall include only</u>:

(i) The election date, hours, ballot title, text, and local election office address and telephone number.

(ii) For proposed district tax or bonded debt increases, the estimated or actual total of district fiscal year spending for the current year and each of the past four years, and the overall percentage and dollar change.

(iii) For the first full fiscal year of each proposed district tax increase, district estimates of the maximum dollar amount of each increase and of district fiscal year spending without the increase.

(iv) For proposed district bonded debt, its principal amount and maximum annual and total district repayment cost, and the principal balance of total current district bonded debt and its maximum annual and remaining total district repayment cost.

(v) Two summaries, up to 500 words each, one for and one against the proposal, of written comments filed with the election officer by 45 days before the election. No summary shall mention names of persons or private groups, nor any endorsements of or resolutions against the proposal. Petition representatives following these rules shall write this summary for their petition. The election officer shall maintain and accurately summarize all other relevant written comments. The provisions of this subparagraph (v) do not apply to a statewide ballot issue, which is subject to the provisions of section 1(7.5) of article V of this constitution.

(c) Except by later voter approval, if a tax increase or fiscal year spending exceeds any estimate in (b)(iii) for the same fiscal year, the tax increase is thereafter reduced up to 100% in proportion to the combined dollar excess, and the combined excess revenue refunded in the next fiscal year. District bonded debt shall not issue on terms that could exceed its share of its maximum repayment costs in (b)(iv). Ballot titles for tax or bonded debt increases shall begin, **"SHALL (DISTRICT) TAXES BE INCREASED (first, or if phased in, final, full fiscal year dollar increase) ANNUALLY...?" or "SHALL (DISTRICT) DEBT BE INCREASED (principal amount), WITH A REPAYMENT COST OF (maximum total district cost),...?"**

(4) Required elections. Starting November 4, 1992, districts must have voter approval in advance for:

(a) Unless (1) or (6) applies, any new tax, tax rate increase, mill levy above that for the prior year, valuation for assessment ratio increase for a property class, or extension of an expiring tax, or a tax policy change directly causing a net tax revenue gain to any district.

(b) Except for refinancing district bonded debt at a lower interest rate or adding new employees to existing district pension plans, creation of any multiple-fiscal year direct or indirect district debt or other financial obligation whatsoever without adequate present cash reserves pledged irrevocably and held for payments in all future fiscal years.

(5) Emergency reserves. To use for declared emergencies only, each district shall reserve for 1993 1% or more, for 1994 2% or more, and for all later years 3% or more of its fiscal year spending excluding bonded debt service. Unused reserves apply to the next year's reserve. [Note: This is partially nullified by the practice of declaring the value of government buildings to be part of the "reserve"—as if they could or would be sold during an emergency.]

(6) Emergency taxes. This subsection grants no new taxing power. Emergency property taxes are prohibited. Emergency tax revenue is excluded for purposes of (3)(c) and (7), even if later ratified by voters. Emergency taxes shall also meet all of the following conditions:

(a) A 2/3 majority of the members of each house of the general assembly or of a local district board declares the emergency and imposes the tax by separate recorded roll call votes.

(b) Emergency tax revenue shall be spent only after emergency reserves are depleted, and shall be refunded within 180 days after the emergency ends if not spent on the emergency.

(c) A tax not approved on the next election date 60 days or more after the declaration shall end with that election month.

(7) Spending limits.

(a) The maximum annual percentage change in state fiscal year spending equals inflation plus the percentage change in state population in the prior calendar year, adjusted for revenue changes approved by voters after 1991. Population shall be determined by annual federal census estimates and such number shall be adjusted every decade to match the federal census.

(b) The maximum annual percentage change in each local district's fiscal year spending equals inflation in the prior calendar year plus annual local growth, adjusted for revenue changes approved by voters after 1991 and (8)(b) and (9) reductions.

(c) The maximum annual percentage change in each district's property tax revenue equals inflation in the prior calendar year plus annual local growth, adjusted for property tax revenue changes approved by voters after 1991 and (8)(b) and (9) reductions.

(d) If revenue from sources not excluded from fiscal year spending exceeds these limits in dollars for that fiscal year, the excess shall be refunded in the next fiscal year unless voters approve a revenue change as an offset. Initial district bases are current fiscal year spending and 1991 property tax collected in 1992. Qualification or disqualification as an enterprise shall change district bases and future year limits. Future creation of district bonded debt shall increase, and retiring or refinancing district bonded debt shall lower, fiscal year spending and property tax revenue by the annual debt service so funded. Debt service changes, reductions, (1) and (3)(c) refunds, and voter-approved revenue changes are dollar amounts that are exceptions to, and not part of, any district base. Voter-approved revenue changes do not require a tax rate change.

(8) Revenue limits.

(a) New or increased transfer tax rates on real property are prohibited. No new state real property tax or local district income tax shall be imposed. Neither an income tax rate increase nor a new state definition of taxable income shall apply before the next tax year. Any income tax law change after July 1, 1992 shall also require all taxable net income to be taxed at one rate, excluding refund tax credits or voter-approved tax credits, with no added tax or surcharge.

(b) Each district may enact cumulative uniform exemptions and credits to reduce or end business personal property taxes.

(c) Regardless of reassessment frequency, valuation notices shall be mailed annually and may be appealed annually, with no presumption in favor of any pending valuation. Past or future sales by a lender or government shall also be considered as comparable market sales and their sales prices kept as public records. Actual value shall be stated on all property tax bills and valuation notices and, for residential real property, determined solely by the market approach to appraisal.

> **(9) State mandates.** Except for public education through grade 12 or as required of a local district by federal law, a local district may reduce or end its subsidy to any program delegated to it by the general assembly for administration. For current programs, the state may require 90 days notice and that the adjustment occur in a maximum of three equal annual installments.

The Taxpayer's Bill of Rights (TABOR) is the most controversial section of the Colorado Constitution—at least from the perspective of many government officials. Three decades after it was enacted by the people, its essential provisions have been eviscerated by the judiciary, the legislature, and the executive.

TABOR's leading purpose is to restrain the nonconsensual growth of government. The purpose is effected in two major ways. First, TABOR allows tax increases only when authorized by the voters. Second, state and local government spending/revenue may grow faster than the rate of inflation plus population growth if and only if the voters give permission.

On the spending front, state government spending has increased sharply since TABOR was enacted. In fiscal years 2021-22, Colorado government state budget will be $34.1 billion,[1] compared to $20.6 billion in 2012-13,[2] or $6.6 billion in 1991-92, the year before TABOR was enacted.[3] Some of that growth was authorized by the voters in 2005, when they passed referendum C to waive spending limits for a five-year period. Some other growth was authorized by the voters in ballot measures that put certain revenue streams—such as new taxes on marijuana and tobacco—outside of TABOR's limits. Many of the spending increases, however, never received consent from the voters.

Colorado government spending has grown much faster than population plus inflation.[4] If state government spending had increased by inflation plus population from 1991-92, the 2021-22 budget would have been 24.9 billion. The actual budget was 37% higher. Or if we start with a baseline of 2012-13, a fiscal year soon after the end of Referendum C's five-year "TABOR time out," the 2021-22 budget would be 28.4 billion. Instead, it is 20% higher.

As for tax increases, since 1992 the voters of Colorado have rejected every proposed state tax increase, sometimes by large margins. Yet in the 2021 session of the general assembly, bills were enacted to:

- Increase gasoline taxes and taxes on delivery services by $200 million. Less than half of that new revenue will be spent on road and highways.[5]
- Eliminate various tax deductions so as to increase state revenues by $372 million annually.[6]
- Order local school districts to impose the largest property tax increase in state history.

The story of the destruction of the 1992 Taxpayer's Bill of Rights is similar to that of the destruction of the original 1876 Constitution's many prohibitions against using taxpayer money to

---

[1] Jesse Paul, *8 big things you need to know about Colorado's $34 billion state budget,* COLORADO SUN, Apr. 7, 2021.
[2] Joint Budget Committee, *Budget in Brief: Fiscal Year 2012-13,* at 3.
[3] Joint Budget Committee, *1991-1992 Appropriations Report,* at 8.
[4] Census bureau estimates for Colorado population were 3,387,199 (1991); 5,192,647 (2012, table 2); and 5,773,714 (2020). The Denver-Boulder-Greeley Consumer Price Index was 125.6 in 1991. By 2012, the local index had been changed to Denver-Lakewood-Aurora, and was 224.6. In 2021, it was 278.6. Legislative Council Staff, *Consumer Price Index, All Items.*
[5] The $200 million figure is the Legislative Council's estimate for fiscal year 2023-24. The Council expects the amount to increase every year thereafter.
[6] Legislative Council estimate for FY 2022-23.

subsidize businesses. Article XI of the original Constitution contained absolute prohibitions on government aid to business and on government's contracting multiyear debt without voter consent. Yet these provisions have been judicially nullified, as will be described in the next chapter.

The path to TABOR

In the late 1970s American voters began to take action against what they perceived to be excessive taxation and spending. California voters in 1978 enacted Proposition 13 to limit property tax increases. In the next election cycle, a dozen states approved tax limits.[7] By 2010, there were 34 tax and expenditures limits (TELs) adopted in the states—some by the legislature, some by the voters.[8]

Figure 28. Vern Bickel founded the Colorado Union of Taxpayers in 1976. Until his death in 1998, he was always in front rank of civic engagement for taxpayer rights.

A 1976 Colorado ballot initiative would have forbidden new taxes or increases in old taxes "without the prior affirmative vote thereon of a majority of the registered electors."[9] A proposed 1978 amendment would have limited government spending increases to inflation plus population growth.[10] Both proposals were handily defeated, partly because the citizen proponents were not well-organized, and were far outspent by opponents.

Nevertheless, the general assembly got the message that many voters were concerned about taxes. California's Proposition 13 had been caused by sharply rising real estate taxes, and so the legislature acted to limit residential property taxes. The legislature referred the Gallagher Amendment to the voters in 1982, and the voters approved it. The Gallagher Amendment ensured that the percentage of the property tax burden paid by residential property

---

[7] David Brunori, Michael Bell, Joseph Cordes & Bing Yuan, *Tax and Expenditure Limitations and Their Effects on Local Finances and Urban Areas, in Urban and Regional Policy and Its Effects* 113 (Brookings Institution, 2008).

[8] Michael J. New, *U.S. State Tax and Expenditure Limitations,* 10 STATE POLITICS & POLICY QUARTERLY 24, 28 (2010).

[9] Legislative Council, Colorado General Assembly, Ballot Information Booklet 41 (1976) ("Blue Book") (proposed Amendment 10).

[10] Legislative Council, Colorado General Assembly, Ballot Information Booklet 3-4 (1978) (proposed Amendment 2).)

did not increase. It was repealed by the voters in 2020, and is discussed in the section on article X, § 3 (ch. 14).

From 1967 until the end of the century, both chambers of the general assembly were under Republican control, except for 1975–76, when public revulsion at president Richard Nixon's Watergate scandal (ch. 5) gave Democrats a one-term majority in the House. While Republican legislatures held the purse strings in the 1970s and 1980s, the size of government in Colorado expanded rapidly, far outpacing inflation and population growth.[11]

Another initiative for citizen votes on taxes was proposed in 1986, and soundly defeated. The 1988 and 1990 elections featured citizen initiatives for what would become the Taxpayer's Bill of Rights (TABOR), to regulate tax and spending increases. The 1990 initiative attracted 49% of voters.

With new language, TABOR returned to the ballot in 1992. Again, opponents heavily outspent proponents. Government officials made hysterical predictions that TABOR would destroy government. Arapahoe County sheriff Patrick Sullivan warned that if TABOR passed, he would have to fire all of the sheriffs' deputies.[12] Governor Roy Romer declared that TABOR would mean that Colorado is "closed for business."[13]

The people of Colorado adopted TABOR—which was Amendment 1 on the 1992 ballot—by a vote 53.7% in favor and 46.3% against.

The 1992 Taxpayer's Bill of Rights was not a novelty in Colorado. The 1876 Constitution had expected the general assembly to steal everything that was not nailed down. Hence, constitutional controls on matters as small as contracts for legislative stationary, and many other restrictions on taxes and spending. *See* chapters 1, 8. Experience led the people to declare many other rules about how the wealth earned by the people would be taxed and spent by the government. *See, e.g.,* chapters 14, 16 (Taxes, Debt, arts. X & XI).

It has been argued that the Colorado Constitution's restrictions on taxes and spending, of which TABOR is one among many, unduly constrain government's ability to act for the general welfare. Others argue that a principal has every right to instruct an agent how to act on behalf of the principal. The people are the sovereign principal, and the government their subordinate agent. COLO. CONST., art. II, §§ 1–3.

The following sections of this chapter explain some key features of how TABOR operates and how Colorado courts have limited TABOR.

---

[11] For example, in the 1970 the state budget was $536,887,473. In 1980 it was $2,295,793,745—327% larger. In the meantime, Colorado's population had grown 31%, from 2,209,596 in 1970 to 2,908,803 in 1980. The purchasing power of one dollar in 1970 was equal to $2.16 in 1980. U.S. Bureau of Labor Statistics, CPI Inflation Calculator. If the 1970 budget had grown by inflation plus population, the 1980 budget would have been $1,588,757,410. The actual budget was 45% higher. The 45% increase came during an economically stagnant decade; while the state government ended the decade 45% richer, most taxpayers did not.

[12] At the time, Sullivan, a Republican, was also Colorado's leading advocate for gun control. Later, the new Arapahoe County Jail was named for him. Still later, he was incarcerated in the jail after he was found to have used his supervisory position over troubled young men to provide them with illegal drugs in exchange for sex. Sadie Gurman, *Ex-sheriff headed to prison in meth-for-sex case,* USA TODAY, June 19, 2014 (Assoc. Pr.).

[13] Fred Holden, *Colorado Tax Limitation: The Power of 1 and a Few More* (information sheet), reprinted from ARVADA COMMUNITY NEWS (July 26, 1999) (Governor Roy Romer asserted that if TABOR passed "we would have to post signs at the borders, 'Colorado is Closed for Business'"); Charles J. Sykes, *After the Freeze: Wisconsin's Taxpayer Bill of Rights,* WISCONSIN INTEREST 7, 10 Winter 2004. Romer also called defeating TABOR the "moral equivalent of defeating the Nazis at the Battle of the Bulge" and called one of its leading advocates, Douglas Bruce, "a terrorist who would lob a hand grenade into a schoolyard full of children."

A. Interpretation by the courts

The Bill of Rights does not contain rights

According to the Colorado Supreme Court, the "Taxpayer's Bill of Rights" is not about rights. Rather, TABOR only regulates legislative power. *Bickel v. City of Boulder*, 885 P.2d 215, 226 (Colo. 1994) (refusing to "analogize alleged violations of Amendment 1 to the taking of property by state and local governments without just compensation").[14]

The purported distinction is absurd. Colorado's Bill of Rights protects citizens from ex post facto laws. The protection is purely a restraint on the type of laws that a legislative body may enact. "No ex post facto law, nor law impairing the obligation of contracts, or retrospective in its operation, or making any irrevocable grant of special privileges, franchises or immunities, shall be passed by the general assembly." Art. II, § 11. The U.S. First Amendment begins with a limit on legislative power: "Congress shall make no law." U.S. CONST., amend. I. The way to protect rights is to enact constitutions and other laws preventing government from violating those rights. Every protection in a Bill of Rights limits the laws that a legislature may enact.

The Taxpayer's Bill of Rights protects the fundamental right of citizens to consent or deny consent to taxation. More broadly, it protects the sovereign right of the people to control government spending and taxation. The violations of these rights led to the British Civil Wars in the 1640s, to the United Kingdom's Glorious Revolution in 1688, and to the American Revolution in 1775. In the United Kingdom, the people reinforced traditional constitutional limits on the monarch taxing or spending without the consent, as expressed by the people's representatives in parliament. According to the people who started and won the American Revolution, only the colonial or state legislatures held the power of the purse; that power belonged neither to the parliament in London nor to the royal colonial governors appointed by the king.

By the 1830s, experience had shown that state legislatures also needed restraints on their taxing and spending. State constitutional reforms and new state constitutions began imposing strict limits on government spending and taxation. *See* chapters 1, 8. The Colorado Taxpayer's Bill of Rights is part of a very long state constitutional law tradition that protects popular sovereignty—a fundamental right specifically declared in the Colorado Bill of Rights. Chapter 2; COLO. CONST, art. II § 2.

When the Colorado supreme court first had to address the Taxpayer's Bill of Rights, the court refused to say its name. Instead, the Taxpayer's Bill of Rights was identified by its 1992 ballot number, "Amendment 1." The court deleted the words "Taxpayer's Bill of Rights" from quotes and replaced them with a bracketed "Amendment 1."[15] The court did reconcile itself to using the name when doing so could be used to bolster an argument in favor of increased government revenue.[16] Eventually, the court steeled itself to the words "Taxpayer's Bill of Rights" in all relevant cases—although not to enforce those words, as will be described below.

---

[14] *See also City of Wheat Ridge v. Cerveny*, 913 P.2d 1110, 1115 (Colo. 1996); *Havens v. Board of County Commissioners of the County of Archuleta*, 924 P.2d 517, 520 (Colo. App. 1996). In a sense, the *Bickel* plaintiffs got their wish. The Colorado Supreme Court has treated TABOR like the constitutional limits on eminent domain, which have also been judicially nullified in large part. See chapter 3 (art. II, §§ 14–15).

[15] *E.g., Bickel*, 885 P.2d at 221 (quoting School District Question 1), 222 (quoting City Question B), 223 (quoting City Question C).

In another case, "TABOR" appeared in a quote, so it was necessary have a footnote spelling out the acronym. The court stated that the "Taxpayer's Bill of Rights" is "another name for Amendment 1." *City of Wheat Ridge v. Cerveny*, 913 P.2d 1110, 115 (Colo. 1996). To the contrary, only the Colorado supreme court believed that "Amendment 1" is an alternative name.

[16] *Zaner v. City of Brighton*, 917 P.2d 280, 284 (Colo. 1996).

"Its preferred interpretation shall reasonably restrain most the growth of government."

TABOR's second sentence provides a rule of interpretation: "Its preferred interpretation shall reasonably restrain most the growth of government." Art. X, § 20(1). If more than one interpretation is plausible, the correct interpretation is the one that reasonably restrains government growth the most. As the sentence indicates, the leading purpose of TABOR is restraint of government growth.

The Colorado supreme court has nullified TABOR's rule of interpretation. According to the court, the "preferred interpretation" of "restrain most" is only to be used when the competing interpretations are equally plausible. *Bickel* at 229; *Nicholl v. E-470 Public Highway Authority*, 896 P.2d 859 (Colo. 1995).

The court only uses "restrain most" when the words can be deployed to favor the government. *City of Wheat Ridge v. Cerveny*, 913 P.2d 1110, 115 (Colo. 1996) (rejecting automatic awards of costs and attorneys' fees for successful TABOR plaintiffs, because "Mandatory awards of attorney fees necessarily increase government spending."); *Bolt v. Arapahoe School District No. 6*, 898 P.2d 525 (Colo. 1995) (rejecting enforcement of certain TABOR provisions because such enforcement would have shrunk the size of government, rather than restrained its growth).

As of 2003, the Colorado supreme court had rendered TABOR's express rule of interpretation "virtually meaningless." Michael R. Johnson, Scott H. Beck, & H. Lawrence Hoyt, *State Constitutional Tax Limitations: The Colorado and California Experiences*, 35 URBAN LAWYER 817, 827 (2003).

Then in 2008, the court announced its own standard of review for the Taxpayer's Bill of Rights: "The presumption of a statute's constitutionality can be overcome only if it is shown that the enactment is unconstitutional beyond a reasonable doubt." *Barber v. Ritter*, 196 P.3d 238, 247-48 (Colo. 2008). The beyond a reasonable doubt standard of review is further discussed in Chapter 33 (Conclusion).

"Most reasonably restrain" and "beyond a reasonable doubt" are very different standards. One is in the Colorado Constitution, and one is not.

Nullification of the constitutional standard of review has enabled the court to manipulate two pairs of categories at the heart of TABOR. The first pair consists of fees and taxes. Taxes require consent and fees do not. With judicial acquiescence, legislative bodies claim that government exactions that are obviously taxes are "fees." Even when the Colorado Constitution specifically says they are "taxes"

The second pair of categories consists of districts and enterprises. "Districts" are TABOR's term of art for any state or local government. Districts must receive voter consent to increase taxes or to increase their rate of spending faster than inflation plus population growth. Government "enterprises" receive less than ten percent of their funding from state or local government. Because of their independence from taxes, they do not need voter consent for rapid revenue growth, nor voter consent to increase the prices they charge their customers. When TABOR was enacted, people imagined that some state colleges might be classified as enterprises if they earned most of their income from tuition, charitable donations, and so on.

The Colorado courts, however, have authorized the creation of fictitious "enterprises" whose income comes entirely from involuntary payments by taxpayers, and which provide no service to those taxpayers.

This chapter will first examine taxes/fees, and then districts/enterprises.

B. Taxes versus Fees

In normal usage, a "fee" is something that is voluntarily provided in exchange for something else. You rent a towel at the city's recreation center, and you pay a fee that covers the cost of the recreation center buying and cleaning towels. Or you pay an entrance fee to use a state park. Because TABOR requires voter consent to impose or raise taxes, but does not control fees, courts have defined "fee" very broadly and "tax" very narrowly. So narrowly that billions of dollars of additional taxes on drivers and hospital patients have been legally classified as fees, for which taxpayer consent was not required.

TABOR did not define "tax," so earlier precedents were applicable. One precedent held that special charges for hookups to a municipal sewer system were not a tax. Sewer charges were to fund the operation of the sewer system, not for general government revenue. The result was not changed by the government setting sewer charges so high that they funded the sewer system and also produced profits that were transferred to general revenue. *Western Heights Land Corp. v. City of Fort Collins*, 146 Colo. 464, 362 P.2d 155 (1961). The same rule was applied to "special assessments" for storm drainage. *Zelinger v. City and County of Denver*, 724 P.2d 1356 (Colo. 1986).

People can choose not to rent a towel at the recreation center, visit a state park, or attend a state college. People do not have a choice about whether to use sewers or storm drainage. Thus, the court of appeals in 1989 held that fees can include involuntary payments. *Bloom v. City of Fort Collins*, 784 P.2d 304 (Colo. App. 1989).

Storm drainage and sewer fees do provide direct benefits to the landowners who pay the fees. The first decision decoupling fees from services came in 1991, the year before TABOR was enacted. A gross receipts tax on airports was not really used to provide government services to airport users. But the revenue was put into a separate account, distinct from general revenue. The court of appeals upheld the arrangement, choosing to "defer to the sound discretion of the government agency imposing such fee." *Westrac, Inc. v. Walker Field, Colo. Pub. Airport Auth.*, 812 P.2d 714 (Colo. App. 1991).

Since the enactment of TABOR, the above precedents have been pushed to their extremes. The government can impose a tax without consent, and get away with calling it a "fee," as long as the government puts the money in a separate account. The so-called fee need not be used to provide a benefit or service to taxpayers who pay the fee.

For example, it was universally agreed that certain rural bridges needed repair. The legislature could have imposed tolls, which genuinely are fees, on users of the bridges, and used the tolls to pay for repair. Alternatively, the legislature could have been more frugal on other spending and used the savings to pay for bridge repair. Or the legislature could have asked voters to raise the gasoline tax. Instead, the legislature raised automobile registration taxes, called them "fees," and dedicated the extra revenue to a "Bridge Enterprise Fund." The vast majority of people who pay auto registration fees never drive over any of the bridges operated by the so-called enterprise. They receive zero benefit from the fees. The system was upheld in *TABOR Foundation v. Colorado Bridge Enterprise*, 353 P.3d 896 (Colo. App. 2014).

At the time the legislature raised automobile registration "fees" so that drivers who never use particular bridges would have to pay for them, the legislature did not imagine that gasoline taxes could be raised without voter consent. Governor Bill Ritter stated that the general assembly had chosen to raise automobile registration "fees" rather than gasoline taxes in order to avoid TABOR's requirement for a vote.[17] The legislature's caution about gasoline taxes was prudent. Gasoline taxes are one of the taxes that the Colorado Constitution specifically identifies as

---

[17] *See* Robert G. Natelson, *The Colorado Taxpayer's Bill of Rights,* INDEPENDENCE INSTITUTE, Issue Paper 3-2016, at 20 n.130 (2016) (discussing 850 KOA radio interview of Ritter by Mike Rosen).

"taxes." In the 1934 election, the voters added section 18 to article X, so that "any excise tax on gasoline . . . be used exclusively for the construction, maintenance, and supervision of the public highways of this state." Art. X, § 18. When the voters in 1936 provided certain revenue streams for an old age pension fund, they specifically forbade use of gasoline taxes for the fund; in doing so declared that gasoline taxes are taxes: "no part of the revenue derived from excise taxes now or hereafter levied, for highway purposes, upon gasoline or other motor fuel, shall be made a part of said old age pension fund." Art. XXIV, § 2(a).

A recent case challenged the Aspen city council's 20 cent "fee" on paper bags. The city justified the fee by pointing to a San Francisco study that the government's cost of disposing of paper bags by hauling them to a landfill was 17 cents per bag. Aspen rounded up to 20 cents, on the theory that it has to haul municipal waste longer distances than San Francisco does. Had the revenue been used simply for waste disposal, the Aspen system would have been a legitimate fee. Instead, much of the money was used to provide cloth bags to residents and non-residents of Aspen, regardless of whether they used paper bags. The revenues were also used for public relations campaigns to tout the Aspen city council's views on recycling. The benefits did not relate to the city's expenses in disposing of paper bags. The Aspen system was upheld by the supreme court. The court held that the 20-cent fee would only be a tax if the plaintiffs had proven beyond a reasonable doubt that the fee bore "no reasonable relationship to Aspen's cost of permitting the use of the bag."

While taxpayers never win TABOR cases in the Colorado supreme court, the Aspen case produced an unusually close 4–3 decision. Justice Coats, joined by chief justice Boatright, wrote a dissenting opinion, and justice Hood dissented separately.

The Coats-Boatright dissent argued that the court's precedent, and common sense, supported "the intuitive and virtually universally-accepted understanding that a charge for no more than the value or cost of some benefit—whether that be in the form of a privilege, a franchise, a license, a permit, or a good or service—provided by the government to a purchaser, or payer, does not amount to raising revenue at all, but is rather in the nature of a sale or direct exchange of things of comparable value, as in any proprietary transaction." Thus, "the mere fact that an exaction is imposed for regulatory purposes, or is earmarked to fund a 'regulatory regime,' cannot change its character as a tax or other revenue-raising exaction."

To the dissenters, it was "obvious that a $0.20 charge can in no way reflect the cost of recycling a single paper grocery bag . . . Rather than the city's general waste reduction program being incidental, in any meaningful sense, to the disposal and recycling of paper grocery bags, it is the latter that is clearly incidental to the former." The charge on grocery bags was a type of "sin tax"—a tax on certain activities that are considered harmful or immoral, such as tobacco use. *See* chapter 31 (Vices?).

Justice Hood's dissent argued that under the court's precedents, the "primary purpose" of a "fee" is "to defray the cost of services provided to the purchaser." Thus, "there must be a meaningful correlation between the class of people charged and the class of people benefitted." The language of the Aspen ordinance clearly indicated that the primary purpose was to confer benefits on "residents, businesses, and visitors," and the "Aspen community"—not benefits on people who paid the grocery bag tax. *Colorado Union of Taxpayers Foundation v. City of Aspen*, 418 P.3d 506 (Colo. 2018).

Had the Aspen city council bothered to ask the voters of Aspen for consent, the ecology-minded residents might well have voted for a straightforward tax to fund waste reduction and recycling education.

In 2019, the legislature presented the voters with Proposition CC, to allow the legislature to retain revenues above the TABOR limit; the legislature promised that the excess funds would be spent on transportation and education. The voters said no.

After the voters indicated their belief that the legislature could take care of roads and highways without even more of the taxpayers' money, the 2021 legislature raised the gasoline tax and imposed new taxes on delivery services. This time, the legislature said that the new taxes were fees.[18] As will be discussed in the next section, many of the new "fees" imposed on drivers and delivery services will be used to provide services to other people, such as subsidizing electric vehicles.

Creation of monopolies

Another means of raising new taxes has been to combine them with the grant of a franchise to a business monopoly. In a ballot measure that did not comply with TABOR's election rules (discussed below), Boulder city voters approved a referendum from the city council to grant a heating and electricity monopoly to a utility corporation. The city would impose a franchise fee on the business, which would pass along the fee in the form of higher heating and electricity charges on all residents of Boulder, who would have no choice but to buy from the city's favored monopoly. The Boulder city council recognized that the monopoly and franchise fee might be found to violate state public utility laws. So as a backup, the referendum said that if the franchise fee were declared illegal, it would be recharacterized as "an occupation or a sales and use tax."

Thus, the referendum involved a large contingent tax, and should have followed TABOR's rules for ballot measures to raise taxes. But the Colorado supreme court held that compliance was not required. According to the court, the ballot measure was "more properly viewed as a ballot issue for the granting of a franchise, rather than one 'for tax or bonded debt increases.'" *Bickel v. City of Boulder*, 885 P.2d 215, 235 (Colo. 1994). The court created a false dichotomy; the referendum was for both a franchise grant and a tax increase.

Cash funds

Within the state budget, there are many cash accounts that are funded by fees. For example, real estate license fees pay the expenses of the realtor regulation. A special fee on gasoline pays for the cleanup of leaking underground storage tanks. Hunting and fishing license fees fund the Colorado division of parks and wildlife. Certain taxes/fees on employment pay for workers compensation.

The government entities that collect and spend these funds are not enterprises. The money they collect *does* count as part of total annual state government revenue. (TABOR's limits on growth of state revenue are discussed below.)

In 2001–04, state general revenues from income taxes and sales taxes declined. Rather than cutting state general spending proportionately, the legislature helped itself to \$442 millions of dollars from 31 cash fee accounts, transferring the cash to the general fund. Once moved into the general fund, the money was spent on things that had nothing to do with the reasons for which the fees had been collected.

The government agencies that had collected the fees were now broke. So, they raised their fees to replenish the funds that the general assembly had raided. The bottom line: money collected as fees (for a particular purpose) was eventually used as a tax (general purpose). As a result of the raid, the people who paid the fees/taxes had to pay increased fees/taxes. The Colorado supreme court held that nothing in the chain of events required the consent of the people.

First, the court correctly held that the raid on the cash funds should not be counted as increased state revenue for purposes of TABOR's revenue caps. The fees had already been

[18] The additional gasoline tax, labeled a "road usage fee" starts at two cents per gallon in fiscal year 2022-23, rises by one cent per gallon annually until hitting eight cents, and is thereafter increased annually for inflation. SB 21-260.

counted against the cap once, in the year when they were collected. To count them as revenue in a later year, when they were transferred to the general fund, would be double counting.

Less plausibly—especially in light of TABOR's interpretive rule—the court held that moving the cash fee funds into general revenue did not turn them into taxes. All that mattered was how they were originally collected, not how they were ultimately spent. Nor did newly increased "fees" (to replenish the funds raided by the general assembly) count as a tax increase, for which voter approval was required. The money was still being ostensibly collected as a "fee"—even though the previous fees had been spent for non-fee purposes. *Barber v. Ritter*, 196 P.3d 238 (Colo. 2008). The legislature raided cash fees again in 2020, taking $42.8 million from 25 cash funds. HB 20-1406; Legislative Council Staff, *Final Fiscal Note: HB 20-1406* (July 27, 2020).

C. Districts vs. Enterprises

TABOR defines a *district* as "the state or any local government, excluding enterprises." Districts include the state of Colorado, "political subdivisions of the state," counties, municipalities, school districts, and special districts. A municipal or county adoption of Home Rule (art. XX) is not an exemption from TABOR. *HCA-HealthOne, LLC v. City of Lone Tree*, 197 P.3d 236 (Colo. App. 2008).

TABOR applies to "districts" but not to "enterprises." The distinction was once clear. An "enterprise" is something that receives less than 10% of its revenue from state or local government. For example, a municipal recreation center pays over 90% of its costs from user fees; the recreation center can raise its prices for memberships, daily passes, or towel rentals whenever it wants. Government entities that are not enterprises are "districts." They may raise taxes only if the voters consent.

However, loose and hostile interpretation of TABOR—the kind of interpretation that is formally forbidden by the "restrain most" text—has allowed many government operations to escape TABOR by being relabeled as enterprises, even though almost all of their income comes from tax revenues.

TABOR defines *enterprise* according to several characteristics. According to the text, one characteristic of an enterprise is being "a government-owned business authorized to issue its own revenue bonds."[19] Revenue bonds are detailed in chapter 16 (Debt, art. XI). A revenue bond pledges a particular income stream (not general revenues) to repay a debt. For example, the municipal recreation center issues bonds to expand its buildings; the bonds are backed only by the recreation center's income from users, and not by the municipality's general revenues.

Early judicial decisions about TABOR enterprises were reasonable. A "business" was judicially defined as "engaging in an activity conducted in the pursuit of benefit, gain or livelihood." *Nicholl v. E-470 Public Highway Authority*, 896 P.2d 859, 868 (Colo. 1995). A business cannot tax; it can only acquire revenues from voluntary transactions. Thus, fact that the E-470 Public Highway Authority could impose taxes meant that it was a district, not an enterprise. *Id.* Subsequently, the general assembly revoked E-470's taxing powers so it could be

---

[19] Enterprises are government businesses. Although they receive certain exemptions from TABOR, they must still comply with other laws that regulate governments, such as the Open Records Act. *Freedom Newspapers, Inc. v. Tollefson*, 961 P.2d 1150 (Colo. App. 1998).

A monograph by the Colorado Municipal League (CML, the lobbying association of city and town governments) argues that the "revenue bonds" rule should be interpreted to include special districts that do not have the authority to issue revenue bonds directly. Instead, the rule should encompass special districts that do not issue revenue bonds, but which can ask a county or municipal government to issue revenue bonds on their behalf. As the CML points out, in 1992, when TABOR was adopted, there were no Colorado government-owned business that issued their own revenue bonds. Colorado Municipal League, *TABOR: A Guide to the Taxpayer's Bill of Rights* 32 (2011) [hereinafter CML].

an enterprise. *Re the Petition of the E-470 Public Hwy. Auth.*, No. 96 CV 946 (Arapahoe Co. D. Ct. 1996).

There is no specific TABOR rule that a government entity be formally declared an enterprise, as long it meets the relevant standards. Thus, the enterprise need not have a corporate identity separate from its parent government. The city government (a municipal corporation) can have within itself an enterprise (the recreation center).

The key characteristic of an enterprise is "receiving under 10% of annual revenue in grants from all Colorado state and local governments combined." Art. X, § 20(2)(d).[20] But this provision has been riddled with loopholes. Some of the loopholes come from the TABOR text, and some from judicial interpretation.

TABOR's 10% limit is for "grants from all Colorado state and local governments combined." So federal grants textually do not count against the limit. By judicial opinion, Colorado government cash grants count, but grants of other property, such as real estate or capital assets, do not. *TABOR Foundation v. Colorado Bridge Enterprise*, 353 P.3d 896 (Colo. App. 2014).

The Great Outdoors Colorado Trust Fund is unquestionably a division of the state government. Because Great Outdoors Colorado (GOCO) was enacted the same year as TABOR, and received more votes, it was reasonable to say that in case of conflict between GOCO and TABOR, GOCO wins. *See* chapter 32 (Natural Resources).

A government entity that receives most its revenue from mandatory fees is, by judicial interpretation, still an enterprise. *Board of County Commissioners, County of Eagle v. Fixed Base Operators, Inc.*, 939 P.2d 464 (Colo. App. 1997) (pass-through of "fees" on airport travelers); *TABOR Foundation v. Colorado Bridge Enterprise*, 353 P.3d 896 (Colo. App. 2014) (pass-through of automobile registration "fee" on automobile owners for use of bridges that they do not use). Similarly, an enterprise need not win customers in the marketplace. Rather, its "customers" can consist entirely of other units of government that are forced to give their money to the alleged enterprise. Colo. Att'y Gen. Op. No. 95-07, Dec. 22, 1995); Colo. Att'y Gen. Op. No. 16-01, Feb. 29, 2016 (describing courts' loose standards for what constitutes an enterprise).

Today, the majority of the state of Colorado's spending has been exempted from TABOR. According to the State Auditor's estimates for fiscal year 2019-20, total state expenditures would be $56,755,336,588. Colorado Office of the State Auditor, *Schedule of TABOR Revenue Fiscal Year 2020* at 13 (Nov. 2020). Of this, over $20 billion of the spending was not counted in the state operating budget. As the legislature's website explains, "Other forms of state spending occur outside of the state budget. For example, federal funds for food assistance programs and some federal and private funding for higher education research projects are not 'appropriated' by the state legislature." Of the 56 billion in state spending, $14,873,800,000 was subject to TABOR's fiscal year spending rules.[21] Thus, only 26% of state spending was even theoretically limited by TABOR.

If we exclude federal and other funds that are not subject to appropriation by the legislature, then for fiscal year 2019-20 the "operating appropriations by department" were $33,630,662,672. Joint Budget Committee, Appropriations Report Fiscal Year 2020-21, 1-18 (2021). The figure does not include spending on capital construction, for which the legislature transferred $3,926,868,000 to the capital construction fund. *Id.* at III-280. This makes total state appropriations $37,557,530,672. Of this $35 billion, 39.6% was subject to TABOR's fiscal year revenue limits.

According to a 2019 Legislative Council memorandum, enterprise revenues exempt from TABOR grew from $742 million in TABOR's first year to $17.9 billion in fiscal year 2017-18.[22]

---

[20] This TABOR rule is codified at C.R.S. § 24-77-102(3).

[21] The preliminary estimate from the State Auditor was slightly different. State Auditor at 13. The final number was published in March 2021.

[22] Matt Bishop, Legislative Council Staff, *State Government Enterprises* (May 20, 2019).

Some of the state spending that is TABOR exempt was lawfully exempted by the voters, as will be described below. Some of the exempt revenue is from genuine enterprises, such as some institutions of higher education, or the lottery proceeds that are granted to Great Outdoors Colorado. And some of the TABOR-exempt revenue is from fictitious enterprises.

The fictitious "Bridge Enterprise Fund" paved the way for the Colorado Healthcare Affordability and Sustainability Enterprise, which receives its income from the Healthcare Affordability and Sustainability Fee. C.R.S. § 25.5-4-402.4. The law imposes a billion dollar annual tax on hospitals.[23] The tax revenue is used to pay for some of Colorado's matching funds for the federal Medicaid program. Medicaid provides medical care for poor people and for many persons well above the poverty line. Pursuant to the "enterprise" statute, hospitals pay the "bed fee," which is a tax on providing care to patients. Hospitals receive the money back as compensation for their care of patients who do not pay their own way—that is, patients on Medicaid. Some hospitals are net losers in the exchange, while others make a profit.

The state tax forces hospitals to raise prices for patients who pay their own way (patients who pay directly, or who have insurance); the tax revenue is then used to pay for the costs of treating patients who do not pay for their own care (those on Medicaid). When governments raise taxes on business provision of services to consumers, businesses usually pass on at least some of the higher costs to the consumers. Thus, some patients are forced to pay extra for their own care in order to subsidize the medical care of other people. This might or might not be good policy, but it looks like a tax, not a fee. By design, the ultimate payer (the patient) receives zero benefit. Indeed, the benefit is earmarked for someone who is definitionally not the payer (other patients).

In a case challenging the new health care taxes, the court of appeals held that none of the plaintiffs had standing. The court acknowledged that in Colorado, taxpayers have standing "to seek to enjoin an unlawful expenditure of public funds." *Barber v. Ritter*, 196 P.3d at 246 (quoting *Nicholl v. E-470 Public Highway Authority*, 896 P.2d 859, 866 (Colo. 1995)). However, a plaintiff must "establish a clear nexus between her status as a taxpayer and the constitutional violation she alleges." *Reeves-Toney v. Sch. Dist. No. 1*, 2019 CO 40, ¶ 28, 442 P.3d 81. "[T]he interest of the *taxpayer* who challenges the constitutionality of government action is her 'economic interest in having h[er] tax dollars spent in a constitutional manner.'" *Id.* at ¶ 23) (quoting *Conrad v. City & Cty. of Denver*, 656 P.2d 662, 668 (Colo. 1982) (brackets in original)).

For the hospital bed tax, the tax was paid by the hospitals, not by the plaintiffs, who were taxpayer organizations and individuals. The hospitals were not complaining about the tax; to the contrary, they had lobbied for it, and they intervened in the case as defendants.

The bed tax was a covert price increase on some patients. The Colorado statute forbids hospitals to disclose the bed tax as a line item on hospital bills. In the view of the court of appeals, hospitals would have had standing to challenge the bed tax, since hospitals paid the bed tax. But hospitals were defending, not challenging, the bed tax.

The plaintiffs argued that their tax dollars *were* involved. True, the tax was first paid by the hospitals. But then it was passed on to patients. Some patients pay hospitals directly, and others pay via insurance. When insurance companies have to pay hospitals more, insurance companies raise premiums for patients. One way or another, patients are getting stuck with at least some of the new hospital taxes.

According to the Colorado Hospital Association brief in the district court:

> The hospital provider fees are not passed through to patients as charges on bills or otherwise. While some of the costs entailed in operating the provider fee may be subsumed in hospital bills generally (like any element of overhead), there is no

[23] For fiscal year 2019-20, the amount was $1,014,762,908. Colorado Healthcare Affordability and Sustainability Enterprise (CHASE), FFY 2019-20 Hospital Group Net Reimbursement (June 19, 2020).

pass-through or linear relationship between the hospital provider fee and hospital charges.

In other words, hospitals do not bill the fee/tax as a line item on hospital bills since the statute outlaws such disclosure. Instead of being a line item in billing, the fee/tax is counted as part of the hospital's "overhead." In the billing to the patient, the fee/tax is charged silently—"subsumed" in "overhead."

To the court of appeals, the indirect nature of the tax pass-through meant that none of the plaintiffs could specifically prove that patients were paying higher hospital bills as a result. Therefore, no plaintiffs had standing. Accordingly, the court could not rule on the merits of whether the new hospital tax violated the Taxpayer's Bill of Rights. *TABOR Foundation v. Colo. Dept. of Health Care Policy and Financing*, 2020 COA 156 (Colo. App. 2020).

Special purpose authorities

Among the units of the Colorado state government are *special purpose authorities*. They are governed by appointed boards and have a certain degree of autonomy. They lack the power to tax directly, but they spend vast amounts of taxpayer money collected by the state. Some of them have the power of eminent domain. Among the largest are the Colorado Housing and Finance Authority, the Water Resources and Power Development Authority, and the Colorado Agricultural Authority. Pursuant to TABOR, these authorities should be classified either as districts or as enterprises, depending on their revenue streams. Many of them receive too much taxpayer revenue to qualify as enterprises, so they should be treated as districts. However, the legislature has declared that the legislatively created special purpose authorities are not government entities at all, and so they can ignore TABOR's spending limits. C.R.S. § 24-77-102(15).

Fictitious enterprises

In 2020, the voters approved the Proposition 117 statutory initiative to require voter consent for the creation of new enterprises with anticipated revenues of over $100 million in their first five years. C.R.S. § 24-77-108. In 2021, the legislature raised the gas tax by calling it a "fee," and imposed new "fees" on delivery services and rental cars. Because of the power of the taxi lobby, Uber and Lyft riders must pay a per-trip tax/fee, but taxi riders need not. The new "fees" will amount to $200.1 million annually for fiscal year 2023-24, the last year for which the legislative council staff's fiscal note calculated a figure.[24] To evade the requirement for a vote on new enterprises with five-year revenues over $100 million, the legislature divided some of the money between one existing enterprise and four new ones. Three of the five "enterprises" are dedicated to subsidizing electric vehicles. In other words, people who drive gasoline automobiles are charged a "road usage fee" and much of the fee revenue is not spent on roads; instead, wealth is transferred to the electric car business and its customers. Some of the money also goes to the Highway Users Trust Fund, which is not an enterprise; it is simply an account for gas taxes dedicated to highways and for federal highways grants.[25]

The dispersal of the revenue is meant to keep any single enterprise from triggering the Proposition 117 requirement for voter consent. In fact, subsection (2) of Proposition 117 states:

---

[24] Legislative Council Staff, *Revised Fiscal Note* (LLS 21-0263) (June 2, 2021).

[25] Community Access Enterprise (to promote adoption of electric vehicles "in an equitable manner"); Clean Fleet Enterprise (to subsidize electric vehicles and fleets); Statewide Bridge and Tunnel Enterprise; Non-attainment Area Air Pollution Mitigation Enterprise (to collect fees on riders and on retail delivery); Clean Transit Enterprise (to subsize electric vehicles for government transit agencies). SB 21-260.

"Revenue collected for enterprises created simultaneously or within the five preceding years serving primarily the same purpose shall be aggregated in calculating the applicability of this section." Thus, the three enterprises dedicated to electric vehicles should be aggregated.

The 1876 Colorado Convention was familiar with fictitious enterprises. Article XV, on corporations, declares: "all fictitious increase of stock or indebtedness shall be void. The stock of corporations shall not be increased except in pursuance of general law, nor without the consent of the persons holding a majority of the stock, first obtained at a meeting held after at least thirty days' notice given in pursuance of law." Art. XV, § 9 (chapter 20).

Fictitious stocks take property from shareholders; fictitious enterprises take property from taxpayers. In both cases, "without the consent of the persons." Fictitious organizations for transferring wealth without consent were outlawed in article XV. They have returned in another form, as the fictious enterprises that nullify the Taxpayer's Bill of Rights.

D. Rights regarding types of taxes

1. Property taxes

Constitutional rules about property taxes are described in chapter 14 (Taxes, art. X). TABOR provides additional protections. TABOR requires voter consent for increases in mill levy rates, forbids new state property taxes, and forbids any district from imposing new or increased taxes on the transfer of property.

Other TABOR protections include providing property taxpayers with accurate information. In Colorado, real estate taxes are calculated starting with the land's full value. From the full value, an assessed value is then determined. The assessment rate changes from year to year, but it is a percentage of the property's full value. In 2020, the assessment rate for business property was 29% and 7.15% for residential property. The mill levy rate is then applied to the assessed value.

For example, suppose a small businessperson owns a store, and the county assessor believes the store's value is \$800,000. The assessed value for taxation would be 29% of that—namely, \$332,000. Assume that the mill levy rate in the county is 75 mills. (A mill is 1/10th of 1%).[26] So for every \$1,000 in assessed value, the business owner pays \$75 annually in property taxes. In the example, the property tax bill is \$17,400 (.075 x \$332,000).

Under TABOR, the governments must inform taxpayers annually about the government's estimated *actual* value of their property. The storeowner in the above example would have to be told that the government thinks the store's value is \$800,000. The government could not misleadingly tell the property owner only that the store is assessed for valuation at \$332,000. Since most people are not sophisticated about property tax calculations, a notice that said only "\$332,000" (and not \$800,000) could mislead the storeowner about the starting number on which her property taxes will be calculated.

If the storeowner believes that the store is worth only \$725,000, the government notice about the \$800,000 valuation puts the storeowner on notice that she might want to appeal the assessment.

Pursuant to TABOR, a notice of actual valuation must be sent annually. Likewise, a property owner may appeal annually.

Before TABOR, the valuation by the county assessor was presumed to be correct. The property owner had the burden of proving otherwise to the appeals board.[27] Now, appeals boards must rule in favor of whoever provides the best evidence. Art. X §20(8)(c).

---

[26] Denver's 2021 rate is 74.195.

[27] CML at 28.

Until TABOR, county assessors could use certain methods to exaggerate the value of a residence. TABOR prohibits these measures, by declaring "Actual value shall be . . . for residential real property, determined solely by the market approach to appraisal." *Id.* In other words, look at the prices for recent home sales in the area.

According to prior rules on property taxation, in article X, § 3, "the actual value of residential real property shall be determined solely by consideration of cost approach and market approach to appraisal." The cost approach to valuation estimates the replacement costs for a home: if the home were destroyed, how much would it cost to rebuild it? Suppose a particular home would sell for $200,000 and would cost $250,000 to rebuild. Whatever the fluctuations in building costs, a home that will sell for only $200,000 is worth $200,000. The fact that rebuilding the home would be expensive does not confer any wealth on the homeowner.

Property taxes are supposed to increase based on wealth. A person who has $250,000 in property wealth will pay 25% more than someone who has $200,000 in such wealth. Under TABOR, a person who has a home that can be sold for $200,000 may not be taxed as if she had a home that would sell for a higher price.

TABOR's "market approach" to assessment ended some assessors' practice of using a partial market approach. In a partial market approach, some comparable sales in the area are excluded—especially mortgage foreclosure sales or tax foreclosure sales. Foreclosures are usually sign of a weak real estate market; foreclosed homeowners could not pay their mortgages or taxes. Foreclosure sales indicate economic distress. The sales also indicate the actual value that buyers are willing to pay for homes in the area. By requiring the market approach, TABOR requires assessors to consider all comparable home sales, including lower-priced ones.

A different type of valuation, the "income approach" already was forbidden for residential property by the constitutional property tax rules in article X, § 3. TABOR provides backup protection to section 3's rule against the income approach. In brief, the income approach values a homeowner's property based on the hypothetical income if the homeowner moved out and leased the property, such as by dividing a single-family home into apartments.[28]

The problem with the income approach, especially for residential property, is that it is hypothetical. A person who *could* abandon her home, subdivide, and rent to multiple tenants is not any wealthier because of hypothetical possible income. Homeowners who are not becoming wealthier from rental income should not be taxed as if they were.

TABOR imposed another limit on property taxes, but that limit has been almost entirely negated. Under TABOR, annual property tax revenues for any given government entity (a "district") can automatically increase at the rate of inflation plus improvements to property (*e.g.*, remodeling a home, adding a second building on business property).[29] In Colorado, property taxes are a major revenue source for county and local governments.

---

[28] For rental property, the income approach can be as follows: look at the price of other recently sold rental properties in the area. Determine the annual rental income for these properties. The ratio is the gross rent multiplier. For example, if an apartment building recently sold for 10 million dollars, and its annual rental income is 1 million dollars, then the gross rent multiplier is 10.

Apply the income approach to a widow living with two grandchildren in her family's old 2,000 square foot home. As a single-family home, the house would be valued at $450,000. Based on average rents in area, the widow could earn $60,000 a year if she moved out and rented her former home to three tenants. The gross rent multiplier is 10, so multiply 10 x $60,000. The widow's home would be assessed at $600,000 under the income approach.

[29] Or for a school district, enrollment growth plus inflation. Art. X § 20(2)(g): "'Local growth' for a non-school district means a net percentage change in actual value of all real property in a district from construction of taxable real property improvements, minus destruction of similar improvements, and additions to, minus deletions from, taxable real property. For a school district, it means the percentage change in its student enrollment."

Suppose that property values in an area are rising rapidly. Property assessments are up sharply. Even while the county's mill levy rate stays the same, property tax revenue soars, because of higher assessments. Can the county keep the extra revenue? Certainly yes, says TABOR—provided that the county asks the voters. TABOR restrains but does forbid growth of government; growth is permitted when the voters choose to allow it.

For many local governments, voters have waived the TABOR property tax revenue limits permanently. In some jurisdictions, the voters were presented with a straightforward permanent waiver, and approved it. In others, voters were presented with a one-time waiver, but buried deep in the text was language that could be interpreted as a permanent waiver. The issue is discussed further, below.

2. Income taxes

The Taxpayer's Bill of Rights provides taxpayers with several protections regarding income taxes. First, TABOR flatly prohibits any "new state real property tax or local district income tax." Art. X, § 20(8)(a). The Colorado Constitution already forbade local income taxes, but Denver evaded the restriction by calling its income tax an "occupational privilege tax" for people who work in Denver. Art. X, § 17 (chapter 14).

Second, TABOR forbids retroactive income tax increases: "Neither an income tax rate increase nor a new state definition of taxable income shall apply before the next tax year." Art. X, § 20(8)(a).

Third, TABOR requires that net taxable income be taxed equally, at the same rate. *Id.* Colorado must have flat income tax, rather than regressive or progressive tax rates. In 1992 Colorado had a flat tax, so TABOR constitutionalized the status quo.

The flat tax rule is for "net taxable income," rather than to gross income. The legislature may increase or reduce deductions from taxable income. To the extent that the changes increase tax revenues, voter consent is required, as described next.

3. Tax policy changes

Tax policy changes can increase government revenue even when tax rates stay the same. For example, if the legislature repeals certain income tax deductions, then taxpayers' next taxable incomes will be higher, and the government will raise more income tax revenue. TABOR requires a vote on all tax policy changes that directly increase a district's net revenue. Art. X, § 20 (4)(a).

In 2009, the supreme court nullified this provision of TABOR. According to the court, if voters have allowed a district to retain excess revenue, then voters have implicitly waived their right to vote on tax policy changes. According to the court, tax policy changes only require a vote only if the new policies would cause a district to exceed its revenue caps. *Mesa County Board of County Commissioners v. State of Colorado*, 203 P.2d 519 (Colo. 2009) . The opinion makes no sense; TABOR separately requires voter approval for revenue increases above the cap, for any reason.

As a result, the general assembly has helped itself to billions of dollars of increased revenue by eliminating or limiting various tax deductions and exemptions. In 2021 the legislature enacted tax policy changes to raise Coloradans' taxes by $372.3 million annually, without asking for consent.[30] Some of the new revenue was offset in reductions of the business personal property tax, by expansion of the Earned Income Tax Credit (EITC, which is partly a tax refund, and partly

[30] The figure is for the total tax increase for fiscal year 2022-23. Net revenues are lower, because of increases in some tax deductions or credits, and by additional spending on EITC "credits," which are in part a spending program, not tax credits.

a welfare program, since persons may receive more money than they paid in income taxes), and by expansion of the Child Tax Credit to cover persons unlawfully present in the United States. EITC spending beyond a refund of income taxes actually paid is not a tax reduction; it is a social welfare program. Even if one counts all the EITC expansion as if it were tax reduction, the tax policy changes raised state revenue by $57.2 million for fiscal year 2023-24. House Bill 21-1311; Ben Murrey, *To keep campaign promise, Polis must veto House Bill 1311*, COMPLETE COLORADO, June 5, 2021.

But since the tax policy change will not cause the state government to exceed its fiscal year spending cap, the precedent of the Colorado supreme prevents voters from having the opportunity to approve it.

4. The court's decision on de minimis exceptions

According to a recent supreme court decision, voter approval is not required for what the court considers to be *de minimis* increases in taxes. The case arose from a statutory adjustment in sales tax exemptions. Certain items are exempt from the state sales tax. Local districts have their own exemptions, which may not exactly match the state exemptions. To simplify sales tax collection by vendors, the legislature in 2013 conformed the Regional Transportation District (RTD) and Scientific and Cultural Facilities District (SCFD) exemptions and the state exemptions, so they were identical. The net effect was to raise RTD and SCFD sales tax revenues by 0.6%, which amounted to only about 1/1,000th of the districts' total revenue.

The supreme court held that voter consent was not needed. The court interpolated into TABOR a de minimis exception. The court pointed to TABOR's "reasonably restrain" language and said that requiring a vote would be unreasonable. There was no evidence that the 2013 sales tax revisions had been enacted for the primary purpose of increasing taxes. *TABOR Foundation v. Regional Transportation District*, 416 P.3d 101 (Colo. 2018). All this was true enough. It is also true that in the legislative choices, about what items to include or exclude from the sales tax, the legislative choices increased the districts' revenues, rather than reducing them or leaving them stable.

5. Preservation of prior limits on taxes and spending

By TABOR's first paragraph, "Other limits on district revenue, spending, and debt may be weakened only by future voter approval." When the voters enacted TABOR in 1992, there were two major "other limits." Pursuant to TABOR, they could be weakened only by the voters.

For the state government, the Arveschoug-Bird statute limited annual increases in general fund appropriations.[31] (As noted above, the general fund comprises less than half of annual state budget and only a quarter of all state government spending.) For local governments, a state statute limited annual property tax growth to 5.5% for counties and for municipalities that are not home rule.

Nevertheless, in 2009 the legislature greatly weakened Arverschoug-Bird, and did not ask the voters for approval. The purported justification was that Arverschoug-Bird was not one of TABOR's "other limits" because it had not been effective in limiting increased general fund spending.[32] The legislative action belies the legislative pretext. If Arverschoug-Bird were not limiting spending, the general assembly would not have bothered to weaken it.

---

[31] The statute was not formally titled Arveschoug-Bird, but it was commonly called by that name, for its sponsors, rep. Steve Arveschoug and sen. Mike Bird.

[32] The legislative rationale was based on an analysis by former supreme court justice Jean Dubofsky. John Tomasic, *Ritter signs budget reform bill, ends reign of Arveschoug-Bird*, COLO. INDEPENDENT, June 3,

In La Plata County, the voters were asked to waive the TABOR revenue caps and assented. The court of appeals held that they had also waived the statutory 5.5 percent limit on property tax revenue increases. *Wilbur v. Board of County Commissioners of the County of La Plata*, 42 P.3d 49 (Colo. App. 2001). Supposedly, they had so agreed because the ballot language said the county could keep revenue "without any other condition or limitation." Adhesion contracts offered by big businesses hide their most extreme waivers of consumer rights among a mass of otherwise reasonable language. So do tax and spending referenda drafted by governments.

E. TABOR revenue caps, formerly important

TABOR's stated purpose is to "reasonably restrain most the growth of government." Therefore, TABOR allows automatic government revenue increases to account for population growth plus inflation. If inflation was 4% and a county's population grew 1%, then the county's budget the next year can automatically increase by 5%. If county officials want to spend more, they can ask the voters for consent.

Opponents of TABOR criticize the revenue caps because they mean that government cannot automatically grow as fast as the economy. For example, if population growth and inflation are each 1%, and the economy grows by 10%, government revenues might rise by 12%. Under TABOR, the government can automatically increase spending by the 2% of inflation plus population growth. Beyond that, the government must ask for consent to increase its size.

The term of art in TABOR is *fiscal year spending*. There are subrules related to employee pensions, reserve accounts, court-ordered damage awards, and sales of government property. A statute provides additional detail for these terms. C.R.S. § 24-77-102.

A particularly important subrule involves pass-throughs of revenue, when one government ("district") collects money and gives it to another. *Id.* The most common example is property taxes. Counties impose their own property taxes. The state imposes its own, smaller, property tax. On top of those, people must pay property taxes for municipalities and for local districts. The most important local districts are school districts. Additionally, there are thousands of other local districts, for water, mining, libraries, fire protection, and many other purposes. Chapter 19 (art. XIV, counties and special districts).

For the convenience of everyone, the county treasurer collects all the property taxes. The county treasurer keeps the property taxes imposed by the county and disburses the other taxes to the relevant government entities: school districts, the state government, municipal governments, and special districts. The revenue counts as fiscal year spending of the recipient government, such as a school district. It does not count as fiscal year spending by the pass-through collector, such as the county government. C.R.S. § 30-28-133(4.3).

TABOR's limits on nonconsensual increases in fiscal year spending are criticized by some advocates who argue that government spending (and hence, the government's ability to control people's personal affairs) must always advance and never retreat. Some people have the opposite view and want to shrink the existing government. TABOR takes a middle ground. The size of the existing government can continue and can account for population growth and inflation. Above the steady state, increases are allowed whenever voters consent.

At least that is the constitutional theory. The practice is different. At the local level, spending caps have been obliterated by voter waivers—some of which were obtained by bait-and-switch ballot measures, as discussed below. On the whole (including in elections with forthright ballot language), Colorado voters have approved hundreds of referenda to allow excess local

---

2009; Colo. Att'y Gen. Op. No. 98-02, Oct. 26, 1998, *modified by* Colo. Att'y Gen. Op. No. 99-05, July 30, 1999; Johnson, Beck & Hoyt at 820; Richard B. Collins, *The Colorado Constitution in the New Century,* 78 U. COLO. L. REVIEW 1265, 1305 (2007).

government spending. In contrast, voters have often been skeptical of the state legislature's referenda to increase its own general revenue spending. Perhaps the difference in electoral outcomes is that local governments have greater credibility with voters.

While TABOR's revenue caps are mostly nonexistent for local government, they still apply at the state level, in a limited sense. As described above, TABOR by its own terms does not apply its revenue caps to outside grants. Federal grants are a large part of state spending, including the grants of Medicaid and for transportation (very broadly defined). Nor are private grants covered, including donations by special interest groups, such as to pay for like-minded staff within an executive office. *See* C.R.S. § 24-77-102(5) & (6) (defining federal and private grants). If the state government passes a federal or private grant to a local government, the money still counts as federal or private, not state.

As also described above, much of the state budget has been offloaded into "enterprises" that are exempt from the TABOR revenue caps.

Additionally, the voters have exempted certain government revenues from TABOR's spending or taxing limits. Here are some of the most important:

A 2000 constitutional amendment exempts some of the value of senior citizens' homes from property taxes. A 2006 supplement to the amendment gave the same exemption to the homes of fully disabled veterans. The legislature may raise or lower the exemption freely. Lowering the exemption has the effect of raising property taxes. Art. X, §3.5 (chapter 14).

The Great Outdoors Colorado (GOCO) amendment was passed by the voters in 1992, the same year as TABOR. It dedicates state lottery revenue to the outdoors, with a transition period to use some funds to finish preexisting capital construction projects, such as prisons. Art. XXVII (chapter 32). The supreme court held that lottery revenue that is given to GOCO by the state government does not count as fiscal year spending. The portions of lottery revenue that were retained for other state building projects did count as fiscal year revenue. *Submission of Interrogatories on Senate Bill 93-74*, 852 P.2d 1 (Colo. 1993).

A 2000 statutory referendum authorized multistate lotteries and required that some of the new revenue be used for school building construction or maintenance. It exempted all lottery proceeds from fiscal year spending rules. C.R.S. § 24-77-103(2.3).

A 2000 constitutional amendment provided for automatic increases in public school spending. The state was required to put certain sums into a "state education fund," and these amounts do not count as fiscal year spending. Art. IX, § 17 (chapter 13).

In 2004 a constitutional amendment greatly raised tobacco taxes, required spending the revenue on particular health programs, and exempted the revenue from fiscal year spending limits. Art. X, § 21 (chapter 31).

In 2008 a constitutional amendment expanded the scope of legalized gambling and exempted the states' new gambling tax revenues from TABOR. Art. XVIII, § 9 (chapter 31).

A 2013 statutory referendum, Proposition AA, exempted marijuana tax revenues. When marijuana tax revenues turned out to be higher than the amounts for which Proposition AA had won voter approval, Proposition BB in 2015 allowed the state to keep the excess.

As the aforesaid votes show, the people are willing to allow state government growth, when presented with specific proposals. Looser or vaguer ballot measures to grow state government faster have usually been rejected.

The latest revenue forecasts from the Legislative Counsel forecast surpluses that will trigger TABOR refunds in the next several years. Given the general assembly's ingenuity in avoiding refunds in the previous decade, taxpayers should not spend any anticipated refund in advance.

Ratchet effects

TABOR has been criticized for having a "ratchet effect" in reducing the size of government. That argument was always inaccurate and has long been irrelevant. Most local governments in Colorado have been exempted from TABOR fiscal year spending limits. For the state government, the fiscal year spending limits apply to less than half the state budget. Their practical effect was mostly eliminated by voter approval of Referendum C in 2005.

A ratchet is "a device consisting of a bar or wheel with a set of angled teeth in which a cog or tooth engages, allowing motion in one direction only." Metaphorically, a ratchet is "a situation or process that is perceived to be changing in a series of irreversible steps."

Opponents of TABOR criticized its "ratchet effect." The epithet incorrectly presumes that TABOR mandates an irreversible shrinkage of government. Indeed, some TABOR opponents can be said to favor a ratchet effect in the other direction: the growth of government must be irreversible.

TABOR's "preferred interpretation shall reasonably restrain most the growth of government." Restraining growth is not shrinkage. Staying steady at a 44-inch waist is not the same as becoming slender. And if a food shortage makes the person's waist decline to 43 inches, it is not "shrinkage" to require that the return to 44 inches might take more than one year.

Here is the alleged ratchet effect for state government: In year one, tax revenues are 15 billion. In year two, inflation plus population growth allow state revenues to increase by 5%, to 15.75 billion. In year three, there is recession and general revenues fall to 14 billion. Because of the 1876 Constitution's balanced budget rule, the legislature can only spend 14 billion, no more. Art. X, § 16 (chapter 14).

The next year, the economy improves. Without any changes in tax rates, tax revenues rise to $16 billion. In the same year, Colorado population increase was 2%, and inflation was 5%. Pursuant to TABOR, state fiscal revenue can automatically increase by 7%. So from a 14 billion base (previous year), the state government can automatically spend 14.98 billion (base + inflation + population growth). As for the extra 1.02 billion, the legislature can refund the excess, or it can ask voters for permission to keep it.

In no case does TABOR shrink government by requiring that one year's spending be less than the previous year's. TABOR does mean that if revenue declines from year 1 to year 2, the automatically allowed increase in spending for year 3 will be calculated from the year 2 base, not the year 1 base. Maybe the voters in year 4 want to keep the billion dollars for themselves, to help them climb out of the personal economic problems caused by the recession. Maybe the voters feel flush and will agree that state government will do a good job spending the billion dollars. The decision is up to the people.

Referendum C

In 2005, the general assembly presented voters a referendum that was touted as a five-year "TABOR time out" to undo the ratchet effect. It did considerably more.

Supported by over 900 tax consumer organizations and opposed by the handful of pro-taxpayer organizations, Referendum C passed with 52 percent in favor.[33] Its companion measure, referendum D, would have started the extra spending early, by borrowing against anticipated revenues in future years. Referendum D was defeated, fortunately; revenues plunged in the Great Recession of 2008–09, so repaying the debt would have been difficult.

The Referendum C ballot text began, "without raising taxes." This was true in the sense that the referendum did not change tax rates. But the result of the referendum was that over the next

---

[33] Codified at C.R.S. § 24-77-103.6.

decade, the legislature kept over 10 billion extra dollars of the taxpayers' money— about $2,000 per person.[34] If government ends up with $2,000 more in taxes per person, that seems like a tax increase.

The ballot measure language promised more spending on education, health care, transportation projects, firefighters, and police officers. Two of the five enumerated services, education and health, received over 98% of the excess revenue.[35]

The legislature used Referendum C money for K-12 education, for the state's voucher program for higher education, and for the state's contribution to Medicaid (a joint state-federal medical welfare program). Yet while the legislature added revenues from Referendum C, it cut other funding for the same programs.

On net, education and health spending grew 11.9%. Spending by the legislature on everything else grew 28.7%.[36] Voters had reason to feel deceived.

Under TABOR, the state government's general fund could increase above the prior year's spending by inflation plus population growth. Referendum C changed that. The new baseline for state spending would be whatever year in the five-year "time-out" had the most revenue. That turned out to be fiscal year 2007–08, just before the Great Recession.

As a result of the new, higher limits, the legislature's fiscal year spending rarely comes close to requiring the legislature to refund excess revenue to the taxpayers. When fiscal year 2014–15 was so prosperous that it appeared that the legislature might have to refund $150 million, the legislature found some accounting tactics to keep all the money.[37] For fiscal year 2019-–20, state spending was $2.6 billion higher than it would have been without Referendum C. Legislative Council Staff, *Report on Referendum C Revenue and Spending FY 2005-06 through FY 2020-21.* (Oct. 15, 2020).

In 2019, the legislature referred Proposition CC to the voters, asking to retain more money above the TABOR cap. The money was promised to be spent on transportation and education. Perhaps memories of what happened with Referendum C in 2005 contributed to the defeat of CC in 2019. It was rejected by 54%.

F. Weakening of enforcement mechanisms

Election rules

TABOR aimed to stop various ploys used by governments to manipulate elections. One common trick was selecting unusual election dates, so that voter turnout would be low. With low turnout, special interest supporters of a tax or spending increase (*e.g.*, government unions) can form a disproportionately high fraction of the electorate.[38]

---

[34] Robert G. Natelson, *The Colorado Taxpayer's Bill of Rights*, INDEPENDENCE INSTITUTE, Issue Paper 3-2016, at 39 (2016)

[35] Colorado Legislative Council, *Report on Referendum C Revenue and Spending FY 2005-6 through FY 2014-14* (Oct. 15, 2014); Kate Watkins, *State Spending Limitations: TABOR and Referendum C*, at 4, fig. 4 (Colo. Legis. Council Staff, July 6, 2009).

[36] Mark Hillman & Amy Oliver, *State Budget Scrutiny Reveals Ref C Shuffle,* INDEPENDENCE INSTITUTE, Issue Backgrounder IB-2007-E, Aug. 2007.

[37] John Frank, *Colorado budget bill eliminates TABOR refunds, slashes spending,* DENVER POST, Mar. 24, 2016.

[38] "Prior to the adoption of TABOR, municipalities routinely called for 'special elections' on bond issues and other fiscal matters during virtually any month of the year." CML at 2. In "the first three general elections held after the adoption of TABOR (1994, 1996, and 1998), municipal tax increase ballot questions enjoyed only a 41 percent success rate. In contrast, tax questions were successful 59 percent of

TABOR aimed to stop this abuse for all ballot measures, not solely for TABOR-related elections. Pursuant to TABOR, "ballot issue" elections must be on: a regular biennial election date (such as the Denver City Council elections that are held in April of odd-numbered years), or on the general election days in even-numbered years (the first Tuesday after the first Monday in November), or in odd-numbered years, on the first Tuesday in November.[39]

Ballot measures to raises taxes or debt must say so at the beginning. The language must be: "SHALL (DISTRICT) TAXES BE INCREASED (first, or if phased in, final, full fiscal year dollar increase) ANNUALLY" or "SHALL (DISTRICT) DEBT BE INCREASED (principal amount), WITH A REPAYMENT COST OF (maximum total district cost)?"

Courts have held that the above language is not required for a measure to extend a tax that was scheduled to sunset. *Bruce v. City of Colorado Springs*, 129 P.3d 988 (Colo. 2006). Nor to long-term debt that is nominally structured as an optional year-to-year obligation.[40]

Some referenda to remove TABOR limits do not tell the voters that they are asking for an exemption from the Taxpayer's Bill of Rights. Instead, they obliquely mention "limitations provided by law."[41]

TABOR tried to limit ballot language abuse but has been only partially successful. The type of ballot language manipulation that still takes place in Colorado is exemplified by Jefferson County's 2019 ballot issue 1A. The measure was a single sentence of 300 words, with the promised benefits loaded at the top. Only the most discerning readers who could make their way through the verbiage to the end would find the indirect statements that, notwithstanding the promises at the beginning of the sentence, the Jefferson County commissioners could spend the extra money on anything they wanted.[42]

In 2021 the legislature amended the election statutes to require that in future TABOR elections, the ballot language must include pro-tax talking points. Ballot measures to reduce state or local taxes must list the three state spending programs that will supposedly be reduced by the measure—even though the proposed tax reduction leaves the relevant legislative body free to adjust spending any way it chooses. Measures to increases taxes must include the language "In order to increase or improve levels of public services," and, if the tax proponents have something specific in mind, they must list the services to be increased. The statute specifically declares that if the tax increases pass, the government has no obligation to actually spend its new revenue on the promised services. C.R.S. § 1-40-106(3). The Blue Book of pro/con ballot information distributed to voters must include information about the estimated tax effects for people in fourteen different income categories. C.R.S. § 1-40-124.5. The obvious purpose is to encourage lower-income voters to support higher taxes, by showing them that other people will pay most of the burdens.

Enforcement lawsuit constriction

TABOR did not rely on government officials faithfully to follow the Constitution by limiting their own powers to tax and spend. Accordingly, TABOR declares itself to be self-executing. It

---

the time when submitted on other election dates." *Id.* at 60. Thus, TABOR was successful in reducing the number of municipal tax increases that were passed only because the election was held on a date designed for voter suppression.

[39] Hence, Tuesday, November 1, cannot be an election day in an even year, but it can be in an odd year.

[40] CML at 38. Discussed further in chapter 16 (art. XI, Debt).

[41] Proposition AA (marijuana taxes). 2013 Colo. Session Laws 1866.

[42] Rob Natelson, *How Colorado officials manipulate ballot language to get what they want: The case of JeffCo Issue 1A,* COMPLETE COLORADO (Oct. 7, 2019). The proposal was defeated at the polls thanks to a sustained public education campaign by opponents. Not every deceptive ballot measure is countered by skeptics who have sufficient resources to inform a large portion of the voters.

does not depend on the general assembly to enact implementing statutes. This is a common practice of modern state constitutional amendments.

Accurately expecting government hostility and noncompliance, TABOR also authorizes citizen lawsuits against violations. To facilitate lawsuits, TABOR provides that enforcement suits shall receive top judicial priority among civil cases. Unlike in federal courts, Colorado legal doctrine has long allowed for taxpayers to have standing to sue against unlawful expenditures of taxpayer money. However, this doctrine has lately been narrowed. According to the Colorado court of appeals opinion about the hospital bed tax, taxpayers did not have standing to sue. The taxes were paid directly by hospitals, who did not sue. While hospitals passed along the tax by raising bills for patients, the pass-along was "subsumed" into the hospitals' accounting for "overhead," rather than presented as line items in patient bills. Because the taxes were imposed on patients indirectly, as overhead charges that affected total bills, taxpayers could not prove that their own money was being extracted to pay the tax, and so they could not challenge the tax's legality. *TABOR Foundation v. Colo. Dept. of Health Care Policy and Financing*, 2020 COA 156 (Colo. App. 2020).

TABOR's encouragement of taxpayer suits has been held not to alter the general rule that local governments, such as counties, do not have standing except when conferred by statute. *Board of Commissioners of the County of Boulder v. City of Broomfield*, 7 P.3d 1033 (Colo. App. 1999), cert. granted (Sept. 11, 2000), cert. denied as improvidently granted (Feb. 5, 2001). By taking local governments out of the picture as plaintiffs, the rule means that pro-taxpayer local governments, who have fulltime lawyers on staff, cannot use those lawyers to fight for taxpayer interests. Meanwhile, other state or local governments can use their own fulltime lawyers to fight against claims that taxpayers' rights have been violated.

To encourage private enforcement, TABOR provides: "Successful plaintiffs are allowed costs and reasonable attorney fees, but a district is not unless a suit against it be ruled frivolous." The supreme court, however, held that awards of attorneys fees and court costs are optional, based on the judge's discretion. Posing as the taxpayers' friend, the court invoked TABOR's "restrain most the growth of government" language and pointed out that if governments always had to pay successful plaintiffs, then government spending would increase. *City of Wheat Ridge v. Cerveny*, 913 P.2d 1110 (Colo. 1996).

The court's purported concern for frugality ignored the obvious fact that a successful suit will typically recover or save amounts of taxpayers' money far in excess of the amount of attorneys fees.

Few private individuals can afford to pay for a lawsuit. Attorneys' pro bono time is finite. By preventing successful private enforcement suits from recovering fees and costs, the court has ensured that many TABOR violations are not challenged.

Local opt out of mandates

As TABOR advocates knew from the experience of other states, state governments try to evade tax or expenditures limits by ordering local governments to perform certain tasks without compensation. TABOR section 9 provides a process for local governments to withdraw from state mandates. They must provide 90 days notice, and the withdrawal must be in three equal annual steps. The process is recorded with the state Department of Local Affairs. C.R.S. § 29-1-304.7.

There are two express exemptions. First, for U.S. Constitution Supremacy Clause reasons, TABOR does not attempt to authorize local governments to escape federal mandates. Second, school districts cannot opt out of mandates.

The Colorado supreme court has invented a third exemption: counties may not opt out. In the court's view, a county is not a TABOR "local district." Rather, it is an agent of the state government; being part of the state government, it cannot opt out of a state mandate. *Romer v.*

Board of County Commissioners for the County of Weld, 897 P.2d 779 (Colo. 1995); *State of Colorado ex rel. Norton v. Board of County Commissioners of Mesa County*, 897 P.2d 788 (Colo. 1995). The court's 1995 reasoning is broad enough so that future courts could eliminate the opt-out entirely. As discussed in chapter 25 (Home Rule, art. XX), the prevailing legal doctrine in the United States is that *all* local governments—including counties, municipalities, and special districts—are agents of the state government. Hence, *Romer* could be extended to any or all of them.

The Kerr litigation

Starting in 2011, several former or current legislators, local officials, and tax consumers litigated a federal lawsuit claiming that the Taxpayer's Bill of Rights violates the Republican Form of Government guarantee of the United States Constitution. U.S. Const. art. IV, § 3 ("The United States shall guarantee to every State in this Union a Republican Form of Government"). In the plaintiffs' view, a republican form of government is one in which a "fully effective legislature" does not need consent to raise taxes or spending. The original plaintiffs were later joined by several school districts.

For a decade, litigation continued about whether the parties have standing to bring the suit. The case raised questions under U.S. Supreme Court doctrine about when state legislators have standing to sue in federal court, when local governments have federal court standing to sue their state, and whether Republican Form of Government claims are justiciable or if instead enforcement of the Guarantee Clause is a matter for Congress.

The case generated an original opinion in U.S. district court for Colorado in 2012, a revised opinion from that same court later that year, a decision by the Tenth Circuit in 2014, Tenth Circuit denial of a petition for rehearing en banc (with dissenters including then-judge Gorsuch), the Tenth Circuit decision being vacated by the U.S. Supreme Court in 2015, another Tenth Circuit decision in 2016 followed by remand to the district court, a district court decision in 2017, and a 2019 Tenth Circuit decision.

Finally, December 2021, the Tenth Circuit decided the case en banc and held 7–2 that the case should be dismissed. *Kerr v. Polis*, No. 17-1192 (10th Cir. Dec. 13, 2021) (en banc). The majority explained the general rule that federal courts do not hear cases against a state brought by a political subdivision of a state unless the underlying law grants political subdivisions a right to sue.

Here, the school district plaintiffs had standing, for they suffered a concrete injury that was redressable through litigation: because of TABOR, they had to spend money to put referenda on the ballot asking for tax increases, rather than being able to raise taxes unilaterally.

However, the plaintiffs had not persuasively shown that the Republican Form of Government Clause in the U.S. Constitution was intended to create a cause of action for political subdivisions to sue their parent state. The same was true for the 1875 Enabling Act (detailed in chapter 1), by which Congress put Colorado on the path to statehood and required Colorado to have a republican form of government.

The original understanding of a "republic" is entirely consistent with direct citizen voting, as shown by practices, political writings, and the dictionaries of the time. Amicus Brief of the Independence Institute and Cato Institute in *Kerr v. Hickenlooper*, no. 12-1445 (10th Cir., Feb. 28, 2013). *See also* Robert G. Natelson, *A Republic, Not a Democracy? Initiative, Referendum, and the Constitution's Guarantee Clause*, 80 TEXAS L. REVIEW 807 (2002). For a contrary view, see Joshua Pens, *Restore The Republic: The Incompatibility Between the Taxpayer's Bill of Rights and the Guarantee Clause*, 87 U. COLO. L. REVIEW 621 (2021).

G. Waivers

One of TABOR's election law rules is: "Except for petitions, bonded debt, or charter or constitutional provisions, districts may consolidate ballot issues and voters may approve a delay of up to four years in voting on ballot issues. District actions taken during such a delay shall not extend beyond that period."

It was argued that the above language means that voter-approved waivers of fiscal year spending limits can last for up to four years. If so, TABOR picked a backhanded way to say so. On the other hand, the argument for the TABOR language having some other meaning made even less plausible claims about what the text meant. The court of appeals held that "voter approved revenue changes" need not be limited in time. *Havens v. Board of County Commissioners of the County of Archuleta*, 58 P.3d 1165 (Colo. App. 2002).

It is often said that 174 of Colorado's 178 school districts have obtained voter exemptions from TABOR's revenue caps.[43] So have 230 of Colorado's 271 municipalities.[44] As have 51 of the 64 counties.[45]

The Colorado supreme court has been very loose in deciding that local voters have chosen to waive all TABOR restraints. The E-470 Public Highway Authority was approved by voters in a 1988 referendum. The court held that the 1988 referendum presciently functioned as a waiver of the TABOR limits that would be enacted by voters in 1992. *Nicholl v. E-470 Public Highway Authority*, 896 P.2d 859 (Colo. 1995).

A 2021 case showed that voter approval for a district retaining excess revenue can be interpreted as voter waiver of their right to vote on the largest property tax increase in Colorado history. *In re Interrogatory on House Bill 21-1164*, 2021 CO 34 (Colo. 2021).

From 1995 to 2006, the Colorado department of education (CDE) issued instructions to school districts about the mill levy rates. In the view of the majority of the court, the instructions were illegal, since they ordered districts to lower their mill levy rates to avoid exceeding TABOR's revenue limits, even though the voters in the district had approved waivers. *Id.* at ¶ 10. In dissent, chief justice Boatright argued that the record on what CDE did and how school districts had responded was too murky. Rather than deciding the issue based on an interrogatory from the general assembly, the court should have waited for a more-developed record from the ordinary process of civil litigation. *Id.* at ¶ 100 (Boatright, C.J., dissenting).

In 2007, the legislature decided that the CDE instructions had been unlawful. School districts were ordered to raise their mill levy rates, but also to grant taxpayers a credit to offset the increased rates. The 2021 bill provided for a 20-year process to fully eliminate the credits and for school districts to raise their mill levies by one mill per year. Cumulatively, the bill will create the largest property tax increase in Colorado history. The increase will be about $90 million in the first year, and $288 million annually in 2040.[46]

The legislative interrogatory to the supreme court asked if the Taxpayer's Bill of Rights stood in the way. A good question, since TABOR requires voter consent for any "mill levy above that for the prior year." Art. X, § 20(4)(a). The majority held that the mill levy increases did not require a vote of the people. Their votes to allow school districts to retain excess revenue had implicitly waived their right to vote on increases on any mill levy, as long as the increased mill levy was no higher than the 1994 level. The majority waxed eloquent about how its decision effectuated the will of the school district voters.

---

[43] Jesse Paul, *Lawmakers can allow school districts to raise property taxes without voter approval, Colorado Supreme Court rules,* COLORADO SUN, May 24, 2021.

[44] Bell Policy Center, *What is Debrucing?* (2019).

[45] Colorado Counties, Inc., *De-Bruced Counties* (Dec. 2019) (listing counties with general waivers of revenue limits and with waivers of the separate 5.5% cap).

[46] Paul, *Lawmakers*, *supra.*

Chief justice Boatright's dissent pointed to the actual text of the revenue limit waivers in 161 of the 174 school districts: "provided, however, that no local or property tax mill levy shall be increased at any time, nor shall any new tax be imposed, without prior consent of the voters." *Id.* at ¶ 83 (Boatright, C.J., dissenting).

> [T]he only issue before the voters—and thus the only issue on which they conceivably could have expressed their intent—was whether TABOR's revenue limit should be waived. In other words, no one knows what the voters intended to do about the mill levy rates in their districts because they were never asked. But, the majority "assume[s] that in voting to waive TABOR's revenue limits, school district voters understood that their votes were predicated on the continuation of the mill levy rates then in effect." Maj. op. ¶ 41 (emphasis added). That is a big assumption—one I am unwilling to make, and in my view, one that the constitution prohibits. With the majority's decision today, voters must now be aware that any vote on revenue limits may act as permission to always maintain applicable tax rates at their current levels. Maj. op. ¶ 42 ("[I]n voting to waive the TABOR revenue limits . . . the voters who authorized those waivers necessarily approved the mill levies in effect at the time they voted.").

Id. at ¶ 84 (brackets in original).

Justice Samour concurred in the majority's result only. He explained that he agreed with much of chief justice Boatright's dissent, but he took a different approach to uphold the legislature's bill. The CDE instructions had been *ultra vires* and therefore illegal. TABOR's rule about any "mill levy above that for the prior year" should be read as applying the most recent prior year of *legal* mill levies. Since the reduced mill levies were illegal, they could not be a "prior year." So TABOR would apply to the last prior year of *legal* mill levies, which justice Samour said was 1994.

Chief justice Boatright replied that even if TABOR could be read as justice Samour preferred, the baseline year for the reset should be 2007, not 1994. "In *Mesa*, we approved of SB 07-199, which froze the mill levy rates in 2007, meaning districts' rates were at least 'legal' since 2007. So, if our reference point is the last 'legal' rate (though I don't agree that our constitution supports such an interpretation), then why wouldn't the current rates serve as the reference point?" *Id.* at ¶ 97, n. 10 (Boatright, C.J., dissenting).

Further reading:

On TABOR specifically, Robert G. Natelson, *The Colorado Taxpayer's Bill of Rights*, INDEPENDENCE INSTITUTE, Issue Paper 3-2016 (2016) (a comprehensive survey of TABOR cases through 2016, from which this chapter is partly adapted and used with permission); Paul Eliason & Byron Luz, *Can Fiscal Rules Constrain the Size of Government? An Analysis of the "Crown Jewel" of Tax and Expenditure Limitations*, 166 J. OF PUBLIC ECONOMICS 115 (2018) (short answer: no); Peter J. Whitmore, *The Taxpayers Bill of Rights: Twenty Years of Litigation*, 42 COLO. LAWYER 35 (2013) (summary of cases); Colorado Municipal League, *TABOR: A Guide to the Taxpayer's Bill of Rights* (2011); Kathleen J. Gebhardt, *Challenges to Funding School Facilities in Colorado*, 83 NEB. L. REVIEW 856 (2005); Michael R. Johnson, Scott H. Beck, & H. Lawrence Hoyt, *State Constitutional Tax Limitations: The Colorado and California Experiences*, 35 URBAN LAWYER 817 (2003).

On tax and expenditure limits in general: Donald Bruce, Elizabeth A. Glass & Matthew C. Harris, *On the Effectiveness of State Tax and Expenditure Policies to Encourage Enterpreneurship*, 8 J. OF ENTREPRENEURSHIP & PUBLIC POLICY (no. 4, 2019); Christine Wen, et al., *Starving Counties, Squeezing Cities: Tax and Expenditure Limits in the U.S.*, 23 J. OF ECONOMIC POLICY REFORM 101 (2018); Steven Deller, et al., *Do Tax and Expenditure*

Limitations Exacerbate Rising Income Inequality? (Wiley Online Library, 2021); Sungho Park, et al., *The Effects of Tax and Expenditure Limitations (TELs) on Municipal Fiscal Outcomes During a Period of Fiscal Distress*, 18 PUBLIC FINANCE & MANAGEMENT 201 (2018); Craig S. Maher, Sungho Park & James Harrold, *The Effects of Tax and Expenditure Limits on Municipal Pension and OPEB Funding During the Great Recession*, 16 SOUTHERN PUBLIC ADMINISTRATION EDUCATION FOUNDATION (no. 2, 2016).

On the *Kerr* litigation: Lee A. Steven, *Kerr v. Polis*, COLO. LAWYER, July 2021.

CHAPTER 16

Public Indebtedness, Article XI

Art. XI, Section 1. No lending or pledging of credit

> Neither the state, nor any county, city, town, township or school district shall lend or pledge the credit or faith thereof, directly or indirectly, in any manner to, or in aid of, any person, company or corporation, public or private, for any amount, or for any purpose whatever; or become responsible for any debt, contract or liability of any person, company or corporation, public or private, in or out of the state.

Q. What part of "no" don't you understand?
A. The whole thing. To me, "no" means "yes," as long as I think I have good motives.

Section 1 employs the most comprehensive, unequivocal words possible in the English language: "directly or indirectly, in any manner . . . for any amount, or for any purpose whatever . . . any debt, contract or liability."

The Colorado supreme court, however, has nullified section 1. The complete prohibition on public credit for any organization "for any purpose whatever" is perverted to allow public credit whenever there is an alleged "public purpose." And the legislative claim that a "public purpose" exists is supposedly entitled to near-absolute judicial deference. The leading cases have often discussed article XI, §§ 1–2 in conjunction, so they are summarized under section 2.

The last case in which a party won a case based on a violation of Section 1 was in 1960. According to a statute, when a group of people attempted to incorporate a town, the expenses of incorporation, such as legal fees and the cost of holding the election, would be borne by the new town, if the voters chose to incorporate. If the voters rejected creating the new town, then the county would pay the expenses. The statute saddling counties with someone else's debt was held to violate Section 1. *Board of County Com'rs of Arapahoe County v. Humes*, 144 Colo. 434, 356 P.2d 910 (1960).

The nullification of section 1 is an important reason that Colorado has become a sanctuary state for immigrants seeking to go on welfare—namely, corporations that seek the welfare privilege of low-cost forced loans from the taxpayers, rather than borrowing money from banks or the bond market at market rates. Because interest income from state and local government bonds is not subject to state or federal taxes, the bond issuers can cut their interest rates by about 2% compared to the free market rate. In effect, there is one rate of interest in Colorado for some of the borrowing by influential businesses and a higher rate for businesses without political clout.

Art. XI, Section 2. No aid to corporations

> Neither the state, nor any county, city, town, township, or school district shall make any donation or grant to, or in aid of, or become a subscriber to, or shareholder in any corporation or company or a joint owner with any person, company, or corporation, public or private, in or out of the state, except as to such ownership as may accrue to the state by escheat, or by forfeiture, by operation or provision of law; and except as to such ownership as may accrue to the state, or to any county, city, town, township, or school district, or to either or any of them, jointly with any person, company, or corporation, by forfeiture or sale of real estate for nonpayment of taxes, or by donation or devise for public use, or by purchase by or on behalf of any or either of them, jointly with any or either of them, under execution in cases of fines, penalties, or forfeiture of recognizance, breach of condition of official bond, or of bond to secure public moneys, or the performance of any contract in which they or any of them may be jointly or severally interested. Nothing in this section shall be construed to prohibit any city or town from becoming a subscriber or shareholder in any corporation or company, public or private, or a joint owner with any person, company, or corporation, public or private, in order to effect the development of energy resources after discovery, or production, transportation, or transmission of energy in whole or in part for the benefit of the inhabitants of such city or town.

Section 2 comprehensively forbids certain government actions. No Colorado government may

- make any donation or
- grant to, or in
- aid of, or
- become a subscriber to,
- shareholder or
- joint owner with
- any corporation or company, public or private, in or out of the state.

There are defined exceptions for gifts of stock to government, fines, and so on.

In 1974, the voters created exceptions for energy development and provision of energy. For example, a municipality could go into business with a private utility; the municipality and utility could create a joint business to provide electricity to the people of the municipality.

In 1972, voters added section 2a, to authorize the general assembly to set up a student loan programs. Because student loans operate "in aid of" public or private educational corporations, the 1972 amendment was the constitutional means to create a specific exception to the general rules of section 2.

Section 2 was based on the bitter experience of government joint ventures with railroads in territorial days. Private profits, public losses. The Convention and the people extrapolated from the railroad example the principle of separating government from participation in businesses. Colorado Convention, *Address to the People of Colorado* (1876) (chapter 1); Donald Wayne Hensel, *A History of the Colorado Constitution in the Nineteenth Century* (Ph.D. thesis in History, U. of Colo., 1957) (available on JSTOR).[1]

Professor Dale Oesterle traces the destruction of the Colorado Constitution's many express limits on corporate welfare and special privileges to the push for the Moffat Tunnel. Dale A. Oesterle, *Lessons on the Limits of Constitutional Language from Colorado: The Erosion of the Constitution's Ban on Business Subsidies*, 73 U. COLO. L. REVIEW 587 (2002).

Denver business leaders had long sought a direct railroad link to the west, ultimately to Salt Lake City. They did not want to have to ship products by rail north to Cheyenne or south to Pueblo to connect with a westward transcontinental line. Likewise, northwest Colorado was abundant in agricultural goods and coal, and wanted a direct rail connection to get them to Denver.

The difficulty was that there was no mountain pass near Denver that was viable for a railroad. That was the reason why the first transcontinental railroad had been built through Cheyenne and not Denver. So a plan was conceived to dig and blast a railroad tunnel through James Peak, in Grand County. From an engineering viewpoint, the plan was viable. After getting through the tunnel, the railroad could head west or southwest to connect to a rail line to Salt Lake City.[2]

The first problem was that the plan was not necessarily economically viable. It was questionable whether a railroad line under James Peak could ever attract enough traffic to pay for itself. That was one reason that no railroad had attempted to build the tunnel.

The second problem was the Colorado Constitution. As the Colorado Convention's *Address to the People* had explained, the Convention had debated corporations extensively, and had chosen a middle course. On the one hand, the Convention rejected government meddling in business operations. Proposals to allow the legislature to set railroad rates, to abolish limited liability for corporate shareholders, or to enact certain banking regulations were all defeated.

On the other hand, the Convention adopted a bevy of provisions to prevent government favoritism to particular businesses. Much of article XV (Corporations) is devoted to the topic. So are the uniform taxation rules in article X, and the prohibitions on special legislation in article V, §§ 25, 34. Indeed, article V's extensive procedural controls and transparency mandates on legislation were created in part to make it difficult for special corporate favors to be inserted into legislation.

Most relevantly for the businessmen who dreamed of taxpayers paying for a tunnel under James Peak, article XI, § 1, forbade governments from going into debt on behalf of business, and § 2 prohibited every level of government in Colorado from going into business with a business.

The Convention well knew that prohibiting government aid to corporate pets would place Colorado at a competitive disadvantage with states where corporate welfare was allowed. The Convention, and then the people of Colorado who ratified the proposed Constitution, decided that Colorado had plenty of natural advantages to attract businesses. The taxpayers did not need to be burdened with paying to attract businesses that needed special favors to be willing to do business in Colorado; the best business climate would be created by a level playing field. "The delegates apparently believed that the loss of some business to other states would be outweighed by the prospect of increased government integrity." Oesterle at 596.

---

[1] Whether for light rail today or canals in the early 19th century, states overspend and overborrow. "By the summer of 1842, eight states and the Territory of Florida were in default on interest payments . . . Ultimately, Mississippi and Florida repudiated their debts outright, and Louisiana, Arkansas, and Michigan repudiated part of their debts. New York, Ohio, and Alabama barely avoided default." John Joseph Wallis, *Constitutions, Corporations, and Corruption: American States and Constitutional Change, 1842 to 1852*, 65 JOURNAL OF ECONOMIC HISTORY 211 (2005).

[2] The connection was ultimately made at Dotsero, in Eagle County.

Separation of business and state can be analogized to separation of church and state. Churches do better, in the long run, when government do not meddle in church affairs. This means that governments treat all churches equally; they attempt to create a free climate where churches can thrive or fail depending on their ability to attract members by choice. Taxpayers do not pay for churches, and no government can give special treatment to a politically influential church.

The Colorado supreme court first enforced section 2 in 1879. During territorial days, before the 1876 Constitution outlawed government using taxpayer funds to go into business with corporations, Boulder County had bought stock in a railroad. Then, after the Constitution had become the law in Colorado, Boulder offered to give the railroad of the stock owned by Boulder, if the railroad would build a line from Longmont to Cheyenne. The Colorado court held the plan unconstitutional. While recognizing that there might be practical advantages to joint ventures of business and government, the court explained that the constitutional prohibition was clear, and that was the end of the matter. *E.g.*, *Colorado Central R.R. v. Lea*, 5 Colo. 192 (1879). Apparently, the rail line made economic sense, for it was later built it without needing any special gifts. Oesterle at 604.

In 1912, advocates of the James Peak tunnel convinced the general assembly to refer a ballot measure to the state to issue bonds and build the tunnel. Voters said no, by 2 to 1. Oesterle at 606.

The next year, the Denver City Charter was amended to allow Denver to issue bonds to pay for two-thirds of the estimated cost of the tunnel. The Moffat Railroad would pay the other third of construction costs directly and would pay the principal and interest on the Denver bonds. After the bonds were retired, the tunnel would become property of the Moffat Railroad. A divided Colorado supreme court held that the proposal violated sections 1 and 2 of article XI. *Lord v. City & County of Denver*, 58 Colo. 1, 143 P. 288 (1914).

Tunnel proponents returned in 1919 with another proposed state constitutional amendment. This time, the bonds would finance not only the James tunnel, but also a tunnel through Monarch Pass and a tunnel through Cumbres Pass. The multitunnel proposal did attract more voters than had a James-only tunnel, but it was still rejected by the voters. Oesterle at 604.

The Moffat Railroad fell into receivership in 1921. *Id.* at 607. Luckily for the taxpayers of Denver, the 1913 plan had been blocked by the supreme court in *Lord*, so taxpayers were not stuck with paying for the bonds that the Moffat Railroad had been expected to pay.

In 1922, the legislature created the Moffat Tunnel Improvement District, consisting of Denver, three West Slope counties, a portion of a fourth, and a six-to-eight-mile-wide strip connecting east and west. The district was given the power to issue bonds and to impose property taxes to pay for the bonds. The Moffat Tunnel would be built and owned by the district, not by a private enterprise. The bonds were to be repaid by the district leasing the tunnel to railroads at below-market rates. The system was upheld by the Colorado supreme court in 1922, rejecting claims that the below-market leases represented a "grant in aid" or "gift" to a railroad in violation of article XI. The court did not address the state debt limits in section 3 of article XI, even though the debts of the Moffat Tunnel Improvement District, a state agency, pushed state debt far over section 3's constitutional limits. *Milheim v. Moffat Tunnel Improvement District*, 72 Colo. 268, 211 P. 649 (Colo. 1922); Oesterle at 608.[3]

Actual lease revenues from Moffat Tunnel, once it was completed, were even lower than the below-market revenues that proponents had expected, necessitating a very long payoff period. Proponents of the Moffat Tunnel Improvement District had promised that the job could be done with a $6.7 million bond. The amount of bonds actually issued was $15.5 million. By 1960, the

---

[3] The U.S. supreme court held that the Moffat program did not violate the Fourteenth Amendment's Due Process of Equal Protection Clauses. *Milheim v. Moffat Tunnel Improvement District*, 262 U.S. 710 (1923).

cost of principal and interest had ballooned to $45 million. ROBERT ATHEARN, THE DENVER & WESTERN RIO GRANDE RAILROAD 267 (1977).[4]

Milheim cleared the way for governments to subsidize businesses by building business facilities, so long as the government retained title to the facility. Thus, Denver could issue bonds to buy to build Mile High Stadium and lease it to professional sports teams. Later, voters approved a special sales tax district to pay for a stadium for the Colorado Rockies baseball team.

In 1998, the Denver Broncos football team threatened to leave town unless they were given another subsidized new stadium. Voters in the Stadium District (Denver metro area) approved extending the baseball sales tax to build another football stadium. The $300 million Broncos bonds were paid off in 2012. Although the taxpayers in the Stadium District paid for the new stadium, the Broncos were given the revenue from sale of naming rights. Their facility is now officially named "Empower Field at Mile High," in honor of Empower Retirement. Previous namesakes were Invesco and Sports Authority.

Oesterle traces the destruction of the Colorado Constitution prohibitions on corporate welfare to a process that began with *Milheim* in 1922 and has continued ever since. The *Milheim* court did not question *Lord*'s stern rejection of the notion that section 2 could be evaded whenever the government action had a public purpose. "If the existence of a public benefit is to . . . take it out of the constitutional prohibition, then the prohibition is utterly nugatory and valueless, as such consideration would exist in every probable case." *Lord*, 58 Colo. at 17–18.

In 1955, the Colorado supreme court took the next step to rendering section 2 "utterly nugatory and valueless." Now, gifts of taxpayer money to private interests would be allowed whenever there was a "valid public purpose." *McNichols v. City and County of Denver*, 131 Colo. 246, 280 P.2d 1096 (1955).

The final step came in 1970, when the supreme court made it clear that courts should not bother examining whether there actually is a valid public purpose. Rather, courts must make "every presumption" in favor of there being a valid public purpose—in the case at bar, for bonds to subsidize an agricultural feed plant. *Allardice v. Adams County*, 476 P.2d 982 (1970).

Before *Allardice*, government bond attorneys, pursuant to *Milheim* and *Lord*, had been careful not to issue bonds that included the condition that if the government defaulted on its bond payments, the bond holders could seize the government property. *Milheim* and *Lord* had suggested that such bonds would violate section 2, but *Allardice* legalized them, and such terms are now routine in Colorado. Oesterle at 611.

Section 2 banned aid to corporations by every form of government that existed in Colorado in 1876: the state, counties, cities, towns, townships, and school districts. Later, new government entities began to be created, such as special districts and special purpose authorities. The court held that section 2 does not apply to them. Created by the state legislature, the Colorado Housing Finance Authority (CHFA), was not part of "the state." Nor was it a special commission or private corporation, neither of which are allowed to tax. Art. V, § 35. The CHFA could not be a private corporation, because corporations may not be created by special act of the legislature. Art. XV, § 1. *In re Interrogatories by Colorado State Senate (Senate Resolution No. 13) Concerning House Bill No. 1247 Fifty-First General Assembly*, 566 P.2d 350 (Colo. 1977) The CHFA was neither fish nor fowl, neither government nor private. In a magical condition, the CHFA and its many imitators are exempt from the constitutional rules that limit corporations and from the constitutional rules that limit government—including the Taxpayer's Bill of Rights. *See* chapter 15.C.

In short, the Colorado Constitution's "ban on business subsidies is nullified. All that is necessary is good lawyering to employ the proper fictions." Oesterle at 615.

---

[4] The first lessee, the Denver & Salt Lake Railroad, defaulted on its lease in 1930, two years after the tunnel opened. The insolvent railroad was purchased by the Denver & Rio Grande Western Railroad, based in Pueblo, which assumed the lease. Oesterle at 609.

Recently, when the City of Colorado Springs gave some city parkland to the Broadmoor Hotel, in exchange for city hiking trail easements on Broadmoor property, the court of appeals refused to consider whether the exchange had been of equal value or was so unequal as to constitute a gift to the Broadmoor. *Save Cheyenne v. City of Colorado Springs*, 2018 COA 18, 425 P.3d 1174 (Colo. App. 2018).

The judicial nullification of sections 1 and 2 borrowed by analogy from the earlier nullification of article V, § 34, which bans general assembly appropriations to private organizations or individuals. The court claimed that such appropriations are lawful whenever the legislature says that they are for a public purpose. *Bedford v. White*, 106 P.2d 469 (1940).

The judicial abrogation of government restraints on taxpayer debt or aid to businesses or private interests was *not* necessary to keep the Constitution up to date. The people chose to amend Article XI for energy and student loans. The most plausible reason they were not asked to add amendments for other debt was that the big businesses that wanted the loans feared the voters would say no.

Art. XI, Section 2a. Student loans authorized

> The general assembly may by law provide for a student loan program to assist students enrolled in educational institutions.

Added by the voters in 1972, section 2a shows that the voters are capable of creating exceptions to section 2 when they see a good reason to do so.

Art. XI, Section 3. Public debt of state

> <u>The state shall not contract any debt by loan in any form, except to provide for casual deficiencies of revenue, erect public buildings for the use of the state, suppress insurrection, defend the state, or, in time of war, assist in defending the United States</u>; and the amount of debt contracted in any one year to provide for deficiencies of revenue shall not exceed one-fourth of a mill on each dollar of valuation of taxable property within the state, and the aggregate amount of such debt shall not at any time exceed three-fourths of a mill on each dollar of said valuation, until the valuation shall equal one hundred millions of dollars, and thereafter such debt shall not exceed one hundred thousand dollars; and the debt incurred in any one year for erection of public buildings shall not exceed one-half mill on each dollar of said valuation; and the aggregate amount of such debt shall never at any time exceed the sum of fifty thousand dollars (except as provided in section 5 of this article), and in all cases the valuation in this section mentioned shall be that of the assessment last preceding the creation of said debt.

This section prohibits "any" state debt, except for certain specified purposes. First, the government may borrow to cover "casual deficiencies"—for example, to pay expenses in February, knowing that tax payments will arrive in April. Second, a limited amount of debt is lawful to erect public buildings, such as by issuing bonds to pay for construction of a courthouse. Finally, debt is allowed for defending he state in dire circumstances. The balanced budget requirement (art. X, § 16) contains an identical exception when necessary to "suppress insurrection, defend the state, or, in time of war, assist in defending the United States."

During the Great Depression, Congress passed the National Industrial Recovery Act, creating federal agency to control wages, prices, and most other economic activity.[5] Part of the act authorized the federal government to loan money to states for highway projects. In a special session called the governor, the Colorado general assembly was considering taking the loan, which was for 10 million dollars, payable at four percent annual interest, for a twenty-year period of repayment. Because "the Senate still entertains doubts as to the constitutionality of said bill," the Colorado senate sent interrogatories to the Colorado supreme court.

The court pointed out that the loan plainly violated section 3. "The state shall not contract any debt by loan in form." The constitution's stated exceptions to the rule obviously did not apply. The court continued:

> We venture the assertion that no man, able to read and understand ordinary English, however otherwise educated or uneducated, wise or foolish, would question for a moment that this bill was a plain violation of the constitutional prohibition, or find any reason to the contrary, save by a resort to profound legal learning and a doubtful application of judicial precedents. Apparently acquiescing in this position the Attorney General and his assistants raise no such question. They say, in effect, that while House Bill No. 6 appears, prima facie, to contract a debt, it does not in fact do so because payment thereof must be made from a "special fund," and in such cases this and other courts, by a course of reasoning here applicable, have held that no debt is thus contracted within the constitutional prohibition.

In re Senate Resolution No. 2, 94 Colo. 101, 114, 31 P.2d 325 (1933).[6]

Although the loan payoff would be from a special fund, the money that went into the fund would simply be some of the tax revenue that that state had been raising for years. If there were a new revenue source to pay the loan, then section 3 might not be violated:

> Since the purpose of section 3 of article XI is to prevent the pledging of revenues of future years, a statute which at the same time it creates a debt, creates the fund to pay it, and which fund would not be otherwise available for general purposes, is clearly outside the constitutional prohibition. If, for example, the state could purchase a machine for making gold out of common clay, and agreed to pay for the contrivance only out of the product, that debt would not be prohibited by said section 3.

Id. at 114-15. Or, as allowed by the court's precedents, "debts for local improvements to be paid for by special assessments . . . In such cases the improvement is paid for solely out of the value which it adds to the property of the taxpayer." *Id.* at 115. The same for loans for public utilities improvement that would be paid solely from the new revenue generated by the improvements. *Id.*

The attorney general had argued that the loan was sustainable as a "continuing appropriation," since the general assembly would have to appropriate payments every year. The court answered:

---

[5] The National Recovery Administration was later unanimously held unconstitutional by the U.S. Supreme Court, because of its standardless delegation of so much power. *A.L.A. Schechter Poultry Corp. v. United States*, 295 U.S. 495 (1935).

[6] At the end of the opinion, the court thanked the attorney general and amici for the excellence of their presentations.

> [A]n appropriation made by one General Assembly to pay for services or materials to be thereafter annually furnished, and which "continues" only because future General Assemblies do not, as well they might, discontinue both consideration and payment, and a "continuing appropriation" by a so-called "irrepealable act" to pay in installments, over a long period of years, for services or materials furnished in toto during the current year, are so different in all essential particulars as to have nothing in common save an arbitrary name. If the latter can be upheld under the cloak of continuing appropriations this constitutional prohibition against contracting debts is construed out of existence, for under that cloak any debt may pass.

Id. at 116.

The legislature and governor had argued that, in the emergency of the Great Depression, the highway program could be considered a debt "to defend the state." The court said no:

> On this question the declarations of the executive and legislative departments of the state government, while probably persuasive, are not binding here. If they were, the Constitution would cease to have even the force of a statute. If the people's "Thou shalt not," can be brushed aside by the simple ipse dixit of their servants thus bound, the mandate is impotent. Such a construction, once adopted, breaks the barrier, and future legislatures, protected by the precedent, might pile up mountains of debt on future generations, resulting in inevitable impoverishment or ruthless repudiation.
>
> . . .
>
> [O]ur Constitution was adopted in 1876. The men who framed it, and those who adopted it, were not without experience, history tells us, of grave economical and industrial emergencies. These must have been in mind when they so acted, but they gave no permission to the legislature to violate their mandate in emergencies. They gave permission to contract "a debt by a loan in any form" to "defend the state" and most of them had lived through a period when strenuous measures were necessary to defend the state and well knew the meaning of the words they used. In all other cases they forbade the consumption of anticipated revenues of future years and limited their lawmakers to the adoption of usual or unusual taxing measures, or a new allocation of revenue already provided. The present emergency must be so met.
>
> . . .
>
> [I]n this jurisdiction, the bulwarks erected in former times still stand unshaken. High dikes are built for great floods.
>
> It has been said, in substance, that this bill, by a "broad" construction, may be squared with the Constitution, and that only by a "narrow" construction can it be made repugnant thereto. That position rests upon an erroneous interpretation of those terms, and follows the popular fallacy that, all interpretation which upholds legislation is broad and all which overthrows it is narrow . . . . [The people's intent in enacting section 3 being clear,] the construction which resorts to technical terms and fine distinctions to frustrate that intent is narrow, and that which imports its common meaning to simple language to effectuate that intent is broad. We must not be frightened by mere words.

Id. 116-19.

The dissent pointed out that loan would be paid by the gas tax that had been enacted in the 1933 regular legislative session. Only a little bit of the gas tax money was currently pledged to other purposes. By the terms of the contract from the federal government, the loan would create a legal obligation only on the fund to which the gas tax revenue would be deposited, and not on state general revenues. *Id.* at 126–26 (Butler, J., dissenting).

Further, wrote the dissent, the court had previously held that the governor's decision about whether to call out the militia to suppress what the governor considers to be an insurrection was not subject to judicial review. (*In re Moyer*, 35 Colo. 159, 85 P. 190 (1904)). Therefore, the court should accept the legislative and gubernatorial declarations about defending the state, unless they were "palpably or obviously false." *Id.* at 137–41.

In the 1934 election, the people adopted a citizen initiative to require that all money raised from automobile and gas taxes "be used exclusively for the construction, maintenance, and supervision of the public highways of this state." Art. X, § 18 (chapter 14).

The next year, the general assembly borrowed $25 million from a federal highway loan program. The bill created a State Highway Fund, to receive the auto and gas taxes. The federal loan would be payable only from the state highway fund, and no other source.

The court upheld the loan. The majority opinion quoted from the 1933 *In re Senate Resolution No. 2*: loans were not restricted by section 3 if the revenue to repay the loan "would not be otherwise available for general purposes." Because of the 1934 constitutional amendment, tax revenue from cars and gas was "not be otherwise available for general purposes." It did not matter that the gas tax was existing revenue, not new revenue. *Johnson v. McDonald*, 97 Colo. 324, 49 P.2d 1017 (1935).

Dissenting, justice Hilliard wrote,

> I admire, while I deplore, the cunning logic that convinces the court that black is white and that there is no difference between heaven and hell. It will be news to our people that the promise of the state to pay twenty-five millions of dollars out of the proceeds—and all of the proceeds—of the various excises having to do with motor vehicles is not a debt. The opinion will disabuse their minds of that fallacy, although it may be that the more obtuse will be unable to perceive why the state should pay out one million dollars of interest annually on obligations which it does not owe . . . Should it come to pass that the excises fail [the auto and gas taxes are not sufficient to repay the loan] there will not be found a lack of plausible gentlemen, mayhap those who have argued here, to call upon the state to perform its plain moral duty and raise and pay that twenty-five millions to protect the good name of the commonwealth. Our history dictates that such will be our policy. Men who dealt with the state and extended it credit in the past well knowing the warrants they received were void and worthless yet were not bowed down with their prospective losses for they knew the good people would not repudiate their claims and thus besmirch their honor. We issued, by constitutional amendment, general obligation bonds to pay those trusting creditors. The buyer of the twenty-five millions of no-debt paper now proposed will feel safe in his belief that it is a debt whether the court thinks so or not. I confess, when I consider the many phases of this problem, that I am embittered, and deeply embittered. The court has worshipped at the shrine of construction, often and here the falsest of gilded gods, and for that sin the sweat of the people shall not fail for more than a generation.
>
> "The Constitution was written to be understood by the voters; its words and phrases were used in their normal and ordinary as distinguished from technical meaning; where the intention is clear there is no room for construction and no excuse for interpolation or addition." *United States v. Sprague*, 282 U. S. 716

(1931).[7] This court has often announced the same wholesome doctrine. *Cf. People ex rel. Seeley v. May*, 9 Colo. 80, 10 P. 641 (1886); *In re Lowrie*, 8 Colo. 499, 19 P. 489 (1886). The Constitution of Colorado ordains that "The State shall not contract any debt by loan in any form." It will be perceived instantly that this permits the state to enter into an irrevocable contract to borrow and pay twenty-five millions of dollars out of our only practicable source of road-building revenue, the proceeds of the motor vehicle excises. The very heavens protest against so monstrous a construction of the document conceived by the people for their protection against rapacity. If this be law, and the court has said it is, there is no limit whatever and the constitutional limitation and prohibition of debt might as well be stricken from the instrument altogether. The language of the Constitution could not have been more imperatively or understandingly phrased. And yet, it is overthrown by niceties so refined as to be nonexistent and logic that destroys both the letter and the spirit.

. . . The true, and the only, special fund rule in connection with debt prohibitions is that an inhibited debt is not created where the bondholders must look for repayment to the enhancement of values, as in the case of local improvement districts, or to earnings and profits, as in the case of so-called revenue bonds, arising out of the operation of publicly owned utilities . . . its basis is simply that the capital of the holders of local improvement district bonds, or of utility bonds, has produced and made possible the enhanced value or earnings with which alone the bonds are to be repaid. The tax load of the people, whether of excise or ad valorem, has not been increased or affected. But where, as here, the imposition of a tax is necessary to discharge the debt the rule fails at once. There is no enhancement of values, there are no earnings or profits, there is simply the creation of an additional and staggering debt to be discharged out of taxes wrung from the people . . .

No debt? The act by its terms is irrepealable. It pledges every penny of future motor vehicle excises to the payment of the euphemistically styled "Revenue Anticipation Warrants." The power of the Federal Constitution is cited by the court to show that come what may these instruments cannot be repudiated . . . The truth is, despite the court's protested adherence to the rule that a debt is created where funds otherwise available for general purposes must be applied in payment, that the debt-prohibiting sections of the Constitution have been discarded by the opinion in this case. As was suggested in the admirable presentation of counsel for the defendant in error [the attorney general, defending the loan], the legislature is now at liberty to set up a "State Excise Corporation," make all (other) excises payable to it, give it power to issue anticipation warrants, and pledge all excises to the end of time to repay them . . .

. . . The individual may be prodigal at his pleasure, pledging his future income to the extent of his credit. But the state of Colorado, it was believed until now, however much its careless or wasteful servants might dissipate its income of the year for the same year, enjoyed constitutional protection against present spoliation of next year's income . . . [T]his court, as did the trial court, has but to announce adherence to the Constitution and its own pronouncements, to save the people from this orgy of exploiting the future . . . I am unable to frustrate this scheme, but I can

---

[7] The *Sprague* rule of constitutional meaning was quoted and cited in *District of Columbia v. Heller*, 554 U.S. 570, 577 (2008). The rule is the most-cited language from the *Heller* case, since it applies to all constitutional interpretation.

> pay modest tribute to the framers of our organic law, who, well advised of the danger, believed they had protected the inarticulate against machinators.

Id. at 357-62 (Hilliard, J., dissenting).

From the perspective of the twenty-first century, professors Richard Collins and Dale Oesterle observe:

> It is interesting to speculate about what state government would look like if the simple debt limits in the 1876 Constitution were respected today. State government would be on a cash basis except for public building projects, which would have to pass a popular vote. Capital leases (long-term leases with an option to purchase) would be construed, as they are in private industry, as long-term loans and would also require a popular vote. If the state government wanted to undertake a major highway project, for example, and annual appropriations over the life of the project would be insufficient to pay for the project, the state would have to save, not borrow, to do the job, or turn the construction over to a private toll company. The state could not incur debt to finance utilities or railroad tunnels or sports stadiums; it would have to turn such enterprises over to private owners who could sell bonds (and stock) to finance construction.

RICHARD COLLINS & DALE A. OESTERLE, THE COLORADO STATE CONSTITUTION 284-85 (1st ed. 2001).

Art. XI, Section 4. Limits on state debt

> In no case shall any debt above mentioned in this article be created except by a law which shall be irrepealable, until the indebtedness therein provided for shall have been fully paid or discharged; such law shall specify the purposes to which the funds so raised shall be applied, and provide for the levy of a tax sufficient to pay the interest on and extinguish the principal of such debt within the time limited by such law for the payment thereof, which in the case of <u>debts contracted for the erection of public buildings and supplying deficiencies of revenue shall not be less than ten nor more than fifteen years</u>, and the funds arising from the collection of any such tax shall not be applied to any other purpose than that provided in the law levying the same, and when the debt thereby created shall be paid or discharged, such tax shall cease and the balance, if any, to the credit of the fund shall immediately be placed to the credit of the general fund of the state.

Usually, one legislature can repeal any act of a previous legislature. But the legislature may not repudiate debts contracted by previous legislatures.

When the legislature borrows money, it must raise taxes sufficiently to pay the interest and principal on the debt. The taxes must sunset when the debt it paid. Borrowing to erect public buildings must be for a term of 10–15 years.

But as explained above, almost all government borrowing is done under the guise of not being "debt," thus evading section 4 and the rest of article XI.

The Taxpayer's Bill of Rights, art. X, § 20, contains additional provisions to effectuate article XI's debt limits.

Art. XI, Section 5. Debt for public buildings

> A debt for the purpose of erecting public buildings may be created by law as provided for in section four of this article, not exceeding in the aggregate three mills on each dollar of said valuation; provided, that before going into effect, such law shall be ratified by the vote of a majority of such qualified electors of the state as shall vote thereon at a general election under such regulations as the general assembly may prescribe.

The modern means for evading Sections 5 (state debts for public buildings) and 6 (local government debt) are certificates of participation. A COP is essentially a type of rent-to-own lease. Suppose the state want to build a new office building to replace an existing state office building. The state conveys the land and building to a business. The business builds a new building and leases it to the state on a year-by-year basis. If the state renews the lease every year, and pays the full rent for 25 years, then at the end of the 25 years the business gives the office building to the State. Because the lease is year-to-year, the state has no formal continuing legal obligation.

A COP amounts to a 25-year mortgage, dressed up a series of year-to-year leases. By using s COP (for which the formal legal obligation is only one year), the state or local government evades all the article XI restrictions on debt, as well as the Taxpayer's Bill of Rights (art. X, § 20) requirement that new debt be put to a vote of the people. *See Glennon Heights, Inc. v. Central Bank & Trust*, 658 P.2d 872 (Colo 1983); *Colorado Criminal Justice Reform Coalition v. Ortiz*, 121 P.3d 288 (Colo. App. 2005).

The total interest payments on a 25-year loan are nearly double the interest amount on a 15-year loan. Taxpayers get stuck paying the extra interest for the unconstitutional 25-year loans.

Art. XI, Section 6. Local government debt limits

> (1) No political subdivision of the state shall contract any general obligation debt by loan in any form, whether individually or by contract pursuant to article XIV, section 18(2)(a) of this constitution except by adoption of a legislative measure which shall be irrepealable until the indebtedness therein provided for shall have been fully paid or discharged, specifying the purposes to which the funds to be raised shall be applied and providing for the levy of a tax which together with such other revenue, assets, or funds as may be pledged shall be sufficient to pay the interest and principal of such debt. Except as may be otherwise provided by the charter of a home rule city and county, city, or town for debt incurred by such city and county, city, or town, no such debt shall be created unless the question of incurring the same be submitted to and approved by a majority of the qualified taxpaying electors voting thereon, as the term "qualified taxpaying elector" shall be defined by statute.
>
> (2) Except as may be otherwise provided by the charter of a home rule city and county, city, or town, the general assembly shall establish by statute limitations on the authority of any political subdivision to incur general obligation indebtedness in any form whether individually or by contract pursuant to article XIV, section 18(2)(a) of this constitution.

> (3) Debts contracted by a home rule city and county, city, or town, statutory city or town or service authority for the purposes of supplying water shall be excepted from the operation of this section.

Section 6 applies to local government the debt rules from sections 4 and 5. Originally, school district debt was in section 7, and municipal debt was in section 8. In 1970, all the local debt provisions were consolidated in section 6.

The water loophole of subsection (3) has no practical validity today since TABOR requires a vote on all local debt.

The judicial precedents allowing state government to borrow money by various means without calling it "debt" apply equally to local borrowing. Thus, certificates of participation (mortgages dressed up as year-to-year leases) are often used by local governments. So when the voters of Jefferson County rejected a ballot measure to construct an expensive new government building, the Jefferson county commissioners built the new Jefferson County Government Center (a/k/a "the Taj Mahal") by using certificates of participation.

An early application of section 6 came in 1883, when Leadville city solicitor Daniel E. Parks took the lead in relieving bankrupt Lake County of a million dollars of debt. The debt was the consequence of "the rascality of early boards of county commissioners," in the words of the Leadville *Herald-Tribune.* Finally, the people "elected men of unimpeachable integrity" to run the county government. The Colorado supreme court held that county debts in excess of the constitutional limit were uncollectable. The Lake County debt cases had national influence in changing 50 years of precedents on local government debt, as was recognized in the leading national treatise, *Dillon on Municipal Corporations*. FRANK HALL, 3 HISTORY OF COLORADO 128 (2008) (1891); FRANK HALL, 4 HISTORY OF COLORADO 543 (1895).

The 1992 Taxpayer's Bill of Rights is sometimes treated as if it were a sharp break from Colorado's past. To the contrary, constraint on government taxing, spending, and borrowing is as old as the 1876 Constitution, and has been reinforced by many subsequent amendments. The debt limits of article XI in the 1876 Constitution helped to begin this enduring tradition.

Art. XI, Section 7. State and political subdivisions may give assistance to any political subdivision

> No provision of this constitution shall be construed to prevent the state or any political subdivision from giving direct or indirect financial support to any political subdivision as may be authorized by general statute.

The original 1876 § 7 restricted school district debt. The new version, adopted in 1970, erases article X's various limits on state aid to local governments.

Art. XI, Secs. 8–10. (repealed)

Section 8 of the original Constitution contained restrictions on local debt.

Section 9 of the original Constitution provided that the debt rules in article XI did not impair the previously contracted debts of local governments, if those debts had been contracted in accordance with the laws of the Colorado Territory.

Winter Olympics

Section 10, enacted by the voters in 1972, forbade taxpayer spending or borrowing in support of the 1976 Winter Olympics, which had been awarded to Colorado. The chief proponent of the 1972 amendment was state representative Dick Lamm (D-Denver), who in 1974 would win his first of three terms as governor, and who has recently retired from a professorship at the University of Denver.

Repeated experience shows that government funding for the Olympics is a financial fiasco. The scale of the fiasco has increased in recent years, but the principle was the same in 1972. Besides that, Colorado voters in 1972 saw no need to subsidize growth in the state. They were already worried that rapid growth was degrading the state's quality of life. The alliance of thrifty voters and environmental voters carried Lamm's initiative to victory. *See* WILLIAM PHILPOTT, VACATIONLAND: TOURISM AND ENVIRONMENT IN THE COLORADO HIGH COUNTRY 267–75 (2014).

The International Olympic Committee (an organization comparable to FIFA in its opacity and bad governance) chose Innsbruck, Austria, as the replacement site. Having hosted the 1964 Winter Olympics, Innsbruck already had most of the necessary facilities. *See* Timothy Sanderson, *1976 Winter Olympics*, COLORADO ENCYCLOPEDIA.

Section 10 was repealed in 1990, as part of the continuing process of removing obsolete provisions of the Constitution, the 1976 Olympics no longer being a threat to Colorado's taxpayers or way of life.

Part IV

Other provisions for good government

CHAPTER 17

Officers and State Personnel, Article XII

Sections 1 through 11 of article XII govern state officers, such as by requiring them to personally attend to their office, not to take bribes, not to receive salaries increases during their term, and to take an oath of allegiance to the U.S. and Colorado Constitutions.

Section 13 was added by amendment, and later split into sections 13 through 15. It creates a state civil service system.

Art. XII, Section 1. When offices expire

> Every person holding any civil office under the state or any municipality therein, shall, unless removed according to law, exercise the duties of such office until his successor is duly qualified; but this shall not apply to members of the general assembly, nor to members of any board or assembly, two or more of whom are elected at the same time. The general assembly may, by law, provide for suspending any officer in his functions pending impeachment or prosecution for misconduct in office.

Persons holding state or municipal offices must perform their duties. Section 1 does *not* authorize an office holder to continue in office past the expiration of his term, even if no replacement has been chosen. *Walsh v. People*, 72 Colo. 406, 211 P. 646 (1922).

For example, in the regular November election for county clerk, the challenger wins. The challenger is scheduled to assume the office in January. But the challenger dies before taking office. The incumbent county clerk holds the office until the expiration of her term in January.

Upon expiration of the old term, the office is vacant. Accordingly, and pursuant to art. 14, § 9, (county officer vacancies), the county commissioners appoint a county clerk to hold office until the next general election. *Gibbs v. People ex rel. Watts*, 66 Colo. 414, 182 P. 894 (1919).

Art. XII, Section 2. Personal attention

> No person shall hold any office or employment of trust or profit, under the laws of the state or any ordinance of any municipality therein, without devoting his personal attention to the duties of the same.

This seems obvious, but Anglo-American history made it necessary to constitutionalize the point. In the United Kingdom until about the middle of the 19th century, it was very common for people who got government offices to pay little or no attention to a job. Such no-show jobs were known as *sinecures.* For example, in the government-run Church of England, a person might be appointed as the priest for a diocese, and thereby be entitled to an annual fixed income. Yet the person might only show up at the particular church to preach a sermon and distribute communion for Christmas and Easter, ignoring the church and its parishioners the rest of the time. When the U.K. parliament first debated railroad regulation in the 1830s, some opponents argued that a railroad commission would be a waste of money, since the commissioners would probably just pocket their salaries and do nothing else. The change in social norms in the U.K. in the 19th century—so that government appointees usually did in fact work fulltime at their jobs—was a key condition for the public's willingness to accept the massive growth of government that began in the 19th century and continues today.

The most significant attempt at enforcement of section 2 was a case involving Lake County district judge Frank Owens, who had moved to Denver and set up a law practice. Supposedly for health reasons, his presence in Lake County was rare. He held court in his Denver law office. After he was re-elected in 1900 (having showed up in Lake County long enough to campaign), the attorney general brought a *quo warranto* petition to remove him from office. *Quo warranto* is Latin for "by what authority?" It is used for the revocation of corporate charters or to contest the title to an office.[1] The supreme court held that Owens' actions were not sufficient for his removal. *People v. Owens*, 29 Colo. 535, 69 P. 515 (1902).

Similarly, when a district attorney during World War II was serving in the armed forces outside of Colorado, a private citizen brought a *quo warranto* action against him. The district court stayed the proceedings against him, for a period until his military service expired, and for three months thereafter. According to the court, the public was not harmed by his absence. The supreme court affirmed the district court. *People ex rel. Flanders v. Neary*, 113 Colo. 12, 154 P.2d 48 (1944).

Art. XII, Section 3. Defaulter in office is disqualified from further office

> No person who is now or hereafter may become a collector or receiver of public money, or the deputy or assistant of such collector or receiver, and who shall have become a defaulter in his office, shall be eligible to or assume the duties of any office of trust or profit in this state, under the laws thereof, or of any municipality

[1] *Quo warranto* proceedings are presently governed by Colo. Rules of Civil Procedure 106. Remedial writs are covered in chapter 10 (Judiciary, art. VI). The historic special forms and pleadings for these writs have been abolished.

> therein, until he shall have accounted for and paid over all public money for which he may be accountable.

If you are supposed to manage the government's money, and you lose the money because of your malfeasance, you cannot hold government office until you pay back the money.

Art. XII, Section 4. Embezzlers, perjurers, and such may not hold office

> No person hereafter convicted of embezzlement of public moneys, bribery, perjury, solicitation of bribery, or subornation of perjury, shall be eligible to the general assembly, or capable of holding any office of trust or profit in this state.

If you are criminally convicted of offenses that indicate your propensity for deceit, you cannot hold public office. By statute, Colorado allows persons with criminal convictions to receive public employment or occupational licenses under certain conditions. C.R.S. § 24-5-101. The statute expressly does not cover the public offices mentioned in section 4.

Art. XII, Section 5. Investigation of state and county treasurers

> The district court of each county shall, at each term thereof, specially give in charge to the grand jury, if there be one, the laws regulating the accountability of the county treasurer, and shall appoint a committee of such grand jury, or of other reputable persons not exceeding five, to investigate the official accounts and affairs of the treasurer of such county, and report to the court the condition thereof. The judge of the district court may appoint a like committee in vacation at any time, but not oftener than once in every three months. The district court of the county wherein the seat of government may be shall have the like power to appoint committees to investigate the official accounts and affairs of the state treasurer and the auditor of state.

District court grand juries are supposed to keep an eye on the county treasurers. Despite the constitutional text, grand juries do not regularly investigate county treasurers.

Art. XII, Section 6. No receiving bribes

> Any civil officer or member of the general assembly who shall solicit, demand or receive, or consent to receive, directly or indirectly, for himself or for another, from any company, corporation or person, any money, office, appointment, employment, testimonial, reward, thing of value or enjoyment or of personal advantage or promise thereof, for his vote, official influence or action, or for withholding the same, or with an understanding that his official influence or action shall be in any way influenced thereby, or who shall solicit or demand any such money or advantage, matter or thing aforesaid for another, as the consideration of his vote, official influence or action, or for withholding the same, or shall give or withhold his vote, official influence or action, in consideration of the payment or promise of such money, advantage, matter or thing to another, shall be held guilty

> of bribery, or solicitation of bribery, as the case may be, within the meaning of this constitution, and shall incur the disabilities provided thereby for such offense, and such additional punishment as is or shall be prescribed by law.

A very broad definition of bribery. Consistent with the 1876 Convention's view that government officials would steal everything they could get away with. Bribery is defined in more detail in C.R.S. § 18-8-301 et seq. Interpreting the federal anti-bribery statute, the Hobbs Act, the U.S. supreme court held that setting up meetings or organizing events is not an "official act" covered by the statute. *McDonnell v. United States*, 136 S.Ct. 2355 (2016).

Art. XII, Section 7. No giving bribes

> (1) Any person who directly or indirectly offers, gives, or promises any money or thing of value or privilege to any member of the general assembly or to any other public officer in the executive or judicial department of the state government to influence him in the performance of any of his public or official powers or duties is guilty of bribery and subject to such punishment therefor as may be prescribed by law.
>
> (2) The offense of corrupt solicitation of members of the general assembly or of public officers of the state or of any political subdivision thereof and any occupation or practice of solicitation of such members or officers to influence their official action shall be defined by law and shall be punished by fine, imprisonment, or both.

Section 6 covers legislators and other public officers receiving bribes, while section 7 covers the persons offering bribes. The criminal statutes implementing section 6 and 7 address both. C.R.S. §§ 18-8-302 & 303.

There have been legislators in the past, who, while serving as legislators, drafted bills for a special interest and were paid for their services. Not a good idea.

Notice the section 7 does *not* require consummation. A person can be convicted for offering a bribe that is rejected.

By statute, state legislators and the governor are prohibited from receiving campaign donations from lobbyists while the legislature is in session. C.R.S. § 1-45-105.5. This reduces the possibility of legislators coercing donations in exchange for votes.

One consequence of the no-solicitation statute is that legislators who intend to run for another office (*e.g.*, U.S. House) often resign from the legislature, because the no-solicitation period, which runs from the beginning of the legislative session until its end in mid-May, may make it impossible for them to raise funds for a viable campaign.

Art. XII, Section 8. Oath or affirmation of civil officers

> Every civil officer, except members of the general assembly and such inferior officers as may be by law exempted, shall, before he enters upon the duties of his office, take and subscribe an oath or affirmation to support the constitution of the United States and of the state of Colorado, and to faithfully perform the duties of the office upon which he shall be about to enter.

As with wedding vows, some people take their oaths seriously, and some do not. The oath for state legislators is separately provided, in art. V, § 2.

A hearing commissioner at the Department of Revenue's Division of Motor Vehicles is not a "civil officer" covered by section 8. The commissioner's "duty was the routine application of a mandatory statute," and he was always subject to the supervision of the director of revenue. The court analogized the commissioner to the state legislator who was also low-level revenue department employee; the legislator's job was not a "civil office," so the legislator was not in violation of the article V, § 8 prohibition on legislators holding civil office. *Campbell v. State, Dept. of Revenue, Division of Motor Vehicles*, 176 Colo. 202, 207–08, 491 P.2d 1385 (1971) (citing *Hudson v. Annear*, 101 Colo. 551, 555, 75 P.2d 587 (1938)).

As for "commissioners in lunacy," who had the power to commit a person to a mental institution, the position was, at most, an "inferior" civil office. The Constitution gave the general assembly the power to enact oath exemptions for inferior officers, and the general assembly had done so by statute. *Isham v. People*, 82 Colo. 550, 262 P. 89 (1927).

The executive director of the department of revenue certainly does need to take the oath. But his failure to do so does not render his acts void, at least when the plaintiff could not show any irregularity in the director's actions that pertained to the plaintiff. *Hedstrom v. Motor Vehicle Div., Dept. of Revenue*, 662 P.2d 173 (Colo. 1983).

Art. XII, Section 9. Where to file oaths

> Officers of the executive department and judges of the supreme and district courts, and district attorneys, shall file their oaths of office with the secretary of state; every other officer shall file his oath of office with the county clerk of the county wherein he shall have been elected.

Failure to file the oath does not mean that the person's acts in office are invalid, if the oath later was properly filed. *People v. Scott*, 116 P.3d 1231 (Colo. App. 2004). A district court judge signed the oath but failed to file it. He was held to still have had authority to carry out his duties, as a "de facto officer." *People v. Stanley*, 170 P.3d 782 (Colo. App. 2007).

Art. XII, Section 10. If a person refuses to qualify for office, the office becomes vacant

> If any person elected or appointed to any office shall refuse or neglect to qualify therein within the time prescribed by law, such office shall be deemed vacant.

For example, a person who refuses to take the oath of office may not assume the office. For some offices, such as sheriff, the office holder must post a bond. Failure to post bond will make the office vacant.

Art. XII, Section 11. Elected officers' terms may not be extended nor salaries raised

> No law shall extend the term of any elected public officer after his election or appointment nor shall the salary of any elected public officer be increased or decreased during the term of office for which he was elected. The term of office of

> any officer elected to fill a vacancy shall terminate at the expiration of the term during which the vacancy occurred.

During a person's term in office, the salary may not be increased, nor may the length of the term be extended. Prospective changes can take effect after the person has been re-elected to a new term. Note also article V, § 6, preventing the general assembly from raising its own salary until there has been an intervening general election.

Art. XII, Section 12. (repealed)

This section of the 1876 Constitution had prohibited duelists and their seconds from holding public office. At the time, it was a good incentive to reduce dueling. Duels were typically fought because of an alleged offense to a person's honor, so section 12 made dueling into a prohibition of holding honorable office. *See generally* UTE FREVERT, MEN OF HONOUR: A SOCIAL AND CULTURAL HISTORY OF THE DUEL (1995).

Section 12 was repealed by the voters in 1990, since dueling has not been a problem for many decades.

Art. XII, Section 13. State personnel system

This section creates a state civil service system. The vast majority of litigation under article XII involves this section.

> (1) Appointments and promotions to offices and employments in the state personnel system shall be made according to merit and fitness, to be ascertained by a comparative analysis of candidates based on objective criteria without regard to race, creed, color, or political affiliation. A numerical or nonnumerical method may be used for the comparative analysis of candidates.
>
> (2)
>
> (a) The state personnel system shall comprise all appointive public officers and employees of the state, except the following:
>
> (I) Members of the public utilities commission, the industrial commission of Colorado, the state board of land commissioners, the Colorado tax commission, the state parole board, and the state personnel board;
>
> (II) Members of any board or commission serving without compensation except for per diem allowances provided by law and reimbursement of expenses;
>
> (III) The employees in the offices of the governor and the lieutenant governor whose functions are confined to such offices and whose duties are concerned only with the administration thereof;
>
> (IV) Appointees to fill vacancies in elective offices;
>
> (V) One deputy of each elective officer other than the governor and lieutenant governor specified in section 1 of article IV of this constitution;
>
> (VI) Officers otherwise specified in this constitution;

(VII) Faculty members of educational institutions and departments not reformatory or charitable in character, and such administrators thereof as may be exempt by law;
(VIII) Students and inmates in state educational or other institutions employed therein;
(IX) Attorneys at law serving as assistant attorneys general;
(X) Members, officers, and employees of the legislative and judicial departments of the state, unless otherwise specifically provided in this constitution;
(XI) Subject to the approval of the state personnel director, the following persons from each principal department: Deputy department heads, chief financial officers, public information officers, legislative liaisons, human resource directors, and executive assistants to the department heads; and
(XII) Subject to the approval of the state personnel director, senior executive service employees.

(b) The total number of employees exempted from the state personnel system pursuant to subparagraphs (XI) and (XII) of paragraph (a) of this subsection (2) shall not exceed an amount equal to one percent of the total number of persons in the state personnel system.

(3) Officers and employees within the judicial department, other than judges and justices, may be included within the personnel system of the state upon determination by the supreme court, sitting en banc, that such would be in the best interests of the state.

(4) Where authorized by law, any political subdivision of this state may contract with the state personnel board for personnel services.

(5) The person to be appointed to any position under the state personnel system shall be one of the six persons ranking highest on the eligible list for such position, or such lesser number as qualify, as determined from the comparative analysis process, subject to limitations set forth in rules of the state personnel board applicable to multiple appointments from any such list.

(6)

(a) Except as set forth in paragraph (b) of this subsection (6), all appointees shall reside in the state, but applications need not be limited to residents of the state as to those positions the state personnel board or the state personnel director determines cannot be readily filled from among residents of this state.

(b) If a position is for work that is to be performed primarily at a location that is within thirty miles of the state border:
(I) Applications for the position are not limited to residents of the state; and
(II) An appointee to the position is not required to be a resident of the state.

(7) The head of each principal department shall be the appointing authority for the employees of his office and for heads of divisions, within the personnel system, ranking next below the head of such department. Heads of such divisions shall be the appointing authorities for all positions in the personnel system within their respective divisions. Nothing in this subsection shall be construed to affect the supreme executive powers of the governor prescribed in section 2 of article IV of this constitution.

(8) Persons in the personnel system of the state shall hold their respective positions during efficient service or until reaching retirement age, as provided by law. They shall be graded and compensated according to standards of efficient service which shall be the same for all persons having like duties. A person certified to any class or position in the personnel system may be dismissed, suspended, or otherwise disciplined by the appointing authority upon written findings of failure to comply with standards of efficient service or competence, or for willful misconduct, willful failure or inability to perform his duties, or final conviction of a felony or any other offense which involves moral turpitude, or written charges thereof may be filed by any person with the appointing authority, which shall be promptly determined. Any action of the appointing authority taken under this subsection shall be subject to appeal to the state personnel board, with the right to be heard thereby in person or by counsel, or both. [In other words, civil service appointees cannot be fired, except for misconduct.]

(9)

(a) The state personnel director may authorize the temporary employment of persons, not to exceed nine months, during which time an eligible list shall be provided for permanent positions. No other temporary or emergency employment shall be permitted under the state personnel system.

(b) Nothing in paragraph (a) of this subsection (9) shall be construed as permitting the appointment of a temporary employee for the purpose of eliminating a permanent position from the state personnel system.

(10) The state personnel board shall establish probationary periods for all persons initially appointed, but not to exceed twelve months for any class or position. After satisfactory completion of any such period, the person shall be certified to such class or position within the personnel system, but unsatisfactory performance shall be grounds for dismissal by the appointing authority during such period without right of appeal.

(11) Persons certified to classes and positions under the classified civil service of the state immediately prior to July 1, 1971, persons having served for six months or more as provisional or acting provisional employees in such positions immediately prior to such date, and all persons having served six months or more in positions not within the classified civil service immediately prior to such date but included in the personnel system by this section, shall be certified to comparable positions, and grades and classifications, under the personnel system, and shall not be subject to probationary periods of employment. All other persons in positions under the personnel system shall be subject to the provisions of this section concerning initial appointment on or after such date.

A civil service system was created by statute in 1907. A 1918 amendment constitutionalized civil service. The wartime veteran's preference was added in 1944. A 1970 amendment split the old section 13 into 13, 14, and 15. It also applied the preference for wartime preference to service during undeclared wars.

Under the civil service system, the governor can appoint department heads (cabinet members) and can also appoint all the staff of the governor's office. The department heads can in turn appoint the staff of their office and can usually appoint the division heads within their department. Everyone else gets appointed by the division heads. *See* C.R.S. § 24-1-108 (part of the Administrative Organization Act of 1968, the foundational statutes for Title 24, regarding operation of the state government).

In other words, executive branch employees below the level of division head are not subject to removal for political reasons. After passing a one-year probationary period, they can only be fired for cause, or because of budget needs. By the regulations created by the state personnel board (section 14), the first people fired because of budget cuts must be the people with the least seniority.

The civil service system does not apply to the legislative or judicial branches, nor to state college faculty. Nor to the lawyers in the office of the attorney general. The number of state employee who are exempt from the state personnel system may not exceed 1%.

The purpose of a civil service system is to protect government employees from political pressure. A clerk for the state patrol should not lose her job depending on which party wins an election.

The supreme court has held that section 13 implicitly forbids state government from hiring outside contractors to perform services previously performed by state employees. *Horrell v. Dep't of Administration*, 861 P.2d 1194 (Colo. 1993) (custodial services at state buildings); *Colorado Assoc. of Public Employees v. Dep't of Highways*, 809 P.2d 988 (Colo. 1991) (highway maintenance); *Colorado Assoc. of Public Employees v. Board of Regents*, 804 P.2d 138 (1990) (CU hospital may not be turned into a nonprofit corporation, because employees would lose their civil service classification).

Art. XII, Section 14. State personnel board

> (1) There is hereby created a state personnel board to consist of five members, three of whom shall be appointed by the governor with the consent of the senate, and two of whom shall be elected by persons certified to classes and positions in the state personnel system in the manner prescribed by law. Each member shall be appointed or elected for a term of five years, and may succeed himself, but of the members first selected, the members appointed by the governor shall serve for terms of one, two, and three years, respectively, and the members elected shall serve for terms of four and five years, respectively. Each member of the board shall be a qualified elector of the state, but shall not be otherwise an officer or employee of the state or of any state employee organization, and shall receive such compensation as shall be fixed by law.
>
> (2) Any member of the board may be removed by the governor for willful misconduct in office, willful failure or inability to perform his duties, final conviction of a felony or of any other offense involving moral turpitude, or by reason of permanent disability interfering with the performance of his duties, which removal shall be subject to judicial review. Any vacancy in office shall be filled in the same manner as the selection of the person vacating the office, and for the unexpired term.

> (3) The state personnel board shall adopt, and may from time to time amend or repeal, rules to implement the provisions of this section and sections 13 and 15 of this article, as amended, and laws enacted pursuant thereto, including but not limited to rules concerning standardization of positions, determination of grades of positions, standards of efficient and competent service, the conduct of competitive examinations of competence, grievance procedures, appeals from actions by appointing authorities, and conduct of hearings by hearing officers where authorized by law.
>
> (4) There is hereby created the department of personnel, which shall be one of the principal departments of the executive department, the head of which shall be the state personnel director, who shall be appointed under qualifications established by law. The state personnel director shall be responsible for the administration of the personnel system of the state under this constitution and laws enacted pursuant thereto and the rules adopted thereunder by the state personnel board.
>
> (5) Adequate appropriations shall be made to carry out the purposes of this section and section 13 of this article.

The state personnel board has five members. Three are appointed by the governor and confirmed by the senate. Two are elected by state employees who are part of the civil service system. Board members may not be state employees or members of a state employee association.

The board may enact regulations about the civil service system.

A department of personnel shall be one of the principal departments of the executive branch. It shall administer the civil service system.

Art. XII, Section 15. Veterans' preferences

Summary: Added by initiative in 1944 and amended several times since. Wartime veterans, disabled veterans, and surviving spouses get preference in hiring, and in protection from layoffs, but not in promotion.

In particular, 5 points for serving in the armed forces during wartime. Ten points if disabled because of wartime service. Five points for the surviving spouse of a veteran or of disabled veteran.

When reducing the number of employees in state government is necessary, people must be laid off by seniority. Lowest seniority gets laid off first. In case of a tie, war veterans get to keep their jobs. War veterans can count their military service years as part of their seniority. No more than 20 years of military service may be so counted. For persons who served fewer than 20 years in the military, no more than 10 years may be counted.

> (1)
>
> (a)
>
> (I) The minimum requirements for a candidate to be placed on an eligible list for a position shall be the same for each candidate for appointment or employment in the state personnel system or in any comparable civil service or merit system of any agency or political subdivision of the state, including any municipality chartered or to be chartered under article XX of this constitution.

(II) If a numerical method is used for the comparative analysis based on objective criteria, applicants entitled to preference under this section shall be given preference in accordance with paragraphs (b) to (e) of this subsection (1). If a nonnumerical method is used, applicants entitled to preference under this section shall be added to the interview eligible list.

(b) Five points shall be added to the comparative analysis score of each candidate who is separated under honorable conditions and who, other than for training purposes, (i) served in any branch of the armed forces of the United States during any period of any declared war or any undeclared war or other armed hostilities against an armed foreign enemy, or (ii) served on active duty in any such branch in any campaign or expedition for which a campaign badge is authorized.

(c) Ten points shall be added to the comparative analysis score of any candidate who has so served, other than for training purposes, and who, because of disability incurred in the line of duty, is receiving monetary compensation or disability retired benefits by reason of public laws administered by the or the veterans administration, or any successor thereto.

(d) Five points shall be added to the comparative analysis score of any candidate who is the surviving spouse of any person who was or would have been entitled to additional points under paragraph (b) or (c) of this subsection (1) or of any person who died during such service or as a result of service-connected cause while on active duty in any such branch, other than for training purposes.

(e) No more than a total of ten points shall be added to the comparative analysis score of any such candidate pursuant to this subsection (1).

(2) The certificate of the department of defense or of the veterans administration, or any successor thereto, shall be conclusive proof of service under honorable conditions or of disability or death incurred in the line of duty during such service.

(3)

(a) When a reduction in the work force of the state or any such political subdivision thereof becomes necessary because of lack of work or curtailment of funds, employees not eligible for preference under subsection (1) of this section shall be separated before those so entitled who have the same or more service in the employment of the state or such political subdivision, counting both military service for which such preference is given and such employment with the state or such political subdivision, as the case may be, from which the employee is to be separated.

(b) In the case of such a person eligible for preference who has completed twenty or more years of active military service, no military service shall be counted in determining length of service in respect to such retention rights. In the case of such a person who has completed less than twenty years of such military service, no more than ten years of service under subsection (1)(b)(i) and (ii) shall be counted in determining such length of service for such retention rights.

(4) The state personnel board and each comparable supervisory or administrative board of any such civil service or merit system of any agency of the state or any such political subdivision thereof shall implement the provisions of this section to assure that all persons entitled to preference in a comparative analysis and retention shall enjoy their full privileges and rights granted by this section.

(5) No person shall receive preference pursuant to this section with respect to a promotional opportunity. Any promotional opportunity that is also open to persons other than employees for whom such appointment would be a promotion, shall be considered a promotional opportunity for the purposes of this section.

(6) [Repealed in 2012.]

(7) This section shall be in full force and effect on and after July 1, 1971, and shall grant veterans' preference to all persons who have served in the armed forces of the United States in any declared or undeclared war, conflict, engagement, expedition, or campaign for which a campaign badge has been authorized, and who meet the requirements of service or disability, or both, as provided in this section. This section shall apply to all public employment opportunities, except as set forth in subsection (5) of this section, conducted on or after such date, and it shall be in all respects self-executing.

Section 15 grants veterans' preferences to persons who served in "any declared war or any undeclared war or other armed hostilities against an armed foreign enemy." The language was added by the people in 1970, because the Vietnam War (1965–73 for Americans) and the Korean War (1950–53) had not been "declared" wars. Congress had voted to authorize military action in both wars but had not declared war on North Korea or North Vietnam.

Indeed, the last time the U.S. Congress exercised its power to declare war was in 1941–42. In response to the December 7, 1941, Japanese attack on Pearl Harbor, Congress declared war on December 8. Several days later, on Dec. 11, Japan's allies Germany and Italy declared war on the United States. Congress declared war on them within hours. Then in 1942, the U.S. declared war on Germany's eastern allies—Hungary, Rumania, and Bulgaria. Since then, the U.S. has fought many different nations, but has never declared war.

The Denver city government adopted a rule that the veterans' preference for undeclared wars applied only to the Vietnam and Korea periods, and nothing else. In the parallel federal law for wartime veterans' preferences, qualifying service includes the period from September 11, 2001, until the June 15, 2004, end of Operation Iraqi Freedom. While the court of appeals agreed that the federal standard for "undeclared war," was not preemptive, the court of appeals said that it was persuasive. Denver's argument that the 1970 amendment applied only to past undeclared wars, and not to future ones, was implausible. *Arthur v. City and County of Denver*, 198 P.3d 1285 (Colo. App. 2008).

CHAPTER 18

Impeachments, Article XIII

Art. XIII, Section 1. House to impeach, Senate to try

The house of representatives shall have the sole power of impeachment. The concurrence of a majority of all the members shall be necessary to an impeachment. All impeachments shall be tried by the senate, and when sitting for that purpose, the senators shall be upon oath or affirmation to do justice according to law and evidence. When the governor or lieutenant-governor is on trial, the chief justice of the supreme court shall preside. No person shall be convicted without a concurrence of two-thirds of the senators elected.

Art. XIII, Section 2. Who may be impeached

The governor and other state and judicial officers, shall be liable to impeachment for high crimes or misdemeanors or malfeasance in office, but judgment in such cases shall only extend to removal from office and disqualification to hold any office of honor, trust or profit in the state. The party, whether convicted or acquitted, shall, nevertheless, be liable to prosecution, trial, judgment and punishment according to law.

Art. XIII, Section 3. Officers who are not impeachable are subject to removal by law

All officers not liable to impeachment shall be subject to removal for misconduct or malfeasance in office in such manner as may be provided by law.

By Jerry Kopel

The charge doesn't have to be "high crimes and misdemeanors." The Colorado Constitution gives a legislator an impeachment reason not available under the U.S. Constitution. It's called "malfeasance in office."

The courts, including Colorado's, have defined "malfeasance" as "doing an act a person should not do at all, that is wholly wrongful and unlawful." However, the Colorado legislature has defined "malfeasance" in much broader terms in C.R.S. §§ 29-1-115, 29-1-608, and other statutes.

In the statutes, "malfeasance" means "knowingly and willfully (1) failing to perform any of the duties imposed upon him by this (article, part, or section) or (2) violating any of its provisions or (3) furnishing false or fraudulent information."

As with any other resolution introduced in the House, a resolution for impeachment would be assigned to a committee, most likely Judiciary or State Affairs. At present, there are no House or Senate rules on impeachments, so there is no House rule allowing the person charged to defend himself or herself. A decision to allow only a limited amount of defense evidence could be lawful on the basis that if the House passes articles of impeachment, the time for all the evidence to be presented is in the trial in the Senate.

The House committee would have to prepare articles of impeachment. There being no special rules for impeachments, there is no requirement that the full committee vote. As long as there is a quorum present, a majority of the quorum is sufficient to pass the resolution to the House floor. At that point, article XIII requires 33 votes in favor to send the resolution to the Senate.

The Senate does not send the House resolution to a Senate committee. The Senate convenes itself to try the matter "upon oath or affirmation to do justice according to law and evidence." Colorado has no rule forbidding a state senator from asking questions directly during the trial.

If a resolution for impeachment is introduced by one member of the House, some of the procedural decisions might be made according to House Rule 46: "Any matter not covered by these rules shall be governed by the decision of the Speaker, subject to the right of appeal by any member as in these rules provided for." The appeal is resolved by a vote of the full House.

The last Colorado impeachment took place in a special session, called by governor Ralph Carr on April 28, 1939. The civil service commissioners could not be removed by the governor under allegations of test fixing and abuse of testing standards. The Colorado supreme court had held in 1925 that the only recourse was impeachment of the civil service commissioners. *Roberts ex rel. Hicks*, 77 Colo. 281, 235 P. 1069 (1925) (applying art. XII, § 13, creating the state civil service system). After the House impeached, the Senate tried and acquitted two members of the civil service commission.

The rules that were adopted are printed in those 1939 House and Senate Special Session Journals and could easily be re-used in any future impeachment.

Notable decisions

- State legislators are *not* subject to impeachment. Each legislative body may replace its head (speaker of the house; president of the senate) by majority vote. Each legislative body likewise has the authority to expel a member by a 2/3 vote. Art. V, § 12; *In re Speakership*, 15 Colo. 520, 25 P. 707 (1891).

- District attorneys are subject to impeachment. *People v. Losavio*, 199 Colo. 212, 606 P.2d 856 (1980)

Chapter 19

Counties, Article XIV

In 1855, the legislature of the territory of Kansas created Arapahoe, El Paso, and Fremont counties. The New Mexico territory and the Utah territory also created counties in their Colorado lands. Even more so than the Kansas-created counties, the New Mexico and Utah territories were aspirational. No territorial government from afar had the practical ability to govern Colorado.

When Colorado became its own territory in 1861, the new territorial legislature divided Colorado into 17 counties. When statehood came in 1876, there were 26 counties.

By 1913, there were 62 normal counties, plus the City and County of Denver, which was carved out of Arapahoe County by the 1902 Home Rule amendment, article XX. The City and County of Broomfield was created in 2001, taking portions of Jefferson, Boulder, and Adams counties. Art. XX, §§ 10–13.

Of the 64 counties, the only two whose boundaries have never changed are Gilpin and Clear Creek. Both are early mining counties in narrow mountain valleys.

County boundaries are specified in C.R.S. title 30, article 5.

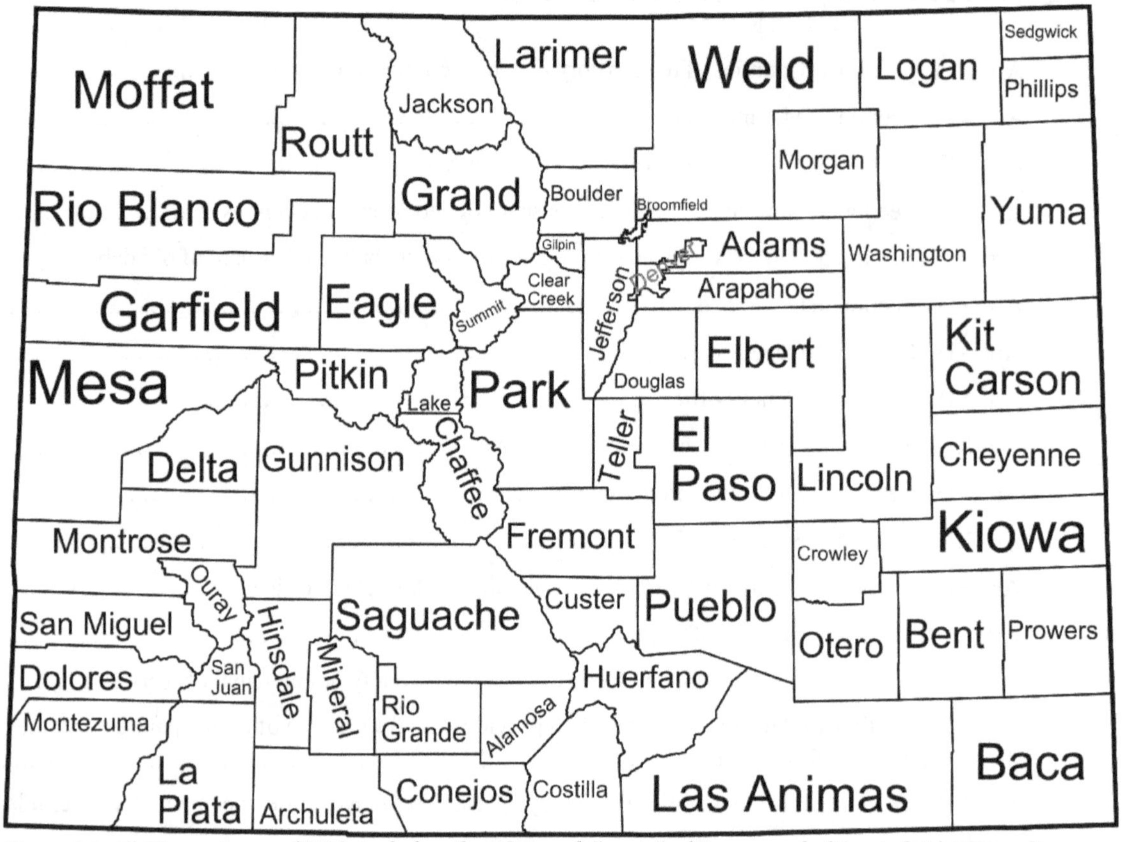

Figure 34. All 64 counties as of 2021, including the "City and County" of Denver and of Broomfield. Wikimedia Commons.

Historic changes in country boundaries can be viewed at https://www.mapofus.org/colorado/.

Art. XIV, Section 1. Counties of the territory become counties of the state

> The several counties of the territory of Colorado as they now exist, are hereby declared to be counties of the state.

"[M]unicipalities and counties exist for convenient administration of government and are merely instruments of state created to carry out will of the state." *Board of County Com'rs of Jefferson County v. City and County of Denver*, 150 Colo. 198, 205, 372 P.2d 152, 156 (1962).

In the 1998 case *Romer v. Board of County Commissioners of Pueblo*, the supreme court granted certiorari to decide a single question: "Does a county department of social services have standing to compel the State Department of Human Services to reduce statewide social services expenditures? We hold that it does not . . . We hold that a county does not have standing to obtain judicial review of the actions of the state department, a superior agency, in order to reduce social services expenditures." 956 P.2d 566 (Colo. 1998).

Nevertheless, Colorado—like most Midwestern states—has a strong tradition of local government, and the general assembly is often hesitant to interfere in county matters.

Art. XIV, Section 2. Moving county seats

> The general assembly shall have no power to remove the county seat of any county, but the removal of county seats shall be provided for by general law, and no county seat shall be removed unless a majority of the registered electors of the county, voting on the proposition at a general election vote therefor; and no such proposition shall be submitted oftener than once in four years, and no person shall vote on such proposition who shall not have resided in the county six months and in the election precinct ninety days next preceding such election.

County seats are listed in C.R.S. § 30-7-101. Election procedures for votes to change county seats are in title 30, article 8. By statute, a county seat change requires a 2/3 majority for a new location. This has been held not to violate section 2's language regarding "a majority of registered electors." *Alexander v. People*, 7 Colo. 155, 2 P. 894 (1883).

No county seat has changed since 1940. Not all county seats are in the largest city within the county; for example, Georgetown is the county seat of Clear Creek County, even though Idaho Springs has a larger population.

Art. XIV, Section 3. Striking off territory from a county

> Except as otherwise provided by statute, no part of the territory of any county shall be stricken off and added to an adjoining county, without first submitting the question to the registered electors of the county from which the territory is proposed to be stricken off; nor unless a majority of all the registered electors of said county voting on the question shall vote therefor.

With the 1974 addition of the first clause, "Except as otherwise provided by statute," Section 3 is a much weaker parallel to the provision in the U.S. Constitution that Congress cannot take away any territory of a state without the consent of the state's legislature. U.S. CONST., art. IV, § 3.

Pre-1974, the Colorado supreme court had ruled that a popular vote is necessary to give territory from one county to another—but the legislature can, without asking for a popular vote, take territory from a county to create a new county. *Frost v. Pfeiffer*, 26 Colo. 338, 58 P.147 (1899) (creating Teller County from parts of El Paso and Fremont).[1]

If the majority of voters in a particular region of a county petition to be annexed by a different county, there must be an election on the proposed annexation. C.R.S. § 30-6-105 et seq.

The original 1902 version of article XX (home rule) had allowed Denver to annex land without the consent of the residents. This was abolished by the Poundstone Amendment, adopted in 1974.[2] The Poundstone Amendment also modified section 3, to permit county boundary changes when "provided by statute." This has been used for some minor adjustments to Denver's

---

[1] Teller County is named for Henry Teller. An 1858 immigrant and mining lawyer, Teller was Colorado's U.S. Senator 1876–1882 and 1885–1909. In-between, he was Secretary of the Interior. Arriving in 1858, Teller was the leading political figure of Colorado's first half-century. Fremont County is named for John C. Frémont, "the Pathfinder," who led several missions of discovery and exploration in Colorado and the West in the 1840s and 1850s. He was elected as California's first U.S. Senator and was the first presidential nominee of the Republican Party, in 1856.

[2] Named for proponent Freda Poundstone, a leading Republican activist.

border. C.R.S. § 30-6-109.7. To build Denver International Airport, Denver was allowed to annex part of Adams County, but only after a favorable vote by the people of Adams County. C.R.S. § 30-6-109.5.

Art. XIV, Section 4. New county shall pay its share of debt from old counties

> In all cases of the establishment of any new county, the new county shall be held to pay its ratable proportion of all then existing liabilities, of the county or counties from which such new county shall be formed.

The general assembly can determine the ratable portion of debt from the old county, or it can choose to defer to the determination of local officials. *In re House Bill No. 231*, 9 Colo. 624, 21 P. 472 (1886).

If the former county has a surplus rather than a debt, the new county does not get a share of the surplus, unless a statute so provides. *Washington County v. Weld County*, 12 Colo. 152, 20 P. 273 (1889).[3]

Art. XIV, Section 5. Part moved from one county to another shall pay its share of old debt

> When any part of a county is stricken off and attached to another county, the part stricken off shall be held to pay its ratable proportion of all then existing liabilities of the county from which it is taken.

If part of a county decides to join another county, they still have to pay their share of the old county's debt.

Art. XIV, Section 6. County commissioners

> In each county having a population of less than seventy thousand there shall be elected, for a term of four years each, three county commissioners who shall hold sessions for the transaction of county business as provided by law; any two of whom shall constitute a quorum for the transaction of business. Two of said commissioners shall be elected at the general election in the year nineteen hundred and four, and at the general election every four years thereafter; and the other one of said commissioners shall be elected at the general election in the year nineteen hundred and six, and at the general election every four years thereafter; provided, that when the population of any county shall equal or exceed seventy thousand, the board of county commissioners may consist of five members, any three of whom shall constitute a quorum for the transaction of business. Three of said commissioners in said county shall be elected at the general election in the year nineteen hundred and four, and at the general election every four years thereafter; and the other two of said commissioners in such county shall be elected at the general election in the year nineteen hundred and six and every four years thereafter; and all of such commissioners shall be elected for the term of four years.

[3] Lewis Ledyard Weld was the first secretary of the Colorado territory.

> This section shall govern, except as hereafter otherwise expressly directed or permitted by constitutional enactment.

All counties—other than Denver and Broomfield, which are both a "city and county"—are governed by elected county commissioners, who serve four-year terms. The number of commissioners in each county is three, except that if the county's population is more than 70,000, the people may choose to have five commissioners. For counties with five commissioners, the terms are staggered, so that at least two seats are decided in every general election. If there are five commissioners, some of them have to be elected in districts, rather than at large. C.R.S. §§ 1-4-205, 30-10-306.5.

Section 6 is why Boulder County, despite having a large population, only has three commissioners. If Boulder County residents were allowed to vote by districts, a Republican might sometimes win a district election outside the city of Boulder.

Statutes for county commissioners are in title 30, articles 10 and 11.

Art. XIV, Section 7. (repealed)

Repealed in 1968, section 7 dealt with pay for county officers. That topic is covered by current section 15.

Art. XIV, Section 8. County officers

> There shall be elected in each county, at the same time at which members of the general assembly are elected, commencing in the year nineteen hundred and fifty-four, and every four years thereafter, one county clerk, who shall be ex officio recorder of deeds and clerk of the board of county commissioners; one sheriff; one coroner; one treasurer who shall be collector of taxes; one county surveyor; one county assessor; and one county attorney who may be elected or appointed, as shall be provided by law; and such officers shall be paid such salary or compensation, either from the fees, perquisites and emoluments of their respective offices, or from the general county fund, as may be provided by law. The term of office of all such officials shall be four years, and they shall take office on the second Tuesday in January next following their election, or at such other time as may be provided by law.

In the 1876 Constitution, county officers were elected to two-year terms. This was changed to four years by a 1954 amendment. The elections are the same year as gubernatorial elections, *i.e.,* not in the presidential election year. The constitutional elected county officers are:

- County clerk. Keeps the records of the county commissioners and is the recorder of deeds and registrar of titles. Manages elections, and reports results to the secretary of state.
- Sheriff. Discussed in the next section.
- Coroner. Issues death certificates. Discussed in section 8.7.
- Treasurer. Collects taxes.
- Assessor. Determines property values for taxation.
- Attorney. May be elected *or* appointed. C.R.S. § 30-11-118 (must be at least 25 years old and a member of the Colorado bar).

- Surveyor. An amendment to allow the surveyor to be elected *or* appointed was rejected by the voters in 2000. 2000 Colo. Laws 2781 (proposing ballot issue to the voters).

County officer salaries are C.R.S. § 30-2-101 et seq. County officers in general are C.R.S. § 30-10-101 et seq.

Art. XIV, Section 8.5. County sheriff qualifications

> The general assembly shall have the authority to establish by law qualifications for the office of county sheriff, including but not limited to training and certification requirements.

Under section 10, the only qualification for being a county officer is being a qualified elector who has lived in the county for at least one year. Added in 1996, section §8.5 allows the legislature to set additional qualifications for sheriffs.[4]

In the English system of government, the second oldest title of office is "sheriff."[5] The Anglo-Saxon word for what we today call a "county" was "shire." The word "sheriff" is a compound of "seyre" (meaning "shire") and "reve" (meaning "bailiff" or "guardian"). The sheriff is therefore the guardian of the county.

England's King Alfred the Great (reigned 871–99) led a guerilla war that expelled oppressive Danish invaders. To restore law and order, Alfred fixed England's county boundaries with greater precision and used the counties to organize national and community self-defense. The sheriff was the pillar of this self-defense system and often the leader of the county militia. The sheriff exercised the authority to summon and command the armed body of the people not only in the militia, but also in several related forms: *posse comitatus*, "hue and cry," and "watch and ward." According to medieval historian Frank Barlow, "[i]t is not unlikely that every freeman had the duty, and right, to bear arms" in Anglo-Saxon times.[6]

When carrying out the duty to bear arms, the freeman would most commonly be under the leadership of the sheriff. The Colorado Constitution (art. II, § 13) recognizes the right to keep and bear arms "in defense of home, person, and property" *and* the right to keep and bear arms "in aid of the civil power when thereto legally summoned"—such as in a *posse comitatus*.

As the county leader of the armed people, "the reeve became the guarantor of the survival of the group."[7] "[T]he people maintained law and order among themselves" because the central government of the king had no practical ability to do so.[8]

By the time of the English settlement of North America, in the early seventeenth century, the office of sheriff had been declining in England for centuries. Justices of the peace were more important.

Colonial Americans took the office of sheriff and revived it in its full Anglo-Saxon glory. Americans began to restore what they considered to be the ancient right of electing sheriffs—a right that had been mostly eroded in England after the Norman Conquest in 1066.

Although the office looked the same on paper on both sides of the Atlantic, there were very significant practical differences, all of which had the effect of elevating the sheriff in America. To begin with, the American colonial sheriff was quite independent of central authority. One reason

---

4 This could not be applied retroactively, during a sheriff's current term. *Jackson v. State,* 966 P.2d 1046 (Colo. 1998).

5 Most of this section is based on David B. Kopel, *The Posse Comitatus and the Office of Sheriff: Armed Citizens Summoned to the Aid of Law Enforcement,* 104 J. CRIM. L. & CRIMINOLOGY 671 (2015).

6 FRANK BARLOW, EDWARD THE CONFESSOR 172 (1970).

7 DAVID R. STRUCKHOFF, THE AMERICAN SHERIFF 3 (1994).

8 *Id.* at 4.

was that unlike the English counties, the American counties were self-governing for almost all practical purposes.

An important American innovation was that the sheriff either had a salary or could only charge fees (*e.g.*, for executing a civil judgment) that were fixed by law. This reform recognized the problem of some of the unsalaried English sheriffs who had used their office for personal enrichment.

The restoration of direct election of sheriffs "encouraged them to adopt an active role, whilst the fact that they were officials of county government helped to give them the opportunity to do so."[9] Election "meant that sheriffs were amongst the first public officials to be elected in any newly settled area and were therefore able to develop their role with little opposition from competing organisations or officials."[10]

Americans came to understand the election of the sheriff as a right of the people.[11] The 1802 Ohio Constitution was the first state constitution to formally specify that sheriffs must be elected.[12] Today, the large majority of American state constitutions require that sheriffs be elected by the people of the county.[13]

Developments in the United States confirmed the importance and independence of sheriffs, whose power came directly from the people. The classic American treatise on sheriff law, written in 1884 by William L. Murfee, observed,

> the sheriff is, in each of the United States, a constitutional officer, recognized *eo nomine* [by that name] as part of the machinery of the state government, and therefore, although it is competent for legislatures to add to his powers or exact from him the performance of additional duties, it is, upon well established legal principles, beyond their powers to circumscribe his common-law functions or to transfer them to other officers.[14]

Consistent with the above history, it has been held that elected county sheriffs have the right to discharge deputies at will. This power cannot be limited by a county ordinance, or even the sheriff's self-imposed limitations. *Williams v. McKee*, 655 Fed. App'x 677 (10th Cir. 2016) (no

---

[9] Steve Gullion, *Sheriffs in Search of a Role*, 142 NEW L.J. 1156, 1157 (1992).

[10] *Id.*

[11] STRUCKHOFF , *supra*, at 23.

[12] *Id.* at 27; OHIO CONST. of 1802, art. VI § 1. The 1836 Constitution of the independent Republic of Texas likewise required election of sheriffs. TEX. CONST. of 1836, art. IV, § 12.

[13] ALA. CONST. art. V, § 138; ARIZ. CONST. art. XII, § 3; ARK. CONST. art. 7, § 46; CAL. CONST. art. XI, §§ 1(b), 4(c); COLO. CONST. art. XIV, § 8; DEL. CONST. art. III, § 22; FLA. CONST. art. VIII, § 1; GA. CONST. art. IX, § 1, para. III; IDAHO CONST. art. XVIII, § 6; ILL. CONST. art. VII, § 4; IND. CONST. art. 6, § 2; KY. CONST. § 99; LA. CONST. art. V, § 27; ME. CONST. art. IX, § 10; MD. CONST. art. IV, § 44; MASS. CONST. art. XIX; MICH. CONST. art. VII, § 4; MISS. CONST. art. V, § 138; NEV. CONST. art. IV, § 32; N.H. CONST. pt. 2, art. 71; N.J. CONST. art. VII, § 2, para. 2; N.M. CONST. art. X, § 2; N.Y. CONST. art. XIII, § 13; N.C. CONST. art. VII, § 2; N.D. CONST. art. VII, § 8; OR. CONST. art. VI, § 6; PA. CONST. art. IX, § 4; S.C. CONST. art. V, § 24; TENN. CONST. art. VII, § 1; TEX. CONST. art. V, § 23; VT. CONST. ch. II, §§ 43, 50; VA. CONST. art. VII, § 4; WASH. CONST. art. XI, § 5; W. VA. CONST. art. IX, § 1; WIS. CONST. art. VI, § 4.

[14] WILLIAM L. MURFEE, A TREATISE ON THE LAW OF THE SHERIFFS AND OTHER MINISTERIAL OFFICERS, at v (St. Louis, F.H. Thomas & Co., 1884); *see also id.* at 22 ("It is competent for the state legislature to impose upon him new duties growing out of public policy and convenience, but it cannot strip him of his time-honored and common-law functions and devolve them upon the incumbents of other offices created by legislative authority."); CLYDE F. SNYDER & IRVING HOWARDS, COUNTY GOVERNMENT IN ILLINOIS 78 (Carbondale: U. of Ill. Pr. 1960) ("[T]he sheriff . . . possesses certain common-law powers and duties of which he cannot be deprived by legislative enactment . . . ." The "common-law powers" are "vested in the sheriff by constitutional implication.") (citing *People v. Clampitt*, 200 N.E. 332 (Ill. 1936); *Cnty. of Edgar v. Middleton*, 86 Ill. App. 3d 502 (1899); *Cnty. of McDonough v. Thomas*, 84 Ill. App. 3d 408 (1899)).

federal constitutional violation in Delta County sheriff Fred McKee firing a deputy for refusing to park the deputy's car, which had a political bumper sticker, away from the jail, because the bumper sticker undermined the public's perception of impartiality). Unlike municipal police officers, sheriffs' deputies are emphatically *not* part of a civil service system.

Today, American sheriffs are elected in all states except Alaska (which has no counties), Hawaii, Rhode Island, and Connecticut (where the office of sheriff was abolished in 2000).

In Colorado, if the county has adopted home rule, as detailed below, it can opt out of the constitutional system for sheriffs, and provide that deputies be covered by civil service. Denver has done so. The Denver sheriff is appointed, not elected, and only has responsibility for the city jail and for security of courts and other government buildings or officers, and for issuing concealed handgun carry permits. Accordingly, there is no Denver sheriff's office. Rather, in Denver, as in Broomfield, the sheriff is merely the head of a department. The Denver sheriff cannot even choose his own undersheriff, who is the second-in-command. Instead, the undersheriff is selected by the civil service system.

The traditional American view is that the legislature may add new duties or powers to the office of sheriff but may not remove any of the sheriff's inherent common law powers or duties.[15] An example of a new duty, not traceable to the common law, is that by Colorado statute, the sheriff is the chief fire warden in his or her county.[16]

In America, the most important traditional responsibility of the sheriff has been keeping the peace. For various aspects of that duty, the sheriff has the authority to summon assistance from armed citizens. Formally, there are four separate prongs to this common law authority, although in practice they can easily overlap. The first prong stems from the English sheriff's duty of keeping "watch and ward," to guard towns, which was given statutory expression under King Richard I (reigned 1189–99). This is the power to arrange watches and patrols, and to require townsfolk to take turns on guard duty. "Ward" was the daytime activity, and "watch" the nighttime activity.

Closely related to "watch and ward" was "hue and cry," the second traditional power. Under English law originating long before the Norman Conquest of 1066, all able-bodied men were obliged to join in the *hutesium et clamor* (hue and cry) to pursue fleeing criminals. Pursuing citizens were allowed to use deadly force if necessary to prevent escape.

The third power of the sheriffs is to summon the *posse comitatus*.

The fourth power is to summon the militia. The use of this military force is supposed to be rare and only for situations that the *posse comitatus* is incapable of resolving.

The sheriff's role as conservator of the peace—with the authority to summon the *posse comitatus*, raise the hue and cry, and administer watch and ward—was straightforwardly recognized in the American colonies. But the changes in the posse began to reflect—and intensify—the ways in which the Americans were reshaping their English legal heritage towards greater self-government and liberty.

Gautham Rao's article *The Federal Posse Comitatus Doctrine* explains: "In its migration to America, however, colonists transformed the *posse comitatus* from an instrument of royal prerogative to an institution of local self-governance."[17] The posse "functioned through, rather than upon, the local popular will."[18] In other words, the Americans brought the posse back to its

---

[15] MURFEE, *supra*, at 22.
[16] C.R.S. § 30-10-512.
[17] Gautham Rao, *The Federal Posse Comitatus Doctrine: Slavery, Compulsion, and Statecraft in Mid-Nineteenth-Century America*, 26 LAW & HIST. REVIEW 1, 10 (2008); *see also* PAULINE MAIER, FROM RESISTANCE TO REVOLUTION 16–20 (1991) (noting, *inter alia*, use of *posse comitatus* to prevent impressment of Americans into the British navy).
[18] Rao, *supra*, at 10.

traditional Anglo-Saxon role, shaking off six centuries of how the Norman Conquest and succeeding monarchs had partially undemocratized the posse and the sheriff.

According to Rao, "[t]he colonists' control of the *posse comitatus*—of the legal means of coercion—all but precipitated the American Revolution."[19] The policies of the government in London had so alienated the Americans that they were no longer willing to enforce what London wanted. The British prime minister, Lord North, recognized the problem: the posse had switched sides. Rather than providing the manpower to enforce parliament's will, the posse was now actively resisting that will. The problem was exacerbated by the fact that most sheriffs leaned Whig (towards citizen rights) rather than Tory (towards the authority of the monarch).

So, at the advice of Lord North and his party, the British government attempted to resort to military coercion of the Americans, and, starting in the fall of 1774, a gun control program designed to disarm them. Forcible disarmament with house-to-house searches by the British redcoats was attempted at Lexington and Concord on the morning of April 19, 1775. The Americans resisted with their personal arms, and the Revolutionary War began.[20]

The *posse comitatus* thrived in nineteenth century America. Senator and diplomat Edward Livingston extolled the posse because "the same ties of property, of family, of love of country and of liberty" which make possemen "effective instruments for the suppression of disorder" also make them "unfit . . . to promote any scheme of usurpation. The people can apprehend no danger to their liberties from such a force."[21]

Citizens served in the posse readily and with pride. It was used for a wide variety of local enforcement, ranging from stopping illegal fishing to suppressing riots. Like jury service, posse service was a mandatory duty of a citizen, one that should be performed as part of free citizen's rights and duties in a self-governing republic. In Colorado, in the nineteenth century and the early twentieth, posses were often summoned for keeping the peace.[22]

The expansion of government, including the much larger number of law enforcement personnel, has made posses less necessary than in the past, but they are still used in modern Colorado. Large posses were summoned in Pitkin County in 1977 after serial killer Ted Bundy escaped from the county courthouse, and in 1994 in Hinsdale County after two criminals on an interstate crime spree murdered sheriff Roger Coursey. In both cases the posses thwarted the criminals' escape.

For less extraordinary situations, at least 17 Colorado county sheriffs have established posses, who are trained by the sheriff's office. They may be armed or unarmed, depending on the discretion of the sheriff, such as requiring posse members to pass the same firearms qualifications standards as deputies. Posse members may use arms from the office armory or supply their own. The posses help sheriffs provide security during county fairs, control roads during weather emergencies, and guard areas in hostage situations, among many other duties. During the September 2013 floods, Larimer County sheriff Justin Smith exercised his authority to temporarily deputize persons in some remote small towns, to prevent looting.

---

[19] *Id.*

[20] William F. Swindler, *"Rights of Englishmen" Since 1776: Some Anglo-American Notes*, 124 U. PENNSYLVANIA L. REVIEW 1083, 1089–91 (1976); David B. Kopel, *How the British Gun Control Program Precipitated the American Revolution*, 6 CHARLESTON L. REVIEW 283 (2012).

[21] EDWARD LIVINGSTON, A SYSTEM OF PENAL LAW FOR THE STATE OF LOUISIANA 209–10 (Lawbook Exchange 2010) (1833). Livingston served as secretary of state for Andrew Jackson, and also as a United States senator for Louisiana and United States representative for two states, New York and Louisiana. Roger J. Champagne, *Livingston, Edward*, *in* 17 ENCYCLOPEDIA AMERICANA 615 (1980).

[22] *See, e.g.,* David B. Kopel, *The Right to Arms in Nineteenth Century Colorado,* 95 DENVER L. REVIEW 329, 431 n.834 (2018) (listing various posse summons).

Art. XIV, Section 8.7. County coroner qualifications

> The general assembly shall have the authority to establish by law qualifications for the office of county coroner, including but not limited to training and certification requirements.

Section 8.7 allows the legislature to set qualifications for coroners.

The office of coroner in England was created in 1194.[23] The office was originally much broader than today, when forensic autopsies are the office's only routine law enforcement role. Historically, coroners presided at some judicial hearings and had arrest powers.[24] Under the common law, coroners had the power to summon a *posse comitatus* or to lead a hue and cry (pursuit of a felon).[25]

The common law peace-keeping powers of coroners have always been affirmed by Colorado statute. The 1861 statutes of Colorado's first territorial legislature stated:

> When any felonious offense shall be committed, public notice thereof shall be immediately given in all public places near where the same was committed, and fresh pursuit shall forthwith be made after every person guilty thereof by sheriffs, coroners, constables, and all other persons who shall be by any of them commanded or summoned for that purpose.

1861 Colo. Session Laws 326.

Likewise, in modern law, coroners and sheriffs both have the authority to summon a *posse comitatus*:

> It is the duty of the sheriffs, undersheriffs, and deputies to keep and preserve the peace in their respective counties, and to quiet and suppress all affrays, riots, and unlawful assemblies and insurrections. For that purpose, and for the service of process in civil or criminal cases, and in apprehending or securing any person for felony or breach of the peace, they, and every coroner, may call to their aid such person of their county as they may deem necessary.

C.R.S. § 30-10-516.

If you receive a *posse comitatus* summons from your county coroner, you should assume that something bad has happened to the county sheriff, and that civil order in the county is near collapse. So do your civic duty and help the coroner.

Art. XIV, Section 9. Vacancies

> In case of a vacancy occurring in the office of county commissioner a vacancy committee of the same political party as the vacating commissioner constituted as

---

[23] Articles of the Eyre, 1 Stats. of the Realm 233, art. 20 (1194).

[24] *See, e.g.*, GEORGE WEBB, THE OFFICE AND AUTHORITY OF A JUSTICE OF PEACE 97–104 (Williamsburg, William Parks 1736).

[25] WEBB, at 253 ("By the Common Law, every Judge of Record, Sheriffs, Coroner, Constable, or other Office to whose office belongs the Conservation of the Peace, may command and take the Aid and Force of Others to pacify Riots, or Affrays.") (citing 28 Edward III, chapter 8 (1355)). The standard citation for historical English statutes means: in the 28th year of the reign of King Edward the Third, this was the 8th statute that was enacted.

> provided by law shall, by a majority vote, fill the vacancy by appointment within ten days after occurrence of the vacancy. If the vacancy committee fails to fill the vacancy within ten days after occurrence of the vacancy, the governor shall fill the same by appointment within fifteen days after occurrence of the vacancy. The person appointed to fill a vacancy in the office of county commissioner shall be a member of the same political party, if any, as the vacating commissioner. In case of a vacancy in any other county office, or in any precinct office, the board of county commissioners shall fill the same by appointment. Any person appointed pursuant to this section shall hold the office until the next general election, or until the vacancy is filled by election according to law.

In other words, county commissioner vacancies are filled the same way as general assembly vacancies: a committee of the vacant commissioner's political party chooses the replacement. Originally, the governor had chosen the replacement county commissioners, but this was changed by amendment in 1978.

Vacancies in all other county offices are filled by appointment by the county commissioners. C.R.S. § 30-10-105. *See also* COLO. CONST., art. XII, § 10 (vacancies on refusal or neglect to qualify for office).

Art. XIV, Section 10. Only qualified electors are eligible for county office

> No person shall be eligible to any county office unless he shall be a qualified elector; nor unless he shall have resided in the county one year preceding his election.

The general assembly may not impose additional statutory requirements for eligibility. *Reale v. Board of Real Estate Appraisers*, 880 P.2d 1205 (Colo. 1994) (statute had said that county assessor must be a licensed real estate appraiser).

As noted above, constitutional amendments now allow the general assembly to set additional qualifications for sheriffs and coroners.

Art. XIV, Section 11. (repealed)

This had required elections for justices of the peace and of constables. These offices are now extinct in Colorado.

Art. XIV, Section 12. General assembly may create other county or municipal officers

> The general assembly shall provide for the election or appointment of such other county officers and such municipal officers of statutory cities and towns as public convenience may require; and their terms of office shall be as prescribed by statute.

Although there were some controversies in the late nineteenth and early twentieth centuries, since section 8 was adopted in its modern form, the general assembly has not enacted any statutes creating additional county officers.

Art. XIV, Section 13. General assembly shall provide laws for creation of municipalities, and their division into up to four classes

> The general assembly shall provide, by general laws, for the organization and classification of cities and towns. The number of such classes shall not exceed four; and the powers of each class shall be defined by general laws, so that all municipal corporations of the same class shall possess the same powers and be subject to the same restrictions.

A "city" has a population of at least 2,001, while a town has fewer. C.R.S. § 31-1-101.

The general assembly has divided the 187 "statutory" cities and towns into four classes, with uniform laws for each class. C.R.S., title 31, articles 1 & 2. Statutory municipalities have no powers beyond what the statutes grant. Any doubt is resolved against the alleged power. *City of Aurora v. Bogue*, 176 Colo. 198, 489 P.2d 1295 (1971); *Town of Eaton v. Bouslog*, 133 Colo. 130, 292 P.2d 343 (1956) (eminent domain).

Article XX allows cities and towns to opt out of the section 13 system, and instead to exercise home rule. In 1940 there were 10 home rule cities and towns. They have steadily increased, numbering 101 by 2018. *See* Sam Mamet, *Overview of Colorado Municipal Home Rule*, COLORADO MUNICIPAL LEAGUE (2018). Becoming "home rule" gives a city or town much greater power. To opt into home rule, a municipality must have a charter, adopted by the voters. A charter is like a constitution for a municipality. Art. XX.

Art. XIV, Section 14. Municipalities created by special laws may choose to come under general law

> The general assembly shall also make provision, by general law, whereby any city, town or village, incorporated by any special or local law, may elect to become subject to and be governed by the general law relating to such corporations.

This covers cities, towns, and villages that were incorporated by charters from the territorial legislature. Today, only Georgetown remains as a section 14 city. All other relevant municipalities have opted into the section 13 system.

Art. XIV, Section 15. County officer compensation and fees

> The general assembly shall fix the compensation of county officers in this state by law, and shall establish scales of fees to be charged and collected by such county officers. All such fees shall be paid into the county general fund.
>
> When fixing the compensation of county officers, the general assembly shall give due consideration to county variations, including population; the number of persons residing in unincorporated areas; assessed valuation; motor vehicle registrations; building permits; military installations; and such other factors as may be necessary to prepare compensation schedules that reflect variations in the

> workloads and responsibilities of county officers and in the tax resources of the several counties.
>
> The compensation of any county officer shall be increased or decreased only when the compensation of all county officers within the same county, or when the compensation for the same county officer within the several counties of the state, is increased or decreased.
>
> County officers shall not have their compensation increased or decreased during the terms of office to which they have been elected or appointed.

Pursuant to section 15, counties are divided into six categories, plus subcategories, with uniform pay for county officers in the same class. C.R.S. § 30-2-102(1.5).[26]

Fees that may be collected by county officers may vary based on a five-tier classification of counties, which applies to fees and nothing else. C.R.S. § 30-1-101 et seq.[27]

These classes for fees and salaries purposes are *not* the same as the four-class system (A, B, C, D) that exists for county court judges, pursuant to article VI.

Table 5. Classification of counties

I-A: Adams, Arapahoe, Boulder, Douglas, El Paso, Jefferson, Larimer, Pueblo, Weld.
I-D: Mesa.
II-A: Eagle, Garfield, La Plata, Routt, Summit.
II-C: Fremont and Pitkin.
III-A: Alamosa, Chaffee, Clear Creek, Gunnison, Moffat, Montrose, Morgan, Park, Rio Blanco, San Miguel, Teller.
III-B: Archuleta, Delta, Gilpin, Logan.
III-C: Otero.
III-D: Grand, Las Animas, Montezuma.
IV-A: Custer, Elbert, Ouray, Prowers.
IV-B: Kit Carson, Lake, Washington, Yuma.
IV-C: Huerfano.
IV-D: Rio Grande.
V-A: Baca, Conejos, Costilla, Lincoln, Mineral, Phillips, San Juan.
V-B: Crowley, Hinsdale.
V-C: Bent, Dolores.
V-D: Cheyenne, Saguache.
VI-B: Sedgwick.
VI-D: Jackson, Kiowa.
C.R.S. § 30-2-102.

---

[26] County Commissioner salaries range from $39,700 (category VI-D) up to $113,490 (category I-A). County Treasurer salaries range from $46,500 up to $144,430.

[27] First class: city and county of Denver.

Second class: Adams, Arapahoe, Boulder, Douglas, El Paso, Jefferson, Pueblo, and Weld.

Third class: Delta, Garfield, Larimer, Las Animas, Logan, Mesa, Montezuma, Montrose, Morgan, and Otero.

Fourth class: Alamosa, Archuleta, Bent, city and county of Broomfield, Chaffee, Cheyenne, Clear Creek, Conejos, Costilla, Crowley, Eagle, Elbert, Fremont, Gilpin, Gunnison, Huerfano, Kit Carson, Lake, La Plata, Lincoln, Ouray, Park, Phillips, Prowers, Rio Grande, Routt, Saguache, San Miguel, Sedgwick, Teller, Washington, and Yuma.

Fifth class: Baca, Custer, Dolores, Grand, Hinsdale, Jackson, Kiowa, Mineral, Moffat, Pitkin, Rio Blanco, San Juan, and Summit.

Art. XIV, Section 16. County home rule

> (1) Notwithstanding the provisions of sections 6, 8, 9, 10, 12, and 15 of this article, the registered electors of each county of the state are hereby vested with the power to adopt a home rule charter establishing the organization and structure of county government consistent with this article and statutes enacted pursuant hereto.
>
> (2) The general assembly shall provide by statute procedures under which the registered electors of any county may adopt, amend, and repeal a county home rule charter. Action to initiate home rule may be by petition, signed by not less than five percent of the registered electors of the county in which home rule is sought, or by any other procedure authorized by statute. No county home rule charter, amendment thereto, or repeal thereof, shall become effective until approved by a majority of the registered electors of such county voting thereon.
>
> (3) A home rule county shall provide all mandatory county functions, services, and facilities and shall exercise all mandatory powers as may be required by statute.
>
> (4) A home rule county shall be empowered to provide such permissive functions, services, and facilities and to exercise such permissive powers as may be authorized by statute applicable to all home rule counties, except as may be otherwise prohibited or limited by charter or this constitution.
>
> (5) The provisions of sections 6, 8, 9, 10, 12, and 15 of article XIV of this constitution shall apply to counties adopting a home rule charter only to such extent as may be provided in said charter.

By adopting home rule, a county can opt out of the article XIV constitutional requirements for what county officers there will be, and how those officers will be chosen.

Section 16 was adopted in 1970. The only counties whose voters have adopted a charter and used the section 16 opt-out are Weld and Pitkin.

The powers of home rule counties are detailed in title 30, article 35, the County Home Rule Powers Act. This includes special rules for bonds, and the authority to create special taxing districts.

Art. XIV, Section 17. Service authorities

This is *one* of the means for creation of special districts. Special districts are discussed in the final section of this chapter.

> (1)
>
> > (a) The general assembly shall provide by statute for the organization, structure, functions, services, facilities, and powers of service authorities pursuant to the following requirements:
> > (b) A service authority may be formed only upon the approval of a majority of the registered electors voting thereon in the territory to be included.
> > (c) The territory within a service authority may include all or part of one county or home rule county or all or part of two or more adjoining counties

or home rule counties, but shall not include only a part of any city and county, home rule city or town, or statutory city or town at the time of formation of the service authority. No more than one service authority shall be established in any territory and, in no event, shall a service authority be formed in the metropolitan area composed of the city and county of Denver, and Adams, Arapahoe, and Jefferson counties which does not include all of the city and county of Denver and all or portions of Adams, Arapahoe, and Jefferson counties.
(d) The boundaries of any service authority shall not be such as to create any enclave.
(e) No territory shall be included within the boundaries of more than one service authority.

(2)

(a) The general assembly shall also provide by statute for:
(b) The inclusion and exclusion of territory in or from a service authority;
(c) The dissolution of a service authority;
(d) The merger of all or a part of two or more adjacent service authorities, except that such merger shall require the approval of a majority of the registered electors voting thereon in each of the affected service authorities; and,
(e) The boundaries of any service authority or any special taxing districts therein or the method by which such boundaries are to be determined or changed; and
(f) The method for payment of any election expenses.

(3)

(a) The general assembly shall designate by statute the functions, services, and facilities which may be provided by a service authority, and the manner in which the members of the governing body of any service authority shall be elected from compact districts of approximately equal population by the registered electors of the authority, including the terms and qualifications of such members. The general assembly may provide that members of the governing body may be elected by a vote of each compact district or by an at-large vote or combination thereof. Notwithstanding any provision in this constitution or the charter of any home rule city and county, city, town, or county to the contrary, mayors, councilmen, trustees, and county commissioners may additionally hold elective office with a service authority and serve therein either with or without compensation, as provided by statute.
(b) A service authority shall provide any function, service, or facility designated by statute and authorized as provided in paragraphs (c) and (d) of this subsection.
(c) All propositions to provide functions, services, or facilities shall be submitted, either individually or jointly, to the registered electors in the manner and form prescribed by law.

(d) Each such function, service, or facility shall be authorized if approved by a majority of the registered electors of the authority voting thereon; but if the service authority includes territory in more than one county, approval shall also require a majority of the registered electors of the authority voting thereon in those included portions of each of the affected counties.

(e) Notwithstanding the provisions of paragraphs (b), (c), and (d) of this subsection, where, upon formation of a service authority, any function, service, or facility is already being provided in at least four counties or portions thereof by a single special district, regional planning commission or metropolitan council, or an association of political subdivisions, the general assembly may provide, without a vote of the registered electors, for assumption by one or more service authorities of such function, service, or facility.

(f) Notwithstanding the provisions of paragraphs (b), (c), and (d) of this subsection, a service authority may contract with any other political subdivision to provide or receive any function, service, or facility designated by statute; but a service authority shall not be invested with any taxing power as a consequence of such contract.

(4)

(a) A service authority shall be a body corporate and a political subdivision of the state.

(b) Any other provision of this constitution to the contrary notwithstanding, any service authority formed under this article and the statutes pursuant thereto may exercise such powers to accomplish the purposes and to provide the authorized functions, services, and facilities of such authority as the general assembly may provide by statute.

(c) Notwithstanding the provisions of article XX of this constitution, any authorized function, service, or facility may be provided exclusively by the authority or concurrently with other jurisdictions as may be prescribed by statute, subject to the provisions of subsections (3)(c), (3)(d), (3)(e), and (3)(f) of this section.

Adopted in 1970 and revised in 2000. Implemented by the Regional Service Authority Act. C.R.S. § 32-7-101 et seq.

Art. XIV, Section 18. Relationships of political subdivisions

Another means for creating districts that span county or municipal boundaries.

(1)

(a) Any other provisions of this constitution to the contrary notwithstanding:

(b) The general assembly may provide by statute for the terms and conditions under which one or more service authorities may succeed to the rights, properties, and other assets and assume the obligations of any other political subdivision included partially or entirely within such authority, incident to the powers vested in, and the functions, services, and facilities authorized to be provided by the service authority, whether vested and authorized at the time of the formation of the service authority or subsequent thereto; and,

(c) The general assembly may provide by statute for the terms and conditions under which a county, home rule county, city and county, home

rule city or town, statutory city or town, or quasi-municipal corporation, or any combination thereof may succeed to the rights, properties, and other assets and assume the obligations of any quasi-municipal corporation located partially or entirely within its boundaries.
(d) The general assembly may provide by statute procedures whereby any county, home rule county, city and county, home rule city or town, statutory city or town, or service authority may establish special taxing districts.

(2)
(a) Nothing in this constitution shall be construed to prohibit the state or any of its political subdivisions from cooperating or contracting with one another or with the government of the United States to provide any function, service, or facility lawfully authorized to each of the cooperating or contracting units, including the sharing of costs, the imposition of taxes, or the incurring of debt.
(b) Nothing in this constitution shall be construed to prohibit the authorization by statute of a separate governmental entity as an instrument to be used through voluntary participation by cooperating or contracting political subdivisions.
(c) Nothing in this constitution shall be construed to prohibit any political subdivision of the state from contracting with private persons, associations, or corporations for the provision of any legally authorized functions, services, or facilities within or without its boundaries.
(d) Nothing in this constitution shall be construed to prohibit the general assembly from providing by statute for state imposed and collected taxes to be shared with and distributed to political subdivisions of the state except that this provision shall not in any way limit the powers of home rule cities and towns.

Also added in 1970. Pursuant to section 18, the general assembly has enacted the Local Marketing Districts Act, C.R.S. title 29, article 25, part 1, which creation of marketing districts for various sorts of business promotion.

Another use of section 18 powers is several special districts joining together to create a self-insurance pool. *Colorado Special Districts Property and Liability Pool v. Lyons*, 277 P.3d 874 (Colo. App. 2012). Or a mass transit system created jointly by a county and several municipalities. *Durango Transp., Inc. v. City of Durango*, 824 P.2d 48 (Colo. App. 1991).

Districts and special districts in Colorado

A bewildering variety of special local governments exist in Colorado. How many governments are there in our state?

To start: number of state governments (1) + number of county governments (64) + number of Colorado municipalities (196 incorporated towns + 73 incorporated cities). This is a total of 336.

But when you add in districts of various sorts, the total number of governments is over 3,000. There are 179 public school districts in Colorado. There are also many *special districts.* The best-known special district is the Regional Transportation District. Another is the Scientific and Cultural Facilities District. Corporate welfare for the Denver Broncos stadium was provided by the Metropolitan Football Stadium District.

There are also mine drainage districts, water and/or sanitation districts, wastewater districts, water conservancy districts, fire and/or rescue districts, parks and/or recreation districts, library districts, hospital districts, cemetery districts, metropolitan districts, general improvement districts, public improvement districts, special improvement maintenance districts, downtown development authorities, urban renewal authorities, and business improvement districts. Plus mass transportation districts, flood control districts, rail districts, mental health care districts, forest improvement districts, health assurance districts, and health service districts. A statewide "New Energy Improvement District" subsidizes the installation of solar panels etc. C.R.S. Title 32 is devoted to special districts.

The Colorado Department of Local Affairs provides an excellent map of some of these districts: https://demography.dola.colorado.gov/CO_SpecialDistrict/. Just southeast of Denver University is the Skyline Fire Protection District. To the south (below Iliff) is the Hi-Lin Water & Sanitation District.[28] North lies the Cherry Creek Corporate Center Metropolitan District.

The Special District Association of Colorado represents the interests of special districts and provides public information and other services. In the state government, the Department of Local Affairs provides many services to special districts, and to counties and municipalities. https://www.colorado.gov/pacific/dola/division-local-government

Critics say that so many districts means that government is out of control. Supporters say that special districts make government more efficient: each special district has a few particular tasks, and no other. Local government can be custom-tailored to create special units dedicated to a project (libraries, fire protection, etc.) with boundaries that fit the needs of a particular project. County and municipality boundaries are convenient for general government, but not for special needs in some areas.

[28] "Lin" is part of the official name, notwithstanding its unorthodox spelling.

CHAPTER 20

Corporations, Article XV

Figure 29. Denver & Rio Grande Railroad train at the Salt Lake City depot, 1915. History Colorado, Denver, Colorado.

Introduction

Corporations were a major concern of the Colorado Convention. When the Convention submitted a proposed constitution to the people for ratification, the Convention also submitted an *Address to the People*. The *Address* explained how the Convention had sought a middle ground:

> Probably no subject has come before the Convention causing more anxiety and concern than the troublesome and vexed question pertaining to corporations. The legislatures of other States have, in most cases, been found unequal to the task of preventing abuses and protecting the people from the grasping and monopolizing tendencies of railroads and other corporations. Experience has shown that positive restrictions on the powers of the legislature in relation to these matters are necessary.
>
> To this end we have provided for the wiping out of all dormant and sham corporations claiming special and exclusive privileges. We have denied the General Assembly the power to create corporations, or to extend or enlarge their chartered rights by special legislation, or to make such rights and privileges irrevocable; but in case it shall be found that the exercise of such rights and privileges proves injurious to the people, then the General Assembly shall have power to alter, revoke or annul such charters, when that can be done without injustice to the corporators.

> We have declared that railroad corporations shall be liable as common carriers, and that to avail themselves of the benefits of future legislation, they must subject themselves to all the provisions and requirements of the Constitution. We have forbidden the consolidation of parallel and competing lines, and of all unjust and unreasonable discriminations between individual in their business with such corporations.
>
> We have carefully guarded the right of eminent domain, requiring a just compensation to be paid in cash when private property is taken [art. II, §§ 14–15, Bill of Rights], and have required all foreign corporations, as a condition of their doing business here, to have one or more known places of business, and an agent or representative within the State, upon whom the process of our courts can be served at any and all times.
>
> We have also retained the jurisdiction of our courts in case of consolidation of a corporation with the State with any foreign corporation, over that part of the corporation property with the limits of this State.
>
> We are aware that these provisions do not cover the whole ground, but it must be remembered that while some of sister States have not gone far enough in placing restrictions on the legislative power, others have gone too far, and have had to recede. We have endeavored to take a middle ground, believing it to be more safe, and in the end that it will give more general satisfaction.[1]

Besides the above, article II (Bill of Rights), article V (legislative powers), article X (tax) and article XI (debt) also have provisions to bar special benefits for favored corporations. No other topic appears in so many articles of the Constitution.

The Colorado Convention delegates had plenty of knowledge about what could go wrong if a corporation could make itself a legislative favorite. In Colorado territory days, some businesses had promised to help develop the territory by building railroads. The territorial and local governments knew that railroads would be essential to Colorado. So, taxpayer funds went to buy subscriptions to the issuance of new stock in railroad corporations, or to guarantee the bonds of would-be railroads. Too often, the railroad corporation went bust, and the taxpayers were stuck.

The Colorado Convention of 1876 met in the aftermath of the worst congressional bribery scandal thus far in American history, caused by a railroad's cozy relationship with government. In 1872, the public learned that a sham construction company called the Crédit Mobilier had milked outrageous fees from the Union Pacific Railroad. The fees went to insiders who controlled both the Crédit Mobilier and the Union Pacific. The Union Pacific had been given the federal government contract to build the Omaha to Utah part of the first transcontinental railroad.[2]

Only three years after the Colorado Constitution was ratified, the Colorado supreme court heard a case arising from Boulder County subscribing $200,000 in stock of the Colorado Central Railroad Company. As chief justice Elbert's opinion explained, "it was undoubtedly the intention of the framers of the Constitution, whether wisely or not, to prohibit, by the fundamental law of the new State, all public aid to railroad companies, whether by donation, grant or subscription, no

---

[1] More text of the *Address to the People of Colorado* is reprinted in chapter 1 (Creation of the State of Colorado).

[2] The Union Pacific built the portion of the transcontinental railroad from Omaha, Nebraska, to Promontory Point, Utah. There, the transcontinental line met Leland Stanford's Central Pacific Railroad, which came from Sacramento, California. On May 10, 1869, the transcontinental joinder was marked with the driving of a Golden Spike.

One of the bribe-takers, sadly, was former speaker of the house and then-vice-president Schuyler Colfax, an Indiana man who had always been a great friend of and advocate for Colorado. Denver's Colfax Avenue is named for him.

matter what might be the public benefit and advantages flowing from the construction of such roads." *Colorado Cent. R. Co. v. Lea*, 5 Colo. 192 (1879).

As the Colorado supreme court later observed, when the Convention met, the taxing of citizens for the benefit of railroads "had become a mania, particularly in the west." *Lord v. City and County of Denver*, 58 Colo. 1, 15, 143 P. 284 (1914) (enforcing art. XI, §§ 1–2, and forbidding Denver to issue bonds to build the Moffat Tunnel for the benefit of the Denver & Salt Lake Railroad.)

As described in chapter 16, the Colorado supreme court since the mid-twentieth century has nullified article XI's constitutional protections against corporate welfare. Today, corporate welfare is permitted whenever the government believes that there will be some economic benefit from the welfare. That is the opposite of what the Constitution says.

Have circumstances changed, making the constitutional concerns no longer relevant? The Colorado Convention was afraid of the oligopoly power of the railroads; at the time, seven corporations owned two-thirds of the nation's rail network. Today, many modern industries, including transportation, are even more concentrated.

Perhaps the concentration is economically efficient. The Colorado Constitution aims to ensure that corporations earn their income legitimately, such as by providing goods or services efficiently—rather than by using political power to transfer money from taxpayers-to-government-to-corporations.

Summary of Article XV

- Corporations must be created by general law, not by special purpose statutes for a particular corporation.
- The general assembly may alter or revoke corporate charters, provided "that no injustice shall be done to the corporators."
- Railroads are common carriers, who must serve all customers. Railroad companies must allow interconnection from other railroads.
- The consolidation of competing, parallel rail lines is forbidden.
- Everyone has an equal right to personal and property transportation by rail. Railroad rates must not make "undue or unreasonable discrimination" among customers.
- The general assembly's power to take property from corporations by eminent domain is the same as the power to take property from individuals. The general assembly may require the corporations not "conduct their business in such manner as to infringe the equal rights of individuals or the general well-being of the state."
- A corporation may not increase the number of shares of stock without majority consent of the shareholders.
- Foreign corporations doing business in Colorado must have a registered agent in Colorado for service of process.
- Street railroads may not be constructed in towns without consent of the local government.
- The legislature may not pass retrospective laws to benefit anyone, including corporations.
- Competing telegraph lines may not be consolidated.
- If a Colorado corporation consolidates with a foreign corporation, the Colorado government does not lose jurisdiction over the Colorado entity.
- Employment contracts may not waive the employee's right to sue a corporation for personal injuries caused by the corporation's negligence.

Art. XV, Section 1. Limitations on prior grants of special privileges (repealed)

Repealed in 2000 as obsolete. The 1876 provision had voided "All existing charter or grants of special or exclusive privileges under which the corporators or grantees shall not have organized and commenced business in good faith at the time of the adoption of this Constitution." In other words, if the territorial government had given a corporation a special privilege, and the corporation had already started operating in good faith in reliance on that privilege, the situation could continue. But if a corporation had not commenced business, then special privileges were revoked.

Art. XV, Section 2. Corporate charters must be created by general law

> No charter of incorporation shall be granted, extended, changed or amended by special law, except for such municipal, charitable, educational, penal or reformatory corporations as are or may be under the control of the state; but the general assembly shall provide by general laws for the organization of corporations hereafter to be created.

Today, Americans are familiar with the neutral system for chartering corporations. If you want to form a corporation, you file some forms with the Colorado secretary of state, pursuant to statutes specifying how to incorporate. If the forms meet the statutory standards, the secretary of state automatically grants the corporate charter.

The above process has been the norm in the United States since the late nineteenth century. It is a great improvement of the process that had prevailed in England, colonial America, and then the early republic. Then, corporations were a much rarer form of business organization. A corporate charter could only be granted by a special act of the legislature, creating a particular corporation. The system forced would-be corporations to buy political influence.

Section 2 constitutionalizes the good government standard of general rules for incorporation. It complements article V, § 25, which prohibits the general assembly from passing certain types of special laws, including for corporations.

Section 2 still allows for special laws to create or manage institutions under state or municipal control, such as the University of Colorado, municipal corporations (cities and towns), and so on.

Art. XV, Section 3. General assembly may revoke, alter or annul charters

> The general assembly shall have the power to alter, revoke or annul any charter of incorporation now existing and revocable at the adoption of this constitution, or any that may hereafter be created, whenever in their opinion it may be injurious to the citizens of the state, in such manner, however, that no injustice shall be done to the corporators.

Art. XV, Section 4. Railroads are common carriers

> All railroads shall be public highways, and all railroad companies shall be common carriers. Any association or corporation organized for the purpose, shall have the right to construct and operate a railroad between any designated points within this state, and to connect at the state line with railroads of other states and territories. Every railroad company shall have the right with its road to intersect, connect with or cross any other railroad.

Railroads in Colorado are common carriers. They must accept any paying customer—subject of course to available capacity, and to customers following the rules of conduct. (*E.g.*, in the 19th century, no smoking in the car reserved for ladies.) The common carriers rule likewise applies to freight.

Railroads cannot prohibit a competing line from crossing their tracks. Nor can railroad A prevent its competitor, railroad B, from building a connection for the A and B tracks.

Section 4 is contrary to the ordinary law of property rights. Normally, a business has no obligation to let a competitor cross its property. Nor is a business required to allow a competitor to connect with the business's own property. As the Colorado Convention recognized, the government can have power to abrogate property rights only when a constitution grants such a power.

Section 4 requires railroads to allow a mechanical connection. It does not require a railroad to enter into a business relationship with another railroad. Nor does it require a railroad to construct a depot at a railroad junction. *Atchison, Topeka & Santa Fe Railroad Company v. Denver & New Orleans Railroad*, 110 U.S. 667 (1884) (Waite, C.J.) (diversity jurisdiction).

Art. XV, Section 5. Consolidation of parallel lines forbidden

> No railroad corporation, or the lessees or managers thereof, shall consolidate its stock, property or franchises with any other railroad corporation owning or having under its control a parallel or competing line.

The 1876 Colorado Constitution preceded the federal 1890 Sherman Antitrust Act. Although the Colorado Constitution has no objection to corporate mergers in general, it does prohibit railroad mergers that directly reduce competition. An implementing statute clarifies that railroad mergers across state lines are permissible. C.R.S. § 40-22-101. For example, a railroad company with a line from Denver to the Kansas border may merge with a connecting line that travels from the Kansas/Colorado border to Topeka, providing single ownership for the Denver to Topeka line.

By a century after statehood, section 5 had become obsolete. In 1976, and even more so thereafter, long distance personal travel was mainly by motor vehicle (including busses) or airplane. Freight shipping by railroad was still important, but relatively less so now that trucks carried goods all over an excellent interstate highway network. There are few if any places in the United States where competing rail lines are economically viable. The number of rail lines that are sustainable based on passenger or freight revenue in any given area is usually one at most.[3]

Federal statutes govern the modern arrangement. Pursuant to the Supremacy Clause of the U.S. Constitution, they preempt any state laws, including state constitutions.

---

[3] With the arguable exception of commuter rail lines in extremely dense areas, such as the tristate area around New York City. But even they are heavily subsidized by general tax revenues.

Art. XV, Section 6. Equal rights of public to transportation

> All individuals, associations and corporations shall have equal rights to have persons and property transported over any railroad in this state, and no undue or unreasonable discrimination shall be made in charges or in facilities for transportation of freight or passengers within the state, and no railroad company, nor any lessee, manager or employee thereof, shall give any preference to individuals, associations or corporations in furnishing cars or motive power.

Railroads are common carriers. Like inns in the common law, they must accept all comers—providing of course that the customers pay their way and follow the rules of decorum. Section 6 simply restates the common law, specifically applied to railroads. *Atchison, Topeka & Santa Fe Railroad Company v. Denver & New Orleans Railroad*, 110 U.S. 667 (1884) (Waite, C.J.); *Bayles v. Kansas Pacific. R. Co.*, 13 Colo. 181, 22 P. 341 (1889).

Section 6 prohibits "undue or unreasonable discrimination" in rates. The section does not prohibit *all* discrimination. For example, a railroad says: If you want to ship freight on one car for a certain distance, the price is X. If you rent five cars, you get a discount; the price per car is 95% of X. If you rent twenty cars, the price per car is 80% of X. The price discrimination is not undue or unreasonable. It reflects the fact that bulk sales reduce overhead costs for suppliers. It is less expensive for a railroad to sell 20 cars at once than to sell 20 cars one at a time.

What is "undue or unreasonable discrimination"? The types of deals that railroads sometimes made with large customers to sell cars at certain quantities for certain rates *and* to deny the customers' competitors the opportunity to buy cars under the same terms.

Art. XV, Section 7. (repealed)

Repealed 2000. Formerly, all railroad and transportation companies in existence as of 1876 must file with the secretary of state a binding affirmation accepting the Colorado Constitution.

Art. XV, Section 8. Corporations may not be exempted from eminent domain

> The right of eminent domain shall never be abridged nor so construed as to prevent the general assembly from taking the property and franchises of incorporated companies, and subjecting them to public use, the same as the property of individuals; and the police power of the state shall never be abridged or so construed as to permit corporations to conduct their business in such manner as to infringe the equal rights of individuals or the general well-being of the state.

State and local special grants to favored corporations are common today. Do such grants "infringe the equal rights of individuals"?

Governments' eminent domain powers are limited by the Bill of Rights, sections 14 and 15. However, the protections have been greatly weakened by judicial interpretation. Chapter 4 (Bill of Rights).

Statutes on eminent domain are C.R.S. § 38-1-101 et seq.

Art. XV, Section 9. Fictitious stock

> No corporation shall issue stocks or bonds, except for labor done, service performed, or money or property actually received, and all fictitious increase of stock or indebtedness shall be void. The stock of corporations shall not be increased except in pursuance of general law, nor without the consent of the persons holding a majority of the stock, first obtained at a meeting held after at least thirty days' notice given in pursuance of law.

Fictitious stock is also known as "watered stock." For example, a corporation makes an initial public offering. Investors buy 100,000 shares, for $10 apiece. If you bought a thousand shares, you own 1% of the corporation. Later, the corporation issues a million new shares, and gives them to people who paid nothing. Under the Colorado Constitution, the new stock is "void" and "fictitious."

The Colorado Constitution protects the rights of legitimate shareholders. No new stock may be issued without their consent. The issuance of such stock without stockholder consent is *ipso facto* invalid. *In re Dreiling*, 233 Bankruptcy Rep. 848 (Bankruptcy Ct., D. Colo. 1999). The implementing statute is C.R.S. § 7-56-202. Stock shares may not be issued in exchange for a promissory note or a promise of future services. *Haselbush v. Alsco of Colo., Inc.*, 161 Colo. 138, 421 P.2d 113 (1966).

Art. XV, Section 10. Foreign corporations must have a Colorado agent

> No foreign corporation shall do any business in this state without having one or more known places of business, and an authorized agent or agents in the same, upon whom process may be served.

Section 10 requires that corporations doing business in Colorado be liable to suit in Colorado state courts.

The mere existence of a Colorado agent for an out-state-corporation does not make the corporation a resident of Colorado. Nor is the county where the agent's office is located a proper venue for a suit against the corporation. *Magill v. Ford Motor Company*, 379 P.3d 1033 (Colo. 2016).

Art. XV, Section 11. No street railroads without municipal consent

> No street railroad shall be constructed within any city, town, or incorporated village, without the consent of the local authorities having the control of the street or highway proposed to be occupied by such street railroad.

As of 1876, a hugely important national issue. Railroads were running lines through densely populated parts of towns, with predictably annoying and sometimes fatal results. Indeed, there were nationwide riots over the problem in July 1877. *See* DAVID O. STOWELL, STREETS, RAILROADS, AND THE GREAT STRIKE OF 1877 (1999).

In 1876, Colorado had relatively little railroad infrastructure compared to most other states. So, the Constitution was proactive against a problem known in other states.

The general assembly may impose restrictions on street railroads, even if those restrictions are not favored by the municipality where the railroad will be built. *City of Denver v. Mercantile Trust Co. of New York*, 201 F. 790 (8th Cir. 1912).[4]

Art. XV, Section 12. No retrospective laws

> The general assembly shall pass no law for the benefit of a railroad or other corporation, or any individual or association of individuals, retrospective in its operation, or which imposes on the people of any county or municipal subdivision of the state, a new liability in respect to transactions or considerations already past.

This has been held to be a mere restatement of the general prohibition on retrospective laws in the Bill of Rights, article II, § 11. *Continental Title Insurance Co. v. District Court*, 645 P.2d 1310, 1314 n.5 (Colo. 1982).

Art. XV, Section 13. No consolidation of telegraph lines

> Any association or corporation, or the lessees or managers thereof, organized for the purpose, or any individual, shall have the right to construct and maintain lines of telegraph within this state, and to connect the same with other lines, and the general assembly shall, by general law, of uniform operation, provide reasonable regulations to give full effect to this section. No telegraph company shall consolidate with, or hold a controlling interest in, the stock or bonds of any other telegraph company owning or having the control of a competing line, or acquire, by purchase or otherwise, any other competing line of telegraph.

This applies to telegraph lines the same constitutional rules as for railroad lines: interconnection must be allowed; no consolidation or shared ownership of competing lines.

Art. XV, Section 14. Consolidating with a foreign corporation does not create an exemption to Colorado law

> If any railroad, telegraph, express or other corporation organized under any of the laws of this state, shall consolidate, by sale or otherwise, with any railroad, telegraph, express or other corporation organized under any laws of any other state or territory or of the United States, the same shall not thereby become a foreign corporation, but the courts of this state shall retain jurisdiction over that part of the corporate property within the limits of the state in all matters which may arise, as if said consolidation had not taken place.

If a Colorado railroad is bought by a corporation based in another state, the Colorado government retains jurisdiction over all railroad property within Colorado.

When a New Jersey waterworks corporation bought a Colorado one, the former Colorado corporation's assets in Colorado were still subject to seizure, if necessary, for judgments by Colorado courts. But for federal diversity jurisdiction and venue purposes, the new corporation

[4] Colorado was part of the Eighth Circuit until 1929, when the Tenth Circuit was created by the Tenth Circuit Reorganization Act.

was a resident of New Jersey only, not Colorado. *Rust v. United Waterworks Co.*, 70 F. 129 (8th Cir. 1895).

Art. XV, Section 15. Employees may not waive employer liability for personal injury caused by employer negligence

> It shall be unlawful for any person, company or corporation to require of its servants or employees, as a condition of their employment or otherwise, any contract or agreement, whereby such person, company or corporation shall be released or discharged from liability or responsibility on account of personal injuries received by such servants or employees while in the service of such person, company or corporation, by reason of the negligence of such person, company or corporation, or the agents or employees thereof, and such contracts shall be absolutely null and void.

Employers may not require would-be employees to sign a liability waiver for injuries caused by the employer's negligence. Section 15 is a departure from contract and property rights, as they were understood at the time. Thus, the departure needed to be expressly authorized by the new Constitution.

Courts did not extend section 15 beyond its text. The Pullman Company manufactured and operated railroad sleeping cars. The Pullman Company paid the Denver & Rio Grande Railroad Company a fee to carry Pullman cars. The Pullman Company operated and collected all the revenue from passengers using the sleeping cars. A Pullman employee, working on a Pullman car that was carried by the Denver & Rio Grande Railroad, could validly waive injury claims against the railroad, which was not his employer. *Denver & Rio Grande Railroad Co. v. Whan*, 39 Colo. 230, 89 P. 39 (1907).

In 1915, the Colorado Workers' Compensation Act was enacted. As a no-fault insurance system, it obviated the need for tort lawsuits by most workers who were injured on the job.

CHAPTER 21

Mining and Irrigation, article XVI

Figure 36. Two miners taking out ore in the tunnel of a gold mine at Eagle River Canyon, Colorado, ca. 1905.

Here is a Land Where Life is Written in Water

At the base of the rotunda of the Colorado State Capitol is an excerpt from the poem *Here is a Land Where Life is Written in Water*, by Colorado's poet laureate, Thomas Hornsby Ferril. Each pair of lines is illustrated by a beautiful mural:

Men shall behold the Water in the Sky,
And Count the Seasons by the Living Grasses.

Then shall the river namers track the sunset,
Singing the long song to the Shining Mountains.

Here shall the melting peaks renew the oxen,
Here firewood is and here shall men build cities.

Water shall sluice the gold yellow as leaves
That fall from silver trees on silent hills.

And men shall fashion glaciers into greenness
And harvest April rivers in the autumn.

Deep in the earth where roots of willows drank
Shall aqueducts be laid to nourish cities.

Water the lightning gave shall give back lightning
and Men shall store the lightning for their use.

Beyond the Sundown is tomorrow's Wisdom
Today is going to be long long ago.

By Jerry Kopel
Every day, legislators, staff, and lobbyists walk through the rotunda on the first floor of the state capitol building. Some view without really seeing the larger-than-life murals dominating the circular walls.

Tourists do stop and study the pictures. Everyone should stop once in a while to read what is written. The poetry is by Thomas Hornsby Ferril, perhaps the greatest poet Colorado has ever produced. As he wrote, "Here is a land where life is written in water."

According to a Gene Amole column in the *Rocky Mountain News*, Ferril was at an all-male party celebrating painter Allen True's new studio in 1935, when hamburgers were delivered, and the banter turned to the subject of water. As Ferril told Amole:

> I began drawing pictures on the hamburger sack, telling Allen he could make murals out of them. He saved the sack and painted the murals. I had agreed to write the poetic texts.
>
> All eight murals were ready to go up in the rotunda in 1938. Allen had painted them in a greenhouse at City Park . . . So I got up early one morning and wrote all the poem at one sitting. The lettering was done by Pascal Quackenbush. When the government money ran out, the generous Boettchers footed the bill. The job was completed in 1940.

In turn, the last panel is dedicated to Charles Boettcher. I was told the amount donated was between $4,000 and $9,000, not a small sum in the 1930s. And no claim to immortality can be greater than to be part of the capitol rotunda.

Ferril (1896–1988) received many literary awards for his work but never the deserved recognition of being a national poet, critics claiming he was too Western. His former home at 2123 Downing Street in Denver—where he lived 88 of his 92 years—is a Landmark for Preservation site containing Ferril's life work.

Trial by Time, one of the many books of poetry by Ferril, published in 1944, contains the poetry written on the rotunda.

Further reading: A. THOMAS TRUSKY, THOMAS HORNSBY FERRIL (1973); For more on this family of Colorado philanthropists, see

Figure 37. Eight photos of Capitol rotunda. Greg Walcher.

Men shall behold the Water in the Sky
and count the Seasons by the living Grasses.

Then Shall the River-namers track the Sunset
Singing the long song to the Shining Mountains.

Here shall the melting Snows renew the Oxen
here Firewood is and here shall men build Cities.

Water shall sluice the Gold yellow as leaves
that fall from Silver Trees on silent Hills.

And Men shall fashion Glaciers into Greenness
and harvest April rivers in the Autumn.

Deep in the Earth where roots of Willows drank
shall Aqueducts be laid to nourish Cities.

Water the lightning gave shall give back lightning
and Men shall store the lightning for their use.

Beyond the Sundown is tomorrow's Wisdom
Today is going to be long long ago.

Figure 30. The Twin Lakes reservoirs, south of Leadville, as seen from Mount Elbert. These glacial lakes were enlarged into reservoirs as part of the Independence Pass Transmountain Diversion System. Some of the water from the Roaring Fork watershed (West Slope) is diverted to the lakes via the Twin Lakes Tunnel. From Twin Lakes, water flows into the Arkansas River watershed (East Slope). The Twin Lakes dam, constructed in 1978, is operated by the U.S. Bureau of Reclamation.

Art. XVI, Section 1. Commissioner of mines

> There shall be established and maintained the office of commissioner of mines, the duties and salaries of which shall be prescribed by law. When said office shall be established, the governor shall, with the advice and consent of the senate, appoint thereto a person known to be competent, whose term of office shall be four years.

Today, the Director of the Department of Natural Resources may also be the Commissioner of Mines. C.R.S. § 34-21-102.

Art. XVI, Section 2. Laws for mine ventilation and employment of children

> The general assembly shall provide by law for the proper ventilation of mines, the construction of escapement shafts, and such other appliances as may be necessary to protect the health and secure the safety of the workmen therein; and shall prohibit the employment in the mines of children under twelve years of age.

Legislative inaction on mine safety is not an option. The legislature "shall" enact appropriate laws.[1]

Statutes on mine safety are at Title 34, articles 20–31. The minimum age for mine work is presently 14, with appropriate training, or in an apprenticeship program, etc. C.R.S. § 8-12-110.

Section 2 does not address maximum working hours for mines. Legislative power to set maximum hours for mines and other hazardous workplaces was added by amendment of article V in 1901. Art. V, § 25a. The amendment was enacted following the Colorado supreme court decision that an 8-hour limit on working days in underground mines and smelters violated miners' rights to acquire property, under Art. II, § 3. *In re Morgan*, 26 Colo. 415, 58 P. 1071 (1899). *Cf. Dalrymple v. Sevcik*, 80 Colo. 297, 251 P. 134 (1926) (statutory requirements for fans and certified foremen in underground coal mines are reasonable exercise of the police power, and not a violation of the Fourteenth Amendment).

Art. XVI, Section 3. Laws for mine drainage

> The general assembly may make such regulations from time to time, as may be necessary for the proper and equitable drainage of mines.

Unlike mine safety, mine drainage is subject on which the legislature "may" act. Mine drainage laws are at Title 34, articles 50 & 51. The statutes establish Mine Drainage Districts, which supervise mine drainage within their jurisdictions.

---

[1] In 1876 the Territorial Legislature had enacted the first mine safety law. General Laws of Colorado, ch. 15, ¶¶ 144–45 (1877). And also a statute forbidding persons under 14 from working in coal mines. *Id.* at ¶ 151.

Art. XVI, Section 4. Teaching of mining and metallurgy

> The general assembly may provide that the science of mining and metallurgy be taught in one or more of the institutions of learning under the patronage of the state.

The result is the Colorado School of Mines (C.R.S. § 23-41-101 et seq.), as well as mining and metallurgy classes at other state institutions of higher education. The School of Mines had been established by the territorial legislature in 1874.[2]

The original 1876 Constitution had encouraged mining by providing a 10-year property tax exemption for mines that had no net income. Former art. X, § 3 (1876).

Further reading on Colorado mining:

Colorado Geological Survey, *Mining History of Colorado* (2001). Two-page summary for gold, silver, molybdenum, uranium, coal, marble, gemstones, gypsum, soda ash, and others.

DANA ECHOHAWK, COLORADO MINING HISTORY RESOURCE GUIDE (Center for Colorado and the West at the Auraria Library, 2013). This modern bibliography includes regional and topical chapters, and guides for further research.

JAMES EDWARD FELL, JR., ORES TO METALS: THE ROCKY MOUNTAIN SMELTING INDUSTRY (2009). Without efficient smelting, the mining of Colorado ores would be economically impossible. It is no exaggeration to say that improvements in smelting in the decades following the Gold Rush saved Colorado.

WILLIAM GILPIN, GUIDE TO THE KANSAS GOLD MINES AT PIKES PEAK, DESCRIBING THE ROUTES, CAMPING PLACES, TOOLS, OUTFITS FROM NOTES OF CAPT. J.W. GUNNISON, TOPOGRAPHICAL ENGINEER. ALSO AN ADDRESS ON THE NEW GOLD MINES, DELIVERED AT KANSAS CITY (Nolie Mumey ed., facsimile reprint 1952) (1859). Colorado's greatest early booster and visionary.

CHARLES WILLIAM HENDERSON, MINING IN COLORADO: A HISTORY OF DISCOVERY, DEVELOPMENT AND PRODUCTION (Washington: U.S. Department of the Interior, 1926).

JOSEPH E. KING, A MINE TO MAKE A MINE: FINANCING THE COLORADO MINING INDUSTRY, 1859–1902 (1977).

MICHAEL NEUSCHATZ, THE GOLDEN SWORD: THE COMING OF CAPITALISM TO THE COLORADO MINING FRONTIER (1986).

OLIN GLENN SAXON, COLORADO AND ITS MINING INDUSTRY (1859–1959) (Denver: Mining and Petroleum Committee, Colorado State Chamber of Commerce, 1959).

LEE SCAMEHORN, HIGH ALTITUDE: A HISTORY OF FOSSIL FUELS IN COLORADO (2002).

DUANE A. SMITH, ROCKY MOUNTAIN MINING CAMPS: THE URBAN FRONTIER (1974).

DUANE A. SMITH, THE TRAIL OF GOLD AND SILVER: MINING IN COLORADO, 1859–2009 (2009).

ELLIOTT WEST, THE CONTESTED PLAINS: INDIANS, GOLDSEEKERS AND THE RUSH TO COLORADO (2000).

Jonathan Wood, *Prospecting for Pollution: The Need for Better Incentives to Clean Up Abandoned Mines*, POLITICAL ECONOMY RESEARCH CENTER (2020).

---

[2] In 1870, the territorial legislature made a controversial $3,800 grant to Episcopal Bishop George M. Randall, to establish an institution for instruction in mining ("Jarvis Hall") at the College of St. John the Evangelist, in Golden. In 1874, the entire institution was transferred to the territory, and renamed the Colorado School of Mines.

Art. XVI, Section 5. Water of streams is public property

> The water of every natural stream, not heretofore appropriated, within the state of Colorado, is hereby declared to be the property of the public, and the same is dedicated to the use of the people of the state, subject to appropriation as hereinafter provided.

In semiarid Colorado, survival has always depended on the wise and sustainable use of water. Without irrigation, Colorado could grow few crops, except near stream beds. Breaking from the common law, the Convention constitutionalized a new system of water law, designed to encourage beneficial use. California had already developed a similar system, but Colorado was the first to constitutionalize it. Colorado's model was later followed by other Western states.

According to section 5, water *that has not already been appropriated* belongs to the people. However, as the next section provides, any unappropriated water may be appropriated by beneficial use.

Art. XVI, Section 6. Priority of appropriation for water rights

> The right to divert the unappropriated waters of any natural stream to beneficial uses shall never be denied. Priority of appropriation shall give the better right as between those using the water for the same purpose; but when the waters of any natural stream are not sufficient for the service of all those desiring the use of the same, those using the water for domestic purposes shall have the preference over those claiming for any other purpose, and those using the water for agricultural purposes shall have preference over those using the same for manufacturing purposes.

Colorado was the first state to constitutionalize the Doctrine of Prior Appropriation.[3] The doctrine repeals the common law of water priority. Under the common law, if water flows through your land, you have the right to that flow, regardless of whether you use it. The common law favors *riparian rights*. The common law was a practical system in Great Britain and the eastern United States, where water is plentiful.

Semiarid Colorado needed to use water efficiently. Unlike the common law, prior appropriation favors the first person to put water to use. In 1872, territorial court chief justice Moses Hallett[4] had explained why Colorado could not follow the common law of water:

---

[3] Some modern articles on the Doctrine of Prior Appropriation: Gregory J. Hobbs, Jr., *Distributive Water Justice: Colorado's Doctrine of Prior Appropriation Incorporates Instream Flow Rights on Behalf of the People*, 22 U. DENVER WATER L. REVIEW 377 (2019) (Supreme court justice and expert on water law); Steven M. Smith, *Instream Flow Rights within the Prior Appropriation Doctrine: Insights from Colorado*, 59 NAT. RESOURCES J. 181 (2019); Lawrence J. MacDonnell, *Prior Appropriation: A Reassessment*, 18 U. DENVER WATER L. REVIEW 228 (2015); Lauren R. Bushong, *How Colorado's Prior Appropriation System Addresses Environmental and Recreational Concerns Without a Public Trust Doctrine*, 18 U. DENVER WATER L. REVIEW 462 (2015); Duane Rudolph, *Why Prior Appropriation Needs Equity*, 18 U. DENVER WATER L. REVIEW 348 (2015); Reed D. Benson, *Alive but Irrelevant: The Prior Appropriation Doctrine in Today's Western Water Law*, 83 U. COLO. L. REVIEW 675 (2012).

[4] James Faulkner Pinkney, *Moses Hallett*, 2 ROCKY MNTN. L. REVIEW 173 (1929-1930) (now the Univ. of Colo. L. Review).

> rules respecting the tenure of property must yield to the physical laws of nature, whenever such laws exert a controlling influence . . . When the lands of this territory were derived from the general [U.S.] government, they were subject to the law of nature, which holds them barren until awakened to fertility by nourishing streams of water, and the purchasers could have no benefit from the grant without the right to irrigate them.

Yunker v. Nichols, 1 Colo. 551 (1871).

"Beneficial use" specifically includes domestic, agriculture, and manufacturing (§ 6) plus mining and drainage (§ 7). These terms are interpreted broadly. *See Lamborn v. Bell*, 18 Colo. 346, 32 P. 989 (1893) ("manufacturing" includes milling).

"Beneficial use" is not limited only to the enumerated items. It also includes land reclamation, and instream flow rights for fishing and wildlife conservation. *State Dept. of Nat. Res. v. Southwest Colo. Water Cons. District*, 671 P.2d 1294 (Colo. 1983) (reclamation); *Colorado River Water Conservancy Dist. v. Colorado Water Conservancy Board*, 197 Colo. 469, 594 P.2d 570 (1979).

Water owned by the Southern Ute Indian Reservation in southwestern Colorado is *not* subject to the requirement of beneficial use. *Winters v. United States*, 207 U.S. 564 (1908) (having natural resources available is essential to the purpose of a reservation, so beneficial use is not required).

Art. XVI, Section 7. Right-of-way for ditches, canals, and flumes

> All persons and corporations shall have the right-of-way across public, private and corporate lands for the construction of ditches, canals and flumes for the purpose of conveying water for domestic purposes, for the irrigation of agricultural lands, and for mining and manufacturing purposes, and for drainage, upon payment of just compensation.

Section 7 gives water users a limited power of eminent domain. Upon payment of just compensation, a water user gets an easement to construct ditches, canals, or flumes (artificial channels, often used for logs). The Private Takings Clause of the Bill of Rights, art. II, § 14, likewise authorizes private eminent domain for water channels.[5]

Section 7 is also used by municipal corporations (towns and cities) for eminent domain for water channels. As discussed in chapter 24 (Home Rule, art. XX), home rule jurisdictions have extraterritorial eminent domain power. They have frequently used that power to take water rights.

Front range cities used eminent domain to divert Western Slope water. Eighty percent of Colorado's population lives east of the Continental Divide, whereas eighty percent of Colorado's water is west of the Divide. Without transmountain diversions, the Front Range could not sustain its current population, and this has been the case for many decades.

Although perhaps self-executing, section 7 is still subject to statutory regulation. *CAW Equities, L.L.C. v. City of Greenwood Village*, 2018 COA 42M, 425 P.3d 1197 (Colo. App. 2018).

---

[5] An especially successful example of irrigation in the 1870s was the Union Colony, in Greeley. Founded by Horace Greeley and Nathan Meeker, the colony was a cooperative agricultural society that built reservoirs, canals, and ditches for water from the Cache la Poudre River. DAVID BOYD, A HISTORY: GREELEY AND THE UNION COLONY (1890).

Art. XVI, Section 8. County commissioners may fix water rates

> The general assembly shall provide by law that the board of county commissioners in their respective counties, shall have power, when application is made to them by either party interested, to establish reasonable maximum rates to be charged for the use of water, whether furnished by individuals or corporations.

County commissioners can set reasonable maximum charges for the use of water, regardless of whether the water seller is an individual or a corporation. The seller may seek judicial review if the rate is allegedly arbitrary or confiscatory. *Montezuma Water & Land Co. v. McCracken*, 62 Colo. 394, 163 P.286 (1917).

As of 1876, government price-fixing was generally disfavored, as a violation of liberty of contract. Accordingly, the authorization of price-fixing for a particular commodity was an appropriate topic to constitutionalize.

A brief overview of Colorado water law

The following is based mainly on P. ANDREW JONES & TOM CECH, COLORADO WATER LAW FOR NON-LAWYERS (2009). Notwithstanding the title, it is very useful for lawyers who are not already water law experts.[6]

In every state except Colorado, water rights are primarily adjudicated by a State Engineer, or some other executive branch office. In Colorado, decisions are made by specialized Water Courts.[7]

Under the English common law of riparian water rights, each riparian right is of equal priority. Thus, rights are correlative; if a drought reduces water flow in a stream, all riparian owners suffer equal diminishment. The quantity of water that a riparian owner may use is not specified; rather the owner may use as much water as is reasonable and beneficial to the riparian land. Water rights are part of the riparian land right and may not be transferred separately. Water may not be diverted outside of its natural watershed. Riparian rights are not lost by nonuse of the water. If the riparian land parcel is subdivided, land that is no longer riparian no longer has any water rights, unless the transfer specifies otherwise.

Colorado and most of the Western U.S. differ in every respect. In the West, the differences began with mining. Water is necessary for mining, but many mines were not on riparian land. If the miners had not been able to acquire water rights, mining, and hence the (non-Indian) settlement of Colorado would have been economically impossible.

Also, the loam soils of the South Platte and Arkansas River basins turned out to be excellent for agriculture—but only if they were irrigated.

Water rights only arise when water is *diverted* and put to *beneficial use*. In current law, some undisturbed natural flows are considered beneficial use, for purposes such as fishing and conservation.

---

[6] For more intricate legal analysis, a useful treatise is JAMES N. CORBRIDGE, JR. & TERESA A. RICE, VRANESH'S COLORADO WATER LAW (rev. ed. 2000). George Vranesh was a leading Colorado water lawyer of the latter 20th century. The 2000 edition consolidates his three-volume treatise into a single, more readable volume, and provides updates. The passage of years makes it less complete than it once was, but still informational.

[7] Created in 1919. 1919 Colo. Sess. Laws 487.

Under prior appropriation, the rule is "first in time, first in right."[8] In other words, the first user acquires the right to as much water from a stream as he is actually uses. Any subsequent user of the remaining water is *junior* to the *senior* water right. If there is a shortage, such as in a drought, the junior users must forego all their water use before senior users must forego any.

Among the states, Colorado has the "purest" version of the prior appropriation doctrine.

Determining priority is not always easy, since rights arise at the time of the first beneficial use, and there was originally no stable system of recording rights.[9] When land is conveyed in Colorado, the typical instrument is a *warranty deed*, by which the seller warrants that the seller has full rights to the land. The warranty deed is usually backed up by *title insurance*; the insurance company will issue the insurance after a straightforward review of land title records in the county clerk's office. In contrast, water rights conveyances almost never have a warranty deed. Instead, the more common conveyance is a *quit claim deed*, by which the seller conveys whatever rights he owns, but makes no guarantee that there are not more senior rights to the water.

The doctrine of prior appropriation aims to discourage waste. A water right exists only to the extent it is put to beneficial use.

Although constitutionalized in 1876, Colorado water law had begun to diverge from riparian doctrine earlier. The first legislature of the Territory of Colorado in 1861 enacted legislation allowing water to be diverted to non-riparian lands.

Certainty of ownership of water rights is impaired by decisions holding that the federal government has implicit "reserved" water rights on federal lands, including Indian reservations, National Forests, National Parks, and Bureau of Land Management land. Since 36% of Colorado is federal land, this can have a major impact on even the most senior water rights. The 2016 Colorado Water Rights Protection Act, C.R.S. § 37-92-310, orders Colorado's State Engineer to refuse to enforce or administer federal water claims that violate Colorado law

In the water-scarce West, interstate conflicts over water rights are common. If Colorado used all the water it wanted, then Kansas might get nothing from rivers that originate in Colorado.

As the only continental state from which all water flows *out*, and none flows *in*, Colorado is ripe for conflict with its neighbors.[10] Interstate conflicts are generally resolved by *interstate compacts*, of which Colorado is party to nine involving water.[11] Disputes arising under the compacts created long-enduring cases and offspring of such cases. For example, Kansas versus Colorado water law cases have been heard seven times by the U.S. supreme court.[12]

Starting in 1881, water rights were administered by the office of the State Engineer. Colorado was the first state to create an office for water management. Today, Colorado is divided into 7 Water Divisions, which are administered by *division engineers* in the Colorado Division of Water Resources, a part of the Department of Natural Resources. The division engineers supervise *river commissioners*—field staff who have the responsibility to open or cut off water flow at *headgates*, so that senior users' flows are protected during times of heavy demand.

---

[8] Based on the equity maxim *Qui priore est in tempore, potior est in jure.*

[9] Starting with the Adjudication Act of 1879, water rights claimants must file a claim in court; if the court finds their claim valid, a decree will be issued.

[10] One partial exception: the Green River starts in Colorado, flows into Wyoming, and then flows back into Colorado, before eventually leaving the state for good.

[11] Colorado River Compact (Calif., Ariz., Nev., N.M. Utah, Wyo., 1922); La Plata River Compact (N.M., 1923); South Platte River Compact (Neb., 1923); Rio Grande Compact (N.M., Tex., 1938); Republican River Compact (Kan., Neb., 1942); Upper Colorado River Compact (N.M., Utah, Wyo., 1948); Arkansas River Compact (Kan., 1949); Costilla Creek Compact (N.M., 1963); Animas-Las Plata Project Compact (N.M., 1969).

[12] *Kansas v. Colorado*, 185 U.S. 125 (1902); *Kansas v. Colorado*, 206 U.S. 46 (1907); *Colorado v. Kansas*, 320 U.S. 383 (1943); *Kansas v. Colorado*, 514 U.S. 673 (1995); *Kansas v. Colorado*, 533 U.S. 1 (2001); *Kansas v. Colorado*, 543 U.S. 86 (2004); *Kansas v. Colorado*, 556 U.S. 98 (2009).

Water rights in Colorado are precious. For example, the value of surface water rights in the South Platte basin is equal to about 6% of the state's total gross domestic product.

Because water rights are fully transferable, and the water need not be kept in its original watershed, water rights naturally flow to whomever will pay the most for them. This is economically efficient. However, it means that agricultural landowners on the eastern plains may sell their water rights to residential developers on the Front Range. The sales are creating a cycle that depopulates the farming communities of the plains.

Some holders of Colorado water rights

Mutual ditch companies. These private companies acquired water rights by being the first to put certain water to beneficial use, by building ditches to divert it. Water rights to the ditch water are proportionate, based on the number of shares of the ditch company held by an individual.

Irrigation districts. An early form of special districts. A majority of landowners in an area may petition their Board of County Commissioners to create an irrigation district in the area. The irrigation district will be governed by directors elected by the landowners. The district may buy and sell water rights. Colorado has 16 irrigation districts, mainly on the plains and the northwest.

Water Conservancy Districts. Pursuant to the Water Conservancy Act of 1937, these districts may be created by decree of a district court. They have the powers to tax and to condemn property by eminent domain. Directors are appointed by the district judge. They may develop water and provide water to customers for a fee. Colorado has about 50 water conservancy districts.

Water Conservation Districts. There are four of these, all created by the legislature. They cover large geographic areas and are intended to play a leading role in water planning, development, and conservation. They are often involved in interstate litigation. Among their functions are to buy up and retire water rights, so that Colorado water usage does not put the state in violation of interstate compacts.

Municipal and other special improvement districts. Governed by a board of directors elected by water users in the area, the districts receive revenue from water fees and from property taxes. They can issue bonds. They are one of the most common types of special districts. As in any special district, property taxes (or user fees) may be much higher than on nearby land that is not part of the district.

Municipalities typically buy water rights for development, but they may also buy rights for recreational water use, such as fishing. As noted, this qualifies as beneficial use.

Colorado Water Conservation Board. Created by the legislature, its purpose is to hold water rights and use them to preserve or augment in-stream flows. For example, if the City of Boulder wishes to preserve Boulder Creek for recreation, it can purchase the senior rights for the creek and dedicate those rights to the CWCB.

The above is a simplified explanation of water rights for surface flows from rivers, creeks, and streams, which are *tributary water*. Water rights also exist for three other types of water: *non-tributary and not non-tributary groundwater*, *designated groundwater*, and *exempt wells*. Wells and subsurface water were not much of an issue until the 1950s, when technology first allowed them to be used for large-scale irrigation. Because groundwater may be connected to tributary waters, the conflicts among various types of water rights can keep lawyers in clover.

Ralph Carr's defense of state rights and water rights

Today Ralph Carr is remembered for his outstanding two terms as governor. He was urged to run for office because of his universally admired record as defender of Colorado water rights. As an assistant attorney general in the 1920s, he had negotiated water compacts with other states. His

U.S. supreme court victory for the Colorado state engineer added to his luster. *Hinderlider v. La Plata River & Cherry Creek Ditch Co.*, 304 U.S. 92 (1938); ADAM SCHRAGER, THE PRINCIPLED POLITICIAN: THE RALPH CARR STORY 10–11 (1938).

When Carr was governor, the Franklin Roosevelt administration proposed the Arkansas Valley Authority Act. The bill was modeled on the Tennessee Valley Authority (TVA), by which the federal government had taken over water in the impoverished valleys and then provided flood control and electricity.

But most Coloradans, including governor Carr, fervently opposed an AVA. It would upset the interstate compacts Colorado had negotiated, destroy water rights in the Arkansas Valley, forbid state management of the Arkansas River without advance federal permission, and subject the people in the valley to an unaccountable federal entity with eminent domain power.

According to Carr, "In short, the whole system of life within these river basins is to be altered and changed to conform with a theory of government which nullifies constitutional rights and leaves individual states stripped of everything but their names . . . Either we are to continue to retain some semblance of state rights and state individuality, or else we are to surrender every power of self-determination."

Carr's relentless leadership and lobbying were so effective that the proposed AVA never came up for a vote in Congress. The defeat of the AVA was one of the biggest successes in Carr's perpetual campaign against the New Deal. SCHRAGER at 65–69.

Further reading: Greg Walcher, *Where Life is Written in Water: Why Water Issues Unite, Divide, and Matter So Much in Colorado*, INDEPENDENCE INSTITUTE, Issue Paper 1-2021 (Mar. 2021) (superb explanation and analysis of current issues, such as sales of agricultural water rights for suburban expansion, troubles caused by invasive tamarisk trees, and much more); Greg Hobbs, Jr., *History of Colorado River Law, Development and Use: A Primer and Look Forward*, paper presented at Hard Times on the Colorado River: Drought, Growth and the Future of the Compact (Univ. of Colo. Law School Summer Conference, June 8-10, 2005); Water Education Colorado, https://www.watereducationcolorado.org/.

CHAPTER 22

Militia, article XVII

Art. XVII, Section 1. Militiamen

> The militia of the state shall consist of all able-bodied male residents of the state between the ages of eighteen and forty-five years; except, such persons as may be exempted by the laws of the United States, or of the state.

This mostly parallels the federal definition of the militia of the United States, originally governed by the 1792 Second Militia Act, and currently codified at 10 U.S.C. § 246.[1] The state militia automatically incorporates the federal exemptions (*e.g.*, chaplains). The state may add additional exemptions.

If you fit the definition, you a member of the militia of the State of Colorado *and* you are a member of the militia of the United States.

Calling Forth

In Colorado, "The governor shall be commander-in-chief of the military forces of the state, except when they shall be called into actual service of the United States. He shall have power to call out the militia to execute the laws, suppress insurrection or repel invasion." COLO. CONST., art. V, § 4.

The U.S. Constitution's Calling Forth Clause grants Congress the power "To provide for calling forth the Militia to execute the Laws of the Union, suppress Insurrections and repel Invasions." Congress has provided for calling forth the militia of the U.S. by enacting a statute delegating the calling forth power the president, and by setting conditions therefor.

The Insurrection Act of 1807, as amended, was invoked by presidents Eisenhower and Kennedy to quash violent resistance to federal court orders for school desegregation. President G.H.W. Bush used the insurrection act to attempt to suppress the Rodney King riots in Los Angeles in 1992. In all these situations, the president called forth the state National Guards (the organized class of the militia) and put them into federal (not state) service.

1

(a) The militia of the United States consists of all able-bodied males at least 17 years of age and, except as provided in section 313 of title 32, under 45 years of age who are, or who have made a declaration of intention to become, citizens of the United States and of female citizens of the United States who are members of the National Guard.

(b) The classes of the militia are--

(1) the organized militia, which consists of the National Guard and the Naval Militia; and

(2) the unorganized militia, which consists of the members of the militia who are not members of the National Guard or the Naval Militia.

Art. XVII, Section 2. Organization, equipment, and discipline shall conform to U.S. army regulations

> The organization, equipment and discipline of the militia shall conform as nearly as practicable, to the regulations for the government of the armies of the United States.

The Constitution grants Congress the powers "to provide for organizing, arming, and disciplining, the Militia, and for governing such Part of them as may be employed in the Service of the United States, reserving to the States respectively, the Appointment of the Officers, and the Authority of training the Militia according to the discipline prescribed by Congress" U.S. CONST., art. I, § 8.

In response to Anti-Federalist fears that Congress would abuse its militia powers by putting every militiaman (most of the able-bodied adult male population) under the power of military courts, the Fifth Amendment guarantees the right to grand jury indictment, "except in cases arising in the land or naval forces, or in the Militia when in actual service in time of War or public danger."

Sections 1 and 2 of article XVII incorporate by reference future federal changes in federal militia law, which then become applicable to the Colorado militia via sections 1 and 2. The Colorado application of a federal change was challenged as violating Colorado's article V, since the change had not been enacted as law by the legislature. The Colorado supreme court, however, held that the specific controls the general, and article XVII creates exceptions to the general article V rules about law-making. *People ex rel. Boatwright v. Newlon*, 77 Colo. 516, 238 P. 44 (1925).

Art. XVII, Section 3. Militia officers

> The governor shall appoint all general, field and staff officers and commission them. Each company shall elect its own officers, who shall be commissioned by the governor; but if any company shall fail to elect such officers within the time prescribed by law, they may be appointed by the governor.

A statute requires that the adjutant general, the highest-ranking officer of the militia, be confirmed by the Senate. C.R.S. § 28-3-105(1). Today, the Adjutant General is the chief executive of the Colorado National Guard. The Colorado National Guard was organized pursuant to an 1879 statute.[2]

Note the guarantee in the U.S. Constitution, art. I, § 8, that even when a state militia is called into federal service, the state controls the appointment of officers.

Art. XVII, Section 4. Armories

> The general assembly shall provide for the safekeeping of the public arms, military records, relics and banners of the state.

---

[2] The Colorado National Guard consists of the Army Guard and the Air Guard, with a total membership of over 5,000. The Colorado National Guard is part of the Colorado Department of Military Affairs. The other part of the department is the Colorado Civil Air Patrol, which is tied to the U.S. Air Force, and has over 2,000 members. RICHARD COLLINS & DALE A. OESTERLE, THE COLORADO STATE CONSTITUTION 340 (2d ed. 2020).

Like mine safety (art. XVI, § 2), armories are a "shall" duty of the legislature.

"Public arms" are government-owned arms that are given or loaned to militiamen who cannot afford their own. Public arms are also a reserve for anyone's arms that are broken during militia service, such as in combat. *See, e.g.*, David B. Kopel & Stephen P. Halbrook, *Tench Coxe and the Right to Keep and Bear Arms in the Early Republic*, 7 WM. & MARY BILL OF RIGHTS J. 347 (1999) (federal public arms program under presidents Jefferson and Madison).

Art. XVII, Section 5. Peacetime exemption for conscientious objectors

> No person having conscientious scruples against bearing arms shall be compelled to do militia duty in time of peace.

The Constitution mandates an exemption for conscientious objectors during peacetime. During wartime, the matter is left to legislative choice.

For the peacetime exemption, the 1876 Constitution included the proviso "provided, such person shall pay an equivalent for such exemption." Paying "an equivalent" is a tax as a substitute for personal service. It was a frequent requirement for conscientious objector exemptions in the laws of many states. In Colorado, the rule was repealed in 2002.

The Colorado Constitution right to keep and bear arms (art. II, § 13) includes two separate purposes: 1. "in defense or home, person, or property" *and* 2. "in aid of the civil power when thereto legally summoned." The second purpose meshes well with article XVII, so that militiamen will have their personal arms available for militia service, if they are called forth.

History of the National Guard

After the War of 1812 ended in 1815, most states, except Massachusetts, were desultory about training their militias.[3] Consequently, civic-minded men created volunteer militia units, most famously the Zouaves. The volunteer militias assembled for military practice and camaraderie. Typically, they received a charter from the state and their officers were granted state military commissions by the governor. During wartime, such as the Mexican War and especially the Civil War, the units volunteered *en masse*. Their units usually entered federal service intact. *See* JERRY COOPER, THE RISE OF THE NATIONAL GUARD: THE EVOLUTION OF THE AMERICAN MILITIA, 1865–1920 (2002); JERRY M. COOPER, THE MILITIA AND THE NATIONAL GUARD IN AMERICA SINCE COLONIAL TIMES: A RESEARCH GUIDE (1993); MARCUS CUNLIFFE, SOLDIERS AND CIVILIANS: THE MARTIAL SPIRIT IN AMERICA 1775–1865, at 177–254 (1968).

Volunteer militias from New York and Massachusetts helped save Washington, D.C., from Confederate invasion during the chaotic period after the attack on Fort Sumter. *Id.* at 252–54.

Toward the end of the Civil War, a new sort of independent state volunteer force arose. These militias usually called themselves the "National Guard." During the latter decades of the nineteenth century, they received official state recognition, financial support, and training. Eventually, they were absorbed into the state governments.

The National Guard soon developed a symbiotic relationship with the National Rifle Association. The NRA's 1871 corporate charter from New York State included the purpose "to promote the introduction of a system of aiming drill and target firing among the National Guard

---

[3] The sections on the National Guard and State Defense forces are from NICHOLAS J. JOHNSON, DAVID B. KOPEL, GEORGE A. MOCSARY, E. GREGORY WALLACE & DONALD J. KILMER, FIREARMS LAW AND THE SECOND AMENDMENT: REGULATION, RIGHTS, AND POLICY (Wolters Kluwer, 3d ed. 2021).

of New York and the militia of other states." JAMES B. TREFETHEN, AMERICANS AND THEIR GUNS 10 (1967). The National Guard Association, an organization dedicated to promoting the interests of the National Guard, held its first convention in 1879, electing NRA co-founder George Wingate as its first president. COOPER, RISE OF THE NATIONAL GUARD at 85-88.

During the first two decades of the twentieth century, the leadership of the two organizations closely overlapped. Russell S. Gilmore, *Crackshots and Patriots: The National Rifle Association and America's Military-Sporting Tradition, 1871–1929* (Ph.D. thesis, University of Wisconsin, 1974).

National Guard units participated in the 1898 Spanish-American War. Although they performed better than had the volunteer independent militias in the wars of 1846 or 1861, deficiencies in the quality of their training were apparent. Congress repealed the Militia Act of 1792 and enacted the Militia Act of 1903. 32 Stat. 775 (1903). It is commonly known as the 'Dick Act" for its sponsor representative Charles W.F. Dick, a major general in the Ohio National Guard. With important revisions five years later, 35 Stat. 399 (1908), the Dick Act remains the foundation of current federal militia law.

The Dick Act gave formal federal recognition and financial support to the National Guard. It defined the "organized militia" of the United States as the National Guard, plus the Naval Militias maintained by some states. 10 U.S.C. § 247(b)(1). The Dick Act definition of the "unorganized militia" is discussed below.

Units of the National Guard are organized by state. When not called into active federal service, guard members are under the command of their state's governor. So, in one sense, the guard is part of the state militia. Over the past century, however, both congressional legislation and judicial decisions have narrowed the distinctions between the National Guard and the regular federal armed forces.

The National Defense Act of 1916 substantially increased federal control over the National Guard, giving it much more the character of a reserve unit of the standing army than a state-controlled militia. 39 Stat. 166 (1916). The 1916 Act asserted federal government veto power over the appointment of National Guard officers, notwithstanding the language in article I, Section 8, "reserving to the States respectively the Appointment of the Officers" of the militia. Proponents said that they were doing no more than what Patrick Henry, at the Virginia constitutional ratifying convention, had warned that they would be able to do. H.R. Rep. No. 297, 64th Cong., 1st Sess. (1916).

According to long-standing Anglo-American common law, a militia cannot be sent into foreign lands without its consent. So, the National Guard could not be ordered into foreign countries. *See* Authority of President to Send Militia into a Foreign Country, 29 U.S. Op. Atty. Gen. 322 (1912) (Calling Forth Clause authorizes federal militia only to suppress insurrections, execute the laws of the union, and repel invasions).

To evade limits on National Guard deployment, a 1933 law created a system of "dual enlistment." Each person who enlists in a state National Guard unit must simultaneously enlist in the National Guard of the United States, which is a part of the United States Army. Any Guard unit can be called up into federal service as part of the regular armed forces. When summoned into federal service, the Guard unit temporarily ceases to be part of the state National Guard. The 1933 federal powers over the National Guard were based on Congress's army power, not the militia power. 48 Stat. 153 (1933); U.S. CONST. art. I, § 8, cl. 12 (granting Congress the power "To raise and support Armies").

Initially, the federalization power was limited. The president could only order the National Guard to active duty in a national emergency. In 1952, Congress repealed the national emergency requirement, and provided that Guard units could not be ordered to active foreign duty without the consent of the governor of the relevant state. Then in 1986, Congress eliminated a governor's power to refuse deployment outside of the United States if the refusal were because of a governor's "objection to the location, purpose, type, or schedule of such active duty." 10 U.S.C. § 12301(f).

The supreme court unanimously upheld the new legislation against a challenge by Minnesota governor Rudy Perpich. *Perpich v. Department of Defense*, 496 U.S. 334 (1990). He claimed that sending the Minnesota Guard to training in Honduras violated states' prerogatives under the Militia Clauses. The Honduran deployment was controversial, because it was related to a Reagan administration campaign against the communist dictatorship in next-door Nicaragua.

Writing for the court, justice Stevens emphasized that "[t]he congressional power to call forth the militia may in appropriate cases supplement its broader power to raise armies and provide for the common defense and general welfare, but it does not limit those powers." *Id.* at 350. Even if Congress only had militia powers, Congress could "discipline the Militia" by sending it outside of the United States for training. *Id.* at 350–51. *Perpich* does not cite or discuss the Second Amendment.

For more on the National Guard, see, in addition to the sources cited above, MICHAEL D. DOUBLER, THE NATIONAL GUARD AND RESERVE: A REFERENCE HANDBOOK (2008).

State Defense Forces

By the U.S. Constitution, "No State shall . . . keep Troops, or Ships of War in time of Peace" without "the consent of Congress." U.S. CONST. art. I, § 10, cl. 3. In 1956 and 1958 statutes, Congress consented for each state, the District of Columbia, the Commonwealth of Puerto Rico and other U.S. territories, to "organize and maintain defense forces" separate from the National Guard. 32 U.S.C. § 109(c).

Colorado is one of the approximately 20 states (plus Puerto Rico) with a statute for a state defense force, although Colorado's SDF is inactive at present.

By federal statute, the units of the state defense forces' may not be "called, ordered, or drafted into the [United States] armed forces," although their individual members are not exempt from being drafted or otherwise called into federal military service. 32 U.S.C. § 109(c), (d). The sizes of the SDFs vary, though each is smaller than a single brigade (3,000 to 5,000 troops) of the United States Armed Forces or National Guard. Many state defense forces focus more on disaster relief and emergency services than on military training.

According to the Colorado State Defense Force Act, all able-bodied male citizens (and males who have declared an intent to naturalize) ages 18 to 64 are subject to SDF duty. There are various occupational exemptions, including police, firefighters, judges, "ministers of the gospel," plus staff at hospitals, prisons, and jails.[4] Conscientious objectors are to be assigned to noncombatant service.

The composition and operation of the SDF is to be determined by the governor, but the SDF may not include members of the US Armed Forces or of the National Guard. Persons who serve in a SDF are entitled to pay at the rate equivalent to a corresponding rank in the US Army, are considered state employees, and as such are entitled to workers' compensation.[5]

The SDF may not serve outside Colorado except: 1. If the Colorado governor chooses to respond to another governor's call to assist forces "who are actually engaged in defending such

---

[4] The ministerial exemption is miswritten. Under the U.S. First Amendment, a ministerial exemption cannot possibly to limited only to those who proclaim, "the gospel" (the Christian "good news").

Another miswriting is section 28-4-112: "No person shall be commissioned or enlisted in such forces who is not a citizen of the United States." This contradicts section 103.5, which includes in the SDF "those who have declared their intention to become citizens of the United States." The section 112 limit is from the original 1986 statute, while section 103.5 was enacted in 2002, and is therefore controlling.

[5] By separate statute, persons serving in a posse comitatus are also covered by worker's compensation. C.R.S. § 8-40-202.

other state." 2. "in fresh pursuit of insurrectionists, saboteurs, terrorists, enemies, or enemy forces beyond the borders of this state into another state." Forces from other states are granted the right of fresh pursuit into Colorado.

Civil organizations, associations, and other groups may *not* be enlisted in the SDF as a unit. State Defense Force Act, C.R.S. § 28-4-104 through 115.

After the Pearl Harbor attack on Dec. 7, 1941, Colorado governor Ralph Carr mobilized the Colorado Home Guard. At the time, this volunteer force had 200 men, and the governor called for 2,000. The Colorado Home Guard protected critical infrastructure, such as utilities, reservoirs, bridges, and tunnels against saboteurs. Air support was provided by private planes based in Colorado Springs. Local defense councils were set up, and gun clubs provided them training. ADAM SCHRAGER, THE PRINCIPLED POLITICIAN: THE RALPH CARR STORY 80–81, 89 (2008).

CHAPTER 23

Miscellaneous, article XVIII

Art. XVIII, Section 1. Homestead and exemption laws

The general assembly shall pass liberal homestead and exemption laws.

Homestead laws

Homestead laws are an early example of affordable housing policy. The federal Homestead Act of 1862 helped millions of Americans earn their way to home ownership. Such laws give a plot of unused government land to a person who earns title by occupying and improving for a term of years—usually by farming or mining.[1] Today, some small towns in the Midwest will give free land to attract residents. Marquette, Kansas, has shown that the strategy can keep a small town alive.

Compared to the nineteenth century, most governments today are not very interested in giving away their own land to help affordable single-family housing.

Homestead exemption laws

Exemption laws protect a part of a person's property from court judgements, other collections, bankruptcy, and so on.[2]

In *Black's Law Dictionary*, "liberal" means "free in giving, generous, not mean or narrow-minded, not literal or strict."

Liberal exemption and homestead laws are another "shall" duty of the general assembly. The general assembly has sometimes ignored this duty. The 1868 territorial legislature had enacted a $2,000 homestead exemption. General Laws of Colorado chs. 46, 59 (1877). The amount was not raised to account for inflation until 1951, even though the value of the dollar began a long-term decline following the creation of the Federal Reserve in 1913. By 1956, $2,000 was equivalent to $772 in 1913 dollars.

The homestead exemption statutes are at C.R.S. § 38-41-201 et seq. The Colorado homestead exemption is $75,000 for an owner-occupied home, or $105,000 if the owner is elderly or disabled. C.R.S. § 38-41-201(1). (Seventy-five thousand dollars in October 2021 was equivalent to $2,657 in January 1913.) The homestead exemption applies to the equity that the owner has already paid for the home—not for the equity held by a mortgage lender.[3]

In Colorado the homestead exemption also includes "burial sites, including spaces in mausoleums, to the extent of one site or space for the debtor and each dependent." This exemption is as old as the statutes of the first Colorado territory legislature, in 1861.

"Liberal" does not mean "foolish." Some other states have allowed a homestead exemption for the entire value of any home. These states have attracted debtors-on-the-run who establish residency by living there for 91 days. (Federal law forbids a longer standard for residency.) They

---

[1] For the history of the 1862 Act, see HAROLD M. HYMAN, AMERICAN SINGULARITY: THE 1787 NORTHWEST ORDINANCE, THE 1862 HOMESTEAD AND MORRILL ACTS, AND THE 1944 G.I. BILL (1986). The federal act's 160-acre grants were sufficient for fertile areas such as eastern Nebraska or Kansas. The 160-acre limit was too small for most Colorado farms to achieve economic viability.

[2] Although the U.S. Constitution grants Congress the enumerated power to create "uniform Laws on the subject of Bankruptcies throughout the United States," U.S. CONST., art. I, § 8, Congress did not exercise this power until 1898. Even today, some aspects of bankruptcy law, including some of the debtor's exemptions, are set by state law.

[3] In the same spirit, Colorado law limits wage garnishment to no more than 25% of a worker's wages. C.R.S. § 5-5-106. Reforming garnishment was a major concern for Rep. Jerry Kopel, who practiced bankruptcy law with his wife Dolores, in the Kopel & Kopel law firm.

buy multi-million-dollar mansions and claim the "no homestead limit" exemption. Thus, they shelter millions of dollars from creditors.

If you take out a mortgage, the contract will almost certainly require you to waive your homestead exemption rights. So the homestead exemption mostly comes into play when the owner's debt arises from a tort action, medical costs, etc. The home will be sold to satisfy the judgement, but the $75,000 homestead exemption will be given to the former homeowner for a fresh start. The $75,000 equity must be kept in a separate account to be immune from creditors. Within the following two years, the money must be used to purchase another home. The homestead exemption follows into the new residence.

Further reading: Joel S. Thompson, *Homestead Marshalling*, 14 COLO. LAWYER 1612 (1985); Dolores Kopel, *Colorado's Homestead Exemption*, 5 COLO. LAWYER 1059 (1976).

Art. XVIII, Section 2. Lotteries prohibited, except when allowed

Covered in chapter 31 (Vices?).

Art. XVIII, Section 3. Arbitration laws

> It shall be the duty of the general assembly to pass such laws as may be necessary and proper to decide differences by arbitrators, to be appointed by mutual agreement of the parties to any controversy who may choose that mode of adjustment. The powers and duties of such arbitrators shall be as prescribed by law.

Yet another type of law that the general assembly "shall" enact. The initial impetus was speedy resolution of disputed mining claims.

Colorado's adoption of the Uniform Arbitration Act is C.R.S. § 13-22-201 et seq.

Art. XVIII, Section 4. Felony definition

> The term felony, wherever it may occur in this constitution, or the laws of the state, shall be construed to mean any criminal offense punishable by death or imprisonment in the penitentiary, and none other.

State statutes are consistent with this definition. Only an offense that could be punished by a sentence in a state "penitentiary" counts. A sentence that can only be served in a county or municipal jail does not count. *Brooks v. People*, 14 Colo. 413, 24 P. 553 (1890). This means that counties, cities, and towns—even if they have home rule—cannot create felonies.

Art. XVIII, Section 5. (repealed)

Repealed in 2008, section 5 of the 1876 Constitution had ordered the legislature to enact laws prohibiting "spurious, poisonous, or drugged spirituous liquors." Making sure that whiskey is not poisonous is a very good activity for government. Based on 132 years of good legislative behavior, the voters determined that the Constitution no longer needed to specify the order to the general assembly.

Art. XVIII, Section 6. Forests

Covered in chapter 32 (Natural Resources).

Art. XVIII, Section 7. Property tax exemption for planting (repealed)

Repealed in 2008, the 1876 section had provided a property tax exemption for the increased value of planted hedges, orchards, and forests. In a sense, section 7 was a companion to the pro-plant spirit of section 6.

Art. XVIII, Section 8. Publication of laws

> The general assembly shall provide for the publication of the laws passed at each session thereof.

The original version had required that statutes be published in Spanish and German until 1900. However, few people requested such statutes.

When my father got a job at the State Archives in the 1950s, his first assignment was burning books, such as unused old editions of the German language statutes.

The rules for publication of session laws are C.R.S. § 24-70-223. According to *Black's Law Dictionary*, "publication" means "Generally, the act of declaring or announcing to the public." BLACK'S LAW DICTIONARY (11th ed. 2019).

Thus, the Colorado Reapportionment Commission, an arm of the general assembly, did *not* have to publish its plans in newspapers. It was sufficient that the commission merely "mailed a hearing schedule and relevant local and statewide maps showing the proposed new legislative districts to the affected county clerks and recorders, Democratic and Republican county chairpersons, and newspapers and radio stations serving the areas in which the hearings were to be held. Technical descriptions of the proposed districts also were sent to clerks and recorders and party chairpersons." *In re Reapportionment of Colorado General Assembly*, 647 P.2d 191, 195 (Colo. 1982). Thanks to amendments adopted in 2018, the present redistricting process offers much more public transparency. Art. V, §§ 44–44.6, 46–48.4.

The Twelve Tables

The publication of laws is an important protection of civil liberty. When ancient Rome overthrew the Tarquin kings and established a republic, the new republican government required that the laws be published. Before that, the laws had been unwritten, to be interpreted by the upper-class priests (*pontifices*). It was easy for the élite to manipulate the system against the public. In the Roman Republic, the most important laws were written on the Twelve Tables.

The Twelve Tables were, literally, twelve bronze tablets containing the basic legal rules, published in the final form in 449 B.C. They were placed in the Forum, so every citizen could easily read them. They were created after extensive public debate and discussion, by a committee of ten (*decemvirs*), which relied in part on Greek law and which made revisions based on public comment by citizens.[4]

---

[4] TITUS LIVIUS, THE EARLY HISTORY OF ROME 192–248 (book 3, *8–*59) (Aubrey de Sélincourt trans., Penguin Books 1971) (first published sometime during the reign of Augustus Caesar).

Thus, the laws were published, readily accessible, and written to be readily understood by an ordinary citizen. Previously, the laws had been closely guarded by a select few who secretly manipulated and misused the law to their own benefit. As one legal historian summarized:

> From an historical point of view, their importance cannot be overrated. The fixing of the brazen tablets, in a conspicuous position in the heart of the city, marks, at a critical period in the infancy of the commonwealth, the successful issue of one of the many struggles of the plebeian element for that equality of rights which was denied them by the patricians, and which it was vain to look for until a preliminary step had been obtained, viz., the withdrawal, from the hands of a dominant caste, of the exclusive knowledge of, and power of perverting to their own ends, those hitherto unwritten usages which had served the purposes of law.[5]

The principle of section 8 is still at issue today. As the laws governing so many aspects of human behavior have proliferated, how many persons can learn all the laws that apply to them, so that they may obey them? *See, e.g.*, HARVEY SILVERGLATE & ALAN M. DERSHOWITZ, THREE FELONIES A DAY: HOW THE FEDS TARGET THE INNOCENT (2011).

Art. XVIII, Section 9. Limited gambling

Covered in chapter 31 (Vices?).

Art. XVIII, Section 9a. Term limits on U.S. senators and representatives

Adopted by initiative in 1990, section 9a created term limits for federal office. State term limits on congressional representatives have been held unconstitutional because article I, sections 2 & 3 of the U.S. Constitution specify the only permissible restrictions on who may serve in Congress. *U.S. Term Limits, Inc. v. Thornton*, 514 U.S. 779 (1995).

The 1990 amendment proponents knew that term limits were being challenged almost everywhere they were enacted. So subsection (3) states the people's wishes that federal representatives abide by term limits even if not legally forced to do so.

The gambling amendment and the term limits amendment were both on the 1990 ballots as proposed "Section 9." When both passed, gambling became section 9 and term limits became section 9a.

A 1994 amendment cut the number of terms for U.S. Representatives from 6 to 3. The amendment also specifically incorporated the severability rule in the recently adopted article XVIII, section 10.

> (1) In order to broaden the opportunities for public service and to assure that members of the United States Congress from Colorado are representative of and responsive to Colorado citizens, no United States Senator from Colorado shall serve more than two consecutive terms in the United States Senate, and no United States Representative from Colorado shall serve more than three consecutive terms in the United States House of Representatives. This limitation on the number of

[5] T. LAMBERT MEARS, Introduction, to THE INSTITUTES OF GAIUS AND JUSTINIAN: THE TWELVE TABLES, AND THE CXVIIITH AND CXXVIITH NOVELS, lvi (The Lawbook Exchange 2004) (1882).

terms shall apply to terms of office beginning on or after January 1, 1995. Any person appointed or elected to fill a vacancy in the United States Congress and who serves at least one half of a term of office shall be considered to have served a term in that office for purposes of this subsection (1). Terms are considered consecutive unless they are at least four years apart.

(2) The people of Colorado hereby state their support for a nationwide limit of twelve consecutive years of service in the United States Senate and six consecutive years of service in the United States House of Representatives and instruct their public officials to use their best efforts to work for such a limit.

(3) The people of Colorado declare that the provisions of this section shall be deemed severable from the remainder of this measure and that their intention is that federal officials elected from Colorado will continue voluntarily to observe the wishes of the people as stated in this section in the event any provision thereof is held invalid. The severability provisions of Section 10 of Article XVIII of the Colorado Constitution apply to this Section 9a.

Art. XVIII, Section 10. Severability of all constitutional provisions

If any provision of any section of any article in this constitution is found by a court of competent jurisdiction to be unconstitutional, the remaining provisions are valid unless the court holds that the valid provisions are so essentially and inseparably connected with, and so dependent upon, the void provision that it cannot be presumed the enactment of the valid provisions would have occurred without the void one; or unless the court determines that the valid provisions, standing alone, are incomplete and not capable of being executed.

Added in 1992 as a tag-along to an amendment that clarified the rights of local approval of gambling in section 9. Courts generally presume that severability is intended, but section 10 makes sure.

Art. XVIII, Section 11. Term limits for local officials

(1) In order to broaden the opportunities for public service and to assure that elected officials of governments are responsive to the citizens of those governments, no nonjudicial elected official of any county, city and county, city, town, school district, service authority, or any other political subdivision of the State of Colorado, no member of the state board of education, and no elected member of the governing board of a state institution of higher education shall serve more than two consecutive terms in office, except that with respect to terms of office which are two years or shorter in duration, no such elected official shall serve more than three consecutive terms in office. This limitation on the number of terms shall apply to terms of office beginning on or after January 1, 1995. For purposes of this Section 11, terms are considered consecutive unless they are at least four years apart.

(2) The voters of any such political subdivision may lengthen, shorten or eliminate the limitations on terms of office imposed by this Section 11. The voters of the state may lengthen, shorten, or eliminate the limitations on terms of office for the state board of education or the governing board of a state institution of higher education imposed by this Section 11.

(3) The provisions of this Section 11 shall apply to every home rule county, home rule city and county, home rule city and home rule town, notwithstanding any provision of Article XX, or Sections 16 and 17 of Article XIV, of the Colorado Constitution.

Added by 1994 initiative. Separate amendments in articles IV and V provide the term limits of most state officers and for the general assembly. This section covers other elected officials. The voters in local governments may lengthen the term limits, or abolish them, as the voters choose. Many votes have chosen to allow three terms instead of two. Local abolition of term limits has been most common for county coroners and sheriffs.

Art. XVIII, Section 12. Term limits enforcement (repealed)

Adopted 1996, held unconstitutional in *Morrissey v. State*, 951 P.2d 911 (Colo. 1998). Repealed 2002.

The former amendment ordered the general assembly to join the other states that had applied to Congress for a convention to propose a U.S. Constitution term limits amendment. Under the U.S. Constitution's art. V, an amendment can be proposed in either of two ways: 1. By two-thirds of each house of Congress, or 2. In a convention proposed by three-fourths of the states.[6] Historically, when the number of states proposing an amendment approaches three-quarters, a reluctant Congress will propose an amendment itself. That is how the Seventeenth Amendment (popular election of Senators) was proposed.

Secondly, former section 12 instructed Colorado's congressional representatives to vote for a term limits amendment.

Third, if a legislator violated the above, the next ballot would have to include the information that the legislator had disregarded voter instructions on term limits.

Art. XVIII, Section 12a. Ballot information on voluntary congressional term limits

To replace section 12 after it was declared unconstitutional, term limits advocates proposed a milder initiative for ballot information about term limits. Upon adoption by the voters, it became section 12a.

It allows congressional candidates to make a formal declaration that they will voluntarily abide by term limits. Or a candidate may voluntarily file a formal declaration that candidate will

---

[6] From colonial days onward, there is an established tradition of states holding conventions. The traditions show how states vote (one state, one vote), the subject matter (limited to whatever a state's legislature or people authorized its delegates to consider), and so on. *See* Robert G. Natelson, *Founding-Era Conventions and the Meaning of the Constitution's "Convention for Proposing Amendments,"* 65 FLA. L. REVIEW 615 (2013).

not take a term limits pledge. If the candidate requests, ballots must include a notice that the candidate has taken the pledge or has chosen not to.

(1) Information for voters about candidates' decisions to term limit themselves is more important than party labeling, therefore, any candidate seeking to be elected to the United States Congress shall be allowed, but not required, to submit to the secretary of state an executed copy of the Term Limits Declaration set forth in subsection (2) of this section not later than 15 days prior to the certification of every congressional election ballot to each county clerk and recorder by the secretary of state. The secretary of state shall not refuse to place a candidate on any ballot due to the candidate's decision not to submit such declaration.

(2) The language of the Term Limits Declaration shall be as set forth herein and the secretary of state shall incorporate the applicable language in square brackets "[ ]" for the office the candidate seeks:

<u>Congressional Term Limits Declaration</u>

Term Limits Declaration One
Part A: I, __________, voluntarily declare that, if elected, I will not serve in the United States [House of Representatives more than 3 terms] [Senate more than 2 terms] after the effective date of the Congressional Term Limits Declaration Act of 1998.

____

Signature by candidate executes Part A Date

Part B: I, __________, authorize and request that the secretary of state place the applicable ballot designation, "Signed declaration to limit service to no more than [3 terms] [2 terms]" next to my name on every election ballot and <u>in all government-sponsored voter education material</u> in which my name appears as a candidate for the office to which Term Limit Declaration One refers.

____

Signature by candidate executes Part B Date

If the candidate chooses not to execute any or all parts of Term Limits Declaration One, then he or she may execute and submit to the secretary of state any or all parts of Term Limits Declaration Two.

Term Limits Declaration Two

Part A: I, __________, have voluntarily chosen not to sign Term Limits Declaration One. If I had signed that declaration, I would have voluntarily agreed to limit my service in the United States [House of Representatives to no more than 3 terms] [Senate to no more than 2 terms] after the passage of the congressional Term Limits Declaration Amendment of 1998.

____

Signature by candidate executes Part A Date

After executing Part A, a candidate may execute and submit the voluntary statement in Part B.

Part B: I, ________, authorize and request that the secretary of state place the ballot designation, "Chose not to sign declaration to limit service to [3 terms] [2 terms]" next to my name on every official election ballot and in all government-sponsored voter education material in which my name appears as a candidate for the office to which Term Limits Declaration Two refers.

____
Signature by candidate executes Part B Date

(3) In the ballot designations in this section, the secretary of state shall incorporate the applicable language in brackets for the office the candidate seeks. Terms shall be calculated without regard to whether the terms were served consecutively.

(4) The secretary of state shall allow any candidate who at any time has submitted an executed copy of Term Limits Declaration One or Two, to timely submit an executed copy of Term Limits Declaration One or Two at which time all provisions affecting that Term Limits Declaration shall apply.

(5) The secretary of state shall place on that part of the official election ballot and in all government-sponsored voter education material, immediately following the name of each candidate who has executed and submitted Parts A and B of Term Limits Declaration One, the words, "Signed declaration to limit service to [3 terms] [2 terms]" unless the candidate has qualified as a candidate for a term that would exceed the number of terms set forth in Term Limits Declaration One. The secretary of state shall place on that part of the official election ballot and <u>in all government-sponsored voter education material</u>, immediately following the name of each candidate who has executed and submitted Parts A and B of Term Limits Declaration Two the words, "Chose not to sign declaration to limit service to [3 terms] [2 terms]".

(6) For the purpose of this section, service in office for more than one-half of a term shall be deemed as service for a full term.

(7) No candidate shall have more than one declaration and ballot designation in effect for any office at the same time and a candidate may only execute and submit Part B of a declaration if Part A of that declaration is or has been executed and submitted.

(8) The secretary of state shall provide candidates with all the declarations in this section and promulgate regulations as provided by law to facilitate implementation of this section as long as the regulations do not alter the intent of this section.

(9) If any portion of this section be adjudicated invalid, the remaining portion shall be severed from the invalid portion to the greatest possible extent and be given the fullest force and application.

Brackets in original.

The biggest effect of section 12a might have come in the 2002 U.S. Senate race. One-term incumbent Wayne Allard (R) was facing a rematch with his 1996 opponent, Ted Strickland (D). At the time, Colorado did not have a widespread system of mail-in voting, so most voters saw the ballot for the first time on election day.

The ballot included that fact that Allard and all the minor party candidates had taken the pledge. Strickland had not pledged and had not requested any term limits information be included on his ballot line. So in a field where all but one candidates had taken the pledge, Strickland stood out. Although Strickland had a six point polling lead before voting began, Allard won the election. Allard fulfilled his pledge and did not run for another term in 2008.

Today, fewer candidates take the pledge, but for those who do, the information is supplied on their ballot line. The secretary of state has stopped distributing pledge information in its voter materials for the public, even Section 12a the Constitution requires voluntary pledges to be included in "in all government-sponsored voter education material."

Art. XVIII, Section 12b. Wildlife trapping forbidden

Covered in chapter 32 (Natural Resources). Adopted 1996.

On the 1996 ballot, there were two proposed Sections 12: the wildlife amendment, and the tough version of the term limits pledge. After both passed, the term limits text was designated section 12, and the wildlife amendment was section 13.

A 2000 amendment changed the section 13 wildlife amendment into section 12b.

Art. XVIII, Section 13. Triskaidekaphobia

Triskaidekaphobia is fear of the number 13. It is fair to say that article XVIII is triskaidekaphobic. While the other Colorado articles have no qualms about a thirteenth section, article XVIII was amended to avoid the allegedly unlucky number.

The same year, 2000, when the voters were being asked to change the section number for the wildlife law, medical marijuana proponents had their own proposed amendment. Of course, they proposed it as section 14.

Art. XVIII, Section 14. Medical marijuana

Covered in chapter 31 (Vices?).

Art. XVIII, Section 15. Minimum wage rate

> Effective January 1, 2007, Colorado's minimum wage shall be increased to $6.85 per hour and shall be adjusted annually for inflation, as measured by the Consumer Price Index used for Colorado. This minimum wage shall be paid to employees who receive the state or federal minimum wage. No more than $3.02 per hour in tip income may be used to offset the minimum wage of employees who regularly receive tips.

Adopted in 2006. Put on the ballot that year partly for the purpose of bolstering Democratic turn-out, and apparently successful in that regard. Implementing statutes are C.R.S. §§ 8-6-106 (Director of the Colorado Dept. of Labor and Employment will announce raises in the minimum wage consistent with art. XVIII, § 15); 8-6-108.5 (1977 statute that unemancipated minors may be paid 15% less than the adult minimum wage).

On January 1, 2021, the Colorado minimum wage automatically increased to $12.32. (Or $9.30 for tipped employees). The actual minimum wage is zero, because a prospective employee who is unable to contribute more than $12 of hourly value to the enterprise will not be hired.

The employer side of the federal Social Security tax is 6.2% and is 1.45% for Medicare. In 2020 the voters adopted a statutory initiative, Proposition 118, for paid family and medical leave. C.R.S. § 8-13.3-401 et seq. The employer share starts at .45%, subject to unlimited future increases by administrative action, without a vote of the people. So an employee's cost to the employer in Colorado would be 8.1% higher than the employee's wages. Thus, job seekers who can contribute at least $12.92 in hourly value have the possibility of being hired in Colorado.

The Consumer Price Index (CPI) is published by the U.S. Department of Labor, Bureau of Labor Statistics. Historically, the Bureau published only a Denver-Boulder-Greeley CPI, not a statewide CPI. The CPI is now calculated for Denver-Aurora-Lakewood. Critics of section 15 point out that it reflects the cost of living in expensive urban area and is a poor guideline for some other parts of the state.

Further reading: Kristin L. Arthur, *Increasing the Minimum Wage Through Direct Democracy*, 94 DENVER L. REVIEW ONLINE (Mar. 28, 2017).

Art. XVIII, Section 16. Personal use of marijuana

Covered in chapter 31 (Vices?)

CHAPTER 24

Amendments and Constitutional Convention, article XIX

Art. XIX, Section 1. Constitutional convention

An enduring constitution must have a system for change. State constitutional conventions were common in the 19th century. Colorado has not needed one, because it has had a functional system for amendment or revision, in section 2 of article XIX.

> The general assembly may at any time by a vote of two-thirds of the members elected to each house, recommend to the electors of the state, to vote at the next general election for or against a convention to revise, alter and amend this constitution; and if a majority of those voting on the question shall declare in favor of such convention, the general assembly shall, at its next session, provide for the calling thereof. The number of members of the convention shall be twice that of the senate and they shall be elected in the same manner, at the same places, and in the same districts. The general assembly shall, in the act calling the convention, designate the day, hour and place of its meeting; fix the pay of its members and officers, and provide for the payment of the same, together with the necessary expenses of the convention. Before proceeding, the members shall take an oath to support the constitution of the United States, and of the state of Colorado, and to faithfully discharge their duties as members of the convention. The qualifications of members shall be the same as of members of the senate; and vacancies occurring shall be filled in the manner provided for filling vacancies in the general assembly. Said convention shall meet within three months after such election and prepare such revisions, alterations or amendments to the constitution as may be deemed necessary; which shall be submitted to the electors for their ratification or rejection at an election appointed by the convention for that purpose, not less than two nor more than six months after adjournment thereof; and unless so submitted and approved by a majority of the electors voting at the election, no such revision, alteration or amendment shall take effect.

A recommendation of the general assembly to the electors to vote at the next general election for or against a constitutional convention pursuant to section 1, is not subject to the governor's veto. *People ex rel. Stewart v. Ramer*, 62 Colo. 128, 160 P. 1032 (1916); *Nesbit v. People*, 19 Colo. 441, 448, 36 P. 221, 223 (1894) ("Article 19 is sui generis; it provides for revising, altering and amending the fundamental law of the state, and is not in pari materia with those provisions of article 5 prescribing the method of enacting ordinary statutory laws.").

Art. XIX, Section 2. Constitutional amendments

(1)

(a) Any amendment or amendments to this constitution may be proposed in either house of the general assembly, and, if the same shall be voted for by two-thirds of all the members elected to each house, such proposed amendment or amendments, together with the ayes and noes of each house thereon, shall be entered in full on their respective journals. The proposed amendment or amendments shall be published with the laws of that session of the general assembly. At the next general election for members of the general assembly, the said amendment or amendments shall be submitted to the registered electors of the state for their approval or rejection, and such as are approved by a majority of those voting thereon or, if applicable the number of votes required pursuant to paragraph (b) of this subsection (I), shall become part of this constitution.

(b) In order to make it more difficult to amend this constitution, a constitutional amendment shall not become part of this constitution unless the amendment is approved by at least fiftyfive percent of the votes casts thereon; except that this paragraph (b) shall not apply to a constitutional amendment that is limited to repealing, in whole or in part, any provision of this constitution. [Added 2016.]

(2) If more than one amendment be submitted at any general election, each of said amendments shall be voted upon separately and votes thereon cast shall be separately counted the same as though but one amendment was submitted; but each general assembly shall have no power to propose amendments to more than six articles of this constitution.

(3) No measure proposing an amendment or amendments to this constitution shall be submitted by the general assembly to the registered electors of the state containing more than one subject, which shall be clearly expressed in its title; but if any subject shall be embraced in any measure which shall not be expressed in the title, such measure shall be void only as to so much thereof as shall not be so expressed.

The 1876 Constitution had allowed to the general assembly in any one session to propose no more than the amendment of one article of the Constitution. This was changed in 1900, to allow a legislative session to propose amendments for up to six articles of the Constitution. The change made it much easier to update the Constitution.

The people by initiative may propose an unlimited number of constitutional amendments in any single election. *People ex rel. Tate v. Prevost*, 55 Colo. 199, 134 P. 129 (1913).

Article XIX, § 2, is the sole source of procedures for the general assembly to propose constitutional amendments. Thus, the general assembly does *not* need to comply with article V, which only applies to legislative enactments. *Nesbit v. People*, 19 Colo. 441, 448, 36 P. 221, 223 (1894). Note that a general assembly proposal for a convention or for amendments must win the support of two-thirds of the total membership in each house, not two-thirds of the members voting.

A legislative referendum for a constitutional amendment must comply with the single-subject rule, but there is no judicial review of single subject compliance unless the amendment is adopted. This contrasts with Title Board and supreme court review of citizen initiatives for proposed amendments, which are subject to pre-election review. *Polhill v. Buckley*, 923 P.2d 119 (Colo. 1996). *See* chapter 9 (Initiative and Referendum).

Part V
New Articles

CHAPTER 25

Home Rule, article XX

Denver thinks she is the State and we frankly admit that she is a large and important part of it . . . Denver is progressive and aggressive; she wants everything in sight and takes what she gets. Denver's singleness of purpose and generous liberality—for Denver—are well-nigh relentless.[1]

Introduction

Ten states, including Colorado, have full home rule. Florida has home rule for everything except taxes. Eight more states have home rule for all counties and some municipalities. National League of Cities, *Local Government Authority*.

Article XX was added by a referred amendment in 1902 and has been further amended. In 1905, the Colorado supreme court held that section 2 applied to Denver as a city, but Denver as a county still had to follow the state constitutional rules for counties—such as an elected board of county commissioners, elected sheriff, and so on. *People ex rel. Miller v. Johnson*, 34 Colo. 143, 86 P. 233 (1905) (Denver cannot deviate from state election dates for county officers). The decision led to the defeat of the Republican justices in subsequent partisan elections. (Colorado judicial elections used to be partisan, as described in chapter 10, Judiciary.) In 1911, the court overruled its precedent, so constitutional county officers disappeared from Denver. *People v. Cassiday*, 50 Colo. 503, 117 P. 357 (1911) (abolition of county form of government in Denver was constitutional). *See also City and County of Denver v. Rinker*, 148 Colo. 441, 366 P.2d 548 (1961) (reaffirming *Cassiday* principles).

Section 6 of the 1902 amendment had allowed cities of the first or second class—the largest cities—to vote to establish home rule. The cities of Pueblo, Colorado Springs, and Grand Junction soon did so.[2]

Section 6 was much expanded by a 1912 citizen initiative. It strengthened home rule and offered it to more municipalities. RICHARD COLLINS & DALE A. OESTERLE, THE COLORADO STATE CONSTITUTION 386–87 (2d ed. 2020).

In 1998 the people adopted sections 10–13, authorizing the creation of the City and County of Broomfield, under the same rules as applicable to Denver.

For a good guide on researching municipal law and legislative history, see Michael Whitlaw, *Municipal Resources*, COLO. LAWYER, July 2021.

The Dillon Rule and its many Colorado exceptions

As a baseline, Colorado follows the Dillon Rule: municipalities and counties are subject to the plenary control of the state legislature.[3] In Colorado, the Dillon Rule has always been tempered by the Constitution:

- Art V, § 35 (general assembly may not delegate "to any special commission, private corporation or association" the supervision of municipal improvements and property, or to levy taxes for "any municipal function whatsoever").

---

[1] Irving Stanton, land office registrar in Pueblo. IRVING W. STANTON, SIXTY YEARS IN COLORADO: REMINISCES AND REFLECTIONS OF A PIONEER OF 1860, 181, 209–10 (Denver 1922) (describing territorial days).

[2] Details of the home rule struggle can be found in CLYDE LYNDON KING, THE HISTORY OF THE GOVERNMENT OF DENVER WITH SPECIAL REFERENCE, TO ITS RELATIONS WITH PUBLIC SERVICE CORPORATIONS (Ph.D. thesis, U. of Penn.) (Forgotten Books, 2016 reprint).

[3] Named for John Forest Dillon, an Iowa Supreme Court justice, Eighth Circuit judge, and law professor. Author of Municipal Corporations (1872), the leading treatise of its time on the subject.

- Art. VI, § 19 (court rules must be uniform).
- Art. X, § 3 (uniformity in taxation, with some exceptions).
- Art. X, § 7 (general assembly may not impose municipal taxes).
- Art. XIV, § 13 (cities and towns may be divided into no more than four classes, and rules within each class must be uniform).
- Art. XIV in general, which puts many aspects county government beyond the general assembly's power to change.
- And of course the home rule provisions in article XX.

Cities and towns with and without home rule

In Colorado law, a *town* has a population of 2,000 or fewer, and a *city* has more. *Statutory cities and towns* derive all their powers from specific state statutes. They are governments of enumerated powers. The general assembly is supreme in their domain, to the extent it wants to be.

There are 12 statutory cities and 160 statutory towns. Home rule been adopted 97 cities.

Counties with and without home rule

County home rule is mainly covered in article XIV, § 16, adopted in 1970. The same year, a new section 9 was added to article XX. It allowed for home rule by every county, city, or town.

Two counties—Weld and Pitkin—have adopted home rule pursuant to these provisions.

The only way to create a "City and County" is by express constitutional text. Denver and Broomfield are the two in this category. Colorado's remaining 60 counties have not adopted home rule.

Bold text and italics within the text below are added by Kopel.

Art. XX, Section 1. City and County of Denver created

> The municipal corporation known as the city of Denver and all municipal corporations and that part of the quasi-municipal corporation known as the county of Arapahoe, in the state of Colorado, included within the exterior boundaries of the said city of Denver as the same shall be bounded when this amendment takes effect, are hereby consolidated and are hereby declared to be a single body politic and corporate, by the name of the "City and County of Denver". By that name said corporation shall have perpetual succession, and shall own, possess, and hold all property, real and personal, theretofore owned, possessed, or held by the said city of Denver and by such included municipal corporations, and also all property, real and personal, theretofore owned, possessed, or held by the said county of Arapahoe, and shall assume, manage, and dispose of all trusts in any way connected therewith; shall succeed to all the rights and liabilities, and shall acquire all benefits and shall assume and pay all bonds, obligations, and indebtedness of said city of Denver and of said included municipal corporations and of the county of Arapahoe; by that name may sue and defend, plead and be impleaded, in all courts and places, and in all matters and proceedings; may have and use a common seal and alter the same at pleasure; may purchase, receive, hold, and enjoy or sell and dispose of, real and personal property; may receive bequests, gifts, and donations of all kinds of property, in fee simple, or in trust for public, charitable, or other purposes; and do all things and acts necessary to carry out the purposes of such gifts, bequests, and donations, with power to manage, sell, lease, or otherwise

dispose of the same in accordance with the terms of the gift, bequest, or trust; **shall have the power, *within or without its territorial limits*, to construct, condemn and purchase, purchase, acquire, lease, add to, maintain, conduct, and operate water works, light plants, power plants, transportation systems, heating plants, and any other public utilities or works or ways** local in use and extent, in whole or in part, and everything required therefore, for the use of said city and county and the inhabitants thereof, and any such systems, plants, or works or ways, or any contracts in relation or connection with either, that may exist and which said city and county may desire to purchase, in whole or in part, the same or any part thereof may be purchased by said city and county which may enforce such purchase by proceedings at law as in taking land for public use by **right of eminent domain, and shall have the power to issue bonds upon the vote of the taxpaying electors**, at any special or general election, in any amount necessary to carry out any of said powers or purposes, as may by the charter be provided.

[The first sentence of the next paragraph was added in 1974]
The provisions of section 3 of article XIV of this constitution and the general annexation and consolidation statutes of the state relating to counties shall apply to the city and county of Denver. Any contiguous town, city, or territory hereafter annexed to or consolidated with the city and county of Denver, under any such laws of this state, in whatsoever county the same may be at the time, shall be detached per se from such other county and become a municipal and territorial part of the city and county of Denver, together with all property thereunto belonging.

The city and county of Denver shall alone always constitute one judicial district of the state.

[The following was added in 1974 by the Poundstone Amendment, then revised in 2002]
Any other provisions of this constitution to the contrary notwithstanding:

No annexation or consolidation proceeding shall be initiated after the effective date of this amendment pursuant to the general annexation and consolidation statutes of the state of Colorado to annex lands to or consolidate lands with the city and county of Denver until such proposed annexation or consolidation is first approved by a majority vote of a six-member boundary control commission composed of one commissioner from each of the boards of county commissioners of Adams, Arapahoe, and Jefferson counties, respectively, and three elected officials of the city and county of Denver to be chosen by the mayor. The commissioners from each of the said counties shall be appointed by resolution of their respective boards.

No land located in any county other than Adams, Arapahoe, or Jefferson counties shall be annexed to or consolidated with the city and county of Denver unless such annexation or consolidation is approved by the unanimous vote of all the members of the board of county commissioners of the county in which such land is located.

All actions, including actions regarding procedural rules, shall be adopted by the commission by majority vote. Each commissioner shall have one vote, including the commissioner who acts as the chairman of the commission. All procedural rules adopted by the commission shall be filed with the secretary of state.

This amendment shall be self-executing.

Article XX was adopted in 1902.

Denver has always had a fraught relationship with the rest of the state. In some states, a large metropolis arose decades after statehood. Chicago and Los Angeles are examples. In contrast, from the beginning of the 1858 Gold Rush until the present, Denver has always been the largest city in Colorado.[4]

Some of what annoyed the rest of the state was Denver's loose stance on morals, including its semiofficial tolerance of brothels, saloons, and gambling dens, notwithstanding statewide laws on the subject.

Denver has also attempted to impose its own version of morality on the rest of the state; for example, according to Denver ordinances at the turn of the 21st century, Denver claimed the right to seize and forfeit without trial the automobiles and firearms of people who were lawfully (under state law) transporting firearms through the city—for example, a licensed hunter from Colorado Springs who was driving through Denver, with an unloaded rifle in the trunk, on the way to a hunting trip in Jackson County.[5]

As noted in chapter 10 (Judiciary, art. VI, § 3), Denver's election machinery and law enforcement were notoriously corrupt, with deleterious consequences for statewide elections. In local elections, the pervasive fraud deprived Denver voters of their article VII right to pure elections. As discussed in chapter 7 (Executive Power, art. IV, § 5), when Progressive governor Davis Waite exercised his statutory right to fire Denver's Police and Fire Commissioners, they responded with an armed take-over of the municipal building, leading to an siege in which governor Waite summoned the state militia.

Continuing conflicts led to the home rule movement for Denver. The movement achieved its first success with the 1902 enactment of article XX. Section 6 was revised in 1912, to put Denver's home rule on clearer constitutional footing, and to allow other cities to choose home rule.

With home rule, Denver can tax, exercise eminent domain, and operate utilities. These latter two powers can also be exercised *outside* the city's boundaries. As a result, the Denver Water Board forcibly acquired considerable water rights, including diversions from the West Slope. Today, much of Denver's water supply comes from West Slope diversions of the Colorado River.

Eminent domain can work in both directions. The Denver Charter generally dedicates city park land to perpetual use as a park unless the voters authorize a change. But the state can still condemn the land for a highway, with no vote by the people of Denver. *Welch v. City and County of Denver,* 141 Colo. 587, 349 P.2d 352 (1960).

Annexations

In accord with section 1 of article XX, Denver was allowed to annex land without the consent of the persons annexed or of their former county, contrary to the safeguards of article XIV, § 3 (no changes in county boundaries without voter consent). The involuntary annexations were held not to violate the Fourteenth Amendment's Equal Protection guarantee. *Board of County Com'rs of Jefferson County v. City and County of Denver*, 150 Colo. 198, 372 P.2d 152 (1962).

The 1974 Poundstone Amendment to section 1 curtailed Denver's ability to annex territory without the consent of the residents of the territory, restoring the rights of Art. XIV, § 3, to persons in territory coveted by Denver. Further, a multicounty Boundary Control Commission

---

[4] To be precise, what we today call "Denver" initially included the rival towns of Auraria and St. Charles. Before 1902, many suburban towns beyond "Denver City" had sprung up, including South Denver, Elyria, Highlands, Montclair, and Globeville. These were all consolidated into Denver in 1902.

[5] This was finally stopped by a preemptive state statute. C.R.S. § 18-12-105.6 (localities may not ban firearms in cars if the firearm is for lawful protection or hunting).

must approve annexations. Pursuant to the text of the Poundstone Amendment, the general assembly may enact minor boundary adjustments. C.R.S. § 30-6-109.7. But when Denver wanted to annex a large swathe of Adams County to build Denver International Airport, a vote of the people of Adams County was necessary.

The eminent domain powers granted to Denver by section 1 are also granted to all home rule cities by section 6, which incorporates section 1 powers. A city's proposed annexation is subject to judicial review for bad faith. For example, when the city of Erie proposed to develop some vacant land, the city of Lafayette attempted to annex it, and to block the development by creating an open space buffer. But the court found Lafayette's open space argument to be a bad faith pretext: The Erie plan already provided some buffer; Lafayette had never previously expressed the slightest interest in the land; and the real purpose was to block the Erie development and thereby prevent an important Lafayette business from relocating. *City of Lafayette v. Town of Erie Urban Renewal Authority,* 434 P.3d 746 (Colo. App. 2018).

Further reading: Franklin J. James & Christopher B. Gerboth, *A Campy Divided: Annexation Battles, the Poundstone Amendment, and Their Impact on Metropolitan Denver, 1941–1988*, COLO. HISTORY 5 (2001).

Art. XX, Section 2. Denver officers

> The officers of the city and county of Denver shall be such as by appointment or election may be provided for by the charter; and the jurisdiction, term of office, duties and qualifications of all such officers shall be such as in the charter may be provided; but the charter shall designate the officers who shall, respectively, perform the acts and duties required of county officers to be done by the constitution or by the general law, as far as applicable. If any officer of said city and county of Denver shall receive any compensation whatever, he or she shall receive the same as a stated salary, the amount of which shall be fixed by the charter, or, in the case of officers not in the classified civil service, by ordinance within limits fixed by the charter; provided, however, no elected officer shall receive any increase or decrease in compensation under any ordinance passed during the term for which he was elected.

Denver must adopt a charter that creates the officers of the city and county and provides their means of selection. Elected officers may not receive salary increases during their term.

A charter is like a constitution for a municipality and must be enforced with equal rigor. *E.g.*, *Hoper v. City and County of Denver*, 173 Colo. 390, 479 P.2d 967 (1971) (proposed charter amendment violated charter's clear title rule); *Tenney v. City and County of Denver*, 119 Colo. 263, 203 P.2d 504 (1949) (Charter said that city employee compensation would be fixed by ordinance; city had no authority to pay moving expenses for new employee, in absence of an ordinance authorizing such type of compensation); *Reed v. Blakley*, 115 Colo. 559, 176 P.2d 681 (1946) (enforcing Denver Charter rule that the Denver Manager of Public Safety and Excise—not the City Council—has the sole power to decide on liquor licenses); *McNichols v. City and County of Denver*, 109 Colo. 269, 124 P.2d 601 (1942) (Mayor cannot evade Charter rules on appointment and compensation of justices of the peace); *Lail v. City and County of Denver*, 88 Colo. 362, 297 P. 512 (1931) (Mayor cannot unilaterally consolidates the offices public trustee, office of clerk and recorder, and ex officio clerk).

Denver's current form of government was adopted by the people in 1916, based on the Cleveland system. It creates the "strong mayor" form of government. That was the typical system in Denver, except for a brief and unsuccessful experiment with "commission government" in the 1910s.

Art. XX, Section 3. Denver charter must put police and fire under civil service

> Immediately upon the canvass of the vote showing the adoption of this amendment, it shall be the duty of the governor of the state to issue his proclamation accordingly. Every charter shall provide that the department of fire and police and the department of public utilities and works shall be under such civil service regulations as in said charter shall be provided.

Denver's fire, police, and public utilities must be under civil service. Section 3 was an understandable provision in light of the massive police corruption in late 19th century Denver. But corruption persisted thereafter.

Civil service protections are important for employees, including police officers, who might otherwise be fired for unjustified reasons. At the same time, civil service laws make it difficult to terminate mediocre or sub-mediocre employees. One can see the results in modern controversies over the use of force by law enforcement. Most problems arise from municipal police departments, where employees usually have civil service protections. In contrast, the deputies of sheriffs' offices are at-will employees, who can be instantly fired. It is easy for a sheriff to use his or her power properly, to get rid of mediocre deputies, or improperly, to fire an employee for a personal grudge.

In Denver and Broomfield, there is no sheriff's "office." Rather, the sheriff heads a mere "department"—a sub-entity that is answerable to the mayor or a mayoral appointee but not to the people. While sheriffs in 62 counties are directly elected by the people, the Denver and Broomfield sheriffs are appointed by the mayor (Broomfield) or an appointee of the mayor (Denver, Manager of Public Safety). The Denver sheriff does not even have the authority to choose his second-in-command, the undersheriff. Denver's undersheriff is a civil servant who rises to the position based on seniority. *See Roybal v. City and County of Denver*, 436 P.3d 604 (Colo. App. 2019) (state statute giving sheriffs power to appoint and dismiss is superseded by home rule city code).

In counties other than Denver and Broomfield, the sheriff's office is the countywide law enforcement agency. However, county sheriffs usually let a municipality's police department take the lead on matters within the municipality. In Denver and Broomfield, the sheriff's department is responsible only for operating the county jail, providing courthouse security, transporting prisoners, and so on. General law enforcement is the responsibility of the Denver or Broomfield police departments.

Art. XX, Section 4. Denver franchises subject to initiative and referendum

> (1) The people of the city and county of Denver are hereby vested with and they shall always have the exclusive power in making, altering, revising or amending their charter.
>
> (2) Deleted by S.C.R.00-005, §1, eff. Dec. 28, 2000.
>
> (3) Deleted by S.C.R.00-005, §1, eff. Dec. 28, 2000.

> (4) Any franchise relating to any street, alley, or public place of the said city and county shall be subject to the initiative and referendum powers reserved to the people under section 1 of article V of this constitution. Such referendum power shall be guaranteed notwithstanding a recital in an ordinance granting such franchise that such ordinance is necessary for the immediate preservation of the public peace, health, and safety. Not more than five percent of the registered electors of a home rule city shall be required to order such referendum. Nothing in this section shall preclude a home rule charter provision which requires a lesser number of registered electors to order such referendum or which requires a franchise to be voted on by the registered electors. If such a referendum is ordered to be submitted to the registered electors, the grantee of such franchise shall deposit with the treasurer the expense (to be determined by said treasurer) of such submission. The council shall have power to fix the rate of taxation on property each year for city and county purposes.

The original section 4 required a popular vote on all city franchises. Many city charters do require such a vote in all circumstances. As amended, section 4 guarantees a right of referendum on franchises if at least 5% of registered voters sign a petition. The vote cannot be evaded by a safety clause.

Section 4 (referendum for franchises) and Section 5 (initiative and referendum for charter amendments and ordinary legislation) were the first Colorado provisions guaranteeing the right of referendum and initiative—preceding the 1910 revision of article V, § 1, by eight years.

Municipal franchises include the grant of monopolies for public utilities. Attempts to grant franchises without a vote required by municipal charter were held void in *Community Tele-Communications, Inc. v. Heather Corp*., 677 P.2d 330 (Colo. 1984) (Cortez city ordinance issuing a cable TV franchise could not override city charter requiring a vote); *Berman v. City and County of Denver*, 120 Colo. 218, 209 P.2d 754 (trolley cars and busses; rejecting prior unconstitutional practices by the city council as creating precedents for new unconstitutional practices).

The power to grant a franchise can be used to regulate the rates charged by a franchisee. *City and County of Denver v. Mountain States Tel. & Tel. Co.*, 67 Colo. 225, 184 P. 604 (1919); *Spears v. Utilities Com'n*, 100 Colo. 369, 67 P.2d 1029 (1937) (PUC had no authority over rates in Denver).

When a Denver water utility's franchise expired, the city refused to renew it, and offered to buy the utility's property for a ruinously low price. If the utility did not agree, Denver would just build its own water utility. None of this violated the U.S. Fourteenth Amendment. *City and County of Denver v. New York Trust Co*., 229 U.S. 123 (1913).

Selling city land or a building to a private buyer is not the grant of a franchise. *Hall v. City and County of Denver*, 115 Colo. 538, 177 P.2d 234 (1946) (selling courthouse that was no longer in use). No vote is needed for a city's acquisition of a sports stadium, which is not a utility. *Ginsberg v. City and County of Denver*, 164 Colo. 572, 436 P.2d 685 (1968) (the beginning of the Denver Broncos turning into a taxpayer-supported business).

Interaction with Public Utilities Commission

Article XXV, which creates the Public Utilities Commission to exercise delegated powers of the general assembly regarding utilities, grants the PUC power over "facilities and service and rates and charges therefor" of public utilities, "wheresoever situate or operating within the State of Colorado, whether within or without a home rule city or home rule town." However, article XXV expressly holds harmless municipalities' reasonable exercise of police and licensing powers, and home rule entities' "power to grant franchises." Article XXV does not apply to municipally owned facilities, such as an electric utility owned by a city.

When Englewood was a statutory city, it granted a franchise to a telephone company. Later, Englewood became home rule, and still later, the franchise expired. The Colorado supreme court held that the telephone company had a state franchise and did not need one from Englewood. The court relied on state statutes that authorized telephone, telegraph, electricity, gas, and pipeline companies to use rights of way on public highways, so long as they do not interfere with highway operation. The statutes also affirmed that *construction* (*e.g.*, erecting telephone poles) required municipal consent. Since the telephone infrastructure had already been built, Englewood could not require the phone company to obtain a city franchise. *City of Englewood v. Mountain States Telephone & Telegraph Co.*, 163 Colo. 400, 431 P.2d 40 (1967).

When a city annexed land where a utility company was already operating pursuant to a PUC certificate of convenience and necessity, the city could not require the utility to obtain a city franchise. But the utility's expansion of facilities (*e.g.*, running new electrical lines to customers) did require a city franchise. *City of Greeley v. Poudre Valley Rural Elec. Ass'n, Inc.*, 744 P.2d 739 (Colo. 1987).

If a utility with a city franchise must pay the city a franchise fee, the state Public Utilities Commission may authorize the utility to raise its rates to recover the cost of the fee—even if the city objects. *City of Montrose v. Public Utilities Com'n of State of Colo.*, 732 P.2d 1181 (Colo. 1987) (not fooled by city's creative accounting that turned the franchise fee into a sort of sales tax; rejecting speculative argument that citizens will be unhappy when they see a line item on their utility bill showing how much the city is extracting from them via the franchise fee).

Interaction with Taxpayer's Bill of Rights

The Taxpayer's Bill of Rights (Art. X, § 20) rules for election dates apply only to elections on fiscal issues. The rules do not restrict the date for a vote on the transfer an electric franchise from one company to another. *Zaner v. City of Brighton*, 917 P.2d 280 (Colo. 1996).

Art. XX, Section 5. Denver charter amendments

> The citizens of the city and county of Denver shall have the exclusive power to amend their charter or to adopt a new charter, or to adopt any measure as herein provided;
>
> It shall be competent for qualified electors in number not less than five percent of the next preceding gubernatorial vote in said city and county to petition the council for any measure, or charter amendment, or for a charter convention. The council shall submit the same to a vote of the qualified electors at the next general election not held within thirty days after such petition is filed; whenever such petition is signed by qualified electors in number not less than ten percent of the next preceding gubernatorial vote in said city and county, with a request for a special election, the council shall submit it at a special election to be held not less than thirty nor more than sixty days from the date of filing the petition; provided, that any question so submitted at a special election shall not again be submitted at a special election within two years thereafter. In submitting any such charter, charter amendment or measure, any alternative article or proposition may be presented for the choice of the voters, and may be voted on separately without prejudice to others. Whenever the question of a charter convention is carried by a majority of those voting thereon, a charter convention shall be called through a special election

> ordinance as provided in section four (4) hereof, and the same shall be constituted and held and the proposed charter submitted to a vote of the qualified electors, approved or rejected, and all expenses paid, as in said section provided.
>
> The clerk of the city and county shall publish, with his official certification, for three times, a week apart, in the official newspapers, the first publication to be with his call for the election, general or special, the full text of any charter, charter amendment, measure, or proposal for a charter convention, or alternative article or proposition, which is to be submitted to the voters. Within ten days following the vote the said clerk shall publish once in said newspaper the full text of any charter, charter amendment, measure, or proposal for a charter convention, or alternative article or proposition, which shall have been approved by majority of those voting thereon, and he shall file with the secretary of state two copies thereof (with the vote for and against) officially certified by him, and the same shall go into effect from the date of such filing. He shall also certify to the secretary of state, with the vote for and against, two copies of every defeated alternative article or proposition, charter, charter amendment, measure or proposal for a charter convention. Each charter shall also provide for a reference upon proper petition therefor, of measures passed by the council to a vote of the qualified electors, and for the initiative by the qualified electors of such ordinances as they may by petition request.
>
> The signatures to petitions in this amendment mentioned need not all be on one paper. Nothing herein or elsewhere shall prevent the council, if it sees fit, from adopting automatic vote registers for use at elections and references.
>
> No charter, charter amendment or measure adopted or defeated under the provisions of this amendment shall be amended, repealed or revived, except by petition and electoral vote. And no such charter, charter amendment or measure shall diminish the tax rate for state purposes fixed by act of the general assembly, or interfere in any wise with the collection of state taxes.
>
> The city council, or board of trustees, or other body in which the legislative powers of any home rule city or town may then be vested, on its own initiative, may submit any measure, charter amendment, or the question whether or not a charter convention shall be called, at any general or special state or municipal election held not less than 30 days after the effective date of the ordinance or resolution submitting such question to the voters.

Pursuant to this 1902 amendment, Denver voters have the right of initiative and referendum, including for charter revisions. In 1910, a subsequent amendment gave initiative and referendum rights to citizens of all municipalities. Art. V, § 1 (9).

In Denver, a petition by 5% of voters is sufficient to put the question of an ordinance, a charter amendment, or a new charter convention the ballot at the next scheduled election. This means any election in which all qualified electors may participate, including a school board election. *Election Commission of City and County of Denver v. McNichols*, 193 Colo. 263, 565 P.2d 937 (1977).

If 10% of voters sign the petition, a special election must be scheduled. The city council may choose to put a competing, alternative, measure on the ballot.

Ballot titles must inform voters. A proposal to switch Denver elections from nonpartisan to party-designated candidates was titled "Repealing Sections Cl. 1 through Cl. 10, inclusive and Cl. 12-2 of the Charter of the City and County of Denver (1960 compilation) and enacting new

Sections Cl. 1 through Cl. 4 concerning municipal elections and officers." This was woefully short of informative. *Hoper v. City and County of Denver*, 173 Colo. 390, 479 P.2d 967 (1971). A charter amendment can include diverse subjects if they are disclosed in the title. *Coopersmith v. City and County of Denver*, 156 Colo. 469, 399 P.2d 943 (1965). But this might not still be valid in light of the 1994 single subject amendment, art. V, § 1(5.5).

Per the text of the penultimate paragraph in section 5, any "measure adopted or defeated" by the people may not be amended, repealed, or revived by a city council. So if the people of Denver adopt an ordinance to decriminalize psylocibin mushrooms, the city council may not change it. Conversely, if they defeat an initiative to legalize heroin, the city council may not legalize it. But note: clever draftsmanship can evade these restrictions, so that what is adopted by a city council is not exactly the same as what was rejected by the voters. And while an initiated ordinance may not be repealed or amended, except by subsequent vote of the people, a separate ordinance might address the same issue, without attempting to override the initiated ordinance.

After adopting a charter for 1902 home rule, the people of Denver held a convention for a new charter in 1904. That charter, as amended through 1911, is available at https://archive.org/details/charterofcitycou00denv.

The current public text of Denver's laws interpolates charter provisions into various places in the Revised Municipal Code. The confusing mash-up is available at: https://www.municode.com/library/co/denver/codes/code_of_ordinances.

Art. XX, Section 6. Municipal home rule

> The people of each city or town of this state, having a population of two thousand inhabitants as determined by the last preceding census taken under the authority of the United States, the state of Colorado or said city or town, are hereby vested with, and they shall always have, power to make, amend, add to or replace the charter of said city or town, which shall be its organic law and **extend to all its local and municipal matters.**
>
> Such charter and the ordinances made pursuant thereto in such matters shall supersede within the territorial limits and other jurisdiction of said city or town any law of the state in conflict therewith.
>
> Proposals for charter conventions shall be submitted by the city council or board of trustees, or other body in which the legislative powers of the city or town shall then be vested, at special elections, or at general, state or municipal elections, upon petition filed by qualified electors, all in reasonable conformity with section 5 of this article, and all proceedings thereon or thereafter shall be in reasonable conformity with sections 4 and 5 of this article.
>
> From and after the certifying to and filing with the secretary of state of a charter framed and approved in reasonable conformity with the provisions of this article, such city or town, and the citizens thereof, shall have the powers set out in sections 1, 4 and 5 of this article, and all other powers necessary, requisite or proper for the government and administration of its local and municipal matters, including power to legislate upon, provide, regulate, conduct and control:
>
>> a. The creation and terms of municipal officers, agencies and employments; the definition, regulation and alteration of the powers,

duties, qualifications and terms or tenure of all municipal officers, agents and employees;

b. The creation of police courts; the definition and regulation of the jurisdiction, powers and duties thereof, and the election or appointment of police magistrates therefor;

c. The creation of municipal courts; the definition and regulation of the jurisdiction, powers and duties thereof, and the election or appointment of the officers thereof;

d. All matters pertaining to municipal elections in such city or town, and to electoral votes therein on measures submitted under the charter or ordinances thereof, including the calling or notice and the date of such election or vote, the registration of voters, nominations, nomination and election systems, judges and clerks of election, the form of ballots, balloting, challenging, canvassing, certifying the result, securing the purity of elections, guarding against abuses of the elective franchise, and tending to make such elections or electoral votes non-partisan in character;

e. The issuance, refunding and liquidation of all kinds of municipal obligations, including bonds and other obligations of park, water and local improvement districts;

f. The consolidation and management of park or water districts in such cities or towns or within the jurisdiction thereof; but no such consolidation shall be effective until approved by the vote of a majority, in each district to be consolidated, of the qualified electors voting therein upon the question;

g. The assessment of property in such city or town for municipal taxation and the levy and collection of taxes thereon for municipal purposes and special assessments for local improvements; such assessments, levy and collection of taxes and special assessments to be made by municipal officials or by the county or state officials as may be provided by the charter;

h. The imposition, enforcement and collection of fines and penalties for the violation of any of the provisions of the charter, or of any ordinance adopted in pursuance of the charter.

It is the intention of this article to grant and confirm to the people of all municipalities coming within its provisions the full right of self-government in both local and municipal matters and the enumeration herein of certain powers shall not be construed to deny such cities and towns, and to the people thereof, any right or power essential or proper to the full exercise of such right.

The statutes of the state of Colorado, so far as applicable, shall continue to apply to such cities and towns, except insofar as superseded by the charters of such cities and towns or by ordinance passed pursuant to such charters.

> All provisions of the charters of the city and county of Denver and the cities of Pueblo, Colorado Springs and Grand Junction, as heretofore certified to and filed with the secretary of state, and of the charter of any other city heretofore approved by a majority of those voting thereon and certified to and filed with the secretary of state, which provisions are not in conflict with this article, and all elections and electoral votes heretofore had under and pursuant thereto, are hereby ratified, affirmed and validated as of their date.
>
> Any act in violation of the provisions of such charter or of any ordinance thereunder shall be criminal and punishable as such when so provided by any statute now or hereafter in force.
>
> The provisions of this section 6 shall apply to the city and county of Denver.
>
> This article shall be in all respects self-executing.

The original section 6, enacted 1902, had authorized cities of the first and second class to ask voters whether to hold a charter convention. A city that adopted a charter would have the same home rule powers as Denver's sections 1, 4, and 5.

A 1912 initiative created the section 6 that remains today. In all home rule municipalities, the rights of initiative and referendum must be guaranteed, pursuant to sections 4 and 5.

The power of home rule over local matters is not derived from the general assembly, but from the Constitution itself. A city council may not use a safety clause to insulate an ordinance from being negated by referendum. *Burks v. City of Lafayette*, 142 Colo. 61, 349 P.2d 692 (1960).

Charter amendments can be initiated by voters or referred by a city council. *Coopersmith v. City and County of Denver*, 156 Colo. 469, 399 P.2d 943 (1965).

Even though home rule provides for plenary powers for home rule governments, annexations by home rule cities may still need to respect some prior arrangements. For example, a city annexed land that had been part of a taxing district for rural transportation. While home rule cities have plenary power over local taxation, the annexation did not invalidate the district's sales tax in the annexed territory. *Wal-Mart Stores, Inc. v. Pikes Peak Rural Transportation Authority,*434 P.3d 725 (Colo. App. 2018).

Case law on conflicts with state law

Nothing in article XX overrides other constitutional provisions that expressly forbid local legislation. *City & County of Denver v. Sweet*, 138 Colo. 41, 329 P.2d 441 (1958) (enforcing art. X, § 17, ban on municipal income taxes) (but note that Denver evaded this by reframing its income tax an "occupational privilege tax" for people who work in Denver).

Section 6 gives home rule entities very broad powers, but only for "local and municipal matters." The phrase is the key to conflicts between state law and home rule laws. Under current doctrine, a subject will fall into one of three categories:

- purely local concern, *e.g.*, speed limits on city-maintained roads;
- purely statewide concern, *e.g.*, election dates for state officers; or
- "mixed" state and local concern, which means most subjects.

There is no formulaic test for mixed subjects. Instead, courts consider many factors including:

- whether there is a need for statewide uniformity;

- the need for intergovernmental cooperation;
- extraterritorial effects of the municipal law;
- history of state or local activity on the subject; and
- relevant constitutional provisions.

The factors help the court decide whether there is "a sufficiently weighty state interest" to override the local law. *City & County of Denver v. State*, 788 P.2d 764 (Colo. 1990).

Some leading cases holding in favor of local control:

- *City & County of Denver v. State* (invalidating statute that prohibited cities from requiring city employees to live in the city);
- *Fraternal Order of Police v. City & County of Denver*, 926 P.2d 582 (Colo. 1996) (general assembly may not require Denver deputy sheriffs to meet the minimum requirements of the statewide Peace Officer Standards and Training [POST] statute; relying on section 6a's specific home rule powers re municipal employees);
- *R.E.N. v. City of Colorado Springs*, 823 P.2d 1359 (Colo. 1992) (allowing city to criminally prosecute juvenile shoplifters for violating city ordinance, even though state Juvenile Code forbids such prosecution);
- *U.S. West Communications, Inc. v. City of Longmont*, 948 P.2d 509 (Colo. 1997) (city required that already-installed overhead utility wires must be buried underground; held not to be preempted by state Public Utilities Commission tariff).

The following cases have upheld state laws preempting local law:

- *Town of Telluride v. Lot 34 Venture, LLC*, 3 P.3d 30 (Colo. 2000) (state statute § 38-12-301-302 outlawed rent control on residential housing);[6]
- *Voss v. Lundvall*, 830 P.2d 1061 (Colo. 1992) (city may not violate statewide Oil and Gas Conservation Act by banning all drilling wells);
- *National Advertising Council v. Department of Highways*, 751 P.2d 632 (Colo. 1998) (state Outdoor Advertising Act against billboards next to interstate highways trumps city's approval of such billboards);[7]
- *City & County of Denver v. Qwest Corp.*, 18 P.3d 748 (Colo. 2001) (state statute allows telecommunications companies to use municipal rights of way, and to ignore city requirement that they obtain a special permit).

Further reading

Lynn A. Baker & Daniel B. Rodriguez, *Constitutional Home Rule and Judicial Scrutiny*, 86 DENVER U.L. REVIEW 1337 (2009).

George Boyle, *Colorado's Municipal System*, 30 COLO. LAWYER 33 (2001)

RICHARD COLLINS & DALE A. OESTERLE, THE COLORADO STATE CONSTITUTION 389-92 (2d ed. 2020).

---

[6] Rent control (limits on price changes in a proposed lease after an old lease has expired) advantages present tenants. According to critics of rent control, forced leasing at submarket prices results in reduced repair and improvement of properties, and the construction of fewer new properties—to the detriment of future tenants and of the area in general.

[7] Billboard prohibition was a special cause of first lady Mrs. Lyndon "Lady Bird" Johnson, as part of her Keep America Beautiful campaign.

PHIL GOODSTEIN, ROBERT SPEER'S DENVER 1904–1920 (2004) (particularly useful for the bibliographies after each chapter with sources on the legal and political fights over home rule).

Grace Heusner, Allison Sloto & Joshua Ulan Galperin, *Defining and Closing the Hydraulic Fracturing Governance Gap,* 95 DENVER L. REVIEW 191 (2017).

Debra S. Kalish, Gerald E. Dahl, Christopher Price, *The Doctrine of Preemption and Regulating Oil and Gas Development*, 38 COLO. LAWYER 47 (Oct. 2009) (cited by many Colorado opinions).

Robert M. Linz, *Researching Colorado Local Government Law*, 38 COLO. LAWYER 101 (Aug. 2009).

Laurie Reynolds, *Home Rule, Extraterritorial Impact, and the Region*, 86 DENVER U.L. REVIEW 1271 (2009).

Howard C. Klemme, *Powers of Home Rule Cities in Colorado*, 36 U. COLO. L. REVIEW 321 (1964).

Art. XX, Section 7. City and county of Denver shall be a single school district

> The city and county of Denver shall alone always constitute one school district, to be known as District No. 1, but its conduct, affairs and business shall be in the hands of a board of education consisting of such numbers, elected in such manner as the general school laws of the state shall provide.
>
> The said board of education shall perform all the acts and duties required to be performed for said district by the general laws of the state. Except as inconsistent with this amendment, the general school laws of the state shall, unless the context evinces a contrary intent, be held to extend and apply to the said "District No. 1".
>
> Upon the annexation of any contiguous municipality which shall include a school district or districts or any part of a district, said school district or districts or part shall be merged in said "District No. 1", which shall then own all the property thereof, real and personal, located within the boundaries of such annexed municipality, and shall assume and pay all the bonds, obligations and indebtedness of each of the said included school districts, and a proper proportion of those of partially included districts.
>
> Provided, however, that the indebtedness, both principal and interest, which any school district may be under at the time when it becomes a part, by this amendment or by annexation, of said "District No. 1", shall be paid by said school district so owing the same by a special tax to be fixed and certified by the board of education to the council which shall levy the same upon the property within the boundaries of such district, respectively, as the same existed at the time such district becomes a part of said "District No. 1", and in case of partially included districts such tax shall be equitably apportioned upon the several parts thereof.

Denver's public schools must comprise a single school district. This overrides the general power of the state legislature to alter school district boundaries at will. Art. IX, § 15. *Board of County Com'rs of Jefferson County v. City and County of Denver*, 150 Colo. 198, 372 P.2d 152 (1962) (allowing involuntarily annexed families to be put under the control of Denver Public Schools).

Election rules for the Denver School Board are at C.R.S. § 22-31-131. The Denver Clerk & Recorder has published a helpful School Board Candidate Quick Guide. The guide is useful not only for school board candidates, but also for cites to key statutes and regulations that apply to many elections.

Section 7 accounts for some of the public resistance to further annexations by Denver. The general perception, which is often accurate, is that the school districts in areas surrounding Denver operate better than the Denver Public Schools.

Art. XX, Section 8. Conflicting constitutional provisions are inapplicable

> Anything in the constitution of this state in conflict or inconsistent with the provisions of this amendment is hereby declared to be inapplicable to the matters and things by this amendment covered and provided for.

However, section 8 can itself be trumped by any future amendment. For example, Denver was not exempt from the 1914 state amendment imposing alcohol prohibition—even though the amendment did not specifically mention Denver. *People ex rel. Carlson v. City Council of City & County of Denver*, 60 Colo. 370, 153 P. 690 (1915).

Art. XX, Section 9. Electors by initiative may adopt, repeal, or amend home rule charter

> (1) Notwithstanding any provision in sections 4, 5, and 6 of this article to the contrary, the registered electors of each city and county, city, and town of the state are hereby vested with the power to adopt, amend, and repeal a home rule charter.
>
> (2) The general assembly shall provide by statute procedures under which the registered electors of any proposed or existing city and county, city, or town may adopt, amend, and repeal a municipal home rule charter. Action to initiate home rule shall be by petition, signed by not less than five percent of the registered electors of the proposed or existing city and county, city, or town, or by proper ordinance by the city council or board of trustees of a town, submitting the question of the adoption of a municipal home rule charter to the registered electors of the city and county, city, or town. No municipal home rule charter, amendment thereto, or repeal thereof, shall become effective until approved by a majority of the registered electors of such city and county, city, or town voting thereon. A new city or town may acquire home rule status at the time of its incorporation.
>
> (3) The provisions of this article as they existed prior to the effective date of this section, as they relate to procedures for the initial adoption of home rule charters and for the amendment of existing home rule charters, shall continue to apply until superseded by statute.
>
> (4) It is the purpose of this section to afford to the people of all cities, cities and counties, and towns the right to home rule regardless of population, period of incorporation, or other limitation, and for this purpose this section shall be self-executing. It is the further purpose of this section to facilitate adoption and

amendment of home rule through such procedures as may hereafter be enacted by the general assembly.

Adopted in 1970, Section 9 allows towns with a population of 2,000 or less to adopt home rule. Second, it allows counties to choose home rule. County home rule—adopted in Weld and Pitkin Counties—is also covered by Art. XIV, § 16.

Section 9 provides that "registered electors" may petition for home rule. This does not conflict with a state statute that petitions for *incorporation* (creation) of a city or town must be signed by landowners. *Malmgren v. Copper Mountain, Inc.*, 873 P.2d 44 (Colo. App. 1994).

Art. XX, Section 10. Creation of city and county of Broomfield

Adopted in 2001, these sections carve the city and county of Broomfield out of other counties and give Broomfield home rule powers like Denver's. The case law on Broomfield mainly concerns disputes over which governments could collect taxes during the transitional period of the creation of the City and County of Broomfield. It is omitted from this chapter.

Boldface below is by Kopel.

> **The city of Broomfield will be detached from the four counties it spans.** The city of Broomfield is a preexisting municipal corporation and home rule city of the state of Colorado, physically situated in parts of Adams, Boulder, Jefferson, and Weld counties. On and after November 15, 2001, all territory in the municipal boundaries of the city of Broomfield shall be detached from the counties of Adams, Boulder, Jefferson, and Weld and shall be consolidated into a single county and municipal corporation with the name "The City and County of Broomfield". Prior to November 15, 2001, the city of Broomfield shall not extend its boundaries beyond the annexation boundary map approved by the Broomfield city council on April 28, 1998, as an amendment to the city of Broomfield 1995 master plan. The existing charter of the said city of Broomfield shall become the charter of the city and county of Broomfield.
>
> **Broomfield has the standard home rule powers.** The city and county of Broomfield shall have perpetual succession; shall own, possess, and hold all real and personal property, including water rights, the right to use water, and contracts for water, currently owned, possessed, or held by the said city of Broomfield; shall assume, manage, and dispose of all trusts in any way connected therewith; shall succeed to all the rights and liabilities of, shall acquire all benefits of, and shall assume and pay all bonds, obligations, and indebtedness of said city of Broomfield and its proportionate share of the general obligation indebtedness and, as provided by intergovernmental agreement, its proportionate share of revenue bond obligations of the counties of Adams, Boulder, Jefferson, and Weld on and after November 15, 2001.
>
> The city and county of Broomfield may sue and defend, plead, and be impleaded in all courts and in all matters and proceedings; may have and use a common seal and alter the same at pleasure; may grant franchises; may purchase, receive, hold, and enjoy, or sell and dispose of real and personal property; may receive bequests, gifts, and donations of real and personal property, or real and personal property in

trust for public, charitable, or other purposes, and do all things and acts necessary to carry out the purposes of such gifts, bequests, donations, and trusts with power to manage, sell, lease, or otherwise dispose of the same in accordance with the terms of the gift, bequest, donation, or trust.

Including extraterritorial eminent domain. The city and county of Broomfield shall have the power within and without its territorial limits to construct, condemn, purchase, acquire, lease, add to, maintain, conduct, and operate water works, water supplies, sanitary sewer facilities, storm water facilities, parks, recreation facilities, open space lands, light plants, power plants, heating plants, electric and other energy facilities and systems, gas facilities and systems, transportation systems, cable television systems, telecommunication systems, and other public utilities or works or ways local in use and extent, in whole or in part, and everything required therefor, for the use of said city and county and the inhabitants thereof; to purchase in whole or in part any such systems, plants, works, facilities, or ways, or any contracts in relation or connection thereto that may exist, and may enforce such purchase by proceedings at law as in taking land for public use by right of eminent domain; and to issue bonds in accordance with its charter in any amount necessary to carry out any said powers or purposes, as the charter may provide and limit. The city and county of Broomfield shall have all of the powers of its charter and shall have all of the powers set out in section 6 of this article, including the power to make, amend, add to, or replace its charter as set forth in section 9 of this article. The charter provisions and procedures shall supersede any constitutional or statutory limitations and procedures regarding financial obligations. The city and county of Broomfield shall have all powers conferred to home rule municipalities and to home rule counties by the constitution and general laws of the state of Colorado that are not inconsistent with the constitutional provisions creating the city and county of Broomfield.

Transition rules. Prior to November 15, 2001, the charter and ordinances of the city of Broomfield shall govern all local and municipal matters of the city. On and after November 15, 2001, the constitutional provisions creating and governing the city and county of Broomfield, the city and county charter adopted in accordance with these constitutional provisions, and the ordinances existing and adopted from time to time shall govern all local and municipal matters of the city and county of Broomfield.

On and after November 15, 2001, the requirements of section 3 of article XIV of this constitution and the general annexation and consolidation statutes of the state relating to counties shall apply to the city and county of Broomfield. On and after November 15, 2001, any contiguous territory, together with all property belonging thereto, hereafter annexed to or consolidated with the city and county of Broomfield under any laws of this state, in whatsoever county the same may be at the time, shall be detached from such other county and become a municipal and territorial part of the city and county of Broomfield.

Boundary control commission to limit nonconsensual annexations. On and after November 15, 2001, no annexation or consolidation proceeding shall be initiated pursuant to the general annexation and consolidation statutes of the state to annex lands to or consolidate lands with the city and county of Broomfield until such proposed annexation or consolidation is first approved by a majority vote of a seven-member boundary control commission. The boundary control commission shall be composed of one commissioner from each of the boards of commissioners of Adams, Boulder, Jefferson, and Weld counties, respectively, and three elected officials of the city and county of Broomfield. The commissioners from each of the said counties shall be appointed by resolution of the respective county boards of commissioners. The three elected officials from the city and county of Broomfield shall be appointed by the mayor of the city and county of Broomfield. The boundary control commission shall adopt all actions, including actions regarding procedural rules, by majority vote. Each member of the boundary control commission shall have one vote, including the commissioner who acts as chairperson of the commission. The commission shall file all procedural rules adopted by the commission with the secretary of state.

Art. XX, Section 11. Broomfield officers

The officers of the city and county of Broomfield shall be as provided for by its charter or ordinances. The jurisdiction, term of office, and duties of such officers shall commence on November 15, 2001. The qualifications and duties of all such officers shall be as provided for by the city and county charter and ordinances, but the ordinances shall designate the officers who shall perform the acts and duties required of county officers pursuant to this constitution or the general laws of the state of Colorado, as far as applicable. All compensation for elected officials shall be determined by ordinance and not by state statute. If any elected officer of the city and county of Broomfield shall receive any compensation, such officer shall receive the same as a stated salary, the amount of which shall be fixed by ordinance within limits fixed by the city and county charter or by resolution approving the city and county budget and paid in equal monthly payments. No elected officer shall receive any increase or decrease in compensation under any ordinance or resolution passed during the term for which such officer was elected.

Just as in Denver, all officers are chosen pursuant to the charter, and not by state statute or other constitutional provisions. No elected officer's compensation may be changed during a term.

Art. XX, Section 12. Schedule for transfer of government to Broomfield

Upon the canvass of the vote showing the adoption of the constitutional provisions creating and governing the city and county of Broomfield, the governor shall issue a proclamation accordingly, and, on and after November 15, 2001, the city of Broomfield and those parts of the counties of Adams, Boulder, Jefferson, and Weld included in the boundaries of said city shall be consolidated into the city and county of Broomfield. The duties and terms of office of all officers of Adams, Boulder, Jefferson, and Weld counties shall no longer be applicable to and shall terminate with regard to the city and county of Broomfield. On and after November 15, 2001, the terms of office of the mayor and city council of the city of Broomfield shall terminate with regard to the city of Broomfield and said mayor and city council shall become the mayor and city council of the city and county of Broomfield. The city council of the city and county of Broomfield, in addition to performing the duties prescribed in the city and county charter and ordinances,

> shall perform the duties of a board of county commissioners or may delegate certain duties to various boards and commissions appointed by the city council of the city and county of Broomfield. The city and county of Broomfield shall be a successor district of the city of Broomfield under section 20 of article X of this constitution. Any voter approval granted the city of Broomfield under section 20 of article X of this constitution prior to November 15, 2001, shall be considered voter approval under said section for the city and county of Broomfield. The city and county of Broomfield shall have the power to continue to impose and collect sales, use, and property taxes that were imposed by the city of Broomfield and the counties of Adams, Boulder, Jefferson, and Weld within the areas where said taxes were imposed on November 14, 2001, until the voters of the city and county of Broomfield approve uniform sales, use, and property taxes within the city and county of Broomfield or approve increased sales, use, or property taxes within the city and county of Broomfield. Any violation of any criminal statutes of the state of Colorado occurring on or before November 14, 2001, shall continue to be prosecuted within the county where the violation originally occurred.

A transition provision, akin to some parts of the 1876 Constitution's Schedule. The City and County of Broomfield can continue to collect the sales taxes from the areas of pre-Broomfield County cities and counties, until the City and County of Broomfield adopts uniform taxes. Crimes that occurred before the creation of the City and County of Broomfield will continue to be prosecuted by the old counties.

Art. XX, Section 13. Broomfield home rule sections are self-executing

> Sections 10 through 13 of this article shall be in all respects self-executing and shall be construed so as to supersede any conflicting constitutional or statutory provision that would otherwise impede the creation of the city and county of Broomfield or limit any of the provisions of those sections. Except as otherwise provided in sections 10 through 13, said sections shall be effective on and after November 15, 2001. After the adoption of the constitutional provisions creating and governing the city and county of Broomfield, the general assembly may appropriate funds, if necessary, in cooperation with the city and county of Broomfield to implement these constitutional provisions at the state level.

The self-executing provision typical of modern constitutional amendments.

CHAPTER 26

Recalls, article XXI

The trinity of the progressive reform movement of the late 19th and early 20th centuries was initiative, referendum, and recall. Initiative and referendum were established by 1910 amendment of section 1 of article V. The recall power was added in 1912. The recall remedy of article XXI is concurrent with other provisions for removal of government employees, such as impeachment (art. XIII). Like initiative and referendum, recall is a fundamental right. Accordingly, the right must be generously construed, and statutory restrictions on the right must be strictly construed. *Bernzen v. City of Boulder*, 186 Colo. 81, 525 P.2d 416 (1974); *Shroyer v. Sokol*, 191 Colo. 32, 550 P.2d 309 (1976).

Art. XXI, Section 1. Right of recall of state officers

Every elective public officer of the state of Colorado may be recalled from office at any time by the registered electors entitled to vote for a successor of such incumbent through the procedure and in the manner herein provided for, which procedure shall be known as the recall, and shall be in addition to and without excluding any other method of removal provided by law.

The procedure hereunder to effect the recall of an elective public officer shall be as follows:

A petition signed by registered electors entitled to vote for a successor of the incumbent sought to be recalled, equal in number to twenty-five percent of the entire vote cast at the last preceding election for all candidates for the position which the incumbent sought to be recalled occupies, demanding an election of the successor to the officer named in said petition, shall be filed in the office in which petitions for nominations to office held by the incumbent sought to be recalled are required to be filed; provided, if more than one person is required by law to be elected to fill the office of which the person sought to be recalled is an incumbent, then the said petition shall be signed by registered electors entitled to vote for a successor to the incumbent sought to be recalled equal in number to twenty-five percent of the entire vote cast at the last preceding general election for all candidates for the office, to which the incumbent sought to be recalled was elected as one of the officers thereof, said entire vote being divided by the number of all officers elected to such office, at the last preceding general election; and such petition shall contain a general statement, in not more than two hundred words, of the ground or grounds on which such recall is sought, which statement is intended

> for the information of the registered electors, and the registered electors shall be the sole and exclusive judges of the legality, reasonableness and sufficiency of such ground or grounds assigned for such recall, and said ground or grounds shall not be open to review.

The recall power is "political in nature," and the voters' decision is not subject to judicial review. *Bernzen v. City of Boulder*, 186 Colo. 81, 525 P.2d 416 (1974).

The threshold of a voter-initiated recall is intentionally very high. The number of registered voters who sign the recall petition must be at least 25% of the number of people who voted in the last election for the office at issue.

Thoughtful use of technology has made it easier for citizens to meet this threshold. The 2013 recall campaign against state senators John Morse (senate president, D-Colo. Springs) and Angela Giron (D-Pueblo County) began with no support from major state or national organizations, including gun rights groups. Usually, when high-quality paid petition gatherers collect signatures, the percentage of valid signatures is 70-80%. The 2013 citizen activists, however, used technology to check attempted signatures on the spot; signers were immediately verified against the database of registered voters in the senate districts. This ensured that the petitions did not include signatures from people outside the relevant senate district, persons who were not registered to vote, etc. Accordingly, the recall petition signatures had an unusually high validity rate.

Art. XXI, Section 2. Recall petitions

> Any recall petition may be circulated and signed in sections, provided each section shall contain a full and accurate copy of the title and text of the petition; and such recall petition shall be filed in the office in which petitions for nominations to office held by the incumbent sought to be recalled are required to be filed.
>
> The signatures to such recall petition need not all be on one sheet of paper, but each signer must add to his signature the date of his signing said petition, and his place of residence, giving his street number, if any, should he reside in a town or city. The person circulating such sheet must make and subscribe an oath on said sheet that the signatures thereon are genuine, and a false oath, willfully so made and subscribed by such person, shall be perjury and be punished as such. All petitions shall be deemed and held to be sufficient if they appear to be signed by the requisite number of signers, and such signers shall be deemed and held to be registered electors, unless a protest in writing under oath shall be filed in the office in which such petition has been filed, by some registered elector, within fifteen days after such petition is filed, setting forth specifically the grounds of such protest, whereupon the officer with whom such petition is filed shall forthwith mail a copy of such protest to the person or persons named in such petition as representing the signers thereof, together with a notice fixing a time for hearing such protest not less than five nor more than ten days after such notice is mailed. All hearings shall be before the officer with whom such protest is filed, and all testimony shall be under oath. Such hearings shall be summary and not subject to delay, and must be concluded within thirty days after such petition is filed, and the result thereof shall be forthwith certified to the person or persons representing the signers of such petition. In case the petition is not sufficient it may be withdrawn by the person or a majority of the persons representing the signers of such petition, and may, within fifteen days thereafter, be amended and refiled as an original

> petition. The finding as to the sufficiency of any petition may be reviewed by any state court of general jurisdiction in the county in which such petition is filed, upon application of the person or a majority of the persons representing the signers of such petition, but such review shall be had and determined forthwith. The sufficiency, or the determination of the sufficiency, of the petition referred to in this section shall not be held, or construed, to refer to the ground or grounds assigned in such petition for the recall of the incumbent sought to be recalled from office thereby.
>
> When such petition is sufficient, the officer with whom such recall petition was filed, shall forthwith submit said petition, together with a certificate of its sufficiency to the governor, who shall thereupon order and fix the date for holding the election not less than thirty days nor more than sixty days from the date of submission of said petition; provided, if a general election is to be held within ninety days after the date of submission of said petition, the recall election shall be held as part of said general election.

Petitions with the requisite number of signers are deemed sufficient unless someone files a protest within 15 days, "setting forth specifically the grounds of such protest." There must be a hearing on the protest within 10 days, and a decision within 30. For state officials, the petitions are filed with the secretary of state. For all other offices, the petition is filed with the county clerk. C.R.S. § 1-12-100.5(5).

By statute, the recall petition must include a statement about the cost of the recall election, a 200 word statement of the reasons for recall, and a 300 word statement by the incumbent against the reasons for recall. Once a recall petition effort begins, the petitioners have 60 days to collect sufficient signatures. C.R.S. §§ 1-12-108(1.5); 31-4-503(2)(a) (municipalities).

Art. XXI, Section 3. Resignations and vacancies

> If such officer shall offer his resignation, it shall be accepted, and the vacancy caused by such resignation, or from any other cause, shall be filled as provided by law; but the person appointed to fill such vacancy shall hold his office only until the person elected at the recall election shall qualify. If such officer shall not resign within five days after the sufficiency of the recall petition shall have been sustained, the governor shall make or cause to be made publication of notice for the holding of such election, and officers charged by law with duties concerning elections shall make all arrangements for such election, and the same shall be conducted, returned and the result thereof declared in all respects as in the case of general elections.
>
> On the official ballot at such elections shall be printed in not more than 200 words, the reasons set forth in the petition for demanding his recall, and in not more than three hundred words there shall also be printed, if desired by him, the officer's justification of his course in office. If such officer shall resign at any time subsequent to the filing thereof, the recall election shall be called notwithstanding such resignation.
>
> There shall be printed on the official ballot, as to every officer whose recall is to be voted on, the words, "Shall (name of person against whom the recall petition is filed) be recalled from the office of (title of the office)?" Following such question

> shall be the words, "Yes" and "No", on separate lines, with a blank space at the right of each, in which the voter shall indicate, by marking a cross (X), his vote for or against such recall.
>
> On such ballots, under each question, there shall also be printed the names of those persons who have been nominated as candidates to succeed the person sought to be recalled; but no vote cast shall be counted for any candidate for such office, unless the voter also voted for or against the recall of such person sought to be recalled from said office. The name of the person against whom the petition is filed shall not appear on the ballot as a candidate for the office.
>
> If a majority of those voting on said question of the recall of any incumbent from office shall vote "no", said incumbent shall continue in said office; if a majority shall vote "yes", such incumbent shall thereupon be deemed removed from such office upon the qualification of his successor.
>
> If the vote had in such recall elections shall recall the officer then the candidate who has received the highest number of votes for the office thereby vacated shall be declared elected for the remainder of the term, and a certificate of election shall be forthwith issued to him by the canvassing board. In case the person who received the highest number of votes shall fail to qualify within fifteen days after the issuance of a certificate of election, the office shall be deemed vacant, and shall be filled according to law.
>
> Candidates for the office may be nominated by petition, as now provided by law, which petition shall be filed in the office in which petitions for nomination to office are required by law to be filed not less than fifteen days before such recall election.

Once a recall petition is certified, the incumbent has five days to resign. If the incumbent resigns, the vacancy is filled in the same manner as any other vacancy. If the incumbent decides to stand and fight, the governor sets a recall election date. If the incumbent resigns any time after the five-day window, the recall election is still held. The recall must be held within 30 to 60 days after the petition is certified, except that it will be held on a general election that is within 90 days, or a county or school district election date within 120 days. C.R.S. § 1-12-111(2).

The recall ballot will include up to 200 words about why the official should be recalled, and up to 300 words why not.

Voters first vote yes/no on the recall. They then vote on a successor, in the eventuality that the yes side prevails on the first question. The recall target cannot be a candidate for successor. *Bernzen v. City of Boulder*, 186 Colo. 81, 525 P.2d 416 (1974).

The right to vote on the successor *cannot* be conditioned on voting on the yes/no recall. Pursuant to Fourteenth Amendment equal protection, a voter may skip the yes/no and still vote on the successor. *In re Hickenlooper*, 312 P.3d 153 (Colo. 2013) (interrogatory to the Colorado supreme court).

If for some reason the winning successor is found to be ineligible for office (*e.g.*, not a U.S. citizen or a district resident), the office is declared vacant, and filled in the same manner as any other vacancy.

Successor candidates can be put on the ballot under statutory procedures (*e.g.*, nominated by a party's central committee), or by petition.

Under the two-step process, persons who want to preserve as much of the status quo as possible can coalesce behind a replacement candidate for #2, who would have many of the same views as the officeholder ousted in #1. The danger of this strategy, however, is that more people may vote in favor of the recall if they find the incumbent to be personally unacceptable and are (via #2) offered a new candidate with similar views. Thus, in the 2013 recalls, the Democratic party did not field alternative candidates in case the Morse or Giron recalls succeeded on question #1.

There is a second way to keep a recall-targeted seat in similar political hands. No later than five days after a recall petition is certified as having enough signatures, the incumbent may resign. The new vacancy is treated the same as a vacancy for any other cause. For state legislative seats, the vacancy is filled by a vote of the party Central Committee for district.

For example: the September 2013 recalls were a surprising success. Senator John Morse's district had been drawn to maximize the chance for Democratic victory in the region. Its core was the Democratic neighborhoods of Colorado Springs, plus Manitou Springs. Morse was narrowly ousted. Senator Giron, of Pueblo, was recalled in a 60%–40% landslide. Recall opponents had outspent the proponents by 9:1, but this was still insufficient to save incumbents who led the way in shoving unpopular gun control measures through the legislature, while refusing to allow many opponents (particularly, county sheriffs) even to testify. Never before or since have members of the general assembly been removed by recall. RICHARD COLLINS & DALE A. OESTERLE, THE COLORADO STATE CONSTITUTION 405 (2d ed. 2020) .

Emboldened, gun rights activists began a recall petition drive against state sen. Evie Hudak. She represented a Lakewood swing district with a close partisan balance, which Hudak had narrowly won in the previous election, the Obama-led Democratic 2012 sweep in Colorado. But since the election, Hudak had caused herself a variety of problems.

In 2013 committee hearings on gun control, while witnesses were testifying about sexual assault and other serious traumas, Hudak was spotted browsing through Facebook. Both major parties routinely send trackers to every general assembly committee hearing to watch for gaffes by the other side.

During a hearing on a bill to prohibit licensed carrying of concealed handguns on state college campuses, witness Amanda Collins had testified about her experience of being raped in a parking garage at the University of Nevada-Reno—just a few feet away from an unoccupied campus police substation.

Condescendingly, Hudak told rape victim Collins that it was a good thing that the university had prevented her from carrying her licensed handgun. Otherwise, the criminal might have taken the handgun away and used it against Collins. The senator's statement was bigoted and ignorant. Undisputed data from the Department of Justice's National Crime Victimization Survey shows that fewer than 1% of defensive gun uses result in the criminal taking the gun.[1] Most relevantly, as Ms. Collins retorted, "He already had a weapon of his own, he didn't need mine."

Although the committee still voted in favor of the campus carry ban on a party-line vote, the furor over Hudak's remarks doomed the bill. By the time the full Senate took up gun control bills later in the week, the sponsor had withdrawn the campus carry ban. In the next election cycle, when gun control advocates announced plans to promote a ballot initiative to ban campus carry, the Democratic party powers firmly told them not to do so, for the initiative would be sure to bring pro-gun voters to the polls, to the detriment of Democrats statewide. However, in 2021, the general assembly authorized bans on licensed carry on higher education campuses, and in much of the rest of the state. *See* chapter 4 (art. II, § 13).

While the recall petition drive for senator Hudak was in progress in December 2013, the senator resigned her seat. The Senate was 18D and 17R, so a Hudak recall would have flipped party control of the Senate. By resigning and thus stopping the recall, Hudak ensured that the

---

[1] GARY KLECK, TARGETING GUNS: FIREARMS AND THEIR CONTROL 167–68 (1997). Since the publication of Kleck's research, no scholar has challenged Kleck's conclusions, data, or methodology. Nevertheless, the myth persists among the misinformed.

Senate would stay Democratic for the 2014 session. Hudak's replacement, appointed by the party central committee, was her former campaign manager, city councilperson Rachel Zenzinger.

After serving in the 2014 general assembly, Zenzinger was defeated in the 2014 general election. She persisted, ran again in 2016 and won.

The 2013 Senate recalls were the exception in Colorado political history. Recalls of state officials are very rare. In subsequent years, big talkers who threatened recalls against state officials have not come remotely close to collecting the requisite number of signatures.

In contrast, recall votes for local officials have occurred with some frequency.

Art. XXI, Section 4. Municipal recall

> No recall petition shall be circulated or filed against any officer until he has actually held his office for at least six months, save and except it may be filed against any member of the state legislature at any time after five days from the convening and organizing of the legislature after his election.
>
> After one recall petition and election, no further petition shall be filed against the same officer during the term for which he was elected, unless the petitioners signing said petition shall equal fifty percent of the votes cast at the last preceding general election for all of the candidates for the office held by such officer as herein above defined.
>
> In any recall election of a state elective officer, if the incumbent whose recall is sought is not recalled, he shall be repaid from the state treasury for the expenses of such election in the manner provided by law. The general assembly may establish procedures for the reimbursement by a local governmental entity of expenses incurred by an incumbent elective officer of such governmental entity whose recall is sought but who is not recalled.
>
> If the governor is sought to be recalled under the provisions of this article, the duties herein imposed upon him shall be performed by the lieutenant-governor; and if the secretary of state is sought to be recalled, the duties herein imposed upon him, shall be performed by the state auditor.
>
> The recall may also be exercised by the registered electors of each county, city and county, city and town of the state, with reference to the elective officers thereof, under such procedure as shall be provided by law.
>
> Until otherwise provided by law, the legislative body of any such county, city and county, city and town may provide for the manner of exercising such recall powers in such counties, cities and counties, cities and towns, but shall not require any such recall to be signed by registered electors more in number than twenty-five percent of the entire vote cast at the last preceding election, as in section 1 hereof more particularly set forth, for all the candidates for office which the incumbent sought to be recalled occupies, as herein above defined.
>
> Every person having authority to exercise or exercising any public or governmental duty, power or function, shall be an elective officer, or one appointed, drawn or designated in accordance with law by an elective officer or officers, or by some board, commission, person or persons legally appointed by an elective officer or

officers, each of which said elective officers shall be subject to the recall provision of this constitution; provided, that, subject to regulation by law, any person may, without compensation therefor, file petitions, or complaints in courts concerning crimes, or do police duty only in cases of immediate danger to person or property.

Nothing herein contained shall be construed as affecting or limiting the present or future powers of cities and counties or cities having charters adopted under the authority given by the constitution, except as in the last three preceding paragraphs expressed.

In the submission to the electors of any petition proposed under this article, all officers shall be guided by the general laws of the state, except as otherwise herein provided.

This article is self-executing, but legislation may be enacted to facilitate its operations, but in no way limiting or restricting the provisions of this article, or the powers herein reserved.

Summary:

- A recall petition may not be filed until the officer "has actually held his office for at least six months." Except against "a member of the state legislature at any time after five days from the convening and organizing of the legislature after his election." By statute, the six-month period also applies to appointees, except appointees to the legislature. C.R.S. §§ 1-12-102(1), 31-4-505 (municipal).

- If the incumbent survives the recall election, no further recalls may be filed during the incumbent's term, unless a new recall petition is signed by registered voters equal to at least 50% of the votes cast in the last election for the officer. By statute, persons who signed the petition for the first recall may not sign the petition for the second recall. C.R.S. §§ 1-12-108(3)(a).

- If the state officer incumbent wins, the state treasury shall repay campaign expenses, according to procedures to be established by the general assembly. The general assembly can establish a similar procedure for local officials. Originally, the recall target could be reimbursed for 100% of campaign expenses. *Passarelli v. Schoettler,* 747 P.2d 867 (Colo. 1987) (city councilman). Pursuant to a 1988 amendment, reimbursement may be limited by statute. Currently, a state official can be reimbursed from the state treasury up to 10 cents per voter for specified expenses. For example, campaign literature and advertising costs are reimbursable, as are legal fees for challenging the petition. The incumbent's lodging and meals while campaigning are not reimbursable, nor are salaries for campaign staff, nor legal expenses related to campaign finance law compliance. County officials can receive up to 40 cents per voter. The rate is the same for municipal officials (from the municipal treasury), but municipalities have the option whether to adopt an ordinance providing for reimbursement. C.R.S. §§ 31-4-504.5 (municipal option).

- "The recall may also be exercised by the registered electors of each county, city and county, city and town of the state, with reference to the elective officers thereof, under such procedure as shall be provided by law."

- Local governments can provide recall procedures but may not set the petition threshold higher than 25%.

- Deep in section 4 is a non-delegation rule. Everyone who exercises government power in Colorado must either be personally subject to recall or must be under the control of someone who is subject to recall. In other words: elected officials are subject to recall. Every other person exercising government power is either: 1. Directly appointed by an elected official; 2. Hired by a person (*e.g.*, a department head) or a board, commission, etc. who is in turn appointed by an elected official. The rule seems to conflict with the constitutionalized state personnel system, art. XII, §§ 13-14. The vast majority of state employees are appointed by division heads, who are two steps removed from the elected governor; division heads are generally appointed by department heads, who gubernatorial appointees.

- The non-delegation rule has a limit: "any person may, without compensation therefor, file petitions, or complaints in courts concerning crimes, or do police duty only in cases of immediate danger to person or property."[2]

- "This article is self-executing, but legislation may be enacted to facilitate its operations, but in no way limiting or restricting the provisions of this article, or the powers herein reserved."

Recall procedures for elected officials are specified in C.R.S. §§ 1-12-101 through 123 (state); 31-4-501 through 507 (municipal); 31-1-906 & 907 (special districts).

According to the Colorado supreme court, the right of recall does not include judges. Pursuant to article VI, §§ 23–25, judges are appointed by an executive officer, and may be removed in certain unusual circumstances. Although judges are subject to retention elections, judges are, arguably, not "elected." *Matter of Title, Ballot Title, and Submission Clause for 2013–2014 #76*, 2014 CO 52, 333 P.3d 76, 84 (Colo. 2014). The case is the supreme court's most recent detailed analysis of the right of recall.

By statutes of questionable constitutionality, recall petitions may not be circulated within 6 months of the end of someone's term, or within 6 months of an election on which the incumbent's office will be on the ballot. C.R.S. § 1-12-102(4) (state); C.R.S. § 31-4-505(3).

---

[2] The latter seems to be a reference to service in a *posse comitatus*, when summoned by an appropriate official. For more on posses, see chs. 4, 6, & 21 (Bill of Rights, § 13; Fighting for Survival; Militia, art. XVII). Some of the summoning officials, such as sheriffs and coroners, are directly elected, but others, such as municipal police officers and (arguably) judges, are far-removed from any elected supervisor.

CHAPTER 27

Old Age Pension, article XXIV

Articles XXII and XXIII. (repealed)

Enacted in 1914, article XXII had prohibited alcohol. It was replaced in 1932 by an article allowing regulated alcohol, while forbidding saloons. As detailed in chapter 31 (Vices?), article XXII was later entirely repealed.

The former article XXIII, enacted in 1918, had involved the publication of legal notices. It required that legal notices be published in "two newspapers of opposite political faith." That is, a Democratic-leaning newspaper and a Republican-leaning newspaper. After World War II, newspapers became less overtly partisan, making article XXIII difficult to apply.

The article was repealed in 1994, and replaced by article V, § 7.3. It requires that information about ballot issues be published in legal newspapers—newspapers that meet the standards for publications of legal notices.

Article XXIV. Introduction

In 1927, the general assembly enacted a statute creating an old age pension fund. Congress enacted a similar statute in 1935, the Social Security Act. Article XXIV was adopted by the voters in 1936, with immediate harmful consequences. The pension fund was allocated 85% of the revenue from the state sales tax, use tax, and liquor tax. It also required federal grants to be directed to the pension fund. The result was disastrous for other welfare programs: unemployment relief, aid to families with dependent children, maternal health care, child health care, and vocational education.

Opponents tried to get article XXIV declared unconstitutional. They argued that it was "statutory" and not "constitutional" in nature, and that its spending directives violated the U.S. Constitution by depriving Coloradans of a republican form of government. The court did not find these arguments persuasive. *In re Interrogatories of Governor*, 99 Colo. 591, 65 P.2d 7 (1937).

Amendments in 1956 fixed many of the problems. Most importantly, the large annual surplus from the pension fund could be transferred to the general fund. § 7. Today, Colorado is the only state that has an old age pension fund in its Constitution.

The implementing statutes are C.R.S. §§ 26-12-112 et seq.

Article XXIV has been held to *not* be self-executing, except for the establishment of the pension fund. *Bedford v. Sinclair*, 112 Colo. 176, 147 P.2d 486 (1944).

Today, the Colorado Old Age Pension (COAP) is a small part of the state budget and does not excite much controversy. As a matter of constitutional drafting, it is interesting to study, since it is the granddaddy of all the amendments that specify government action at a statutoryish level of detail.

Art. XXIV, Section 1. Old age pension fund created

A fund to be known as the old age pension fund is hereby created and established in the treasury of the state of Colorado.

Art. XXIV, Section 2. Revenue for fund

There is hereby set aside, allocated and allotted to the old age pension fund sums and money as follows:

(a) Eighty-five percent of all net revenue accrued or accruing, received or receivable from any and all excise taxes now or hereafter levied upon sales at retail, or any other purchase transaction; together with eighty-five percent of the net revenue derived from any excise taxes now or hereafter levied upon the storage, use, or consumption of any commodity or product; together with eighty-five percent of all license fees imposed by article 26 of title 39, Colorado Revised Statutes, and amendments thereto; provided, however, that no part of the revenue derived from excise taxes now or hereafter levied, for highway purposes, upon gasoline or other motor fuel, shall be made a part of said old age pension fund.

(b) Eighty-five percent of all net revenue accrued or accruing, received or receivable from taxes of whatever kind upon all malt, vinous, or spirituous liquor, both intoxicating and non-intoxicating, and license fees connected therewith.

(c) Deleted by 2006, S.C.R.06-002, § 1, eff. Dec. 31, 2006.

(d) All grants in aid from the federal government for old age assistance.

(e) Deleted by 2006, S.C.R.06-002, § 1, eff. Dec. 31, 2006.

(f) Such other money as may be allocated to said fund by the general assembly.

Art. XXIV, Section 3. Eligibility for pension

Every citizen of the United States who has been a resident of the state of Colorado for such period as the general assembly may determine, who has attained the age of sixty years or more, and who qualifies under the laws of Colorado to receive a pension, shall be entitled to receive the same; provided, however, that no person

> otherwise qualified shall be denied a pension by reason of the fact that the person is the owner of real estate occupied by the person as a residence; nor for the reason that relatives may be financially able to contribute to the person's support and maintenance; nor shall any person be denied a pension for the reason that the person owns personal property which by law is exempt from execution or attachment; nor shall any person be required, in order to receive a pension, to repay, or promise to repay, the state of Colorado any money paid to the person as an old age pension.

Colorado-resident U.S. citizens at least 60 years old are eligible for the pension. The general assembly can set further qualifications. Means-testing is allowed, although certain things may not be included in the means test. Persons may not be denied because they own real estate, or because there are family members who could support them.

Following a 1970 U.S. supreme court case, the implementing statute was amended to allow legal resident aliens to receive the pension. C.R.S. § 26-2-111; *Gonzales v. Shea*, 318 F. Supp. 572 (D. Colo. 1970), *vacated & remanded* 403 U.S. 927 (1971) (in light of the recent decision in *Graham v. Richardson*, 403 U.S. 365 (1971)).

As a general rule, Congress has very broad discretion to discriminate against legal resident aliens, and states have virtually none—except for self-government matters such as voting and eligibility for employment in government jobs involving the exercise of discretion.

The residency requirement of section 3 has been removed in the current implementing statute, following a Colorado supreme court decision that a residency requirement of longer than the time necessary to process an application was unconstitutional under the Fourteenth Amendment's Equal Protection Clause. *Jeffrey v. Colorado Dept. of Social Services*, 592 P.2d 874 (Colo. 1979).

Art. XXIV, Section 4. Fund to be administered by state board of public welfare

> The state board of public welfare, or such other agency as may be authorized by law to administer old age pensions, shall cause all moneys deposited in the old age pension fund to be paid out as directed by this article and as required by statutory provisions not inconsistent with the provisions hereof, after defraying the expense of administering the said fund.

Payments will be administered by the state board of public welfare, or a successor agency, currently the Department of Human Services.

Art. XXIV, Section 5. Protection of revenue streams for pension fund

> The excise tax on sales at retail, together with all license fees levied by article 26 of title 39, Colorado Revised Statutes, and amendments thereto, are hereby continued in full force and effect beyond the date on which said taxes and license fees would otherwise expire, and shall continue until repealed or amended; provided, however, that no law providing revenue for the old age pension fund shall be repealed, nor shall any such law be amended so as to reduce the revenue provided for the old age pension fund, except in the event that at the time of such repeal or amendment, revenue is provided for the old age pension fund in an

amount at least equal to that provided by the measure amended or repealed during the calendar year immediately preceding the proposed amendment or repeal.

No law providing revenue for the old age pension fund shall be repealed, unless the law provides an equivalent source of revenue.

Art. XXIV, *Section 6. Basic minimum award*

(a) Beginning on the effective date of this article, every person entitled to and receiving an old age pension from the state of Colorado under any former law or constitutional provision shall be entitled to receive the basic minimum award hereinafter provided for, without being required to make a new application therefor, and such basic minimum award shall be paid each month thereafter, so long as he remains qualified, to each person receiving an old age pension at the time of the adoption of this article, and such basic minimum award shall likewise be paid to each person who hereafter becomes qualified to receive an old age pension; subject, however, to the provisions of this article relating to net income from other sources.

(b) From and after the effective date of this article, the basic minimum award payable to those persons qualified to receive an old age pension shall be one hundred dollars monthly, provided, however, that the amount of net income, from whatever source, that any person qualified to receive a pension may have shall be deducted from the amount of the pension award unless otherwise provided by law.

(c) The state board of public welfare, or such other agency as may be authorized by law to administer old age pensions, shall have the power to adjust the basic minimum award above one hundred dollars per month if, in its discretion, living costs have changed sufficiently to justify that action.

By the text, the basic minimum award is $100 monthly. This may be reduced to the extent that the recipient has income from any other source. The state board of public welfare has the discretion to increase the basic minimum award, based on increased cost of living.

In the original 1936 article, the minimum payment was $45. It was raised to $100 in 1956. As of 2020, the monthly minimum payment was $821. To be eligible, an individual must have resources (not including a home) of less than $2,000. The individual must first apply for federal welfare (Supplemental Security Income, SSI). Colorado Old Age Pension (COAP) payments are reduced by whatever amounts the recipient receives from SSI and/or private pensions. COAP recipients who receive the full amount are typically single women with no record of employment outside the home. RICHARD COLLINS & DALE A. OESTERLE, THE COLORADO STATE CONSTITUTION 416 (2d ed. 2020).

Art. XXIV, Section 7. Revenues remaining after payment of basic minimum award to be transferred to health and medical care fund

(a) All the moneys deposited in the old age pension fund shall be first available for payment of basic minimum awards to qualified recipients, and no part of said fund

> shall be transferred to any other fund until such basic minimum awards shall have been paid.
>
> (b) Any moneys remaining in the old age pension fund after full payment of such basic minimum awards shall be transferred to a fund to be known as the stabilization fund, which fund shall be maintained at the amount of five million dollars, and restored to that amount after any disbursements therefrom. The state board of public welfare, or such other agency as may be authorized by law to administer old age pensions, shall use the moneys in such fund only to stabilize payments of basic minimum awards.
>
> (c) Any moneys remaining in the old age pension fund, after full payment of basic minimum awards and after establishment and maintenance of the stabilization fund in the amount of five million dollars, shall be transferred to a health and medical care fund. The state board of public welfare, or such other agency as may be authorized by law to administer old age pensions, shall establish and promulgate rules and regulations for administration of a program to provide health and medical care to persons who qualify to receive old age pensions and who are not patients in an institution for tuberculosis or mental disease; the costs of such program, not to exceed ten million dollars in any fiscal year, shall be defrayed from such health and medical care fund; provided, however, all moneys available, accrued or accruing, received or receivable, in said health and medical care fund, in excess of ten million dollars in any fiscal year shall be transferred to the general fund of the state to be used pursuant to law.

Once the old age pension fund has paid the basic minimum award to all eligible recipients, the surplus shall be transferred to a stabilization fund. The stabilization fund should have $5 million dollars, to be replenished as needed. This is reserved for payments towards the basic minimum award.

Once the $5 million stabilization fund is full, and the basic minimum awards have been paid, the surplus shall be transferred to a health and medical care fund. From this fund, up to $10 million shall be used to provide medical care to persons who qualify to receive old age pensions. COAP provides medical care to individuals 60–64 who do not qualify for the federal Medicaid program (a means-tested federal/state medical welfare program). At age 65, they become eligible for Medicare, which is not means-tested.

Extra money exceeding the annual $10 million shall be transferred to the general fund.

Art. XXIV, Section 8. Fund is inviolate

> All moneys deposited in the old age pension fund shall remain inviolate for the purpose for which created, and no part thereof shall be transferred to any other fund, or used or appropriated for any other purpose, except as provided for in this article.

Money deposited in the old age pension fund shall remain inviolate for the purpose for which it was created. Except that, pursuant to section 7, the vast majority of the money that is deposited in the old age pension fund soon passes into the general fund. Today, COAP is minor part of the state budget, except that much state revenue first flows into the COAP fund, on its way to the general fund.

CHAPTER 28

Public Utilities, article XXV

> In addition to the powers now vested in the General Assembly of the State of Colorado, all power to regulate the facilities, service and rates and charges therefor, including facilities and service and rates and charges therefor within home rule cities and home rule towns, of every corporation, individual, or association of individuals, wheresoever situate or operating within the State of Colorado, whether within or without a home rule city or home rule town, as a public utility, as presently or as may hereafter be defined as a public utility by the laws of the State of Colorado, is hereby vested in such agency of the State of Colorado as the General Assembly shall by law designate.
>
> Until such time as the General Assembly may otherwise designate, said authority shall be vested in the Public Utilities Commission of the State of Colorado; provided however, nothing herein shall affect the power of municipalities to exercise reasonable police and licensing powers, nor their power to grant franchises; and provided, further, that nothing herein shall be construed to apply to municipally owned utilities.

Added in 1954, this article creates a Public Utilities Commission. By statute, public utilities include electricity, gas, water, trash pickup and disposal, intrastate communications (telephone, telegraph, cable), common carriers (intrastate busses, railroads, and air), plus pipelines. C.R.S. § 40-1-103.

Article XXV expressly does not affect article V, § 35, which forbids state regulation of municipal utilities within the boundaries of the municipality. By judicial interpretation, the exemption also applies to county utilities. *City of Durango v. Durango Transport, Inc.*, 807 P.2d 1152 (Colo. 1991).

Thanks to article XXV, the general assembly does have authority to regulate privately-owned (nongovernment) utilities in home rule cities. RICHARD COLLINS & DALE A. OESTERLE, THE COLORADO STATE CONSTITUTION 417-18 (2d ed. 2020).

Statutes on public utilities are in title 40, articles 1-7. PUC Rules are part of the Colorado Code of Regulations and are available on the PUC website.

The purpose of a public utilities commission is to regulate utilities in the public interest, so they provide reliable and nondiscriminatory service at the lowest price consistent with earning a reasonable rate of return. When government officials order utilities to spend more, the extra cost is passed on to consumers. The consumers pay for all the extra spending and for utility profits on top of that (the rate of return). The extra spending is not necessarily in the interest of the utility's captive customers. Consumer participation in PUC hearings is difficult, partly because the intricacy of PUC procedures means that consumers will need a lawyer with utility law expertise. The expert lawyers, however, tend to focus their practice on the income side of the question—namely, representing parties with an interest in higher utility rates. For a case study of some challengers' partial success in a pro-consumer intervention see, Lili Valis, *Coalition of Ratepayers Case Study*, INDEPENDENCE INSTITUTE, Issue Paper (Fall 2018) (ratemaking for Colorado Energy Plan and for the Rush Creek Wind Farm).

CHAPTER 29

Political Speech and Spending Controls, article XXVIII

Article XXVIII was enacted by the voters in 2002. In 2008, it was amended by the voters to severely restrict campaign contributions by holders of sole-source government contracts, in sections 15–17. The 2008 amendments were soon held to violate the First Amendment.

Article XXVIII is the most complicated part of the Colorado Constitution. The text is detailed and intricate. Lawyers advising clients on campaign finance issues must also be aware of the many judicial decisions, some of them finding article XXVIII partially unconstitutional under the U.S. First Amendment. Additionally, the lawyer must understand the related state statutes and regulations. Colorado election law can be a rewarding specialty, but it is perilous for dilettantes. Make sure to know it well lest you inadvertently get clients in trouble.

Further reading:

- A political organization must put its relevant financial information on a secretary of state website called TRACER ("Transparency in Contribution and Expenditure Reporting").
- A political organization may only terminate itself if its TRACER balance is zero.Fair Campaign Practices Act. C.R.S. title 1, article 45. The statutes copy much language from article XXVIII, but also cover additional matters.
- Secretary of state campaign finance regulations. Dep't of State, 8 Colo. Code Regs. 1505–06.Secretary of state, Colorado Campaign and Political Finance Manual (rev. Jan. 2021). The manual includes reprints of relevant statutes and regulations.
- Secretary of state, Campaign Finance webpage. A tremendous amount of helpful information, including links to campaign finance training classes, audio of continuing legal education on campaign finance, and much more. The training here is a good starting point for the practice of campaign finance law.

Bolded subsection headings below are by Kopel.

Art. XXVIII, Section 1. Purposes and findings

> The people of the state of Colorado hereby find and declare that large campaign contributions to political candidates create the potential for corruption and the appearance of corruption; that large campaign contributions made to influence election outcomes allow wealthy individuals, corporations, and special interest groups to exercise a disproportionate level of influence over the political process; that the rising costs of campaigning for political office prevent qualified citizens from running for political office; that because of the use of early voting in Colorado timely notice of independent expenditures is essential for informing the electorate; that in recent years the advent of significant spending on electioneering communications, as defined herein, has frustrated the purpose of existing campaign finance requirements; that independent research has demonstrated that the vast majority of televised electioneering communications goes beyond issue discussion to express electoral advocacy; that political contributions from corporate treasuries are not an indication of popular support for the corporation's political ideas and can unfairly influence the outcome of Colorado elections; and that the interests of the public are best served by limiting campaign contributions,

establishing campaign spending limits, providing for full and timely disclosure of campaign contributions, independent expenditures, and funding of electioneering communications, and strong enforcement of campaign finance requirements.

Section 1 articulates the compelling state interests in the speech restrictions that follow.

Art. XXVIII, Section 2. Definitions

For the purpose of this article and any statutory provisions pertaining to campaign finance, including provisions pertaining to disclosure:

(1) "Appropriate officer" means the individual with whom a candidate, candidate committee, political committee, small donor committee, or issue committee must file pursuant to section 1-45-109 (1), C.R.S., or any successor section.

(2) "Candidate" means any person who seeks nomination or election to any state or local public office that is to be voted on in this state at any primary election, general election, school district election, special district election, or municipal election. "Candidate" also includes a judge or justice of any court of record who seeks to be retained in office pursuant to the provisions of section 25 of article VI. A person is a candidate for election if the person has publicly announced an intention to seek election to public office or retention of a judicial office and thereafter has received a contribution or made an expenditure in support of the candidacy. A person remains a candidate for purposes of this article so long as the candidate maintains a registered candidate committee. A person who maintains a candidate committee after an election cycle, but who has not publicly announced an intention to seek election to public office in the next or any subsequent election cycle, is a candidate for purposes of this article.

(3) "Candidate committee" means a person, including the candidate, or persons with the common purpose of receiving contributions or making expenditures under the authority of a candidate. A contribution to a candidate shall be deemed a contribution to the candidate's candidate committee. A candidate shall have only one candidate committee. A candidate committee shall be considered open and active until affirmatively closed by the candidate or by action of the secretary of state.

(4) "Conduit" means a person who transmits contributions from more than one person, directly to a candidate committee. "Conduit" does not include the contributor's immediate family members, the candidate or campaign treasurer of the candidate committee receiving the contribution, a volunteer fund raiser hosting an event for a candidate committee, or a professional fund raiser if the fund raiser is compensated at the usual and customary rate.

(5)

(a) **"Contribution" is anything of value given to a candidate.** "Contribution" means:

(I) The payment, loan, pledge, gift, or advance of money, or guarantee of a loan, made to any candidate committee, issue committee, political committee, small donor committee, or political party;

(II) Any payment made to a third party for the benefit of any candidate committee, issue committee, political committee, small donor committee, or political party;

(III) The fair market value of any gift or loan of property made to any candidate committee, issue committee, political committee, small donor committee or political party;

(IV) Anything of value given, directly or indirectly, to a candidate for the purpose of promoting the candidate's nomination, retention, recall, or election.

(b) **"Contribution" doesn't include volunteer time.** "Contribution" does not include services provided without compensation by individuals volunteering their time on behalf of a candidate, candidate committee, political committee, small donor committee, issue committee, or political party; a transfer by a membership organization of a portion of a member's dues to a small donor committee or political committee sponsored by such membership organization; or payments by a corporation or labor organization for the costs of establishing, administering, and soliciting funds from its own employees or members for a political committee or small donor committee.

(6) **All time is part of one "election cycle" or the next.** "Election cycle" means either:

(a) The period of time beginning thirty-one days following a general election for the particular office and ending thirty days following the next general election for that office;

(b) The period of time beginning thirty-one days following a general election for the particular office and ending thirty days following the special legislative election for that office; or

(c) The period of time beginning thirty-one days following the special legislative election for the particular office and ending thirty days following the next general election for that office.

(7) **"Electioneering communication" is any distributed speech that mentions a candidate by name within 30 days before a primary or 60 days before a general election.**

(a) "Electioneering communication" means any communication broadcasted by television or radio, printed in a newspaper or on a billboard, directly mailed or delivered by hand to personal residences or otherwise distributed that:

(I) Unambiguously refers to any candidate; and

(II) Is broadcasted, printed, mailed, delivered, or distributed within thirty days before a primary election or sixty days before a general election; and

(III) Is broadcasted to, printed in a newspaper distributed to, mailed to, delivered by hand to, or otherwise distributed to an audience that includes members of the electorate for such public office.

(b) **But not what the media does, and not communications by an organization to its members.** "Electioneering communication" does not include:

(I) Any news articles, editorial endorsements, opinion or commentary writings, or letters to the editor printed in a newspaper, magazine or other periodical not owned or controlled by a candidate or political party;

(II) Any editorial endorsements or opinions aired by a broadcast facility not owned or controlled by a candidate or political party;

(III) Any communication by persons made in the regular course and scope of their business or any communication made by a membership organization solely to members of such organization and their families;

(IV) Any communication that refers to any candidate only as part of the popular name of a bill or statute.

(8) **"Expenditure" includes all spending of money for expressly advocating about the election of a candidate or a ballot issue.**

(a) "Expenditure" means any purchase, payment, distribution, loan, advance, deposit, or gift of money by any person for the purpose of expressly advocating the election or defeat of a candidate or supporting or opposing a ballot issue or ballot question. An expenditure is made when the actual spending occurs or when there is a contractual agreement requiring such spending and the amount is determined.

(b) **But not spending by the media, nor spending for organizational communications to members.** "Expenditure" does not include:

(I) Any news articles, editorial endorsements, opinion or commentary writings, or letters to the editor printed in a newspaper, magazine or other periodical not owned or controlled by a candidate or political party;

(II) Any editorial endorsements or opinions aired by a broadcast facility not owned or controlled by a candidate or political party;

(III) Spending by persons, other than political parties, political committees and small donor committees, in the regular course and scope of their business or payments by a membership organization for any communication solely to members and their families;

(IV) Any transfer by a membership organization of a portion of a member's dues to a small donor committee or political committee sponsored by such membership organization; or payments made by a corporation or labor organization for the costs of establishing, administering, or soliciting funds from its own employees or members for a political committee or small donor committee.

(9) **An "independent expenditure" is an expenditure that is not coordinated with a candidate.** "Independent expenditure" means an expenditure that is not controlled by or coordinated with any candidate or agent of such candidate. Expenditures that are controlled by or coordinated with a candidate or candidate's agent are deemed to be both contributions by the maker of the expenditures, and expenditures by the candidate committee.

(10) **"Issue committee" is any group of two or more people associated for the major purpose of supporting or opposing a ballot issue, and which receives or spends at least $200.**

(a) "Issue committee" means any person, other than a natural person, or any group of two or more persons, including natural persons:

(I) That has a major purpose of supporting or opposing any ballot issue or ballot question; or

(II) That has accepted or made contributions or expenditures in excess of two hundred dollars to support or oppose any ballot issue or ballot question.

(b) **An "issue committee" is not one of the other entities elsewhere covered by article XXVIII, such as candidate committees.** "Issue committee" does not include political parties, political committees, small donor committees, or candidate committees as otherwise defined in this section.

(c) An issue committee shall be considered open and active until affirmatively closed by such committee or by action of the appropriate authority.

(11) **"Person" includes entities that are not natural persons.** "Person" means any natural person, partnership, committee, association, corporation, labor organization, political party, or other organization or group of persons.

(12) A **"political committee" is two or more people who spend at least $200 to support or oppose a candidate. It does not include political parties, candidate committees, or issue committees.**

(a) "Political committee" means any person, other than a natural person, or any group of two or more persons, including natural persons that have accepted or made contributions or expenditures in excess of $200 to support or oppose the nomination or election of one or more candidates.

(b) "Political committee" does not include political parties, issue committees, or candidate committees as otherwise defined in this section.

(c) For the purposes of this article, the following are treated as a single political committee:

(I) All political committees established, financed, maintained, or controlled by a single corporation or its subsidiaries;

(II) All political committees established, financed, maintained, or controlled by a single labor organization; except that, any political committee established, financed, maintained, or controlled by a local unit of the labor organization which has the authority to make a decision independently of the state and national units as to which candidates to support or oppose shall be deemed separate from the political committee of the state and national unit;

(III) All political committees established, financed, maintained, or controlled by the same political party;

(IV) All political committees established, financed, maintained, or controlled by substantially the same group of persons.

(13) "Political party" means any group of registered electors who, by petition or assembly, nominate candidates for the official general election ballot. "Political party" includes affiliated party organizations at the state, county, and election district levels, and all such affiliates are considered to be a single entity for the purposes of this article, except as otherwise provided in section 7.

(14) **Small donor committees are a type of political committee. They receive donations of no more than $50 annually from members. (The classic small donor committee is an arm of a union.)**

(a) "Small donor committee" means any political committee that has accepted contributions only from natural persons who each contributed no more than fifty dollars in the aggregate per year. For purposes of this section, dues transferred by a membership organization to a small donor committee sponsored by such organization shall be treated as pro-rata contributions from individual members.

(b) "Small donor committee" does not include political parties, political committees, issue committees, or candidate committees as otherwise defined in this section.

(c) For the purposes of this article, the following are treated as a single small donor committee:

(I) All small donor committees established, financed, maintained, or controlled by a single corporation or its subsidiaries;

(II) All small donor committees established, financed, maintained, or controlled by a single labor organization; except that, any small donor committee established, financed, maintained, or controlled by a local unit of the labor organization which has the authority to make a decision independently of the state and national units as to which candidates to support or oppose shall be deemed separate from the small donor committee of the state and national unit;

(III) All small donor committees established, financed, maintained, or controlled by the same political party;

(IV) All small donor committees established, financed, maintained, or controlled by substantially the same group of persons.

(15) "Unexpended campaign contributions" means the balance of funds on hand in any candidate committee at the end of an election cycle, less the amount of all unpaid monetary obligations incurred prior to the election in furtherance of such candidacy.

All of the above definitions are very broad. So broad that specific language was needed to exempt writing a letter to the editor of a local newspaper.

Art. XXVIII, Section 3. Contribution limits

(1) Except as described in subsections (2), (3), and (4) of this section, no person, including a political committee, shall make to a candidate committee, and no candidate committee shall accept from any one person, aggregate contributions for a primary or a general election in excess of the following amounts:

(a) **Individuals can give $500 or $200, depending on the office, to a candidate in the primary, and a similar donation in the general election.** Five hundred dollars to any one:

(I) Governor candidate committee for the primary election, and governor and lieutenant governor candidate committee, as joint candidates under C.R.S., or any successor section, for the general election;

(II) Secretary of state, state treasurer, or attorney general candidate committee; and

(b) Two hundred dollars to any one state senate, state house of representatives, state board of education, regent of the university of Colorado, or district attorney candidate committee.

(2) **Small donor committees can give $5,000 or $2,000 in the primary and again in the general election.** No small donor committee shall make to a candidate committee, and no candidate committee shall accept from any one small donor committee, aggregate contributions for a primary or a general election in excess of the following amounts:

(a) Five thousand dollars to any one:

(I) Governor candidate committee for the primary election, and governor and lieutenant governor candidate committee, as joint candidates under 1-1-104, C.R.S., or any successor section, for the general election;

(II) Secretary of state, state treasurer, or attorney general candidate committee; and

(b) Two thousand dollars to any one state senate, state house of representatives, state board of education, regent of the university of Colorado, or district attorney candidate committee.

(3) **Contributions to or by political parties are capped.**

(a) No political party shall accept aggregate contributions from any person, other than a small donor committee as described in paragraph (b) of this subsection (3), that exceed three thousand dollars per year at the state, county, district, and local level combined, and of such amount no more than twenty-five hundred dollars per year at the state level;

(b) No political party shall accept aggregate contributions from any small donor committee that exceed fifteen thousand dollars per year at the state, county, district, and local level combined, and of such amount no more than twelve thousand, five hundred dollars at the state level;

(c) No political party shall accept contributions that are intended, or in any way designated, to be passed through the party to a specific candidate's candidate committee;

(d) In the applicable election cycle, no political party shall contribute to any candidate committee more than twenty percent of the applicable spending limit set forth in section 4 of this article.

(e) Any unexpended campaign contributions retained by a candidate committee for use in a subsequent election cycle shall be counted and reported as contributions from a political party in any subsequent election for purposes of paragraph (d) of this subsection (3);

(4) **Corporations and unions cannot make donations to candidate, except via small donor committee or a political committee as a conduit for donations from members or employees.**

(a) It shall be unlawful for a corporation or labor organization to make contributions to a candidate committee or a political party, and to make expenditures expressly advocating the election or defeat of a candidate; except that a corporation or labor organization may establish a political committee or small donor committee which may accept contributions or dues from employees, officeholders, shareholders, or members.

(b) **But ideological corporations can just spend their own money, rather than having to create small donor or political committees.** The prohibition contained in paragraph (a) of this subsection (4) shall not apply to a corporation that:

(I) Is formed for the purpose of promoting political ideas and cannot engage in business activities; and

(II) Has no shareholders or other persons with a claim on its assets or income; and

(III) Was not established by and does not accept contributions from business corporations or labor organizations.

(5) **Political committees can receive no more than $500 from a member in a two-year period.** No political committee shall accept aggregate contributions or pro-rata dues from any person in excess of five hundred dollars per house of representatives election cycle.

(6) **Candidate committees cannot give money to other candidates.** No candidate's candidate committee shall accept contributions from, or make contributions to, another candidate committee, including any candidate committee, or equivalent entity, established under federal law.

(7) No person shall act as a conduit for a contribution to a candidate committee.

(8) **Candidate committees can borrow money from banks under standard terms, and the loan does not count as a contribution.** Notwithstanding any other section of this article to the contrary, a candidate's candidate committee may receive a loan from a financial institution organized under state or federal law if the loan bears the usual and customary interest rate, is made on a basis that assures repayment, is evidenced by a written instrument, and is subject to a due date or amortization schedule. The contribution limits described in this section shall not apply to a loan as described in this subsection (8).

(9) **All covered committees must keep their funds in a separate bank account.** All contributions received by a candidate committee, issue committee, political committee, small donor committee, or political party shall be deposited in a financial institution in a separate account whose title shall include the name of the committee or political party. All records pertaining to such accounts shall be maintained by the committee or political party for one-hundred eighty days following any general election in which the committee or party received contributions unless a complaint is filed, in which case they shall be maintained until final disposition of the complaint and any consequent litigation. Such records shall be subject to inspection at any hearing held pursuant to this article.

(10) **No committee can receive a cash contribution of more than $100 or spend more than $100 in cash.** No candidate committee, political committee, small donor committee, issue committee, or political party shall accept a contribution, or make an expenditure, in currency or coin exceeding one hundred dollars.

(11) **Nobody can be reimbursed for a contribution to a committee.** No person shall make a contribution to a candidate committee, issue committee, political committee, small donor committee, or political party with the expectation that some or all of the amounts of such contribution will be reimbursed by another person. No person shall be reimbursed for a contribution made to any candidate committee, issue committee, political committee, small donor committee, or political party, nor shall any person make such reimbursement except as provided in subsection (8) of this section.

(12) **No contributions from non-citizens, foreign governments, or foreign corporations not authorized to do business in Colorado.** No candidate committee, political committee, small donor committee, or political party shall knowingly accept contributions from:

(a) Any natural person who is not a citizen of the United States;

(b) A foreign government; or

(c) Any foreign corporation that does not have the authority to transact business in this state pursuant to article 115 of title 7, C.R.S., or any successor section.

(13) **Contribution limits are indexed for inflation.** Each limit on contributions described in subsections (1), (2), (3)(a), (3)(b) and (5) of this section, and subsection (14) of section 2, shall be adjusted by an amount based upon the percentage change over a four year period in the United States bureau of labor statistics consumer price index for Denver-Boulder-Greeley, all items, all consumers, or its successor index, rounded to the nearest lowest twenty-five dollars. The first adjustment shall be done in the first quarter of 2007 and then every four years thereafter. The secretary of state shall calculate such an adjustment in each limit and specify the limits in rules promulgated in accordance with article 4 of title 24, C.R.S., or any successor section.

Contribution limits are set quite low. As section 1 indicates, the intent is to disable a candidacy that is dependent on a small number of wealthy donors. For example, in 1968 Minnesota Democratic senator Eugene McCarthy challenged incumbent president Lyndon Johnson, focusing mainly on McCarthy's opposition to the Vietnam War. President Johnson of course had the vast resources of the mainstream Democratic party behind him. McCarthy had plenty of youthful, idealistic volunteers, who cut their hippie tresses and went "Clean for Gene" to be more persuasive to voters they contacted. Although Johnson won the New Hampshire primary, McCarthy did unexpectedly well, and a few days after the primary, Johnson announced that he would not seek reelection.

McCarthy's campaign was financed by a few very wealthy donors. According to McCarthy he could not have run in 1968 if the federal campaign finance limits, enacted in 1974, had been in effect. Along with New York senator James Buckley, McCarthy sued to have the 1971 Federal Campaign Act and its 1974 amendments declared unconstitutional. They won a partial victory in the U.S. Supreme Court. *Buckley v. Valeo*, 474 U.S. 1 (1976).

Art. XXVIII, Section 4. Voluntary spending limits

(1) Candidates may certify to the secretary of state that the candidate's candidate committee shall not exceed the following spending limits for the applicable election cycle:

(a) Two and one-half million dollars combined for a candidate for governor and governor and lieutenant governor as joint candidates under 1-1-104 C.R.S., or any successor section;

(b) Five hundred thousand dollars for a candidate for secretary of state, attorney general, or treasurer;

(c) Ninety thousand dollars for a candidate for the state senate;

(d) Sixty-five thousand dollars for a candidate for the state house of representatives, state board of education, regent of the university of Colorado, or district attorney.

(2) Candidates accepting the campaign spending limits set forth above shall also agree that their personal contributions to their own campaign shall be counted as political party contributions and subject to the aggregate limit on such contributions set forth in section 3 of this article.

(3) Each candidate who chooses to accept the applicable voluntary spending limit shall file a statement to that effect with the secretary of state at the time that the candidate files a candidate affidavit as currently set forth in section 1-45-110(1), C.R.S., or any successor section. Acceptance of the applicable voluntary spending limit shall be irrevocable except as set forth in subsection (4) of this section and shall subject the candidate to the penalties set forth in section 10 of this article for exceeding the limit.

(4) If a candidate accepts the applicable spending limit and another candidate for the same office refuses to accept the spending limit, the accepting candidate shall have ten days in which to withdraw acceptance. The accepting candidate shall have this option of withdrawing acceptance after each additional non-accepting candidate for the same office enters the race.

(5) The applicable contribution limits set forth in section 3 of this article shall double for any candidate who has accepted the applicable voluntary spending limit if:

(a) Another candidate in the race for the same office has not accepted the voluntary spending limit; and

(b) The non-accepting candidate has raised more than ten percent of the applicable voluntary spending limit.

(6) Only those candidates who have agreed to abide by the applicable voluntary spending limit may advertise their compliance. All other candidates are prohibited from advertising, or in any way implying, their acceptance of voluntary spending limits.

(7) Each spending limit described in subsection (1) of this section shall be adjusted by an amount based upon the percentage change over a four year period in the United States bureau of labor statistics consumer price index for Denver-Boulder-Greeley, all items, all consumers, or its successor index, rounded to the nearest lowest twenty-five dollars. The first adjustment shall be done in the first quarter of 2007 and then every four years thereafter. The secretary of state shall calculate such an adjustment in each limit and specify the limits in rules promulgated in accordance with article 4 of title 24 C.R.S., or any successor section.

Campaigns can adopt voluntary spending limits, and so advertise the adoption. If candidate A adopts the limits and candidate B (in the same race) does not, then the contribution limits to candidate A are doubled.

Art. XXVIII, Section 5. Independent expenditures

> (1) **If you make independent expenditures for or against a candidate of more than $1,000 in a year, you must report it to the secretary of state.** Any person making an independent expenditure in excess of one thousand dollars per calendar year shall deliver notice in writing to the secretary of state of such independent expenditure, as well as the amount of such expenditure, and a detailed description of the use of such independent expenditure. The notice shall specifically state the name of the candidate whom the independent expenditure is intended to support or oppose. Each independent expenditure in excess of one-thousand dollars shall require the delivery of a new notice. Any person making an independent expenditure within thirty days of a primary or general election shall deliver such notice within forty-eight hours after obligating funds for such expenditure.
>
> (2) Any person making an independent expenditure in excess of one thousand dollars shall disclose, in the communication produced by the expenditure, the name of the person making the expenditure and the specific statement that the advertisement of material is not authorized by any candidate. Such disclosure shall be prominently featured in the communication.
>
> (3) Expenditures by any person on behalf of a candidate for public office that are coordinated with or controlled by the candidate or the candidate's agent, or political party shall be considered a contribution to the candidate's candidate committee, or the political party, respectively.
>
> (4) This section 5 applies only to independent expenditures made for the purpose of expressly advocating the defeat or election of any candidate.

In compliance with U.S. supreme court decisions on the First Amendment, section 6 does not prohibit independent expenditures. Such expenditures must be reported to the secretary of state.

Independent expenditures may not be coordinated with the candidate. However, clever operatives can find workarounds. For example, in the final days of the general election for the U.S. Senate in 2014, senator Mark Udall's campaign manager, Alan Salazar, tweeted details from Udall's internal polling. The tweets were of course readable by any Twitter user. They were especially useful to the independent groups that were spending money on Udall's behalf, since they implicitly informed the groups about which demographics should be targeted for more advertising.

Independent expenditures are only controlled by section 5 if they are "for the purpose of expressly advocating the defeat or election of any candidate." In other words, "Vote against John Hickenlooper" is covered. "Call Hickenlooper's office and tell them that you are disappointed with his sleazy ethics" is not.

N.B.: Spending that merely mentions a candidate's name (and which contains no express advocacy) within 60 days of a general election or 30 days of a primary is separately controlled by section 2(7).

Art. XXVIII, Section 6. Electioneering communications

> **Electioneering communications (defined in section 2(7)) must be reported to the secretary of state.**
> (1) Any person who expends one thousand dollars or more per calendar year on electioneering communications shall submit reports to the secretary of state in accordance with the schedule currently set forth in 1-45-108(2), C.R.S., or any successor section. Such reports shall include spending on such electioneering communications, and the name, and address, of any person that contributes more than two hundred and fifty dollars per year to such person described in this section for an electioneering communication. In the case where the person is a natural person, such reports shall also include the occupation and employer of such natural person. The last such report shall be filed thirty days after the applicable election.
>
> (2) Notwithstanding any section to the contrary, it shall be unlawful for a corporation or labor organization to provide funding for an electioneering communication; except that any political committee or small donor committee established by such corporation or labor organization may provide funding for an electioneering communication.

Electioneering communications must be reported; donors over $250 annually must also be reported, along with the name of the donor's employer. If you give $500 to an independent committee in support of a candidate who is opposed by angry trolls, expect the trolls to contact your employer.

Art. XXVIII, Section 7. Disclosure

> The disclosure requirements relevant to candidate committees, political committees, issue committees, and political parties, that are currently set forth in section 1-45-108, C.R.S., or any successor section, shall be extended to include small donor committees. The disclosure requirements of section 1-45-108, C.R.S., or any successor section, shall be extended to require disclosure of the occupation and employer of each person who has made a contribution of one hundred dollars or more to a candidate committee, political committee, issue committee, or political party. For purposes of this section and 1-45-108, C.R.S., or any successor section, a political party shall be treated as separate entities at the state, county, district, and local levels.

Separately from section 6, section 7 requires disclosure of name and employer for anyone who contributes $100 or more.

Art. XXVIII, Section 8. Filings

> The secretary of state shall promulgate rules relating to filing in accordance with article 4 of title 24, C.R.S., or any successor section. The rules promulgated pursuant to this section shall extend section 1-45-109, C.R.S., or any successor section to apply to small donor committees.

File the required reports with the secretary of state.

Art. XXVIII, Section 9. Secretary of state enforcement

(1) **Secretary of state will keep records of forms filed under article XXVIII.** The secretary of state shall:

(a) Prepare forms and instructions to assist candidates and the public in complying with the reporting requirements of this article and make such forms and instructions available to the public, municipal clerks, and county clerk and recorders free of charge;

(b) Promulgate such rules, in accordance with article 4 of title 24, C.R.S., or any successor section, as may be necessary to administer and enforce any provision of this article;

(c) Prepare forms for candidates to declare their voluntary acceptance of the campaign spending limits set forth in section 4 of this article. Such forms shall include an acknowledgment that the candidate voluntarily accepts the applicable spending limit and that the candidate swears to abide by those spending limits. These forms shall be signed by the candidate under oath, notarized, filed with the secretary of state, and available to the public upon request;

(d) Maintain a filing and indexing system consistent with the purposes of this article;

(e) Make the reports and statements filed with the secretary of state's office available immediately for public inspection and copying. The secretary of state may charge a reasonable fee for providing copies of reports. No information copied from such reports shall be sold or used by any person for the purpose of soliciting contributions or for any commercial purpose;

(f) **If somebody files a complaint against a secretary of state candidate, the secretary of state turns the complaint over to the attorney general.** Refer any complaints filed against any candidate for the office of secretary of state to the attorney general. Any administrative law judge employed pursuant to this section shall be appointed pursuant to part 10 of article 30 of title 24, C.R.S., or any successor section. Any hearing conducted by an administrative law judge employed pursuant to subsection (2) of this section shall be conducted in accordance with the provisions of section 24-4-105, C.R.S., or any successor section.

(2) **Anyone can file a complaint with the secretary of state within 180 days of the alleged violation. The secretary of state must turn the complaint over to an administrative law judge, who must rule on an expedited schedule. A prevailing complainant gets attorneys fees. ALJ decisions may be appealed to the court of appeals.**

(a) Any person who believes that a violation of section 3, section 4, section 5, section 6, section 7, or section 9(1)(e), of this article, or of sections 1-45-108, 1-45-114, 1-45-115, or 1-45-117 C.R.S., or any successor sections, has occurred may file a written complaint with the secretary of state no later than one hundred eighty days after the date of the alleged

> violation. The secretary of state shall refer the complaint to an administrative law judge within three days of the filing of the complaint. The administrative law judge shall hold a hearing within fifteen days of the referral of the complaint, and shall render a decision within fifteen days of the hearing. The defendant shall be granted an extension of up to thirty days upon defendant's motion, or longer upon a showing of good cause. If the administrative law judge determines that such violation has occurred, such decision shall include any appropriate order, sanction, or relief authorized by this article. The decision of the administrative law judge shall be final and subject to review by the court of appeals, pursuant to section 24-4-106(11), C.R.S., or any successor section. The secretary of state and the administrative law judge are not necessary parties to the review. The decision may be enforced by the secretary of state, or, if the secretary of state does not file an enforcement action within thirty days of the decision, in a private cause of action by the person filing the complaint. Any private action brought under this section shall be brought within one year of the date of the violation in state district court. The prevailing party in a private enforcement action shall be entitled to reasonable attorneys fees and costs.
>
> (b) The attorney general shall investigate complaints made against any candidate for the office of secretary of state using the same procedures set forth in paragraph (a) of this subsection (2). Complainant shall have the same private right of action as under paragraph (a) of this subsection (2).
>
> (c) **If an issue committee establishes a separate bank account for spending on a ballot issue, ALJ subpoenas cannot rummage through the committee's other materials.** A subpoena issued by an administrative law judge requiring the production of documents by an issue committee shall be limited to documents pertaining to contributions to, or expenditures from, the committee's separate account established pursuant to section 3(9) of this article to support or oppose a ballot issue or ballot question. A subpoena shall not be limited in this manner where such issue committee fails to form a separate account through which a ballot issue or ballot question is supported or opposed.

Private individuals can file a complaint with the secretary of state, who must refer it to an administrative law judge.

Art. XXVIII, Section 10. Penalties

> (1) **Penalties are 2x to 5x the amount involved.** Any person who violates any provision of this article relating to contribution or voluntary spending limits shall be subject to a civil penalty of at least double and up to five times the amount contributed, received, or spent in violation of the applicable provision of this article. Candidates shall be personally liable for penalties imposed upon the candidate's committee.
>
> (2) **Fifty dollars per day for late filings.**

(a) The appropriate officer shall impose a penalty of fifty dollars per day for each day that a statement or other information required to be filed pursuant to section 5, section 6, or section 7 of this article, or sections 1-45-108, 1-45-109 or 1-45-110, C.R.S., or any successor sections, is not filed by the close of business on the day due. Upon imposition of a penalty pursuant to this subsection (2), the appropriate officer shall send the person upon whom the penalty is being imposed proper notification by certified mail of the imposition of the penalty. If an electronic mail address is on file with the secretary of state, the secretary of state shall also provide such notification by electronic mail. Revenues collected from fees and penalties assessed by the secretary of state or revenues collected in the form of payment of the secretary of state's attorney fees and costs pursuant to this article shall be deposited in the department of state cash fund created in section 24-21-104(3), C.R.S., or any successor section.

(b) **Penalties for late filing may be appealed to an ALJ, who may reduce the penalty if the violator proves good cause.**

(I) Any person required to file a report with the secretary of state and upon whom a penalty has been imposed pursuant to this subsection (2) may appeal such penalty by filing a written appeal with the secretary of state no later than thirty days after the date on which notification of the imposition of the penalty was mailed to such person's last known address in accordance with paragraph (a) of this subsection (2). Except as provided in paragraph (c) of this subsection (2), the secretary shall refer the appeal to an administrative law judge. Any hearing conducted by an administrative law judge pursuant to this subsection (2) shall be conducted in accordance with the provisions of section 24-4-105, C.R.S., or any successor section. The administrative law judge shall set aside or reduce the penalty upon a showing of good cause, and the person filing the appeal shall bear the burden of proof. The decision of the administrative law judge shall be final and subject to review by the court of appeals pursuant to section 24-4-106 (11), C.R.S., or any successor section.

(II) If the administrative law judge finds that the filing of an appeal brought pursuant to subparagraph (I) of this paragraph (b) was frivolous, groundless, or vexatious, the administrative law judge shall order the person filing the appeal to pay reasonable attorney fees and costs of the secretary of state in connection with such proceeding.

(c) Upon receipt by the secretary of state of an appeal pursuant to paragraph (b) of this subsection (2), the secretary shall set aside or reduce the penalty upon a showing of good cause.

(d) Any unpaid debt owing to the state resulting from a penalty imposed pursuant to this subsection (2) shall be collected by the state in accordance with the requirements of section 24-30-202.4, C.R.S., or any successor section.

> (3) **You can't overturn an election result because somebody violated the rules.** Failure to comply with the provisions of this article shall have no effect on the validity of any election.

Violators must be heavily fined. The daily fines for failure to file a report can become quite hefty for a small committee that ceased operations in March, but ineptly failed to file the required notice of closure with the secretary of state until December.

Art. XXVIII, Section 11. Conflicting statutes are inapplicable

> Any provisions in the statutes of this state in conflict or inconsistent with this article are hereby declared to be inapplicable to the matters covered and provided for in this article.

An abundance of caution clause expressly superseding any conflicting statute.

Art. XXVIII, Section 12. Certain conflicting statutes are repealed

> Sections 1-45-103, 1-45-105.3, 1-45-107, 1-45-111, and 1-45-113 are repealed.

Express repeal of certain conflicting statutes.

Art. XXVIII, Section 13. Implementing legislation

> The provisions of this article shall take effect on December 6, 2002, and be applicable for all elections thereafter, except that the provisions of this article concerning sole source government contracts shall take effect on December 31, 2008. Legislation may be enacted to facilitate its operation, but in no way limiting or restricting the provisions of this article or the powers herein granted.

Implementing statutes may not narrow the scope of article XXVIII.

Art. XXVIII, Section 14. Severability

> If any provision of this article or the application thereof to any person or circumstances is held invalid, such invalidity shall not affect other provisions or applications of the article which can be given effect without the invalid provision or application, and to this end the provisions of this article are declared to be severable.

The usual abundance of caution severability clause.

Art. XXVIII, Section 15. Sole source government contractors

A 2008 initiative tried to address the problem of sole source government contracts given as a reward for political influence. But the text violated the U.S. First Amendment, such as by forbidding political contributions by family members of sole source government contractors—and even for two years after the contract ended. *Dallman v. Ritter*, 225 P.3d 610 (Colo. 2010).

> Because of a presumption of impropriety between contributions to any campaign and sole source government contracts, contract holders shall contractually agree, for the duration of the contract and for two years thereafter, to cease making, causing to be made, or inducing by any means, a contribution, directly or indirectly, on behalf of the contract holder or on behalf of his or her immediate family member and for the benefit of any political party or for the benefit of any candidate for any elected office of the state or any of its political subdivisions.

Art. XXVIII, Section 16. Sole source government contractor reporting

Also enacted in 2008, section 16 was a public reporting and disclosure law about sole source government contracts. The Colorado supreme court conceded that some parts of sections 15 and 16 were constitutional. But the court held these were not severable, because the remaining provisions were "so incomplete or riddled with omissions" that they could not be salvaged. *Dallman v. Ritter*, 225 P.3d 610 (2010).

> To aid in enforcement of this measure concerning sole source contracts, the executive director of the department of personnel shall promptly publish and maintain a summary of each sole source government contract issued. Any contract holder of a sole source government contract shall promptly prepare and deliver to the executive director of the department of personnel a true and correct "Government Contract Summary," in digital format as prescribed by that office, which shall identify the names and addresses of the contract holders and all other parties to the government contract, briefly describe the nature of the contract and goods or services performed, disclose the start and end date of the contract, disclose the contract's estimated amount or rate of payment, disclose the sources of payment, and disclose other information as determined by the executive director of the department of personnel which is not in violation of federal law, trade secrets or intellectual property rights. The executive director of the department of personnel is hereby given authority to promulgate rules to facilitate this section.

Art. XXVIII, Section 17. Sole source government contractor enforcement

The last of the three 2008 amendments on sole source government contract fell along with other two. The provisions that complied with the U.S. First Amendment were not severable, because the remaining provisions were "so incomplete or riddled with omissions" that they could not be salvaged. *Dallman v. Ritter*, 225 P.3d 610 (2010).

In the text below, subsection (2) gets at the heart of what the 2008 amendments were trying to address: favored government contracts for favored political contributors.

> (1) Every sole source government contract by the state or any of its political subdivisions shall incorporate article XXVIII, section 15, into the contract. Any person who intentionally accepts contributions on behalf of a candidate committee, political committee, small donor committee, political party, or other entity, in violation of section 15 has engaged in corrupt misconduct and shall pay restitution to the general treasury of the contracting governmental entity to compensate the governmental entity for all costs and expenses associated with the breach, including costs and losses involved in securing a new contract if that becomes necessary. If a person responsible for the bookkeeping of an entity that has a sole source contract with a governmental entity, or if a person acting on behalf of the governmental entity, obtains knowledge of a contribution made or accepted in violation of section 15, and that person intentionally fails to notify the secretary of state or appropriate government officer about the violation in writing within ten business days of learning of such contribution, then that person may be contractually liable in an amount up to the above restitution.
>
> (2) Any person who makes or causes to be made any contribution intended to promote or influence the result of an election on a ballot issue shall not be qualified to enter into a sole source government contract relating to that particular ballot issue.
>
> (3) The parties shall agree that if a contract holder intentionally violates section 15 or section 17(2), as contractual damages that contract holder shall be ineligible to hold any sole source government contract, or public employment with the state or any of its political subdivisions, for three years. The governor may temporarily suspend any remedy under this section during a declared state of emergency.
>
> (4) Knowing violation of section 15 or section 17(2) by an elected or appointed official is grounds for removal from office and disqualification to hold any office of honor, trust or profit in the state, and shall constitute misconduct or malfeasance.
>
> (5) A registered voter of the state may enforce section 15 or section 17(2) by filing a complaint for injunctive or declaratory relief or for civil damages and remedies, if appropriate, in the district court.

Statutory changes in 2019

The text of Article XXVIII was quite harsh on citizen activists, who, unlike many major party candidates, did not have ready access to expensive teams of election lawyers to navigate the article XXVIII intricacies. The citizen complaint procedure made harassment easy. For example, a parent of a schoolchild "placed various advertisements in some type of periodical or newspaper critiquing 'Common Core' education curricula and standardized testing programs . . . . [D]ays after placing these advertisements, a superintendent of the relevant school district filed a complaint against plaintiff because she allegedly, inter alia, did not register as a political committee, and thus, violated Colorado's campaign finance laws." *Holland v. Williams*, 457 F. Supp. 3d 979, 988-89 (D. Colo. 2018); Nick Sibilla & John Kerr, *Can't Afford a Lawyer? No Free Speech for You: Colorado campaign finance regulations censor ordinary citizens*, REASON,

Dec. 19, 2016. Caught between the text of article XXVIII and the legal mandates of the First Amendment, the general assembly eventually acted reform statutes in 2019.

The *Holland* court found that the private enforcement mechanism of section 9(2)(a) facially violated the First and Fourteenth Amendments of the U.S. Constitution. In response, Senate Bill 19-232_created new enforcement procedures: the complaint is reviewed by the Elections Division of the secretary of state's office. The Deputy Secretary of State (a political appointee of the Secretary) can override the Division's decision. A live complaint then goes to an Administrative Law Judge. ALJs are employees of the Office of Administrative Courts, which is part of the Department of Personnel & Administration; but here, the ALJ functions as a mere hearing officer. The deputy secretary presently asserts the authority to overturn the ALJ's decision. Thereafter, a case can be appealed to the court of appeals. Other revisions changed the statute of limitations to 180 days after the complainant "knew or should have known" of the violation. Respondents have a ten-day grace period to file missing form(s). Membership lists or data lists of the accused must be kept confidential and are not subject to the Open Records Act. Private complainants cannot appear before the hearing officer but may ask for permission to file an amicus brief. The secretary may issue advisory opinions; reliance on an advisory opinion is an affirmative defense.

House Bill 19-1318 defined a "small-scale issue committee" as a ballot issue committee that spends less than $5,000 to support or oppose a ballot issue. If the small-scale committee spends less than $200, it does not have to file any forms or disclosures. If it spends $201 to $5,000 in an election cycle, it must register. But it need not file reports about donors or expenditures.

Issue committees and small-scale issue committees are prohibited from accepting contributions from natural persons who are not U.S. citizens, from foreign governments, or from foreign corporations that lack the authority to transact business in Colorado. If a person solicits funds for an independent expenditure committee six months or less before the person declares his candidacy for an office, the independent expenditure committee is treated as if it were part of the candidate's treasury.

If a corporation, union, or independent expenditure committee gives $10,000 to anyone for the purposes of making an independent expenditure, the donor must provide the recipient with a document including the following information: For-profit corporations must provide the name and address of every beneficial owner. Non-profits must disclose all donors of more than $5,000 in the preceding 12 months whose donations were earmarked for independent expenditures or electioneering communications. The names of natural persons may be redacted if the person signs an affidavit, in a form provide by the secretary of state, that the person believes he or she is reasonably probable to be harmed, threatened, harassed, or to suffer reprisal.

Victims of frivolous, vexatious, or harassment complaints may ask a district court for attorneys' fees and costs.

Senate Bill 19-068 expanded restrictions to include the entire period between a primary and the general election, even when the primary is more than 60 days before the general election.

Summaries of leading decisions

Good faith defense

The private enforcement system of section 9 and the government enforcement system of section 10 are independent, and do not overlap. The "applicable provisions do not create a good faith defense," but an ALJ still has discretion in assessing the penalty. *Patterson Recall Committee, Inc. v. Patterson*, 209 P.3d 1210 (Colo. App. 2009) (committee to recall a county commissioner stopped filing reports, but did not formally dissolve itself after its recall petition signatures were ruled insufficient; fine was upheld).

In 2017, the legislature enacted a limited good faith defense, but that was repealed in 2019. The 2017 revisions to C.R.S. § 1-45-109(4)(c) had provided that when a complaint was filed under article XXVIII, §9(2)(a), the secretary of state had to give email notice to the targeted committee. The committee could request a postponement of the ALJ hearing and would have 15 business days to amend the allegedly defective report. If the committee cured all the problems, then the committee would not be fined, *if the committee proved* that it was acting in good faith or was in substantial compliance.

"Major purpose" and "issue committee" are not vague

The terms "a major purpose" and "issue committee" in article XXVIII are not unconstitutionally vague, even under the particularly strict test for vagueness that is applied in First Amendment cases. A think tank that devotes substantial effort to speaking out on a ballot measure is not an "issue committee." This factual finding was based on "the length of time the Independence Institute had been in existence, its original purpose, its organizational structure, the various issues with which it had been involved, and the amount of money expended on the radio ads in proportion to its annual budget." *Independence Institute v. Coffman*, 209 P.3d 1130 (Colo. App. 2008).

Home rule unimpaired

Article XXVIII does not apply to home rule counties and municipalities that have their own laws on the matters covered in article XXVIII. These need not be more stringent than article XXVIII. Colo. Att'y Gen. Op. No. 03-01, Jan. 13, 2003. Complaints are processed by the municipal clerk.

Attorney's fees are only for petitioners, not respondents

A respondent who wins before an ALJ may not be awarded attorney's fees even when the private claims made against respondent were groundless, frivolous, and vexatious. The plain language of the Constitutional provision created a non-reciprocal enforcement right in favor of the complainant, and only the legislature or the people have power to correct that result. *McGihon v. Cave*, 2016 COA 78, 410 P.3d 647 (Colo. App. 2016).

Statute of limitations of 180 days

The old violation-based 180-day statute of limitations to file a complaint began anew every time an excess contribution was made. In one case, a complaint about a $350 contribution was filed within the 180 day statute of limitations. The contribution in isolation was lawful. There were also many prior contributions by the donor to the recipient that were by now outside the reach of the statute of limitations. The ALJ must still consider the facts of the prior contributions in determining whether the $350 contribution was unlawful because it exceeded the allowable aggregate. The alleged excessive contributor was the governor-elect's inaugural committee, which was, arguably, a political committee. The alleged excessive recipient was his candidate committee, which had just helped him win gubernatorial election. In other words, money raised for the inaugural was used to pay off campaign expenses, and the inaugural committee's total contributions to the candidate committee exceeded the permissible aggregate. *Lambert v. Ritter Inaugural Committee, Inc.*, 218 P.3d 1115 (Colo. App. 2009).

Contributions received after a candidate election, and which are not spent for election purposes, must still be disclosed

Coloradans for a Better Future (CBF) bought radio ads in the 2012 Republican primary for CU regent; they criticized one candidate and supported another.

After the election was over, Coloradans for a Better Future wanted to terminate itself. The termination was handled by an attorney pro bono. Was the pro bono work an in-kind contribution that had to be reported under article XXVIII? The supreme court held that article XXVIII's contribution rules apply only to "any candidate committee, issue committee, political committee, small donor committee or political party." CBF, in contrast, was a "political organization."

Under Colorado's Fair Campaign Practices Act statute, donated services, such as pro bono legal work, only count as a "contribution" when they are behalf of a "candidate committee." Pro bono services for other entities (*e.g.*, issue committees, political organizations) are not reportable contributions. *Coloradans for a Better Future v. Campaign Integrity Watchdog*, 2018 CO 6, 409 P.3d 350 (2018).

Clear constitutional language trumps the blue book

The Committee for the American Dream was a political committee of the Colorado Homebuilders Association. CAD bought television ads that criticized state senator John Kefalas by name but did not expressly advocate for or against his re-election. CAD reported the spending but did not identify the spending as being for the purpose of opposing the Kefalas election.

CAD was relying on the blue book, the voter guide prepared by the non-partisan staff of the general assembly. The blue book is distributed to every voter for a general election. It explains the content of ballot issues and summarizes the pro and con arguments. The blue book for proposed Article XXVIII stated that the article would not apply to advertisements not "specifically urging the election or defeat of the candidate."

However, section 2(7)(a) of article XXVIII defines "electioneering communication" as "any communication broadcasted by television . . . that unambiguously refers to any candidate . . . and is broadcasted . . . sixty days before a general election . . . to an audience that includes members of the electorate for such public office." Although the blue book is very important in interpreting ambiguous language in a ballot measure, the language of article XXVIII was not ambiguous. Accordingly, CAD was fined for not disclosing that its television advertising expenditures were for the Kefalas Senate election. *Colorado Citizens for Ethics in Government v. Committee for American Dream*, 187 P.3d 1207 (Colo. App. 2008).

Exemptions for ideological corporations

Corporations and labor unions may not spend money from their treasury to give to a candidate, or to expressly advocate for or against the election of the candidate. Instead, they must establish a political committee or a small donor committee to receive contributions from employees or members. Only the committees may give to campaigns or independently advocate in candidate races. Art. XXVIII, §§ 3(4)(a), 6(2) §.

There is an exception for corporations that exist for the purpose of ideological advocacy. To be exempt, the ideological corporation must have been "formed for the purpose of promoting political ideas and cannot engage in business activities." It must have no shareholders or other persons with claims on its assets or income. And it may not accept contributions from business corporations or labor unions. *Id.* at § 3(4)(b). The exemption is required by First Amendment caselaw. *See Federal Election Commission v. Massachusetts Citizens for Life, Inc.*, 479 U.S. 238 (1986) (*MCFL*).

The Colorado Right to Life Committee is such a corporation. Mostly. Yet it has received $50 annually in contributions from a corporation. It has earned several hundred dollars annually from selling goods (*e.g.*, bumper stickers), from renting its mailing list, and from a program by which members signed up for long distance telephone services from a particular company and the company gave some of the revenue to CRL. CRL annual income from member donations was over $100,000.

The secretary of state urged that the "not engaged in business" provision of article XXVIII must be applied strictly. The Tenth Circuit disagreed, because every circuit court to construe *MCFL* has found that ideological corporations with *de minimis* business income or corporate contributions are still entitled to the exemption. *Colorado Right to Life Committee, Inc. v. Coffman*, 498 F.3d 1137 (10th Cir. 2007).

Union campaigning

A statewide teacher's union and a local teachers' union organized their members, and volunteers from other unions, to walk door-to-door, distribute literature, and communicate with voters, in support of the state senate candidacy of Bob Bacon. The organizing was conducted by union members who were paid by the unions to do full-time political work. This was not an "expenditure" that needed to be reported, because there is an exemption for "any communication solely to members and their families." Art. XXVIII, § 2(8)(b)(III).

The paid union staff did communicate with nonmembers, "creating postcards intended to be sent to nonmembers, and sending letters and making phone calls to nonmembers to recruit nonmembers for the walks supporting Bacon." However, the petitioners failed to prove that the unions made any expenditure in doing so. They could not prove that postcards had actually been sent to nonmembers, and they could not prove that the phone calls to nonmembers had resulted in expenditures.

The "membership communication exemption" had to be construed broadly, to comply with the First Amendment. Although a contrary interpretation was plausible, "As the Supreme Court has directed us, when the First Amendment is at issue, the tie goes to the speaker rather than to censorship and regulation."

In dissent, Justice Coats wrote that the majority had overread the membership communication exception. The majority rule allows "for partisan political campaign activities by paid union staff, as long as any direct contact with potential voters is left to union volunteers . . . [T]he majority's 'exception' virtually swallows the proscription itself, converting words of prohibition into a license for union campaigning . . . For my part, I am quite convinced that article XXVIII's proscription of all political expenditures by unions and corporations comports with the dictates of the First Amendment. If the majority doubts this proposition, it should strike down article XXVIII as a violation of the Supremacy Clause rather than simply rewriting it."

Also dissenting, Justice Eid cited supreme court precedent indicating that union spending for political activities could be restricted to a special segregated fund. It was permissible to ban the use of the union's general treasury for these activities. Justices Eid and Coats joined each other's dissents. *Colorado Educ. Ass'n v. Rutt*, 184 P.3d 65 (Colo. 2008).

Justice Eid's opinion had some validity when it was written in 2008, but it later became untenable after the U.S. supreme court's *Citizens United* decision, which held that unions and corporations may freely make independent expenditures from their own treasuries. *Citizens United v. Federal Election Commission*, 558 U.S. 310 (2010).

Use of union dues for politics without consent

The secretary of state promulgated an administrative rule that unions could only use a member's dues for political activity if the member affirmatively consented in writing each year. Several unions of government employees sued. The district court issued a preliminary injunction that was upheld on appeal.

For the union to obtain written consent would take two to three months and cost up to four dollars per member. The U.S. supreme court had upheld the use of union dues for politics, even when union membership was a mandatory condition of employment. According to the court, putting the burden on the employee to opt out was sufficient constitutional protection of the employee's rights. *See, e.g.*, *Abood v. Detroit Bd. of Educ.*, 431 U.S. 209 (1977). *Abood* and its progeny had created a floor of employee rights. The court of appeals turned the floor into a ceiling. According to the court of appeals, a government may not establish greater protection for employees.

The court of appeals was particularly concerned by the requirement for annual renewal of consent, since that seemed to presume that the employee dissented. The court did not find the rule facially invalid. Instead, it was invalid as applied to the particular plaintiffs in the context of the 2006 election, since the rule had been announced too close to the election. *Sanger v. Dennis*, 148 P.3d 404 (Colo. App. 2006).

In 2018, the U.S. supreme court over-ruled *Abood*. According to the majority, the First Amendment forbids governments to mandate that a worker's income will automatically be transferred to a political organization without the worker's consent. *Janus v. American Federation of State, County, and Municipal Employees, Council 31*, 138 S.Ct. 2448 (2018).

Under previous practice in Colorado, employees who are compelled to join unions and who do not want to have their money spent on politics must request a refund of the political portion of their dues. The opt-out request must be in writing and must be made every year. Usually, the period when opt-out is allowed is fairly short—for public school teachers, a few weeks in the early fall. These practices became illegal under *Janus*.

Taxpayer dollars may be used to promote pro-government information

Using school district funds, the Douglas County School Board commissioned a report that favorably analyzed the district's reform efforts. This was not a violation of article XXVIII, because none of the money was used to advocate for anyone's election. *Keim v. Douglas County School District*, 399 P.3d 722 (Colo. 2015).

Media exemption may not exclude documentaries

Citizens United is a nonprofit corporation that produces political films. Its 2014 half-hour film *Rocky Mountain Heist* critically described how a group of several very wealthy men—including Jared Polis, Tim Gill, and others—had effectively invested their money over a period of years to make Colorado Democratic. The production and marketing budget for the film was $773,975. The film mentioned current candidates for office by name, and it included scenes of events in which people advocated for or against the election of political candidates.

Accordingly, *Rocky Mountain Heist* and the advertising therefor were "electioneering communications" and "independent expenditures" under article XXVIII. Thus, Citizens United was required to file reports with the secretary of state and to disclose all of its donors of more than $250 (and their employers).

The Tenth Circuit held that Citizens United was entitled to a preliminary injunction based on the First and Fourteenth Amendments.

At oral argument, the secretary of state said that the donor disclosure only applied to donors whose gifts were earmarked specifically for *Rocky Mountain Heist.* However, as the court noted, the secretary's concession at oral argument did not provide protection against a private complaint.

Under federal election law, as administered by the Federal Election Commission (FEC), Citizens United has been determined to be entitled to the "press exemption" under federal law. However, the text of the press exemptions in article XXVIII (8)(b) (and C.R.S. § 1-45-103(10)) is narrower than the "press exemption" in federal election law, as interpreted by the FEC.

Following U.S. supreme court precedent, the Tenth Circuit applied "exacting scrutiny" to article XXVIII's discrimination among different types of media. Exacting scrutiny is a specialized standard developed for some First Amendment issues; it is weaker than strict scrutiny but stronger than intermediate scrutiny.

Given that Citizens United was an established media company—having produced 25 video documentaries in the past decade—the secretary of state could articulate no persuasive reason for article XXVIII's discrimination.

Article XXVIII provides exemptions for express advocacy in media *content* but not in media *advertising.* A *Denver Post* editorial titled "We are voting for John Hickenlooper and urge you to do so the same" is exempt. But the *Post* would not be exempted for a radio ad that said "Buy our Sunday edition and learn why you should vote for John Hickenlooper."

So the Citizens United *advertising* for its movie was still legitimately covered by article XXVIII, to the extent that the advertising contained scenes of express advocacy. *Citizens United v. Gessler*, 773 F.3d 200 (10th Cir. 2014).

Riddle v. Hickenlooper

742 F.3d 922 (10th Cir. 2014)

Summary: For a Colorado House of Representatives race, an individual can donate $400 to a candidate: $200 in the primary and $200 in the general election. Even if the candidate has no opposition in the primary, the primary contributions may still be made. Of course, an unopposed candidate can spend money during the primary season to appeal to voters with an eye on the general election. Or the candidate can just save the money and spend it during the general election.

Under Colorado statutory law, minor parties (*e.g.*, Greens, Libertarians) may not hold a primary when only one candidate is seeking the nomination for an office. Persons who run as independent candidates in the general election do not run in primaries.

Thus, in the course of an election cycle, a Democratic or Republican candidate for the Colorado House of Representatives can receive $400 from an individual, but other candidates can receive only $200.

In 2010, former Democrat Kathleen Curry ran as an independent against a Democrat and Republican for House District 61. Several of her donors brought a federal civil rights lawsuit under 42 U.S.C. § 1983. The Tenth Circuit unanimously ruled in their favor on Equal Protection grounds. Having done so, the panel felt no need to address the plaintiff's separate claim under the First Amendment.

GORSUCH, Circuit Judge, concurring

I confess some uncertainty about the level of scrutiny the Supreme Court wishes us to apply to this contribution limit challenge, but I harbor no question about the outcome we must reach. My colleagues are surely right that, as applied, Colorado's statutory scheme offends the Constitution's equal protection guarantee, whatever plausible level of scrutiny we might deploy. At the same time, it's no less clear to me that, with a little effort, Colorado could have achieved its stated policy objectives (and might still) without offending the national charter.

. . . [I]n the particular situation we face, major party contributors can channel twice as much money to their favorite candidate in the general election as minor party contributors can. The minor party contributors who bring this equal protection challenge suggest (at least in places) that we should consider applying strict scrutiny to this particular aspect of Colorado's statutory scheme. They say that contributing in elections implicates a fundamental liberty interest, that Colorado's scheme favors the exercise of that fundamental liberty interest by some at the expense of others, and for this reason warrants the most searching level of judicial scrutiny.

For my part, I don't doubt this line of argument has much to recommend it. The trouble is, we have no controlling guidance on the question from the Supreme Court. And in what guidance we do have lie some conflicting cues. No one before us disputes that the act of contributing to political campaigns implicates a "basic constitutional freedom," one lying "at the foundation of a free society" and enjoying a significant relationship to the right to speak and associate — both expressly protected First Amendment activities. *Buckley v. Valeo*, 424 U.S. 1, 25 (1976) (per curiam). Even so, the Court has yet to apply strict scrutiny to contribution limit challenges—employing instead something pretty close but not quite the same thing. See *id.* (using a "closely drawn" rather than a strict scrutiny standard); *Davis v. FEC*, 554 U.S. 724, 740 n.7 (2008); *Republican Party of N.M. v. King* No. 12-2015, slip op. at 8-9 (10th Cir. Dec. 18, 2013).

Some have questioned whether contribution limits should be subject to strict scrutiny. *See, e.g., Randall v. Sorrell*, 548 U.S. 230, 266-67 (2006) (Thomas, J., concurring in the judgment); *Buckley*, 424 U.S. at 241-45 (Burger, C.J., concurring in part and dissenting in part) . . .

Of course, all these teachings have come in the context of First Amendment challenges to contribution limits—and in this appeal we are asked to decide a Fourteenth Amendment claim. In the Fourteenth Amendment's equal protection context, the Supreme Court has clearly told us to apply strict scrutiny not only to governmental classifications resting on certain inherently suspect grounds (paradigmatically, race) but also governmental "classifications affecting fundamental rights." *Clark v. Jeter*, 486 U.S. 456, 461 (1988) . . .

To these questions, I can imagine this (potential) reply. The plaintiffs before us don't complain that Colorado's contribution limits violate their First Amendment rights because, say, the limits are too low for everyone. Instead, they complain that the State's contribution limits violate the Fourteenth Amendment's equal protection guarantee by discriminating against minor party contributors. And whatever level of scrutiny should apply to equal infringements of the right to contribute in the First Amendment context, the strictest degree of scrutiny is warranted under Fourteenth Amendment equal protection doctrine when the government proceeds to discriminate against some persons in the exercise of that right. On this account, there is something distinct, different, and more problematic afoot when the government selectively infringes on a fundamental right. *Cf. Davis*, 554 U.S. at 743-44 (suggesting that even in the First Amendment context "imposing different contribution . . . limits on candidates vying for the same seat" may call out for especially heightened scrutiny).

To be sure, Colorado tries a separate line of defense, suggesting that its discriminatory contribution scheme is justified not only because of corruption but also because of cost. Under Colorado law, major party candidates must always participate in primaries. Even when unchallenged. Meanwhile, under Colorado law minor parties may not conduct primaries when only one candidate seeks the nomination. Because even unchallenged primaries can be expensive, the State reasons, major party candidates who face no challenge for the nomination need and deserve more money than similarly situated minor party counterparts.

This argument bears no shortage of curiosities, but consider just these two. First, can a state really justify unequal treatment because of a "problem" of its own creation? After all, to the extent unchallenged major party candidates may incur more costs because they have to participate in primaries (an essential factual premise for which Colorado has identified no evidence in our record), that's only because state statutory law requires them to do so.

Second, what does the State's proffered rationale have to do with the rule it seeks to defend? Even if we accept for argument's sake the notion that major party candidates "need" more money to secure their parties' nominations because of the primary election process, that speaks only to the primary election. Meanwhile, the challenge in this case focuses on the fact Colorado's regulatory regime allows major party contributors greater influence in the general election. The State's rationale and rule just don't jibe: it supplies a possible rationale for higher contribution limits for major party candidates at the primary election stage but the challenge in this case focuses on the fact the State effectively allows higher contributions to major party candidates at the general election stage.

When it really comes down to it, the only reason I can imagine for Colorado's challenged regulatory scheme is a bald desire to help major party candidates at the expense of minor party candidates. Whether that rationale could save Colorado's scheme seems to me highly doubtful. Of course, the Supreme court has suggested that states may enact "reasonable election regulations" designed to foster a two-party system. *Timmons v. Twin Cities Area New Party*, 520 U.S. 351, 367 (1997). But the court has never gone so far as to suggest the states may pursue that interest by discriminating against contributors based on their political allegiances. *Cf. id.* (a state's interest in a two-party system "does not permit [it] to completely insulate the two-party system from minor parties' or independent candidates' competition and influence").

Neither has Colorado had the audacity to suggest that we should uphold its regime on this basis — and when deciding whether a law satisfies strict scrutiny or *Buckley*'s slightly less demanding standard, this court is obliged to assess the law only in light of the interests the State has sought to pursue, not those it hasn't. *See, e.g., Nixon v. Shrink Mo. Gov't PAC*, 528 U.S. 377, 387-88 (2000).

Having said this much, it is worth pausing to emphasize what isn't said in these pages. Nothing in what I've suggested or what the court holds intimates that Colorado must adopt a per-election-cycle rather than a per-election approach to the regulation of campaign contributions. The State represents that its constitution requires some sort of statutory scheme regulating campaign contributions on a per-election basis (disaggregating primary and general election contributions and capping them separately) rather than on a per-cycle basis (aggregating the two steps in one overall contribution limit).

If we strike down its current statutory regime, Colorado says it worries its constitutional command may be imperiled too. But such fears are misplaced. The fact that Colorado's current statutory per-election scheme runs afoul of the federal equal protection guarantee doesn't mean all will. The federal government regulates campaign contributions on a per-election basis and manages to do so without any of the discrimination found in Colorado statutory law. Perhaps the State might follow this model or some other. What we hold today is limited but no less essential for it: a state cannot adopt contribution limits that so clearly discriminate against minority voices in the political process without some "compelling" or "closely drawn" purpose—and Colorado has articulated none.

CHAPTER 30

Ethics in Government, article XXIX

Article XXIX came from Colorado Common Cause, as did article XXVIII. The latter, involving campaign speech regulations, is discussed in chapter 29.

For enforcement procedures, article XXIX is an improvement over article XXVIII. Article XXIX has an expeditious method to weed out frivolous complaints. It provides for an independent commission with expertise to make decisions.

However, in substance article XXIX is far too inclusive. Drafts were distributed to sympathetic lawyers, who pointed out some of the problems with its overbroad language. Nevertheless, Common Cause went ahead and put the draft on the ballot, while failing to correct the numerous identified problems. Although Common Cause is generally dedicated to "good government," its behavior with article XXIX was irresponsible.

In the general election, the core targets of article XXIX (lobbyists who take legislators out to lunch and pick up the tab) apparently decided that fighting the proposal was hopeless. Nobody made a significant effort to explain to the voters that article XXIX was very overbroad. Article XXIX (2006) is in the same spirit as the grossly excessive sole source government contractors amendments from 2010 (art. XXVIII, §§ 15–17). Both addressed genuine problems, both were part of Colorado's efforts since 1876 to thwart government corruption, and both took good principles beyond logical extremes. As justice Felix Frankfurter wrote in another context, article XXIX's policy "is to burn down the house to roast a pig." *Butler v. Michigan*, 352 U.S. 380, 383 (1957).

Art. XXIX, Section 1. Purposes and findings

(1) The people of the state of Colorado hereby find and declare that:

(a) The conduct of public officers, members of the general assembly, local government officials, and government employees must hold the respect and confidence of the people;

(b) They shall carry out their duties for the benefit of the people of the state;

(c) They shall, therefore, avoid conduct that is in violation of their public trust or that creates a justifiable impression among members of the public that such trust is being violated;

(d) Any effort to realize personal financial gain through public office other than compensation provided by law is a violation of that trust; and
(e) To ensure propriety and to preserve public confidence, they must have the benefit of specific standards to guide their conduct, and of a penalty mechanism to enforce those standards.

(2) The people of the state of Colorado also find and declare that there are certain costs associated with holding public office and that to ensure the integrity of the office, such costs of a reasonable and necessary nature should be born by the state or local government.

Art. XXIX, Section 2. Definitions

As used in this article, unless the context otherwise requires:

(1) "Government employee" means any employee, including independent contractors, of the state executive branch, the state legislative branch, a state agency, a public institution of higher education, or any local government, except a member of the general assembly or a public officer.

(2) "Local government" means county or municipality.

(3) "Local government official" means an elected or appointed official of a local government but does not include an employee of a local government.

(4) "Person" means any individual, corporation, business trust, estate, trust, limited liability company, partnership, labor organization, association, political party, committee, or other legal entity.

(5) "Professional lobbyist" means any individual who engages himself or herself or is engaged by any other person for pay or for any consideration for lobbying. "Professional lobbyist" does not include any volunteer lobbyist, any state official or employee acting in his or her official capacity, except those designated as lobbyists as provided by law, any elected public official acting in his or her official capacity, or any individual who appears as counsel or advisor in an adjudicatory proceeding.

(6) "Public officer" means any elected officer, including all statewide elected officeholders, the head of any department of the executive branch, and elected and appointed members of state boards and commissions. "Public officer" does not include a member of the general assembly, a member of the judiciary, any local government official, or any member of a board, commission, council or committee who receives no compensation other than a per diem allowance or necessary and reasonable expenses.

Section 2 provides ordinary definitions of "Government employee", "Local government", "Local government official", "Person" (natural or legal), "Professional lobbyist", and "Public officer."

Art. XXIX, Section 3. Gift ban

(1) No public officer, member of the general assembly, local government official, or government employee shall accept or receive any money, forbearance, or forgiveness of indebtedness from any person, without such person receiving lawful consideration of equal or greater value in return from the public officer, member of the general assembly, local government official, or government employee who accepted or received the money, forbearance or forgiveness of indebtedness.

(2) No public officer, member of the general assembly, local government official, or government employee, either directly or indirectly as the beneficiary of a gift or thing of value given to such person's spouse or dependent child, shall solicit, accept or receive any gift or other thing of value having either a fair market value or aggregate actual cost greater than fifty dollars ($50) in any calendar year, including but not limited to, gifts, loans, rewards, promises or negotiations of future employment, favors or services, honoraria, travel, entertainment, or special discounts, from a person, without the person receiving lawful consideration of equal or greater value in return from the public officer, member of the general assembly, local government official, or government employee who solicited, accepted or received the gift or other thing of value.

(3) The prohibitions in subsections (1) and (2) of this section do not apply if the gift or thing of value is:

(a) A campaign contribution as defined by law;

(b) An unsolicited item of trivial value less than fifty dollars ($50), such as a pen, calendar, plant, book, note pad or other similar item;

(c) An unsolicited token or award of appreciation in the form of a plaque, trophy, desk item, wall memento, or similar item;

(d) Unsolicited informational material, publications, or subscriptions related to the recipient's performance of official duties;

(e) Admission to, and the cost of food or beverages consumed at, a reception, meal or meeting by an organization before whom the recipient appears to speak or to answer questions as part of a scheduled program;

(f) Reasonable expenses paid by a nonprofit organization or other state or local government for attendance at a convention, fact-finding mission or trip, or other meeting if the person is scheduled to deliver a speech, make a presentation, participate on a panel, or represent the state or local government, provided that the non-profit organization receives less than five percent (5%) of its funding from for-profit organizations or entities;

(g) Given by an individual who is a relative or personal friend of the recipient on a special occasion.

(h) A component of the compensation paid or other incentive given to the recipient in the normal course of employment.

> (4) Notwithstanding any provisions of this section to the contrary, and excepting campaign contributions as defined by law, no professional lobbyist, personally or on behalf of any other person or entity, shall knowingly offer, give, or arrange to give, to any public officer, member of the general assembly, local government official, or government employee, or to a member of such person's immediate family, any gift or thing of value, of any kind or nature, nor knowingly pay for any meal, beverage, or other item to be consumed by such public officer, member of the general assembly, local government official or government employee, whether or not such gift or meal, beverage or other item to be consumed is offered, given or paid for in the course of such lobbyist's business or in connection with a personal or social event; provided, however, that a professional lobbyist shall not be prohibited from offering or giving to a public officer, member of the general assembly, local government official or government employee who is a member of his or her immediate family any such gift, thing of value, meal, beverage or other item.
>
> (5) The general assembly shall make any conforming amendments to the reporting and disclosure requirements for public officers, members of the general assembly and professional lobbyists, as provided by law, to comply with the requirements set forth in this section.
>
> (6) The fifty-dollar ($50) limit set forth in subsection (2) of this section shall be adjusted by an amount based upon the percentage change over a four-year period in the United States bureau of labor statistics consumer price index for Denver-Boulder-Greeley, all items, all consumers, or its successor index, rounded to the nearest lowest dollar. The first adjustment shall be done in the first quarter of 2011 and then every four years thereafter.

The general rule is that no government employee *or their spouses or dependent children* can ever receive any gift, in any form. The ban does not apply if the total value of the gifts given by a donor in a given year is less than $50. The limit is adjusted by the Consumer Price Index and as of 2021 was $65.

Lobbyists cannot give anything, ever, except campaign contributions. Not even a Diet Coke when the lobbyist notices that a government employee's child is thirsty. However, if the lobbyist is married to a government employee, the lobbyist may give gifts to their children, and even pay for their food.

Educational organizations such as the Independence Institute or the Sierra Club can give government employees free copies of their books, monographs, etc. But not if the government employee asks to receive the written material.

If a government employee is invited to speak at a luncheon, she can eat the lunch.

A non-profit organization can pay the travel expenses for a government employee to appear on a panel. To be eligible, the nonprofit may not receive more than 5% of its total funding from for-profit entities.

Personal gifts to friends and family are allowed "on a special occasion." So, if you are the friend of a government employee's child, you can give the child a $100 gift for high school graduation. But the child's aunt cannot give her nephew her used car, absent a special occasion.

Gifts in the normal course of employment are allowed. Therefore, if a charter school has a surplus at the end of the year, it can pay the teachers a year-end bonus.

Art. XXIX, Section 4. Lobbying limits on former state officials

> No statewide elected officeholder or member of the general assembly shall personally represent another person or entity for compensation before any other statewide elected officeholder or member of the general assembly, for a period of two years following vacation of office. Further restrictions on public officers or members of the general assembly and similar restrictions on other public officers, local government officials or government employees may be established by law.

Statewide elected officeholders and members of the general assembly cannot become registered paid lobbyists until at least two years after they have left office. The intent is to prevent a legislator in his final term from passing legislation favorable to an interest group, and then being hired as a lobbyist for that group.

Art. XXIX, Section 5. Independent ethics commission

> (1) There is hereby created an independent ethics commission to be composed of five members. The purpose of the independent ethics commission shall be to hear complaints, issue findings, and assess penalties, and also to issue advisory opinions, on ethics issues arising under this article and under any other standards of conduct and reporting requirements as provided by law. The independent ethics commission shall have authority to adopt such reasonable rules as may be necessary for the purpose of administering and enforcing the provisions of this article and any other standards of conduct and reporting requirements as provided by law. The general assembly shall appropriate reasonable and necessary funds to cover staff and administrative expenses to allow the independent ethics commission to carry out its duties pursuant to this article. Members of the commission shall receive no compensation for their services on the commission.
>
> (2)
>
> (a) Members of the independent ethics commission shall be appointed in the following manner and order:
>
> (I) One member shall be appointed by the Colorado senate;
> (II) One member shall be appointed by the Colorado house of representatives;
> (III) One member shall be appointed by the governor of the state of Colorado;
> (IV) One member shall be appointed by the chief justice of the Colorado supreme court; and
> (V) One member shall be either a local government official or a local government employee appointed by the affirmative vote of at least three of the four members appointed pursuant to subparagraphs (I) to (IV) of this paragraph (a).
>
> (b) No more than two members shall be affiliated with the same political party.

(c) Each of the five members shall be registered Colorado voters and shall have been continuously registered with the same political party, or continuously unaffiliated with any political party, for at least two years prior to appointment to the commission.

(d) Members of the independent ethics commission shall be appointed to terms of four years; except that, the first member appointed by the Colorado senate and the first member appointed by the governor of the state of Colorado shall initially serve two year terms to achieve staggered ending dates.

(e) If a member is appointed to fill an unexpired term, that member's term shall end at the same time as the term of the person being replaced.

(f) Each member shall continue to serve until a successor has been appointed, except that if a member is unable or unwilling to continue to serve until a successor has been appointed, the original appointing authority as described in this subsection shall fill the vacancy promptly.

(3)

(a) Any person may file a written complaint with the independent ethics commission asking whether a public officer, member of the general assembly, local government official, or government employee has failed to comply with this article or any other standards of conduct or reporting requirements as provided by law within the preceding twelve months.

(b) The commission may dismiss frivolous complaints without conducting a public hearing. Complaints dismissed as frivolous shall be maintained confidential by the commission.

(c) The commission shall conduct an investigation, hold a public hearing, and render findings on each non-frivolous complaint pursuant to written rules adopted by the commission.

(d) The commission may assess penalties for violations as prescribed by this article and provided by law.

(e) There is hereby established a presumption that the findings shall be based on a preponderance of evidence unless the commission determines that the circumstances warrant a heightened standard.

(4) Members of the independent ethics commission shall have the power to subpoena documents and to subpoena witnesses to make statements and produce documents.

(5) Any public officer, member of the general assembly, local government official, or government employee may submit a written request to the independent ethics commission for an advisory opinion on whether any conduct by that person would constitute a violation of this article, or any other standards of conduct or reporting requirements as provided by law. The commission shall render an advisory opinion pursuant to written rules adopted by the commission.

Article XXIX is enforced by the five-member Independent Ethics Commission. The commission does not have to comply with the Colorado Open Meetings Law because it is not a "any state public body." It is "separate and distinct from the executive and legislative branches." *Dunafon v. Krupa*, 2020 COA 149, 477 P.3d 785, 790 (Colo. App. 2020); C.R.S. § 24-6-402 (2)(a).

The governor, house, senate, and chief justice each appoint one member. The fifth member is chosen by the other four. No more than two members shall be affiliated with the same political party. Members must have been registered Colorado voters for at least two years. They serve four-year staggered terms.

Anyone can file a complaint. The complaint must be about something that happened, including failure to file a report, within the preceding 12 months.

Government employees can ask for advisory opinions about whether a proposed action is lawful.

Art. XXIX, Section 6. Penalties

> Any public officer, member of the general assembly, local government official or government employee who breaches the public trust for private gain and any person or entity inducing such breach shall be liable to the state or local jurisdiction for double the amount of the financial equivalent of any benefits obtained by such actions. The manner of recovery and additional penalties may be provided by law.

The donor and recipient must each pay double the equivalent of the financial benefit unlawfully conferred.

Art. XXIX, Section 7. Counties and municipalities can adopt their own rules

> Any county or municipality may adopt ordinances or charter provisions with respect to ethics matters that are more stringent than any of the provisions contained in this article. The requirements of this article shall not apply to home rule counties or home rule municipalities that have adopted charters, ordinances, or resolutions that address the matters covered by this article.

All local governments can opt out by adopting more stringent restrictions. Home rule governments can opt out just by having some rules on gifts, even if less stringent.

Art. XXIX, Section 8. Conflicting statutes are inapplicable

> Any provisions in the statutes of this state in conflict or inconsistent with this article are hereby declared to be preempted by this article and inapplicable to the matters covered by and provided for in this article.

Art. XXIX, Section 9. Implementing legislation

> Legislation may be enacted to facilitate the operation of this article, but in no way shall such legislation limit or restrict the provisions of this article or the powers herein granted.

The website of the Colorado Independent Ethics Commission is https://iec.colorado.gov/. The Commission's opinions are available at https://iec.colorado.gov/opinions. There is a helpful topical index, https://iec.colorado.gov/opinions/opinions-indexed-by-topic.

The plain language of article XXIX forbids giving a college scholarship to the child of a firefighter. To avoid this absurd result, the Commission adopted the absurd position that the scholarship is not "gift" but instead is a payment in exchange for future performance: that the recipient will attend the school offering the scholarship.

The commission likewise construed "special occasion" (when friends or relatives can give gifts to public employees or their families) to "not necessarily mean events that are rare or unusual. A special occasion may occur on a regular basis, such as a weekly meal with friends or family."[1]

Likewise, inheritances (which are gifts, since the dead cannot exchange contractual consideration[2]) are allowed because they "do not raise any ethical issues." *See* Position statement 08-01 (initial determinations on scholarships, special occasions, and inheritances).

"Special discounts" are allowed if broadly available—for example, the American Automobile Association offers discounted memberships to all state government employees.

State university professors can receive examination copies of textbooks as long as the professor did not ask for it; if the professors does ask for the examination copy, the copy is the property of the university, not the professor. Position statement 09-01.

Reimbursement for travel expenses is covered by seven subcategories of IEC rules, depending on who is doing the reimbursing.

The commission's rulings on the above issues have not been challenged, perhaps because they represent results that article XXIX's proponents favored and would have provided for in article XXIX had the proponents drafted the article competently.

Attorneys employed by state government, or advising state employees, should consult the IEC rules carefully. The same is true for attorneys working with local governments, which may have their own rules.

Article XXIX has been weaponized by Democratic and Republican partisans. Whatever minor problems it solved regarding free lunches for legislators are far outweighed by the harm it has done in making perilous the ordinary activities of apolitical government employees. *See* Miller Hudson, *Ethics commission or kangaroo court?*, COLO. POLITICS, June 12, 2020.

---

[1] *Cf. The Incredibles* (2004 film):

Dash: But Dad always said our powers were nothing to be ashamed of, our powers made us special.
Helen: Everyone's special, Dash.
Dash: Which is another way of saying no one is.

[2] But see the Grateful Dead folk tales (from which the band took its name): a person performs an act of kindness for a deceased person—such as arranging for a decent burial. Later, the decedent appears to the person, and performs an impossible feat for the person's benefit. GORDON HALL GEROULD, THE GRATEFUL DEAD: THE HISTORY OF A FOLK STORY (1908).

Part VI
Special Topics

CHAPTER 31

Vices? Alcohol, Marijuana, Gambling, and Tobacco

This chapter looks at the constitutional treatment of four things that have sometimes been considered vices that should be prohibited—and which are today treated as lucrative sources of tax revenue. The chapter first covers alcohol, which was once prohibited by constitutional amendment, the now-repealed article XXII. Tobacco is very severely taxed by article X, § 21, added in 2004 and made more severe in 2016. Lotteries and similar games of pure chance, such as bingo, used to prohibited, but then were legalized for civil society fundraisers; today, over two dozen state lottery games harvest funds from gamblers. The lotteries have the worst odds of any form of legal gambling. Limited, small-stakes casino gambling was relegalized by article XVIII, section 9; later, the stakes and scope were greatly expanded. Relegalization of medical marijuana and later of adult use were also accomplished by amendments to article XVIII.

As you read the constitutional language below, observe how the amendments' drafters go into statutoryish detail to constrain legislative resistance to the amendments' purposes. Compare and contrast the provisions about the different subjects regarding what sort of safeguards they impose.

Art. XXII. Alcohol

In 1914, the people of Colorado adopted article XXII, forbidding the manufacture or sale of intoxicating liquors starting in 1916, except for medical or sacramental purposes. A proposed federal counterpart, the Eighteenth Amendment, was ratified by the Colorado general assembly in 1919, and was adopted nationally later in the year. Colorado's prohibition amendment was repealed in 1932. National prohibition was repealed the next year by the Twenty-First Amendment.

During Prohibition, the legislature defined beer with alcohol content of less than 1.6% (3.2 proof) as not being intoxicating. This helped the Coors Brewing Company, in Golden.

The 1932 change to article XXII legalized alcohol manufacture, sale and distribution "wholly within the state of Colorado." Subject to federal law, the Colorado activities had to be "by or through such agencies and under such regulations as may hereafter be provided by statutory laws of the state of Colorado; but no such laws shall ever authorize the establishment or maintenance of any saloon."

Slowly compliant, the general assembly enacted regulatory legislation three years later, in 1935. Originally, the forbidden "saloon" was defined broadly—so that only hotels, restaurants, and private clubs could serve alcohol. *E.g.*, *City & County of Denver v. Gushurt*,, 120 Colo. 465, 210 P.2d 616 (1949) (installation of shuffleboards in a restaurant not allowed; upholding liquor code provision that a restaurant with a liquor license may conduct no business other than "the sale of meals, foods, drinks and tobaccos, or hotel business").

Later, the understanding of a lawful tavern (which is not an illegal "saloon") was broadened to include establishments that sell "sandwiches and light snacks." C.R.S. §§ 12-47-409 (beer and wine license), -412 (tavern license), 414 (retail gaming tavern license). *Cf.* -410 (bed & breakfast may give complimentary drinks to guests).

Figure 31. Leadville saloon.

Like many Midwestern states, Colorado had special alcohol rules for young adults 18–20: they could buy 3.2 beer, but not any other form of alcohol. Grocery stores and gas stations could sell 3.2, but not other alcohol.

The law encouraged young drinkers to stick with low alcohol drinks. Such beer is intoxicating, but on a volumetric basis, much less so than the alternatives. The benefits were lost when Colorado and other states fell into line with a new federal highway funding law in the late 1980s. To maintain full federal highway funding, states had to raise their drinking age for all alcohol to 21. *South Dakota v. Dole*, 483 U.S. 203 (1987) (chapter 5). With all alcohol now equally illegal, young adults shifted to more easily concealable and highly concentrated hard liquor. Because high school students often procure illegal alcohol from friends or relatives a few years older, the federal "incentive" also shifted high school consumption away from weak beer, and towards the most potent forms of alcohol.

Article XXII has been repealed, as part of removal of obsolete language from the state constitution.

Art. X, Section 21. Tobacco taxes for health-related purposes

The first constitutional tobacco tax was adopted in 2004. The revenues from the taxes are exempt from constitutional TABOR limits, and the spending is on autopilot, beyond legislative supervision. The amendment reflects voter skepticism that the legislature would spend all the new anti-tobacco revenue on anti-tobacco and other programs favored by the amendment's proponents.

Statutory tobacco taxes are at C.R.S. § 39-28-102.5 & 103.5, & 39-28.5-102.5. The bolded headings below are added by Kopel. Bolding of constitutional text is also by Kopel.

> **Findings**
> (1) The people of the state of Colorado hereby find that tobacco addiction is the leading cause of preventable death in Colorado, that Colorado should deter children and youth from starting smoking, that cigarette and tobacco taxes are effective at preventing and reducing tobacco use among children and youth, and that tobacco tax revenues will be used to expand health care for children and low

income populations, tobacco education programs and the prevention and treatment of cancer and heart and lung disease.

Additional taxes

(2) There are hereby imposed the following additional cigarette and tobacco taxes:

(a) Statewide cigarette tax, on the sale of cigarettes by wholesalers, at the rate of three and two-tenths cents per cigarette (64 cents per pack of twenty); and

(b) A statewide tobacco products tax, on the sale, use, consumption, handling, or distribution of tobacco products by distributors, at the rate of twenty percent of the manufacturer's list price.

Existing taxes may never be repealed by the general assembly

(3) The cigarette and tobacco taxes imposed by this section shall be in addition to any other cigarette and tobacco taxes existing as of the effective date of this section on the sale or use of cigarettes by wholesalers and on the sale, use, consumption, handling, or distribution of tobacco products by distributors. Such existing taxes and their distribution shall not be repealed or reduced by the general assembly.

Exemption from constitutional spending limits

(4) All revenues received by operation of subsection (2) shall be excluded from fiscal year spending, as that term is defined in section 20 of article X of this constitution, and the corresponding spending limits upon state government and all local governments receiving such revenues.

Revenues allocated to medical aid for low-income people (65%), anti-tobacco programs (16%), medical research (16%), & other specified uses (3%).

(5) The revenues generated by operation of subsection (2) shall be appropriated annually by the general assembly only in the following proportions and for the following health related purposes:

(a) Forty-six percent (46%) of such revenues shall be appropriated to increase the number of children and pregnant women enrolled in the children's basic health plan above the average enrollment for state fiscal year 2004, add the parents of enrolled children, and expand eligibility of low income adults and children who receive medical care through the "Children's Basic Health Plan Act", article 19 of title 26, Colorado Revised Statutes, or any successor act, or through the "Colorado Medical Assistance Act", article 4 of title 26, Colorado Revised Statutes, or any successor act.

(b) Nineteen percent (19%) of such revenues shall be appropriated to fund comprehensive primary care through any Colorado qualified provider, as defined in the "Colorado Medical Assistance Act," article 4 of title 26, Colorado Revised Statutes, or any successor act, that meets either of the following criteria:

(I) Is a community health center as defined in section 330 of the U.S. public health services act, or any successor act; or

(II) At least 50% of the patients served by the qualified provider are uninsured or medically indigent as defined in the "Colorado Medical Assistance Act," article 4 of title 26, Colorado Revised Statutes, or any successor act, or are enrolled in the children's

basic health plan or the Colorado medical assistance program, or successor programs.
Such revenues shall be appropriated to the Colorado department of health care policy and financing, or successor agency, and shall be distributed annually to all eligible qualified providers throughout the state proportionate to the number of uninsured or medically indigent patients served.

(c) Sixteen percent (16%) of such revenues shall be appropriated for school and community-based and statewide tobacco education programs designed to reduce initiation of tobacco use by children and youth, promote cessation of tobacco use among youth and adults, and reduce exposure to second-hand smoke. Such revenues shall be appropriated through the "Tobacco Education, Prevention and Cessation Act", part 8 of article 3.5 of title 25, Colorado Revised Statutes, or any successor act.

(d) Sixteen percent (16%) of such revenues shall be appropriated for the prevention, early detection, and treatment of cancer and cardiovascular and pulmonary diseases. Such revenues shall be appropriated to the prevention services division of the Colorado department of public health and environment, or successor agency, and shall be distributed statewide with oversight and accountability by the Colorado state board of health created by article 1 of title 25, Colorado Revised Statutes.

(e) Three percent (3%) of such revenues shall be appropriated for health related purposes to provide revenue for the state's general fund, old age pension fund, and municipal and county governments to compensate proportionately for tax revenue reductions attributable to lower cigarette and tobacco sales resulting from the implementation of this tax.

The general assembly may never reduce prior spending in the above categories.

(6) Revenues appropriated pursuant to paragraphs (a), (b), and (d) of subsection (5) shall be used to supplement revenues that are appropriated by the general assembly for health related purposes on the effective date of this section, and shall not be used to supplant those appropriated revenues.

If there is a declared fiscal emergency, the legislature can use the revenue for any health-related purpose.

(7) Notwithstanding any other provision of law, the general assembly may use revenue generated under this section for any health related purpose and to serve populations enrolled in the children's basic health plan and the Colorado medical assistance program at their respective levels of enrollment on the effective date of this section. Such use of revenue must be preceded by a declaration of a state fiscal emergency, which shall be adopted only by a joint resolution, approved by a two-thirds majority vote of the members of both houses of the general assembly and the governor. Such declaration shall apply only to a single fiscal year.

Nothing else in Colorado law limits how high and fast the spending can rise.

(8) Revenues appropriated pursuant to subsections (5) and (7) of this section shall not be subject to the statutory limitation on general fund appropriations growth or any other spending limitation existing in law.

(9) This section is effective January 1, 2005.

The specific taxes required by section 20 are enacted at C.RS. §§ 39-28-102.5 & 39-28-103.5.

Figure 32. Joe Onorfio, proprietor of Onorfio Music Company—for decades the state's best instrument store, on South Broadway in Denver. History Colorado-Denver, Colorado.

Whatever one thinks of the policy merits of the 2004 constitutional citizen initiative, it was not a corrupt bargain between the government and the big tobacco companies.

Article X, § 21 can be contrasted with the 1998 Master Settlement Agreement between big tobacco, Colorado, and 45 other states. The big three tobacco companies had been accused in state attorney general lawsuits of deceiving consumers, enticing minors to smoke, and other misdeeds. The various small tobacco companies, such as discounters, were not sued. The attorneys general and big tobacco reached a mutually beneficial agreement: the tobacco market would be restructured to give a perpetual oligopoly to big tobacco—in exchange for the oligopoly giving state governments a perpetual share of their revenue stream.

To the surprise of some anti-tobacco advocates, many state governments, Colorado included, did not use all the new tobacco profits for anti-smoking programs, medical treatment of persons with tobacco-related diseases and so on. Rather, tobacco revenue was soon being spent by the general funds.

The profit-sharing arrangement was structured to permanently cap the already-small market share of the little companies. The little companies had not engaged in the misdeeds of big three. The deal cut by big tobacco and big government was for their mutual enrichment, to the detriment of third parties—the consumer and the small businesses. *See, e.g.*, Mark Hillman (former Colo. state treasurer), *Unconstitutional Cartel*, WALL STREET JOURNAL, Sept. 20, 2005.

In 2020, the general assembly, the governor, and Philip Morris worked together to craft Proposition EE, a statutory referendum to raise tobacco taxes even further, to stringently tax vaping—which is based on eggplant and not tobacco—and to spend the extra revenue on particular programs.

Philip Morris and the political branches entered into a price-fixing agreement. Usually, price-fixing is illegal in the United States. It a violation of the Sherman Antitrust Act and often results in criminal prosecution. However, price-fixing is not an antitrust law violation when the government does it.[1] Philip Morris agreed not to fight Proposition EE in the general election. In exchange, the governor and legislative proponents of proposition EE agreed to impose price-fixing to eliminate businesses that compete with Philip Morris on price. Proposition EE created a minimum price for a pack of cigarettes. That state-enforced minimum just happened to be about the same price as a pack of Philip Morris cigarettes. Packs from discount companies used to be about two dollars less than the Philip Morris price. Now, price competition is forbidden. *See* Ben Murrey, *Democrat deal on Prop EE benefits big tobacco, squeezes small biz*, COMPLETE COLORADO, Jan. 28, 2021.

---

[1] Or as former president Richard Nixon said, "Well, when the president does it . . . that means that it is not illegal." *Transcript of David Frost's Interview with Richard Nixon 1977*, ASHBROOK CENTER, Teaching American History (2006) (ellipses for pause in the original).

Art. XVIII, Section 2. Lotteries prohibited, except when allowed

Article XVIII is the "Miscellaneous" article of the Constitution. It contains sections on homestead laws, gambling, arbitration, forests, leg-hold traps, minimum wage, and marijuana. The majority of its sections are covered in chapter 23. The environmental sections are in chapter 32. This chapter covers article XVIII's four sections on gambling and marijuana.

The 1876 Constitution gave the legislature "no power to authorize lotteries or gift enterprises for any purpose." Rather, the legislature "shall pass" laws to prevent the sale of tickets within the state. A "gift enterprise" is a type of lottery, in which the "gift" is distributed by chance.

In 1949, the legislature enacted a statute allowing regulated gambling on horse races, later expanded to include greyhound races. The statute did not violate the constitutional ban on lotteries, because lotteries are games of chance, whereas betting on horse races involves skill. *Ginsberg v. Centennial Turf Club*, 126 Colo. 471, 251 P.2d 926 (1952).

In 1959, the voters decided to authorize bingo and lotto games as regulated fundraisers by a wide variety of civil society groups. Bingo statutes, administered by the secretary of state, are at C.R.S. § 24-21-601 et seq.

A 1975 statute augmented horse and dog racing by allowing "sweepstakes races." These were multistage games in which bettors first bet on the finish of a horse or dog race (a game of skill), and then winners advanced to a second stage where further winnings were distributed by chance. This violated the constitutional prohibition on lotteries. *In re Interrogatories Sweepstakes Races Act*, 196 Colo. 353, 585 P.2d 595 (1978).

In 1980 the voters authorized the legislature to create a state lottery. State lottery statutes are C.R.S. § 24-35-201 et seq.

According to the constitutional text for the Colorado lottery, the revenues would be spent on the outdoors—except if the legislature provided otherwise by statute. The legislature soon shifted lottery revenue into capital construction for the state government. In response, the people in 1992 enacted Amendment XXVI, "Great Outdoors Colorado," appropriating lottery revenue to conservation and recreation. Colorado is the only state that allocates lottery revenue to the outdoors.

Meanwhile, the Colorado lottery, governed by the Colorado Lottery Commission (appointed by the governor and confirmed by the senate) has grown to 28 games. While there are many ways to gamble—slot machines, table games, sports bets—state lotteries offer the worst odds by far. For example, in a roulette game in a casino, the player bets which slot a ball will land within a spinning wheel. The betting involves no skill. On the average, a gambler's return on investment is about 95%. In other words, if you play many times, for every $100 you gamble you will come home with $95. The casino will take your other $5. Sports betting has a similar return on investment.[2] State lottery return on investment is usually closer to 50%. Spend $100, come home

---

[2] A typical roulette wheel has alternating red and black slots for numbers 1 through 36, plus two green slots, 0 and 00. If the bettor picks the right number, 1 through 36, the bettor is paid at 35:1 odds. If the ball lands on green 0 or 00, then all bets lose, and the house collects all the money. The green 0 and 00 provide the house with its edge, which is 2/38 = 5.3%. Other bets are available in roulette, such a red or black (2:1 payoff) or 1–12, 13–24, or 25–36 (3:1 payoff). If not for the green 0 and 00, all these bets would, in the long run, return to the gamblers the amount of money gambled. The 0 and 00 create the house's gross revenues.

Sports betting is typically at 11:10 odds. In other words, if you bet $11 and your team beats the spread, the casino will give you $21 (a $10 payoff for risking $11). If your team doesn't beat the spread, the casino keeps your $11. The 11:10 ratio provides the casino's gross revenues—a certain profit for the casino, as

with $50, in the long run. Notably, the Colorado Lottery's website does not disclose the return on investment for its games.

Section 2 does not apply to casino gambling in three municipalities, which is legalized and regulated pursuant to section 9.

In the constitutional text below, bolded headings are by Kopel.

No lotteries for any purpose, except sometimes

(1) The general assembly shall have no power to authorize lotteries for any purpose; except that the conducting of such games of chance as provided in subsections (2) to (4) of this section shall be lawful on and after January 1, 1959, and the conducting of state-supervised lotteries pursuant to subsection (7) of this section shall be lawful on and after January 1, 1981.

Bingo and lotto legalized for civil organizations

(2) No game of chance pursuant to this subsection (2) and subsections (3) and (4) of this section shall be conducted by any person, firm, or organization, unless a license as provided for in this subsection (2) has been issued to the firm or organization conducting such games of chance. The secretary of state shall, upon application therefor on such forms as shall be prescribed by the secretary of state and upon the payment of an annual fee as determined by the general assembly, issue a license for the conducting of such games of chance to any bona fide chartered branch or lodge or chapter of a national or state organization or to any bona fide religious, charitable, labor, fraternal, educational, voluntary firemen's or veterans' organization which operates without profit to its members and which has been in existence continuously for a period of five years immediately prior to the making of said application for such license and has had during the entire five-year period a dues-paying membership engaged in carrying out the objects of said corporation or organization, such license to expire at the end of each calendar year in which it was issued.

(3) The license issued by the secretary of state shall authorize and permit the licensee to conduct games of chance, restricted to the selling of rights to participate and the awarding of prizes in the specific kind of game of chance commonly known as bingo or lotto, in which prizes are awarded on the basis of designated numbers or symbols on a card conforming to numbers or symbols selected at random and in the specific game of chance commonly known as raffles, conducted by the drawing of prizes or by the allotment of prizes by chance.

Regulations for bingo and lotto

(4) Such games of chance shall be subject to the following restrictions:

---

long as the spread is set to attract equal numbers of wagers on both teams. Astute sports bettors may identify (or think they have identified) anomalies where the betting line (*e.g.* "Broncos +4.5") is mistaken. If the gambler is correct, then the odds shift in bettor's favor. The same is true in horse racing; the odds for any given horse are adjusted based on how much money is being wagered in favor of that horse, compared to other horses in the race. To the extent that the bettor can identify odds anomalies due to misjudgments by the other bettors, the gambler can profit in the long run.

If blackjack is played correctly with basic strategy, and without counting cards, the gamblers will in the long run come home with 98% of the money they gambled. Counting cards, if done perfectly, can raise the player's rate of return to 102%. In brief, when a partially dealt deck is rich in Aces and 10-cards (K, Q, J, 10), the gambler increases the bet. To defeat counting, casinos deal from a large deck, consisting of six or more regular decks, and reshuffle frequently.

> (a) The entire net proceeds of any game shall be exclusively devoted to the lawful purposes of organizations permitted to conduct such games.
> (b) No person except a bona fide member of any organization may participate in the management or operation of any such game.
> (c) No person may receive any remuneration or profit for participating in the management or operation of any such game.

(5) Subsections (2) to (4) of this section are self-enacting, but laws may be enacted supplementary to and in pursuance of, but not contrary to, the provisions thereof.

(6) The enforcement of this section shall be under such official or department of government of the state of Colorado as the general assembly shall provide.

General assembly may establish a lottery. Revenues will be spent on the outdoors. Unless the legislature enacts a statute to spend it on something else.
(7) Any provision of this constitution to the contrary notwithstanding, the general assembly may establish a state-supervised lottery. Unless otherwise provided by statute, all proceeds from the lottery, after deduction of prizes and expenses, shall be allocated to the conservation trust fund of the state for distribution to municipalities and counties for park, recreation, and open space purposes.

Art. XVIII, Section 9. Gambling

Enacted in 1990, section 9 legalized small stakes casino gambling in three historic mountain towns. As sold to the voters, the ballot measure would help preserve historic Central City, Black Hawk, and Cripple Creek by allowing low-stakes gambling ($5 maximum bet) in historic buildings. For example, an ice cream parlor could have a couple slot machines.

However, regulatory capture was almost immediate. The misnamed Limited Gaming Control Commission allowed casinos to evade several of the constitutional rules. For example, the Constitution specified that no more than 50% of the space on a floor could be used for gambling. But by the Commission's regulation, the square footage includes only gaming tables, and not the aisles between the tables.

Any new construction of casinos was supposed to conform to the historic WWI architecture of the old mining towns. With local connivance, the requirement was flagrantly ignored in Black Hawk—the Ameristar casino and hotel tower being especially egregious.

During the 1990s, several ballot issues proposed expanding casino gambling to other cities; they were rejected overwhelmingly.

By a 2008 amendment, the maximum bet was raised to $100, and additional casino games were permitted. Then a 2020 amendment removed any cap.

The original 1992 amendment had legalized slot machines plus $5 blackjack. In 2008 roulette and craps were added. Then in 2020, all games became legal.

Additionally casino-centric sports betting and horse race betting were authorized. The casinos in Black Hawk, Central City, and Cripple Creek may offer online or in-person sports or horserace betting. National online betting companies do so via contractual relationships with the casinos.

The bolded section headings are by Kopel.

(1) Any provisions of section 2 of this article XVIII or any other provisions of this constitution to the contrary notwithstanding, limited gaming in the City of Central, the City of Black Hawk, and the City of Cripple Creek shall be lawful as of October 1, 1991.

Limited gaming control commission

(2) The administration and regulation of this section 9 shall be under an appointed limited gaming control commission, referred to in this section 9 as the commission; said commission to be created under such official or department of government of the state of Colorado as the general assembly shall provide by May 1, 1991. Such official or the director of the department of government shall appoint the commission by July 1, 1991. The commission shall promulgate all necessary rules and regulations relating to the licensing of limited gaming by October 1, 1991, in the manner authorized by statute for the promulgation of administrative rules and regulations. Such rules and regulations shall include the necessary defining of terms that are not otherwise defined. There shall be a. It shall be in an executive department of government, as specified by the general assembly. The governor will appoint the commissioners. They will make gaming regulations.

Restrictions: historic architecture, amount of floor space for gambling

(3) Limited gaming shall be subject to the following:

(a) Limited gaming shall take place only in the existing Colorado cities of: the City of Central, county of Gilpin, the City of Black Hawk, county of Gilpin, and the City of Cripple Creek, county of Teller. Such limited gaming shall be further confined to the commercial districts of said cities as said districts are respectively defined in the city ordinances adopted by: the City of Central on October 7, 1981, the City of Black Hawk on May 4, 1978, and the City of Cripple Creek on December 3, 1973.

(b) Limited gaming shall only be conducted in structures which conform, as determined by the respective municipal governing bodies, to the architectural styles and designs that were common to the areas prior to World War I and which conform to the requirements of applicable respective city ordinances, regardless of the age of said structures.

(c) No more than thirty-five percent of the square footage of any building and no more than fifty percent of any one floor of such building, may be used for limited gaming.

(d) Limited gaming operations shall be prohibited between the hours of 2:00 o'clock a.m. and 8:00 o'clock a.m., unless such hours are revised as provided in subsection (7) of this section.

(e) Limited gaming may occur in establishments licensed to sell alcoholic beverages.

Terms defined

(4) As certain terms are used in regards to limited gaming:

(a) "Adjusted gross proceeds" means the total amount of all wagers made by players on limited gaming less all payments to players; said payments to players being deemed to include all payments of cash premiums, merchandise, tokens, redeemable game credits, or any other thing of value.

(b) "Limited gaming" means the use of slot machines and the card games of blackjack and poker, each game having a maximum single bet of five dollars, unless such games or single bets are revised as provided in subsection (7) of this section

(c) "Slot machine" means any mechanical, electrical, video, electronic, or other device, contrivance, or machine which, after insertion of a coin, token, or similar object, or upon payment of any required consideration whatsoever by a player, is available to be played or operated, and which, whether by reason of the skill of the player or application of the element of chance, or both, may deliver or entitle the player operating the machine to receive cash premiums, merchandise, tokens, redeemable game credits, or any other thing of value other than unredeemable free games, whether the payoff is made automatically from the machines or in any other manner.

Distribution of revenue

(5)

Casinos can be taxed up to 40% of their adjusted gross proceeds. The money goes to a limited gaming fund that in the state treasury. (The current AGP tax is 20%.)

(a) Up to a maximum of forty percent of the adjusted gross proceeds of limited gaming shall be paid by each licensee, in addition to any applicable license fees, for the privilege of conducting limited gaming. Subject to subsection (7) of this section, such percentage shall be established annually by the commission according to the criteria established by the general assembly in the implementing legislation to be enacted pursuant to paragraph (c) of this subsection (5). Such payments shall be made into a limited gaming fund that is hereby created in the state treasury.

The formula below applies, at most, to the first $5 of a wager. Wagers above that amount are covered by section (7).

(b)

The limited gaming fund pays the expenses of the commission.

(I) From the moneys in the limited gaming fund, the state treasurer is hereby authorized to pay all ongoing expenses of the commission and any other state agency, related to the administration of this section 9. Such payment shall be made upon proper presentation of a voucher prepared by the commission in accordance with statutes governing payments of liabilities incurred on behalf of the state. Such payment shall not be conditioned on any appropriation by the general assembly.

Whatever is left over is distributed as follows: 50% state general fund; 28% state historical fund; 12% Gilpin and Teller County Commissioners; 10% to Central City, Black Hawk, and Cripple Creek municipalities

(II) At the end of each state fiscal year, the state treasurer shall distribute the balance remaining in the limited gaming fund, except for an amount equal to all expenses of the administration of this section 9 for the preceding two-month period, according to the following guidelines and subject to the distribution criteria provided in subsection (7) of this section: fifty percent shall be transferred to the state general fund or such other fund as the general assembly shall provide; twenty-eight percent shall be transferred to the state historical fund, which fund is hereby created in the state treasury; twelve percent shall be distributed to the governing bodies of Gilpin county and Teller county in proportion to the gaming revenues generated in each county; the remaining ten percent shall be distributed to the governing bodies of the cities of: the City of Central, the City of Black Hawk, and the City of Cripple Creek in proportion to the gaming revenues generated in each respective city.

For the state historical fund, 20% of the revenue must be used for historic preservation and restoration in the three cities. The remaining 80% is for historic preservation and restoration statewide, as the general assembly shall determine.
(III) Of the moneys in the state historical fund, from which the state treasurer shall also make annual distributions, twenty percent shall be used for the preservation and restoration of the cities of: the City of Central, the City of Black Hawk, and the City of Cripple Creek, and such moneys shall be distributed, to the governing bodies of the respective cities, according to the proportion of the gaming revenues generated in each respective city. The remaining eighty percent in the state historical fund shall be used for the historic preservation and restoration of historical sites and municipalities throughout the state in a manner to be determined by the general assembly.

(c) & (d). Repealed.
(e) The general assembly shall enact provisions for the special licensing of qualifying nonprofit charitable organizations desiring to periodically host charitable gaming activities in licensed gaming establishments.

Severability
(f) If any provision of this section 9 is held invalid, the remainder of this section 9 shall remain unimpaired.

(6)

(a) Except as provided in paragraph (e) of this subsection (6), limited gaming shall not be lawful within any city, town, or unincorporated portion of a county which has been granted constitutional authority for limited gaming within its boundaries unless first approved by an affirmative vote of a majority of the electors of such city, town, or county voting thereon. The question shall first be submitted to the electors at a general, regular, or special election held within thirteen months after the effective date of the amendment which first adds such city, county, or town to those authorized for limited gaming pursuant to this constitution; and said election shall be conducted pursuant to applicable state or local government election laws.
(b) If approval of limited gaming is not obtained when the question is first submitted to the electors, the question may be submitted at subsequent elections held in accordance with paragraph (d) of this subsection (6); except that, once approval is obtained, limited gaming shall thereafter be lawful within the said city, town, or unincorporated portion of a county so long as the city, town, or county remains among those with constitutional authority for limited gaming within their boundaries.

(c) Nothing contained in this subsection (6) shall be construed to limit the ability of a city, town, or county to regulate the conduct of limited gaming as otherwise authorized by statute or by this constitution.

(d)

(I) The question submitted to the electors at any election held pursuant to this subsection (6) shall be phrased in substantially the following form: "Shall limited gaming be lawful within __________?"

(II) The failure to acquire approval of limited gaming in the unincorporated portion of a county shall not prevent lawful limited gaming within a city or town located in such county where such approval is acquired in a city or town election, and failure to acquire such approval in a city or town election shall not prevent lawful limited gaming within the unincorporated area of the county in which such city or town is located where such approval is acquired in an election in the unincorporated area of a county.

(III) If approval of limited gaming is not acquired when the question is first submitted in accordance with this subsection (6), the question may be submitted at subsequent elections so long as at least four years have elapsed since any previous election at which the question was submitted.

(e) Nothing contained in this subsection (6) shall be construed to affect the authority granted upon the initial adoption of this section at the 1990 general election, or the conduct and regulation of gaming on Indian reservations pursuant to federal law.

(f) For purposes of this subsection (6), a "city, town, or county" includes all land and buildings located within, or owned and controlled by, such city, town, or county or any political subdivision thereof. "City, town, or county" also includes the city and county of Denver.

Below is the 2008 amendment expanding the types of games and raising the maximum bet to $100.

(7)

(a) Through local elections, the voters of the cities of Central, Black Hawk, and Cripple Creek are authorized to revise limits on gaming that apply to licensees operating in their city's gaming district to extend:

(I) Hours of limited gaming operation;

(II) Approved games; and

(III) Single bets.

(b) Limited gaming tax revenues attributable to the operation of this subsection (7) shall be deposited in the limited gaming fund. The commission shall annually determine the amount of such revenues generated in each city.

(c) From gaming tax revenues attributable to the operation of this subsection (7), the treasurer shall pay:

(I) Those ongoing expenses of the commission and other state agencies that are related to the administration of this subsection (7);

(II) Annual adjustments, in connection with distributions to limited gaming fund recipients listed in subsection (5)(b)(II) of this section, to reflect the lesser of six percent of, or the actual percentage of, annual growth in gaming tax revenues attributable to this subsection (7); and

(III) Of the remaining gaming tax revenues, distributions in the following proportions:

(A) Seventy-eight percent to the state's public community colleges, junior colleges, and local district colleges to supplement existing state funding for student financial aid programs and classroom instruction programs; provided that such revenue shall be distributed to institutions that were operating on and after January 1, 2008, in proportion to their respective full-time equivalent student enrollments in the previous fiscal year;

(B) Ten percent to the governing bodies of the cities of Central, Black Hawk, and Cripple Creek to address local gaming impacts; provided that such revenue shall be distributed based on the proportion of gaming tax revenues, attributable to the operation of this subsection (7), that are paid by licensees operating in each city; and

(C) Twelve percent to the governing bodies of Gilpin and Teller Counties to address local gaming impacts; provided that such revenue shall be distributed based on the proportion of gaming tax revenues, attributable to the operation of this subsection (7), that are paid by licensees operating in each county.

(d) After July 1, 2009, the commission shall implement revisions to limits on gaming as approved by voters in the cities of Central, Black Hawk, or Cripple Creek. The general assembly is also authorized to enact, as necessary, legislation that will facilitate the operation of this subsection (7).

(e) If local voters in one or more cities revise any limits on gaming as provided in paragraph (a) of this subsection (7), any commission action pursuant to subsection (5) of this section that increases gaming taxes from the levels imposed as of July 1, 2008, shall be effective only if approved by voters at a statewide election held under section 20(4)(a) of article X of this constitution.

Exemption from Taxpayer's Bill of Rights

(f) Gaming tax revenues attributable to the operation of this subsection (7) shall be collected and spent as a voter-approved revenue change without regard to any limitation contained in section 20 of article X of this constitution or any other law.

Figure 33. Denver gambling den, ca. 1900. History Colorado - Denver, Colorado.

Art. XVIII, Section 14. Medical marijuana

As you read section 14 (medical use) and section 16 (adult use), note the differences in what is allowed or not—for example age limits, quantities, and taxes. Section 14 was enacted in 2000, and section 16 in 2012. Can you see some drafting differences, based on what marijuana proponents had learned in the interim? Among the improvements are that section 16 had explanatory headers for its subsections.

The medical marijuana ballot initiative had a complicated history. In the 1998 election, the proponents, Coloradans for Medical Rights, fought with the secretary of state over whether sufficient signatures had been submitted, and whether the secretary of state had employed the proper method of randomly sampling signatures. Shortly after the 1998 general election, the supreme court ruled that—although the measure had appeared on the 1998 ballot—votes would not be counted. Instead, the measure would be voted on the 2000 ballot. Thus, the 2000 ballot measure included language (from 1998) ordering various state officials to perform certain acts in 1999. *See In the Matter of Statement of Sufficiency For 1997–98 # 40 (Medical Use of Marijuana)*, 968 P.2d 112 (Colo. 1998); Ron Bain, *Marijuana controversy continues*, DENVER POST, July 30, 2000.

Bolded headings below are by Kopel.

Definitions

(1) As used in this section, these terms are defined as follows:

(a) "Debilitating medical condition" means:

(I) Cancer, glaucoma, positive status for human immunodeficiency virus, or acquired immune deficiency syndrome, or treatment for such conditions;

(II) A chronic or debilitating disease or medical condition, or treatment for such conditions, which produces, for a specific patient, one or more of the following, and for which, in the professional opinion of the patient's physician, such condition or conditions reasonably may be alleviated by the medical use of marijuana: cachexia; severe pain; severe nausea; seizures, including those that are characteristic of epilepsy; or persistent muscle spasms, including those that are characteristic of multiple sclerosis; or

(III) Any other medical condition, or treatment for such condition, approved by the state health agency, pursuant to its rule making authority or its approval of any petition submitted by a patient or physician as provided in this section.

(b) “Medical use” means the acquisition, possession, production, use, or transportation of marijuana or paraphernalia related to the administration of such marijuana to address the symptoms or effects of a patient’s debilitating medical condition, which may be authorized only after a diagnosis of the patient’s debilitating medical condition by a physician or physicians, as provided by this section.

(c) “Parent” means a custodial mother or father of a patient under the age of eighteen years, any person having custody of a patient under the age of eighteen years, or any person serving as a legal guardian for a patient under the age of eighteen years.

(d) “Patient” means a person who has a debilitating medical condition.

(e) “Physician” means a doctor of medicine who maintains, in good standing, a license to practice medicine issued by the state of Colorado.

(f) “Primary care-giver” means a person, other than the patient and the patient's physician, who is eighteen years of age or older and has significant responsibility for managing the well-being of a patient who has a debilitating medical condition.

(g) “Registry identification card” means that document, issued by the state health agency, which identifies a patient authorized to engage in the medical use of marijuana and such patient’s primary care-giver, if any has been designated.

(h) “State health agency” means that public health related entity of state government designated by the governor to establish and maintain a confidential registry of patients authorized to engage in the medical use of marijuana and enact rules to administer this program.

(i) “Usable form of marijuana” means the seeds, leaves, buds, and flowers of the plant (genus) cannabis, and any mixture or preparation thereof, which are appropriate for medical use as provided in this section, but excludes the plant’s stalks, stems, and roots.

(j) "Written documentation" means a statement signed by a patient's physician or copies of the patient's pertinent medical records.

Affirmative defense for patients and care-givers

(2)

(a) Except as otherwise provided in subsections (5), (6), and (8) of this section, a patient or primary care-giver charged with a violation of the state's criminal laws related to the patient's medical use of marijuana will be deemed to have established an affirmative defense to such allegation where:

(I) The patient was previously diagnosed by a physician as having a debilitating medical condition;

(II) The patient was advised by his or her physician, in the context of a bona fide physician-patient relationship, that the patient might benefit from the medical use of marijuana in connection with a debilitating medical condition; and

(III) The patient and his or her primary care-giver were collectively in possession of amounts of marijuana only as permitted under this section.

This affirmative defense shall not exclude the assertion of any other defense where a patient or primary care-giver is charged with a violation of state law related to the patient's medical use of marijuana.

(b) Effective June 1, 1999, it shall be an exception from the state's criminal laws for any patient or primary care-giver in lawful possession of a registry identification card to engage or assist in the medical use of marijuana, except as otherwise provided in subsections (5) and (8) of this section.

(c) It shall be an exception from the state's criminal laws for any physician to:

(I) Advise a patient whom the physician has diagnosed as having a debilitating medical condition, about the risks and benefits of medical use of marijuana or that he or she might benefit from the medical use of marijuana, provided that such advice is based upon the physician's contemporaneous assessment of the patient's medical history and current medical condition and a bona fide physician-patient relationship; or

(II) Provide a patient with written documentation, based upon the physician's contemporaneous assessment of the patient's medical history and current medical condition and a bona fide physician-patient relationship, stating that the patient has a debilitating medical condition and might benefit from the medical use of marijuana.

No physician shall be denied any rights or privileges for the acts authorized by this subsection.

(d) Notwithstanding the foregoing provisions, no person, including a patient or primary care-giver, shall be entitled to the protection of this section for his or her acquisition, possession, manufacture, production, use, sale, distribution, dispensing, or transportation of marijuana for any use other than medical use.

(e) Any property interest that is possessed, owned, or used in connection with the medical use of marijuana or acts incidental to such use, shall not be harmed, neglected, injured, or destroyed while in the possession of state or local law enforcement officials where such property has been seized in connection with the claimed medical use of marijuana. Any such property interest shall not be forfeited under any provision of state law providing for the forfeiture of property other than as a sentence imposed after conviction of a criminal offense or entry of a plea of guilty to such offense. Marijuana and paraphernalia seized by state or local law enforcement officials from a patient or primary care-giver in connection with the claimed medical use of marijuana shall be returned immediately upon the determination of the district attorney or his or her designee that the patient or primary care-giver is entitled to the protection contained in this section as may be evidenced, for example, by a decision not to prosecute, the dismissal of charges, or acquittal. **[But see decisions below, limiting part (2)(e).]**

Patient registry

(3) The state health agency shall create and maintain a confidential registry of patients who have applied for and are entitled to receive a registry identification card according to the criteria set forth in this subsection, effective June 1, 1999.

(a) No person shall be permitted to gain access to any information about patients in the state health agency's confidential registry, or any information otherwise maintained by the state health agency about physicians and primary care-givers, except for authorized employees of the state health agency in the course of their official duties and authorized employees of state or local law enforcement agencies which have stopped or arrested a person who claims to be engaged in the medical use of marijuana and in possession of a registry identification card or its functional equivalent, pursuant to paragraph (e) of this subsection (3). Authorized employees of state or local law enforcement agencies shall be granted access to the information contained within the state health agency's confidential registry only for the purpose of verifying that an individual who has presented a registry identification card to a state or local law enforcement official is lawfully in possession of such card.

(b) In order to be placed on the state's confidential registry for the medical use of marijuana, a patient must reside in Colorado and submit the completed application form adopted by the state health agency, including the following information, to the state health agency:

(I) The original or a copy of written documentation stating that the patient has been diagnosed with a debilitating medical condition and the physician's conclusion that the patient might benefit from the medical use of marijuana;

(II) The name, address, date of birth, and social security number of the patient;

(III) The name, address, and telephone number of the patient's physician; and

(IV) The name and address of the patient's primary care-giver, if one is designated at the time of application.

(c) Within thirty days of receiving the information referred to in subparagraphs (3)(b)(I)-(IV), the state health agency shall verify medical information contained in the patient's written documentation. The agency shall notify the applicant that his or her application for a registry identification card has been denied if the agency's review of such documentation discloses that: the information required pursuant to paragraph (3)(b) of this section has not been provided or has been falsified; the documentation fails to state that the patient has a debilitating medical condition specified in this section or by state health agency rule; or the physician does not have a license to practice medicine issued by the state of Colorado. Otherwise, not more than five days after verifying such information, the state health agency shall issue one serially numbered registry identification card to the patient, stating:

(I) The patient's name, address, date of birth, and social security number;

(II) That the patient's name has been certified to the state health agency as a person who has a debilitating medical condition, whereby the patient may address such condition with the medical use of marijuana;

(III) The date of issuance of the registry identification card and the date of expiration of such card, which shall be one year from the date of issuance; and

(IV) The name and address of the patient's primary care-giver, if any is designated at the time of application.

(d) Except for patients applying pursuant to subsection (6) of this section, where the state health agency, within thirty-five days of receipt of an application, fails to issue a registry identification card or fails to issue verbal or written notice of denial of such application, the patient's application for such card will be deemed to have been approved. Receipt shall be deemed to have occurred upon delivery to the state health agency, or deposit in the United States mails. Notwithstanding the foregoing, no application shall be deemed received prior to June 1, 1999. A patient who is questioned by any state or local law enforcement official about his or her medical use of marijuana shall provide a copy of the application submitted to the state health agency, including the written documentation and proof of the date of mailing or other transmission of the written documentation for delivery to the state health agency, which shall be accorded the same legal effect as a registry identification card, until such time as the patient receives notice that the application has been denied.

(e) A patient whose application has been denied by the state health agency may not reapply during the six months following the date of the denial and may not use an application for a registry identification card as provided in paragraph (3)(d) of this section. The denial of a registry identification card shall be considered a final agency action. Only the patient whose application has been denied shall have standing to contest the agency action.

(f) When there has been a change in the name, address, physician, or primary care-giver of a patient who has qualified for a registry identification card, that patient must notify the state health agency of any such change within ten days. A patient who has not designated a primary care-giver at the time of application to the state health agency may do so in writing at any time during the effective period of the registry identification card, and the primary care-giver may act in this capacity after such designation. To maintain an effective registry identification card, a patient must annually resubmit, at least thirty days prior to the expiration date stated on the registry identification card, updated written documentation to the state health agency, as well as the name and address of the patient's primary care-giver, if any is designated at such time.

(g) Authorized employees of state or local law enforcement agencies shall immediately notify the state health agency when any person in possession of a registry identification card has been determined by a court of law to have willfully violated the provisions of this section or its implementing legislation, or has pled guilty to such offense.

(h) A patient who no longer has a debilitating medical condition shall return his or her registry identification card to the state health agency within twenty-four hours of receiving such diagnosis by his or her physician.

(i) The state health agency may determine and levy reasonable fees to pay for any direct or indirect administrative costs associated with its role in this program.

Quantities allowed

(4)

(a) A patient may engage in the medical use of marijuana, with no more marijuana than is medically necessary to address a debilitating medical condition. A patient's medical use of marijuana, within the following limits, is lawful:

(I) No more than two ounces of a usable form of marijuana; and

(II) No more than six marijuana plants, with three or fewer being mature, flowering plants that are producing a usable form of marijuana.

(b) For quantities of marijuana in excess of these amounts, a patient or his or her primary care-giver may raise as an affirmative defense to charges of violation of state law that such greater amounts were medically necessary to address the patient's debilitating medical condition.

Prohibitions

(5)

(a) No patient shall:

(I) Engage in the medical use of marijuana in a way that endangers the health or well-being of any person; or

(II) Engage in the medical use of marijuana in plain view of, or in a place open to, the general public.

(b) In addition to any other penalties provided by law, the state health agency shall revoke for a period of one year the registry identification card of any patient found to have willfully violated the provisions of this section or the implementing legislation adopted by the general assembly.

Special limits on minors
(6) Notwithstanding paragraphs (2)(a) and (3)(d) of this section, no patient under eighteen years of age shall engage in the medical use of marijuana unless:

(a) Two physicians have diagnosed the patient as having a debilitating medical condition;

(b) One of the physicians referred to in paragraph (6)(a) has explained the possible risks and benefits of medical use of marijuana to the patient and each of the patient's parents residing in Colorado;

(c) The physicians referred to in paragraph (6)(b) has provided the patient with the written documentation, specified in subparagraph (3)(b)(I);

(d) Each of the patient's parents residing in Colorado consent in writing to the state health agency to permit the patient to engage in the medical use of marijuana;

(e) A parent residing in Colorado consents in writing to serve as a patients primary care-giver;

(f) A parent serving as a primary care-giver completes and submits an application for a registry identification card as provided in subparagraph (3)(b) of this section and the written consents referred to in paragraph (6)(d) to the state health agency;

(g) The state health agency approves the patient's application and transmits the patient's registry identification card to the parent designated as a primary care-giver;

(h) The patient and primary care-giver collectively possess amounts of marijuana no greater than those specified in subparagraph (4)(a)(I) and (II); and

(i) The primary care-giver controls the acquisition of such marijuana and the dosage and frequency of its use by the patient.

Governor to designate registry agency
(7) Not later than March 1, 1999, the governor shall designate, by executive order, the state health agency as defined in paragraph (1)(g) of this section.[3]

General assembly to enact anti-fraud statutes
(8) Not later than April 30, 1999, the general assembly shall define such terms and enact such legislation as may be necessary for implementation of this section, as well as determine and enact criminal penalties for:

---

[3] The governor designated the Colo. Dept. of Public Health and Environment.

(a) Fraudulent representation of a medical condition by a patient to a physician, state health agency, or state or local law enforcement official for the purpose of falsely obtaining a registry identification card or avoiding arrest and prosecution;

(b) Fraudulent use or theft of any person's registry identification card to acquire, possess, produce, use, sell, distribute, or transport marijuana, including but not limited to cards that are required to be returned where patients are no longer diagnosed as having a debilitating medical condition;

(c) Fraudulent production or counterfeiting of, or tampering with, one or more registry identification cards; or

(d) Breach of confidentiality of information provided to or by the state health agency.

Application process
(9) Not later than June 1, 1999, the state health agency shall develop and make available to residents of Colorado an application form for persons seeking to be listed on the confidential registry of patients. By such date, the state health agency shall also enact rules of administration, including but not limited to rules governing the establishment and confidentiality of the registry, the verification of medical information, the issuance and form of registry identification cards, communications with law enforcement officials about registry identification cards that have been suspended where a patient is no longer diagnosed as having a debilitating medical condition, and the manner in which the agency may consider adding debilitating medical conditions to the list provided in this section. Beginning June 1, 1999, the state health agency shall accept physician or patient initiated petitions to add debilitating medical conditions to the list provided in this section and, after such hearing as the state health agency deems appropriate, shall approve or deny such petitions within one hundred eighty days of submission. The decision to approve or deny a petition shall be considered a final agency action.

No insurance reimbursement
(10)

(a) No governmental, private, or any other health insurance provider shall be required to be liable for any claim for reimbursement for the medical use of marijuana.

(b) Nothing in this section shall require any employer to accommodate the medical use of marijuana in any work place.

Self-executing
(11) Unless otherwise provided by this section, all provisions of this section shall become effective upon official declaration of the vote hereon by proclamation of the governor, pursuant to article V, section (1)(4), and shall apply to acts or offenses committed on or after that date.

Notable decisions

Section 14 did not repeal anti-marijuana laws, but instead created an affirmative defense for medical marijuana users and caregivers. The constitutional affirmative defense has four elements. The general assembly enacted an affirmative defense with seven elements for caregivers: (1) to have the caregiver registration card in possession; (2) maintain a list of patients; and (3) grow the marijuana plants in an enclosed and locked space. C.R.S. § 25-1.5-106(8)(a)(II). The court of appeals held the statute unconstitutional. The Constitution did not authorize the legislature to add more elements to the affirmative defense. *People v. Cox*, 2021 COA 68 (Colo. App. 2021).

If law enforcement incorrectly seizes someone's medical marijuana, they do not have to return it (despite section 2(e)), because the act of return would force the officer to violate the federal Controlled Substances Act. *People v. Crouse*, 2017 CO 5, 388 P.3d 39 (Colo. 2017).

But a burglar can be required to pay restitution for the value of marijuana stolen from a dispensary. The burglar would only be delivering money, and not a controlled substance. *People In Interest of D.M.*, 2019 COA 56M, 444 P.3d 834 (Colo. App. 2019).

When sheriffs' deputies destroyed medical marijuana plants, in contravention of state law, the owner had no cause of action under 42 U.S.C. § 1983, since the owner had no federal right to the property. Nor is there a cause of action under state law against the sheriff's office. *Young v. Larimer County Sheriff's Office*, 356 P.3d 939 (Colo. App. 2014).

Legality under Colorado law did not prevent the federal Drug Enforcement Agency (DEA) from forfeiting a medical marijuana cultivation warehouse pursuant to the federal "crack house" statute. *In re Rent-Rite Super Kegs West Ltd.*, 484 Bankruptcy Rep. 799 (2012).

A state court probation condition against committing any new "offense" can include prohibition on medical marijuana use that is lawful under state law but forbidden by federal law. *People v. Watkins*, 282 P.3d 500 (Colo. App. 2012).

Physicians may recommend the use of medical marijuana but may not prescribe it. *Colorado Medical Board v. McLaughlin*, 425 P.3d 1187 (Colo. App. 2018).

To raise the affirmative defense of medical necessity allowing cultivation of 7 to 29 plants, a physician's certification must be obtained beforehand. A certification following an arrest is not allowed. *People v. Fioco*, 342 P.3d 530 (Colo. App. 2014).

Note that section 14 does not set up a detailed system for retail sales. Instead, section 14 simply creates affirmative defenses. The growth of medical marijuana retail stores was the result of regulatory decisions to allow caregivers to have a large number of patients. In contrast, later-enacted section 16, on personal use of marijuana, does set up comprehensive regulation of retail sales.

Art. XVIII, Section 16. Personal use of marijuana

(1) Purpose and findings.

(a) In the interest of the efficient use of law enforcement resources, enhancing revenue for public purposes, and individual freedom, the people of the state of Colorado find and declare that the use of marijuana should be legal for persons twenty-one years of age or older and taxed in a manner similar to alcohol.

(b) In the interest of the health and public safety of our citizenry, the people of the state of Colorado further find and declare that marijuana should be regulated in a manner similar to alcohol so that:

(I) Individuals will have to show proof of age before purchasing marijuana;

(II) Selling, distributing, or transferring marijuana to minors and other individuals under the age of twenty-one shall remain illegal;
(III) Driving under the influence of marijuana shall remain illegal;
(IV) Legitimate, taxpaying business people, and not criminal actors, will conduct sales of marijuana; and
(V) Marijuana sold in this state will be labeled and subject to additional regulations to ensure that consumers are informed and protected.

(c) In the interest of enacting rational policies for the treatment of all variations of the cannabis plant, the people of Colorado further find and declare that industrial hemp should be regulated separately from strains of cannabis with higher delta-9 tetrahydrocannabinol (THC) concentrations.

(d) The people of the state of Colorado further find and declare that it is necessary to ensure consistency and fairness in the application of this section throughout the state and that, therefore, the matters addressed by this section are, except as specified herein, matters of statewide concern.

(2) Definitions. As used in this section, unless the context otherwise requires,

(a) "Colorado Medical Marijuana Code" means article 43.3 of title 12, Colorado Revised Statutes.

(b) "Consumer" means a person twenty-one years of age or older who purchases marijuana or marijuana products for personal use by persons twenty-one years of age or older, but not for resale to others.

(c) "Department" means the department of revenue or its successor agency.

(d) "Industrial hemp" means the plant of the genus cannabis and any part of such plant, whether growing or not, with a delta-9 tetrahydrocannabinol concentration that does not exceed three-tenths percent on a dry weight basis.

(e) "Locality" means a county, municipality, or city and county.

(f) "Marijuana" or "marihuana" means all parts of the plant of the genus cannabis whether growing or not, the seeds thereof, the resin extracted from any part of the plant, and every compound, manufacture, salt, derivative, mixture, or preparation of the plant, its seeds, or its resin, including marihuana concentrate. "Marijuana" or "marihuana" does not include industrial hemp, nor does it include fiber produced from the stalks, oil, or cake made from the seeds of the plant, sterilized seed of the plant which is incapable of germination, or the weight of any other ingredient combined with marijuana to prepare topical or oral administrations, food, drink, or other product.

(g) "Marijuana accessories" means any equipment, products, or materials of any kind which are used, intended for use, or designed for use in planting, propagating, cultivating, growing, harvesting, composting, manufacturing, compounding, converting, producing, processing, preparing, testing, analyzing, packaging, repackaging, storing, vaporizing, or containing marijuana, or for ingesting, inhaling, or otherwise introducing marijuana into the human body.

(h) "Marijuana cultivation facility" means an entity licensed to cultivate, prepare, and package marijuana and sell marijuana to retail marijuana stores, to marijuana product manufacturing facilities, and to other marijuana cultivation facilities, but not to consumers.

(i) "Marijuana establishment" means a marijuana cultivation facility, a marijuana testing facility, a marijuana product manufacturing facility, or a retail marijuana store.

(j) "Marijuana product manufacturing facility" means an entity licensed to purchase marijuana; manufacture, prepare, and package marijuana products; and sell marijuana and marijuana products to other marijuana product manufacturing facilities and to retail marijuana stores, but not to consumers.

(k) "Marijuana products" means concentrated marijuana products and marijuana products that are comprised of marijuana and other ingredients and are intended for use or consumption, such as, but not limited to, edible products, ointments, and tinctures.

(l) "Marijuana testing facility" means an entity licensed to analyze and certify the safety and potency of marijuana.

(m) "Medical marijuana center" means an entity licensed by a state agency to sell marijuana and marijuana products pursuant to section 14 of this article and the Colorado Medical Marijuana Code.

(n) "Retail marijuana store" means an entity licensed to purchase marijuana from marijuana cultivation facilities and marijuana and marijuana products from marijuana product manufacturing facilities and to sell marijuana and marijuana products to consumers.

(o) "Unreasonably impracticable" means that the measures necessary to comply with the regulations require such a high investment of risk, money, time, or any other resource or asset that the operation of a marijuana establishment is not worthy of being carried out in practice by a reasonably prudent businessperson.

(3) Personal use of marijuana. Notwithstanding any other provision of law, the following acts are not unlawful and shall not be an offense under Colorado law or the law of any locality within Colorado or be a basis for seizure or forfeiture of assets under Colorado law for persons twenty-one years of age or older:

(a) Possessing, using, displaying, purchasing, or transporting marijuana accessories or one ounce or less of marijuana.

(b) Possessing, growing, processing, or transporting no more than six marijuana plants, with three or fewer being mature, flowering plants, and possession of the marijuana produced by the plants on the premises where the plants were grown, provided that the growing takes place in an enclosed, locked space, is not conducted openly or publicly, and is not made available for sale.

(c) Transfer of one ounce or less of marijuana without remuneration to a person who is twenty-one years of age or older.

(d) Consumption of marijuana, provided that nothing in this section shall permit consumption that is conducted openly and publicly or in a manner that endangers others.

(e) Assisting another person who is twenty-one years of age or older in any of the acts described in paragraphs (a) through (d) of this subsection.

(4) Lawful operation of marijuana-related facilities. Notwithstanding any other provision of law, the following acts are not unlawful and shall not be an offense under Colorado law or be a basis for seizure or forfeiture of assets under Colorado law for persons twenty-one years of age or older:

(a) Manufacture, possession, or purchase of marijuana accessories or the sale of marijuana accessories to a person who is twenty-one years of age or older.

(b) Possessing, displaying, or transporting marijuana or marijuana products; purchase of marijuana from a marijuana cultivation facility; purchase of marijuana or marijuana products from a marijuana product manufacturing facility; or sale of marijuana or marijuana products to consumers, if the person conducting the activities described in this paragraph has obtained a current, valid license to operate a retail marijuana store or is acting in his or her capacity as an owner, employee or agent of a licensed retail marijuana store.

(c) Cultivating, harvesting, processing, packaging, transporting, displaying, or possessing marijuana; delivery or transfer of marijuana to a marijuana testing facility; selling marijuana to a marijuana cultivation facility, a marijuana product manufacturing facility, or a retail marijuana store; or the purchase of marijuana from a marijuana cultivation facility, if the person conducting the activities described in this paragraph has obtained a current, valid license to operate a marijuana cultivation facility or is acting in his or her capacity as an owner, employee, or agent of a licensed marijuana cultivation facility.

(d) Packaging, processing, transporting, manufacturing, displaying, or possessing marijuana or marijuana products; delivery or transfer of marijuana or marijuana products to a marijuana testing facility; selling marijuana or marijuana products to a retail marijuana store or a marijuana product manufacturing facility; the purchase of marijuana from a marijuana cultivation facility; or the purchase of marijuana or marijuana products from a marijuana product manufacturing facility, if the person conducting the activities described in this paragraph has obtained a current, valid license to operate a marijuana product manufacturing facility or is acting in his or her capacity as an owner, employee, or agent of a licensed marijuana product manufacturing facility.

(e) Possessing, cultivating, processing, repackaging, storing, transporting, displaying, transferring or delivering marijuana or marijuana products if the person has obtained a current, valid license to operate a marijuana testing facility or is acting in his or her capacity as an owner, employee, or agent of a licensed marijuana testing facility.

(f) Leasing or otherwise allowing the use of property owned, occupied or controlled by any person, corporation or other entity for any of the activities conducted lawfully in accordance with paragraphs (a) through (e) of this subsection.

(5) Regulation of marijuana.

(a) Not later than July 1, 2013, the department shall adopt regulations necessary for implementation of this section. Such regulations shall not prohibit the operation of marijuana establishments, either expressly or through regulations that make their operation unreasonably impracticable. Such regulations shall include:

(I) Procedures for the issuance, renewal, suspension, and revocation of a license to operate a marijuana establishment, with such procedures subject to all requirements of article 4 of title 24 of the Colorado Administrative Procedure Act or any successor provision;

(II) A schedule of application, licensing and renewal fees, provided, application fees shall not exceed five thousand dollars, with this upper limit adjusted annually for inflation, unless the department determines a greater fee is necessary to carry out its responsibilities under this section, and provided further, an entity that is licensed under the Colorado Medical Marijuana Code to cultivate or sell marijuana or to manufacture marijuana products at the time this section takes effect and that chooses to apply for a separate marijuana establishment license shall not be required to pay an application fee greater than five hundred dollars to apply for a license to operate a marijuana establishment in accordance with the provisions of this section;

(III) Qualifications for licensure that are directly and demonstrably related to the operation of a marijuana establishment;

(IV) Security requirements for marijuana establishments;

(V) Requirements to prevent the sale or diversion of marijuana and marijuana products to persons under the age of twenty-one;

(VI) Labeling requirements for marijuana and marijuana products sold or distributed by a marijuana establishment;

(VII) Health and safety regulations and standards for the manufacture of marijuana products and the cultivation of marijuana;

(VIII) Restrictions on the advertising and display of marijuana and marijuana products; and

(IX) Civil penalties for the failure to comply with regulations made pursuant to this section.

(b) In order to ensure the most secure, reliable, and accountable system for the production and distribution of marijuana and marijuana products in accordance with this subsection, in any competitive application process the department shall have as a primary consideration whether an applicant:

(I) Has prior experience producing or distributing marijuana or marijuana products pursuant to section 14 of this article and the Colorado Medical Marijuana Code in the locality in which the applicant seeks to operate a marijuana establishment; and

(II) Has, during the experience described in subparagraph (I), complied consistently with section 14 of this article, the provisions of the Colorado Medical Marijuana Code and conforming regulations.

(c) In order to ensure that individual privacy is protected, notwithstanding paragraph (a), the department shall not require a consumer to provide a retail marijuana store with personal information other than government-issued identification to determine the consumer's age, and a retail marijuana store shall not be required to acquire and record personal information about consumers other than information typically acquired in a financial transaction conducted at a retail liquor store.

(d) The general assembly shall enact an excise tax to be levied upon marijuana sold or otherwise transferred by a marijuana cultivation facility to a marijuana product manufacturing facility or to a retail marijuana store at a rate not to exceed fifteen percent prior to January 1, 2017 and at a rate to be determined by the general assembly thereafter, and shall direct the department to establish procedures for the collection of all taxes levied. Provided, the first forty million dollars in revenue raised annually from any such excise tax shall be credited to the Public School Capital Construction Assistance Fund created by article 43.7 of title 22, C.R.S., or any successor fund dedicated to a similar purpose. Provided further, no such excise tax shall be levied upon marijuana intended for sale at medical marijuana centers pursuant to section 14 of this article and the Colorado Medical Marijuana Code.

(e) Not later than October 1, 2013, each locality shall enact an ordinance or regulation specifying the entity within the locality that is responsible for processing applications submitted for a license to operate a marijuana establishment within the boundaries of the locality and for the issuance of such licenses should the issuance by the locality become necessary because of a failure by the department to adopt regulations pursuant to paragraph (a) or because of a failure by the department to process and issue licenses as required by paragraph (g).

(f) A locality may enact ordinances or regulations, not in conflict with this section or with regulations or legislation enacted pursuant to this section, governing the time, place, manner and number of marijuana establishment operations; establishing procedures for the issuance, suspension, and revocation of a license issued by the locality in accordance with paragraph (h) or (i), such procedures to be subject to all requirements of article 4 of title 24 of the Colorado Administrative Procedure Act or any successor provision; establishing a schedule of annual operating, licensing, and application fees for marijuana establishments, provided, the application fee shall only be due if an application is submitted to a locality in accordance with paragraph (i) and a licensing fee shall only be due if a license is issued by a locality in accordance with paragraph (h) or (i); and establishing civil penalties for violation of an ordinance or regulation governing the time, place, and manner of a marijuana establishment that may operate in such locality. A locality may prohibit the operation of marijuana cultivation facilities, marijuana product manufacturing facilities, marijuana testing facilities, or retail marijuana stores through the enactment of an ordinance or through an initiated or referred measure; provided, any initiated or referred measure to prohibit the operation of marijuana cultivation facilities, marijuana product manufacturing facilities, marijuana testing facilities, or retail marijuana stores must appear on a general election ballot during an even numbered year.

(g) Each application for an annual license to operate a marijuana establishment shall be submitted to the department. The department shall:

(I) Begin accepting and processing applications on October 1, 2013;

(II) Immediately forward a copy of each application and half of the license application fee to the locality in which the applicant desires to operate the marijuana establishment;

(III) Issue an annual license to the applicant between forty-five and ninety days after receipt of an application unless the department finds the applicant is not in compliance with regulations enacted pursuant to paragraph (a) or the department is notified by the relevant locality that the applicant is not in compliance with ordinances and regulations made pursuant to paragraph (f) and in effect at the time of application, provided, where a locality has enacted a numerical limit on the number of marijuana establishments and a greater number of applicants seek licenses, the department shall solicit and consider input from the locality as to the locality's preference or preferences for licensure; and

(IV) Upon denial of an application, notify the applicant in writing of the specific reason for its denial.

(h) If the department does not issue a license to an applicant within ninety days of receipt of the application filed in accordance with paragraph (g) and does not notify the applicant of the specific reason for its denial, in writing and within such time period, or if the department has adopted regulations pursuant to paragraph (a) and has accepted applications pursuant to paragraph (g) but has not issued any licenses by January 1, 2014, the applicant may resubmit its application directly to the locality, pursuant to paragraph (e), and the locality may issue an annual license to the applicant. A locality issuing a license to an applicant shall do so within ninety days of receipt of the resubmitted application unless the locality finds and notifies the applicant that the applicant is not in compliance with ordinances and regulations made pursuant to paragraph (f) in effect at the time the application is resubmitted and the locality shall notify the department if an annual license has been issued to the applicant. If an application is submitted to a locality under this paragraph, the department shall forward to the locality the application fee paid by the applicant to the department upon request by the locality. A license issued by a locality in accordance with this paragraph shall have the same force and effect as a license issued by the department in accordance with paragraph (g) and the holder of such license shall not be subject to regulation or enforcement by the department during the term of that license. A subsequent or renewed license may be issued under this paragraph on an annual basis only upon resubmission to the locality of a new application submitted to the department pursuant to paragraph (g). Nothing in this paragraph shall limit such relief as may be available to an aggrieved party under section 24-4-104, C.R.S., of the Colorado Administrative Procedure Act or any successor provision.

(i) If the department does not adopt regulations required by paragraph (a), an applicant may submit an application directly to a locality after October 1, 2013 and the locality may issue an annual license to the applicant. A locality issuing a license to an applicant shall do so within ninety days of receipt of the application unless it finds and notifies the applicant that the applicant is not in compliance with ordinances and regulations made pursuant to paragraph (f) in effect at the time of application and shall notify the department if an annual license has been issued to the applicant. A license issued by a locality in accordance with this paragraph shall have the same force and effect as a license issued by the department in accordance with paragraph (g) and the holder of such license shall not be subject to regulation or enforcement by the department during the term of that license. A subsequent or renewed license may be issued under this paragraph on an annual basis if the department has not adopted regulations required by paragraph (a) at least ninety days prior to the date upon which such subsequent or renewed license would be effective or if the department has adopted regulations pursuant to paragraph (a) but has not, at least ninety days after the adoption of such regulations, issued licenses pursuant to paragraph (g).

(j) Not later than July 1, 2014, the general assembly shall enact legislation governing the cultivation, processing and sale of industrial hemp.

(6) Employers, driving, minors and control of property.

(a) Nothing in this section is intended to require an employer to permit or accommodate the use, consumption, possession, transfer, display, transportation, sale or growing of marijuana in the workplace or to affect the ability of employers to have policies restricting the use of marijuana by employees.

(b) Nothing in this section is intended to allow driving under the influence of marijuana or driving while impaired by marijuana or to supersede statutory laws related to driving under the influence of marijuana or driving while impaired by marijuana, nor shall this section prevent the state from enacting and imposing penalties for driving under the influence of or while impaired by marijuana.

(c) Nothing in this section is intended to permit the transfer of marijuana, with or without remuneration, to a person under the age of twenty-one or to allow a person under the age of twenty-one to purchase, possess, use, transport, grow, or consume marijuana.

(d) Nothing in this section shall prohibit a person, employer, school, hospital, detention facility, corporation or any other entity who occupies, owns or controls a property from prohibiting or otherwise regulating the possession, consumption, use, display, transfer, distribution, sale, transportation, or growing of marijuana on or in that property.

(7) Medical marijuana provisions unaffected. Nothing in this section shall be construed:

(a) To limit any privileges or rights of a medical marijuana patient, primary caregiver, or licensed entity as provided in section 14 of this article and the Colorado Medical Marijuana Code;

(b) To permit a medical marijuana center to distribute marijuana to a person who is not a medical marijuana patient;

(c) To permit a medical marijuana center to purchase marijuana or marijuana products in a manner or from a source not authorized under the Colorado Medical Marijuana Code;

(d) To permit any medical marijuana center licensed pursuant to section 14 of this article and the Colorado Medical Marijuana Code to operate on the same premises as a retail marijuana store; or

(e) To discharge the department, the Colorado Board of Health, or the Colorado Department of Public Health and Environment from their statutory and constitutional duties to regulate medical marijuana pursuant to section 14 of this article and the Colorado Medical Marijuana Code.

(8) Self-executing, severability, conflicting provisions. All provisions of this section are self-executing except as specified herein, are severable, and, except where otherwise indicated in the text, shall supersede conflicting state statutory, local charter, ordinance, or resolution, and other state and local provisions.

(9) Effective date. Unless otherwise provided by this section, all provisions of this section shall become effective upon official declaration of the vote hereon by proclamation of the governor, pursuant to section 1(4) of article V.

The constitutional right to cultivation must take place "in an enclosed, locked space," not "openly or publicly." Section 16(3)(b). The implementing statute makes it illegal to grow marijuana "on land that the person owns, occupies, or controls." C.R.S. § 18-18-406(3)(a)(I). To comply with the Constitution, the statute had to be interpreted so that it did not apply to the "land" within one's enclosed residence or garage. *People v. Garcia-Gonzalez*, 2020 COA 166, 478 P.3d 1288 (Colo. App. 2020).

The States of Nebraska and Oklahoma attempted to sue Colorado over the injuries they suffered from Colorado's relegalization of adult use, such as increased law enforcement expenses for highway patrols to catch automobiles taking marijuana out of Colorado. Under the U.S. Constitution, "Controversies between two or more States" must be brought in the U.S. supreme court's original jurisdiction. U.S. CONST., art. III, § 2, cl. 1. According to the court's current precedent, a *State v. State* complaint may only be filed if the court grants leave. The court denied leave. *Nebraska v. Colorado*, 136 S.Ct. 1034 (2016). Justices Thomas and Alito dissented; they argued that article III's text gives the court no discretion to refuse to accept complaint filings in *State v. State* cases.

Meanwhile, some private parties and Colorado county officials filed suit in federal district court, alleging specific harms from relegalization. The Tenth Circuit held that none of the alleged equitable or other claims stated a valid claim for relief—except that some of the private parties did have a claim for specific harms, such as odors from nearby grow operations. The federal Racketeer Influenced and Corrupt Organizations Act (RICO) specifically defines marijuana growing as a type of "racketeering," and creates a private cause of action. 18 U.S.C. § 1964(c) (citizen suits authorized). Nebraska and Oklahoma were not allowed to intervene. Although the nominal defendant was governor John Hickenlooper in his official capacity, the suit was in effect against the state of Colorado, and only the U.S. Supreme Court can hear *State v. State* suits. *Safe Streets Alliance v. Hickenlooper*, 859 F.3d 865 (10th Cir. 2017).

Further reading: Sam Kamin, *Colorado Marijuana Regulation Five Years Later: Have We Learned Anything at All?* 96 DENVER L. REVIEW 221 (2019); Rachel Allen, *Local Government Regulation of Personal Marijuana Grows*, 94 DENVER L. REVIEW ONLINE article 18 (2017); John M. Husband, *Off-Duty Medical Marijuana Use Not Protected Under Lawful Activities Statute*, 42 COLO. LAWYER 103 (July 2013) (explaining cases holding that Colo. statute against employers firing employees for lawful activities outside of work does not apply to marijuana use, since marijuana is federally illegal); Angela Dillis, Sietse Goffard, Jeffery Miron, & Erin Partin, *The Effect of State Marijuana Legalizations: 2021 Update*, CATO INSTITUTE Policy Analysis no. 908 (Feb. 2, 2021) (state legalizations have had only minor effects for good or ill).

CHAPTER 32

Natural Resources, articles XVIII, XXVI, XXVII

Roxborough State Park.

Art. XVIII, Section 6. Forests

> The general assembly shall enact laws in order to prevent the destruction of, and to keep in good preservation, the forests upon the lands of the state, or upon lands of the public domain, the control of which shall be conferred by congress upon the state.

This is the first conservation provision in any state constitution. Part of the original 1876 Constitution, the forests section is an early example of Colorado's conservation ethos. That ethos is likewise manifest in the 1992 Great Outdoors Colorado amendment (art. XXVII), which makes Colorado the only state in the nation to dedicate lottery revenue to the outdoors.

Notwithstanding the "shall" language, state forest protection laws were not enacted until later in the 19th century. Current forestry laws are at C.R.S. § 36-7-101 et seq. Next door to the forests in section 6, the now-repealed section 7 of article XVIIII had provided a property tax exemption for increased land values arising from the planting of forests, orchards, or hedges—another example of Colorado's ethos of responsible stewardship.

Art. XVIII. Section 12b. Wildlife trapping prohibited

This section prohibits taking wildlife by snares (rope traps), instant kill body-gripping traps, or poison. There are limited exemptions for government, ranching, and farming. The section does not apply to birds and most rodents.

(1) It shall be unlawful to take wildlife with any leghold trap, any instant kill body-gripping design trap, or by poison or snare in the state of Colorado.

(2) The provisions of subsection (1) of this section shall not prohibit:

(a) The taking of wildlife by use of the devices or methods described in subsection (1) of this section by federal, state, county, or municipal departments of health for the purpose of protecting human health or safety;

(b) The use of the devices or methods described in subsection (1) of this section for controlling:

(I) wild or domestic rodents, except for beaver or muskrat, as otherwise authorized by law; or

(II) wild or domestic birds as otherwise authorized by law;

(c) The use of non-lethal snares, traps specifically designed not to kill, or nets to take wildlife for scientific research projects, for falconry, for relocation, or for medical treatment pursuant to regulations established by the Colorado wildlife commission; or

(d) The use of traps, poisons or nets by the Colorado division of wildlife to take or manage fish or other non-mammalian aquatic wildlife.

(3) Notwithstanding the provisions of this section 12, the owner or lessee of private property primarily used for commercial livestock or crop production, or the employees of such owner or lessee, shall not be prohibited from using the devices or methods described in subsection (1) of this section on such private property so long as:

(a) such use does not exceed one thirty day period per year; and

(b) the owner or lessee can present on-site evidence to the division of wildlife that ongoing damage to livestock or crops has not been alleviated by the use of non-lethal or lethal control methods which are not prohibited.

(4) The provisions of this section 12 shall not apply to the taking of wildlife with firearms, fishing equipment, archery equipment, or other implements in hand as authorized by law.[1]

(5) The general assembly shall enact, amend, or repeal such laws as are necessary to implement the provisions of this section 12, including penalty provisions, no later than May 1, 1997.

(6) As used in this section, unless the context otherwise requires:

(a) The term "taking" shall be defined as provided in section 33-1-102(43), C.R.S., on the date this section is enacted.

---

[1] Subsection (4) was not formally necessary, because section 12b's stated application in subsection (1) does not involve subsection (4) activities. Still, subsection (4) was prudently included by advocates for proposed section 12b, to assure voters that it would not interfere with hunting and fishing.

(b) The term "wildlife" shall be defined as provided in section 33-1-102(51), C.R.S., on the date this section is enacted.

Enacted as a 1996 citizen initiative, section 12b was criticized for being a constitutional amendment, rather than a statute. Proponents worried the legislature would dilute a statute.

Subsection (4) follows the style of the original Constitution by specifying the types of laws the general assembly "shall" enact.

One of the exemptions is for government employees "for the purpose of protecting human health or safety." It might be wondered why nongovernment persons are forbidden from protecting human health and safety— neither their own nor their families'.

The text specifically does not apply to "rodents." The text does prohibit poisoning other land mammals and reptiles. A program to poison rodents, namely prairie dogs, caused incidental poisoning of snakes and rabbits, who sometimes inhabit vacant prairie dog dens. The court of appeals interpreted sections 12b to not forbid incidental poisoning. The court did hold that an animal rights organization had standing to sue, based on the pleaded specific harms of reduced wildlife enjoyment by members of the organization who observe, trap, and relocate prairie dogs. *Rocky Mountain Animal Defense v. Colorado Div. of Wildlife*, 100 P.3d 508 (Colo. App. 2004).

In contrast, a different court of appeals panel held that there is no private cause of action under section 12b. *Prairie Dog Advocates v. City of Lakewood*, 20 P.3d 1203 (Colo. App. 2000). In the Colorado's court of appeals, three-judge panels need not follow the precedents of previous three judge panels. But in federal courts of appeal, such as the Tenth Circuit, which covers Colorado and six adjacent states, a three-judge panel is bound to follow the precedent of a prior panel.

Under section 12b, coyotes may not be poisoned or trapped. As a result, they have become more common in metro Denver.

Article XXVI. Nuclear detonations

Art. XXVI, Section 1. Nuclear detonations regulated

No nuclear explosive device may be detonated or placed in the ground for the purpose of detonation in this state except in accordance with this article.

Art. XXVI, Section 2. Voter approval required for detonations

Before the emplacement of any nuclear explosive device in the ground in this state, the detonation of that device shall first have been approved by the voters through enactment of an initiated or referred measure authorizing that detonation, such measure having been ordered, proposed, submitted to the voters, and approved as provided in section 1 of article V of this constitution.

Art. XXVI, Section 3. Indemnification with absolute liability

Before the detonation or emplacement for the purpose of detonation of any nuclear explosive device, a competent state official or agency designated by the governor shall first have certified that sufficient and secure financial resources exist in the form of applicable insurance, self-insurance, indemnity bonds, indemnification agreements, or otherwise, without utilizing state funds, to compensate in full all parties that might foreseeably suffer damage to person or property from ground

> motion, ionizing radiation, other pollution, or other hazard attributable to such detonation. Damage is attributable to such detonation without regard to negligence and without regard to any concurrent or intervening cause.

Art. XXVI, Section 4. Self-executing

> This article shall be in all respects self-executing; but, the general assembly may by law provide for its more effective enforcement and may by law also impose additional restrictions or conditions upon the emplacement or detonation of any nuclear explosive device.

Art. XXVI, Section 5. Severability

> If any provision of this article, or its application in any particular case, is held invalid, the remainder of the article and its application in all other cases shall remain unimpaired.

Section 3 applies and advances beyond the common law doctrine of ultrahazardous activity. Persons engaged in ultrahazardous activity (paradigmatically, dynamite blasting) can be held liable for resulting damages, regardless of their having acted with the highest standard of care.

Section 3 goes even further, by requiring nuclear detonators to prove in advance that they have the resources to pay any judgement for damages. Section 3 also goes further by awarding damages without consideration of concurrent or intervening causes. For example, if someone snuck into a deep cavern to watch the explosion, the person's survivors could still sue for wrongful death, with no adjustment in the award to account for the effect of the decedent's gross negligence.

Arguably, article XXVI is federally preempted (via the Supremacy Clause, U.S. Const. art. VI) as to any nuclear explosions authorized by the United States Atomic Energy Commission, which is to say all of them.

As a deterrent to nuclear explosions without voter approval, article XXVI appears to have been perfectly successful. There have been no nuclear blasts within the continental United States since 1973.

Background

In 1969, the federal Atomic Energy Commission detonated a nuclear bomb 8,000 feet underground in Garfield County to liberate natural gas reserves. In 1973, three bombs, all at least a mile underground, were detonated in Rio Blanco County for the same purpose. The AEC suggested that several thousand similar detonations would be necessary for natural gas development. James P. Sterba, *Atom-Test Blast Set in Colorado*, N.Y. TIMES, May 15, 1973.

Opponents of the program raised safety concerns, while proponents pointed to the AEC's record on peaceful uses of atomic energy.

Distrustful of the federal government, Coloradans adopted article XXVI in 1974. It requires voter approval for any underground nuclear detonations in the state.

Subsequently, much milder forms for extraction of deep underground natural gas reserves have been developed. Namely, horizontal hydraulic fracturing—an advancement of a technique first used in Texas in the late 1940s. It relies on water pressure and lubrication rather than explosions. In the long run, by thwarting the peaceful use of atomic explosions, article XXVI helped spur the growth of fracking.

A constitutional caste system

According to a 1982 Colorado supreme court opinion, some parts of the Constitution deserve careful judicial attention ("fundamental") and others do not:

> The Colorado Constitution does not restrict itself to addressing only those areas deemed fundamental. Rather, it contains provisions which are both equally suited for statutory enactment, e.g., Mining and Irrigation, Colo. Const. Art. XVI, and Nuclear Detonations, Colo. Const. Art. XXVI; as well as those deemed fundamental to our concept of ordered liberty, e.g., Freedom of Elections, Colo. Const. Art. II, Sec. 5. Thus, under the Colorado Constitution, fundamental rights are not necessarily determined by whether they are guaranteed explicitly or implicitly within the document.

Lujan v. Colorado State Bd. of Educ., 649 P.2d 1005 (Colo. 1982).

The privileging of some justices' favorite parts of the Constitution over disfavored ones has been endemic in the Colorado supreme court. Much of article X (taxes) and article XI (debt) have been judicially nullified. The Colorado supreme court has underenforced or obliterated three sections of the Bill of Rights, four sections of the constitutional restrictions on the general assembly, and other constitutional provisions. *See* chapter 33 (Conclusion).

The powers of the judicial branch are delegated powers of the people of Colorado. The Colorado Constitution specifies the scope and rules of the delegation. Coloradans have decided that certain matters are too important to be "suited for statutory enactment." For example, the immense power of an atomic explosion must be authorized by a vote of the people; taxation must be by express consent; aliens have arms rights and property rights; morally controversial activities such as gambling, smoking, alcohol, or marijuana will be allowed (or not) according to terms set by the people.

The *Lujan* dicta denigrate article XVI (mining and water) as not "fundamental." Without water, life is impossible. When water is scarce, as in semiarid Colorado, people cannot live in a common society if they cannot agree on who has what rights to which water. By necessity since the early territorial days, Coloradans created a law of water rights that contradicted hundreds of years of common law. The new legal system was fundamental to Coloradans' ability to live together—and to live at all. Thanks to article XVI, the essential principles of Colorado's innovative and fundamental water laws were guaranteed as a foundation of the new State of Colorado.

The four water sections of article XVI are terse. None are longer than two sentences (three if you say that a semicolon separates two sentences). Of course, the people can amend article XVI anytime they choose, and change the system of water rights. Through all the changes in Colorado from 1876 to 2021, article XVI has served the people so well that it has never been amended.

Fundamental indeed.

Like the water sections of article XVI, the mining sections have never needed amendment. Mining was the *sine qua non* for the survival of Colorado. In the early Gold Rush, placer mining predominated. Then came hard rock mining. By 1876, soft rock mining, such as coal, was increasing. Later, underground extraction of oil and gas became part of the boom-and-bust cycle.

The 1875–76 Colorado Convention could not have foreseen the future importance of oil. As the time, crude oil was considered filthy and troublesome. Nobody knew how useful refined oil could be.

The Colorado Convention did know that the mining was the beating heart of the Colorado economy, so the Constitution set forth some essentials for mining: the general assembly *shall* enact laws for mine safety and child labor. Two sections of article XVI provide that the general assembly "may" enact some other laws related to mining: mine ventilation, and establishment of a school of mines.

Some constitutional provisions say "shall" and others say "may." According to the text of the Colorado Constitution, the nonfundamental provisions are the ones with "may." Although the Constitution calls out the importance of certain topics, the general assembly retains full discretion; it may act, or not.

Quo warranto? By what authority?

Some contracts are terse, and others lengthy. The contract that Colorado courts are obligated to uphold is the Colorado Constitution in its entirety. The most authoritative expression of the will of the sovereign—of the people —is constitutional enactment. Courts derive all their authority from delegation by the people. Courts lack lawful authority to selectively underperform their duties to enforce parts of the contract that they disagree with. As the U.S. supreme court said, "we know of no principled basis on which to create a hierarchy of constitutional values." *Valley Forge Christian College v. Americans United for Separation of Church and State, Inc.*, 454 U.S. 464, 484 (1982).

While all of a constitution is equal in authority, the enforcement of some parts is left to different branches. The judicial branch is not the final arbiter of everything—as decisions of the judicial branch have often recognized. For example, the United States Senate decides, with finality, the official journal and records of the Senate. *National Labor Relations Board v. Noel Canning*, 573 U.S. 513 (2014). In disputes over foreign affairs, the federal courts usually let the legislative and executive branches battle it out.

Likewise in Colorado, the governor has the final say in whether to issue a pardon for all convictions that are pardonable. COLO. CONST. art. IV, § 7. There is no room for judicial review over the wisdom of the governor's decision. The Colorado supreme court has repeatedly recognized that it is ill-equipped to take over taxes and spending for Colorado public schools. Indeed, that was the ultimate point that the *Lujan* court was making. *Lobato* was in the same spirit.

The *Lujan* court's error was not the judicial modesty about the judicial branch's ability to supervise a wholesale revamping of the public school system. Rather, the error was the arrogant presumption that the court has the authority to separate constitutional sections into higher and lower classes. The text of the Constitution itself does the sorting. The less important, non-mandatory provisions say "may."

Article XXVI says "shall" four times. The word "may" is used once to describe what may not be done. Two other uses of "may" encourage but do not mandate further legislation by the general assembly.

With clarity, the people of Colorado have created fundamental law regulating nuclear detonations in the State. Nuclear detonations are not small matters. The "shall" commands of article XXVI are simple to understand. Unlike the complexity of school finance, it is very easy to tell whether a proposed explosion is or is not a nuclear explosion for which article XXVI requires the advance consent of the people. There is no good reason for article XXVI to be assigned to some category of inferior, less important, underenforced constitutional text.

Article XXVII. Great Outdoors Colorado

In 1982, the voters approved an amendment to article XVIII, which had banned lotteries other than tightly regulated charitable fundraisers. Proponents of the new state lottery promised that the revenue would be used for parks and open space. Yet in 1983, the general assembly allocated half the new revenue to the Capital Construction Fund. In 1988, the legislature decided that the permissible state lottery also included electronic lotto and that most of the new revenue would be spent on to prison construction.

The public response was article XXVII, enacted by the voters in 1992. It requires that most revenue from the state lottery be used for enhancement of outdoor recreation, wildlife, open space, and outdoor education.

Explanations follow certain sections.

Art. XXVII, Section 1. Great Outdoors Colorado Program

(1) The people of the State of Colorado intend that the net proceeds of every state-supervised lottery game operated under the authority of article XVIII, Section 2 shall be guaranteed and permanently dedicated to the preservation, protection, enhancement and management of the state's wildlife, park, river, trail and open space heritage, except as specifically provided in this article. Accordingly, there shall be established the Great Outdoors Colorado Program to preserve, protect, enhance and manage the state's wildlife, park, river, trail and open space heritage. The Great Outdoors Colorado Program shall include:

(a) Wildlife program grants which:
(I) Develop wildlife watching opportunities;
(II) Implement educational programs about wildlife and wildlife environment;
(III) Provide appropriate programs for maintaining Colorado's diverse wildlife heritage;
(IV) Protect crucial wildlife habitats through the acquisition of lands, leases or easements and restore critical areas;

(b) Outdoor recreation program grants which:
(I) Establish and improve state parks and recreation areas throughout the State of Colorado;
(II) Develop appropriate public information and environmental education resources on Colorado's natural resources at state parks, recreation areas, and other locations throughout the state;
(III) Acquire, construct and maintain trails and river greenways;
(IV) Provide water for recreational purposes through the acquisition of water rights or through agreements with holders of water rights, all in accord with applicable state water law;

(c) A program to identify, acquire and manage unique open space and natural areas of statewide significance through grants to the Colorado Divisions of Parks and Outdoor Recreation and Wildlife, or municipalities, counties, or other political subdivision of the State, or non-profit land conservation organizations, and which will encourage cooperative investments by other public or private entities for these purposes; and

(d) A program for grants to match local investments to acquire, develop and manage open space, parks, and environmental education facilities, and which will encourage cooperative investments by other public or private entities for these purposes.

Art. XXVII, Section 2. Trust fund created

A fund to be known as the Great Outdoors Colorado Trust Fund, referred to in this article as the "Trust Fund," is hereby created and established in the Treasury of the State of Colorado.

The year after GOCO was enacted, the general assembly specified that since GOCO took so much money that had formerly been available to the general fund, all incidental management costs of GOCO had to be paid by GOCO, and not by the general fund. C.R.S. § 33-60-105.

Art. XXVII, Section 3. Trust fund revenues

(1) Beginning with the proceeds from the fourth quarter of the State's Fiscal Year 1992-1993, all proceeds from all programs, including Lotto and every other state-supervised lottery game operated under the authority of Article XVIII, Section 2 of the Colorado Constitution, whether by the Colorado Lottery Commission or otherwise (such programs defined hereafter in this Article as "Lottery Programs"), net of prizes and expenses of the state lottery division and after a sufficient amount of money has been reserved, as of the end of any fiscal quarter, to ensure the operation of the lottery for the ensuing fiscal quarter (such netted proceeds defined hereafter in this Article as "Net Proceeds") are set aside, allocated, allotted, and continuously appropriated as follows, and the Treasurer shall distribute such proceeds no less frequently than quarterly, as follows:

(a) Repealed by S.C.R. 02-006, § 1, eff. Dec. 20, 2002.
(b) For each quarter including and after the first quarter of the State's Fiscal Year 1998-1999:

(I) Forty percent to the Conservation Trust Fund for distribution to municipalities and counties and other eligible entities for parks, recreation and open space purposes;
(II) Ten percent to the Division of Parks and Outdoor Recreation for the acquisition, development and improvement of new and existing state parks, recreation areas and recreational trails; and
(III) All remaining Net Proceeds in trust to the Board of the Trust Fund, provided, however, that in any state fiscal year in which the portion of the Net Proceeds which would otherwise be given in trust to the State Board of the Trust Fund exceeds the amount of $35 million, to be adjusted each year for changes from the 1992 Consumer Price Index--Denver, the Net Proceeds in excess of such amount or adjusted amount shall be allocated to the General Fund of the State of Colorado.

(c) Repealed by S.C.R. 02-006, § 1, eff. Dec. 20, 2002.
(d) Repealed by S.C.R. 02-006, § 1, eff. Dec. 20, 2002.
(e) Repealed by S.C.R. 02-006, § 1, eff. Dec. 20, 2002.

(2) From July 1, 1993, the following sums of money and property, in addition to Net Proceeds as set forth in Section 3(1) above, are set aside, allocated, allotted, and continuously appropriated in trust to the Board of the Trust Fund:

(a) All interest derived from moneys held in the Trust Fund;

(b) Any property donated specifically to the State of Colorado for the specific purpose of benefitting the Trust Fund, including contributions, grants, gifts, bequests, donations, and federal, state, or local grants; and

(c) Such other moneys as may be allocated to the Trust Fund by the General Assembly.

Money is allocated to the Great Outdoors Colorado Trust Fund, the Division of Parks and Recreation (a unit of the Department of Natural Resources), and the Conservation Trust Fund (via which the Department of Local Affairs distributes grants to local governments for conservation, C.R.S. § 29-21-101). Net proceeds above $35 million (in 1992 inflation-adjusted dollars) go to the general fund.

The repealed subsections of section 3 were transitional, to continue paying off existing capital construction projects that were dependent on lottery revenue.[2]

Art. XXVII, Section 4. Trust fund inviolate

All moneys deposited in the Trust Fund shall remain in trust for the purposes set forth in this article, and no part thereof shall be used or appropriated for any other purpose, nor made subject to any other tax, charge, fee or restriction.

Art. XXVII, Section 5. Trust fund spending

(1)

(a) Expenditures from the Trust Fund shall be made in furtherance of the Great Outdoors Colorado Program, and shall commence in State Fiscal Year 1993-94. The Board of the Trust Fund shall have the duty to assure that expenditures are made for the purposes set forth in this section and in section 6, and that the amounts expended for each of the following purposes over a period of years be substantially equal:

(I) Investments in the wildlife resources of Colorado through the Colorado Division of Wildlife,[3] including the protection and restoration of crucial wildlife habitats, appropriate programs for maintaining Colorado's diverse wildlife heritage, wildlife watching, and educational programs about wildlife and wildlife environment, consistent with the purposes set forth in Section 1(1)(a) of this article;

(II) Investments in the outdoor recreation resources of Colorado through the Colorado Division of Parks and Outdoor Recreation, including the State Parks System, trails, public information and environmental education resources, and water for recreational

---

[2] Issues related to the phase-out were addressed in *In re Great Outdoors Colorado Trust Fund*, 913 P.2d 533 (Colo. 1996).

[3] This unit of the Department of Natural Resources that administers the state program for hunting and fishing, including habitat conservation. Its present name is Colorado Parks and Wildlife.

facilities, consistent with the purposes set forth in Section 1(1)(b) of this article;

(III) Competitive grants to the Colorado Divisions of Parks and Outdoor Recreation and Wildlife, and to counties, municipalities or other political subdivisions of the state, or non-profit land conservation organizations, to identify, acquire and manage open space and natural areas of statewide significance, consistent with the purposes set forth in Section 1(1)(c) of this article; and

(IV) Competitive matching grants to local governments or other entities which are eligible for distributions from the conservation trust fund, to acquire, develop or manage open lands and parks, consistent with the purposes set forth in Section 1(1)(d) of this article;

(b) Provided, however, that the State Board of the Great Outdoors Colorado Trust Fund shall have the discretion (a) to direct that any portion of available revenues be reinvested in the Trust Fund and not expended in any particular year, (b) to make other expenditures which it considers necessary and proper to the accomplishment of the purposes of this amendment.

(2) All funds provided to state agencies from the Trust Fund shall be deemed to be custodial in nature, and the expenditure of those funds shall not be subject to legislative appropriation or restriction.

The state board can choose to reinvest its revenue in a given year, rather than spend it. It can "make other expenditures which it considers necessary and proper to the accomplishment of the purposes of this amendment." Trust Fund expenditures "shall not be subject to legislative appropriation or restriction."

In 1999, an opinion by new Democratic attorney general Ken Salazar withdrew and replaced an opinion by previous Republican attorney general Gale Norton. The new opinion stated that the GOCO board, and not the state treasurer, had the default power of how to invest. Colo. Att'y Gen. Op. No. 99-06, 1999 WL 33100124 (July 30, 1999).

Art. XXVII, Section 6. State board to administer trust fund

(1) There shall be established a State Board of the Great Outdoors Colorado Trust Fund. The Board shall consist of two members of the public from each congressional district, a representative designated by the State Board of Parks and Outdoor Recreation, a representative designated by the Colorado Wildlife Commission, and the Executive Director of the Department of Natural Resources. The public members of the Board shall be appointed by the Governor, subject to the consent of the Senate, for terms of four years—provided, however, that when the first such members are appointed, one of the public members from each congressional district shall be appointed for a two-year term, to assure staggered terms of office thereafter. At least two members shall reside west of the Continental Divide. At least one member shall represent agricultural interests. The public members of the board shall be entitled to a reasonable per diem compensation to be determined by the Board plus their actual expenses for each meeting of the Board or a committee

of the Board. The Board's composition shall reflect, to the extent practical, Colorado's gender, ethnic and racial diversity, and no two of the representatives of any one congressional district shall be members of the same political party. Members of the Board shall be subject to removal as provided in Article IV, Section 6 of this constitution.

(2) The Board shall be responsible for, and shall have the power to undertake the following actions:

(a) To direct the Treasurer to disburse expendable income from the Trust Fund as the Board may determine by resolution, and otherwise to administer the Trust Fund, provided, however, that the Board shall not have the power to acquire any interest in real property other than (I) temporarily to hold real property donated to it and (II) to acquire leased office space;

(b) To promulgate rules and regulations as are necessary or expedient for the conduct of its affairs and its meetings and of meetings of any committees and generally for the administration of this article, provided, however, that such rules and regulations shall give the public an opportunity to comment on the general policies of the Board and upon specific grant proposals before the Board;

(c) To cause to be published and distributed an annual report, including a financial report, to the citizens, the Governor and the General Assembly of Colorado, which will set out the Board's progress in administering the funds appropriated to it, and the Board's objectives and its budget for the forthcoming year, and to consult with the General Assembly from time to time concerning its objectives and its budget;

(d) To administer the distribution of grants pursuant to Sections 1(1)(c), 1(1)(d), 5(1)(a)(III), and 5(1)(a)(IV) of this article, with the expense of administering said grants to be defrayed from the funds made available to the program elements of said sections;

(e) Commencing July 1, 1993, to determine what portions, if any, of moneys allocated to the Trust Fund should be invested in an interest-bearing Trust Fund account by the Treasurer of the State of Colorado, to remain in the Trust Fund and available for expenditure in future years;

(f) To employ such staff and to contract for such office space and acquire such equipment and supplies and enter into such other contracts as it may consider necessary from time to time to accomplish its purposes, and to pay the cost thereof from the funds appropriated to the Board under this article, provided, however, that to the extent it is reasonably feasible to do so the Board shall (I) contract with the Colorado Department of Natural Resources or other state agency for necessary administrative support and (II) endeavor to keep the level of administrative expense as low as may be practicable in comparison with its expenditures for the purposes set forth in Section 1 of this article, and the Board may contract with the State Personnel Board or any successor thereof for personnel services.

> (3) The Board shall be a political subdivision of the state, and shall have all the duties, privileges, immunities, rights, liabilities and disabilities of a political subdivision of the state, provided, however, that its organization, powers, revenues and expenses shall not be affected by any order or resolution of the general assembly, except as provided in this constitution. It shall not be an agency of state government, nor shall it be subject to administrative direction by any department, commission, board, bureau or agency of the state, except to the extent provided in this constitution. The Board shall be subject to annual audit by the state auditor, whose report shall be a public document. The Board shall adopt rules permitting public access to its meetings and records which are no less restrictive than state laws applicable to state agencies, as such laws may be amended from time to time. The Board members, officers and directors of the Board shall have no personal liability for any actions or refusal to act by the Board as long as such action or refusal to act did not involve willful or intentional malfeasance or gross negligence.

The state board of the Great Outdoors Colorado trust fund is comprised of:

- two members of the public from each congressional district,
- a representative designated by the State Board of Parks and Outdoor Recreation,
- a representative designated by the Colorado Wildlife Commission, and
- the executive director of the Department of Natural Resources.

Public members are appointed by the governor, confirmed by the senate, and serve for staggered 4-year terms. There must be at least two members from west of the Continental Divide, and one from agriculture. To the extent practical, members shall reflect Colorado's gender, ethnic and racial diversity. If more than one member is from the same congressional district, they must be of different political parties.

The board may hire staff and may make rules for the conduct of its affairs. The board may not acquire any interest in real property except for: 1. Leased office space; 2. Temporary holding of donated real property.

The board is a political subdivision of the state. It is not subject to anyone's control, except as provided in the Constitution. The board must have open meetings and an annual audit by the state auditor, and must publish reports.

Art. XXVII, Section 7. No effect on water law

> Nothing in this article shall affect in any way whatsoever any of the provisions under Article XVI of the State Constitution of Colorado, including those provisions related to water, nor any of the statutory provisions related to the appropriation of water in Colorado.

So existing water users did not have to worry that their water rights would be taken away when upstream land was purchased for conservation.

Art. XXVII, Section 8. Lottery proceeds must supplement and not replace spending for the Department of Natural Resources

> The people intend that the allocation of lottery funds required by this article of the constitution be in addition to and not a substitute for funds otherwise appropriated

> from the General Assembly to the Colorado Department of Natural Resources and its divisions.

Section 8 keeps the general assembly from cutting existing appropriations in year one of GOCO. But it does not stop the legislature from freezing appropriations at their 1992 levels and making GOCO responsible for nominal funding increases to keep up with inflation.

Art. XXVII, Section 9. Eminent domain prohibited

> No moneys received by any state agency pursuant to this article shall be used to acquire real property by condemnation through the power of eminent domain.

None of the Great Outdoors money, including money granted to local governments, can be used to acquire real property by eminent domain. This helps keep GOCO non-coercive. You don't have to pay for GOCO unless you are foolish enough to buy lottery tickets. And GOCO won't take your property unless you want to sell.

Yet when the town of Silverthorne initiated condemnation proceedings to take people's land to make a public trail, the landowners were not allowed to present evidence that Silverthorne was using GOCO money to pay for the condemnation. The court held that GOCO's enactment did not change long-standing precedent that the target of a condemnation cannot raise the defense of the condemner's illegal source of funds *Town of Silverthorne v. Lutz*, 2016 COA 17, 370 P.3d 368 (Colo. App. 2016).

Art. XXVII, Section 10. Payment in lieu of taxes

> Any acquisitions of real property made by a state agency pursuant to this article shall be subject to payments in lieu of taxes to counties in which said acquisitions are made. Such payments shall be made from moneys made available by the Trust Fund, and shall not exceed the rate of taxation for comparable property classifications.

When the state acquires formerly private property in a county, the county can no longer tax that property. *See* art. X, § 4 (intergovernmental tax immunity). Historically, the state has given the county a sum of money equivalent to the property tax that the county could have imposed. These gifts are called *payments in lieu of taxes* (PILT). The federal government has a similar PILT program for federal property. When a state agency acquires property pursuant to Great Outdoors, it must make PILT. The PILT shall come from the trust fund. The payment system is C.R.S. § 33-60-104.5.

Art. XXVII, Section 11. Effective date

> This article shall become effective upon proclamation by the governor, and shall be self-implementing. This article shall apply to each distribution of net proceeds from the programs operated under the authority of Article XVIII, Section 2 of the Colorado Constitution, whether by the Colorado Lottery Commission or otherwise, made after July 1, 1993 and shall supersede any provision to the contrary in Article XVIII, Section 2 [state lottery] or any other provision of law.

Article XXVII was enacted in 1992, the same year as TABOR. Since the former got more votes, the supreme court decided that lottery revenues for GOCO are mostly exempt from TABOR's fiscal year spending rules. *In re Interrog. on S.B. 93-74*, 852 P.2d 1 (Colo. 1993). By subsequent statutes, lottery revenues are completely exempt. C.R.S. § 22-54-117, 24-77-102(17).

CHAPTER 33

Conclusion

The Colorado Constitution is magnificent. Our Constitution is based on natural rights and popular sovereignty. Pursuant to the text of our Constitution, the people rule—yet that a majority can never violate anyone's natural rights, many of which are enumerated in the Constitution. The Colorado Constitution is a near-perfect frame of government for a constitutional republic.

On controversial issues such as lotteries, casinos, alcohol, tobacco, and marijuana, the people of Colorado have changed their minds, and changed the Constitution accordingly. Since 1910 with the rights of initiative and referendum, the people of Colorado have directly exercised their lawmaking powers, especially when the sovereign people's agents (government officials) have undermined the people's rights. Some amendments to the Constitution that were proposed by citizens as initiatives have been foolish. So were some of the amendments proposed by the general assembly as referenda. Any body with legislative power, including the people, sometimes acts wisely and sometimes otherwise. Through the Colorado Constitution, the people have exercised "their sole and exclusive right of governing themselves."

A longstanding problem of government is misuse of government power to give certain businesses or workers special benefits. *See, e.g.*, Statute of Monopolies, 21 James I, c. 3 (1623) (forbidding the monarch to grant monopolies). *See generally*, Steven G. Calabresi & Larissa C. Leibowitz, *Monopolies and The Constitution: A History Of Crony Capitalism*, 36 HARVARD JOURNAL OF LAW & PUBLIC POLICY 983 (2013).

After 1776, experience showed that even in the United States—where terse state constitutions declared the best principles of republican government—big business and big government would still conspire to transfer wealth to themselves from consumers and small businesses. Therefore, Colorado's 1876 Constitution was replete with rules against special favors for corporations and with rules for equality of treatment in general, including uniformity of taxation. The primary rules were backed up by other rules on legislative procedure, on taxation by consent, and against government debt. Many constitutional protections were fortified by later amendments, including

Give A Vote to Every Legislator (GAVEL, 1988) and the Taxpayer's Bill of Rights (TABOR, 1992). Chapters 8, 15.

Our state Constitution guarantees that businesses will compete on a level playing field. Bigger companies with political clout cannot receive special tax exemptions or subsidies. Nor can the government use eminent domain to take property from a small business and convey it to a big business.

Although few people like taxes, all Coloradans knows that the taxes they pay—including the taxes to service government borrowing—are by consent, authorized by the people through the Constitution's specified processes.

A person who simply read the Colorado Constitution would expect today's Colorado to be the copacetic state described above. The reality is different. In practice, Colorado is only partially the constitutional republic guaranteed by our Constitution. In this concluding chapter, I explore some of the reasons why the government Coloradans live under is sometimes a far cry from the good and fair government our Constitution guarantees, and I offer some suggestions about how Coloradans can begin to address the problem.

About seven percent of the Colorado Constitution has been nullified by the state government, including the judiciary

There are 356 sections of the Colorado Constitution, including the two preambles. Of these, 28 are not presently treated as law by one of more branches of the Colorado state government. Looking on the bright side, this means that the state government is mostly obeying about 93% of the Constitution.

This book has suggested that the following constitutional sections have been partially or fully negated:

- Schedule, § 20. Colorado presidential electors shall be chosen by the direct vote of the people of Colorado.
- Art. II, § 11. No irrevocable special privileges.
- Art. II, § 13. Right to keep and bear arms may not "be called in question."
- Art. II, § 14. "Private property shall not be taken for private use."
- Art. V, § 1. Referendum may only be barred for "laws necessary for the immediate preservation of the public peace, health, or safety.
- Art. V, § 7. General assembly regular sessions limited to "one hundred and twenty calendar days."
- Art. V, § 21. Bills must contain a single subject.
- Art. V, § 25. No special legislation for businesses.
- Art. V, § 28. No extra compensation to government employees or contractors.
- Art. V, § 31. "All bills for raising revenue shall originate in the house of representatives."
- Art. V, § 34. "No appropriation shall be made for charitable, industrial, educational or benevolent purposes to any person, corporation or community not under the absolute control of the state."
- Art. IX, § 8. "[N]or shall any distinction or classification of pupils be made on account of race or color."
- Art. X, § 3. "Each property tax levy shall be uniform upon all real and personal property."

- Art. X, § 9. "The power to tax corporations and corporate property, real and personal, shall never be relinquished or suspended."
- Art. X, § 10. "All corporations in this state, or doing business therein, shall be subject to taxation."
- Art. X, § 18. Gasoline and auto registration taxes shall "be used exclusively for the construction, maintenance, and supervision of the public highways of this state."
- Art. X, § 20. Taxpayer's Bill of Rights. Ten separate clauses put out of operation by judicial decision.
- Art. XI, § 1. No pledging government credit "in any manner" for any person or corporation.
- Art. XI, § 2. No donations or grants to any person or corporation.
- Art. XI, § 3. State "shall not contract any debt by loan in any form," with specified exceptions.
- Art. XI, § 4. Debt for "the erection of public buildings . . . shall not be less than ten nor more than fifteen years."
- Art. XI, § 5. Debt for "erecting public buildings . . . shall be ratified by the vote of a majority of" electors.
- Art. XI, § 6. Local government debt must be approved by a majority of voters.
- Art. XII, § 5. District courts shall annually charge grand juries to investigate county treasurer accounts.
- Art. XVIII, § 9. Casinos shall be allowed only in buildings with pre-World War I style architecture. "No more than thirty-five percent of the square footage of any building and no more than fifty percent of any one floor of such building, may be used for limited gaming."
- Art. XXVII, § 9. No Great Outdoors Colorado money may be used for eminent domain.
- Art. XVIII, § 12a. Congressional candidates' decision on voluntary term limits pledge must appear in all government-sponsored voter education material.
- Art. XXIX, § 3. Government employees and their families may only receive gifts from friends or family "on a special occasion."

Although the 28 negated sections involve diverse topics, 16 of the sections cluster around a broad issue: undoing the work of the Convention and the people that "had protected the inarticulate against machinators." *Johnson v. McDonald*, 97 Colo. 324, 362, 49 P.2d 1017 (1935). The Colorado supreme court has negated the Constitution's restraints on taxing, spending, and borrowing without consent; the Constitution's limit on eminent domain; the Constitution's requirements for uniformity of taxation; and the Constitution's rule against special legislation. State and local government corporate welfare deals routinely violate multiple sections of the Constitution. Favored businesses get tax abatements and other special, irrevocable privileges. Everyone else is burdened with more taxes and debt to pick up the slack. The construction industry and the debt industry profit handsomely when governments take out 25-year loans to erect buildings, without consent of the taxpayers, and in defiance of the constitutional requirement that government building loans to be 15 years or less so that taxpayers are not burdened with excessive interest. Because the Colorado supreme court has in effect repealed much of Article XI, which had strongly limited public indebtedness, today's profligate governments have burdened future governments, future taxpayers, and Colorado's future with many billions of dollars of debt. Almost all of the debt was accumulated without consent of the voters, with machinations designed to deny the voters their constitutional right to choose whether to authorize debt.

In Colorado, judicial nullification of sections of the Constitution has been accomplished in diverse ways. The most brazen form, discussed next, is simply to declare that the Constitution means the opposite of what it plainly says.

Nullification from the bench

As chapter 5 detailed, ever since 1798 Kentucky Resolution against the Alien & Sedition Acts, nullification has been a mechanism of the vertical separation of powers in America's federal system. While states cannot actually nullify federal law, their refusal to participate in federal law enforcement can render some federal laws much less effective within a state—such as with fugitive slave enforcement in the 1850s. More recently, the voters of Colorado in 2012, against the opposition of virtually the entire governing class, relegalized adult use of marijuana. Federal statutes notwithstanding, the people prevailed.

Other chapters in this book have examined a different type of nullification: the nullification of the state Constitution by government officials. For example, the Colorado constitution mandates: "The state shall not contract any debt by loan in any form." Art. XI, § 3. Yet the Colorado supreme court says that the prohibition on "debt by loan in any form" does not apply if the loan is secured by a portion of the government's revenue that is placed in a separate account. *Johnson v. McDonald*, 97 Colo. 324, 49 P.2d 1017 (1935).

The Constitution insists: "Neither the state, nor any county, city, town, township, or school district shall make any donation or grant to, or in aid of, or become a subscriber to, or shareholder in any corporation or company or a joint owner with any person, company, or corporation, public or private, in or out of the state." The Colorado supreme court, however, has announced that this does not apply when there is a "valid public purpose," and courts must make "every presumption" that there is. *Allardice v. Adams County*, 476 P.2d 982 (1970) (government bonds to build an agricultural feed plant for Ralston Purina).

The 1988 GAVEL Amendment limited regular legislative sessions of "one hundred twenty calendar days," with no exceptions. Art. V, § 7. In 2010, the court defined "calendar days" exactly the way that other speakers of the English language do. *People v. Zhuk*, 239 P.3d 437, 437–38 (Colo. 2010) (December 3 to December 17 is "fourteen calendar days").

Yet in 2020, the Colorado supreme court asserted that "calendar days" was "ambiguous" and then chose to "defer" to a House and Senate Joint Rule that allowed the legislature in 2020 and 2021 to extend the length of its regular session far beyond 120 calendar days. *In re Interrogatory on House Joint Resolution 20-1006*, 2020 CO 23 (2020).

What the court did to article XI, starting in 1922, it has also done to the Taxpayer's Bill of Rights, starting with the court's 1994 announcement that a Bill of Rights is not a Bill of Rights, and that the court would ignore the rule of interpretation expressly mandated by the Bill of Rights. *Bickel v. City of Boulder*, 885 P.2d 215, 226 (Colo. 1994).

As nullification takes hold over time, the actual text of the Constitution becomes minuscule in the court's opinions. The attention shifts to the precedents allowing further violations of the constitutional text. Consider section 1 of article XI. The text is so broad and unequivocal that almost every case involving government debt on behalf of business could be decided simply by quoting the text:

> Neither the state, nor any county, city, town, township or school district shall lend or pledge the credit or faith thereof, directly or indirectly, in any manner to, or in aid of, any person, company or corporation, public or private, for any amount, or for any purpose whatever; or become responsible for any debt, contract or liability of any person, company or corporation, public or private, in or out of the state.

The Convention wrote and the people ratified the most comprehensive language they could: "directly or indirectly, in any manner . . . public or private, for any amount, or for any purpose whatever." Yet government debt on behalf of business and other private interests is routine in Colorado.

In U.S. Constitution interpretation, there is lively debate over original public meaning versus other methods that give judges more freedom to make their own judgments about wise policy. However, the Colorado Constitution opinions criticized in this book have purported to be textualist. They have not articulated any theory that authorizes court to issue decisions contrary to plain constitutional text. Empirically speaking, there seem to be many decisions that are based on some theory other than textualism. Whatever those theories are, they have not been mentioned in the court's opinions.

Rules of judicial review

Some of the dismantling of the Colorado Constitution has taken place under the court's chosen standards of review. First, the court will only hold a law unconstitutional if it is so proven beyond a reasonable doubt. Second, the court will defer to the judgment of other branches that a law is constitutional, even when the other branches have never made any such judgement.

Statutes must be proven unconstitutional beyond a reasonable doubt

The Colorado supreme court's rule is that someone challenging a statute must prove it is unconstitutional beyond a reasonable doubt. The rule applies even within the Bill of Rights sections of the Constitution, although some sections in article II have been favored with different standards copied from U.S. Constitution case law. Beyond a reasonable doubt was announced as early as *Alexander v. People*, 7 Colo. 155, 2 P. 894, 896 (1883).[1]

Court of appeals judge Briggs explained the problems with beyond a reasonable doubt. *United Air Lines, Inc. v. City & Cty. of Denver*, 973 P.2d 647, 655–59 (Colo. App. 1998) (Briggs, J., specially concurring). Obviously, the standard

> resembles nothing so much as the presumption of innocence and burden of proof involved in a criminal case—an evidentiary burden of proof.
>
> The purpose of a constitutional analysis is of course not to make factual findings. Some underlying factual disputes may have to be resolved. However, no heightened standard of proof applies, and the ultimate purpose is still the resolution of a constitutional challenge through legal analysis.
>
> Even when the challenge is to the constitutionality of a legislative enactment as applied, the "evidence" required for the legal analysis is often undisputed, consisting of no more than the legislative enactment, a factual context, and perhaps some uncontested legislative history.
>
> . . .
>
> [T]he court's ultimate degree of certainty, or firmness of conviction, in a conclusion resolving a constitutional challenge does not result from the evidence, or "proof," presented. It results from the force, or persuasiveness, of legal argument.

---

[1] By art. XIV, § 9, "no county seat shall be removed unless a majority of the qualified electors of the county, voting on the proposition, vote therefore." The *Alexander* court stated that the Constitution does not create rules by negative implication. The Constitution set a minimum standard, and the legislature had discretion to set a higher standard. The beyond a reasonable doubt remark was dicta.

> . . .
>
> [T]he deference to which a co-equal branch of government is entitled appears and disappears, case by case, depending on the nature of the constitutional right or classification asserted. While it may be appropriate to vary the standard of review in a constitutional analysis on such bases, it is unclear why the respect and sensitivity to which each branch of government is entitled should be anything less than invariable.

Id. at 657-58.

Judge Briggs traces the beyond a reasonable doubt language to "an extremely sensitive and cautious [U.S.] Supreme Court" opinion from 1827. That court wrote, "It is but a decent respect due to the wisdom, the integrity, and the patriotism of the legislative body, by which any law is passed, to presume in favor of its validity, until its violation of the constitution is proved beyond a reasonable doubt." *Id* at 659 (quoting *Ogden v. Saunders*, 25 U.S. (12 Wheat.) 213, 270 (1827)). As judge Briggs points out, the U.S. supreme court abandoned such language long ago. *Id.* The U.S. court today employs a wide variety of standards of review for different part of the Constitution; although the modern rules can be criticized, they at least avoid the problem of trying to turn a criminal law trial evidence rule into a rule of legal analysis.

Moreover, the U.S. court's occasional use of such language was never a formal methodology for the court. The main popularizer of beyond a reasonable doubt rule in constitutional law was Harvard professor James Bradley Thayer, a Progressive who disliked judicial review per se, and whose influential article could provide little supporting precedent from federal or state courts. *See* Hugh Spitzer, *"Unconstitutional Beyond A Reasonable Doubt"—A Misleading Mantra that Should Be Gone for Good*, 96 WASHINGTON L. REVIEW ONLINE art. 5 (2021); James B. Thayer, *The Origin and Scope of the American Doctrine of Constitutional Law*, 7 HARVARD L. REVIEW 129 (1893).

As judge Briggs stated, well-reasoned appellate opinions uphold the moral power of courts. "What is important in the final analysis, constitutional or otherwise, is that appellate courts articulate principles and standards that are needed and useful. It is debatable whether requiring any heightened degree of deference is either . . . Even if both, requiring that a constitutional challenge rest on 'proof beyond a reasonable doubt' is neither." 973 P.2d at 659.

In the 2018 RTD sales tax case, the plaintiffs asked the Colorado supreme court to replace "beyond a reasonable doubt" with a standard requiring a "plain showing." The court declined to do so, since it said the plaintiffs would lose under either standard. *TABOR Foundation v. Regional Transportation District*, 416 P.3d 101 (Colo. 2018) (chapter 15).

When the court granted certiorari in the Aspen grocery bag tax case, it asked the parties to address whether "beyond a reasonable doubt" should be replaced with "preponderance of the evidence." The preponderance standard means "more likely than not." By 4–3, the court again said that plaintiffs would lose either way. *Colorado Union of Taxpayers Foundation v. City of Aspen*, 418 P.3d 506 (Colo. 2018).

The beyond a reasonable doubt standard upends the constitutional order. Rather than the Colorado Constitution being supreme, legislative acts are made supreme. If the standard means what it says, legislative enactments are immune from constitutional enforcement except in the rare circumstances when the proof meets that same overwhelming standard that would be necessary to convict a person of a crime. Finding that a legislative body exceeded constitutional limits should not require such an extreme standard. Indeed, the cases when the court does find a law unconstitutional, the pro/con arguments and evidence tend to be less overwhelming than "beyond a reasonable doubt.[2]

Deference to popular sovereignty

One theory in favor of beyond a reasonable doubt is the people's supremacy. The people have all the sovereignty. Except for the portion of their sovereignty that they delegated to the federal government by ratifying the U.S. Constitution, the people have plenary power. Therefore the people, acting through their elected legislature, can do whatever they want, except to the extent that their Constitution forbids it. The people being supreme, the Constitution should only very rarely be construed to thwart the people's will.

The justification has three weaknesses. First, in Colorado, the Constitution comes directly from the people, ratified by them on July 1, 1876, and then amended by direct vote. Statutes enacted by the general assembly are further removed from the people and therefore are not as directly expressive of their will.

Second, the "will" of the people includes their long-term will that the worst of their transient desires be thwarted. As U.S. supreme court justice David Brewer put it, "Constitutions . . . represent the deliberate judgment of the people as to the provisions and restraints which, firmly and fully enforced, will secure to each citizen the greatest liberty and utmost protection. They are rules proscribed by Philip sober to control Philip drunk." David E. Bernstein, *Philip Sober Controlling Philip Drunk:* Buchanan v. Warley *in Historical Perspective*, 51 VANDERBILT L. REVIEW 797 (1998) (quoting David J. Brewer, *An Independent Judiciary as the Salvation of the Nation*, in NEW YORK STATE BAR ASSOCIATION, PROCEEDINGS OF THE NEW YORK STATE BAR ASSOCIATION 37 (1893)).

In Colorado, the court does not defer to the people's sovereignty. Constitutional amendment is the strongest, highest level at which the people express their decision about what the law shall be. The Colorado supreme court has treated with disdain the people's enactment of the Taxpayer's Bill of Rights, starting with the refusal in early decisions even to say its name. *See* chapter 15. Thus, the theory of deference to the people cannot be a present-day justification for the beyond a reasonable doubt rule in Colorado.

Deference to the legislature

A different argument for beyond a reasonable doubt is the "presumption that public officials, in the discharge of their duties, have acted lawfully; and the fact, of which the courts take judicial notice, that members of the General Assembly have taken an oath to support the state Constitution. Hence follows the presumption that they have not passed an act which violates the fundamental law." *In re Senate Resolution No. 2*, 94 Colo. at 112.

The presumption has been accurate at some points in history for some legislators. For the presumption to be true, legislators would have to read the section(s) of the state Constitution that pertain to the bills being voted on. In a legislative body where many members vote on bills they never read, it seems unlikely that they always look into what the Constitution says.

Coloradans did *not* create a Constitution based on the presumption that state legislators would obey their oaths. Just the opposite. The legislature was viewed as a necessary evil that would be

---

[2] "[I]n practice the court's standard is usually far lower than what it would allow a jury to apply in a criminal case." Daniel J. Domenico, *The Constitutional Feedback Loop: Why No State Institution Typically Resolves Whether a Law is Constitutional and What, If Anything, Should Be Done About It*, 89 DENVER U. L. REVIEW 161, 192 (2011). Indeed, the fact that there are dissents in some cases holding a law unconstitutional shows that some reasonable people (the dissenting justices) did not believe that all "reasonable doubt" had been dispelled.

inclined to legislate for special benefits for itself and others. Hence the lengthy Colorado Constitution, written to hem in the legislature from every angle. *See, e.g.*, chapters 1, 8. In Colorado, constitutional text and history indicate skepticism about the notion that legislation was enacted by legislators who knew or adhered to the Colorado Constitution.

Former solicitor general Daniel Domenico, now a United States district court judge, explained in a 2011 article how the general assembly actually treats questions of constitutionality. In the Colorado system as it currently exists, *nobody* makes a decision about whether a law is constitutional. Instead, the legislature, the executive, and the judiciary each purport to defer to another branch's decision about constitutionality. Domenico wrote:

> It is hardly novel to note that the federal and state constitutions are the supreme law of their respective domains. In practice, however, that supremacy may be largely theoretical.
>
> . . .
>
> Although legislators, judges, and executive branch officials, including governors and attorneys general, take oaths to defend the state and federal constitutions, rarely will any of the institutions of state government prevent a statute whose constitutionality they question—or even doubt—from going into or remaining in effect. Instead, they will defer to the statute over the constitution.
>
> . . .
>
> [T]he courts, the Attorney General's Office, the general assembly, and the governor . . . each . . . takes a deferential view of the constitutional questions they face, applying a high burden of persuasion on anyone posing the question. Each of these institutions thus will typically enact, sign, enforce, defend, and uphold a law about which they may harbor even fairly serious constitutional doubts. Only when those doubts cross a high threshold will one of these institutions seek to impose the stated superiority of the constitution.
>
> . . .
>
> [T]he current situation can, and often does, create something of a feedback loop: the judiciary and attorney general defer to the policy branches' judgments, and the policy branches take that deference into account in making their judgments, and thus, in effect, give themselves deference. Rarely does anyone in these institutions ask the fundamental question, "Is this law constitutional?" Instead, in most instances, they give laws the benefit of the doubt over the ostensibly supreme constitution.
>
> . . .
>
> . . . Every institution, in other words, asks not whether a law is constitutional, but whether it is clearly or undoubtedly unconstitutional. This results in a feedback loop: the attorney general and the courts will defer to the policy branches' constitutional judgments, but the policy branches then take that deference into account in making that judgment themselves. The former two institutions assume the policy branches have asked the constitutional question and will uphold the law even if their independent judgment is that the law is probably (though not undoubtedly) unconstitutional. Meanwhile, the policy branches look to how the courts will assess the constitutional question, and thus do not directly ask the constitutional question, but essentially ask whether the others will block the law if they enact it.

Daniel J. Domenico, *The Constitutional Feedback Loop: Why No State Institution Typically Resolves Whether a Law is Constitutional and What, If Anything, Should Be Done About It*, 89 DENVER U. L. REVIEW 161, 162–63, 189 (2011).

The advice the general assembly receives from its in-house lawyers, the office of legislative legal services (OLLS), "appears to make this feedback loop explicit." *Id.* at 190. The OLLS advises legislators about whether bills are constitutional or not. In the words of OLLS, "OLLS legal memoranda generally resolve doubts about whether the general assembly has authority to enact a particular piece of legislation in favor of the general assembly's plenary power." *Id.* at 182 (citing Memorandum from Office of Legislative Legal Servs. to Keith King, Colo. House Representative (Apr. 7, 2004)). In other words, unless there is no doubt that a bill would be unconstitutional, the legislature's legal staff "generally" will tell the legislature that it can do as it wills.

The OLLS accurately advises legislators how the courts would consider the question of constitutionality: "If enacted, the [law in question] would be presumed constitutional and, if challenged, the [law] would have to be proven unconstitutional beyond a reasonable doubt." *Id.* (quoting and adding brackets, Memorandum from Office of Legislative Legal Servs. to Sue Windels, Colo. State Senator 2 (Mar. 28, 2007)). Domenico summarizes:

> Thus, it seems that the question the legislature is asking is not whether the law is unconstitutional, or even whether it is clearly unconstitutional, but whether there are doubts about whether the courts will uphold the law. Thus, the deference the courts grant the legislature itself becomes part of the policy branches' analysis, and they ask not whether the law is constitutional, but whether the courts will uphold it . . . [T]hese are very different things in our deferential world.

Id. at 190.

Domenico argues that the Colorado attorney general has little choice in the matter, given that the attorney general is the lawyer for the state government. In Domenico's view, the attorney general, as counsel to the government, can do no more than offer its clients predictions about whether courts will find the clients' actions unconstitutional. The attorney general cannot advise its clients that a proposed action actually *is* unconstitutional.

Similarly, Domenico argues that more robust judicial review of constitutionality would be inappropriate because judges are not democratically elected. However, federal courts, and Colorado state courts applying the U.S. Constitution, already hear many cases where the government bears the burden of proving constitutionality.[3] For some but not all provisions of the Colorado Bill of Rights, the Colorado court has voluntarily adopted the U.S. Constitution rule putting the burden of proof on the government. In some other U.S. Constitution cases, challengers win when they make a "plain showing" that a law is unconstitutional.[4] That is a rigorous standard, but not a nearly impossible one.

Domenico suggests legislators and executives should make their own decisions about whether a proposed government action actually *is* constitutional. They should not rely solely on only attorneys' predictions about what highly deferential courts will do.

---

[3] When fundamental rights—such as freedom of speech, the right to keep and bear arms, and rights against discrimination on the basis of race or sex—are affected, the government bears the burden of proving that the restrictive statute is constitutional. The judicial review of the restriction on fundamental rights is called "heightened scrutiny." The rigor of heightened scrutiny of whether the government has met its burden of proof varies, depending on the restriction. The major tests are "intermediate scrutiny" and "strict scrutiny." Both of these have varieties, and there are sometimes other tests, such as "exacting scrutiny." The key point is that the government bears the burden of proof.

[4] *See, e.g., United States v. Morrison,* 529 U.S. 598, 607 (2000) (whether Congress exceeded its powers "To regulate commence . . . among the several States") ("Due respect for the decisions of a coordinate branch of Government demands that we invalidate a congressional enactment only upon a plain showing that Congress has exceeded its constitutional bounds.").

What to do?

Some remedies that haven't worked

Before 1966 Colorado elected judges in partisan elections. Thereafter, judges are appointed by the governors and mayors, with finalists chosen by commissions. Art. VI (chapter 10). Judicial nullification had taken place under both systems.

Sixteen of the 28 nullified sections of the Colorado Constitution involve the government improperly taking A's property to give it to B. If we count each nullified provision of the Taxpayer's Bill of Rights separately, then the figure would be 25 out of 37. Regardless of the exact figure one uses, the problem of judicial nullification in Colorado is most of all a problem of government financial favoritism to the politically powerful: taking small business property by eminent domain to give it to big business, special and nonuniform tax laws for powerful businesses, unauthorized debt that benefits contractors and governments and leaves taxpayers stuck with the burden, taxation without consent so government officials can buy themselves popularity by distributing the fruits of other people's labor.

Some persons believe that the problems could be solved by more government involvement in business, and perhaps by turning big businesses into state entities. These hopes are unrealistic. First, the experience with the Taxpayer's Bill of Rights demonstrates that the creation of state "enterprises" worsens the problem of nonconsensual wealth transfers to the powerful.

Second, we are already a long way on the path to some big businesses becoming *de facto* arms of the government. It will not be surprising if the next big increase in tobacco taxes is structured as a "fee" to be collected by Philip Morris and to further push the corporation's competitors out of the market.

One attempt to address the broad problem of money in politics has been constitutional amendments to control some political inputs: severe restrictions on political spending and speech, and on gifts to government employees. Arts. XXVIII, XXIX. Yet the intricate political speech and spending controls widen the advantage of sophisticated and wealthy political actors, who can afford to hire compliance lawyers, whereas citizen activists must try to figure out things themselves. Article XXIX's gift rules are extremely overbroad, unenforceable as written, and pointlessly interfere with normal citizen interactions with government employees. *See* chapters 29, 30.

The more effective way to reduce money in politics would simply be to obey the Colorado Constitution, so that governments cannot redistribute billions of dollars from taxpayers to special interests. If you leave huge cheese wheels all over your floor, you will inevitably have lots of mice, regardless of the perceived strength of your anti-mouse measures. As long as Colorado governments are conduits for wealth transfer from taxpayers to special interests, special interests will invest in politics—one way or another—because the return on investment is so large.

The Colorado supreme court could solve the problem almost immediately by over-ruling its nullificatory precedents on article X, article XI, and eminent domain. The court could return to is proper role of deciding cases according to the supreme law of the Colorado Constitution. It is true that existing contracts providing special tax waivers or subsidies to corporations would have to honored. Art. II, § 11 (no impairment of the obligation of contracts). Even so, a judicial decision that no new corporate welfare contracts would be upheld—because they are plainly illegal according to the text of our Constitution—would begin to unwind the government's role as the middleman in taking from the inarticulate and giving to the machinators.

However, hoping that a majority of the Colorado supreme court will undo its nullification of many sections of our state Constitution may be as unrealistic as hoping that the legislative and executive branches will take seriously their oaths to support the Constitution.

If none of the branches of our state government will consistently obey and enforce our Colorado Constitution, what can Coloradans do?

Know your rights and duties

A first step for Coloradans is to know the text of their Constitution. That is one reason I wrote this book and created a Colorado Constitution class at the University of Denver. "Knowledge will forever govern ignorance: And a people who mean to be their own Governors, must arm themselves with the power which knowledge gives." James Madison to W.T. Barry, Aug. 4, 1822, *in* THE PAPERS OF JAMES MADISON, 2 RETIREMENT SERIES 555 (David B. Mattern et al. eds., 2013). If you do not know your constitutional rights, then you do not know to defend them.

A constitution reminds people of their rights. When the government flouts the constitution, the text shows the government's lawlessness. However disdainfully the text may be treated by the government, the words of constitutions can still live in people's hearts and minds.

For example, the Equal Protection Clause of the U.S. Fourteenth Amendment was judicially nullified from the late 19th century until the 1930s. Although the U.S. supreme court may have upheld government power to forcibly segregate black people into inferior train cars and schools, and to outlaw many voluntary interracial interactions, the court could not erase the text that every person is entitled to "the equal protection of the laws."

Some courts in the 1970s wrote opinions asserting that the Second Amendment right of the people to keep and bear arms is a right that belongs to the government, not the people, or is a right that belongs only to the National Guard.[5] Earlier, some courts had adopted the theory that the First Amendment allows the government to punish people for speech criticizing the government—so long as the government does not censor the speech in advance. *See, e.g.*, *Patterson v. Colorado*, 205 U.S. 454 (1907) (excerpted in chapter 4).

Notwithstanding the judicial opinions, many Americans did exercise their rights to freedom of speech, to keep and bear arms, and to freely associate with people of any color. Sometimes these rights were exercised in defiance of state or local laws to the contrary. Americans were breaking the law in the sense that they were violating statutes, but these statutes were themselves illegal because they contradicted the natural, essential, and inalienable rights secured to everyone by the U.S. Constitution.

Remember the inherent limits on Colorado government power

As stated in the memo quoted above, the office of legislative legal services believes that the Colorado general assembly has plenary power. The Colorado supreme court's beyond a reasonable doubt rule seems to presume that governments start with unlimited power. Yet the Colorado Constitution provides for a different system of government.

After describing the boundaries of the state, the Colorado Constitution begins by stating three rules of Colorado Constitution government.

- "All political power is vested in and derived from the people; all government, of right, originates from the people, is founded upon their will only, and is instituted solely for the good of the whole." Art. II, § 1.
- "The people of this state have the sole and exclusive right of governing themselves." Art. II, § 2.

[5] *See, e.g.,* David B. Kopel, *The Second Amendment in the Tenth Circuit: Three Decades of (Mostly) Harmless Error*, 86 DENVER U. L. REVIEW 901 (2009).

- "All persons have certain natural, essential and inalienable rights, among which may be reckoned the right of enjoying and defending their lives and liberties; of acquiring, possessing and protecting property; and of seeking and obtaining their safety and happiness." Art. II, § 3.

Starting at the moment of inception, the government created by the Colorado Constitution was of limited power. Our government was born without the power to invade the natural, essential, and alienable rights that are older than the government itself.

The Colorado state government has a birthday, August 1, 1876, when president Grant signed the proclamation of statehood. Natural, essential, and inalienable rights have existed since long before 1876, or 1776.

Rights that are "unalienable" cannot be alienated; it is impossible to surrender such rights to a government. Therefore, the natural, essential, and inalienable rights were never surrendered to the new Colorado state government.

The sovereign people of Colorado, acting in the fullness of their power, created a government of limited power. The government was never granted the power to take away "natural, essential and inalienable rights, among which may be reckoned the right of enjoying and defending their lives and liberties; of acquiring, possessing and protecting property; and of seeking and obtaining their safety and happiness."

The section 3 listed rights are "among" the "natural, essential and unalienable rights." There are many others. "The enumeration in this constitution of certain rights shall not be construed to deny, impair or disparage others retained by the people." Art. II, § 28.

By our Constitution, many government offices have been created or abolished. Natural rights can never be abolished. Any Colorado government that purported to abolish one would be exercising power that was never granted. It would be an act of usurpation, not an act of lawful authority.

Remember your solemn promises

Although governors, legislators, and judges may ignore or evade Colorado's highest laws, you can still adhere to our Constitution. The oath or affirmation to defend the Colorado Constitution is taken by all Colorado government officials, by many government employees, and by every licensed attorney in Colorado. That some oath takers become oath breakers is no reason for others to follow their bad examples—just as one person's infidelity to marriage vows is no excuse for other married couples to ignore their own vows.

Constitutional oaths or affirmations are vows that the exercise of one's powers will comply with the Colorado Constitution. Power may come from one's position as an elected official, a government employee, or an attorney at law.

If you are a legislator, you have the unlimited power, and the duty, to oppose all legislative acts contrary to your judgment of what the Colorado Constitution allows. Indeed, the Colorado supreme court pretends that every legislator already does so. You can at least make the court's assumption a little closer to reality.

Elsewhere in state or local government, within your discretion, you can choose to adhere to the Colorado Constitution. As a local official, you follow the Constitution and therefore decide not to take property from the little guy so that big business can use it, even if the courts refuse to enforce the constitutional laws against eminent domain abuse. You can prioritize the enforcement of laws that comply with the Constitution over those that do not.

As a voter and an active citizen, you can give your support to the candidates who are most loyal to the Constitution. This is not a matter of "progressive" versus "conservative," which are often inaccurate labels anyway. Some self-proclaimed progressives are regressives who want to go backward to the times before the Declaration of Independence, to repudiate the eternal truths of natural rights, consent of the governed, and the legal equality of all. Some self-proclaimed conservatives reject the prudence, caution, skepticism, and tradition of true conservatism, and are easy prey for authoritarians and personality cults.

Constitutionalists bear true allegiance to the Declaration of Independence, the United States Constitution, and their state Constitution. The allegiance may sometimes result in "left-wing" outcomes, and sometimes "right-wing" ones. The first question the constitutionalist asks is not which "side" benefits from a proposal, but what the Constitution says.

Nevertheless, persist

It can feel discouraging to have to keep fighting in the twenty-first century over matters that were intended to be settled with finality by the 1876 adoption of the Constitution. Colorado's Founders created a beautiful state constitution in 1876, yet by the early 20th century, Colorado was among the worst-governed states in the Union. Reformers fought back, starting by securing the rights of initiative and referendum in 1910, and then using those rights to enact further reforms. *See* chapter 9. Some of these reforms endured, whereas others were undone by the legislature in conjunction with the supreme court, which grew more aggressive about excising portions of the Constitution. Reformers persisted, including in the GAVEL-GOCO-TABOR period of 1988–92. The cycle of citizen reform and judicial nullification continues today.

Don't give up. Learned helplessness emboldens wrongdoers. The Founders of the state of Colorado persevered through hard times. *See* chapter 6. Civic engagement by constitutionalists is essential. Otherwise the immense powers of government will be exercised by persons who imagine they have the power to invade natural rights and who evade the constitutional limit on their powers.

We do not have angels to govern us, observed James Madison. Federalist 51. Madison hoped that independent courts would be "an impenetrable bulwark" of constitutional rights. 1 ANNALS OF CONGRESS 457 (June 8, 1789) (Joseph Gales ed., 1843). However, in Colorado, the courts often give a broad construction to the powers of the persons in the government and a narrow construction to the natural, essential, and inherent rights of the people, which precede the government and of a higher origin and importance. *Cf. In re Senate Resolution No. 2*, 94 Colo. 101, 114, 31 P.2d 325 (1933) (criticizing arguments for a narrow construction of article XI).

Colorado's state and local governments, including the appellate courts, have sometimes been unreliable friends, and even active foes, of the Colorado Constitution.

Our Colorado Constitution needs more friends. Perhaps you will choose to be one of them.

Table of Authorities

U.S. SUPREME COURT CASES

OTHER FEDERAL CASES

COLORADO SUPREME COURT CASES

COLORADO COURTS OF APPEALS AND OTHER COLORADO CASES

CASES FROM OTHER STATES

UNITED STATES CONSTITUTION

COLORADO CONSTITUTION

List may not include the main textbook entry on a section. See Table of Contents for main discussion of each section

COLORADO STATUTES

COLORADO STATE AND LOCAL GOVERNMENT DOCUMENTS

BOOKS AND THESES

MONNETT, JOHN H., THE BATTLE OF BEECHER ISLAND AND THE INDIAN WAR OF 1867–1869 (1992).......163, 165, 168, 170, 171

MORRIS, THOMAS D., FREE MEN ALL: THE PERSONAL LIBERTY LAWS OF THE NORTH, 1780–1861 (1974) 121

MUIR, WILLIAM TRAIN, LAWS OF THE NEVADA MINING DISTRICT 1861 (1962) 145

MURFEE, WILLIAM L., A TREATISE ON THE LAW OF THE SHERIFFS AND OTHER MINISTERIAL OFFICERS (1884)........457-58

NAGLE, P.G., GLORIETA PASS (1999)........157

NATELSON, ROBERT G., THE ORIGINAL CONSTITUTION: WHAT IT ACTUALLY SAID AND MEANT (2014) ...102

NEUSCHATZ, MICHAEL, THE GOLDEN SWORD: THE COMING OF CAPITALISM TO THE COLORADO MINING FRONTIER (1986)........486

NOEL, THOMAS J., COLORADO: A HISTORICAL ATLAS (2015)........29, 30, 143, 171, 328

OAKES, JAMES, THE SCORPION'S STING: ANTISLAVERY AND THE COMING OF THE CIVIL WAR (2014).......154

OATS, STEPHEN B., CONFEDERATE CAVALRY WEST OF THE RIVER (1961)........155

PAPERS OF JAMES MADISON, 2 RETIREMENT SERIES (David B. Mattern et al. eds, 2013)........649

PARKHILL, FORBES, THE LAW GOES WEST (1956)........182

PARRINGTON, VERNON LOUIS, MAIN CURRENTS IN AMERICAN THOUGHT: THE BEGINNINGS OF CRITICAL REALISM IN AMERICA, 1860–1920 (1930)........174

PASCOE, PEGGY, WHAT COMES NATURALLY: MISCEGENATION LAW AND THE MAKING OF RACE IN AMERICA (2010)........123

PERKIN, ROBERT L., THE FIRST HUNDRED YEARS 1859–1959: AN INFORMAL HISTORY OF DENVER AND THE ROCKY MOUNTAIN NEWS (1959)........328

PETERSON, JOHN ALTON, UTAH'S BLACK HAWK WAR (1998)........153, 173-74

PHILPOTT, WILLIAM, VACATIONLAND: TOURISM AND ENVIRONMENT IN THE COLORADO HIGH COUNTRY (2014)........434

PROPST, NELL BROWN, THE SOUTH PLATTE TRAIL: STORY OF COLORADO'S FORGOTTEN PEOPLE (rev. ed. 1984)........143, 154, 158, 160, 162-69

PRUCHA, FRANCIS PAUL, AMERICAN INDIAN TREATIES: THE HISTORY OF A POLITICAL ANOMALY (1994) 143, 152, 168, 175, 177

REHNQUIST, WILLIAM, ALL THE LAWS BUT ONE: CIVIL LIBERTIES IN WARTIME (2000)........91

REID, JOHN PHILLIP, POLICING THE ELEPHANT: CRIME, PUNISHMENT, AND SOCIAL BEHAVIOR ON THE OVERLAND TRAIL (1997)........158

REMINI, ROBERT V., THE BATTLE OF NEW ORLEANS: ANDREW JACKSON AND AMERICA'S FIRST MILITARY VICTORY (1999)........45

RESÉNDEZ, ANDRES, THE OTHER SLAVERY: THE UNCOVERED STORY OF INDIAN ENSLAVEMENT IN AMERICA (2016)........100

RICHARDSON, ALBERT D., BEYOND THE MISSISSIPPI: FROM THE GREAT RIVER TO THE GREAT OCEAN: LIFE AND ADVENTURE ON THE PRAIRIES, MOUNTAINS, AND PACIFIC COAST (1867)........177, 181-82

RIGHT, JAMES EDWARD, THE POLITICS OF POPULISM: DISSENT IN COLORADO (1974)........239

ROBERT, HENRY MARTIN, ROBERT'S RULES OF ORDER (1876)........217, 231

ROMMEN, HEINRICH A., THE NATURAL LAW: A STUDY IN LEGAL AND SOCIAL HISTORY AND PHILOSOPHY (Liberty Fund 1998) (1st pub. 1936, as *Die Ewige Wiederkehr des Naturrechts*)........52

RONZIO, RICHARD A., SILVER IMAGES OF COLORADO: DENVER AND THE 1866 BUSINESS DIRECTORY (1986) 143, 180

RUSSELL, CARL P., FIREARMS, TRAPS AND TOOLS OF THE MOUNTAIN MEN (2011)........55, 173

SAXON, OLIN GLENN, COLORADO AND ITS MINING INDUSTRY (1859–1959) (Denver: Mining and Petroleum Committee, Colorado State Chamber of Commerce, 1959)........486

SCAMEHORN, LEE, HIGH ALTITUDE: A HISTORY OF FOSSIL FUELS IN COLORADO (2002)........486

SCHECHTER, HAROLD, MAN-EATER: THE LIFE AND LEGEND OF AN AMERICAN CANNIBAL (Amazon Pub. 2015)........18

SCHRAGER, ADAM, THE PRINCIPLED POLITICIAN: THE RALPH CARR STORY (2008)........36, 492, 498

SHACHTMAN, TOM, HOW THE FRENCH SAVED AMERICA: SOLDIERS, SAILORS, DIPLOMATS, LOUIS XVI, AND THE SUCCESS OF A REVOLUTION (2017)........153

SHAKESPEARE, WILLIAM, MACBETH (1623)........291

SILBERNAGEL, ROBERT, TROUBLED TRAILS: THE MEEKER AFFAIR AND THE EXPULSION OF UTES FROM COLORADO (2011)........176

SCHOLARLY ARTICLES AND MONOGRAPHS

Kalish, Debra S., Gerald E Dahl, & Christopher Price, *The Doctrine of Preemption and Regulating Oil and Gas Development*, 38 COLO. LAWYER 47 (Oct. 2009) 531

Kamin, Sam, *Colorado Marijuana Regulation Five Years Later: Have We Learned Anything at All?* 96 DENVER L. REVIEW 221 (2019) 621

Kates, Don B., Jr., *The Second Amendment and the Ideology of Self-Protection*, 9 CONSTITUTIONAL COMMENTARY 100 (1992). 92

Klemme, Howard C., *Powers of Home Rule Cities in Colorado*, 36 U. COLO. L. REVIEW 321 (1964) 531

Kopel, David B. & Hunter Hovenga, *The National Popular Vote Violates the Colorado Constitution*, DENVER L. REVIEW FORUM (22-Sept.-2020) 25

Kopel, David B. & Joseph G.S. Greenlee, *The Federal Circuits' Second Amendment Doctrines*, 61 ST. LOUIS U. L.J. 193 (2017). 75

Kopel, David B. & Michael Krause, *The Drug War on Human Rights and Civil Liberties*, Occasional Paper # 8 from the Liberal Institute of the Friederich Naumann Foundation (Potsdam, Germany: 2004) 131

Kopel, David B. & Stephen P. Halbrook, *Tench Coxe and the Right to Keep and Bear Arms in the Early Republic*, 7 WM. & MARY BILL OF RIGHTS J. 347 (1999) 495

Kopel, David B. & Trevor Burrus, *Sex, Drugs, Alcohol, Gambling, and Guns: The Synergistic Constitutional Effects*, 6 ALBANY GOV'T L. REVIEW 306 (2013) 130

Kopel, David B., Clayton Cramer & Scott Hattrup, *A Tale of Three Cities: The Right to Bear Arms in State Courts*, 68 TEMPLE LAW REVIEW 1177 (1995) 77, 81

Kopel, David B., *How the British Gun Control Program Precipitated the American Revolution*, 6 CHARLESTON L. REVIEW 283 (2012) 459

Kopel, David B., *Lyman Trumbull: Author of the Thirteenth Amendment, Author of the Civil Rights Act, and the First Second Amendment Lawyer*, 47 LOYOLA U. CHI. L.J. 1117 (2016) 91, 315

Kopel, David B., *Red Flag Laws: Proceed with Caution*, 45 (Alabama) LAW & PSYCHOLOGY REVIEW 39 (2021) 133

Kopel, David B., *The Brady Bill Comes Due: The Supreme Court Saves Federalism*, 9 GEORGE MASON CIVIL RIGHTS & CIVIL LIBERTIES L.J. 189 (1999) 129

Kopel, David B., *The First Amendment Guide to the Second Amendment*, 81 TENN. L. REVIEW 417 (2014) 50

Kopel, David B., *The Natural Right of Self-Defense:* Heller*'s Lesson for the World*, 59 SYRACUSE L. REVIEW 235 (2008) 50

Kopel, David B., *The Posse Comitatus and the Office of Sheriff: Armed Citizens Summoned to the Aid of Law Enforcement*, 104 J. CRIM. L. & CRIMINOLOGY 761 (2014) 76, 121, 456

Kopel, David B., *The Right to Arms in Nineteenth Century Colorado*, 95 DENVER L. REVIEW 329 (2018) 141, 185, 459

Kopel, David B., *The Second Amendment in the Tenth Circuit: Three Decades of (Mostly) Harmless Error*, 86 DENVER U. L. REVIEW 901 (2009) 649

Kopel, David B., *The Supreme Court's Thirty-five Other Second Amendment Cases*, 18 ST. L.U. PUBLIC L. REVIEW 99 (1999). 60

Kopel, David, B., *The Licensing of Concealed Handguns for Lawful Protection: Support from Five State Supreme Courts*, 68 ALBANY LAW REVIEW 305 (2005) 77

Kopel, Dolores, *Colorado's Homestead Exemption*, 5 COLO. LAWYER 1059 (1976) 501

Kube, Robyn W., *Access at Last: The Use of Private Condemnation*, 29 COLO. LAWYER 77 (Feb. 2000) ..82

Larkin, Elizabeth A., *Judicial Selection Methods: Judicial Independence and Popular Democracy*, 79 DENVER U.L. REVIEW 65 (2001) 311

Lawson, Gary, Guy I. Seidman & Robert G. Natelson, *The Fiduciary Foundations of Federal Equal Protection*, 94 BOSTON U. L. REVIEW 415 (2014) 95

Lidstone, Herrick K., & Jeremy Schupbach, *How the Colorado General Assembly Works*, 45 COLO. LAWYER 33 (Dec. 2016) 217

Linz, Robert M., *Researching Colorado Local Government Law*, 38 COLO. LAWYER 101 (Aug. 2009) 531

Luna, Joshua J., *Bail Reform in Colorado: A Presumption of Release*, 88 UNIV. OF COLO. L. REVIEW 1067 (2017) 88

Lund, Nelson, *The Constitution, the Supreme Court, and Racial Politics*, 12 GA. ST. U. L. REVIEW 1129 (1996) 125

Lynchings: By Year and Race, UMKC (University of Missouri at Kansas City) 184

NEWSPAPERS, MAGAZINES, OTHER

UNITED STATES GOVERNMENT DOCUMENTS

Statutes at Large

U.S. Code

Other

OTHER STATE CONSTITUTIONS AND STATUTES

TREATIES

Indian nations

Other nations

Index

Note: This index is generated by Microsoft Word and collects uses of words or phrases. The index is not conceptual.

C

D

L

M

N

O

P

S

T

U

V

W

www.ingramcontent.com/pod-product-compliance
Lightning Source LLC
LaVergne TN
LVHW082002200926
848481LV00010B/2791